Exploring
Sport
and
Exercise
Psychology

Exploring
Sport
and
Exercise
Psychology

Second Edition

Edited by
Judy L. Van Raalte
Britton W. Brewer

AMERICAN PSYCHOLOGICAL ASSOCIATION • WASHINGTON, DC

First printing, March 2002
Second printing, April 2003

Published by
American Psychological Association
750 First Street, NE
Washington, DC 20002
www.apa.org

To order
APA Order Department
P.O. Box 92984
Washington, DC 20090-2984

Tel: (800) 374-2721; Direct: (202) 336-5510
Fax: (202) 336-5502; TDD/TTY: (202) 336-6123
Online: www.apa.org/books/
Email: order@apa.org

In the U.K., Europe, Africa, and the Middle East, copies may be ordered from
American Psychological Association
3 Henrietta Street
Covent Garden, London
WC2E 8LU England

Typeset in Futura and New Baskerville by EPS Group Inc., Easton, MD

Printer: Port City Press, Baltimore, MD
Cover Designer: Minker Design, Bethesda, MD
Technical/Production Editor: Casey Ann Reever

The opinions and statements published are the responsibility of the authors, and such opinions and statements do not necessarily represent the policies of the American Psychological Association.

Library of Congress Cataloging-in-Publication Data
Exploring sport and exercise psychology / edited by Judy L. Van Raalte, Britton W. Brewer.—2nd ed.
   p. cm.
   Includes bibliographical references and index.
   ISBN 1-55798-886-2
   1. Sports—Psychological aspects.   2. Exercise—Psychological aspects.
I. Van Raalte, Judy L.   II. Brewer, Britton W.
[DNLM: 1. Sports—psychology.   2. Exercise—psychology.   QT 260 E965 2002]
QV706.4.E96 2002
796'.01—dc21

2002020856

British Library Cataloguing-in-Publication Data
A CIP record is available from the British Library.

Printed in the United States of America

In memory of Peter Van Raalte (1937–2000)

Contents

Contributors

Mark B. Andersen, PhD, School of Human Movement, Recreation, and Performance, Victoria University, Melbourne, Victoria, Australia

Patrick H. F. Baillie, PhD, Forensic Assessment and Outpatient Services, Calgary Health Region, Alberta, Canada

Beth C. Bock, PhD, Department of Psychiatry and Human Behavior, Miriam Hospital and Brown Medical School, Centers for Behavioral and Preventive Medicine, Providence, RI

Britton W. Brewer, PhD, Department of Psychology, Springfield College, Springfield, MA

Kevin L. Burke, PhD, Department of Health and Kinesiology, Georgia Southern University, Statesboro

Matthew M. Clark, PhD, ABPP, Department of Psychiatry and Psychology, Mayo Clinic, Rochester, MN

Karen D. Cogan, PhD, Center for Sport Psychology and Performance Excellence, Department of Psychology, University of North Texas, Denton

Nicole Damarjian, PhD, Department of Kinesiology, University of Connecticut, Storrs

Steven J. Danish, PhD, Life Skills Center, Department of Psychology, Virginia Commonwealth University, Richmond

David A. Dzewaltowski, PhD, Department of Kinesiology and Research and Extension Office of Community Health, Kansas State University, Manhattan

T. David Elkins, PhD, Department of Psychiatry and Human Behavior, University of Mississippi Medical Center, Jackson

Paul A. Estabrooks, PhD, Department of Kinesiology and Research and Extension Office of Community Health, Kansas State University, Manhattan

Robert J. Fazio, PhD, Department of Psychology, Virginia Commonwealth University, Richmond

Daniel Gould, PhD, Department of Exercise and Sport Sciences, University of North Carolina–Greensboro

Christy Greenleaf, PhD, Department of Kinesiology, Health Promotion, and Recreation, University of North Texas, Denton

Nancy C. Gyurcsik, PhD, Department of Kinesiology and Research and Extension Office of Community Health, Kansas State University, Manhattan

Kate F. Hays, PhD, The Performing Edge, Toronto, Ontario, Canada

Judy A. Johnston, MS, RD/LD, Department of Preventive Medicine, Research and Extension Office of Community Health, Kansas State University, School of Medicine, Wichita

Douglas P. Jowdy, PhD, Head, Sport and Exercise Psychology Program, Argosy University, Phoenix, AZ

Thad R. Leffingwell, PhD, Department of Psychology, Oklahoma State University, Stillwater

Michael J. Mahoney, PhD, Department of Psychology, University of North Texas, Denton, and Saybrook Graduate School and Research Center, San Francisco, CA

Bess H. Marcus, PhD, Psychiatry and Human Behavior, Centers for Behavioral and Preventive Medicine, Brown University, Providence, RI

Sean C. McCann, PhD, Head, Sport Psychology Department, Coaching and Sport Sciences Division, U.S. Olympic Committee, Colorado Springs, CO

Penny McCullagh, PhD, Department of Kinesiology and Physical Education, California State University, Hayward

Andrew W. Meyers, PhD, Department of Psychology, University of Memphis, TN

William P. Morgan, EdD, Department of Kinesiology, Exercise Psychology Laboratory, University of Wisconsin, Madison

Melissa A. Napolitano, PhD, Miriam Hospital and Brown Medical School, Behavioral and Preventive Medicine, Providence, RI

Valerie C. Nellen, PhD, Department of Psychology, Virginia Commonwealth University, Richmond

John M. Noble, PhD, School of Health, Physical Education, and Recreation, University of Nebraska, Omaha

Bruce C. Ogilvie, PhD, Professor Emeritus, Department of Psychology, San Jose State University, Los Gatos, CA

Susanna S. Owens, PhD, Department of Psychology, Virginia Commonwealth University, Richmond

Frank M. Perna, PhD, Department of Psychiatry, Boston Medical Center, MA

Albert J. Petitpas, EdD, Psychology Department and Director of the National Football Foundation Center for Youth Development through Sport, Springfield College, Springfield, MA

Trent A. Petrie, PhD, Center for Sport Psychology and Performance Excellence, Department of Psychology, University of North Texas, Denton

Bernadine M. Pinto, PhD, Miriam Hospital and Brown Medical School, Centers for Behavioral and Preventive Medicine, Providence, RI

Wes Sime, PhD, Health and Human Performance, University of Nebraska, Lincoln

Robert N. Singer, PhD, Department of Exercise and Sport Sciences, University of Florida, Gainesville

Robert J. Smith, PhD, psychologist in private practice, Waltham, MA

Ronald E. Smith, PhD, Department of Psychology, University of Washington, Seattle

Frank L. Smoll, PhD, Department of Psychology, University of Washington, Seattle

Jim Taylor, PhD, Alpine Taylor Consulting, San Francisco, CA

Judy L. Van Raalte, PhD, Department of Psychology, Springfield College, Springfield, MA

Robert S. Weinberg, PhD, Department of Physical Education, Health and Sport Studies, Miami University, Oxford, OH

Maureen R. Weiss, PhD, Kinesiology Program, Curry School of Education, University of Virginia, Charlottesville

James P. Whelan, PhD, Department of Psychology, University of Memphis, TN

Jean M. Williams, PhD, Department of Psychology, University of Arizona, Tucson

Gregory S. Wilson, PEd, Department of Human Kinetics and Sport Studies, University of Evansville, IN

Leonard Zaichkowsky, PhD, School of Education, Boston University, MA

Samuel Zizzi, EdD, Department of Sport and Exercise Psychology, West Virginia University, Morgantown

Foreword

Future historians of psychology are likely to view the 20th century as a formative period during which some of the major themes in the profession were first developed. One of those themes has been the relationship between the mind and the body. That relationship has been a central issue in psychology since its emergence as a separate discipline. Indeed, it is not coincidental that psychology's conceptual parents—philosophy and physiology—represented the polar extremes of this contrast. The mind–body dichotomy became an issue primarily because of the difficulties in conceptualizing an interaction between metaphysical and physical realms. This separation, technically termed *dualism,* has been prevalent in Western civilization since the times of Pythagoras and became formalized and enshrined by René Descartes. Dualism became an intractable problem: How was it possible for a nonmaterial mind to influence the material substance of the body? And how did the experiences of that body make their way from the physical to the mental realm? Proposed answers to questions like these have taken a variety of forms, each of which has had its share of adherents and detractors in the history of psychology.

In the second half of the 19th century, influential pioneers in psychology defined their work and the field itself as studies of consciousness. The pendulum of focus was on the mind's side of the dichotomy. As Wilhelm Wundt's voluntarism and E. B. Titchener's structuralism gave way to the post-Darwinian tradition of functionalism, however, the pendulum moved toward the bodily side. The rise of behaviorism marked the beginning of an anti-mind era, and this was the dominant position in North American psychology for the first half of the 20th century. Private events were largely banished from experimental psychology, and the "black box" of mental life was deemed unimportant to the allegedly "real science" of studying functional relations between stimulus (input) and response (output). The pendulum began its return journey around 1955 and, in the 1970s, psychology and other disciplines were in the throes of a sweeping "cognitive revolution." Beginning with studies in cybernetics and information processing, the cognitive sciences gained momentum and voice. The paradigms of connectionism and constructivism became second and third waves in the cognitive revolution, and the pendulum seemed destined toward the mind side again.

But something else happened. It was an unexpected and, in many ways, unprecedented something. The pendulum of focus broke out of its fixed path of alternations between mind and body. Instead of swinging in a straight line of separation between these two poles, the pendulum began swinging toward a circle that connected mind and body in an integrative way. Signs of this new development were popping up everywhere. The "dry look" in neurobiology, which had likened the brain and nervous system to an electronic circuit board, began to give way to the "wet look" of a nervous system literally bathed in fluids that connected it with the body. Respected brain scientists like Roger Sperry, who had previously endorsed an interactionist position on mind–body relations, began to encourage a new position that moved beyond the Cartesian assumption of dualism. The tradition of rationalist supremacy, which had placed reason above and in control of the body and its passions, was challenged by research emphasizing the power and pervasiveness of emotion in attention, perception, learning, and memory.

George Lakoff, Mark Johnson, and Antonio Damasio were among a creative group of theorists and researchers who documented that the body is in the mind no less than the mind is in the body. Developmental psychologists showed that infants used their bodily movements to establish communicative channels with their caregivers long before their development of language. Esther Thelen introduced the "new look" in motor development, showing how children display complex and dynamic self-organizing processes that defy any meaningful segregation of brain and body. The doctrine of cerebral primacy, which assumed that development and evolution were led by the head, receded in the face of evidence that body and brain development are integrated phenomena. Health psychology and sport psychology came to be recognized as legitimate and promising specializations that reflected this more integrative view.

The body is back, and so is the mind. They are not separate realms. They never were. It may be a long time before people develop a more adequate vocabulary and language habits to address the complexity of body–brain processes, but I believe it is promising that recently steps have been taken toward liberating ourselves from the chains of dualism that have enslaved philosophy for more than two millennia and psychology for more than a century. There is still a long way to go, of course, but this should be an inspiring rather than daunting realization. Psychology is at the beginning of a new era, which promises to be filled with exciting insights that cannot be anticipated. To use the terminology now popular in the sciences of complexity, psychology is in the midst of a phase transition, in which old patterns of order are in the process of being incorporated (literally, embodied) into new patterns.

Dualistic notions about mind and body will not go away quickly or easily, and it is important that we realize the likelihood that dualistic conceptualizations probably served valuable functions in the early stages of reflective inquiry and psychological science. As tempting and popular as it may be to engage in "Descartes bashing," it is wise to respect the roles that traditions play in all evolutions of our thinking. Philosopher Thomas Kuhn is best known for his work on the structure of scientific revolutions, but he was equally emphatic about the role of essential tensions in the development of knowledge. Revolutions require traditions as the targets of their revolts. Changes require enduring stabilities to define them. Recognizing this is central to the appreciation that all development is fundamentally dialectical—that is, that it emerges out of the interaction of contrasts. The embodiment of mind and the return of the body to psychology are developments that have emerged out of a series of long-standing contrasts regarding mind, body, and their possible relationships. New paradigms are now appearing that integrate and elaborate in ways that will break new ground in theory, research, and practice. And one of the areas in which such integrations and elaborations are particularly apparent is that of exercise and sport psychology. This volume represents a major contribution to that area, and I am honored to contribute to it.

To appreciate the significance of this volume, one must realize what it represents in the context of the emerging specializations of exercise and sport psychology. One does not have to go too far back to see why the range and depth of this volume are a welcome and timely contribution. The pioneering works of Norman Triplett in the 1890s and of Coleman Roberts Griffith in the 1920s have been around for close to a century, and yet the field of sport psychology has remained —until very recently—an undernourished specialization. For the first three quarters of the 20th century, psychological studies of exercise and sport were rarely undertaken and even less frequently reported. Things began to change in the 1970s, however, and have continued accelerating since then. A popular rise in health consciousness among the public has encouraged that development. The "movement movement" placed new demands on psychologists interested in incorporating the body into their services.

It is interesting to reflect on exercise and sport psychology only a quarter of a century ago. Exercise was the domain of exercise scientists, and it was considered an esoteric interest. Neighborhood health clubs were rare and little used. Those exercise facilities that did exist were neither high-tech nor fashionable, and their clientele were few and predominantly male. Bicycle lanes, running and walking paths, and fitness equipment were very difficult to find. Shopping malls did not abound with stores selling athletic apparel, running shoes, and home gyms. In North America, at least, sport was largely ignored by psychology. There were no trained specialists in sport psychology, no training programs, and relatively few researchers or practitioners. There were a few psychologists, however, who found themselves focusing more and more on sport. They began to write about the multiple roles of sport in society and the impact of an audience or competitor on athletic performance, the contributions of sports involvement to children's personality development, the existence of biases and preconceptions about women's involvement in exercise and sport, and the effects of hypnosis on athletic training and sports performance. In those days there was precious little literature—either experimental or case study—to inform and assist practitioners interested in offering psychological services to athletes or in recommending exercise or movement to their clients. Practitioners were essentially on their own in shaping their services. Many important lessons were learned and, fortunately, many were conveyed in forms that eventually made them more accessible to the growing numbers of practicing exercise and sport psychologists.

Today there are a growing number of training programs that incorporate exercise and sport psychology as important elements in the preparation of mental health professionals. The era of "talking heads" psychotherapy is evolving to reflect a deep and working appreciation of embodiment in all human experiencing. How does the practitioner do this? How do psychologists help their clients to appreciate the significance of their bodies in their psychological lives? How do we assess their attitudes toward their bodies, eating, exercise, dance, touch, and so on?

How do we individualize recommendations for healthy activities that bring joy as well as fitness into their lives? How do we teach children to develop a relationship with sports, movement, and themselves that sings with a sense of sublime delight at their capacities for "being bodily?" How do we help athletes to enjoy and optimally express their gifts and their hard work in their performances? What are the needs of special populations that may be challenged? And how do we encourage and participate in research and the training of psychologists who are interested in questions such as these?

These are among the issues addressed in this second edition of the present volume. Here the reader has a well-balanced range of chapters on basic themes and contemporary issues in exercise and sport psychology. The authors are highly respected specialists, including some of the pioneers in the field, and all share invaluable knowledge and experience. The topics addressed are core themes, such as assessment, motivation, imagery, cognitive strategies, intensity regulation, hypnosis, exercise therapy, assessment, psychological problems, referral practices, work with children and special populations, professional training, certification, clinical practice, and ethics. This volume represents a wealth of expertise and information that will be invaluable to anyone interested in serving athletes or clients who choose to explore exercise as a path toward well-being. This is a contemporary classic, and it deserves wide readership and practical application.

Michael J. Mahoney

Preface

In preparing the first edition of this book, we attempted to survey the broad and ever-expanding field of sport and exercise psychology. We wanted to develop a highly readable text that would serve as a resource for professionals and students who were interested in learning more about the theoretical, empirical, and applied aspects of the field. To accomplish our goal, we enlisted experts across the diverse array of essential topics in sport and exercise psychology to write chapters.

For the second edition, we have made an effort to update the book with developments in the field that have occurred in the years since the first edition was published, to provide coverage of emerging areas of sport and exercise psychology, and to address important topics that were not included in the first edition. To guide our efforts in revising the book, we read reviews of the first edition, consulted with colleagues, and obtained feedback and suggestions from members of SPORTPSY, an online sport psychology discussion group. The input from these sources, as well as the thoughtful work of the chapter authors, has resulted in a significantly updated and revised book. Specifically, the second edition features an abundance of new references and case examples and three new chapters addressing implementation of comprehensive sport psychology interventions, modeling, and promotion of physical activity through community development.

The second edition retains the focus of the first edition on providing an overview of the field of sport and exercise psychology, connecting theory and practice, and discussing important practical issues related to credentialing and training. We hope that this new edition will provide readers with a strong foundation in sport and exercise psychology and serve as a springboard for further exploration of the field.

Acknowledgments

We undertook the editing of this second edition with high expectations. Through the efforts of a large group of talented people, our aspirations were fulfilled. We are indebted to the chapter authors, who worked diligently to ensure that they included the most current information available, met deadlines, made revisions, made further revisions, and produced outstanding chapters. Preparing this second edition was simplified by the invaluable advice and words of wisdom we received from several experienced authors and colleagues. Jean Williams and Kate Hays were particularly helpful in this regard.

We would again like to thank our mentors, Darwyn Linder and Paul Karoly, who taught us the basics and continue to support and inspire us. Our appreciation extends to our colleagues and students at Springfield College, especially Al Petitpas, who has been unflagging in his advocacy for our scholarly endeavors over the past decade, and Ruth Brennan, Bryan Gross, and Miki Oyler, who managed a mountain of information and facilitated communication with chapter authors.

We must also thank the dedicated professionals at APA Books who made this book possible. In particular, we are grateful to Gary VandenBos, whose strong support fueled the second edition, and to Susan Reynolds, Vanessa Downing, and Casey Reever, whose vision and editorial expertise kept the project on a steady course. We also appreciate the thoughtful feedback we received from the anonymous reviews.

Finally, we thank our families, who remained supportive throughout the preparation of this volume.

Exploring
Sport
and
Exercise
Psychology

Introduction to Sport and Exercise Psychology

Britton W. Brewer and Judy L. Van Raalte

Physical activity is a salient aspect of human experience across the lifespan. Competitive and recreational sport leagues exist for children, adolescents, adults, and seniors. Exercise has been identified as an important part of a healthy lifestyle for young and old alike. Given the centrality of physical activity to contemporary living, it is not surprising that psychologists have become interested in sport and exercise behavior. This interest has given rise to sport and exercise psychology, an emerging field that offers an abundance of exciting opportunities for research and practice in an inherently interesting domain of human behavior (Hays, 1995; Singer, Hausenblas, & Janelle, 2001; Taylor, 1991).

As is the case with many subfields of psychology, sport and exercise psychology encompasses a wide variety of clinical, educational, and research activities. A sport and exercise psychologist might work with athletes at the U.S. Olympic Training Center, use exercise therapeutically with clients, or conduct workshops for parents and youth sport coaches. Although there may be no "typical" sport and exercise psychologist, there are several issues and content areas with which all practicing sport and exercise psychologists should be familiar. This book is designed to acquaint psychologists, psychologists-in-training (i.e., students), and other mental health practitioners interested in sport and exercise psychology with basic interventions, clinical issues, special populations, and professional issues in the field.

The primary purpose of this chapter is to provide an introduction to the growing field of sport and exercise psychology. Historical foundations, research trends, current controversies, client populations, and applied settings of the field are described. After summarizing the history and current status of the field, an overview of the book is presented.

A Brief History of Sport and Exercise Psychology in the United States

Despite the popular misconception of the field as a novel area of inquiry, sport and exercise psychology has a rich history. Although the investigation of psychological factors associated with exercise is a relatively recent phenomenon (Gill, 1986, 1987), scientists have been studying psychological aspects of sport for more than 100 years (Wiggins, 1984). Examination of the evolution of sport and exercise psychology contributes to an enhanced understanding of the field as it stands today.

At the end of the 19th and the beginning of the 20th century, several theoretical and empirical works addressing sport-related topics appeared in the psychological literature (Wiggins, 1984). Notable among these writings were Norman Triplett's (1897) study of audience effects on cycling performance, which is considered the first experiment in social psychology (West & Wicklund, 1980), and American Psychological Association (APA) founding president G. Stanley Hall's (1908) report extolling the psychological benefits of physical education.

On the heels of these early developments, Coleman Griffith established what is regarded as the first sport psychology laboratory in North America in 1925 at the University of Illinois. Griffith conducted research on psychological aspects of sport performance, such as psychomotor learning, personality, and motivation. He also developed course work in sport psychology and later served as sport psychologist for the Chicago Cubs baseball team (Kroll & Lewis, 1970).

Despite Griffith's advances in the 1920s and 1930s, interest in sport psychology in the 1940s and 1950s was restricted primarily to a growing core of motor learning researchers in physical education departments. It was not until the 1960s and 1970s that sport psychology began to flourish as a discipline, as evidenced by the emergence of textbooks, professional organizations, and scholarly journals devoted to the field (Wiggins, 1984; Williams & Straub, 2001). Popular sport-specific research topics during this period included personality, arousal/anxiety, performance enhancement interventions (e.g., relaxation, imagery), achievement motivation, causal attributions, aggression, and team cohesion (Cox, Qiu, & Liu, 1993).

Building on the developments of the 1960s and 1970s, the field expanded further in the 1980s and 1990s. During these decades, major trends included the investigation of psychological aspects of exercise (Browne & Mahoney, 1984; Rejeski & Thompson, 1993) and the application of the growing knowledge base to assist sport participants in achieving maximal performance (Browne & Mahoney, 1984). Reflecting these trends, the *Journal of Sport Psychology* became the *Journal of Sport and Exercise Psychology* (Gill, 1986, 1987) in 1988, and the Association for the Advancement of Applied Sport Psychology (AAASP) was founded in 1985 (Williams & Straub, 2001). Two journals focusing on applied issues in sport psychology, *The Sport Psychologist* and the *Journal of Applied Sport Psychology*, debuted in 1987 and 1989, respectively. The first recognition of sport and exercise psychology by mainstream psychology occurred in 1987 with the formation of Division 47 (Exercise and Sport Psychology) of the APA (Williams & Straub, 2001). In 1991, a process for certifying sport and exercise psychology consultants was implemented by AAASP.

Current Status of Sport and Exercise Psychology

Although its early history was dominated by the efforts of physical educators, sport and exercise psychology has evolved into an interdisciplinary field, involving both sport scientists and psychologists. From an initial focus on sport performance as the primary outcome of interest, sport and exercise psychology has broadened considerably. Performance enhancement remains an important area of research and applied work, but improvement of the quality of sport and exercise participants' involvement in physical activity has emerged as an emphasis of researchers and practitioners (Hays, 1995; Williams & Straub, 2001). Although collegiate, professional, and elite amateur athletes have traditionally been the main recipients of sport and exercise psychology interventions, professionals in the field have expanded the horizon to include youth sport competitors, adult recreational sport participants, masters athletes, and other underserved populations (Murphy, 1995; Singer et al., 2001). In keeping with the widening range of populations targeted for intervention, sport and exercise psychology research and practice have extended beyond the playing field and the laboratory to a host of other venues, including schools, health clubs, sports medicine clinics, counseling centers, and private practice offices.

As a result of continued expansion over the past four decades, sport and exercise psychology has experienced growing pains. In particular, because the field encompasses professionals of varying educational background, issues of training, credentialing, and ethics have come to the fore. Debate is centered on the training needed to become a sport and exercise psychologist, competencies required to be labeled a sport and exercise psychologist, and standards of ethical professional conduct in sport and exercise psychology (Hays, 1995; Murphy, 1995; Silva, 2001; Taylor, 1991).

Overview of This Book

As mentioned above, this book is intended to present an overview of the wide array of issues of potential interest to prospective and current sport and exercise psychology practitioners. The book is designed to serve as a resource with theoretical and practical suggestions related to the practice of sport and exercise psychology. The parts of the book are organized around three questions frequently asked about the field: What specifically do sport and exercise psychologists do? With whom do sport and exercise psychologists work? What does one need to do to become a sport and exercise psychologist? Chapter authors have adopted a scholarly yet practical approach in answering these critical questions. Where available empirical data are limited or nonexistent, gaps in the knowledge base are acknowledged, and sound recommendations for practice based on professional experience are provided.

The first three parts of the book, Performance Enhancement, Promoting Well-Being, and Clinical Issues, pertain primarily to what practitioners in sport and exercise psychology do. Part I, Performance Enhancement, addresses various cognitive–behavioral interventions designed to facilitate optimal sport performance. Interventions such as goal setting, imagery, cognitive strategies, intensity regulation, modeling, and hypnosis are commonly considered the "meat and potatoes" of sport and exercise psychology. For each intervention, a theoretical rationale for using the intervention is provided, empirical support for the intervention is reviewed, and practical suggestions for implementing the intervention are given. Although the interventions featured in this part are presented in individual chapters, professionals would most likely use them in combination in an integrated psychological skills training program, as described in the chapter on developing comprehensive sport psychology intervention programs that concludes this part. Part I is most appropriate for practitioners interested primarily in assisting athletes to achieve favorable outcomes in sport tasks.

Reflecting the current breadth of sport and exercise psychology, Part II, Promoting Well-Being, deals with psychological applications intended to enhance the physical and mental health of both athletes and the general population. Chapter 9, "Exercise Initiation, Adoption, and Maintenance in Adults" describes interventions designed to increase exercise behavior in the general population, an issue with enormous public health ramifications. Immediately following, and complementing, this chapter is "Promotion of Physical Activity Through Community Development," which describes why community interventions are effective in promoting exercise and how community exercise interventions can best be implemented. Demonstrating the versatility of physical activity as a medium for promoting well-being, "Guidelines for Clinical Application of Exercise Therapy for Mental Health" (chapter 11) considers the use of exercise to treat psychological problems. The remaining chapters in Part II, "Counseling Interventions in Applied Sport Psychology" (chapter 12) and "Teaching Life Skills Through Sport" (chapter 13), use developmental perspectives to examine ways in which sport participation can produce favorable psychosocial consequences. Both of these chapters provide further evidence of how sport and exercise psychology is concerned with outcomes beyond sport performance.

Part III of the book, Clinical Issues, addresses aspects of practice that have been largely ignored in the sport and exercise psychology literature. That there has been little coverage of clinical issues such as assessment, psychopathology, and referral may seem surprising to practitioners with clinical training, but it is probably attributable to the fact that the field has traditionally been a subdiscipline of physical education rather than psychology. Chapter 14, "Assessment in Sport and Exercise Psychology," serves as a logical point of departure for this part, because consultation with sport and exercise participants often begins with assessment. In addition to identifying assessment instruments that are particularly useful in work with athlete clients, the chapter examines issues in applying traditional methods of psychological assessment to the sport and exercise milieu. "Psychopathology in Sport and Exercise" (chapter 15) and "Referral Processes in Sport Psychology" (chapter 16) follow the chapter on assessment, highlighting two possible outcomes of assessment: identification of pathological behavior in sport and exercise participants and recognition of the need to refer some clients to other professionals. The chapters in this part are especially relevant to practitioners who lack clinical training or professional experience with sport and exercise populations.

Part IV, Working With Specific Populations, focuses on the individuals with whom sport and exercise psychology practitioners work. Chapters present detailed information on several typical client populations in the field (Murphy, 1995). Special considerations for working with children ("Youth Sports as a Behavior Setting for Psychosocial Interventions," chapter 17), intercollegiate sport participants ("Helping College Student–Athletes In and Out of Sport," chapter 18), and professional or elite amateur athletes ("Working With Elite Athletes," chapter 19) are outlined. The last chapter in this part, "Diversity in Sport," addresses possible influences of selected individual difference factors (i.e., gender, race and ethnicity, sexual orientation, and physical disability status) on sport and exercise psychology consultation.

The fifth and final part of the book, Professional Issues, addresses what an individual aspiring to become a sport and exercise psychologist needs to know and do. In particular, issues central to the professionalization of sport and exercise psychology are explored. Chapters tackle the controversial issues of training ("Education for Becoming a Sport and Exercise Psychologist," chapter 21), credentialing ("Certification in Sport and Exercise Psychology," chapter 22), and ethics ("Ethics in Sport and Exercise Psychology," chapter 24) that confront the field (Hays, 1995; Murphy, 1995; Silva, 2001). Readers may be surprised to learn that the majority of training programs in sport and exercise psychology are in departments of physical education, that certification procedures in sport and exercise psychology are currently in place, and that several unique ethical challenges can occur in sport and exercise psychology practice. Helpful "nuts-and-bolts" suggestions for diversifying a practice to include work with sport and exercise participants are given in "Incorporating Sport and Exercise Psychology Into Clinical Practice" (chapter 23). In "Sport and Exercise Psychology: A Positive Force in the New Millennium," the chapter that concludes both the part and the book, anticipated trends in the field are examined.

Conclusion

Sport and exercise psychology is a growing field with a rich history. As a domain of research and practice, sport and exercise psychology is becoming increasingly diversified. The second edition of *Exploring Sport and Exercise Psychology* is designed to reflect this diversity and serve as a resource for professionals and students interested in the field.

References

Browne, M. A., & Mahoney, M. J. (1984). Sport psychology. *Annual Review of Psychology, 35*, 605–625.

Cox, R. H., Qiu, Y., & Liu, Z. (1993). Overview of sport psychology. In R. N. Singer, M. Murphey, & L. K. Tennant (Eds.), *Handbook of research on sport psychology* (pp. 3–31). New York: Macmillan.

Gill, D. L. (1986). A prospective view of the *Journal of Sport (and Exercise) Psychology. Journal of Sport Psychology, 8*, 164–173.

Gill, D. L. (1987). *Journal of Sport and Exercise Psychology. Journal of Sport Psychology, 9*, 1–2.

Hall, G. S. (1908). *Physical education in colleges: Report of the National Education Association.* Chicago: University of Chicago Press.

Hays, K. F. (1995). Putting sport psychology into (your) practice. *Professional Psychology: Research and Practice, 26*, 33–40.

Kroll, W., & Lewis, G. (1970). America's first sport psychologist. *Quest, 13*, 1–4.

Murphy, S. M. (1995). Introduction to sport psychology interventions. In S. M. Murphy (Ed.), *Sport psychology interventions* (pp. 1–15). Champaign, IL: Human Kinetics.

Rejeski, W. J., & Thompson, A. (1993). Historical and conceptual roots of exercise psychology. In P. Seragian (Ed.), *Exercise psychology: The influence of physical exercise on psychological processes* (pp. 3–35). New York: Wiley.

Silva, J. M. (2001). Current trends and future directions in sport psychology. In R. N. Singer, H. A. Hausenblas, & C. M. Janelle (Eds.), *Handbook of sport psychology* (2nd ed., pp. 823–832). New York: Wiley.

Singer, R. N., Hausenblas, H. A., & Janelle, C. M. (2001). Prologue: A brief history of research in sport psychology. In R. N. Singer, H. A. Hausenblas, & C. M. Janelle (Eds.), *Handbook of sport psychology* (2nd ed., pp. vii–xix). New York: Wiley.

Taylor, J. (1991). Career direction, development, and opportunities in applied sport psychology. *The Sport Psychologist, 5*, 266–280.

Triplett, N. (1897). The dynamogenic factors in pacemaking and competition. *American Journal of Psychology, 9*, 507–553.

West, S. G., & Wicklund, R. A. (1980). *A primer of social psychology theories.* Monterey, CA: Brooks/Cole.

Wiggins, D. K. (1984). The history of sport psychology in North America. In J. Silva & R. Weinberg (Eds.), *Psychological foundations of sport* (pp. 9–22). Champaign, IL: Human Kinetics.

Williams, J. M., & Straub, W. F. (2001). Sport psychology: Past, present, and future. In J. M. Williams (Ed.), *Applied sport psychology: Personal growth to peak performance* (4th ed., pp. 1–12). Mountain View, CA: Mayfield.

Part I

Performance Enhancement

2 Comprehensive Sport Psychology Services

Mark B. Andersen

Sport psychology service delivery is a complex process. No one formula can provide effective and meaningful interventions for all athletes and teams in all situations. Nevertheless, sport psychologists should be familiar and comfortable with some important components of consultation as they embark on work with athletes (see also Poczwardowski, Sherman, & Henschen, 1998). These components include factors that affect the start of service delivery, assessment, goal setting, and the termination process.

Starting Out

Sport psychology services for athletes and coaches begin in many ways. A sport psychologist working for a university intercollegiate athletics department may begin services through coaches who want their athletes to participate in group sessions on mental preparation for competition; through athletes approaching the psychologist who is observing practice; through self-, coach, or sports medicine referral; through chance encounters in hallways; or through the many ways people make contact in universities (many sport psychologists also teach in higher education). However that first contact is made, the next point in service delivery is to explore the presenting concern.

The "manifest" presenting issue is the first reason the athlete or coach gives for wanting service. That issue may be performance anxiety

(Sherman & Poczwardowski, 2000), coach–athlete communication problems (one of the most common presenting concerns; Burke, 1997), career transitions (Lavallee & Andersen, 2000), or any one of many other issues athletes may have. In many cases, what you see is what you get. The first presenting problem *is* the problem. In other cases, however, the presenting concern is really more of a means to an end. And that end is for athletes to get up the nerve to discuss what is really troubling them. If there is a "latent" presenting issue, it may contain more negative emotional valence than the manifest one, such as depression (Cogan, 2000), victimization, or confusion about sexuality. Henschen (1998) called the latent concern "the issue behind the issue," because the manifest issue, just as in manifest and latent contents in psychodynamic dream analysis, is often only the surface of a deeper and more personal problem.

Unfortunately, it is not always easy to find a presenting concern. Athletes are sent to sport psychologists by coaches with nothing much more to go on than "the coach wanted me to see you" (see Andersen, 2000, for how such an awkward start to service delivery might proceed). In such a case, exploration of the athlete's experiences will have to be done to find out how the psychologist could be helpful. When some focus for the work with the psychologist has been established, two questions about "match" usually follow. First, Do the presenting concerns of the athlete and the skills and knowledge of the sport psychologist match? That is, Does the sport psychologist have the "gear" to help the athlete? If the answer is no, then the psychologist should offer the athlete an appropriate referral (see Van Raalte & Andersen, chapter 16, this volume). If the answer is yes, then the second question of match arises: Can we work together? The answer to that question is not as easy to answer as the previous one. Whether two people can work together is determined by multiple issues such as rapport building, transference and countertransference, theoretical orientations, interpersonal styles, and time. It takes time to build a relationship, and relationships are at the core of service delivery. Probably no single factor in service delivery is more important to positive outcome than the quality of the relationship between the sport psychologist and the athlete (see Petitpas, Danish, & Giges, 1999).

It may take weeks to answer the question of working together. For some sport psychologists and athletes who really hit it off, however, the question may be answered more quickly.

Preconceptions and Expectations

The negative perceptions that some athletes have about psychology and psychological services (Van Raalte, Brewer, Brewer, & Linder, 1992) can greatly affect the possibility of an effective working relationship. In the first meeting, the sport psychologist may need to spend time directly addressing some potential anxieties about the work (e.g., "I'll have to talk about my mother"; "The sport psychologist is going to see right through me"; "I'm going to have to dredge up my entire childhood"). Setting athletes at ease can occur directly by letting them know what is *not* expected. It is also beneficial to lay out what service delivery will be about. The following is an example of a sport psychologist setting the stage for a working relationship with a diver and discussing some anxieties the athlete may have about their work together:

> My job here is to talk to athletes about how things are going for them and see if there are ways we can work together to make their athletic involvement more enjoyable and to help with some of the mental aspects of training and competition. What I usually like to do is first hear about you, how you got into diving, what in diving really makes you happy, what's a pain in the butt, how things are going with teammates and coaches, and so forth. And everything we talk about is just between you and me. Nothing we say to each other has to go outside this room unless you want it to. Later, I'd like to tell you a bit about some of the work I've done with other athletes so you can get a feel for what we do around here. How does that sound? (Andersen, 2000, p. 6)

The sport psychologist in this example has communicated a simple plan, telling the athlete that any negative preconceptions will not eventuate and that working together for the happiness and well-being of the athlete is the core of what the service is all about. Thus, the message is, "Expect that we will be in a collaborative effort to help make your sporting experience even better than it already is."

Later in this first meeting, the sport psychologist can turn to more specific expectations. Toward the end of the session, the psychologist may sum up what has been discussed so far. This process of retelling the athletes' stories serves several purposes: (a) It lets athletes know they have been heard and understood, (b) it gives athletes the chance to fill in any gaps or correct psychologist misperceptions about their stories, and (c) it sets the stage for the psychologist to make suggestions about how they might work together as a team. Finally, the sport psychologist can start to lay out a potential plan of action with the athlete's help (e.g., relaxation, goal setting, self-talk monitoring). Whatever the plan is, it will stem from the athlete's story and the psychologist's assessment based on his or her theoretical orientation. A plan helps foster positive expectations about the future, and those positive expectations are also part of the treatment package.

Assessment

Plans do not appear in a formulaic manner from a sport psychology cookbook. As stated previously, they stem from the athlete's story and the theoretical orientation of the psychologist. Theoretical orientations place a framework around the athlete's story that leads psychologists to assessments and ultimately to plans of action that play themselves out in the context of the working alliance. Assessment will differ depending on which theory guides the psychologist. For example, behaviorists do not usually probe for information on intrapsychic conflict (Wolpe, 1973). They would look for and assess the important variables involved in understanding and changing behavior. A psychologist oriented toward rational–emotive behavior therapy (e.g., Ellis, 1994) would look for stories that indicate maladaptive thinking, and the assessment (and the resulting plan) would most likely be solidly grounded in cognitive theory. Psychodynamically oriented psychologists (e.g., Strean & Strean, 1998) would look for stories about relationships, how past early experiences influence present functioning, and how transference and countertransference work in the psychologist–athlete dyad and in other relationships in the athlete's life (e.g., with coaches, teammates, and parents). In this case, the intervention, or plan, would be "insight" oriented. Theory drives assessment, but some features of assessment also can apply to several theoretical orientations.

Assessment Instruments

The sport psychology literature is filled with a panoply of assessment tools, most of them in the "paper-and-pencil" category. These instruments can be used to assess competitive state and trait anxiety, physical self-description, mood, life events, sport motivation, and so forth. Most of these instruments have been used primarily in research settings. However, applied sport psychologists often find that standardized assessment tools are useful to help athletes talk about themselves. Especially with a taciturn or laconic athlete, it can be helpful to have an assessment tool that the athlete has completed, so the psychologist can say, "You know, this questionnaire is saying that when you are in pressure situations you seem to. . . . Does that sound like you?" Having a third-party data source (the assessment tool) can encourage quiet athletes to fill in the details of their stories.

One important shortcoming of assessment tools in sport psychology is that most have not been related to or calibrated with meaningful variables such as performance, functionality, and quality of life (Sechrest, McKnight, & McKnight, 1996). For example, in a recent book on measurement and assessment in sport psychology, the word *calibration* does not appear (Duda, 1998). Thus, if one finds an average six-point drop in cognitive anxiety on the Competitive State Anxiety Inventory–2 (CSAI–2; Martens, Burton, Vealey, Bump, & Smith, 1990) after an intervention, one still does not know how such a change translates into behavior (e.g., performance). Is that change large enough to produce a meaningful difference in performance? But the really big question is, Is that change due to the intervention worth paying for? For more information on assessment and psychometrics in sport psychology, see McCann, Jowdy, and Van Raalte, chapter 14, this volume.

Field Assessment

Sport psychologists operate in a world that is looser, in terms of temporal and spatial parameters, than their colleagues in typical counseling and clinical psychology settings (Andersen, Van Raalte, & Brewer, 2001). Sport psychologists are out on the playing fields, in the gym, at poolside, on the bus to a game, and in the sports medicine clinic with injured athletes. Observing athletes and coaches in these social and competitive situations supplies a wealth of data for assessment (e.g., how players perform at home versus away games, how coach behavior changes from practice to competition, how group dynamics work for or against team performance). This familiarity has its advantages (e.g., a lot of data on the athlete's world) and disadvantages (e.g., boundary issues, dual-role challenges). See Hays and Smith (chapter 23), Andersen (chapter 18), and Baillie and Ogilvie (chapter 19), this volume, for further discussion of boundary issues in sport and exercise psychology.

Needs Assessment

When developing a sport psychology intervention with an athlete or team, it is particularly important to identify their needs rather than to assume that they should be provided with a particular preselected service or intervention such as precompetition mental preparation, goal setting, or anxiety management training. A needs assessment discussion with a coach might begin by asking her to talk about the strengths and weaknesses of her team collectively and her players individually. Invariably, the stories will have psychological components that give entry points to let coaches know how the sport psychologist may be helpful for their specific needs. It is probably wise to keep in mind that "the consumer is always right." The coaches and the athletes are the experts. They know what they need, and it is the job of sport psychologists to help them express those needs (i.e., tell their stories) and then to provide services directed at fulfilling those needs and helping them get better at what they do.

Goal Setting

Goal setting has repeatedly shown itself to be an effective technique for initiating and maintaining behavior change. This section is not on goal setting for athletes, however, it is about the goals sport psychologists set for themselves and the athletes. When a sport psychologist and an athlete get together, goal setting has probably already begun on several conscious and unconscious levels. The athlete may have a conscious goal of getting over prerace anxiety and an unconscious one of finding someone to love and care for him. The psychologist may have a goal of securing another paying client or of connecting with someone who will admire her. Of course, some of these goals are never stated, or even fully understood, but they are goals nonetheless. Like the goals in a formal goal-setting exercise, they motivate behavior (see Marchant, 2000; Weinberg, chapter 3, this volume).

The goals of comprehensive sport psychology service delivery are the overall goals of service itself. Why are sport psychologists in the sport psychology game? What are sport psychologists trying to accomplish? What outcomes do we hope to bring about when the athlete leaves us for the last time? Recently, a colleague, an exercise physiologist, was in a meeting with other exercise physiologists. The meeting was called, in part, to determine goals for the exercise physiology unit (actually, they wanted to formulate a solid rationale for the existence of the unit). Many suggestions were made for improving athlete training, improving performance, and increasing medal counts at the Olympics—all ideas closely linked with the sentiments of *citius, altius,* and *fortius.* The psychologist then stood up and said, "I think our main mission is to try and make athletes and coaches happy." When asked to explain further, he said,

We offer a service aimed at helping athletes get better at their sports, but the final measure of all our efforts is whether the coaches and athletes are pleased with the service. Are they happy with how we have interacted with them? Are they happy with the information and suggestions we have offered? Performance outcome on any given day is mercurial, and even though performance improvements are definitely linked to happiness, the real measure of how we are doing our jobs is whether the athletes and coaches are happy with us and what we offer and want to come back.

What this colleague said is directly applicable to sport psychology services.

The goals of a sport psychologist can also have a dark side. Some students and practitioners drop names of clients, are looking for fame, want to rub shoulders with the internationally elite, and work hard at making athletes dependent on them. In these cases, the goal-setting program is focused on promoting the needs of sport psychologists at the expense of the needs of the athletes and coaches with whom they work. Careful examination of the goals (both manifest and latent) of sport psychologists is necessary. Comprehensive care of athletes and coaches requires comprehensive scrutiny of the main tools of service: the personality and character of the caregiver. The mode of such scrutiny is supervision. Supervision in sport psychology is too broad to cover here, but the central issue is that comprehensive care of athletes involves a net (i.e., the supervisor) for psychologists when they are unsure of how to proceed or are in psychological trouble themselves (Andersen, Van Raalte, & Brewer, 2000; Andersen, Van Raalte, & Harris, 2000; Van Raalte & Andersen, 2000). The main goal of supervision is always the care and welfare of the athlete; no program of athlete service delivery is truly comprehensive without supervision.

Getting With the Program

Once the athletes' or coaches' stories have been constructed to the point where the sport psychologist can begin to see adaptive and maladaptive patterns of behavior and thinking, the question becomes what sorts of interventions (e.g., relaxation, goal setting) and at what levels (e.g., individual, team, organizational) will help. Regardless of theoretical orientation, the development of a cooperative two-way relationship between the psychologist and the athlete serves as the foundation for any intervention. Central to the success of interventions is the evolving of a "we," a kind of collaborative empiricism where sport psychologist and athlete (or coach, or team) are involved in a joint "investigation" of some phenomena (e.g., the athlete's behavior) in an effort to understand and change those phenomena in a manner that leaves the client with more and better resources for the future, and probably makes the client happier.

A variety of interventions are available for sport psychologists to use in congruence with their theoretical orientations and their comprehension of athletes' stories (e.g., cognitive skill development, somatic techniques, educational group [team] interventions, personal counselling, psychotherapy, family interventions). The number and kinds of interventions are legion. Before using any intervention, it is essential to have a clear picture of the situation from the athlete's point of view and to fully understand the context of the situation. Without a complete picture, a psychologist may choose an intervention doomed to fail. For example, a young athlete says he is terribly anxious before races to the point of being physically sick. The sport psychologist therefore prescribes relaxation. The athlete enthusiastically embraces relaxation and practices diligently every night (he really likes his sport psychologist, which fuels his adherence). Before the next race, he throws up, just as in the past, and it happens in the next race, too. The problem is that the psychologist did not engage the athlete in a collaborative effort. If the discussion between the two had gone further, the sport psychologist may have learned that when the athlete performed poorly, his father would not speak to him for days and would even leave the room when the athlete entered. No amount of relaxation was going to compensate for what the boy felt when he was denied his father's love.

Another reason to be cautious about intervening too quickly is that if the intervention fails, the athlete may not return for further consultation. Many athletes have significant time constraints, and if work with a sport psychologist seems unproductive, they will find something else to do. Partly because of the stigma attached to seeing a sport psychologist (Linder, Brewer, Van Raalte, & DeLange, 1991), athletes often attempt to solve their problems themselves. They may try suggestions from teammates, parents, and coaches and also may read assorted books, articles, and Web sites. Thus, the "obvious" intervention (e.g., relaxation) may have already been tried. It is useful for sport psychologists to discuss in detail with the athlete what solutions for the problem have already been attempted. If an intervention does fail, all is not lost.

A failed intervention is fertile ground for further collaborative efforts to find a solution.

Although the ideal sport psychology interventions are generally developed through extensive discussion with teams or athletes, some occasions do warrant the quick fix, or "Band-Aid," intervention. For example, the "sport psyching" team at the New York City Marathon works with athletes in the three hours immediately before the race. Interactions with sport psychologists are typically 5 to 10 minutes. Runners are often overwhelmed by the prospect of the upcoming marathon. The gift of a piece of the finish line tape to serve as inspiration during the race, some suggestions for positive self-talk, and friendly reassurance —all quick fixes—can be useful sport psychology interventions for competition situations.

Termination

Comprehensive care has a beginning (intake, story telling, assessment), a middle (treatment, intervention), and an end (termination). Often, sport psychology service has a "built-in" termination time, especially for those who work with university teams (e.g., the athlete graduates and moves on). In some cases, termination occurs after two or three sessions because the athlete got what he needed, learned a new skill, and returned to his sport a bit more sure of himself. In these cases, termination is relatively easy and painless. In cases in which a long-term close relationship exists between psychologist and athlete, termination brings up several issues for both parties.

Sport psychologists are in the business of working with athletes for a variety of reasons. A common thread among practitioners is the desire to help others, and most psychologists are helpful to their clients. There comes a time, however, when the athlete does not need more help, and that is the time for termination. It is the job of sport psychologists to put themselves out of their jobs. How sport psychologists go about leaving their jobs requires some care. Psychologists and clients, because they have been in close, collaborative relationships, form attachments to each other in the dance of transference and countertransference. Letting go, for either party, may be difficult, may be tinged with anger or sadness, or may be a time of client regression (Quintana, 1993).

Keeping an athlete in one's care when the athlete is not benefiting is unethical. Fortunately, this type of nontermination is not common.

More usual is the situation in which the psychologist and the athlete feel some sadness and loss but generally are happy with the work they have done together. Under supervision, psychologists can get help with their own feelings and thoughts about the termination process.

Preparing the athlete for termination should begin early in service delivery, with conversations about the goals of the work, the repeated assessment of those goals, and once the goals are reached, the establishment of new goals or the initiation of termination. Recounting for the athlete all the gains made and letting the athlete know how the psychologist feels and thinks about their time together can help the termination process along.

With early preparation, adverse reactions to ending relationships may be substantially reduced. Many sport psychologists offer a gradual "weaning" type of termination. For example, instead of attending once-a-week sessions, athletes may start to attend every other week, then monthly, and then on an as-needed, or "booster-shot," basis, so there is no defined termination point.

Conclusion

There is no formula for comprehensive care of athletes. The topics presented and discussed in this chapter (i.e., how to get started, assessment, interventions, termination) provide an overview of some of the more important elements necessary for constructing sport psychology interventions. The other chapters in this part of the book provide in-depth coverage of goal setting, imagery, cognitive strategies, arousal regulation, observational learning, and hypnosis. Continued thought, research, and discussion are warranted to create comprehensive sport psychology interventions that best serve the needs of athletes and coaches.

References

Andersen, M. B. (2000). Beginnings: Intakes and the initiation of relationships. In M. B. Andersen (Ed.), *Doing sport psychology* (pp. 3–16). Champaign, IL: Human Kinetics.

Andersen, M. B., Van Raalte, J. L., & Brewer, B. W. (2000). When sport psychology consultants and graduate students are impaired: Ethical and legal issues in training and supervision. *Journal of Applied Sport Psychology, 12,* 134–150.

Andersen, M. B., Van Raalte, J. L., & Brewer, B. W. (2001). Sport psychology service delivery: Staying ethical while keeping loose. *Professional Psychology: Research and Practice, 32,* 12–18.

Andersen, M. B., Van Raalte, J. L., & Harris, G. (2000). Supervision II: A case study. In M. B. Andersen (Ed.), *Doing sport psychology* (pp. 167–180). Champaign, IL: Human Kinetics.

Burke, K. L. (1997). Communication in sports: Research and practice. *Journal of Interdisciplinary Research in Physical Education, 2,* 39–52.

Cogan, K. (2000). The sadness in sport: Working with a depressed and suicidal athlete. In M. B. Andersen (Ed.), *Doing sport psychology* (pp. 121–137). Champaign, IL: Human Kinetics.

Duda, J. L. (Ed.). (1998). *Advances in sport and exercise psychology measurement.* Morgantown, WV: Fitness Information Technology.

Ellis, A. (1994). The sport of avoiding sport and exercise: A rational–emotive behavior therapy perspective. *The Sport Psychologist, 8,* 248–261.

Henschen, K. P. (1998). The issue behind the issue. In M. A. Thompson, R. A. Vernacchia, & W. E. Moore (Eds.), *Case studies in sport psychology: An educational approach* (pp. 27–34). Dubuque, IA: Kendall/Hunt.

Lavallee, D., & Andersen, M. B. (2000). Leaving sport: Easing career transitions. In M. B. Andersen (Ed.), *Doing sport psychology* (pp. 249–260). Champaign, IL: Human Kinetics.

Linder, D. E., Brewer, B. W., Van Raalte, J. L., & DeLange, N. (1991). A negative halo for athletes who consult sport psychologists: Replication and extension. *Journal of Sport and Exercise Psychology, 13,* 133–148.

Marchant, D. (2000). Goal setting for professional sport. In M. B. Andersen (Ed.), *Doing sport psychology* (pp. 93–103). Champaign, IL: Human Kinetics.

Martens, R., Burton, D., Vealey, R., Bump, L., & Smith, D. (1990). The development of the Competitive State Anxiety Inventory–2 (CSAI–2). In R. Martens, R. S. Vealey, & D. Burton (Eds.), *Competitive anxiety in sport* (pp. 117–190). Champaign, IL: Human Kinetics.

Petitpas, A. J., Danish, S. J., & Giges, B. (1999). The sport psychologist–athlete relationship: Implications for training. *The Sport Psychologist, 13,* 344–357.

Poczwardowski, A., Sherman, C. P., & Henschen, K. P. (1998). A sport psychology service delivery heuristic: Building on theory and practice. *The Sport Psychologist, 12,* 191–207.

Quintana, S. M. (1993). Toward an expanded and updated conceptualization of termination: Implications for short-term, individual psychotherapy. *Professional Psychology: Research and Practice, 24,* 426–432.

Sechrest, L., McKnight, P., & McKnight, K. (1996). Calibration of measures for psychotherapy outcome studies. *American Psychologist, 51,* 1065–1071.

Sherman, C. P., & Poczwardowski, A. (2000). Relax! . . . It ain't easy (or is it?). In M. B. Andersen (Ed.), *Doing sport psychology* (pp. 47–60). Champaign, IL: Human Kinetics.

Strean, W. B., & Strean, H. S. (1998). Applying psychodynamic concepts to sport psychology practice. *The Sport Psychologist, 12,* 208–222.

Van Raalte, J. L., & Andersen, M. B. (2000). Supervision I: From models to doing. In M. B. Andersen (Ed.), *Doing sport psychology* (pp. 153–166). Champaign, IL: Human Kinetics.

Van Raalte, J. L., Brewer, B. W., Brewer, D. D., & Linder, D. E. (1992). NCAA Division II college football players' perceptions of an athlete who consults a sport psychologist. *Journal of Sport and Exercise Psychology, 14,* 273–282.

Wolpe, J. (1973). *The practice of behavior therapy* (2nd ed.). New York: Pergamon Press.

Goal Setting in Sport and Exercise: Research to Practice

Robert S. Weinberg

My goal is to improve my average golf score from 85 to 80.

* * *

My objective is to reduce my unforced errors in tennis matches from 30 to 20.

* * *

Our goal is to go to the state championships.

* * *

I want to be able to bench press 200 pounds.

These statements are just a few examples of different types of goals that athletes set in an attempt to improve their performance. Sport psychologists do not typically have a problem getting athletes to set goals, unlike some other psychological tasks. Rather, they have difficulty getting athletes to set the right kind of goals, that is, goals that enhance motivation. Athletes typically do not need to be convinced that goals are important, but they may need instruction in setting the most effective types of goals and developing a goal-setting program that works.

This chapter takes a research-to-practice approach to help individuals involved in sport and exercise learn more about effective goal setting. The chapter begins with definitions of different types of goals, a discussion of goal-setting theory, and the latest goal-setting research. From this research, principles of effective goal setting are identified, methods of designing a goal-setting program are presented, and common problems and ways to overcome them are discussed.

The Concept of Goal Setting

By definition, a *goal* is that which an individual is trying to accomplish; it is the object or aim of an action. For example, in most goal-setting studies, the term refers to attaining a specific level of proficiency in a task, usually within a specified time limit (Locke, Shaw, Saari, & Latham, 1981). From a practical point of view, goals focus on standards of excellence, such as improving free-throw percentage by 5 points, losing 10 pounds, lowering the time in the mile run by 4 seconds, or improving batting average by 20 points. In addition, these goals would have to be reached within a given time frame, such as by the end of the season or within a certain number of days, weeks, or months.

In sport and exercise, the types of goals set by participants and coaches vary in degree of specificity and difficulty in measuring success. This variation has led sport psychologists to distinguish between outcome, performance, and process goals. *Outcome goals* usually refer to winning and losing, such as a goal to come in first place in the swim meet or to win the state championship. Thus, achieving the goal depends, at least in part, on the ability and play of the opponent. *Performance goals* refer to an athlete's actual performance in relation to his or her own standard of excellence. For example, athletes may wish to improve their first-serve percentage from 50% to 60%, knock off two seconds in the 400-meter medley, or improve their high jump from 6 feet 4 inches to 6 feet 10 inches. All of these goals are under the control of the athlete and are not dependent on winning and losing as with outcome goals. *Process goals* refer to how an athlete performs a particular skill; thus, athletes often focus on these goals in practice. For example, a process goal in tennis might be to bend one's knees when hitting a low shot and in baseball it might be to keep the bat straight up when waiting for the pitch (of course, percentages can be placed on these process goals to make them more specific). Although cases can be made to focus on one type of goal or another, all three types of goals can be effective in enhancing performance and having a positive effect on behavior.

Goal-Setting Theory

Much of the early work on goal setting originated from two major sources, one academic and one organizational. The academic source extends back to the early 1960s and focuses on the associated concepts of intention, task set, and level of aspiration (for a review, see Ryan, 1970). The organizational line of research can be traced to the work of Taylor (1911/1967), in which the concept of task (a specific assignment or goal given to a worker each day) eventually led to the application of goal setting in the form of management-by-objectives programs now widely used in industrial settings (Ordiorne, 1978).

Using these early sources as building blocks, Locke and his colleagues (Locke, 1966, 1968, 1978; Locke et al., 1981; Locke & Latham, 1990) developed a theory of goal setting that has served as the stimulus for literally hundreds of studies in industrial and organizational settings and, more recently, in sport and exercise settings. The basic assumption of goal-setting theory is that task performance is regulated directly by the conscious goals that individuals are trying for on a task. In essence, goals are immediate regulators of human action. Goals operate largely through internal comparison processes and require internal standards against which to evaluate ongoing performance.

According to the theory, difficult goals result in a higher level of performance and effort than easy goals, and specific difficult goals result in a higher level of performance than no goals or generalized goals of "do your best." In addition, the theory states that a person's goals mediate how performance is affected by monetary incentives, time limits, knowledge of results, participation in decision making, degree of commitment, and competition. Locke argued that, although goals can influence behavior, no simple correlation between goals and behavior can be assumed, because people make errors, lack the ability to attain their objectives, or subconsciously subvert their conscious goals. Note that, although most research on the relationship between goal setting and performance has been to test the propositions put forth by Locke, other theories have been developed. These include cognitive mediation theory (Garland, 1985); goal orientation theory (Nicholls, 1984a, 1984b; Maehr & Braskamp, 1986); and the competitive goal-setting model (Burton, 1992), which is discussed later in the chapter.

Goal Setting and Task Performance in Industrial Settings

Research on goal setting as a motivational strategy has proliferated so rapidly in the past 25 years that reviews have often used the statistical technique of meta-analysis to aggregate findings across studies (e.g.,

Locke & Latham, 1990; Mento, Steel, & Karren, 1987; Tubbs, 1991). The most tested aspect of Locke's theory revolves around the relationship of goal difficulty/specificity and performance. As previously mentioned, Locke (1966, 1968) argued that specific, difficult, challenging goals lead to higher levels of task performance than do easy goals, no goals, or "do your best" goals. Locke and Latham reviewed 201 studies (more than 40,000 participants). Of these studies, 91% supported Locke's initial hypothesis. These results were found by using approximately 90 different tasks in both laboratory and field settings, which demonstrates the robustness and generalness of the findings.

A second core aspect of Locke's goal-setting theory is a linear relationship exists between degree of goal difficulty and performance. The only exception is when participants reach the limits of their ability at high goal difficulty levels; in such cases, performance levels off. Three separate meta-analyses of the empirical studies testing the relationship between goal difficulty and performance have been done (Chidester & Grigsby, 1984; Mento, Steel, & Karren, 1987; Tubbs, 1991). Results from these meta-analyses have revealed effect sizes ranging from 0.52 to 0.82. In addition, of the 192 studies reviewed, 175 (91%) provided support for harder goals producing higher levels of task performance than do easy goals. Thus, the goal difficulty/specificity and performance relationships found in industrial settings provide one of the most consistent and robust patterns of findings in the social science literature.

Goal Setting in Sport and Exercise

Although considerable research has been conducted on goal setting in industrial and organizational settings, only in the past 10 to 15 years have sport and exercise psychology researchers begun to examine the topic. A systematic and concerted effort to study this relationship began with the publication of Locke and Latham's (1985) article on the application of goal setting to sports. Locke and Latham suggested that goal setting could work even better in sports than in business because the measurement of an individual's performance is typically more objective in sports than in organizational settings. Following the emphasis in industrial psychology, goal-setting research in sport and exercise has focused on the areas of goal specificity, goal difficulty, and goal proximity.

These areas have been investigated using a variety of skill and physical fitness tasks, such as the number of sit-ups that can be done in 3 minutes, basketball skills, lacrosse, circuit training, and swimming. However, results have been equivocal; some studies have demonstrated support for goal-setting effectiveness and others have not (for detailed reviews, see Burton, 1992; Weinberg, 1992, 1994). An example of the inconsistent findings is found in a study by Burton (1989), which investigated the effects of specific or general goals on fundamental basketball skills (e.g., dribbling, shooting, footwork) of varying complexity. Results indicated that setting specific goals, as compared with general goals, enhanced performance. However, performance was not enhanced on all tasks, and, in fact, higher performance was evidenced on tasks of low complexity than on tasks of high complexity.

Despite the somewhat mixed results in sport and exercise settings, it would be premature and inappropriate to conclude that goal setting is a less powerful technique than has been suggested by the industrial and organizational psychology literatures. Weinberg (1994) argued that the inconsistent findings are at least in part because of the different methodologies used in sport and exercise settings along with variables that mediate the relationship between goal setting and performance. Some of the methodological and design considerations include spontaneous goal setting in control groups, participant motivation and commitment, task characteristics, and competition among participants. Furthermore, athletes and exercise participants are simply different in their motivations and perform under different task conditions than do participants in other goal-setting studies. Thus, it is incumbent on sport and exercise researchers to investigate the conditions under which goal-setting techniques are most effective.

Along these lines, the perceived effectiveness of goal setting was demonstrated in surveys conducted with leading sport psychology consultants working with U.S. Olympic athletes. Results revealed that goal setting was one of the most often used psychological interventions in individual, athlete–coach, and group consultations (Gould, Tammen, Murphy, & May, 1989; Sullivan & Nashman, 1998). In addition, results from Orlick and Partington's (1988) extensive study of Canadian Olympic athletes also demonstrate the use of goal setting as athletes reported daily goal setting as part of their regular training regimen. Furthermore, a recent review (Burton, Naylor, & Holliday, 2001) found that 44 of 56 (78.6%) published goal-setting studies conducted in sport and exercise settings found moderate to strong goal-setting effects.

Overall, it seems that goal setting is an extremely powerful technique for enhancing performance. For example, several intervention studies conducted across athletic seasons revealed that setting specific, attainable, moderately difficult goals led to higher levels of performance than that found in equivalent control conditions (Kingston & Hardy, 1997; Swain & Jones, 1995; Weinberg, Stitcher, & Richardson, 1994). In addition, recent studies using athlete populations (e.g., Burton, Weinberg, Yukelson, & Weigand, 1998; Filby, Maynard, & Graydon, 1999; Weinberg, Burke, & Jackson, 1997; Weinberg, Burton, Yukelson, & Weigand, 2000) as well as a meta-analysis (Kyllo & Landers, 1995) have demonstrated that the goal-setting literature in sport and exercise settings reveals certain consistencies:

- Almost all athletes use some type of goal setting to enhance performance and find these goals to be moderately to highly effective.
- Athletes using multiple goal strategies exhibit the best performances.
- Athletes and coaches are not systematic in writing down their goals.
- The primary reason for setting goals is to provide direction and focus.
- Major barriers to achieving goals include lack of time, stress, fatigue, academic pressures, and social relationships.
- Goals should be moderately difficult, challenging, and realistic.
- Athletes should focus on process as opposed to outcome goals.
- Athletes should use both short-term and long-term goals.
- Goal commitment and acceptance is important in keeping motivation high over time.
- Action plans facilitate the effective implementation of goal-setting strategies.

Thus, it is clear from research and professional practice literature that, as with most sport psychology techniques, goal setting can be effective in enhancing performance. However, these research studies have revealed that goal setting is not a foolproof method that can be easily implemented without some careful thought and planning. As a result, individuals who attempt to implement goal-setting programs in sport and exercise situations should be knowledgeable professionals with a firm understanding of the goal-setting process. It is especially important that each practitioner possess a keen understanding of his or her individual circumstances (e.g., type of sport, individual personalities of participants) to implement goal-setting programs most effectively.

Explanations for the Effectiveness of Goal Setting

Two general categories of explanations have been advanced to explain how goals influence performance. These explanations are known as the mechanistic view and the cognitive view.

Mechanistic Explanation

The mechanistic explanation for the effectiveness of goals on enhancing performance was put forth by Locke and colleagues (Locke et al., 1981). They argued that goals influence performance in four distinct ways: (a) directing attention, (b) mobilizing effort, (c) enhancing persistence, and (d) developing new learning strategies. One way that goals can influence performance is by directing an individual's attention to the task and the relevant cues in the athletic or exercise environment. In fact, college and Olympic athletes have reported that the most important reason they set goals is to focus attention on the task at hand (Weinberg, Burton, Yukelson, & Weigand, 1993; Weinberg et al., 2000). For example, if a basketball player sets a goal to improve his field goal percentage, foul shot percentage, rebounds, and assists, then undoubtedly he would focus his attention in these specific game areas. In essence, the basketball player's attention is focused on important elements of his game that need to be improved.

In addition to focusing attention, goals also increase effort and persistence by providing feedback in relation to one's progress. For example, a long-distance runner may not feel like putting in the required mileage day after day or may feel bored with the repetitive routine of training. But by setting short-term goals and seeing progress toward her long-term goal, motivation can be maintained on a day-by-day basis as well as over time. Similarly, losing 60 pounds might seem like an impossible task for an obese person who has been overweight much of his life. However, by setting a goal to lose two pounds a week and charting this subgoal accomplishment, the individual can stay motivated and persist with the weight loss program for the time required.

The final mechanism by which goals can influence performance is through the development of relevant learning strategies. That is, when goals are set, strategies should be put in place by coaches or athletes to help reach the goals. This is one of the areas in which both coaches and athletes could be more diligent and detailed in designing strategies to meet goals. For example, if a basketball player has a goal to improve her free-throw percentage from 70% to 75%, she might invoke the strategy of shooting an extra 100 free throws each day or of changing her preshot routine or even changing her mechanics of shooting. In any case, new strategies are developed to help the player obtain her free-throw shooting goal.

Cognitive Explanation

A more recent explanation of how goals influence performance comes from the work of Garland (1985), Burton (1989, 1992), and Pierce and Burton (1998). These researchers argued that such psychological states as anxiety, confidence, and satisfaction affect one's goal setting and subsequent performance. For example, Burton (1989) claimed that athletes who set outcome goals that are based on winning and losing will experience more anxiety and less confidence in competitive settings because their goals are really not under their control. That is, if a swimmer sets a goal to come in first in a race and breaks her personal best by 2 seconds but only places third in the race, she would not be satisfied with her performance. This could result in increased anxiety and decreased confidence because the swimmer has little control over the outcome. Conversely, a swimmer who sets a goal to reduce his swimming time by 2 seconds can feel confident about his performance if he reaches this goal even if he comes in third.

This cognitive explanation for the effects of goal setting on performance was supported in a study of intercollegiate swimmers (Burton, 1989). Specifically, swimmers participated in a five-month goal-setting program that emphasized the setting of performance goals (referenced against one's own self-improvement) versus outcome goals focused on winning or place of finish. Results indicated that swimmers who had high ability to set performance goals were less anxious and exhibited better performance compared with those with low ability. Not only do these results demonstrate the importance of setting performance goals, but they also suggest that proper goal setting is a psychological skill that needs to be learned and practiced.

Another cognitive explanation of how goals relate to behavior and performance—goal orientation theory—has been championed by several psychologists (Dweck, 1986; Maehr & Braskamp, 1986; Nicholls, 1984a, 1984b) as well as by sport and exercise psychologists (Duda, 1992; Roberts, 1992). Goal orientation theory predicts that an individual's achievement goals and perceived ability interact to affect achievement-related behaviors. Specifically, it is suggested that an individual's goal perspective will affect self-evaluations of demonstrated ability, expended effort, and attributions for success and failure. In turn, these cognitions are assumed to influence achievement-related affect, strategies, and subsequent behaviors such as performance, task choice, and persistence.

Research has identified two major goal perspectives: ego orientation and task orientation. Individuals with ego orientations derive their notions of ability from success and failure. In essence, their competence is other-referenced, with the goal being to outdo others rather than simply improving. Conversely, individuals with task orientations derive their perceptions of ability and competence from improvements in their own performance. That is, competence is seen as self-referenced, with personal improvement and effort viewed as critical to their perception of ability. Thus, task-oriented individuals will tend to set goals that are realistic, because they are focused on self-improvement rather than the performance of others. These two goal perspectives are not seen as independent. For example, research has indicated that elite athletes are high in both task and ego orientations (Duda & Whitehead, 1998). In summary, research on goal perspectives underscores the notion that individuals' perceptions of ability depend largely on their subjective interpretation of success and failure. This, in turn, affects goal-directed behavior in sport and exercise environments. For example, if an athlete is primarily task-oriented then practices should be set up to focus on personal improvement. If an athlete is outcome-oriented then adding competition on top of personal improvement would help enhance motivation of the group.

Goal-Setting Principles

It is apparent from the theoretical and empirical research reviewed that goal setting can enhance performance and personal growth in sport and exercise environments. It is misleading to think, however, that all types of goals are equally effective in achieving these ends. For example, as already noted, goal orientation theory would predict that athletes and exercisers who have a task orientation would set more realistic goals, persist more in the face of failure, and have more control of reaching their goals than would individuals with a predominantly ego orientation. But as recent research (Filby et al., 1999; Kingston & Hardy,

---

Exhibit 3.1

Goal-Setting Principles

1. Set specific goals.
2. Set realistic, but challenging, goals.
3. Set both long- and short-term goals.
4. Set goals for practice and competition.
5. "Ink it, don't think it."
6. Develop goal achievement strategies.
7. Set performance goals.
8. Set individual and team goals.
9. Provide support for goals.
10. Provide for goal evaluation.

1997; Weinberg et al., 2000) indicates, it is how these different goals interact that is the crucial factor, not just having one or the other type of goal. Furthermore, not only is the orientation of the participation important, but so is the motivational climate created by the teacher or coach (Ntoumanis & Biddle, 1999). Specifically, it has been found that task-oriented climates encourage more adaptive motivational patterns such as increased effort and positive attitudes of participants.

The key, therefore, is to structure goal-setting programs to make them consistent with the basic principles derived from the organizational and sport psychology literatures as well as from professional practice knowledge of sport and exercise psychologists working in field settings. But it is important to keep in mind that the effectiveness of any motivational technique is dependent on the interaction of the individuals and the situation in which the individuals are placed. Thus, the goal-setting principles listed in Exhibit 3.1 and discussed subsequently should be considered within this context.

Set Specific Goals

One of the most consistent findings from the goal-setting literature is that specific goals produce higher levels of task performance than no goals or general "do your best" goals (Weinberg & Weigand, 1993). Athletes often hear coaches and teachers tell participants simply to "go out and do your best." Although this type of instruction can be motivating, it is not as powerful in enhancing motivation and performance as is encouraging participants to go out and achieve a specific goal.

Furthermore, when giving performers specific goals, it is important that the goals be measurable and put in behavioral terms. For example, telling a tennis player to improve her first-serve percentage would not be as helpful as telling her to improve her percentage from 50% to 60% by tossing the ball out in front. This gives the player a specific goal to shoot for and a way to measure whether she achieved the goal. To take an exercise example, it does not help much to tell an individual taking a weight training class that the goal is to become stronger. Rather, a specific goal of increasing the amount he can bench press by 25% over the next three months would be more useful.

Set Realistic But Challenging Goals

Another of the consistent findings from the research literature is that goals should be challenging and difficult, yet attainable (Locke & Latham, 1990). Goals that are too easy do not present a challenge to the individual, which leads to less than maximum effort. This, in turn, might result in being satisfied with a mediocre performance instead of extending oneself to reach one's potential. Conversely, setting goals that are too difficult and unrealistic will often result in failure. This can lead to frustration, lowered self-confidence and motivation, and decreased performance. For example, many high school and college athletes have goals and aspirations of becoming professional athletes. Unfortunately, fewer than 1% will ever reach this goal (Coakley, 1997); thus, the majority of these athletes are doomed to fail and may develop motivational problems. This is not to say that athletes should not strive to do their best or aspire for a professional career. Rather, a realistic look at one's abilities and chances of success are needed within the context of that dream goal of becoming a professional athlete. Thus, the secret is to find a balance between setting oneself up for failure and pushing oneself to strive for success. In this middle ground reside challenging, realistic, attainable goals.

Those who have been athletes, coaches, and teachers understand that striking this balance between goal difficulty and achievability is no easy task. For example, it is critical for sport psychologists to know the capabilities and motivation of athletes when attempting to help them set realistic goals. Sometimes this is a trial-and-error process. Sport and exercise professionals can help athletes in goal setting by offering concrete suggestions for challenging goals. If it becomes apparent that the goals are too easy or too hard, then immediately begin to set more realistic and challenging goals.

Set Short- and Long-Term Goals

Sport and exercise participants often focus on long-term or seasonal goals, such as winning the state championship or losing 30 pounds in six months. However, research has shown that both short- and long-term goals are necessary to keep motivation and performance high over time (Weinberg et al., 1993, 2000). Short-term goals are important because they can provide feedback concerning progress toward the long-term goal. This feedback can serve a motivational function and allow adjustment of goals either upward or downward, depending on the situation. Short-term goals by their nature allow sport and exercise participants to focus on improvement in small increments, which may make goals seem more attainable than an otherwise seemingly impossible long-term goal.

For example, a swimmer getting ready for the Olympic Games calculated that he would have to cut 2 seconds off his time in the 200-meter backstroke if he were to win a medal in the upcoming games. Two seconds is an enormous amount of time in a short race, and the swimmer felt that this seemed impossible. However, instead of focusing on the long-term goal, he broke up the goal into manageable short-term goals. Specifically, the Olympic Games were two years away, so he figured he would have to knock off 1 second per year. Furthermore, given that there are 12 months in a year, he figured he would have to knock off .08 seconds each month. Finally, because there are four weeks in a month, he would have to shave off .02 seconds each week. The swimmer felt he could do this! Thus, achieving short-term weekly goals of reducing his time by .02 seconds became his goal. The result: a gold medal in the backstroke by John Nabor.

Although short-term goals are obviously important, long-term goals are also necessary. Long-term goals provide the direction and final destination for sport and exercise participants and sometimes act as a dream goal. In essence, they keep the focus on where to end up. If progress toward this goal is not fast enough or if it is ahead of schedule, then the long-term goal can be adjusted to be in tune with the new short-term goals. A good way to envision the interaction of short- and long-term goals is to think of a staircase with the long-term goal at the top, the present level of performance at the bottom, and a sequence of progressively linked short-term goals connecting the top and bottom of the stairs.

Set Goals for Practice and Competition

One of the mistakes often made in setting goals is focusing solely or predominantly on competition goals. This does not imply that setting competitive goals is inappropriate; rather, it suggests that practice goals should not be forgotten (Bell, 1983). With the emphasis placed on winning in most competitive sports, it is no wonder that competition goals that focus on competitive outcomes are predominant. However, for most sports, daily practices encompass much more time commitment than do competitions. This is especially the case in sports that usually have only a few important meets, such as gymnastics, figure skating, and track and field; the rest of the time is spent on practice, practice, practice. Moreover, most athletes report that it is easier to "get up" and be motivated for a game or match, whereas additional motivation is needed for daily practice (Gould, 1998).

Practice goals could focus on both performance and nonperformance outcomes. Some typical practice goals could include getting to practice on time, giving teammates positive reinforcement and encouragement, displaying leadership behaviors, and achieving certain performance standards for specific drills. For example, a basketball player might set a goal of hitting 10 consecutive free throws at the end of practice. This practice goal can serve several purposes. First, it will help the player focus on his free-throw shooting and possibly develop different strategies to improve his free-throw percentage (e.g., preshot routine). Second, as the player gets closer to hitting 10 in a row, the pressure starts to build because he certainly does not want to miss after making 8 or 9 in a row and then have to start all over. This creates a sense of pressure that will help transfer to the pressure of real game situations. Third, research indicates that practice goals are as important (if not more important) than competition goals (Filby et al., 1999).

"Ink It, Don't Think It"

Several sport psychologists (e.g., Gould, 1998; Weinberg et al., 2000) have emphasized the importance of writing down and recording goals. Not only should goals be written down, they should also be recorded in a place where they can be easily seen. This can be done in several ways, such as putting goals (as well as goal progress) on a bulletin board outside a swimming pool, with a graph recording the number of miles that each swimmer has completed each week. Or athletes can write their goals on an index card before each practice. The key is not simply that the goals are written down; rather, it is that the goals are available and remain salient to each individual. Often, coaches will go through elaborate goal-setting procedures with their athletes at the beginning of the season, writing down all sorts of goals that are then placed in a drawer never to be looked at again. Coaches and sport and exercise psychologists should record goals and find a highly visible spot to keep them fresh in the participant's mind (some athletes post them in their locker or on their bedroom mirror at home).

Develop Goal Achievement Strategies

In Locke's (1968) seminal work, he proposed that one of the mechanisms underlying the effectiveness of goals in enhancing performance is the development of relevant learning strategies. Unfortunately, this aspect of goal setting is often neglected, as goals are set without a solid series of strategies identified to achieve them. Setting goals without also setting appropriate strategies for achievement is like setting a goal to drive from New York to Los Angeles in four days but forgetting to bring a map.

A sport example highlighting the importance of goal achievement strategies begins with a softball player who sets a goal to improve her batting average 25 points from last season. How is she going to accomplish this goal? At this point, the setting of relevant learning strategies comes into play. The player might decide to change her stance and move further back in the batter's box to get a better look at the ball. She may change her routine while in the on-deck circle and use some imagery before she gets up to bat. Or she may decide she needs to lift more weights to build up her upper-body strength. The key is that some learning strategy (or strategies) needs to be identified and incorporated into the daily training regimen so that the player can actively pursue the goal of improving her batting average.

Prioritize Process, Performance, and Outcome Goals

As noted previously, it is extremely important for individuals to set goals that are based on their own levels of performance rather on the outcome of winning and losing. Unfortunately, given the emphasis society places on competition and winning, it is often difficult not to focus on the final score or outcome of a competition. The ironic thing about this focus on outcome goals is that sport psychologists working with elite athletes have found that the best way to win a championship or gold medal is to focus on performance or process goals (Kingston & Hardy, 1997; Orlick & Partington, 1988). Too much emphasis placed on outcome goals (i.e., winning) at the time of the competition can increase competitive anxiety. This anxiety can result in athletes focusing on the consequences of their success or failure ("What will my coach and friends think about me if I lose?") instead of remaining focused on the task at hand.

Once again, the key point is not that outcome goals are inappropriate; rather, problems arise when individuals focus on outcome goals to the exclusion of performance and process goals. In fact, as most coaches will confirm, if athletes meet performance goals, then the outcome goal of winning will usually take care of itself. For example, if a basketball team meets its goals in the areas of assists, field goal percentage, rebounds, and foul shooting percentage, then its chances of winning increase dramatically. Some research (Weinberg et al., 1993) has indicated that fun (along with performance and outcome goals) was one of the top three goals of collegiate athletes. Mixing in some fun in the practices and games can help keep motivation high and enhance persistence over the long haul.

Set Individual and Team Goals

Coaches of team sports often ask, "Should I have my players set individual goals in addition to team goals?" It depends on the nature of the individual goals. That is, there is a place for individual goals within a team sport, as long as the individual goals do not conflict with team goals (Weinberg et al., 2000). Thus, if a hockey player wants to score 30 goals throughout the season, this goal has the potential to be in conflict with team goals if the player becomes more concerned with scoring goals than helping the team win. In basketball, even a point guard's goal to increase her assists per game could backfire if she starts to look exclusively to pass the ball and turns down good opportunities for her own shots. However, if athletes meet their individual goals, theoretically, these achievements should help team success as well. Thus, sport psychologists should be cautious when athletes set individual goals, making sure they contribute to overall team goals.

Provide Support for Goals

The psychological literature has provided strong evidence for the notion that social support is an important factor in keeping people motivated and persistent, especially when there are obstacles preventing goal attainment (Albrecht & Adelman, 1984; Cohen, 1988). Similarly, research (Hardy, Richman, & Rosenfeld, 1991) has reinforced the critical role that significant others can play in helping individuals achieve their goals. For example, in fitness settings, it has been shown that spousal support is an important factor affecting exercise adherence (Dishman, 1988). As a result, participants in exercise programs aimed at increasing fitness and losing weight should try to involve their spouses in the program by informing them of the goals of the participant and suggesting ways in which a spouse can support the participant's achievement of these goals. Similarly, a volleyball coach who is trying to emphasize performance goals with her athletes may enlist the help of parents, teachers, and friends to provide support for these goals rather than focusing on winning.

One of the most important ways for sport psychologists, coaches, teammates, or parents to provide goal support is to show genuine concern for and interest in athletes, students, and exercisers. It is important to be aware of the goals of individuals and to ask them about the progress they are making. Moreover, encouraging participants to strive toward their goals, but also being a sympathetic listener when they are struggling to meet their goals, goes a long way to keep up spirits and motivation.

Provide for Goal Evaluation

One of the most overlooked aspects of formal goal-setting programs is the evaluation component. As Locke and colleagues (1981) found, evaluative feedback is essential if goals are to be effective in enhancing performance. Therefore, it is critical to provide individuals with feedback on the effectiveness of their goals, and goal evaluation strategies should be continuously implemented throughout the goal-setting process. For example, many performance goals based on statistics such as batting average, runs batted in, steals, and runs scored are readily available to a baseball player. But these statistics are not always evaluated throughout the season to adjust goals chosen at the start of the season —and they should be. Periodic goal evaluation meetings should be scheduled between the player and the coach or the player and the sport

Figure 3.1

Goal Evaluation Card

Stroke	Specific Goal	Strategy	Short-Term Goal	Target Date
Serve	Improve first-serve percentage from 50% to 60%	Hit an extra 50 serves in practice	Improve first-serve percentage to 55% over the next three matches	Achieve 60% first serve by end of the season

psychologist to assess current performance in relation to a player's goals. In this way, goals can be reevaluated and adjusted to provide new motivation and commitment for the players.

In addition, some goals (e.g., more subjective) are more difficult to monitor and evaluate than other goals (e.g., more objective). Gould (1998) provided some examples of how to evaluate such subjective goals. For instance, an athlete may have a goal to improve concentration during practice. To evaluate this goal, the coach could give the player a weekly report card rating his practice concentration on a scale of 1 (poor) to 10 (excellent). Similarly, an injured player may have a goal to go to a rehabilitation clinic three times a week and do range-of-motion exercises and light lifting for 1 hour each time. Attendance could be posted at the rehabilitation center, and the athletic trainer could note how long the athlete performed the prescribed exercises each session. Figure 3.1 is a sample goal evaluation card that is designed for tennis but can be modified for other activities.

Designing a Goal-Setting System

The principles of goal setting and the supporting research should provide a good start to setting productive goals for participants. But following is an overview of the "nuts-and-bolts" of a goal-setting system with three unique stages.

Planning Stage

An effective coach, instructor, or trainer does not want to enter a physical activity setting unprepared. Preparation and planning are essential. The key elements to making this stage work include the following:

- *Assess each individual's needs and abilities.* For athletes, this step could be done in the off-season or preseason; for exercisers, it should be done as quickly as possible at the beginning of the physical activity program.
- *Set the goals based on the needs and abilities assessment.* It is important that goals be set in different areas—the focus should not be only on individual or team skills. For example, goals may focus on enjoyment, playing time, psychological skills, or fitness. It is important to set goals in diverse areas because students, athletes, and exercisers participate in sport and physical activity for a variety of reasons (e.g., skill improvement, weight loss, fun, winning).
- *Plan goal strategies.* After goals are set, plan specific strategies to be put in place over the next season or next program to help participants achieve their goals.

Meeting Stage

Once the planning stage is complete, move to the meeting phase. In this phase, basic goal-setting information and principles are given to participants, specific goals are set, and strategies are decided on.

- *Provide basic goal-setting information.* At the initial meeting, provide participants with basic information about goals, including the principles discussed previously. This information will help them set their own specific goals.
- *Meet individually with all participants.* After participants have reviewed the goal-setting information, it is a good idea to meet individually with all participants to decide on specific goals. Meet with the entire team if team goals are being set.
- *Plan goal achievement strategies.* Help participants choose strategies to reach their goals. (This step is forgotten often but is very important.) For example, if a basketball player has a goal to increase her free-throw percentage from 70% to 75%, specific strategies need to be introduced to help the athlete achieve this goal.

Evaluation Stage

The stage that is probably most difficult for practitioners is the evaluation phase. Many people get all jazzed up about setting goals at the outset of a competitive season or program, but then they lose steam and sight of these goals over time. Here are some tips for the evaluation phase of the program to maintain focus on the goals set at the outset.

- *Plan for goal evaluation procedures.* This is a difficult part of the goal-setting process, and coaches and instructors should plan carefully for goal evaluation. For example, do not plan to re-evaluate goals at the busiest time of the year. Also, someone should be assigned to keep track of goal progress (e.g., a team manager). A physical educator may schedule performance or skill tests periodically to monitor goal progress. In any case, the feedback process costs the instructor or coach little time.
- *Provide for goal reevaluation.* Depending on the nature of the program, the coach or instructor should meet with individuals regarding their progress toward meeting goals. If individuals are exceeding their original goals, new, more difficult, ones should be set. Conversely, if participants are not reaching their goals (e.g., due to injury or other external factors), the goals may need to be pushed back. In any case, feedback from the instructor or coach and constant reevaluation of goals help the participant stay on track and focused.
- *Provide support and encouragement.* Throughout the season or sessions, the coach or instructor should ask participants about their goals and encourage their progress. Showing enthusiasm about the goal-setting process supports the participants and keeps them motivated to fulfill their goals.

Common Problems When Setting Goals

This chapter thus far has focused on the research and practice concerning the effectiveness of goal-setting strategies. Although goals can help improve performance and change behavior, it is not always easy to implement goal-setting programs in sport and exercise settings. In fact, athletes, coaches, exercise leaders, and applied sport psychologists face some common problems when attempting to use goal-setting programs. By understanding and anticipating these problems, they can soften potential negative effects.

Failing to Monitor Goal Progress and Readjust Goals

Often, individuals are excited about setting goals and set many goals at the start of a program. But as time passes, these goals are often forgotten or at least "put on the back burner." Situations can occur that throw people off course in meeting their goals, such as an injury. Therefore it is critical that athletes and sport psychologists or coaches schedule regular meetings specifically for goal evaluation. For example, a marathon runner may have a goal of running 50 miles a week for four months in training. But after six weeks, due to illness and business obligations, it becomes obvious to the runner that she will not be able to meet these goals. Instead of losing motivation and possibly quitting, new goals could be established based on her current level of fitness and performance. For example, the weekly training mileage goal could be reduced to 30 miles for two weeks and then increased again to 40 or 50 miles for the remainder of the training.

Failing to Recognize Individual Differences

One of the most common errors in any psychological intervention in sport and exercise settings is not recognizing individual differences. As noted previously, for example, individuals may differ in their goal orientations (i.e., task vs. ego), which could make a significant difference in the specific goals that are effective for them. Research (Giannini, Weinberg, & Jackson, 1988) has indicated that goal effectiveness is maximized when goal orientations and specific types of goals are matched. Thus, task-oriented individuals are most motivated by goals focusing on self-improvement, whereas ego-oriented individuals are most motivated by goals that focus on winning and losing.

Failing to Set Specific Measurable Goals

Probably the most frequent problem when helping participants in sport and exercise settings is the failure to set specific and measurable goals. Individuals seem to have a propensity for simply setting general goals such as "improving my passing in soccer" or "improving my overall fitness level." For example, if a baseball pitcher has a goal to improve his "pick off" move to first base, the coach could rate the pitcher in practice and game situations using a scale of 1 (not at all improved) to 5 (much improved). Not only does the scale help the pitcher set a specific goal, it also helps him focus on his pick off move because he knows the coach will be carefully evaluating him.

Setting Too Many Goals at the Start

As noted previously, individuals get excited at the start of goal-setting programs and often "bite off more than they can chew." This is especially the case for those with little experience in goal-setting techniques. It is not the number of goals per se that causes the problem; rather, it is monitoring and tracking these goals across time that becomes extremely difficult and time consuming. Therefore, particularly when working with individuals with little goal-setting experience, it is useful to set only a couple of high-priority goals. For example, for a person just starting an exercise program, a simple goal of exercising three or four times a week for 20 to 30 minutes each time would be sufficient.

Summary

This chapter focuses on the effectiveness of setting goals in sport and exercise environments. A goal is defined as attaining a specific level of proficiency in a task, usually within a specified time period, and a distinction is made between subjective and objective goals. Locke's theory of goal setting, which indicates that specific, difficult, challenging goals lead to higher levels of task performance than do easy goals, no goals, or "do your best" goals, is presented. More recent research investigating the relationship between goal and performance in sport and exercise settings has also found support for the effectiveness of setting goals, although the findings are not as robust as those in the industrial literature.

It has been hypothesized that goals directly influence behavior by orienting performer attention to important elements of the task, increasing effort and persistence, and facilitating the development of relevant learning strategies. Goals also can influence behavior more indirectly through changes in cognitions (e.g., self-confidence) and anxiety and can be mediated by goal orientation (i.e., task vs. ego orientation). Basic goal-setting principles based on the literature are presented, including setting specific goals, setting realistic and challenging goals, setting both short- and long-term goals, setting performance goals, writing down goals, providing support for goals, and providing for goal evaluation. Remember that the effectiveness of any goal-setting program will in large part rely on the interactions among the coach, exercise leader, or sport psychologist and the participants. In essence, individual differences and environmental considerations should always be taken into account when setting goals.

References

Albrecht, J. L., & Adelman, M. B. (1984). Social support and life stress: New directions for communication research. *Human Communications Research, 2,* 3–22.

Bell, K. F. (1983). *Championship thinking: The athlete's guide to winning performance in all sports.* Englewood Cliffs, NJ: Prentice-Hall.

Burton, D. (1989). Winning isn't everything: Examining the impact of performance goals on collegiate swimmers' cognitions and performance. *The Sport Psychologist, 32,* 105–132.

Burton, D. (1992). The Jekyll/Hyde nature of goals: Reconceptualizing goal setting in sport. In T. Horn (Ed.), *Advances in sport psychology* (pp. 267–297). Champaign, IL: Human Kinetics.

Burton, D., Naylor, S., & Holliday, B. (2001). Goal setting in sport. In R. Singer, H. Hausenblas, & C. Janelle (Eds.), *Handbook of Sport Psychology* (pp. 497–528). New York: John Wiley & Sons.

Burton, D., Weinberg, R. S., Yukelson, D., & Weigand, D. (1998). The goal effectiveness paradox in sport: Examining the goal practices of collegiate athletes. *The Sport Psychologist, 12,* 404–418.

Chidester, J. S., & Grigsby, W. C. (1984). A meta-analysis of the goal setting performance literature. In A. Pearce & R. B. Robinson (Eds.), *Proceedings of the 44th Annual Meeting of the Academy of Management* (pp. 202–206). Ada, OH: Academy of Management.

Coakley, J. (1997). *Sport in society. Issues and controversies* (5th ed.). St. Louis, MO: Times Mirror/Mosby College.

Cohen, S. (1988). Psychosocial models of the role of social support in the etiology of physical disease. *Health Psychology, 7,* 269–297.

Dishman, R. K. (1988). *Exercise adherence: Its impact on public health.* Champaign, IL: Human Kinetics.

Duda, J. L. (1992). Motivation in sport settings: A goal perspective approach. In G. C. Roberts (Ed.), *Motivation in sport and exercise* (pp. 57–92). Champaign, IL: Human Kinetics.

Duda, J. L., & Whitehead, J. (1998). Measurement of goal perspectives in the physical domain. In J. L. Duda (Ed.), *Advances is sport and exercise psychology measures* (pp. 21–48). Morgantown, WV: Fitness Information Technology.

Dweck, C. S. (1986). Motivational processes affecting learning. *American Psychologist, 41,* 1040–1048.

Filby, C. D., Maynard, I. W., & Graydon, J. K. (1999). The effect of multiple-goal strategies on performance outcomes in training and competition. *Journal of Applied Sport Psychology, 11,* 230–246.

Garland, H. (1985). A cognitive mediation theory of task goals and human performance. *Motivation and Emotion, 9,* 345–367.

Giannini, J., Weinberg, R. S., & Jackson, A. (1988). The effects of master, competitive and cooperative goals on the performance of simple and complex basketball skills. *Journal of Sport and Exercise Psychology, 10,* 408–417.

Gould, D. (1998). Goal setting for peak performance. In J. Williams (Ed.), *Applied sport psychology: Personal growth to peak performance* (2nd ed., pp. 182–196). Mountain View, CA: Mayfield.

Gould, D., Tammen, V., Murphy, S., & May, J. (1989). An examination of U.S. Olympic sport psychology consultants and the services they provide. *The Sport Psychologist, 3*, 300–312.

Hardy, C. V., Richman, J. M., & Rosenfeld, L. B. (1991). The role of social support in the life stress/injury relationship. *The Sport Psychologist, 5*, 128–139.

Kingston, K., & Hardy, L. (1997). Effects of different types of goals on processes that support performance. *The Sport Psychologist, 11*, 277–293.

Kyllo, L. B., & Landers, D. M. (1995). Goal setting in sport and exercise: A research synthesis to solve the controversy. *Journal of Sport and Exercise Psychology, 17*, 117–137.

Locke, E. A. (1966). The relationship of intentions to level of performance. *Journal of Applied Psychology, 50*, 60–66.

Locke, E. A. (1968). Toward a theory of task motivation incentives. *Organizational Behavior and Human Performance, 3*, 157–189.

Locke, E. A. (1978). The ubiquity of the technique of goal setting in theories of and approaches to employee motivation. *Academy of Management Review, 3*, 594–601.

Locke, E. A., & Latham, G. P. (1985). The application of goal setting to sports. *Journal of Sport Psychology, 7*, 205–222.

Locke, E. A., & Latham, G. P. (1990). *A theory of goal setting and task performance*. Englewood Cliffs, NJ: Prentice-Hall.

Locke, E. A., Shaw, K. N., Saari, L. M., & Latham, G. P. (1981). Goal setting and task performance. *Psychological Bulletin, 90*, 125–152.

Maehr, M. L., & Braskamp, L. (1986). *The motivation factor: A theory of personal development*. Lexington, MA: Heath.

Mento, A. J., Steel, R. P., & Karren, R. J. (1987). A meta-analytic study of the effects of goal setting on task performance: 1966–1984. *Organizational Behavior and Human Decision Processes, 39*, 52–83.

Nicholls, J. G. (1984a). Achievement motivation: Conception of ability, subjective experience, task choice and performance. *Psychological Review, 91*, 328–346.

Nicholls, J. G. (1984b). Conception of ability and achievement motivation. In R. Ames & C. Ames (Eds.), *Research on motivation in education: Vol. 1. Student motivation* (pp. 39–73). New York: Academic Press.

Ntoumanis, N., & Biddle, S. J. H. (1999). A review of motivational climate in physical activity. *Journal of Sport Sciences, 17*, 643–655.

Odiorne, G. S. (1978). MBO: A backward glance. *Business Horizons, 21*(5), 14–24.

Orlick, T., & Partington, J. (1988). Mental links to excellence. *The Sport Psychologist, 2*, 105–130.

Pierce, B. E., & Burton, D. (1998). Scoring a perfect 10: Investigating the impact of goal-setting styles on a goal-setting program for female gymnasts. *The Sport Psychologist, 12*, 156–168.

Roberts, G. C. (1992). Motivation in sport and exercise: Conceptual constraints and consequence. In G. C. Roberts (Ed.), *Motivation in sport and exercise* (pp. 3–30). Champaign, IL: Human Kinetics.

Ryan, T. A. (1970). *Intentional behavior: An approach to human motivation*. New York: Ronald Press.

Taylor, F. W. (1967). *The principles of scientific management*. New York: Norton. (Originally published 1911)

Tubbs, M. E. (1991). Goal setting: A meta-analytic examination of the empirical evidence. *Journal of Applied Psychology, 71*, 474–483.

Sullivan, P. A., & Nashman, H. W. (1998). Self-perceptions of the role of USOC sport psychologists in working with Olympic athletes. *The Sport Psychologist, 12*, 95–103.

Swain, A., & Jones, G. (1995). Effects of goal setting interventions on selected basketball skills: A single subject design. *Research Quarterly for Exercise and Sport, 66,* 51–63.

Weinberg, R. S. (1992). Goal setting and motor performance: A review and critique. In G. C. Roberts (Ed.), *Motivation in sport and exercise* (pp. 177–198). Champaign, IL: Human Kinetics.

Weinberg, R. S. (1994). Goal setting and performance in sport and exercise settings: A synthesis and critique. *Medicine and Science in Sport and Exercise, 26,* 469–477.

Weinberg, R. S., Burke, K., & Jackson, A. W. (1997). Coaches' and players' perceptions of goal setting in junior tennis: An exploratory investigation. *The Sport Psychologist, 11,* 426–439.

Weinberg, R. S., Burton, D., Yukelson, D., & Weigand, D. (1993). Goal setting in competitive sport: An exploratory investigation of practices of collegiate athletes. *The Sport Psychologist, 7,* 275–289.

Weinberg, R. S., Burton, D., Yukelson, D., & Weigand, D. (2000). Perceived goal setting practices of Olympic athletes: An exploratory investigation. *The Sport Psychologist, 14,* 280–296.

Weinberg, R. S., Stitcher, T., & Richardson, P. (1994). Effects of a seasonal goal setting program on lacrosse performance. *The Sport Psychologist, 8,* 166–175.

Weinberg, R. S., & Weigand, D. (1993). Goal setting in sport and exercise. A reaction to Locke. *Journal of Sport and Exercise Psychology, 15,* 88–95.

Imagery Training for Peak Performance

Daniel Gould, Nicole Damarjian, and Christy Greenleaf

Carolyn is a highly talented professional golfer. She plays well during practice rounds but does not seem to be able to play up to her potential during tournaments. To enhance her confidence, her coach recommends that she imagine herself executing each shot perfectly before she actually swings. Although skeptical, Carolyn tries this in her next tournament. She finds it difficult to control the "pictures" in her mind and sees herself making mistakes. Frustrated, Carolyn sees little immediate improvement in her game, decides that she is not good at imagery, and retreats to the driving range to hit balls.

* * *

Alan is the new basketball coach at Bacon Academy and decides that he will develop an imagery training program for his team. Every day, after 2 hours of hard practice, Alan has his team lie down and imagine themselves going through various plays outlined in practice. As the season progresses, Alan notices more and more resistance from some of his players with regard to the imagery training. He overhears them complain that they want to go home and eat supper after a workout, not sit in the dark and daydream. Besides, they do not know why they are doing all this "mental stuff" anyway. The team never did imagery last year with Coach Shea, and he led them to a conference championship. Concerned about losing credibility with his team, Alan decides to drop the imagery program.

* * *

Lauren is an elite gymnast. Six weeks before the Olympic tryouts, she sprains her ankle on a dismount. The athletic trainer assures both Lauren and her coach that the injury is minor and that with proper rest and rehabilitation she should be completely recovered in time for the tryouts. Two weeks later, Lauren returns to her normal practice schedule, but she continues to hesitate before her dismounts. Both her sport psychologist and coach encourage her to replay past successful dismounts in her mind to overcome the fear she has developed as a result of her recent fall. Lauren half-heartedly does as they suggest but is not truly committed to imagery training. She feels foolish and self-conscious in front of her teammates and insists that her ankle is still not fully recovered.

"Wait a minute," you say, "Everything I have ever heard or read about sport psychology says that imagery works." After all, Hank Aaron used it to become the all-time home run leader in major league baseball, golf great Jack Nicklaus religiously does it before every shot, and what about all those Olympic athletes who report the usefulness of imagery in enhancing their performance? How can it be suggested that imagery does not work?

To begin with, it should be made clear that we believe in the power of imagery and its value as a psychological skill for enhancing athletic performance. As is conveyed in this chapter, research has clearly demonstrated the efficacy of imagery as a psychological change mechanism in sports. However, stories such as those discussed earlier are not uncommon. Many well-meaning athletes like Carolyn assume that psychological skills such as imagery can be developed overnight to produce immediate performance improvements. When the expected results are not achieved, athletes falsely conclude that imagery does not work. Still, other athletes like Lauren do not fully understand what imagery is or how it can help them achieve their goals. They never truly commit to an imagery training program, and as a result, they fail to gain performance benefits. This is why it is important for coaches like Alan to ensure that their teams understand what imagery is and how it can be used to enhance sport performance.

This chapter is designed to provide sport psychologists and coaches with a comprehensive and practical overview of imagery theory, research, and intervention. Specifically, the following six areas are addressed:

1. the nature of imagery and how it can enhance sport performance
2. theories and models explaining the relationship between imagery and performance

3. evidence of the importance and utility of imagery training programs
4. general guidelines for using imagery
5. recommendations on how to implement an imagery training program
6. problems and pitfalls often made in imagery training programs, as well as ways in which they can be avoided.

What Is Imagery, and How Can It Enhance Sport Performance?

Imagery can be defined as a process by which sensory experiences are stored in memory and internally recalled and performed in the absence of external stimuli (Murphy, 1994). It is important to understand that imagery involves the use of all senses, including sight, touch, taste, sound, smell, and body awareness. Body awareness is especially important in sports, in which the feel of the movement is important.

Assume, for example, that a swimmer is using imagery to prepare mentally for a conference meet in the next month. She imagines herself swimming confidently and strongly. She smells the chlorine of the pool as she waits for the race to begin. She sees herself dive into the water. She feels the power in her kick as she pushes herself past her competitors. She hears water splashing and her teammates cheering her on. By incorporating all of the appropriate senses, this athlete is able to more vividly imagine many aspects of her upcoming race.

With an appropriate training program, imagery skills can increase self-awareness, facilitate skill acquisition and maintenance, build self-confidence, control emotions, relieve pain, regulate arousal, and enhance preparation strategies (Martin, Moritz, & Hall, 1999; Murphy & Jowdy, 1992). However, before outlining specific guidelines for setting up an imagery training program, it is important to summarize the theories that explain why and how imagery works as well as the research examining the relationship between imagery and performance.

Theoretical Explanations for the Relationship Between Imagery and Performance

To effectively use imagery, sport psychologists and coaches must have an understanding of the mechanisms underlying the relationship between imagery and performance. Traditionally, two main theories have been forwarded within the sport psychology literature: (a) the psychoneuromuscular theory and (b) the symbolic learning theory.

Psychoneuromuscular Theory

Psychoneuromuscular theory (Jacobson, 1932) proposes that imagery duplicates the actual motor pattern being rehearsed, although the neuromotor activation is of smaller magnitude when compared with actual physical practice. This neuromuscular activation is thought to be sufficient enough to enhance the motor schema in the motor cortex. Vealey and Greenleaf (1998) referred to this as "muscle memory." For example, Suinn (1972) monitored muscle activity in the legs of skiers as they imagined a downhill run. He found that the electrical patterns in the muscles closely approximated those expected if the person had actually been skiing.

Unfortunately, not all research has been able to replicate Suinn's (1972) results or to show support for the psychoneuromuscular theory. In a meta-analysis of 60 mental practice studies, Feltz and Landers (1983) concluded that it is doubtful that imagery effects result in low-level muscular–impulse activity. Furthermore, research in experimental psychology has suggested that the effects of imagery are more a function of operations within the central nervous system than muscular activity during imagery (Kohl & Roenker, 1983). In other words, imagery may function more at the higher levels of information processing than at the lower muscular levels. The muscular responses found may merely be an effect mechanism rather than a cause of performance changes.

Symbolic Learning Theory

In contrast to psychoneuromuscular theory, symbolic learning theory (Sackett, 1934) contends that imagery effects are more often due to the opportunity to practice symbolic elements of a specific motor task than to the muscle activation itself. In other words, imagery functions by helping athletes develop a "mental blueprint" to guide overt performance. Support for the symbolic learning theory has come from two areas of research. First, several studies have shown that imagery is more effective for tasks that have a high cognitive component as opposed to a high motor component (Ryan & Simons, 1981). Second, motor learning theories contending that early stages of learning are primarily cognitive are compatible with the notion that imagery will have its greatest effects during the early stages of learning.

Informational and Motor Process Theories of Imagery

Although much of the imagery literature in sport psychology is based on the psychoneuromuscular and symbolic learning theories, Murphy and Jowdy (1992) suggested that researchers look beyond traditional theories and investigate the relevance of imagery theories developed in other areas, such as cognitive and clinical psychology. Two such theories are Lang's (1977, 1979) bio-informational theory and Ahsen's (1984) triple-code model of imagery.

Lang's (1977, 1979) bio-informational theory is based on the assumption that an image is a functionally organized, finite set of propositions regarding the relationship and description of stimulus and response characteristics. Stimulus propositions describe the content of the scenario to be imagined. For example, they may include the weather conditions of a particular tennis match or the pin position of a particularly difficult golf hole. Response propositions describe the imager's response to the imagined scenario, for example, a kinesthetic awareness of any muscular changes while performing. It is important to note that, according to bio-informational theory (Lang, 1977, 1979), for imagery rehearsal to influence performance, both stimulus and response propositions must be activated. Rather than conceptualizing an image as merely a stimulus in the athlete's mind to which he or she responds, this theory suggests that images also contain "response scenarios" that enable athletes to access the appropriate motor program and effectively alter athletic performance.

Similar to Lang's bio-informational theory, Ahsen's (1984) triple-code model of imagery also recognizes the primary importance of psychophysiological processes in the imagery process. However, Ahsen's theory goes one step further, to incorporate the personal meaning that an image has for an individual. According to the triple-code model, three essential parts of imagery must be understood by both theorists and clinicians. These include the image itself, the somatic response to the image, and the meaning of the image. For example, a sprinter imagines that she is successfully qualifying for the 100-meter race in the Olympics. Her arousal level increases as she imagines running the race and achieving her life-long dream. In addition, she attaches a great sense of personal pride and satisfaction to the image of this accomplishment. Both the image itself and the somatic response to the image are analogous to Lang's (1977, 1979) stimulus and response propositions. However, no other theory or model of imagery has addressed the importance of the meaning that an individual attaches to a particular image. (See Murphy & Jowdy, 1992, and Suinn, 1993, for more detailed reviews of imagery theories.)

Psychological States Notion

Although most imagery theories focus on improving performance through information processing and motor control processes, it is important to recognize that imagery is also thought to influence athletic performance through its effect on other psychological states, such as self-efficacy or confidence, motivation, and anxiety. For example, in his classic theory of self-efficacy, Bandura (1977) proposed that an important source of efficacy information is the modeling of vicarious experiences and that imagery is an excellent way to reinforce modeled acts and mentally learn from others' experiences. Several studies have linked imagery use and levels of self-confidence (Callow, Hardy, & Hall, 1998; Moritz, Hall, Martin, & Vadocz, 1996). Moritz and colleagues (1996), for instance, found that highly confident athletes used more mastery and arousal control imagery than athletes with low confidence. Imagery may also enhance performance via increased intrinsic motivation. Martin and Hall (1995) found that beginning golfers in an imagery intervention practiced more and set higher goals, thus exhibiting higher levels of intrinsic motivation than those in a control group. Furthermore, widely used multimodal stress management techniques—such as Meichenbaum's (1985) stress management training, Smith's (1980) cognitive–affective stress management training, and Suinn's (1972) visuomotor behavioral rehearsal—feature imagery as a means of reducing anxiety. Moreover, a review of these programs shows that they have been successful in helping athletes control anxiety and enhance sport performance (Gould & Udry, 1994). Imagery thus influences important psychological states such as confidence and anxiety, which in turn influence athletic performance.

Applied Model of Imagery Use in Sport

Martin and colleagues (1999) developed an applied model of how imagery is used in sport (see Figure 4.1), including aspects of both bioinformational theory and the triple-code model. Although it does not

Figure 4.1

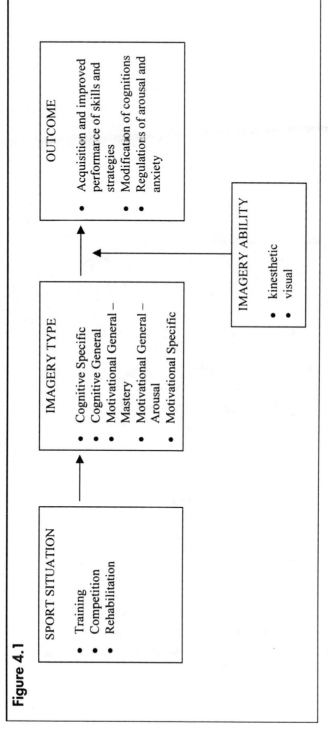

An applied model of mental imagery use in sport. Reprinted with permission from K. Martin, S. Moritz, & C. Hall, 1999. Imagery use in sport: A literature review and applied model. *The Sport Psychologist, 13*(3), 248.

attempt to explain the underlying mechanisms for why and how imagery affects performance, this applied model provides a useful framework for imagery uses within sport. The model consists of four central components, including (a) the sport situation, (b) the type of imagery used, (c) imagery ability, and (d) the outcomes of imagery use.

In addition, the model outlines five types of imagery based on Paivio's (1985) framework of imagery functions. *Cognitive-specific* imagery involves an athlete imaging specific sport skills, such as a basketball free throw. The *cognitive-general* type of imagery refers to imagery of competitive strategies, such as the use of a diamond defense in field hockey. *Motivational general-mastery* imagery involves imaging oneself coping effectively and mastering challenging situations, for example, a tennis player may imagine himself being confident and positive going into a tough match. The *motivational general-arousal* type of imagery refers to imagery focused on various arousal experiences, such as anxiety and relaxation, associated with sport competition. For example, a shooter may imagine that she is feeling physically calm and relaxed during her setup. *Motivation-specific* imagery focuses on imaging oneself working toward and achieving specific goals, such as achieving a personal best time.

Martin and colleagues (1999) suggested three outcomes associated with imagery use based on previous research, including skill and strategy, learning and performance; modifying cognitions; and regulating arousal and competitive anxiety. Based on a review of imagery literature, they concluded that cognitive-specific imagery is most effective for skill and strategy learning and performance, whereas motivational general-mastery and motivational-specific imagery are more effective for modifying cognitions. Furthermore, imagery, combined with other behavioral stress management strategies, is effective for regulating arousal and competition anxiety. In addition to examining outcomes of imagery use, Martin and colleagues also focused on specific sport situations for imagery use, including training, competition, and rehabilitation.

Although research is needed to further develop and test imagery theories and models, given the current state of knowledge, imagery is thought to influence sport performance in several ways. First, although newer theories and most sport psychologists who design imagery programs for athletes still recommend emphasizing kinesthetic feelings of movements, it is doubtful that imagery works through neuromuscular activation. It is more likely that yet unexplored, higher levels of information processing are involved. Second, it is clear that imagery facilitates performance by providing extra opportunities for an athlete to develop symbolic elements of motor tasks. Third, more recent theories and models of imagery stress the importance of emphasizing stimulus propositions, response propositions, and the personal meaning of the image to the performer. Fourth, imagery influences important psychological states, such as confidence and anxiety. Fifth, different types of imagery can be used in various sport situations to influence skill and strategy learning and performance, modify cognitions, and regulate arousal and anxiety.

Imagery Research

The research studies examining the relationship between imagery and athletic performance can be categorized into four main areas: (a) mental practice studies, (b) precompetition imagery intervention research, (c) imagery use studies, and (d) mediating variable studies.

Mental Practice Studies

The majority of mental practice studies are concerned with the effects of mental practice on the learning and performance of motor skills. In these studies, *mental practice* is typically defined as mental rehearsal of a given task or performance without any associated overt actions. Although mental practice may or may not include the use of imagery, the overlap between the two areas warrants a discussion of the findings.

The standard methodology used in mental practice studies involves a between-subjects, pretest–posttest design with four groups: physical practice only, mental practice only, both physical and mental practice, and no practice. For example, Rawlings, Rawlings, Chen, and Yilk (1972) examined the effects of mental practice on a pursuit rotor task. At the onset of the study, all participants were introduced to the task and received 25 practice trials. Following these trials, participants differed in their practice methods. Group 1 received physical practice only, Group 2 received no practice, and Group 3 received mental practice only (imagery and visualization). After an 8-day training period, all participants were retested on the pursuit rotor task for 25 more trials. The results showed that the mental practice group improved considerably over the course of the experiment, almost to the extent that the physical practice group did. In contrast, the no-practice group showed little if any improvement.

On the basis of a meta-analysis of 60 mental practice studies, Feltz and Landers (1983) suggested that mental practice is better than no practice at all. Furthermore, in a comprehensive review of the literature, Weinberg (1981) stated that

> Mental practice combined and alternated with physical practice is more effective than either physical or mental practice alone. In addition, physical practice is superior to mental practice. Mental practice should not replace physical practice, but rather it can be used as a valuable addition to physical practice. (p. 203)

This literature supports the belief that the ideal training program combines both physical and mental practice.

Precompetition Imagery Intervention Research

Unlike mental practice studies, imagery intervention studies involve the use of imagery or mental rehearsal immediately before performance. They examine the effectiveness of imagery to prepare an athlete who is about to perform. Unfortunately, however, studies in this area have generated more questions than answers.

For example, several studies have suggested that imagery rehearsal before performance can benefit performance on some tasks compared with a situation in which no imagery rehearsal is used (see Murphy & Jowdy, 1992, for a detailed review). Shelton and Mahoney (1978) found that 15 male weight lifters who were asked to use their favorite "psyching-up" strategy before a test of hand strength showed significantly greater improvement over baseline than did 15 male weight lifters who were asked to improve their performance but given a distracting cognitive task during preperformance. This type of research is problematic for two reasons. First, such designs do not specify the type of mental rehearsal that facilitates performance. Although each athlete may report having used imagery, this may mean different things to different athletes. Second, this research does little to improve understanding of how imagery interventions influence performance. It fails to address the important and often elusive question about what mechanisms underlie the relationship between imagery and performance.

In addition to these problems, several studies have failed to find a positive relationship between imagery and performance. For example, Weinberg, Gould, Jackson, and Barnes (1980) examined three mental preparation strategies and their effects on a tennis-serve task. Participants were divided into one of four conditions: (a) using imagery to prepare for serving, (b) making positive self-efficacy statements, (c) using attentional focus, and (d) preparing as they normally would (the control group). The results showed that none of the cognitive strategies used increased performance over the control condition.

Murphy and Jowdy (1992) have suggested that these mixed results may be due to several variables, including task, individual difference, and physiology. With regard to the task variables, it is possible that imagery rehearsal may be a more effective strategy for some types of tasks than for others. Perhaps imagery rehearsal is more effective with predominantly cognitive as opposed to motor tasks, for example. It is also important to examine individual-difference variables. Some individuals may, for example, have a higher quality of imagery and thus experience greater improvements in performance. Furthermore, how does imagery influence certain physiological variables (e.g., electromyogram, electroencephalogram, and heart rate), and how does this help to explain changes in performance? Overall, although showing that an imagery-performance relationship often exists, the precompetition imagery intervention studies have been methodologically weak. Future research in this area needs to include better intervention descriptions and manipulation checks.

Imagery Use Studies

Another area of imagery research has focused on the incidence of imagery use among athletes, that is, when, where, and why do athletes use imagery? Athletes use imagery in conjunction with practice, competition, and rehabilitation (Martin et al., 1999), as well as in environments outside of practice and competition, such as school, home, and work (Salmon, Hall, & Haslam, 1994). Athletes tend to use imagery more before competition than in association with practice situations (Barr & Hall, 1992; Hall, Rodgers, & Barr, 1990; Munroe, Giacobbi, Hall, & Weinberg, 2000; Salmon et al., 1994). Munroe, Hall, Simms, and Weinberg (1998) found that imagery use differed across the duration of competitive seasons of athletes from 10 sports. Cognitive-general imagery and motivation-specific imagery were used increasingly as the competitive season progressed. In addition, changes in imagery use across the competitive season depended on the sport.

Munroe and colleagues (2000) interviewed 14 athletes from seven sports to examine where, when, why, and what athletes image. Athletes reported using imagery for both practice and competition situations and indicated that they used imagery during and outside of practice and before, during, and after competition. Athletes in this study indicated that they found imagery to be most effective during practice and before competitions. Athletes reported several reasons for using imagery, many corresponding to the types of imagery described by Paivio (1985) and Martin and colleagues (1999). Athletes reported using imagery for developing skills (cognitive-specific); executing skills and developing and executing strategies (cognitive-general); generating motivation related to performance and outcome (motivational-specific); regulating excitement, control, and relaxation (motivational general-arousal); being mentally tough, focused, and confident (motivational general-mastery); and getting into flow states.

Mediating Variables Studies

The final area of research to be discussed focuses on a variety of possible mediating variables and their influence on the imagery–performance relationship. For example, some researchers have examined the influence of imagery ability on performance. Primarily, imagery ability has been defined by the level of vividness and controllability that athletes have over their imagery. *Vividness* refers to the clarity and reality in an athlete's image, whereas *controllability* refers to the athlete's ability to influence the content of the image. Several correlational studies have found that more successful performers have a higher quality of imagery (Highlen & Bennett, 1983; Meyers, Cooke, Cullen, & Liles, 1979). As stated previously, it is important to consider individual differences in imagery ability when conducting this type of research.

Another possible mediating variable relates to the correctness of an athlete's imagery. For example, Woolfolk, Parrish, and Murphy (1985) used a golf-putting task to determine the effects of imagery correctness on performance. The results showed that participants in the negative-imagery condition performed significantly worse than participants in the positive-imagery and control conditions.

A final mediating variable relates to imagery perspective. Some athletes imagine themselves from an *internal* perspective (i.e., they are inside their body actually experiencing the imagined sensations), whereas others imagine themselves from an *external* perspective (i.e., they are a spectator watching the performance). Although some researchers have found an internal perspective to be associated with higher levels of performance (Mahoney & Avener, 1977), others have found no difference in performance for those with internal- versus external-imagery perspectives (Mumford & Hall, 1985). Recent research (Hardy, 1997; Hardy & Callow, 1999; White & Hardy, 1995) has suggested that an external-imagery perspective is good for imaging tasks in which form is important, whereas an internal-imagery perspective is good for imaging open-skilled tasks in which perception is important for performance. In addition, kinesthetic imagery is thought to be beneficial regardless of the imagery perspective used.

This brief review of the sport and motor performance imagery research shows that this area of investigation is not without problems. More carefully controlled and methodologically sound research is certainly needed. On a more positive note, when combined with physical practice, imagery has been shown to facilitate sport performance. However, this research also demonstrates that imagery does not work for all tasks, with all people, in all situations. Although improved research will clarify on what tasks, with whom, and in what situations imagery works best, it is clear that simply asking athletes to imagine themselves performing better will not guarantee beneficial effects. Sport psychologists and coaches must make informed imagery prescriptions that are guided by an understanding of imagery research and theory as well as those sport psychological guidelines identified for the effective use of imagery.

Guidelines for Using Imagery

From the research conducted thus far, many practical applications have been suggested to help coaches and athletes use imagery as a performance enhancement tool. Similarly, some sport psychologists (Harris & Harris, 1984; Martens, 1987; Orlick, 1986, 1990; Vealey & Greenleaf, 1998) who have had extensive experience in using imagery rehearsal with athletes have been able to derive several useful guidelines for those practitioners or athletes interested in implementing such techniques, the most important of which are subsequently discussed.

Practice Imagery on a Regular Basis

Unfortunately, many coaches and athletes believe that psychological skills such as imagery do not require the same practice that physical skills require. For example, consider the story of Carolyn at the beginning of this chapter. She half-heartedly attempts to use imagery to enhance her golf game. She never truly commits to practicing imagery and becomes frustrated when she fails to realize immediate performance gains. Mental skills are like physical skills: Becoming proficient with the use of imagery requires a commitment throughout the training season. It is unrealistic to think that either a physical or mental skill will be effective in a competitive situation when it is never practiced at any other time. Ideally, then, imagery training should become an integral part of daily practice.

Use All Senses to Enhance Image Vividness

The more senses incorporated into imagery, the more vivid and effective it will be (Harris & Harris, 1984; Orlick, 1986). Many athletes assume that imagery is synonymous with visualization. Although visualization can be an important component of imagery rehearsal, it is important to draw from senses other than sight to increase the quality of imagery, especially in physical activities such as sports. For example, a skier may wish to familiarize herself with an upcoming race course. In addition to "seeing" the course, she also needs to experience the kinesthetic feeling of passing through a particularly tough gate, feeling the wind, and hearing the ski edges slash through the snow. This helps the athlete develop positive feelings as well as a sense of confidence when entering the upcoming event.

Develop Imagery Control

In addition to improving image clarity, it is also important that athletes be able to control the content of their images. Is an athlete's image positive and self-enhancing or negative and self-defeating? As previously discussed, negative imagery can have a detrimental effect on performance. As a sport psychologist or coach, it is important to know the extent to which individual athletes are able to influence the content of their imagery. For example, if a tennis player consistently imagines his serves going into the net, then it may be important to provide specific exercises to strengthen his ability to control his imagery. Fortunately, with practice, most athletes can learn to control the content of their imagery.

Use Internal and External Perspectives

As stated previously, some athletes imagine themselves from the perspective that they are inside their bodies actually experiencing the imagined sensations, whereas others imagine themselves from the perspective of watching their performance on a movie screen. Some researchers have suggested that an internal-imagery perspective is superior to an external-imagery perspective because of the importance of kinesthetic awareness in sport performance (Mahoney & Avener, 1977). However, recent research has suggested the use of external imagery with tasks in which form is important and internal imagery with tasks in which perception and decision making are important (Hardy, 1997; Hardy & Callow, 1999; White & Hardy, 1995). It is possible, for example, that external imagery enhances sport performance by building athletes' self-confidence. As a sport psychologist or coach, you may suggest an internal or external perspective, or both, depending on the needs of the individual athlete and the specific sport demands.

Facilitate Imagery Through Relaxation

Research suggests that imagery combined with relaxation is more effective than imagery alone (Weinberg, Seabourne, & Jackson, 1981). It is thought that the use of relaxation strategies (e.g., passive progressive relaxation or deep breathing) before imagery rehearsal clears athletes' minds of possible distractions and, therefore, allows them to better concentrate on their imagery. The combination of relaxation and imagery training is especially helpful with athletes who are just developing their imagery skills. Unlike athletes who are highly proficient with imagery, less skilled imagers tend to be more easily distracted because their imagery skills are not yet automatic. The purpose of this chapter is not to review relaxation techniques; however, readers can refer to Taylor and Wilson's chapter on arousal regulation (chapter 6, this volume) for more specific relaxation strategies that may be used with imagery.

Develop Coping Strategies Through Imagery

Although positive imagery is generally preferred over negative imagery, there are occasions when negative imagery can also be helpful. If athletes always imagine themselves performing perfectly, then they are almost ensured to set themselves up for failure. Therefore, it is important that athletes learn to cope with adversity as well as success. For example, a baseball player may wish to imagine that he strikes out the first few times at bat, only to come back with a critical hit in the late innings. Coping imagery can help athletes turn a poor performance around. However, such imagery is not recommended for use just before a competitive event. Coping imagery may be best used in the off-season and should not be done too frequently. When athletes are preparing for an important competitive event, it is best to have them imagine themselves performing successfully rather than unsuccessfully.

Use Imagery in Practice and Competition

Imagery rehearsal should be used in practice sessions as well as before competition. Imagery can help an athlete get in the right "zone," both mentally and physically, to optimize training. As an example, imagery can help direct an athlete's attention to specific practice goals. It can also help an athlete who may not be motivated to practice on a given day. Many athletes find it difficult to get up for practice in the off-season. Imagery of arousal-producing situations (e.g., losing to a rival) can be used to help motivate athletes to train hard for competitions that may be months away. In addition, the quality of imagery will improve if it is used daily in practice and, thus, it will serve to better help athletes during the pressures of competition.

Not only is imagery helpful in preparing for competition, but it should also be used frequently during practice. For example, after a mistake, coaches could instruct athletes to mentally correct the problems through imagery before making their next attempts. Likewise, after performing correctly, athletes can take a moment to imagine the look and feel of the correct response. Similarly, when demonstrating, coaches should ask athletes to imagine the skill that was demonstrated before they execute a response. Also, when teaching new offensive or defensive plays to team-sport athletes, coaches should instruct athletes to visualize the correct flow of movement of the team's play. Note, however, that the effective use of imagery during practices does not typically mean that one stops play or instruction for a special 5- or 10-minute imagery session. Rather, coaches should repeatedly ask athletes to "imagine" for very short periods (3 to 10 seconds) as a part of the normal coaching and instructional procedures.

Use Videotapes or Audiotapes to Enhance Imagery Skills

Some athletes find videotapes or audiotapes helpful to develop and reinforce constructive imagery. Although several audiotapes exist on the market, athletes can also make their own tapes to help guide them through an imagery session. If athletes or sport psychologists record tapes, they can then incorporate the same cues in the tapes that are used during physical practice. For example, if a swimmer uses the cue word *punch* to instruct herself to explode off the turn, then this same cue should be used during imagery rehearsal.

Videotapes can also be used to help athletes develop their imagery skills. "Success tapes" can be made with clips of athletes' actual practices or competitions in which they have performed well. An athlete's favorite music can be dubbed onto the tape to serve as a cue to trigger excellent performance in the future. For example, the 1998 U.S. women's ice hockey team used an imagery tape of season highlights interspersed with Muhammad Ali clips to create positive feelings of confidence before their gold medal–winning game. For situations in which it is not practical for athletes to watch a videotape (e.g., at a competitive venue), they can listen to music on a portable stereo headset to help trigger feelings of success.

Use Triggers or Cues to Facilitate Imagery Quality

Triggers or cues are important components of imagery rehearsal. For some athletes, triggers are words or phrases that help them to focus on appropriate cues during imagery. Triggers may also include specific sensory experiences, such as how a given technique or movement feels kinesthetically. Triggers can involve any of the five senses. The key point is that whatever trigger or cue an athlete uses, it must be able to conjure up the appropriate image.

Emphasize Dynamic Kinesthetic Imagery

Another way to enhance the quality of imagery is to have athletes focus particular attention on the kinesthetic feel of a movement. Some athletes also find it useful to actually move during imagery rehearsal. For example, a sprinter may assume a starting position and then imagine blasting from the blocks en route to a record time. A golfer may stand "at address" and actually swing a golf club while imagining the ball traveling through the air and landing close to the hole. With dynamic imagery, the actual movement of the activity often helps athletes to recall more clearly the sensations associated with their performance.

Imagine in Real Time

Sometimes athletes find it helpful to slow down play during imagery, particularly to analyze techniques or patterns of play. Other times they may find it useful to speed up images. It is important to emphasize, however, that because an athlete does not execute techniques in slow motion or in a faster-than-normal speed, the bulk of imagery should be in real time (i.e., the speed at which athletes actually perform). In this way, imagery practice will replicate the actual conditions of play.

Use Imagery Logs

Imagery logs, or notebooks, can serve a variety of purposes. For instance, they can assist athletes in monitoring imagery practice and progress. Different imagery exercises can be recorded along with the extent to which the athlete feels that each exercise was helpful. Imagery logs can also be used to describe previous best performances in an effort to identify better triggers or cues for imagery rehearsal. Overall, imagery logs increase athletes' awareness with regard to the practice they devote to imagery as well as the effectiveness of this practice.

Developing an Imagery Training Program

Having established specific guidelines for using imagery, we now address how to best implement an imagery training program with athletes. Although no two imagery programs are alike, it is important to incorporate the following four phases.

Phase 1: Awareness, Realistic Expectations, and Basic Education

Many coaches are eager to try all that imagery training has to offer. Unfortunately, their efforts are often undermined because of the lack of understanding that many athletes have regarding what imagery is as well as how it can enhance performance. Consider the story of Alan at the beginning of this chapter. After attending a coaching education seminar, he decided to implement an imagery training program with his high school boys basketball team. Although his intentions were good, he failed to educate his team on basic imagery principles and to convince them of the importance of imagery training to their basketball success. As a result, his players questioned the purpose of all this "mental stuff" and never made a commitment to it during practice.

Before implementing any imagery training program, it is critical that sport psychologists and coaches explain what imagery is and address any possible misconceptions that athletes may have. For example, some athletes may look to imagery training as a quick and easy solution to complex performance problems. This thinking is consistent with the desire for instant gratification so prevalent in Western society today. In reality, however, developing and refining imagery skills requires the same systematic practice that physical skills require.

Another common misconception that many athletes hold with regard to imagery training is that it is not useful. It is evident both from the claims of athletes in the popular press (which should be conveyed to athletes) and from a growing body of research that imagery training can have a positive influence in helping athletes achieve their potential. Although imagery training certainly cannot solve all problems, it has helped many athletes reach higher levels of performance.

Because the media attention surrounding sport psychology is often associated with elite performers, many falsely assume that mental skills such as imagery are only for top-ranked amateur or professional athletes. In reality, imagery training can help athletes of all ability levels to achieve their potential. Imagery rehearsal can be used in conjunction with physical training to enhance skill acquisition in any less experienced athlete.

Overall, athletes must be aware of the importance of imagery for performance success if they are to develop a commitment to a training program (Martens, 1987). However, sport psychologists and coaches must be cautious to avoid unrealistic expectations about the effectiveness of imagery. Promises of dramatic performance improvements will set up for failure even the best designed program and undermine the credibility of imagery training.

Therefore, before actually implementing a program, sport psychologists and coaches should hold a brief introductory meeting to explain to athletes what imagery is and how it has helped other athletes in the past. If possible, sport psychologists and coaches should provide examples of successful athletes who have used imagery in the same sport for which the athletes are training. For example, Alan could have conveyed to his basketball team how Bill Russell, one of the best all-time basketball players and winner of 11 National Basketball Association championships, used imagery to execute new plays and build self-confidence (Russell & Branch, 1979). Stories such as this help to establish credibility and respect in the minds of athletes. It lets them know the coach or sport psychologist can speak their language and relate imagery skills to their specific individual needs (Orlick & Partington, 1987; Partington & Orlick, 1987; Ravizza, 1988).

In addition to explaining how imagery can enhance sport performance (e.g., building self-confidence or learning a particular play or
strategy), it is also important to stress in the introductory meeting the
need to practice imagery on a regular basis. During preseason, many
coaches and athletes are enthusiastic about the prospects of an imagery
training program. However, as the season progresses and time demands
and pressures increase, imagery training is often reduced to a handful
of brief meetings added on to an already demanding practice schedule.
Coaches and athletes must view imagery training as an integral part of
practice. Sport psychologists should emphasize that imagery training
will not take away from physical practice but instead will enhance it.

Phase 2: Imagery Skill Evaluation and Development

Once athletes are aware of the value of imagery training, have realistic
expectations, and have received basic education, their specific imagery
skills should be evaluated and developed. Several methods can be used
for evaluating imagery ability. One is to administer a psychological skills
inventory, such as the Sport Imagery Questionnaire discussed by Vealey
and Greenleaf (1998). This questionnaire was originally created by Martens (1982) to measure an athlete's ability to experience each of the
five senses as well as various emotional or mood states. Another way to
evaluate imagery ability is to guide an athlete through an imagery exercise and, afterward, discuss the quality of the images. Several aspects
of the athlete's images in such an evaluation should be considered: (a)
Were the images vivid and controllable? (b) Were they experienced
from an internal or external perspective? (c) Was the athlete able to
feel the physical movements while imaging? and (d) Were images under
the athlete's control? It is important to remember that, just as individual
athletes differ in physical ability, they also differ in their ability to image.

When a sport psychologist or coach recognizes an athlete's
strengths and weaknesses with regard to imagery, he or she can determine which specific practice strategies are most appropriate. In general,
imagery training is designed to enhance the vividness and controllability
of an athlete's imagery. Martens (1987) recommended that a sport imagery training program consist of three steps: (a) sensory awareness
training, (b) vividness training, and (c) controllability training.

Sensory Awareness Training

The first step in Martens's (1987) sport imagery training program is to
have athletes become more aware of their sport experiences. The more

athletes are consciously aware of what they see, hear, and feel, the more likely that they will be able to mentally re-create these experiences through imagery. For example, following a successful practice or competition, an athlete may wish to make note of the various sensations associated with that performance in an effort to identify specific cues that will enhance the quality of imagery in the future.

Vividness Training

After athletes have gained a greater sense of awareness with regard to their sport experiences, Martens (1987) suggested they should work to develop and refine the vividness of their images. This step can be accomplished with a variety of exercises. For example, if athletes have very poor imagery skills, then the sport psychologist or coach might recommend that they start with a simple exercise, such as imagining the details of their bedroom or a piece of equipment associated with their sport (e.g., a football or running shoes). As their imagery skills develop, they can begin to imagine more complex skills associated with their sport performance. Also, athletes may find it helpful to practice in a relaxed environment, free of any possible distractions. As discussed previously, many athletes use relaxation techniques before imagery rehearsal to better focus their attention. There is no limit to the exercises that athletes can do to enhance the vividness of their images. It requires only a little imagination and creativity.

Controllability Training

The final step of Martens's (1987) sport imagery training program involves learning to control and manipulate images. Similar to vividness training, if athletes have poor imagery skills, it is important to begin with a simple exercise in a quiet setting before moving to a more complex, sport-specific exercise. Assume, for example, that a basketball player has difficulty controlling the content of his images. When he tries to imagine himself hitting a 3-point shot, he is unable to visualize the ball going into the basket. In this situation, a sport psychologist or coach may want to suggest that the athlete try a more simple exercise, such as simply imagining that he is dribbling the ball from a stationary position. As he becomes more proficient with this exercise, he can gradually work toward controlling images of more complex basketball skills (e.g., layups, 8-foot jumpshots, 16-foot jumpshots, and then 3-point shots).

It is also important to remind athletes to be patient with themselves at first and not expect too much too soon. This is apparent from comments by Sylvie Bernier, an Olympic champion in springboard diving:

> It took me a long time to control my images and perfect my imagery, maybe a year, doing it every day. At first I couldn't see myself, I always saw everyone else, or I would see my dives wrong all the time. I would get an image of hurting myself, or tripping on the board, or I would "see" something done really bad. As I continued to work at it, I got to the point where I could feel myself doing a perfect dive and hear the crowd yelling at the Olympics. But it took me a long time. (quoted in Orlick, 1990, p. 68)

Regardless of whether an athlete is working on sensory awareness, image vividness, or image control, imagery is a skill like any other, requiring consistent effort to attain a high level of proficiency.

Overall, it is important to remember that individuals differ in their ability to image. Therefore, it is important that within any training program, athletes are evaluated with regard to their imagery ability. Once athletes' strengths and weaknesses are recognized, an imagery program can be tailored to fit the individual needs of a team or athlete.

Phase 3: Using Imagery

Once athletes have developed and evaluated their imagery skills, it is important that they be reminded to continue to use them on a regular basis. Coaches are in the best position to remind athletes to use imagery and can do so with any number of strategies. For example, Mike White, former University of Illinois football coach, made a large meeting room available to his team in the hotel on the nights before games. This "imagery room" was used on a voluntary basis, and players went to this dark, quiet place to mentally prepare themselves. As previously emphasized, coaches should also incorporate the use of imagery in instructional settings by having athletes visualize demonstrations, correct mistakes, and learn new offensive and defensive strategies. Coach support and involvement is essential for a successful imagery training program. Players should also spend time visualizing themselves performing successfully and achieving their goals.

Phase 4: Imagery Evaluation, Adjustment, and Refinement

The final step in any successful imagery training program involves evaluating whether or not the program is meeting its established objectives (Weinberg & Williams, 1998), as well as determining what further adjustments and refinements are needed. For example, assume a 12-week training program has been designed to help a high school soccer team develop and refine their imagery skills. Before implementing the program, the coach or sport psychologist should evaluate current ability levels and assign appropriate exercises for each player. Midway through the season, the athletes' imagery ability should be reevaluated (e.g., with Martens's, 1982, sport imagery questionnaire) to determine how much, if any, progress has been made. For those athletes who have shown little improvement, individual meetings should be scheduled to identify possible problems. Depending on the individual situation, a new strategy may be suggested for future practice. Those athletes who are improving would simply be encouraged to continue with their current strategies, to log imagery effectiveness, and to explore new ways of using imagery.

If an imagery training program is meeting its established objectives, then the sport psychologist or coach can continue with confidence. However, if the program is not meeting its objectives, it is critical to examine the situation to determine why. What obstacles are preventing the program from reaching its goals, and how can these obstacles be overcome? Without critically examining an imagery training program, some athletes may falsely conclude that they are poor imagers when, in fact, they were using inappropriate strategies to develop their imagery skills. Program evaluations provide important feedback on what strategies are effective and for whom they are effective. In addition, they provide an opportunity to alter strategies that may not be effective.

In summary, no two imagery training programs are identical. Each is designed to meet the unique characteristics and needs of the athlete or team for whom it is intended. However, within an individual training program, it is important to include each of the four phases outlined. For any training program to be effective, the athletes must understand that imagery is a skill that requires consistent effort over time to develop. Furthermore, during the training process, it is necessary to evaluate progress and make whatever adjustments are necessary to ensure that the program is meeting its desired objectives.

Summary

Imagery, a process by which sensory experiences are stored in memory and internally recalled and performed in the absence of external stimuli, is a powerful performance enhancement technique studied and used by sport psychologists. Several imagery theories and models focus on explaining how imagery influences performance, as well as how athletes can use imagery. Based on research and practical experience, several guidelines have been suggested to help those practitioners and athletes interested in implementing imagery rehearsal to enhance athletic performance. Several common problems involving the actual implementation of an imagery training program are addressed, and specific suggestions are made about how to best handle them. When implementing an imagery training program, it is important to incorporate the four specific phases outlined in this chapter.

Overall, it is important to remember that imagery is like any physical skill in that it requires systematic practice to develop and refine. Individual athletes differ in their ability to image; therefore, those who have low ability must be encouraged to remain patient. Imagery is not a magical cure for performance woes. It is, however, an effective tool that—when combined with practice and commitment—can help athletes reach their personal and athletic potentials.

References

Ahsen, A. (1984). ISM: The triple code model for imagery and psychophysiology. *Journal of Mental Imagery, 8,* 15–42.

Bandura, A. (1977). Self-efficacy: Toward a unifying theory of behavioral change. *Psychological Review, 84,* 191–215.

Barr, K., & Hall, C. (1992). The use of imagery by rowers. *International Journal of Sport Psychology, 23,* 243–361.

Callow, N., Hardy, L., & Hall, C. (1998). The effect of a motivational-mastery imagery intervention on the sport confidence of three elite badminton players. *Journal of Applied Sport Psychology, 10,* S135.

Feltz, D. L., & Landers, D. M. (1983). The effects of mental practice on motor skill learning and performance: A meta-analysis. *Journal of Sport Psychology, 5,* 25–57.

Gould, D., & Udry, E. (1994). Psychological skills for enhancing performance: Arousal regulation strategies. *Medicine and Science in Sports and Exercise, 26,* 478–485.

Hall, C. R., Rodgers, W. M., & Barr, K. A. (1990). The use of imagery by athletes in selected sports. *The Sport Psychologist, 4,* 1–10.

Hardy, L. (1997). Three myths about applied consultancy work. *Journal of Applied Sport Psychology, 9,* 277–294.

Hardy, L., & Callow, N. (1999). Efficacy of external and internal visual imagery perspectives for the enhancement of performance on tasks in which form is important. *Journal of Sport and Exercise Psychology, 32,* 95–112.

Harris, D. V., & Harris, B. L. (1984). *The athlete's guide to sport psychology: Mental training for physical people.* New York: Leisure Press.

Highlen, P. S., & Bennett, B. B. (1983). Elite divers and wrestlers: A comparison between open and closed-skilled athletes. *Journal of Sport Psychology, 5,* 390–409.

Jacobson, E. (1932). Electrophysiology of mental activities. *American Journal of Psychology, 44,* 677–694.

Kohl, R. M., & Roenker, D. L. (1983). Mechanism involvement during skill imagery. *Journal of Motor Behavior, 15,* 179–190.

Lang, P. J. (1977). Imagery in therapy: An information processing analysis of fear. *Behavior Therapy, 8,* 862–886.

Lang, P. J. (1979). A bio-information theory of emotional imagery. *Psychophysiology, 16,* 495–512.

Mahoney, M. J., & Avener, M. (1977). Psychology of the elite athlete: An exploratory study. *Cognitive Therapy and Research, 3,* 361–366.

Martens, R. (1982, September). *Imagery in sport.* Paper presented at the Medical and Scientific Aspects of Elitism in Sport Conference, Brisbane, Australia.

Martens, R. (1987). *Coaches guide to sport psychology.* Champaign, IL: Human Kinetics.

Martin, K. A., & Hall, C. R. (1995). Using mental imagery to enhance intrinsic motivation. *Journal of Sport and Exercise Psychology, 17,* 54–69.

Martin, K. A., Moritz, S. E., & Hall, C. R. (1999). Imagery use in sport: A literature review and applied model. *The Sport Psychologist, 13,* 245–268.

Meichenbaum, D. (1985). *Stress innoculation training.* Elmsford, NY: Pergamon Press.

Meyers, A. W., Cooke, C. J., Cullen, J., & Liles, L. (1979). Psychological aspects of athletic competitors: A replication across sports. *Cognitive Therapy and Research, 3,* 361–366.

Moritz, S. E., Hall, C. R., Martin, K. A., & Vadocz, E. (1996). What are confident athletes imaging? An examination of image content. *The Sport Psychologist, 10,* 171–179.

Mumford, P., & Hall, C. (1985). The effects of internal and external imagery on performing figures in figure skating. *Canadian Journal of Applied Sport Sciences, 10,* 171–177.

Munroe, K., Giacobbi, P. R., Hall, C., & Weinberg, R. (2000). The four W's of imagery use: Where, when, why, and what. *The Sport Psychologist, 14,* 119–137.

Munroe, K., Hall, C., Simms, S., & Weinberg, R. (1998). The influence of type of sport and time of season on athletes' use of imagery. *The Sport Psychologist, 12,* 440–449.

Murphy, S. M. (1994). Imagery interventions in sport. *Medicine and Science in Sports and Exercise, 26,* 486–494.

Murphy, S., & Jowdy, D. (1992). Imagery and mental rehearsal. In T. Horn (Ed.), *Advances in sport psychology* (pp. 221–250). Champaign, IL: Human Kinetics.

Orlick, T. (1986). *Psyching for sport: Mental training for athletes.* Champaign, IL: Leisure Press.

Orlick, T. (1990). *In pursuit of excellence: How to win in sport and life through mental training.* Champaign, IL: Leisure Press.

Orlick, T., & Partington, J. (1987). The sport psychology consultant: Analysis of critical components as viewed by Canadian athletes. *The Sport Psychologist, 1,* 4–7.

Partington, J., & Orlick, T. (1987). The sport psychology consultant: Olympic coaches' views. *The Sport Psychologist, 1,* 95–102.

Paivio, A. (1985). Cognitive and motivational functions of imagery in human performance. *Canadian Journal of Applied Sport Sciences, 10,* 22–28.

Ravizza, K. (1988). Gaining entry with athletic personnel for season-long consulting. *The Sport Psychologist, 2,* 243–254.

Rawlings, E. I., Rawlings, I. L., Chen, C. S., & Yilk, M. D. (1972). The facilitating effects of mental rehearsal in the acquisition of rotary pursuit tracking. *Psychonomic Science, 26,* 71–73.

Russell, B., & Branch, T. (1979). *Second wind.* New York: Ballantine Books.

Ryan, E. D., & Simons, J. (1981). Cognitive demand imagery and frequency of mental practice as factors influencing the acquisition of mental skills. *Journal of Sport Psychology, 15,* 1–15.

Sackett, R. S. (1934). The influences of symbolic rehearsal upon the retention of a maze habit. *Journal of General Psychology, 13,* 113–128.

Salmon, J., Hall, C., & Haslam, I. (1994). The use of imagery by soccer players. *Journal of Applied Sport Psychology, 6,* 116–133.

Shelton, T. O., & Mahoney, M. J. (1978). The content and effect of "psyching-up" strategies in weight lifters. *Cognitive Therapy and Research, 2,* 275–284.

Smith, R. E. (1980). A cognitive–affective approach to stress management training for athletes. In C. Nadeau, W. Halliwell, K. Newell, & G. C. Roberts (Eds.), *Psychology of motor behavior and sport: 1979* (pp. 54–72). Champaign, IL: Human Kinetics.

Suinn, R. (1972). Removing emotional obstacles to learning and performance by visuomotor behavioral rehearsal. *Behavior Therapy, 3,* 308–310.

Suinn, R. (1993). Imagery. In R. N. Singer, M. Murphey, & L. K. Tennant (Eds.), *Handbook of research on sport psychology* (pp. 492–510). New York: Macmillan.

Vealey, R., & Greenleaf, C. (1998). Seeing is believing: Understanding and using imagery in sport. In J. M. Williams (Ed.), *Applied sport psychology: Personal growth to peak performance* (3rd ed., pp. 237–269). Mountain View, CA: Mayfield.

Weinberg, R. S. (1981). The relationship between mental preparation strategies and motor performance: A review and critique. *Quest, 33,* 195–213.

Weinberg, R. S., Gould, D., Jackson, A., & Barnes, P. (1980). Influence of cognitive strategies on tennis serves of players of high and low ability. *Perceptual and Motor Skills, 50,* 663–666.

Weinberg, R. S., Seabourne, T. G., & Jackson, A. (1981). Effects of visuo-motor behavior rehearsal, relaxation, and imagery on karate performance. *Journal of Sport Psychology, 3,* 228–238.

Weinberg, R. S., & Williams, J. M. (1998). Integrating and implementing a psychological skills training program. In J. M. Williams (Ed.), *Applied sport psychology: Personal growth to peak performance* (3rd ed., pp. 329–358). Mountain View, CA: Mayfield.

White, A., & Hardy, L. (1995). An in-depth analysis of the uses of imagery by high-level slalom canoeists and artistic gymnasts. *The Sport Psychologist, 12,* 387–403.

Woolfolk, R., Parrish, W., & Murphy, S. M. (1985). The effects of positive and negative imagery on motor skill performance. *Cognitive Therapy and Research, 9,* 235–241.

Cognitive Strategies in Sport and Exercise Psychology

Jean M. Williams and Thad R. Leffingwell

More than 15 years have passed since Straub and Williams (1984) heralded the emergence of the field of cognitive sport psychology and more than 25 years since Mahoney's (1977) landmark paper advocating a cognitive skills approach to the understanding and improvement of sport performance. Today, cognitive approaches to enhancing athletic performance dominate sport psychologists' research and intervention strategies (Strean & Roberts, 1992; Whelan, Mahoney, & Meyers, 1991).

Cognitive approaches in sport psychology have been broadly and loosely defined, including techniques such as goal setting, imagery and mental rehearsal, attention control, and cognitive anxiety management. Other chapters in this book deal with many of these topics. This chapter focuses primarily on the relationship of one's thoughts to sport performance and approaches to altering thinking for the enhancement of sport performance and enjoyment. We briefly discuss less conventional interventions based on theoretical challenges to the assumptions of the cognitive model. The chapter concludes with a brief discussion of the relationship between cognitions and exercise behavior, attention, and anxiety.

Cognitions and Sport Performance

What athletes think about themselves, their performance, specific situations, and so forth directly affects their feelings and behaviors. Unfortunately, what athletes say to themselves is not always conducive to good performance, and all too often, it is at the root of poor performance. Although many athletes and sport psychologists believe the best performances occur with no conscious thinking—"automatic" performance—it is probably unrealistic to expect athletes to shut off all thinking during every performance (Zinsser, Bunker, & Williams, 2001). We should not blame thinking itself for poor performance but should instead blame inappropriate or misguided thinking (Bell, 1983). The critical question to answer for improved performance is not whether to think but what, when, and how to think.

Several research studies have supported the notion that successful athletes use different cognitive strategies than do less successful athletes (see Greenspan & Feltz, 1989, or Williams & Krane, 2001, for a more thorough review). Highlen and Bennett (1979) found that wrestlers who qualified for an elite national team reported fewer negative self-thoughts than did nonqualifiers, but they reported no differences in cognitive coping resources such as positive self-thoughts or rationalizing. Similarly, Gould, Weiss, and Weinberg (1981) found that more successful collegiate wrestlers had fewer self-doubts and more match-related thoughts before competition than less successful wrestlers. All of the researchers reported higher self-confidence for the more successful athletes. These results indicate that more successful athletes utilize more appropriate thoughts and experience less negativity and self-doubt compared with even slightly less successful athletes (e.g., Olympic qualifiers vs. nonqualifiers).

Recent qualitative studies have examined the differences in cognitions and affect before and during best and worst performances for elite Olympic wrestlers. Gould, Eklund, and Jackson (1992a, 1992b) found that the wrestlers reported positive expectancies and heightened commitment before their best performances. In contrast, before their worst performances, the athletes reported negative, irrelevant, or irregular thought patterns. In terms of their thoughts during competition, the wrestlers reported task-focused thinking, including task-specific self-talk during their best performances and several ineffective thoughts during their worst performances, including task-irrelevant and negative thoughts. In another qualitative study, Gould, Finch, and Jackson (1993) investigated the stress-coping strategies of U.S. national champion figure skaters. The two most common strategies used by these highly successful athletes included (a) rational thinking and self-talk and (b) positive focus and orientation. Although causality cannot be inferred from these studies, they suggest that successful athletes use more effective cognitive strategies than less successful athletes, indicating that interventions to enhance effective cognitions (e.g., more positive, rational, task focused) may prove effective at enhancing performance.

Cognitive—Behavioral Interventions

The high-pressure situations of competitive sport may represent an ideal environment for fostering irrational or distorted thinking styles. Irrational self-defeating beliefs are roadblocks to self-direction and achievement in sport and exercise settings. In addition to interfering with good, consistent performance, these self-defeating beliefs can interfere with motivation to participate and may result in individuals avoiding the competitive arena (Ellis, 1982). Sport psychologists use several cognitive—behavioral techniques to help athletes become aware of irrational or inappropriate thinking styles and to combat or counter this thinking, ultimately creating habits of effective thinking. These techniques are typically derived from and resemble clinical interventions based on the cognitive model, including rational—emotive therapy (Ellis, 1977), cognitive therapy (Beck, 1970), and cognitive—behavioral modification (Meichenbaum, 1977). Dobson and Block (1988) described three important assumptions of the cognitive model: (a) Cognitive activity can affect behavior (including sport performance), (b) cognitive activity can be altered, and (c) cognitive change can facilitate desired behavioral change. This section of the chapter discusses common types of distorted thinking and how to identify and refute irrational or distorted thinking in sport.

Irrational and Distorted Thinking

Ellis (1982) identified four general irrational beliefs that may interfere with athletes reaching their potential. These four beliefs are (a) "I *must* do well in sport, and if I don't, I am an incompetent, worthless person"; (b) "I *must* do well to gain the love and approval of others, and if I don't, it is *horrible*"; (c) "Everyone *must* treat me with respect and fairness at all times"; and (d) "The conditions of my life *must* be arranged so that I get what I want easily and quickly." In addition to these irrational beliefs, athletes may have several cognitive distortions that can interfere with effective performance (Gauron, 1984). Irrational beliefs and distorted thinking patterns interfere with performance by providing the athlete with faulty information about the competitive environment, resulting in misdirected attention, emotional distress such as excessive anxiety, or lowered self-concept. Gauron (1984) identified the following list of distorted thinking styles that athletes commonly use:

- *Perfectionism.* Athletes and coaches often get caught up in demanding perfection. This unrealistic expectation leads to excessive pressure and undermines effective coping. Ellis (1982) differentiated between perfectionist *desires,* which may lead to championship performance, and perfectionist demands and commands, which have "probably wrecked more athletic attempts than any other self-sabotaging factor" (p. 30). Perfectionistic attitudes can also lead to a negative self-concept and a fear-of-failure syndrome due to self-imposed negative consequences when less-than-perfect performances occur.
- *Catastrophizing.* When athletes hold beliefs that include horrible consequences when expectations are not met, they often exaggerate potential consequences of imagined or real negative events. Catastrophizers may expect the worst in every situation —often worse than reality or previous experience would suggest. This expectation can contribute to actual negative outcomes.
- *Self-worth depends on achievement.* Many athletes view their value as individuals relative to their degree of athletic success. This perception is particularly damaging for young athletes who perceive their self-worth and worth to others, particularly their parents, as depending on their participation and success in sports. This perception clearly increases the pressure to perform, contributes to low and unstable self-worth, and can interfere with the fun of participation in sport.
- *Personalization.* Athletes sometimes exhibit a self-defeating tendency to personalize everything. These athletes tend to overestimate their personal responsibility for every failure and mistake. For example, their missed free throw in the final seconds of the game "caused the team to lose." Over time, this misperception clearly contributes to a low self-concept, elevated performance anxiety, and even decreased motivation and commitment.
- *Fallacy of fairness.* Unfortunately, "fairness" often translates simply to wanting one's own way versus what someone else (e.g., the coach) thinks is fair, or best, for the group. Perceptions of unfair

treatment may interfere with interpersonal relations, appropriate focus of attention, and the ability to cope with adversity.

- *Blaming.* Although some athletes may overpersonalize, others excessively attribute failure externally, for example, to coaches, conditions, or officials. This type of thinking allows athletes relief from all responsibility, which is counter to good performance and effective coping. Athletes need to realistically and rationally evaluate performance outcomes and to accept responsibility when it is appropriate to do so (Orbach, Singer, & Price, 1999).
- *Polarized thinking.* Athletes are often tempted to view situations and people in absolute terms, that is, in black and white. This type of distorted thinking often represents itself as labeling selves or others in simple, unidimensional terms, such as *losers, cheaters,* or *unbeatable.* These irrational labels contribute to performance expectancies and can directly influence performance.
- *One-trial generalizations.* Athletes may sometimes use a single incident to define expectancies for future performances. For example, a college basketball player stated, "We are a second-half basketball team" after his team played its first two games of the season. This kind of irrational generalization interferes with good performance, proper preparation, and appropriate focus. In this example, that team could underemphasize the importance of their play in the first half of a game and thus fail during that half to make adjustments and take advantage of opportunities.

Identifying and Modifying Irrational and Distorted Thinking

Athletes are often unaware of the irrational beliefs or distorted thinking underlying emotional conflicts and performance difficulties. Identifying these distortions represents the first, and most important, step toward modifying maladaptive thinking styles and enjoying the benefits of rational thinking. Coaches and sport psychologists can help identify ineffective thinking by paying close attention to the athlete's attributions and evaluations following performances, particularly poor performances. Often, teachable moments occur just after important competitions, when the athlete has a greater awareness of cognitions before and during competition and may be more open to learning. Also, because athletes often learn distorted thinking patterns from their coaches, coaches in particular must be aware of their own irrational beliefs and the way they model distorted thinking for the athletes.

Silva (1982) identified three phases for implementing cognitive restructuring interventions with athletes: identification, cognitive restructuring, and pairing. In the *identification phase*, the sport psychologist and the athlete attempt to define the boundaries of the affected behavior and the irrational beliefs or self-defeating verbalizations present in the situation. This identification can be accomplished through conversation, journal writing, or actually performing the skill and verbalizing thoughts in the presence of the sport psychologist. During the *restructuring phase*, the athlete is convinced of the inappropriateness of the thoughts, and more effective replacement thoughts are created. Silva emphasized that the effectiveness of the intervention depends on recognizing the need to change. In the *pairing phase*, the athlete uses self-instructional imagery and verbal cues to facilitate the application of new thinking patterns into actual performance. The athletes should practice the imagery several times a day to make the new thoughts automatic.

Ellis and Harper (1975), Beck (1970), and Meichenbaum (1977) emphasized the importance of underlying beliefs in maintaining automatic thoughts. They recommended challenging these underlying beliefs as a vehicle for long-term change in thinking patterns. Beck suggested purposefully acting counter to identified irrational beliefs as a way of experiencing new thinking and feeling. For example, an athlete who uses excessive criticism and self-abuse after every mistake may try to smile and be overtly self-complimentary after a few mistakes to experience the consequences (i.e., thoughts, feelings, and performance) associated with this new behavior.

Athletes, coaches, sport psychologists, and parents can benefit from substituting rational for irrational thinking during all phases of training and competition. If athletes have a particularly difficult irrational belief to rid themselves of, they may benefit from daily affirmation statements counter to the belief. For example, an athlete may use the affirmation "I want to play great today, but my worth as a person does not depend on how I play." Physically relaxing may increase the effectiveness of attempts to counter irrational beliefs. As mentioned previously, most irrational beliefs create anxiety and tension, thus decreasing receptivity to more effective, rational thoughts.

If doubt exists about whether a belief is irrational or ineffective, Steinmetz, Blankenship, Brown, Hall, and Miller (1980) suggested the following criteria to evaluate the belief:

- Are the beliefs based on objective reality?
- Are they helpful to you?

- Are they useful in reducing interpersonal conflicts?
- Do they help you reach your goals?
- Do they reduce emotional conflict?

If the athlete answers no to any of these questions, the belief is likely irrational or counterproductive, and the individual will benefit from modifying it.

Irrational beliefs are well-entrenched in sport: "No pain, no gain," "Give 110% all the time," "Practice makes perfect," and "Winning isn't everything—it's the only thing." Sometimes athletes or coaches believe that modifying some types of irrational thinking (e.g., perfectionism, self-worth depends on achievement) threatens competitiveness or drive. More likely, modifying irrational beliefs enhances performance by helping athletes stay relaxed, task focused, positive, and motivated (Zinsser et al., 2001).

Meta-analytic reviews of sport psychology intervention research have concluded that cognitive interventions such as cognitive restructuring do, in fact, improve the performance of athletes (Greenspan & Feltz, 1989; Meyers, Whelan, & Murphy, 1996). Greenspan and Feltz found that researchers reported positive results in all 11 studies of cognitive restructuring interventions. Greenspan and Feltz cautioned that causality could be inferred from only a few of these studies and expressed concern that perhaps journals publish studies with only positive results, causing an overestimation of the effectiveness of sport psychology interventions, including cognitive restructuring. The meta-analysis by Meyers, Whelan, and Murphy calculated a greater effect size for cognitive restructuring interventions ($n = 4$, $d = .79$, $SD = .36$; n = number of studies, d = effect size, SD = standard deviation) than that found for goal setting ($n = 3$, $d = .54$, $SD = .15$), mental rehearsal ($n = 28$, $d = .57$, $SD = .75$), and relaxation interventions ($n = 25$, $d = .73$, $SD = 1.65$). These authors also concluded that cognitive restructuring interventions improve performance. Although published studies of the effectiveness of cognitive restructuring interventions are limited in number and practically nonexistent with elite athletes, they have reliably demonstrated effectiveness at improving sport performance.

Self-Talk

Broadly defined, *self-talk* occurs whenever an individual thinks, whether making statements internally or externally. We are most concerned with athletes' self-statements that direct attention ("focus"), label the self or others ("I am a choker"), judge performances ("great shot"), and contribute to or undermine good performance. Self-talk serves as the vehicle for making perceptions and beliefs conscious, thereby providing the key to gaining cognitive control (Zinsser et al., 2001). The beliefs and thinking styles discussed previously are often manifested in self-talk, and self-talk is an effective access point for altering these beliefs and styles of thinking.

Several studies have documented the utility of self-talk in competitive sport. Highlen and Bennett (1983) found that divers qualifying for the Pan American Games used more positive self-instruction self-talk and less praising self-talk during competition than nonqualifiers. More successful divers also reported using self-talk more during training and competition. Orlick and Partington (1988) found that successful Olympic athletes often used positive self-statements as part of a well-developed precompetition plan.

In contrast, self-doubt characterized athletes with an ineffective focus of attention. Similarly, the studies by Gould and colleagues (1992a, 1992b) of Olympic wrestlers indicated that self-talk was a common technique for fostering positive expectancies and appropriately focusing attention on the task.

A study of observed self-talk and behavioral assessments with junior tennis players found that negative self-talk was associated with losing (Van Raalte, Brewer, Rivera, & Petitpas, 1994). These results implicated negative self-talk as a contributor to poorer performance, but they failed to show a relationship of positive self-talk to better performance. The authors concluded that the tennis players may have internalized their positive self-talk; thus, the researchers could not observe it as readily as negative self-talk. A later study with adult tennis players (Van Raalte, Cornelius, Brewer, & Hatten, 2000) failed to replicate these findings. Negative self-talk did not predict performance, whereas "positive self-talk use had a positive effect on the performance of only one player, seemed to have a detrimental effect on two players' performances, and was unrelated to 15 players' performances" (p. 351). The researchers also found that tennis match circumstances (e.g., point outcome, serving status) predicted the use of negative self-talk for all the players and the use of positive self-talk for only some of the players.

An experimental investigation of three different types of positive self-talk—task-relevant statements, mood words, and positive self-statements—demonstrated positive performance effects with cross country skiers for all three experimental conditions compared with a control condition that used the self-talk normally used by the skiers (Rushall, Hall, Roux, Sasseville, & Rushall, 1988). Other experimental studies investigating the effects of positive self-monitoring have suggested that positive self-statements may be more effective than negative ones at improving both golfing and bowling performance (Johnston-O'Connor & Kirschenbaum, 1986; Kirschenbaum, Ordman, Tomarken, & Holtzbauer, 1982; Kirschenbaum, Owens, & O'Connor, 1998). Several studies have found that positive self-talk led to better performance than negative self-talk for subjects completing fairly simple, closed-skill tasks (Dagrou, Gauvin, & Halliwell, 1992; Schill, Monroe, Evans, & Ramanaiah, 1978; Van Raalte et al., 1995). Self-talk has also been recommended for use in maintaining exercise behavior (Buffone, Sachs, & Dowd, 1984; Gauvin, 1990).

In contrast, some descriptive studies using self-report of self-talk content found no difference in the content of self-talk between more and less successful athletes (Rotella, Gansneder, Ojala, & Billings, 1980) or between an athlete's best or worst performances (Dagrou, Gauvin, & Halliwell, 1991). Overall, however, the preceding studies provide evidence in support of the hypothesis that both positive self-talk and self-confidence are associated with better, or at least, no worse, performances. It appears that, in general, a positive self-concept, high self-confidence, a task-relevant focus of attention, and less self-doubt relate to better performance. Self-talk that detracts from any of these conditions probably inhibits performance. This section offers suggestions for identifying and modifying self-talk.

Uses for Self-Talk

Self-talk serves a variety of different uses in sport. For example, individuals can use self-talk to correct habits, focus attention, modify activation, and build and maintain self-confidence.

Correcting Bad Habits

Athletes can use self-talk when trying to correct well-learned skills or habits. Often, bad habits are "automatic" in technique, and self-talk can help consciously "override" this automaticity. The content of the self-talk may range from a description of an entire motion (e.g., "swing back, step, hit, follow through") to a single cue word for minor changes (e.g., "turn" or "push"). When using self-talk for changing technique, the self-talk *must* focus on desirable movements, *not* unwanted movements. For example, if a golfer wants to shift weight on the downswing, appropriate self-talk would be "shift" *not* "don't hang back." This type of self-talk is appropriate for the learning or corrective stage, but it may not be necessary once skills are learned or during actual competitive performance if the correct actions occur automatically, that is, without prompting.

Self-Talk for Focusing Attention

Athletes can use self-talk for effectively focusing attention during practice or competition. Athletes can use self-statements or cue words to focus attention in the present moment ("right now" or "be here") and on task-specific cues ("track the ball" or "pick your target"). These cues are used to maintain focus and to refocus when an athlete has lost appropriate focus. For example, Landin and Hebert (1999) found skilled tennis players improved their volleying performance after they were taught a two-word ("split, turn") self-talk sequence timed to specific reactions and movement on the court. The players attributed the success of the self-talk intervention to its directing their attentional focus.

Self-Talk for Modifying Activation

Athletes can modify their activation level by using self-statements to decrease or increase their physical arousal. These self-statements may include relaxing cues (e.g., "easy," "quiet," "relax") or energizing cues (e.g., "go," "get up," "pumped"). For greater effectiveness, athletes should pick cues that have the best emotional content for them. These cues can help to establish optimal activation before and during competition or can help modify it when not appropriate.

Self-Talk for Self-Confidence

Self-statements affect self-confidence either positively or negatively. Self-talk that reflects negative expectancies and excessive self-doubt undermines self-confidence. Although many perceived sources of self-confidence exist outside of an athlete's control—performance outcomes, expectations of others, or talent—the athlete alone controls self-talk. Occasionally, self-statements about negative expectancies can self-motivate and mobilize effort, but problems with self-confidence can arise if this theme of self-statements dominates the athlete's self-talk content. Thus, self-criticism is best restricted to performance or behavior (e.g., "I hit a bad shot"), and not the self (e.g., "I am a terrible golfer. I'll never amount to anything."). In addition, self-statements before and during competition should most often contain positive expectancies of outcome to maintain effort and motivation. Such self-statements, however, should stop short of fostering unwarranted, excessive optimism. Kirschenbaum, O'Connor, and Owens (1999) found that golfers can be overly optimistic and thereby have such positive illusions about their skill and control that they make poor decisions (e.g., overly aggressive shot selection on challenging holes). An intervention that taught more conservative and realistic shot selection led to better performance.

Identifying Self-Talk

To determine whether self-talk needs changing, athletes must first have an awareness of the content of their self-statements and the effect the self-talk has on performance (Meichenbaum, 1977). Athletes must become aware of not only negative and self-defeating self-talk, but also positive and facilitating self-talk. A simple paper-clip exercise can help many athletes increase awareness of the frequency of their negative self-talk. Have the athlete carry some paper clips in a pocket and then transfer a paper clip to a different pocket each time a negative self-statement occurs. Often, athletes become motivated to change because of their amazement at the number of paper clips shifted and the adverse consequences of the self-talk.

Retrospection
Athletes reflect on performances in which they performed particularly well or poorly in an effort to recall thoughts and feelings before and during these performances. For maximal effectiveness, athletes should use this technique as soon after a performance as possible to not forget important aspects of the performance. Often, watching a videotape of the performance can aid more accurate and thorough recall. If sport psychologists observe the performance, they can give specific prompts to help athletes recall significant moments before, during, or after a performance. For athletes who have little awareness of their self-talk, retrospection may not work.

Imagery
Athletes skilled in imagery can vividly recreate past performances to help recall thoughts and feelings. The reliving of the performance through imagery helps athletes become more aware of self-talk they had and the effects of the self-statements on their emotions and performance.

Observation

For athletes who frequently say their self-talk out loud, the sport psychologist can help raise the awareness of self-talk by observing and recording verbalized self-talk during performance. Ideally, sport psychologists should collect information about athletes' verbalizations, the situations in which they occurred and, if possible, the performance consequences. Armed with these data, sport psychologists can more effectively raise athletes' awareness of the content and frequency of their self-talk. Also, this technique provides sport psychologists with data about the actual effects of self-talk on performance. For example, if a tennis player wins most of the points following negative verbalizations, the sport psychologist may reconsider working with the athlete to alter those self-statements. If the observed self-statements improve performance but damage self-esteem or self-confidence, the sport psychologist may choose different strategies to help the athlete get the same performance effects without long-term consequences for self-concept. This technique has the major drawback of being effective only for verbalized, observable self-statements. (See Van Raalte et al., 1994 and 2000 for a prototype of an observation scale that sport psychologists could use to help identify and categorize self-talk and gestures.)

Self-Talk Log

Often, athletes claim to be unaware of the content or frequency of verbalizations during performance. These athletes cannot accurately recall self-talk through retrospection or imagery. Daily record keeping in a self-talk log can effectively increase awareness. The log should include the situation in which the self-talk occurred (e.g., in the locker room, after a foul was called against the athlete, just before a big point); the content of the self-statements (e.g., "Don't choke," "I can't believe you did that"); and the consequence of the self-talk, expressed in terms of performance consequences (e.g., double fault), emotional consequences (e.g., frustration, anger), or both. The self-talk log has several advantages. It usually creates the greatest awareness of self-talk by providing the most accurate and thorough identification of self-talk. It also provides for the best identification of the situations triggering the self-talk and the consequences of the self-talk. If possible, athletes should occasionally carry a small tape recorder during practice to provide immediate documentation of verbalizations, whether said out loud or merely thought. The sport psychologist can also encourage the athlete to record the situation triggering the self-talk and the behavioral and emotional consequences of the self-talk.

Modifying Self-Talk

Once the preceding techniques raise awareness of self-talk and identify potentially facilitating and self-defeating thoughts, the athlete and the sport psychologist can use other techniques to modify self-talk. Assuming the athletes have an appropriate awareness of their self-talk and sufficient motivation to make changes, the sport psychologist can use the following techniques to facilitate self-talk modification: stopping thoughts, changing negative thoughts to positive thoughts, countering, and reframing. Without commitment to change by the athlete, attempts at using the techniques to modify self-talk will probably prove futile.

Even with commitment to change and appropriate practice, some athletes may not have success with cognitive techniques. When this problem occurs, the sport psychologist may need to look for underlying factors that contribute to the athlete's difficulty at altering ineffective self-talk. For example, athletes with low self-esteem and low self-concepts may lack sufficient confidence to believe constructive self-talk or to believe that they deserve to succeed and have good things happen to them. When this type of situation exists, sport psychologists, assuming they are qualified, may need to focus attention on issues directly related to self-esteem and self-concept.

Thought Stoppage

After the athlete has identified specific self-statements or patterns of self-talk that need elimination, the technique of thought stoppage can help minimize this self-talk (Meyers & Schleser, 1980). Thought stoppage involves the use of a trigger or cue to interrupt unwanted thoughts when they occur. This trigger can be verbal (e.g., the word *stop*), visual (e.g., a piece of tape on a tennis racquet or imagining a red stop light), or physical (e.g., snapping of the fingers). Athletes can use almost any trigger they choose, as long as it does not interfere with performance and it is applied consistently. This technique immediately interrupts the unwanted thoughts and, with practice, may effectively control negative self-talk. By stopping negative self-statements before they lead to negative feelings and behaviors, athletes experience relief from self-imposed negativity. With consistent use of thought stoppage, the need for the technique should decrease because the frequency of the unwanted negative self-talk decreases. Some concerns about the use of thought stoppage are discussed in more detail in the section on alternative approaches.

Change Negative Thoughts to Positive Thoughts

Increased use of positive self-talk may help athletes reduce negative self-talk. Negative, or counterproductive, thoughts can be immediately followed by positive thoughts that encourage or appropriately direct attention. For example, if the athlete says, "I hate playing for this coach," she might follow that statement with "I may not enjoy this coach as much as my old coach, but I can learn a lot from her."

Use of this technique has several advantages over thought stoppage alone. Athletes who doubt their ability to stop negative thoughts from occurring may accept that they can at least replace that thought with a more constructive one. If athletes experience more early success in using the cognitive change techniques, they might persevere longer in trying to change faulty thinking habits. Furthermore, substituting with a positive thought may negate, or at least minimize, the effect of the negative thought.

One way to help athletes successfully implement this technique is to have them list their typical negative self-statements on a sheet of paper and then opposite each statement write an appropriate positive self-statement that they might immediately substitute the next time they make the statement. Because negative thoughts often occur when an individual is under stress and overactivated physiologically (Zinsser et al., 2001), the sport psychologist may want to suggest that the athlete say the positive self-statement after the exhalation of a deep breath (see Taylor, chapter 6, this volume, for a discussion of arousal regulation).

Countering

Changing negative self-statements to positive ones will likely not change behavior as long as the athlete still believes in the negative statements (Bell, 1983). If athletes are encouraged to only "be nicer to themselves," we cannot expect more than superficial and short-term effects. Countering represents a useful technique for challenging the athlete's belief in the negative statement, thereby facilitating the acceptance of the constructive self-statement.

Countering is a process of internal debate, using facts, reason, and rational thinking to counter self-defeating thoughts. Bell (1983) suggested that when athletes believe in negative self-statements, they need to build a case against that belief to effectively make changes in self-talk and performance. When using countering, the athlete gathers evidence from a variety of sources to refute the negative belief. For example, an athlete may perceive heightened activation during competition as a sign of fear and weakness: "My heart is pounding so hard. I'm going to choke. I'm such a wimp." The athlete can counter these self-defeating statements by using evidence from past experiences with heightened activation. "My heart is pounding hard, but that's natural, happens to everybody. It is a sign that this is important and exciting. I have come through in these situations before, and I can do it now." In this situation, encouraging athletes to say "I am not nervous" or "I am calm" would not be sufficient, particularly when athletes have evidence available that they *are* nervous (e.g., a pounding heart).

Reframing

Some individuals, athletes included, tend to view the world in narrow, rigid terms. Gauron (1984) recommended the technique of reframing for changing an athlete's frame of reference, or view, of the world. Often, athletes can change negative self-statements to positive by changing their perspective. For example, athletes concerned about competing against a much higher ranked opponent ("I'm going to really embarrass myself") can reframe this concern as an opportunity to assess their skill ("I'm going to see how good I've gotten and where I need improvement"). Similarly, an athlete who has the self-talk "I'm feeling tense and nervous" can reframe the statement to "I'm excited and ready." Hanton and Jones (1999) found that swimmers who perceived their precompetitive anxiety symptoms as debilitative improved their performance after they were taught a self-talk reframing intervention to reinterpret their anxiety symptoms as facilitative. Additional research support for the positive effects of reframing comes from a study that compared the mental preparation of teams who met or exceeded their goals in the 1996 Olympic Games with that of teams that failed to meet their expectations (Gould, Guinan, Greenleaf, Medbery, & Pederson, 1999). Gould and colleagues found that members of the more successful teams reported that they were able to reframe negative events in a positive light.

Coaches can use reframing to focus their teams or to affect morale. For example, if a team loses several successive games, the coach may emphasize the value of the "learning experience." After a big win, coaches often say, "That game is behind us, we have to focus on the next one." Such reframing attempts help to maintain a proper perspective on competition as well as positive versus negative self-statements.

Bell's (1983) caution regarding the importance of knowing the beliefs underlying negative statements bears repeating. If an athlete reframes the situation, thus changing the self-talk, but the belief that caused the negative statement remains, behavior change is unlikely. For the greatest effectiveness, the sport psychologist and athlete should use a combination of thought stoppage, changing negative thoughts to positive thoughts, reframing, and countering when attempting to modify negative, unwanted, or self-defeating self-talk.

Alternative Approaches

The preceding section described interventions for identifying and modifying cognitions for enhancing sport performance as well as the fundamental assumptions underlying their use. These assumptions are receiving significant challenges from cognitive and behavioral psychologists, and sport psychologists should consider these challenges when implementing and evaluating their interventions. This section describes two relevant challenges to cognitive intervention: the ironic effects of thought suppression and acceptance-based approaches to change.

Ironic Processes

Wegner and colleagues have described and investigated a theory of ironic processes of mental control (Wegner, 1994, 1997), and Janelle (1999) discussed the implications for this theory to sport applications (see Taylor, 1999, and Hall, Hardy, & Gammage, 1999, for commentaries). According to the theory, merely attempting to suppress unwanted thoughts can have the paradoxical effect of making unwanted thoughts hyperaccessible during and after suppression and can result in greater effects on mood than when no attempt is made to suppress the thought. A "monitoring process" can become triggered that actively searches for signs of the unwanted cognitive content and brings it into consciousness when detected. This effect may be even greater in stressful situations that increase cognitive load, such as sport competition or artificial situations created in the lab. For example, Wegner, Ansfield, and Pilloff (1998) found that golfers overshot the hole the most when they received instructions both to be particularly careful to *not* hit the ball past the hole and to remember a six-digit number so that they could repeat it after the putt. Thus, the use of thought stoppage during competition may be detrimental to performance. Further research with competitive athletes is necessary before conclusions about the utility of thought stoppage in practice and competition can be drawn.

Acceptance Approaches

From the perspective of radical behaviorism and behavior analytic psychology, the assumption of the cognitive model on thoughts as causes of both emotion and behavior (performance) can be challenged. According to this perspective, thoughts (and feelings) are behaviors and hold no special causal position in understanding behavior. Clinical applications of this approach have focused on acceptance of unwanted thoughts and feelings as a mechanism of behavior change and improved performance, challenging the notions of cause and change underlying the techniques described in this chapter (Hayes & Hayes, 1994; Hayes, Wilson, Gifford, Follette, & Strohsal, 1996). Consistent with Wegner's ironic process theory, fearing negative thinking, believing it to be the cause of future bad behavior or ineffective performance, and attempting to change it are seen as the problems, not the solution.

Little and Simpson (2000) developed an innovative sport application of this approach and investigated an acceptance-based intervention with intercollegiate softball players. In their intervention, the athletes were educated that negative thoughts, loss of self-confidence, and the like should be treated as "informational nuggets" that signal reduction in reinforcement due to ineffective or inconsistent performance. They were instructed that these thoughts are a consequence of behavioral contingencies rather than a cause of future behavior, and attempts to eliminate or alter such thoughts must be avoided. In contrast, the athletes were instructed to accept such thoughts and turn their attention to task-specific behaviors and environmental cues. Little and Simpson found promising performance results and found the athletes to be receptive to the intervention.

Although Wegner's model and acceptance-based approaches are intriguing and worthy of future research, it is too early to make strong recommendations for widespread use of similar interventions or discarding traditional cognitive interventions. It is important, however, for sport psychologists to recognize when they deliver and evaluate interventions, alternatives do exist.

Cognitions and Endurance Performance

Investigations of optimal cognitions for enhancing endurance performance have focused on attentional focus, specifically "associative" and "dissociative" cognitive strategies. Associative cognitions direct attention toward task-related cues (e.g., strategy, pace) and physical sensations that result from the exercise (e.g., breathing, leg muscle fatigue). Dissociative cognitions refer to thoughts that have nothing to do with exercising (e.g., relationships, spiritual matters, math problems).

Since Morgan and Pollock's (1977) original work in this area, several studies have investigated the effect of associative and dissociative strategies on endurance performance. In general, researchers have found that experienced endurance athletes, such as elite marathoners, choose associative strategies as their dominant attentional focus (Masters & Lambert, 1989; Morgan & Pollock, 1977; Silva & Appelbaum, 1989) and most effective strategy for improving performance (Clingman & Hilliard, 1990; Spink & Longhurst, 1986). The opposite occurred for inexperienced individuals; they used dissociative strategies the most and found them the most effective at improving performance (Fillingim & Fine, 1986; Gill & Strom, 1985; Pennebaker & Lightner, 1980; Rejeski & Kenney, 1987; Spink, 1988).

Summarizing 20 years of research on associative and dissociative cognitive strategies, Masters and Ogles (1998) concluded that associative strategies are recommended for faster performance in competition but that dissociative strategies may be useful during training. Morgan (1984), however, recommended that association should be the method of choice even during training because it is more efficient and entails less risk for injury, but dissociative strategies can be selectively used to cope with a particularly stressful portion of an endurance performance. Since Morgan's recommendation, one intervention study demonstrated that a mental training program could be used to increase associative thought content for marathoners (Schomer, 1987).

Cognitions, Anxiety, and Attentional Focus

Cognitive techniques can provide important interventions for dealing with anxiety and maintaining appropriate attentional focus. Cognitions play an important role in the way athletes experience stress and anxiety (Lazarus & Folkman, 1984; Smith, 1980). The cognitive appraisals of the demands of a situation, the importance of meeting the demands, and the individual's ability to meet the demands of the situation mediate the athlete's anxiety responses. For example, Mahoney and Avener (1977) found that more successful gymnasts tended to constructively use their elevated activation (i.e., physiological arousal), and less successful gymnasts approached near panic states by combining activation with self-defeating thoughts. Clearly, distorted thinking habits can create excess anxiety in practice and competitive situations. When an athlete experiences excess stress and anxiety, maintaining a proper attentional focus becomes more difficult, with attention often becoming narrow and internally directed toward worry, self-doubt, and other task-irrelevant thoughts (Nideffer, 1993). Thus, ineffective thinking can hinder good performance in two ways: by (a) creating excess anxiety and accompanying physiological changes, possibly moving activation out of the athlete's optimal level, and by (b) misdirecting attention away from an effective attentional focus, inhibiting good concentration.

Many of the techniques discussed previously in this chapter can be useful for maintaining optimal levels of anxiety and maintaining appropriate attentional focus. Thought stoppage, changing negative thoughts to positive thoughts, countering, and reframing can be used to intervene effectively when anxiety-provoking thoughts occur. Self-talk in the form of cue words can be used effectively to both modify activation (e.g., "relax," "easy") and focus attention (e.g., "see the ball," "be here now").

Conclusion

Cognitive behavioral techniques will continue to dominate sport psychology performance enhancement interventions in the future (Meyers et al., 1996). After interviewing four leading sport psychology practitioners, Newburg (1992) concluded that a primary goal in applied sport psychology is to teach effective thinking, the use of good thoughts, during competition. This recommendation represents a worthy and challenging goal.

The popularity and usefulness of cognitive behavioral techniques are not limited to the field of sport psychology and enhancement of sport performance (Dobson & Block, 1988). Once individuals learn to use the techniques discussed in this chapter to modify ineffective thinking, the techniques can be applied in a variety of situations to enhance the personal growth of athletes and their performance in academic and other nonsport situations. For example, enhancing and maintaining self-esteem is one area where the use of cognitive–behavioral techniques has occurred (Branden, 1994; McKay & Fanning, 1994). By fostering healthy self-esteem in athletes, sport psychologists can enhance the personal growth and development of athletes as well as their performance.

In conclusion, cognitive self-control techniques often challenge the sport psychologist who attempts to teach them and the athlete who tries to use them. Like most habits, thought patterns frequently resist change. Before implementing any changes, emphasize an awareness of ineffective thoughts, their consequences, and when appropriate, the underlying beliefs that contribute to the thoughts. Cognitive techniques require skill, practice, and patience by both the sport psychologist and the athlete for maximal effectiveness.

Although we believe that sufficient support exists for the concepts and interventions addressed in this chapter, we concur with individuals who challenge sport psychology researchers and practitioners to continue testing the efficacy of these interventions, particularly when used with elite athletes (Greenspan & Feltz, 1989; Morgan, 1994; Meyers et al., 1996; Smith, 1989). Only through careful, theory-based intervention and testing will the field of applied sport psychology advance as a profession and a science.

References

Beck, A. T. (1970). Cognitive therapy. *Behavior Modification, 1*, 184–200.

Bell, K. F. (1983). *Championship thinking: The athlete's guide to winning performance in all sports.* Englewood Cliffs, NJ: Prentice-Hall.

Branden, N. (1994). *The six pillars of self-esteem.* New York: Bantam.

Buffone, G. W., Sachs, M. L., & Dowd, E. T. (1984). Cognitive–behavioral strategies for promoting adherence to exercise. In M. L. Sachs & G.W. Buffone (Eds.), *Running as therapy: An integrated approach* (pp. 198–214). Lincoln: University of Nebraska Press.

Clingman, J. M., & Hilliard, D. V. (1990). Race walkers quicken their pace by tuning in, not stepping out. *The Sport Psychologist, 4*, 25–32.

Dagrou, E., Gauvin, L., & Halliwell, W. (1991). La preparation mentale des athletes invoiriens: Practiques cournantes at perspectives de rescherche [The mental preparation of athletes: current practices and research perspectives]. *International Journal of Sport Psychology, 22*, 15–34.

Dagrou, E., Gauvin, L., & Halliwell, W. (1992). Effets du langage positif, negatif, et neutre sur la performance motrice [Effects of positive, negative, and neutral language on motor performance]. *Canadian Journal of Sport Sciences, 17*, 145–147.

Dobson, K. S., & Block, L. (1988). Historical and philosophical bases of the cognitive–

behavioral therapies. In K. S. Dobson (Ed.), *Handbook of cognitive–behavioral therapies* (pp. 3–34). New York: Guilford.

Ellis, A. (1977). Rational–emotive therapy: Research data that support the clinical and personality hypothesis of RET and other modes of cognitive behavior therapy. *The Counseling Psychologist, 7,* 2–42.

Ellis, A. (1982). Self-direction in sport and life. *Rational Living, 17,* 27–33.

Ellis, A. E., & Harper, R. A. (1975). *A new guide to rational living.* Englewood Cliffs, NJ: Prentice-Hall.

Fillingim, R. B., & Fine, M. A. (1986). The effects of internal versus external information processing on symptom perception in an exercise setting. *Health Psychology, 5,* 115–123.

Gauron, E. F. (1984). *Mental training for peak performance.* Lansing, NY: Sport Science Associates.

Gauvin, L. (1990). An experiential perspective on the motivational features of exercise and lifestyle. *Canadian Journal of Sport Sciences, 15,* 51–58.

Gill, D. L., & Strom, E. H. (1985). The effect of attentional focus on performance of an endurance task. *International Journal of Sport Psychology, 16,* 217–223.

Gould, D., Eklund, R. C., & Jackson, S. A. (1992a). 1988 U.S. Olympic wrestling excellence: I. Mental preparation, precompetitive cognition, and affect. *The Sport Psychologist, 6,* 358–382.

Gould, D., Eklund, R. C., & Jackson, S. A. (1992b). 1988 U.S. Olympic wrestling excellence: II. Thoughts and affect occurring during competition. *The Sport Psychologist, 6,* 383–402.

Gould, D., Finch, L. M., & Jackson, S. A. (1993). Coping strategies used by national champion figure skaters. *Research Quarterly for Exercise and Sport, 64,* 453–468.

Gould, D., Guinan, D., Greenleaf, C., Medbery, R., & Pederson, K. (1999). Factors affecting Olympic performance of athletes and coaches from more and less successful teams. *The Sport Psychologist, 13,* 371–394.

Gould, D., Weiss, M., & Weinberg, R. (1981). Psychological characteristics of successful and nonsuccessful Big Ten wrestlers. *Journal of Sport Psychology, 3,* 69–81.

Greenspan, M. J., & Feltz, D. L. (1989). Psychological interventions with athletes in competitive situations: A review. *The Sport Psychologist, 3,* 219–236.

Hall, C. R., Hardy, J., & Gammage, K. L. (1999). About hitting golf balls in the water: Comments on Janelle's (1999) article on ironic processes. *The Sport Psychologist, 13,* 221–224.

Hanton, S., & Jones, G. (1999). The effects of a multimodal intervention program for swimmers: II. Training the butterflies to fly in formation. *The Sport Psychologist, 13,* 22–41.

Hayes, S. C., & Hayes, D. (Eds.). (1994). *Acceptance and Change.* Reno, NV: Context Press.

Hayes, S. C., Wilson, K. G., Gifford, E. V., Follette, V. M., & Strohsal, K. (1996). Experiential avoidance and behavioral disorders: A functional dimensional approach to diagnosis and treatment. *Journal of Consulting and Clinical Psychology, 64,* 1152–1168.

Highlen, P. S., & Bennett, B. B. (1979). Psychological characteristics of successful and nonsuccessful elite wrestlers: An exploratory study. *Journal of Sport Psychology, 1,* 123–137.

Highlen, P. S., & Bennett, B. B. (1983). Elite divers and wrestlers: A comparison between open- and closed-skill athletes. *Journal of Sport Psychology, 5,* 390–409.

Janelle, C. M. (1999). Ironic mental control processes in sport: Implications for sport psychologists. *The Sport Psychologist, 13,* 201–220.

Johnston-O'Connor, E. J., & Kirschenbaum, D. S. (1986). Something succeeds like success: Positive self-monitoring for unskilled golfers. *Cognitive Therapy and Research, 6,* 335–342.

Kirschenbaum, D. S., O'Connor, E. A., & Owens, D. (1999). Positive illusions in golf: Empirical and conceptual analyses. *Journal of Applied Sport Psychology, 11,* 1–27.

Kirschenbaum, D. S., Ordman, A. M., Tomarken, A. J., & Holtzbauer, R. (1982). Effects of differential self-monitoring and level of mastery on sports performance: Brain power bowling. *Cognitive Therapy and Research, 6,* 335–342.

Kirschenbaum, D. S., Owens, D., & O'Connor, E. A. (1998). Smart golf: Preliminary evaluation of a simple, yet comprehensive, approach to improving and scoring the mental game. *The Sport Psychologist, 12,* 271–282.

Landin, D., & Hebert, E. P. (1999). The influence of self-talk on the performance of skilled female tennis players. *Journal of Applied Sport Psychology, 11,* 263–282.

Lazarus, R. S., & Folkman, S. (1984). *Stress, appraisal, and coping.* New York: Springer.

Little, L. M., & Simpson, T. L. (2000). An acceptance-based performance enhancement intervention for collegiate athletes. In M. J. Dougher (Ed.), *Clinical behavior analysis* (pp. 231–244). Reno, NV: Context Press.

Mahoney, M. J. (1977, October). *Cognitive skills and athletic performance.* Paper presented at the annual meeting of the Association for the Advancement of Behavior Therapy, Atlanta, GA.

Mahoney, M. J., & Avener, M. (1977). Psychology of the elite athlete: An exploratory study. *Cognitive Therapy and Research, 1,* 135–141.

Masters, K. S., & Lambert, M. J. (1989). The relations between cognitive coping strategies, reasons for running, injury, and performance of marathon runners. *Journal of Sport and Exercise Psychology, 11,* 161–170.

Masters, K. S., & Ogles, B. M. (1998). Associative and dissociative strategies in exercise and running: 20 years later, what do we know? *The Sport Psychologist, 12,* 253–270.

McKay, M., & Fanning, P. (1994). *Self-esteem* (2nd ed.). Oakland, CA: New Harbinger.

Meichenbaum, D. (1977). *Cognitive–behavior modification.* New York: Plenum Press.

Meyers, A. W., & Schleser, R. A. (1980). A cognitive–behavioral intervention for improving basketball performance. *Journal of Sport Psychology, 3,* 69–73.

Meyers, A. W., Whelan, J. P., & Murphy, S. M. (1996). Cognitive behavioral strategies in athletic performance enhancement. In M. Hersen, R. M. Eisler, & P. M. Miller (Eds.), *Progress in behavior modification: Vol. 30* (pp. 137–164). Pacific Grove, CA: Brooks/Cole.

Morgan, W. P. (1984). Mind over matter. In W. F. Straub & J. M. Williams (Eds.), *Cognitive sport psychology* (pp. 311–316). New York: Sport Science Associates.

Morgan, W. P. (1994). *Forty years of progress: Sport psychology in exercise and sports medicine. American College of Sports Medicine—40th Anniversary lectures.* Indianapolis, IN: American College of Sports Medicine.

Morgan, W. P., & Pollock, M. L. (1977). Psychologic characterization of the elite distance runner. *Annals of the New York Academy of Sciences, 301,* 382–403.

Newburg, D. (1992). Performance enhancement: Toward a working definition. *Contemporary Thought on Performance Enhancement, 1,* 10–25.

Nideffer, R. M. (1993). Concentration and attention control training. In J. M. Williams (Ed.), *Applied sport psychology: Personal growth to peak performance* (pp. 243–261). Mountain View, CA: Mayfield.

Orbach, I., Singer, R., & Price, S. (1999). An attribution training program and achievement in sport. *The Sport Psychologist, 13,* 69–82.

Orlick, T., & Partington, J. (1988). Mental links to excellence. *The Sport Psychologist, 2,* 105–130.

Pennebaker, J. W., & Lightner, J. M. (1980). Competition of internal and external information in an exercise setting. *Journal of Personality and Social Psychology, 39,* 165–174.

Rejeski, W. J., & Kenney, E. (1987). Distracting attentional focus from fatigue: Does task complexity make a difference? *Journal of Sport Psychology, 9,* 66–73.

Rotella, R. J., Gansneder, B., Ojala, D., & Billings, J. (1980). Cognitions and coping strategies of elite skiers: An exploratory study of young developing athletes. *Journal of Sport Psychology, 2,* 350–354.

Rushall, B. S., Hall, M., Roux, L., Sasseville, J., & Rushall, A. C. (1988). Effects of three types of thought content instructions on skiing performance. *The Sport Psychologist, 2,* 283–297.

Schill, T., Monroe, S., Evans, R., & Ramanaiah, N. (1978). The effects of self-verbalizations on performance: A test of the rational–emotive position. *Psychotherapy: Theory, Research, and Practice, 15,* 2–7.

Schomer, H. H. (1987). Mental strategy training programme for marathon runners. *International Journal of Sport Psychology, 18,* 133–151.

Silva, J. M., & Appelbaum, M. E. (1989). Association–dissociation patterns of United States Olympic marathon trial contestants. *Cognitive Therapy and Research, 13,* 185–192.

Silva, J. S. (1982). Competitive sport environments: Performance enhancement through cognitive intervention. *Behavior Modification, 6,* 443–463.

Smith, R. E. (1980). A cognitive–affective approach to stress management training for athletes. In C. H. Nadeau, W. R. Halliwell, K. M. Newell, & G. C. Roberts (Eds.), *Psychology of motor behavior and sport* (pp. 54–72). Champaign, IL: Human Kinetics.

Smith, R. E. (1989). Applied sport psychology in an age of accountability. *Journal of Applied Sport Psychology, 1,* 166–180.

Spink, K. S. (1988). Facilitating endurance performance: The effect of cognitive strategies and analgesic suggestions. *The Sport Psychologist, 2,* 97–104.

Spink, K. S., & Longhurst, K. (1986). Cognitive strategies and swimming performance: An exploratory study. *Australian Journal of Science and Medicine in Sport, 18,* 9–13.

Steinmetz, J., Blankenship, J., Brown, L., Hall, D., & Miller, G. (1980). *Managing stress before it manages you.* Palo Alto, CA: Bull.

Straub, W. F., & Williams, J. M. (1984). *Cognitive sport psychology.* Lansing, NY: Sport Science Associates.

Strean, W. B., & Roberts, G. C. (1992). Future directions in applied sport psychology research. *The Sport Psychologist, 6,* 55–65.

Taylor, J. (1999). Isn't it ironic? Or irony is in the unconscious eye of the beholder. *The Sport Psychologist, 13,* 225–230.

Van Raalte, J. L., Brewer, B. W., Lewis, B. P., Linder, D. E., Wildman, G., & Kozimor, J. (1995). Cork! The effects of positive and negative self-talk on dart throwing performance. *Journal of Sport Behavior, 18,* 50–57.

Van Raalte, J. L., Brewer, B. W., Rivera, P. M., & Petitpas, A. J. (1994). The relationship between observable self-talk and competitive junior tennis players' match performance. *Journal of Sport & Exercise Psychology, 16,* 400–415.

Van Raalte, J. L., Cornelius, A. E., Brewer, B. W., & Hatten, S. J. (2000). The antecedents and consequences of self-talk in competitive tennis. *Journal of Sport and Exercise Psychology, 22,* 345–356.

Wegner, D. M. (1994). Ironic processes of mental control. *Psychological Bulletin, 16,* 34–52.

Wegner, D. M. (1997). When the antidote is the poison: Ironic mental control processes. *Psychological Science, 8,* 148–150.

Wegner, D. M., Ansfield, M., & Pilloff, D. (1998). The putt and the pendulum: Ironic effects of the mental control of action. *Psychological Science, 9*, 196–199.

Whelan, J. P., Mahoney, M. J., & Meyers, A. W. (1991). Performance enhancement in sport: A cognitive behavioral domain. *Behavior Therapy, 22*, 307–327.

Williams, J. M., & Krane, V. I. (2001). Psychological characteristics of peak performance. In J. M. Williams (Ed.), *Applied sport psychology: Personal growth to peak performance* (4th ed., pp. 162–178). Mountain View, CA: Mayfield.

Zinsser, N., Bunker, L. K., & Williams, J. M. (2001). Cognitive techniques for improving performance and building confidence. In J. M. Williams (Ed.), *Applied sport psychology: Personal growth to peak performance* (4th ed., pp. 284–311). Mountain View, CA: Mayfield.

Intensity Regulation and Sport Performance

Jim Taylor and Gregory S. Wilson

As the day of the competition arrives and the event approaches, intensity assumes the central role in precompetitive preparation (Taylor, 2000). Intensity is the most critical factor before competitive performance because, no matter how confident, motivated, or technically or physically prepared athletes are to perform, if the body is not at an optimal level of intensity, accompanied by the requisite physiological and psychological changes, they will simply not be able to perform their best. Because of the impact of intensity on performance, a critical responsibility of athletes before competition is to attain a level of intensity that will enable them to perform at their highest level.

Applied practitioners can play a significant role in this process at several levels. First, consultants can help athletes understand how intensity influences their performances, both positively and negatively. Second, practitioners can assist athletes in identifying their ideal level of intensity. Third, they can help athletes clarify situations in which intensity may shift away from their ideal. Fourth, consultants can provide athletes with the skills to adjust their intensity before and during competition so that athletes are able to maintain their intensity at their ideal level.

This chapter is organized to lead readers to an in-depth understanding of intensity, how it affects athletic performance, and what applied practitioners can do with athletes to help them attain ideal intensity for competition. First, a clarification of what is *intensity* is offered and why this particular term is used in place of terms such as *arousal* or *anxiety*. Second, the chapter provides a discussion of the latest theoretical formulations and empirical findings associated with intensity. Third, an understanding of the nature of intensity as experienced by athletes is presented with attention placed on the symptoms and causes of over- and underintensity. Fourth, the issue of identifying ideal intensity is delineated in which practitioners are shown how to assist athletes in specifying what level of intensity is best for them to perform successfully. Finally, the chapter examines a variety of cognitive, physiological, and general interventions that can be used to regulate intensity before competition.

What Is Intensity?

In previous research and applied writings, other terms have been used synonymously with *intensity*, including *arousal, anxiety,* and *nervousness* (Landers & Boutcher, 1986; Silva & Hardy, 1984; Spielberger, 1972). However, these latter terms are not best suited for use with athletes. The term *arousal* has sexual connotations that can distract athletes from its real meaning and value. Using this term with athletes, particularly with youthful competitors, often produces a comical or anxious reaction that interferes with athletes appreciating and understanding its importance to competitive preparation. The terms *anxiety* and *nervousness* are typically perceived negatively and as states to be avoided. The term *intensity* does not have these limitations. Rather, intensity is viewed by athletes as a positive and important contributor to optimal competitive performance.

The issue of defining intensity has been a point of contention for decades (Borkovec, 1976; Cannon, 1928; Neiss, 1988; Spielberger, 1966). For the purposes of applied practitioners, Zaichkowsky and Takenaka (1993) provided the most detailed and parsimonious conceptualization of *intensity*: a multidimensional construct that performs an energizing function of the mind and body. They have suggested that intensity has three critical qualities that affect performance. First, a physiological activation that includes heart rate, glandular and cortical activity, and blood flow takes place (Landers & Boutcher, 1986; Zaichkowsky & Takenaka, 1993). Second, behavioral responses are evident in terms of motor activity, including changes in coordination, pace, and idiosyncratic behavioral reactions to the physiological alterations. Third, cognitive and emotional responses are also exhibited in terms of valenced evaluations of the physiological and behavioral manifestations of intensity and the accompanying emotional reactions to those evaluations.

Athletes experience intensity in a range from very low, as in a deep sleep, to very high, as in extreme fear (Sonstroem, 1984). Intensity may be experienced by athletes positively as increased confidence, motivation, strength, stamina, agility, and sensory acuity (Carver & Scheier, 1986). It may also be experienced negatively as fear, dread, muscle tension, breathing difficulty, loss of coordination, and other inhibiting manifestations (Eysenck & Calvo, 1992).

Theoretical and Empirical Perspectives on Intensity

Three primary theoretical explanations for the relationship between intensity and athletic performance have been developed: the inverted-U hypothesis (Yerkes-Dodson, 1908), the individual zone of optimal functioning model (Hanin, 1980), and the catastrophe theory (Hardy & Fazey, 1987). A fourth theory, reversal theory, has emerged recently to add to the latest multidimensional conceptualizations of intensity (Apter, 1984; Kerr, 1997); however, this theory has not been empirically tested or validated.

Inverted-U Hypothesis

The inverted-U hypothesis, also referred to as the Yerkes–Dodson Law, was the first and is still the most recognized, hypothesis to attempt to explain the relationship between intensity and performance (Weinberg, 1990). Yerkes's and Dodson's (1908) original conceptualization of this idea was used as an explanation for the relationship between performance and stimulus intensity they discovered in an experiment involving maze discrimination in rats. They found that increases in intensity produced commensurate improvements in performance, but only up to a specified point, after which greater intensity inhibited performance. Hence, when performance was plotted against intensity, a curvilinear relationship in the shape of an inverted-U resulted.

Oxendine (1970) further popularized the basic tenets of the inverted-U hypothesis by suggesting that intensity is sport specific. Oxendine suggested that, although moderate levels of intensity were appropriate for most motor tasks, the optimal level of intensity was dependent on the specific sport task to be performed. For example, gross motor activities involving speed and strength (e.g., shot put, weight lifting) would benefit from high levels of intensity for optimal sport performances, whereas low levels of intensity would predict success for athletic performances in which fine muscle movements, steadiness, coordination, and general concentration (e.g., golf, diving) were essential (Billing, 1980).

However, despite the intuitive appeal of the inverted-U hypothesis, extant empirical research does not support its premise (Fazey & Hardy, 1988; Gould & Krane, 1992; Kleine, 1990; Neiss, 1988;). Its original premise has often been misinterpreted (Wilson, 1999), and recent research examining the claim that optimal intensity levels are influenced by motor skill (i.e., fine or gross) has not supported Oxendine's contention (Imlay, Carda, Stanbrough, & O'Connor, 1995; Krane & Williams, 1994).

Possibly the most important criticism of the inverted-U hypothesis is that it implies that only moderate levels of intensity are appropriate for all athletes and does not account for individual differences in the way athletes respond to the stress of competition (Fazey & Hardy, 1988; Kleine, 1990; Raglin & Hanin, 2000). From an applied perspective, research has demonstrated that individual differences between athletes on similar tasks must also be considered by applied practitioners (Ebbeck & Weiss, 1988; Gould & Tuffey, 1996; Morgan, O'Connor, Sparling, & Pate, 1987; Raglin, Wise, & Morgan, 1990; Wilson & Raglin, 1997). Furthermore, individual differences in attentional processing (Nideffer, 1989), cognitive appraisal (Landers & Boutcher, 1986), trait anxiety (Spielberger, 1989), confidence, motivation, and investment in the activity (Taylor, 2000), as well as physical individual differences such as level of conditioning, general health, fatigue, and injuries, must be considered. As a result of the inability of the inverted-U hypothesis to explain these individual differences, alternative models based on research with athletes have been developed to explain differences in optimal intensity.

Individual Zone of Optimal Functioning Model

In response to these concerns about the inverted-U hypothesis, Hanin (1986) developed the individual zones of optimal function (IZOF) model. Originally the individual optimum zone model (Cratty & Hanin, 1980), this paradigm was later redefined as the zone of optimal function model (Hanin, 1986) before becoming the current IZOF model (Hanin, 2000).

Cratty and Hanin (1980) noted that the original idea of individual differences among athletes was derived from numerous assessments of precompetition intensity in elite Soviet athletes. Data gathered from Soviet rowers, skiers, gymnasts, and ski jumpers supported the premise of anxiety as a significant factor in sport performance on an individual level, but these findings did not support an association between intensity and sport performance on a group level (Raglin & Hanin, 2000). For example, regardless of sport, some athletes performed best at very low levels of intensity, whereas others were successful at very high levels of intensity.

Hence, a significant difference between the IZOF model and the inverted-U hypothesis exists in the optimal range of intensity. Whereas the inverted-U hypothesis suggests that successful performances may be obtained only when athletes perform under states of moderate intensity, the IZOF model contends that athletes differ markedly in their individual level of optimal intensity (Gould & Tuffey, 1996). Moreover, the optimal intensity zone may range anywhere from very low to very high depending on the unique characteristics of the individual athlete (Ebbeck & Weiss, 1988). For instance, Raglin and Turner (1992) reported in a study of college track-and-field athletes that 51% of men and 48% of women in their sample reported successful performances when intensity levels were high, whereas in a study of youth track-and-field athletes, Wilson and Raglin (1997) found 26% of the participants performed best with high levels of intensity. Hence, the optimal level of intensity is considered to be highly individualistic (Hanin, 2000).

Although the IZOF model has received considerable support (Ebbeck & Weiss, 1988; Gould & Krane, 1992; Morgan et al., 1987; Raglin, Wise, & Morgan, 1990; Raglin & Morris, 1994; Raglin & Turner, 1992; Wilson, 1998; Wilson & Raglin, 1997), some aspects of the model have been criticized. For example, although the ability to accurately recall intensity has been questioned (Gould, Tuffey, Hardy, & Lochbaum, 1993; Krane, 1993), research has documented high positive correlations between actual precompetition levels of intensity and precompetition levels of intensity recalled postcompetition (Imlay et al., 1995; Raglin & Turner, 1992; Wilson, Raglin, & Harger, 2000). Also, the mechanism responsible for individual differences in optimal intensity levels, for example, why two athletes in the same sport with similar amounts of experience would perform best at different levels of intensity, has not been fully explained (Gould & Tuffey, 1996; Jones, 1995).

The difficulty in conceptualizing and measuring the multifaceted psychophysiological states of performance is substantial (Hanin, 2000). This has led some sport psychologists (Fazey & Hardy, 1988; Gould et al., 1993; Hardy, 1990; Martens, Vealey, & Burton, 1990) to question the unidimensional conceptualizations of the IZOF model and to propose theories that involve multiple factors that may affect sport performance.

Catastrophe Theory

In response to the emerging multidimensional views of the relationship between intensity and athletic performance, more complex theories have been developed that suggest an interaction of cognitive, somatic, and self-confidence components within an individual athlete (Martens et al., 1990). Using a mathematically based model, Hardy (1990, 1996) has suggested that these components exert an interactive three-dimensional influence on performance.

Catastrophe theory proposes that the impact of physiological arousal on performance depends on an athlete's level of cognitive anxiety (Fazey & Hardy, 1988). Weinberg and Gould (1999) suggested that anxiety consists of a cognitive component that involves worry and apprehension and a somatic component that relates to the degree of physical activation that an athlete experiences. For example, in competitive situations in which physiological activation is high, further increases in cognitive anxiety will have a debilitating effect on performance. However, in cases in which physiological activation is low, increases in cognitive anxiety may act to enhance performance by bringing the athlete into his or her optimal range of intensity (Edwards & Hardy, 1996). Hence, performance decrements occur only under conditions of high physiological activation and high cognitive anxiety. When this happens, "catastrophe" occurs, resulting in a rapid and dramatic deterioration in performance (Cox, 1998).

Although limited support (Edwards & Hardy, 1996; Hardy, Parfitt, & Pates, 1994; Woodman, Albinson, & Hardy, 1997) has been found for the catastrophe model, several investigators have criticized its basic assumptions (Krane, 1993; Krane, Joyce, & Raefeld, 1994). It has been questioned whether the interactive effects of the cognitive, somatic, and self-confidence components are stable characteristics within an athlete or whether they are subject to situational influences (Gill, 1994). Moreover, Gould and Tuffey (1996) have suggested that more specific affective components of anxiety may exist, which has led some theorists (Hanin, 2000) to state that research may need to examine a wider range of emotions that influence sport performance. Furthermore, Woodman et al. (1997) admitted that the catastrophe theory has not been able to account for successful performances that occur under conditions of high cognitive anxiety in some athletes (e.g., Raglin & Turner, 1992; Wilson & Raglin, 1997).

Reversal Theory

Based on research conducted by Apter and colleagues (1984, 2001), reversal theory has been applied to sport settings (Kerr, 1997). Reversal theory takes into account an athlete's interpretation of physical activation (Jones, 1995). That is, high intensity levels are beneficial if an athlete perceives high physical activation as positive. However, if intensity is perceived as negative, it can have a debilitating effect on performance. Therefore, for successful performances to occur, athletes must view their intensity as positive rather than negative (Kerr, 1997).

In addition, reversal theory suggests that shifts in perceptions of intensity occur throughout the duration of a competition (Kerr, 1989). For example, an athlete may begin a competition feeling confident and motivated about his or her performance and interpret the accompanying intensity as beneficial. However, as the competition progresses and the athlete performs poorly, a shift can take place in an athlete's perception of the intensity, and the same level of intensity is viewed as negative. For this reason, reversal theory suggests that perceptions of intensity are not static but rather are constantly changing throughout a competition.

Unfortunately, reversal theory is primarily a descriptive model with no empirical support. Weinberg and Gould (1999) have suggested that it is too early to draw conclusions regarding the efficacy of reversal theory. However, Hanin (2000) has noted that the role of changing emotions, as purported by reversal theory, may be important in understanding individual perceptions of intensity by athletes.

Understanding the Experience of Intensity

A primary goal of applied practitioners is to assist the athletes with whom they work in identifying and attaining their optimal level of intensity. It is first necessary to gain a greater awareness of the experience of intensity for athletes. This experience involves the symptoms and causes of overintensity and underintensity.

Overintensity

Symptoms

As alluded to previously, intensity can be manifested in three ways: physically, behaviorally, and psychologically (Hanin, 2000; Jones, 1995; Kerr, 1997). The most apparent symptoms are physical reactions that include extreme muscle tension, shaking muscles, difficulty breathing, and excessive perspiration (Landers & Boutcher, 1986). Other more subtle physical symptoms include fatigue and a decrease in motor coordination. Behaviorally, symptoms include an increase in pace during competition, generalized agitation, an increase in performance-irrelevant or superstitious behaviors, tense body language, and a decrease in competitive performance (Eysenck & Calvo, 1992). Psychological symptoms of overintensity include negative self-talk (e.g., "I know I will screw up"), irrational thinking (e.g., "If I perform poorly, everyone will hate me"), decline in motivation, overnarrowing of concentration (Nideffer & Sagal, 1998), and emotional feelings of fear and dread (Elko & Ostrow, 1991; Hamilton & Fremouw, 1985).

It is important for applied practitioners to educate athletes to also recognize the less overt indications of overintensity. Some relevant symptoms include stomach butterflies, mistakes during precompetitive preparation, an extreme narrowing of concentration, and a shift from performance-relevant thoughts to negative or performance-irrelevant thoughts.

Causes

Causes of overintensity may be characterized as psychological, social, or situational. Landers and Boutcher (1986) provided a conceptual framework for important psychological influences on intensity. They specified five areas of cognitive appraisal that lead to a negative intensity reaction: (a) the demands of the situation, (b) the individual's resources for effectively managing the demands, (c) the consequences of the situation, (d) the meaning that is placed on the consequences, and (e) recognition of bodily reactions. For example, Richard, a talented 18-year-old freshman pitcher for a highly ranked NCAA Division I baseball team who has been named the starter for the final game of the College World

Series, perceives that the requirements of his starting role in such an important game (i.e., demands) are greater than his ability (i.e., resources) to perform successfully. He believes that he will fail in his performance (i.e., consequences) and that his failure will disappoint his family and ruin his chances of a professional career (i.e., meaning).

Lack of confidence may also contribute to overintensity. Athletes who do not believe they will be successful and yet are required to perform will perceive the situation as threatening and will experience this as overintensity (Weinberg & Gould, 1999). These perceptions, in turn, interfere with the ability of athletes to perform at their highest level. Hanin (2000) supported this view by suggesting that emotional reactions and intensity are influenced by athletes' appraisals of the likelihood of achieving their goals. Edwards and Hardy (1996) reported that athletes whose confidence increased perceived their anxiety to be more facilitative to their competitive performances.

A severe manifestation of lack of confidence is irrational thinking, in which athletes develop extreme and often harmful cognitions about their performance. For example, a downhill ski racer inspecting the course comes to a difficult high-speed turn that she doubts she can negotiate. She sees a tree that would be in her path if she is unable to make the turn and thinks, "That tree has my name on it."

Another intrapersonal cause of overintensity involves focusing on the outcome of the competition rather than its process. Whether the outcome is positive (e.g., "If I win, people will expect me to always win") or negative (e.g., "If I lose, I will let the whole town down"), considering the consequences of a performance adds unnecessary pressure and detracts from a proper competitive focus that allows for optimal performance.

Social causes of overintensity are derived primarily from expectations of significant others in the lives of athletes, including parents, coaches, friends, community, and media. Overintensity results from the perception that if athletes do not live up to the socially derived expectations, they will not be loved and supported, which is a direct threat to their self-esteem (Krohne, 1980; Passer, 1982; Smith, Smoll, & Curtis, 1978).

Environmental variables may also exacerbate the overintensity reaction. Factors such as unfamiliarity with the situation, the occurrence of unexpected events, and worry over uncontrollable aspects of the competitive situation can cause overintensity by producing feelings of uncertainty and helplessness.

Underintensity

Symptoms

Because of the inherent pressures associated with competition, under-intensity is not a common occurrence (Williams & Harris, 1998). How-ever, it may be evident in some athletes and in some competitive situations. As with overintensity, underintensity can manifest itself physically, behaviorally, and psychologically.

Physical symptoms of underintensity include low levels of heart rate, respiration, and adrenaline. These changes are exhibited in the form of low energy and feelings of lethargy. Behaviorally, underintensity can be seen as a decrease in pace during competition, generalized lethargy, "let-down" body language, a reduction in performance-relevant behaviors (e.g., routines), an oversensitivity to external distractions, and a decline in competitive performance. Psychological symptoms include a loss of motivation to compete, difficulty narrowing concentration, and a generalized feeling of "not being all there."

Causes

Unlike overintensity, underintensity is less influenced by social and situational factors and may be characterized primarily as having psychological and physical causes. Overconfidence is a significant psychological cause of underintensity. Athletes who are overconfident believe that they will win easily with little effort. As a result, they do not activate their physiological system (e.g., heart rate, respiration, adrenaline) that will enable them to do just that. A lack of interest or motivation to compete or an absence of fun or enthusiasm will also produce underintensity.

Athletes who lack the desire to perform will not feel the need to activate themselves physiologically. In addition, Csikszentmihalyi (1975) suggested that athletes who perceive that their ability exceeds the demands of the competitive situation will experience boredom, which is a form of underintensity. Social and situational contributors to underintensity include lack of emphasis by coaches or an unimportant game. Fatigue from overtraining or overcompeting, sleeping difficulties, and competitive stress are physical causes of underintensity. Other physical causes of underintensity include nutritional deficiencies and injuries. Athletes experiencing these physical causes generally will not have the physiological resources to activate their body when needed.

Identifying and Assessing Ideal Intensity

As already suggested, no one ideal intensity level exists for all athletes. Ideal intensity involves optimal levels of physiological and cognitive activity for each individual athlete. Furthermore, it is not something that athletes will automatically reach in all competitions. Rather, intensity is determined by numerous personal, sport, social, and situational variables over which athletes have little awareness and even less control (Schmidt & Wrisberg, 2000). The goal, then, of applied practitioners in working with athletes on intensity regulation is (a) to teach them to monitor their level of intensity and (b) to show them how they can effectively attain and maintain their ideal intensity.

As the IZOF (Hanin, 2000) model and catastrophe (Fazey & Hardy, 1988) theory indicate, all athletes have a level of intensity with which they are able to perform their best. Hanin suggests two methods for assessing ideal intensity. First, athletes can measure their level of intensity before each performance throughout a competitive season. Once they have achieved a personal best performance, the level of intensity can be identified and a range of intensity can be established (Hanin, 1986; Raglin & Hanin, 2000). However, Hanin and Syrja (1995) have noted that this method presents several logistical problems. Because intensity must be measured until an outstanding performance occurs, the length of time may be great. Self-ratings of intensity may also be too invasive and may distract from precompetitive and competitive activities (Harger & Raglin, 1994; McCann, Murphy, & Radeke, 1992). As a result of these potential hindrances, Hanin (2000) developed an indirect method based on an athlete's ability to recall feelings before competition. In this method, athletes recall the level of intensity experienced immediately before their best performance, and a range or zone is developed through this retrospection.

An important finding of IZOF research is the ability of athletes to successfully predict precompetition levels of anxiety up to 48 hours before competition. Results from these studies have found significant correlations between predicted and actual precompetition intensity, ranging from .60 to .80 (Hanin, 1986; Morgan et al., 1987, Morgan, O'Connor, Ellickson, & Bradley, 1988; Raglin & Turner, 1992; Wilson, 1998; Wilson & Raglin, 1997). The ability to predict precompetition levels of intensity is important because it may be used as a reference point for intervention with athletes (Hanin, 1986, 2000). For example, this information may provide a marker of an athlete's perceptions about an upcoming competition, because it represents the extent to which the athlete views the situation as threatening (Raglin & Hanin, 2000). Hence, deviations from the optimal intensity zone may indicate which intervention would be most beneficial (Hanin, 2000). However, it is also important to remember that simply being in one's optimal zone of intensity does not guarantee sport success. Many other factors, including psychological, emotional, and physical variables, can affect an athlete's level of performance (Hanin, 2000).

As catastrophe theory asserts, two types of intensity affect the intensity–performance relationship: physiological and cognitive (Fazey & Hardy, 1988). Although catastrophe theory has not yet received extensive empirical support, it provides a broad base for intervention, has strong intuitive appeal, and is consistent with the experiences of applied practitioners. Consequently, keeping in mind the as-yet unproven nature of catastrophe theory, it can be used as a model to assist athletes in identifying their ideal and nonideal levels of physiological and cognitive intensity (Taylor, 2000; Weinberg, 1988).

Using a tool such as an intensity identification form (see Exhibit 6.1), applied practitioners can ask the following questions about athletes' ideal intensity: (a) Before and during a successful competition,

Exhibit 6.1

Intensity Identification Form

Directions: In the space below, indicate the psychological and situational factors that impact your intensity and the quality of your competitive performances. At the bottom, summarize the positive and negative performance factors that distinguish your best and worst performances.

Best Performances	Worst Performances
Physical feelings	
Thoughts	
Emotions	
Social influences	
Competition site	
Event	
Competitive level	

Positive Performance Factors

Negative Performance Factors

how did their body feel (e.g., heart pounding and sweating or calm and at ease? The athletes should be specific in describing their physiological condition.), (b) What were their thoughts and emotions at the time (e.g., positive and excited or neutral and calm)? and (c) What social influences are present or absent during successful performances (e.g., family, coaches, and friends)? The same questions should then be asked for poor performances. What typically emerges is a consistent pattern of physiological, cognitive, and social activity that is associated with ideal and nonideal intensity and the corresponding quality of competitive performance. At the bottom of the form, athletes can summarize the factors that are associated with successful and unsuccessful performance. In rare instances, athletes are unable to find a difference in intensity between successful and unsuccessful performances. In these cases, athletes should look for other psychological or physical factors that can account for the differences.

The purpose of this exercise is to create an understanding in athletes of what their body feels like, what they are thinking and feeling, and with whom they are interacting when they perform well and poorly. The goal of intensity identification is to make athletes aware of these differences before they compete so they can take active steps to reproduce those factors associated with good performance through the use of intensity regulation.

Intensity Regulation

When athletes have identified their ideal and nonideal levels of intensity, they must learn how to regulate their intensity so when the time of competition arrives, they will have the ability to actively shift their intensity to its ideal level. Intensity interventions can be implemented cognitively, physiologically, and situationally, and also at various times as the competition approaches (e.g., during training and precompetitive preparation). Note that cognitive interventions are most effectively used as preventive measures, whereas physiological and situational interventions are best used immediately before and during competition to alleviate undesirable changes in intensity.

Cognitive Interventions for Intensity Regulation

This section addresses a variety of cognitive techniques that may be used to regulate intensity. These techniques can be used during practice sessions and before competitions as a means of preventing nonideal intensity. They can also be applied immediately before competitions to attain ideal intensity. This section is divided into three segments: (a) regulation of overintensity, (b) regulation of underintensity, and (c) general techniques to regulate intensity.

Regulation of Overintensity

Cognitive reappraisal. As the model presented by Landers and Boutcher (1986) indicates, overintensity is most often caused by negative, inaccurate, or extreme cognitive appraisal of a situation. Consequently, a good place to begin controlling overintensity is at its source, that is, by altering that appraisal process (Kerr, 1997). A fundamental aspect of the faulty appraisal process that leads to overintensity is the perception on the part of athletes that they do not have the ability to cope effectively with the five areas of appraisal (i.e., demands, resources, consequences, meaning, and recognition of bodily reactions). This evaluation indicates a basic lack of confidence in their ability. Thus, by developing their confidence, athletes may inhibit overintensity at its source by re-evaluating the situation positively and accurately.

Applied practitioners can assist athletes in rationally assessing an upcoming competition by discussing the five appraisal areas with them individually and as a group. Often, athletes, particularly those who are young or less experienced, become so overwhelmed by the approaching competition that they lose perspective and are simply not able to evaluate the situation objectively. This may lead to irrational thinking, which further increases intensity (Ellis, 1962). Typically, by being shown another way of viewing the situation, athletes are able to recognize the extremity of their thinking and accept a more realistic perspective, which then results in a shift in their intensity to an ideal level (Heyman, 1984).

Applied practitioners can also use this approach in addressing the social causes of overintensity. Assessing athletes' perceptions of others' expectations and then intervening when appropriate can effectively diminish the negative effects of social influences, thus reducing overintensity and improving competitive performance.

All of these interventions have the effect of altering debilitating intensity in several ways. They can offer athletes new perspectives that make competition less threatening. These strategies can change the attitudes that cause overintensity. Finally, they can restructure the perceptions of the intensity symptoms so that athletes see them as positive and facilitating (Kerr, 1990).

Self-talk. At a more direct level, negative, worrying, or irrational self-talk, such as "I know I will fail," "I am so scared," or "I am going to break every bone in my body," are typically found in athletes experiencing overintensity. Applied practitioners can intervene on self-talk by using cognitive restructuring techniques, including thought stopping and positive litanies. For example, athletes can be taught to say "Positive" when a negative thought occurs. Negative thoughts can then be replaced by positive statements, such as "I will try my hardest and play my best." Developing a series of positive self-statements (e.g., "I love to compete," "I am a great athlete," or "I always think and talk positively") can help athletes train themselves to be more positive. These strategies increase athletes' awareness of unproductive thinking and show them how to develop more positive and constructive ways of thinking about situations. For additional intervention techniques for developing confidence, see chapter 5 by Williams and Leffingwell in this volume.

Familiarization. Hanin (2000) indicated that the athletes' environment has a substantial impact on competitive performance. He suggested in his IZOF model that intensity is a function of the appraisals that athletes make about their environment and how athletes respond to their environment. He further indicated that maladaptive responses to the environment are caused by an incomplete understanding of the relevant factors associated with the situation.

Unfamiliarity may occur in several ways. Lack of knowledge of the physical environment in which athletes compete may cause overintensity. The best solution for this particular problem is to give athletes an opportunity to familiarize themselves with the competitive setting, ideally through practice or preliminary competition in the competitive arena. In the absence of direct experience practicing or competing in that setting, enabling athletes to attend another competition at the site or simply allowing them to walk around the setting may be helpful. Athletes may then combine this observational experience of the setting with mental imagery to see themselves competing there in the days before the actual competition. In addition to any firsthand experience at the setting, it can be useful for coaches or some of the athletes who have been there previously to describe some of the critical physical aspects of the setting to newcomers.

These same strategies may also be used to assist athletes in familiarizing themselves with other aspects of the competitive setting. For example, an upcoming meet is the biggest competition in which members of a track-and-field team have competed. It is important for the applied practitioner to familiarize these athletes with factors such as media coverage before the event, training and competitive schedules, transportation, typical activity on the infield, audience responses, access to the locker rooms, and the location of the warm-up areas. Developing a mentoring system with more experienced athletes is one useful tool to assist athletes in becoming more familiar with relevant aspects of a competition.

Anticipating unexpected events. Another cause of overintensity is the occurrence of unexpected events before and during competitions. The most effective means of handling this problem is to prevent or minimize unexpected incidences from occurring. This does not mean that all problems can be prevented from arising during a competition. Rather, the goal is to prevent the unexpected problems that cause overintensity.

This may be achieved in two steps. First, in a meeting with athletes, the applied practitioner can have them identify everything that can go wrong at a competition. Then, the practitioner can ask them to propose solutions to these occurrences (see Exhibit 6.2). Even though difficulties will still arise, instead of panicking and raising intensity to a debilitating level, athletes will recognize that a problem has occurred and have a plan for solving the problem; thus, stress is not generated, and intensity remains at a healthy level.

Exhibit 6.2

Expecting the Unexpected

Directions: A variety of unexpected situations and how to deal with them have been provided. In the space below, identify specific unexpected situations that you may encounter and how to deal with them.

Unexpected	Plan
Late arrival to competition	Have shortened precompetitive routine.
Forget clothing or accessory	Pack extra gear.
Broken equipment	Have backup equipment properly prepared.
No place to practice	Have alternative physical warm-up routine.
Bad weather or conditions	Stay relaxed and focused; stay warmed up.
Change in schedule	Repeat precompetitive routine.
Different opponent	Stay calm; reassess strategy.

Focusing on controllable events. Athletes, like other people, spend considerable time worrying about things over which they have little control (Bandura, 1986). Not only is this a fruitless endeavor, it is a stressful one. Much of what occurs in the competitive sports world is outside of the control of athletes. Moreover, only one thing is truly within their control—themselves. As such, they should focus only on themselves, specifically, what they need to do to perform their best (see Exhibit 6.3).

Applied practitioners can play a meaningful role in helping athletes maintain focus on controllable factors. When practitioners hear athletes worrying about things outside of their control, they should ask athletes some questions. Is this something that is within your control? If so, what can you do to relieve the problem? At this point, the practitioner should help the athlete develop a plan. If not, what part of the situation can you control? At this point, the practitioner should have the athlete focus on what can be controlled and assist him or her in finding a way to alleviate the problem.

Exhibit 6.3

Controllable and Uncontrollable Factors

Directions: A variety of controllable and uncontrollable factors have been provided. In the space below, identify specific controllable and uncontrollable factors that you may encounter.

Controllable Factors	Uncontrollable Factors
Your behavior	Others' attitudes, thoughts, emotions, behavior
Physical condition	Competitors' performances
Motivation/effort	
Coaches	
Attitude	
Family	
Thoughts	
Officials	
Emotions	
Opponent selection	
Equipment	
Competition conditions	
Preparation	
Weather	
Performance	

Regulation of Underintensity

Underintensity, although less likely to occur, can have dramatic negative effects on competitive performance. As a result, applied practitioners should create an awareness of underintensity and teach athletes how to address this phenomenon when it occurs (Caudill, Weinberg, & Jackson, 1983; Williams & Harris, 1998).

Let-down self-talk, such as "I have this competition won" and "I quit," are commonly associated with feelings of underintensity (Caudill, Weinberg, & Jackson, 1983; Williams & Harris, 1998). These types of self-talk produce a physiological decline in intensity, which directly interferes with effective performance. This self-talk needs to be replaced with high-energy self-talk that will raise physiological intensity to an ideal level (Edwards & Hardy, 1996). For example, the statements just given could be replaced with "Finish strong" and "Keep at it."

Physiological Interventions for Intensity Regulation

Despite their best efforts to achieve ideal intensity by cognitive means, due to situational and social aspects of competition, many athletes will still experience nonideal intensity. Consequently, it is important for applied practitioners to provide athletes with simple and practical techniques to use before and during competition that will enable them to attain ideal intensity.

Regulation of Overintensity

Breathing. Perhaps the simplest, and yet most important, technique that can reduce intensity is breathing (Williams & Harris, 1998). It is common to see athletes taking short, choppy breaths before a competition. With overintensity, the breathing system contracts, so athletes get an inadequate supply of oxygen. This can cause fatigue, loss of coordination, and tense muscles, all of which can seriously impair performance. Athletes can counteract this problem by taking deep, rhythmic breaths, which replenishes their oxygen supply and reduces overintensity, thus enabling them to perform their best.

Breathing also has psychological ramifications. A significant problem with overintensity is that athletes tend to become focused on negative symptoms such as muscle tension and stomach butterflies. By taking slow, deep breaths, athletes can alleviate some of these symptoms, thereby increasing self-confidence and general feelings of well-being. In addition, focusing on breathing takes the focus off some of the negative feelings associated with overintensity.

Muscle relaxation. One of the most uncomfortable manifestations of overintensity is muscle tension (Landers & Boutcher, 1986). Tight muscles inhibit coordination, interfere with quality performance, and increase the likelihood of injury. As a result, applied practitioners can teach athletes practical techniques to relax muscles.

One strategy is passive relaxation, which is described in Exhibit 6.4. It involves deep breathing and a "tension-draining" process. This relaxation method usually works for all but the most tense athletes. These athletes often try to get their muscles to relax by shaking them and willing them to relax, but the tension is so great that this does not work.

Exhibit 6.4

Passive Relaxation Script

Imagine there are drain plugs on the bottom of your feet. When you open them, all the tension will drain out of your body, and you will become very, very relaxed. Take a slow, deep breath. Now, undo those plugs. Feel the tension begin to drain out of your body—down from the top of your head, past your forehead, your face, and your jaw. You're becoming more and more relaxed. The tension drains out of your jaw and down past your neck. Now your face and your neck are warm and relaxed and comfortable. Take a slow, deep breath.

The tension continues to drain out of your upper body, past your shoulders, upper arms, and forearms, and out of your hands. Now your shoulders, arms, and hands are warm, relaxed, and comfortable. Take a slow, deep breath.

The tension continues to drain out of your upper body, past your chest and upper back, down past your stomach and lower back. Your upper body is becoming more and more relaxed. There is no more tension left in your upper body. Now your entire upper body is warm and relaxed and comfortable. Take a slow, deep breath.

The tension continues to drain out of your lower body, past your buttocks and down past your thighs and your knees. Your lower body is becoming more and more relaxed. The tension drains out of your calves. There is almost no more tension left in your body, and the last bit of tension drains past your ankles, the balls of your feet, and your toes. Now do a brief survey of your body from head to toe to ensure that there is no more tension left in your body. Your entire body is warm, relaxed, and comfortable. Now replace the plugs so that no tension can get back in. Take a slow, deep breath. Feel the calm and relaxation envelop you. Enjoy that feeling, and remember what it feels like to be completely relaxed.

A technique that directly affects this symptom of overintensity is progressive relaxation (Jacobson, 1938), which involves tightening and relaxing major muscle groups (see Exhibit 6.5).

Progressive relaxation has value for athletes at two levels. First, athletes are often so accustomed to being tense that they are simply not aware of their level of muscle tension and how it affects their competitive performances. The process of tightening and relaxing muscles teaches athletes to discriminate between the states of tension and relaxation. When this recognition occurs, athletes are more sensitive to their body's signals and better able to respond effectively to nonideal levels of intensity (Weinberg & Gould, 1999).

As with any technique, the muscle awareness and control that develops from progressive relaxation takes practice. As a result, applied practitioners or coaches can facilitate this process by making progressive relaxation a part of practice. For example, it can be an enjoyable and beneficial part of the cooldown at the end of each training session.

Smiling. The final physiological intervention for overintensity to be discussed is so basic it is surprising that it is so effective. Athletes whose intensity levels are too high should simply smile. This technique was described several years ago by a sport psychologist who was working with a professional tennis player who became frustrated and angry during an on-court practice session as she struggled to improve a weak part of her game. She became so tense that she could not perform at all. Purely on a whim, the sport psychologist told her to smile. As you can imagine, smiling was the last thing she wanted to do, and she expressed those feelings quite emphatically. However, with persistence—and to appease the sport psychologist—she formed a big smile. The sport psychologist told her to hold the smile. Within 2 minutes, a remarkable transformation occurred. As she held the smile, the tension in her shoulders disappeared; the wrinkle in her brow went away; and her body, which had been hunched and closed, began to rise and open up. She went on to have a productive practice in which she was able to overcome her earlier difficulties.

The sport psychologist was curious as to why smiling had such a dramatic effect. By examining research on the effects of smiling, he discovered several causes of this phenomenon. First, people are conditioned to associate smiling with happiness and feeling good. Second, smiling changes blood flow through the brain and causes the release of neurochemicals that have a relaxing effect (Zajonc, 1985). Third, it is difficult to think and feel in a way that is contrary to what the body is

Exhibit 6.5

Progressive Relaxation Script

Progressive relaxation involves tightening and relaxing major muscle groups. You will focus on four major muscle groups: legs and buttocks, chest and back, arms and shoulders, face and neck. To start, tense the muscles in your legs and buttocks for 5 seconds, then release. Take a long, slow, deep breath. Feel the difference between the tension and the relaxation. Repeat this process in your legs and buttocks.

Tense the muscles in your chest and back for 5 seconds, then release. Take a long, slow, deep breath. Feel the difference between the tension and the relaxation. Repeat this process in your chest and back.

Tense the muscles in your arms and shoulders for 5 seconds, then release. Take a long, slow, deep breath. Feel the difference between the tension and the relaxation. Repeat this process in your arms and shoulders.

Tense the muscles in your face and neck for 5 seconds, then release. Take a long, slow, deep breath. Feel the difference between the tension and the relaxation. Repeat this process in your face and neck.

Tense the muscles in your entire body for 5 seconds, then release. Take a long, slow, deep breath. Feel the difference between the tension and the relaxation. Repeat this process in your entire body.

Now do a mental checklist to make sure that every muscle is relaxed. Your feet are relaxed, calves, thighs, buttocks, stomach, back, chest, arms, shoulders, neck, and face. Every muscle in your body is completely relaxed.

expressing. As such, it is difficult to be frustrated, angry, and tense when smiling.

Regulation of Underintensity

Physical activity. Fundamentally, intensity is the amount of physiological activity experienced by an athlete. As a result, the most direct way to increase intensity is through vigorous physical activity. The most effective type of physical activity depends on the particular sport, but any form of running, jumping, or active movement should be sufficient. The bottom line is to get the heart pumping and the blood flowing.

High-energy body language. Internal physiological activity can be effectively activated with external physiological activity such as high-energy body language. Athletes who pump their fist, slap their thighs, and give high fives to their teammates are using this technique to increase their intensity. Athletes in many sports, such as Reggie Miller (basketball), Maurice Greene (track), and Venus Williams (tennis), use high-energy body language to maintain ideal intensity.

General Interventions for Intensity Regulation

In addition to cognitive and physiological techniques, several general performance enhancement strategies also can be beneficial to many aspects of mental preparation for athletes. Some of these interventions are discussed next, in terms of how they can be used to regulate intensity and affect athletes both cognitively and physiologically.

Mental Imagery

Considerable research has indicated that mental imagery can have a distinct physiological effect on athletes (for a review, see Feltz & Landers, 1983). Consequently, athletes can use mental imagery to adjust intensity before a competition (Caudill et al., 1983). High-energy images of intense competition, strong effort, and success will raise physiological activity. Calming images of relaxing scenes, peace, and tranquility will reduce intensity. Further discussion on the use of imagery in sport and exercise psychology is presented in chapter 4, by Gould, Damarjian, and Greenleaf, in this volume.

Keywords. A common trap that athletes fall into is that they get so absorbed in the heat of competition that they forget to do the things they need to do to perform their best. In particular, athletes forget to monitor and adjust their intensity. A useful tool to maintain an awareness of intensity is to develop meaningful keywords (see Exhibit 6.6).

Applied practitioners can encourage athletes to identify keywords and place them in visible settings, such as their bedroom, locker room, or weight room. Athletes can also place the keywords on their equip-

---

Exhibit 6.6

Intensity Keywords

Directions: A variety of intensity keywords have been provided. In the space below, identify other intensity keywords you can use.

Psych Down	Psych Up
Breathe	Go for it
Loose	Charge
Relax	Attack
Calm	Positive
Easy	Hustle
Focus	Punch it
Trust	Commit
Cool down	Fire up

ment so, during competition, they will see the keywords and remember to monitor and adjust their intensity.

Music. Music can have a profound emotional and physiological effect on people. It can cause people to feel happy, sad, inspired, and angry. It can also excite or relax people. Although this relationship has not been studied empirically in the sports world, many well-known athletes use music to help them regulate their intensity before competition.

Applied practitioners can assist athletes in selecting the style of music that is most appropriate for their intensity needs. For example, athletes who need to increase their intensity should listen to high-energy music. In contrast, those who need to lower intensity should listen to relaxing music.

Situational Interventions for Intensity Regulation

Intensity can also be influenced by situational interventions, in which athletes use the time and space before a competition to achieve ideal intensity. Situational strategies influence intensity by controlling environmental and preparatory factors that affect intensity. By effectively managing time, setting, and preparation before competition, athletes are able to identify and gain control over situational contributors to intensity.

Precompetition Management

On the day of a competition, the time that athletes spend before they compete is the most crucial period of competitive preparation. What athletes think, feel, and do before they compete will dictate how they perform. This precompetitive time can ensure ideal intensity, which leads to quality performance. Athletes should have three goals before they compete. Their equipment should be ideally prepared. Their body should be properly warmed up and at ideal intensity. They should be mentally prepared, most notably with ideal levels of confidence and focus. Applied practitioners can ensure total preparation by asking athletes four questions (see Exhibit 6.7) about their precompetitive environment:

- *Where should you stay at the competition site?* Where athletes can best accomplish their precompetitive preparation depends largely on their attentional style (Nideffer & Sagal, 1998). Athletes who are overly sensitive to external distractions should isolate themselves from the typical activity of the competition site. This reduces the

Exhibit 6.7

Precompetitive Management Plan

Directions: Respond to each question below as it relates to your precompetitive preparation. Then apply this information to your precompetitive routine.

Where should you stay at the competition site?
What must you do to be totally prepared?
Who can assist you with your preparation?
Who and what can interfere with your preparation?

likelihood that environmental distractions such as other competitors, coaches, and officials will interfere with their precompetitive preparations. In contrast, athletes who are overly sensitive to internal distractions should stay around the activity of the competition site. By doing so, they are drawn out of their internal focus by the activity and are less likely to dwell on negative or irrelevant thoughts that could inhibit their precompetitive preparation.

- *What must you do to be totally prepared?* Three primary areas for preparation need to be considered in response to this question: equipment, physical, and mental. For each of these areas, specific methods should be developed to ensure total preparation. Then, athletes should develop precompetitive routines (discussed in the next section) to combine the many preparation strategies into a cohesive plan that is most effective for the particular competition site.

- *Who can assist you with your preparation?* Athletes may interact with many people at the competition site during precompetitive preparation, including coaches, teammates, family, friends, and fans. Some of these people are important to precompetitive preparation, and some are not. For example, Weiss and Friedrichs (1988) reported that when coaches provided frequent positive reinforcement and social support, teams performed at a higher level. The applied practitioner can assist athletes in identifying those individuals who will facilitate their precompetitive preparation.

- *Who and what can interfere with your preparation?* Some people and information, such as chatty teammates, family, unwanted competition information, and results of earlier competitions, may interfere with athletes' precompetitive preparation. Athletes may be distracted from relevant precompetitive focus, and their precompetitive efforts may be inhibited (Magill, 1998; Nideffer, 1989). These distractions need to be identified and actively avoided. In addition, athletes should develop plans to deal with these people and situations.

Precompetitive Routines

Considerable research has demonstrated that precompetitive routines are an effective means of controlling intensity and enhancing the consistency and quality of performances (Boutcher & Crews, 1987; Cohn, Rotella, & Lloyd, 1990; Ravizza & Osborne, 1991). As a result, routines are an important part of precompetitive preparation and are useful to athletes in attaining and maintaining ideal intensity.

Routines are valuable for many reasons. They ensure completion of every key aspect of precompetitive preparation. They enhance familiarity of situations because the routines and the associated preparation become familiar to the athletes. They decrease the likelihood of unexpected events occurring by giving athletes greater control over precompetitive events. Routines develop consistency of thought, feeling, and behavior. They increase feelings of control over the competitive environment. Routines raise confidence and reduce intensity. By developing and implementing an effective precompetitive routine, regardless of the importance of the competition, athletes will condition their minds and bodies into thinking and feeling that this is just another competition in which they will perform their best.

Routines versus rituals. Superstitious behavior is a common phenomenon among athletes. This behavior is the rigid adherence to precompetitive actions that athletes imbue with importance to their performances, yet serve no practical function in preparation for the competition. Often, athletes develop a series of activities that appear to be routines, but they are, in fact, superstitious rituals (Vernacchia, McGuire, & Cook, 1992). It is important for applied practitioners to be able to distinguish between the two to assist athletes in developing effective routines and ensuring maximum preparation.

The goal of routines is to totally prepare athletes for competition. Everything done in precompetitive routines serves a specific and necessary function in the preparation for competition. Also, routines are flexible and can be adapted to unique aspects of each competitive situation. In contrast, rituals involve anything that does not serve a specific purpose in preparation for the competition. In addition, rituals are inflexible, and athletes believe that they *must* be done or they will not perform well. It is important that applied practitioners show athletes that they control their routines but that rituals control them.

Routine content. Each athlete's precompetitive routine should comprise every factor that can influence competitive performance, for example, meals, physical warm-up, equipment, technical warm-up, and mental preparation. A useful means of identifying all the factors is for applied practitioners to discuss with athletes what they do to prepare for a competition. Team sport athletes must deal with the added dimension of team precompetitive routines (e.g., a football offensive-unit running plays). These athletes must manage their precompetitive time effectively to meet their individual and team precompetitive needs.

Early-morning routine. Precompetitive preparation begins as soon as athletes awaken in the morning. This early-morning preparation sets the tone for the day and ensures that the athletes are physically and mentally ready for later preparation. Before athletes get out of bed, they should use mental imagery to rehearse their performance in the upcoming competition. Athletes can also use some of the intensity regulation techniques already discussed to begin the movement to ideal intensity. These techniques set the stage for the competitive performance by generating positive feelings and focus.

Arrival at competition site. A similar preparation process should be conducted on arrival at the competition site. Similar to the early-morning routine that involves mental and physical preparation, this procedure is aimed at further readying athletes for the upcoming competition. Athletes should again use mental imagery to produce the feelings associated with good competitive performance. Imagery, keywords, and other intensity regulation techniques may also be used to direct focus and to begin the move toward ideal intensity.

A more vigorous physical warm-up is also necessary, with the emphasis on a further shift toward ideal intensity. For technical sports such as tennis, golf, and baseball, this phase should be accompanied by technical warm-up, in which proper technique is rehearsed and reinforced. Initial physical and technical warm-up should be slow and gentle as the body warms up. Once the initial warm-up is completed, the preparation should be rehearsed with increasing focus and intensity aimed at simulating competitive conditions. This "priming" effect makes it easier for athletes to attain their ideal focus and intensity when the competition begins.

Final preparation routine. This last stage of the athletes' precompetitive routine ensures that complete readiness is attained just before the competition. Any adjustments to equipment should be made. As with the previous routines, emphasis is placed on fine-tuning the athletes mentally and physically to their optimal state of readiness. Final mental preparation involves using mental imagery to review their performance, repeating keywords to narrow and maintain focus on the competition, and using intensity regulation exercises that will enable the athletes to reach ideal intensity as they approach the competition. Final physical preparation includes last-minute physical warm-up and technical fine-tuning.

The goal of the three levels of precompetitive preparation is that when athletes begin competition, they are ready both mentally and physically to perform their very best. How each of these factors is accomplished is what makes a routine personal to each athlete. Once athletes have established the necessary components of the routine, applied practitioners can assist them in establishing their own personalized precompetitive routine that satisfies their individual needs and style (see Exhibit 6.8).

Exhibit 6.8

Precompetitive Routine

Directions: List the precompetition activities that will help you prepare to perform your very best.

Early morning
  1. Physical:
  2. Mental:

Arrival at competition site
  1. Physical:
  2. Mental:

Before competition
  1. Equipment:
  2. Physical:
  3. Mental:

Summary

When the time of the competition arrives, intensity becomes the most important factor, because if the body is not optimally prepared, athletes will not be able to perform their best. Some level of intensity is necessary for optimal performance, but too much or too little intensity can hurt performance. Moreover, there is no one ideal intensity level for every athlete. Some athletes perform best at low intensity, others perform best at moderate intensity, and others perform best at high intensity. This relationship is influenced by personal, sport, social, and situational factors.

Overintensity is characterized by muscle tension, breathing difficulty, negative self-talk, loss of coordination, and feelings of fear and dread. Overintensity is caused by lack of confidence; extreme or inaccurate cognitive appraisals of the competition; and unfamiliar, expected, or uncontrollable events before the competition. Underintensity is caused by overconfidence, lack of motivation, fatigue, and high ability combined with low demands. Athletes experience underintensity as feelings of lethargy and low energy, an absence of alertness and interest, and problems narrowing concentration before and during a competition.

Applied practitioners should assess athletes' intensity levels when they are performing well versus poorly to help them understand and attain their ideal intensity. Overintensity can be lessened cognitively by building self-confidence, countering inaccurate or extreme thinking, assisting athletes in rationally assessing the upcoming competition, making unfamiliar situations more familiar, planning for unexpected events, and helping athletes focus only on controllable events. Overintensity can be regulated physiologically with the use of breathing, progressive relaxation, and smiling.

Underintensity may be increased by exercising to raise physiological activity, stopping let-down thinking, and using high-energy thinking and talking. General techniques to regulate intensity include mental imagery, keywords, and listening to music. Finally, situational interventions that can be used to regulate intensity include precompetition management and precompetitive routines.

References

Apter, M. J. (1984). Reversal theory and personality: A review. *Journal of Research in Personality, 18,* 265–288.

Apter, M. J. (Ed.). (2001). *Motivational styles in everyday life: A guide to reversal theory.* Washington, DC: American Psychological Association.

Bandura, A. (1986). *Social foundations of thought and action.* Englewood Cliffs, NJ: Prentice-Hall.

Billing, J. (1980). An overview of task complexity. *Motor Skills: Theory Into Practice, 4,* 18–23.

Borkovec, T. D. (1976). Physiological and cognitive processes in the regulation of arousal. In G. E. Schwartz & D. Shapiro (Eds.), *Consciousness and self-regulation: Advances in research* (Vol. 1, pp. 261–312). New York: Plenum.

Boutcher, S. H., & Crews, D. J. (1087). The effect of a preshot attentional routine on a well-learned skill. *International Journal of Sport Psychology, 18,* 30–39.

Cannon, W. B. (1928). The mechanism of emotional disturbance of bodily function. *New England Journal of Medicine, 198,* 877–884.

Carver, C. S., & Scheier, M. F. (1986). Functional and dysfunctional response to anxiety: The interaction between expectancies and self-focused attention. In R. Schwartz (Ed.), *Self-related cognitions in anxiety and motivation* (pp. 111–141). Hillsdale, NJ: Erlbaum.

Caudill, D., Weinberg, R., & Jackson, A. (1983). Psyching-up and track athletes. A preliminary investigation. *Journal of Sport Psychology, 5,* 231–235.

Cohn, P. J., Rotella, R. J., & Lloyd, J. W. (1990). Effects of a cognitive behavioral intervention on the preshot routine and performance in golf. *The Sport Psychologist, 4,* 33–47.

Cox, R. H. (1998). *Sport psychology: Concepts and applications* (4th ed.). Boston: McGraw-Hill.

Cratty, B. J., & Hanin, Y. L. (1980). *The athlete in the sports team.* Denver, CO: Love.

Csikszentmihalyi, M. (1975). *Beyond boredom and anxiety.* San Francisco, CA: Jossey-Bass.

Ebbeck, V., & Weiss, M. R. (1988). The arousal–performance relationship: Task characteristics and performance measures in track and field athletics. *The Sport Psychologist, 2,* 13–27.

Edwards, T., & Hardy, L. (1996). The interactive effects of intensity and direction of cognitive and somatic anxiety and self-confidence upon performance. *Journal of Sport and Exercise Psychology, 18,* 296–312.

Elko, P. K., & Ostrow, A. C. (1991). Effects of a rational–emotive education program on heightened anxiety levels of female collegiate gymnasts. *The Sport Psychologist, 5,* 235–255.

Ellis, A. (1962). *Reason and emotion in psychotherapy.* New York: Lyle Stuart.

Eysenck, M. W., & Calvo, M. S. (1992). Anxiety and performance: The Processing Efficiency Theory. *Cognition and Emotion, 6,* 409–434.

Fazey, J., & Hardy, L. (1988). *The inverted-U hypothesis: A catastrophe for sport psychology?* (BASS Monograph 1). Leeds, UK: White Line Press.

Feltz, D. L., & Landers, D. M. (1983). The effects of mental practice on motor skill learning and performance: A meta-analysis. *Journal of Sport Psychology, 5,* 25–57.

Gill, D. L. (1994). A sport and exercise psychology perspective on stress. *Quest, 46,* 20–27.

Gould, D., & Krane, V. (1992). The arousal–athletic performance relationship: Current status and future directions. In T. S. Horn (Ed.), *Advances in sport psychology* (pp. 119–141). Champaign, IL: Human Kinetics.

Gould, D., & Tuffey, S. (1996). Zones of optimal functioning research: A review and critique. *Anxiety, Stress and Coping, 9,* 53–68.

Gould, D., Tuffey, S., Hardy, L., & Lochbaum, M. (1993). Multidimensional state anxiety and middle distance running performance: An exploratory examination of

Hanin's (1980) zones of optimal functioning hypothesis. *Journal of Applied Sport Psychology, 5,* 89–95.

Hamilton, S. A., & Fremouw, W. J. (1985). Cognitive–behavioral training for college basketball free-throw performance. *Cognitive Therapy and Research, 9,* 479–483.

Hanin, Y. L. (1980). A study of anxiety in sports. In W. F. Straub (Ed.), *Sport psychology: An analysis of athlete behavior* (pp. 236–249). Ithaca, NY: Mouvement.

Hanin, Y. L. (1986). State–trait research in sports in the USSR. In C. D. Spielberger & R. Diaz-Guerrero (Eds.), *Cross-cultural anxiety* (Vol. 3, pp. 45–64). Washington, DC: Hemisphere.

Hanin, Y. L. (2000). Individual zones of optimal functioning (IZOF) model: Emotions–performance relationships in sport. In Y. L. Hanin (Ed.), *Emotions in sport* (pp. 65–89). Champaign, IL: Human Kinetics.

Hanin, Y. L., & Syrja, P. (1995). Performance affect in junior ice hockey players: An application of the individual zones of optimal functioning model. *The Sport Psychologist, 9,* 169–187.

Hardy, L. (1990). A catastrophe model of performance in sport. In J. G. Jones & L. Hardy (Eds.), *Stress and performance in sport* (pp. 81–106). Chichester, England: Wiley.

Hardy, L. (1996). Testing the predictions of the cusp catastrophe model of anxiety and performance. *The Sport Psychologist, 10,* 140–156.

Hardy, L., & Fazey, J. (1987, June). *The inverted-U hypothesis: A catastrophe for sport psychology.* Paper presented at the annual meeting of the North American Society for the Psychology of Sport and Physical Activity, Vancouver, Canada.

Hardy, L., Parfitt, G., & Pates, J. (1994). Performance catastrophes in sport: A test of the hysteresis hypothesis. *Journal of Sport Sciences, 12,* 327–334.

Harger, G. J., & Raglin, J. S. (1994). Correspondence between actual and recalled precompetition anxiety in collegiate track and field athletes. *Journal of Sport and Exercise Psychology, 16,* 206–211.

Heyman, S. R. (1984). Cognitive interventions: Theories, applications, and cautions. In W. F. Straub & J. M. Williams (Eds.), *Cognitive sport psychology* (pp. 289–303). Lansing, NY: Sport Science Associates.

Imlay, G. J., Carda, R. D., Stanbrough, M. E., & O'Connor, P. J. (1995). Anxiety and performance: A test of optimal function theory. *International Journal of Sport Psychology, 26,* 295–306.

Jacobson, E. (1938). *Progressive relaxation.* Chicago: University of Chicago Press.

Jones, G. (1995). Competitive anxiety in sport. In S. J. H. Biddle (Ed.), *European perspectives on exercise and sport psychology* (pp. 128–153). Leeds, UK: Human Kinetics.

Kerr, J. H. (1989). Anxiety, arousal and sport performance: An application of reversal theory. In D. Hackfort & C. C. Spielberger (Eds.), *Anxiety in sports: An international perspective* (pp. 137–151). New York: Hemisphere.

Kerr, J. H. (1990). Stress and sport: Reversal theory. In G. Jones & L. Hardy (Eds.), *Stress and performance in sport* (pp. 107–132). Chichester, England: Wiley.

Kerr, J. H. (1997). *Motivation and emotion in sport: Reversal theory.* East Sussex, UK: Psychology Press.

Kleine, D. (1990). Anxiety and sports performance: A meta-analysis. *Anxiety Research, 2,* 113–131.

Krane, V. (1993). A practical application of the anxiety–athletic performance relationship: The zone of optimal function hypothesis. *The Sport Psychologist, 7,* 113–126.

Krane, V., Joyce, D., & Raefeld, J. (1994). Competitive anxiety, situational criticality, and softball performance. *The Sport Psychologist, 8,* 58–72.

Krane, V., & Williams, J. M. (1994). Cognitive anxiety, somatic anxiety and confidence in track and field athletes: The impact of gender, competitive level, and task characteristics. *International Journal of Sport Psychology, 25,* 203–217.

Krohne, H. W. (1980). Parental child-rearing behavior and the development of anxiety and coping strategies in children. In I. G. Sarason & C. D. Spielberger (Eds.), *Stress and anxiety* (Vol. 7, pp. 243–272). Washington, DC: Hemisphere.

Landers, D. M., & Boutcher, S. H. (1986). Arousal–performance relationships. In J. M. Williams (Ed.), *Applied sport psychology: Personal growth to peak performance* (pp. 163–184). Palo Alto, CA: Mayfield.

Magill, R. A. (1998). *Motor learning: Concepts and applications* (5th ed.). Boston: McGraw-Hill.

Martens, R., Vealey, R. S., & Burton, D. (1990). *Competitive anxiety in sport.* Champaign, IL: Human Kinetics.

McCann, S. C., Murphy, S. M., & Radeke, T. D. (1992). The effect of performance setting and individual differences on the anxiety–performance relationship for elite cyclists. *Anxiety and Stress in Coping, 5,* 117–187.

Morgan, W. P., O'Connor, P. J., Ellickson, K. A., & Bradley, P. W. (1988). Personality structure, mood states, and performance in elite male distance runners. *International Journal of Sport Psychology, 19,* 247–263.

Morgan, W. P., O'Connor, P. J., Sparling, P. B., & Pate, R. R. (1987). Psychological characteristics of elite female distance runners. *International Journal of Sports Medicine, 8,* 124–131.

Neiss, R. (1988). Reconceptualizing arousal: Psychological states in motor performance. *Psychological Bulletin, 103,* 345–366.

Nideffer, R. M. (1989). Anxiety, attention, and performance in sports: Theoretical and practical considerations. In D. Hackfort & C. D. Spielberger (Eds.), *Anxiety in sports: An international perspective* (pp. 117–136). New York: Hemisphere.

Nideffer, R. M., & Sagal, M-S. (1998). Concentration and attentional control training. In J. M. Williams (Ed.), *Applied sport psychology: Personal growth to peak performance* (3rd ed., pp. 296–315). Mountain View, CA: Mayfield.

Oxendine, J. B. (1970). Emotional arousal and motor performance. *Quest, 13,* 23–32.

Passer, M. W. (1982). Psychological stress in youth sports. In R. A. Magill, M. J. Ash, & F. L. Smoll (Eds.), *Children in sport* (2nd ed., pp. 153–177). Champaign, IL: Human Kinetics.

Raglin, J. S., & Hanin, Y. L. (2000). Competitive anxiety. In Y. L. Hanin (Ed.), *Emotions in sport* (pp. 93–111). Champaign, IL: Human Kinetics.

Raglin, J. S., & Morris, M. J. (1994). Precompetition anxiety in women volleyball players. A test of ZOF theory in a team sport. *British Journal of Sports Medicine, 28,* 47–52.

Raglin, J. S., & Turner, P. E. (1992). Predicted, actual and optimal precompetition anxiety in adolescent track and field athletes. *Scandinavian Journal of Medicine and Science in Sports, 2,* 148–152.

Raglin, J. S., Wise, K., & Morgan, W. P. (1990). Predicted and actual pre-competition anxiety in high school girl swimmers. *Journal of Swimming Research, 6,* 5–8.

Ravizza, K., & Osborne, T. (1991). Nebraska's 3 R's: One-play-at-a-time preperformance routine for collegiate football. *The Sport Psychologist, 5,* 256–265.

Schmidt, R. A., & Wrisberg, C. A. (2000). *Motor learning and performance* (2nd ed.). Champaign, IL: Human Kinetics.

Silva, J. M., & Hardy, C. J. (1984). Precompetitive affect and athletic performance. In W. F. Straub & J. M. Williams (Eds.), *Cognitive sport psychology* (pp. 79–88). Lansing, NY: Sport Science Associates.

Smith, R. E., Smoll, F. L., & Curtis, B. (1978). Coaching behaviors in Little League baseball. In F. L. Smoll & R. E. Smith (Eds.), *Psychological perspectives in youth sports* (pp. 173–201). Washington, DC: Hemisphere.

Sonstroem, R. J. (1984). An overview of anxiety in sport. In J. M. Silva, III & R. S. Weinberg (Eds.), *Psychological foundations of sport* (pp. 104–117). Champaign, IL: Human Kinetics.

Spielberger, C. D. (1966). Theory and research on anxiety. In C. D. Spielberger (Ed.), *Anxiety and behavior* (pp. 3–22). New York: Academic Press.

Spielberger, C. D. (1972). *Anxiety: Current trends in theory and research* (Vol. 1). New York: Academic Press.

Spielberger, C. D. (1989). Stress and anxiety in sports. In D. Hackfort & C. D. Spielberger (Eds.), *Anxiety in sports: An international perspective* (pp. 3–17). New York: Hemisphere.

Taylor, J. (2000). *Prime sport: Triumph of the athlete mind.* New York: Universe.

Vernacchia, R., McGuire, R., & Cook, D. (1992). *Coaching mental excellence.* Dubuque, IA: Brown & Benchmark.

Weinberg, R. S. (1988). *The mental advantage: Developing your psychological skills in tennis.* Champaign, IL: Leisure Press.

Weinberg, R. S. (1990). Anxiety and motor performance: Where to from here? *Anxiety Research, 2,* 227–242.

Weinberg, R. S., & Gould, D. (1999). *Foundations of sport and exercise psychology.* Champaign, IL: Human Kinetics.

Weiss, M. R., & Friedrichs, W. D. (1988). The influence of leader behaviors, coach attributes, and institutional variables on performance and satisfaction of collegiate basketball teams. *Journal of Sport Psychology, 8,* 332–346.

Williams, J. M., & Harris, D. V. (1998). Relaxation and energizing techniques of regulation of arousal. In J. M. Williams (Ed.), *Applied sport psychology: Personal growth to peak performance* (3rd ed., pp. 219–236). Mountain View, CA: Mayfield.

Wilson, G. S. (1999). Do physical educators correctly interpret the anxiety and performance relationship? Reevaluating current research. *The Chronicle for Physical Education in Higher Education, 10,* 2–3.

Wilson, G. S. (1998). Gender differences in levels of precompetition and postcompetition anxiety response and individual ratings of performance in collegiate cross-country runners. *International Sports Journal, 1,* 49–56.

Wilson, G. S., & Raglin, J. S. (1997). Optimal and predicted anxiety in 9–12-year-old track and field athletes. *Scandinavian Journal of Medicine and Science in Sports, 2,* 253–258.

Wilson, G. S., Raglin, J. S., & Harger, G. J. (2000). A comparison of the STAI and CSAI–2 in five day recalls of precompetition anxiety in collegiate track and field athletes. *Scandinavian Journal of Medicine and Science in Sports, 10,* 51–54.

Woodman, T., Albinson, J. G., & Hardy, L. (1997). An investigation of the zones of optimal functioning hypothesis within a multidimensional framework. *Journal of Sport and Exercise Psychology, 19,* 131–141.

Yerkes, R. M., & Dodson, J. D. (1908). The relation of strength of stimulus to rapidity of habit formation. *Journal of Comparative Neurology of Psychology, 18,* 459–482.

Zaichkowsky, L., & Takenaka, K. (1993). Optimizing arousal level. In R. N. Singer, M. Murphey, & L. K. Tennant (Eds.), *Handbook of research on sport psychology* (p. 511–527). New York: Macmillan.

Zajonc, R. B. (1985). Emotion and facial efference: A theory reclaimed. *Science, 228,* 15–21.

Observational Learning: The Forgotten Psychological Method in Sport Psychology

Penny McCullagh and Maureen R. Weiss

This chapter illuminates the exciting possibilities of observational learning techniques in sport contexts. Numerous publications highlight the role of observational learning, or modeling, on skill acquisition, psychological responses, and behavior change in physical activity contexts (McCullagh, 1993; McCullagh & Weiss, 2001; McCullagh, Weiss, & Ross, 1989; Weiss, Ebbeck, & Wiese-Bjornstal, 1993; Williams, Davids, & Williams, 1999). Despite its effectiveness, modeling is usually omitted from sport psychology textbooks or receives scant attention. In this chapter, we advocate observational learning as a viable psychological method for modifying thoughts, emotions, and behaviors in a variety of sport contexts. As applied researchers over the past 20 years, we believe that observational learning has been neglected in favor of "sexier" psychological methods such as imagery, relaxation, and self-talk. We hope this chapter will help convince researchers and practitioners *not to forget* observational learning as an effective tool for psychological interventions.

First, three case studies of individuals who encounter challenges in the areas of performance, self-confidence, and anxiety are discussed. Next, an overview of the theoretical underpinnings of modeling is given to help explain why modeling works so effectively. Three sections, which correspond directly to the three case studies, follow in which empirical research on observational learning is discussed as it relates to performance, developmental, and rehabilitation issues. The case studies are revisited to explore possible modeling interventions based on the theory and research we communicated.

Case Studies

Makaila

Makaila is an experienced archer and has been working with the same coach for the past four years. The coach seems to know her abilities and psychological make-up fairly well, but both athlete and coach have recently expressed concern about a couple of issues. Makaila seems to have hit a slump, and her performance has remained the same or declined slightly over the past three months. Also, she has expressed concern about competing against a particular archer who she will be forced to face in a tournament in two months. The coach approaches the sport psychology consultant who has been working with the team about potential interventions that might aid Makaila in her dilemma.

Harrison

When he was younger, 10-year-old Harrison enjoyed swimming and other water activities. He was pretty good at a variety of swimming strokes and felt confident among his peers. He liked the feel of the water on hot summer days, and playing at the local pool was an activity he shared with his friends. All of that changed one day. During swim lessons one morning, a boy from another group decided to play a gag on Harrison. The boy approached Harrison from behind, grabbed him, and shoved his head under water. Not knowing what was happening to him, Harrison started to panic. He flailed under the water, and he was seized by desperate anxiety. Although the instructor rescued Harrison in sufficient time, the event was so traumatic that he climbed up the ladder of the pool, picked up his towel, and walked home. He has not gone near a pool since that time—three years ago.

Felicia

Felicia was highly recruited by top collegiate basketball programs. She could hardly wait to test her skills against highly competitive opponents. Felicia's first season was a rousing success. She worked her way from the bench to the starting five and was a key contributor in several late-game wins that propelled the team to the NCAA tournament. In a game early in her sophomore season, Felicia stole an errant pass and glided down the court for an uncontested layup. When she came down after making the shot, Felicia felt herself landing awkwardly and an excruciating pain shot through her leg. After being helped off the floor, she learned that she had torn her anterior cruciate ligament. Following surgery, Felicia immersed herself in physical rehabilitation outlined by her physician and athletic trainer. Although she observed gains in physical landmarks, she sorely misses being part of the team and cannot seem to discard her constant pessimism and despair. Her defeatist outlook is stimulating thoughts of quitting basketball altogether.

Theoretical Approaches to Observational Learning

Providing demonstrations has long been recognized as an important means for helping individuals learn or modify skills and behaviors. Bandura's (e.g., 1977a, 1977b, 1986, 1997) social cognitive and self-efficacy theories have acknowledged modeling "to be one of the most powerful means of transmitting values, attitudes and patterns of thought and behavior" (1986, p. 47). What are the mechanisms underlying the effectiveness of modeling? Why does is work?

According to Bandura, four processes govern observational learning: attention, retention, production, and motivation. The attention process requires that observers selectively attend to task-salient features to glean the essential parameters necessary for successful reproduction of modeled behaviors. Paying attention, however, does not ensure accurate production of demonstrated behavior; one must remember what was modeled. Observed behaviors can be retained as visual or verbal representations. Coaches and teachers often induce both types of coding or rehearsal methods. For example, a tennis instructor may say "scratch your back with the racquet" to induce verbal coding of movement or "think about the ball toss going up straight as an arrow" to induce imaginal coding. Selective attention to and ability to remember salient task features are insufficient for successful modeling to occur. Observers must translate their cognitive representation of modeled actions to motor performance that approximates that of the model. Finally, without motivation or desire to emulate observed actions, one's attention, retention, and production skills are moot. Depending on the motivation of the observer, modeled acts may or may not be attempted.

It is difficult to discuss theoretical approaches to observational learning without referring to self-efficacy theory (Bandura, 1977a, 1997). *Self-efficacy* is defined as an individual's conviction that he or she can successfully execute the behaviors necessary to produce a desired outcome. According to Bandura, self-efficacy beliefs are a major basis for action, and they exert influence on an individual's choice of activities, effort, and persistence in achievement situations. Efficacy beliefs are derived from four major sources of information: mastery experiences, vicarious experiences, verbal persuasion, and affective or physiological states. All four of these sources relate directly to modeling techniques. Mastery experiences may include watching oneself perform successfully on videotape or in a mirror as ballet dancers do (i.e., self-modeling) or receiving guided assistance to re-enact modeled skills (i.e., participant modeling). Vicarious experiences include watching others execute a skill or behavior, whether they be competent adults (i.e., correct or mastery models) or similar-age peers (i.e., learning or coping models). Verbal persuasion and physiological states have also been linked to modeling techniques in the form of cognitive modeling, model self-talk, and emotive models.

Thus, observational learning and self-efficacy go hand in hand. Observational learning is a key source of efficacy beliefs that, in turn, influence thoughts, emotions, and behaviors. The central processes of observational learning are shown in Figure 7.1. Specifically, attention and retention characterize the cognitive processes that mediate the re-

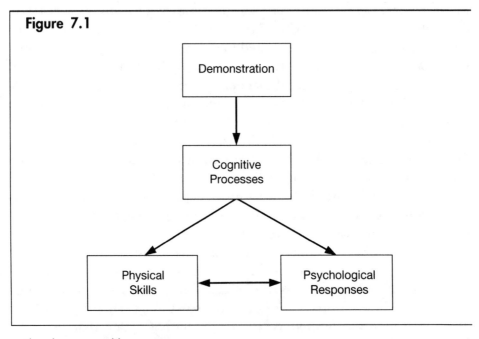

Figure 7.1

The observational learning process.

lationship between observing a demonstration and attempts to match motor performance (i.e., physical skills) to that of the model. Psychological responses (e.g., self-confidence, anxiety) are also influenced by individuals' perceptions of characteristics of the model or demonstration. The double-headed arrow between motor skill and psychological responses reflects the essential role of self-efficacy and motivation in enacting observed skills, as well as the influence of successful performance on psychological outcomes such as self-efficacy, affective responses, and motivated behavior.

Modifying Physical Skills and Psychological Responses

Several variables are salient when discussing observational learning as a method for modifying physical skills (i.e., performance) and psychological responses (e.g., self-efficacy), including model type, self-observation, and imagery. The first two variables represent characteristics of the model (i.e., the person who demonstrates behaviors), whereas imagery represents augmented information associated with the content of the demonstration itself. (For a discussion of other model and demonstration characteristics relevant to acquiring skills and behaviors, readers are directed to McCullagh & Weiss, 2001.)

Model Type

The skill level of the model is one of the most important factors to consider when designing modeling interventions. When choosing someone to demonstrate a physical skill, the first inclination is to select a model that can execute the behavior flawlessly (i.e., a correct model). However, an alternative method is to expose observers to a model who is attempting to learn the skill and has not yet achieved exemplary performance (i.e., a learning model). McCullagh and Caird (1990) compared these model types with college students attempting to learn a laboratory timing skill and found that a learning model was more effective than watching someone execute the skill without errors, but only if observers were privy to feedback given to the model. Hebert and Landin (1994) extended this study to a complex sport skill (tennis forehand). Participants received feedback about their own performance, watched a learning model and heard the instructor's feedback to the model, received a combination of both treatments, or received no demonstrations or feedback. The combination of treatments led to the best performance, whereas the learning model participants produced performance similar to that achieved by receiving feedback about one's own skill execution. Collectively, these findings imply that, if it is impossible for the coach or teacher to give individualized feedback, participants can learn from peers who are practicing the skill, especially if the coach is providing them with informational or corrective feedback.

Why are learning models so effective? Lee, Swinnen, and Serrien (1994) suggested that observers spend more cognitive effort when they watch learning models who are receiving feedback than when they watch correct models. They have to concentrate and process the error information as they watch someone who is learning and receiving feedback. Furthermore, higher self-efficacy may be invoked when learners watch similar others persist and master skills for which they have experienced prior difficulty (McCullagh & Weiss, 2001). Thus, the skill level of both the model and the observer are important considerations when deciding who should demonstrate. For the novice, seeing elite athletes perform skills perfectly may have a negative impact on self-efficacy, motivation, and performance because of perceived dissimilarity between the observer and model.

The type of model can also have an impact on psychological variables other than self-efficacy. Although not designed as a modeling study, Rejeski and Sanford (1984) examined affective responses of college women after watching a tolerant or intolerant model exercising. The tolerant model responded with little overt distress to the exercise demands whereas the intolerant model grimaced and made the exercise session look difficult. Model type clearly influenced observers' perceptions, because those who watched an intolerant model reported greater negative affect and perceived exertion than those who watched a tolerant model. This research suggests that you may want to choose your exercise partner carefully if you want to have a positive experience.

Self-Observation

When we think of using demonstrations to modify behaviors, we usually think of watching others perform. However, in today's highly technical society it is easy to create images on videotapes or computers and to view oneself as the model. Dowrick (1999) conducted considerable research on self-observation modeling techniques and has delineated three types of self-observation: videotape feedback, self-modeling, and feedforward. *Videotape feedback* entails having an individual execute skills and behaviors that are played back on a video monitor. The coach and sport psychology consultant may view these tapes with the performer to make corrective comments. *Self-modeling* is defined by Dowrick as "an intervention procedure using the observation of oneself engaged in adaptive behavior" (p. 23). This type of self-observation usually requires editing of original videotapes or images. *Feedforward* shows individuals executing behaviors beyond what they have actually achieved. This technique might show new skills that are beyond the observer's repertoire and could be used to impart technical information or enhance motivation.

Although limited research on self-observation has been conducted in sport psychology, some applied studies reveal promise in this area. Halliwell (1990) reported positive changes in confidence and performance when he developed music videos showing highlights of games of professional hockey players who were returning from injury or experiencing performance slumps. Maile (cited in Franks & Maile, 1991) reported a remarkable 26% performance increase over a 25-week intervention period in which a weight lifter was shown videos of herself lifting more weight than previously achieved (i.e., feedforward). McCullagh (see Balf, 1996; Livermore, 1996) used self-observation techniques with some Olympic archers to provide information about upcoming competitions and as a source of self-efficacy information. Finally, Starek and McCullagh (1999) examined the effectiveness of self versus peer modeling on learning, self-efficacy, and anxiety of novice adult swimmers and found that individuals performed better after watching themselves than after viewing a peer, although neither anxiety nor self-efficacy were modified.

Self-modeling is being used in numerous applied sport situations. The San Francisco Giants baseball team installed a high-tech digital video system that is less cumbersome than videotape so that players can go immediately behind the dugout and see their own performance or that of opponents. A video coach helps select and construct appropriate replays so players can see themselves under almost any situation. Other professional teams are also using video in an attempt to enhance player performance (Evangelista, 2000).

Imagery and Modeling as Vicarious Experiences

Imagery is widely used by coaches, athletes, and sport psychology consultants for improving physical skills, altering emotional responses, and enhancing self-efficacy. Most sport psychology textbooks espouse the benefits of imagery, such as "evidence from scientific experiments in support of imagery . . . is impressive and clearly demonstrates the value of imagery in learning and performing motor skills" (Weinberg & Gould, 1999, p. 268). Martin, Moritz, and Hall (1999) noted that imagery has primarily been examined relative to its influence on learning and performing physical skills as well as on the regulation of arousal or anxiety. They also pointed out that many imagery studies are confounded with multiple treatments. McCullagh and Ram (2000) reviewed imagery studies conducted over the past 10 years and found that more than half of the studies used live demonstrations, videotapes, or photographs to induce the imagery intervention. Thus, many imagery studies may be confounded by the use of modeling techniques.

The primary difference between modeling and imagery is the type of stimulus used. In modeling studies, external stimuli such as live demonstrations or videotapes are typically shown to observers. The observer then cognitively encodes and rehearses this information before producing a response. With imagery interventions, no external stimulus is provided. Instead, performers create an internal image based on their own previous experiences. Once the image is encoded, modeling and imagery may share similar cognitive processes (Feltz & Landers, 1983). For example, observers may rehearse modeling and imagery stimuli in the same fashion, and modeling and imagery may be influenced by similar motivational goals.

A study by Rushall (1988) vividly demonstrates the similarities between modeling and imagery techniques. Rushall used a covert modeling procedure with a world-ranked wrestler experiencing low confidence in international competitions. In covert modeling, initially other models are imagined, and then gradually the participant becomes the model who is imagined. Eventually, modeled behaviors are practiced under real-world circumstances. The intervention was successful; the wrestler reduced his negative self-statements and improved in performance. Rushall concluded,

> Once *imagery* recall and skill had been developed, the fictional *model* was gradually replaced with features of the athlete himself. Once the athlete had been successfully substituted into the *modeled* situations, he reported using the *modeling* procedure on his own. The *imagery* procedure and behavior strategy development methods were adopted as part of his competition preparation procedures, and the original problem behaviors were removed to his satisfaction. (p. 139, italics added)

The easy interchange between modeling and imagery terms clearly demonstrates the similarity in cognitive processes underlying intervention procedures.

Observational learning researchers have proposed conceptual models that encompass observer (developmental factors), demonstration (augmented information, model type), and rehearsal (verbal, imaginal) variables that affect behavioral and psychological responses (e.g., McCullagh et al., 1989). In a similar vein, Martin et al. (1999) recognized that variables that affect imagery effectiveness lacked conceptual organization for sport psychology research and practice. They proposed a model of imagery that identified four critical factors: sport situation, imagery type, imagery ability, and outcomes. Distinct parallels can be drawn between the factors in their imagery model and those of observational learning models. For example, they suggest that imagery can influence several outcomes, such as the acquisition of skills, modification of cognitions, and regulation of arousal (i.e., informational and motivational purposes). These are the same purposes for which modeling interventions are used. Readers are encouraged to examine their model of imagery, because there may be some benefit in attempting to merge the imagery and modeling literatures.

Developmental Issues

Because Bandura's (1977b, 1986) social–cognitive theory highlights the essential role of attention, retention, production, and motivation processes, the developmental level of the observer is a crucial factor to consider when designing modeling interventions. Research on motor performance shows that children do not fully mature in selective attention, visual processing speed, and control processes (i.e., labeling, rehearsal, and organization) until about age 12 (Gallagher, French, Thomas, & Thomas, 1996). Child novices possess less sport-specific knowledge than do child experts, who demonstrate less sophisticated cognitive representations than do adult experts (e.g., McPherson, 1999; Nevett & French, 1997). Knowledge base is associated with the ability to use self-regulated learning strategies to produce successful motor skill execution. According to Schunk (1989, 1998), modeling is a primary method of influencing self-regulatory development, whereby individuals activate and sustain cognitions (e.g., organizing information, self-efficacy), behaviors (e.g., setting goals, self-reinforcement), and emotions (e.g., feeling pride in one's work) toward achieving a goal.

Children's Modeling of Motor Skills

Research on children's modeling of motor skills consistently points to cognitive and physical developmental differences. Weiss and colleagues (McCullagh, Stiehl, & Weiss, 1990; Weiss, 1983; Weiss, Ebbeck, & Rose, 1992; Weiss & Klint, 1987) demonstrated that a "show-and-tell" model, which simultaneously shows and verbalizes essential performance elements, is especially effective with younger children who do not selectively attend to task-relevant cues or engage spontaneously in rehearsal strategies. Requiring verbal rehearsal of the modeled skills before performing them was also an important strategy for successful skill production. Wiese-Bjornstal and Weiss (1992), using a biomechanical analysis to quantify child–model differences, found that children's recognition, recall, and physical enactment of a novel softball pitch increased with repeated exposures to the model and availability of verbal cues. These results and others (e.g., Bouffard & Dunn, 1993) support Schunk's (1998) contention that modeling is a viable psychological method for enhancing children's self-regulation skills (e.g., selective attention, verbal self-instruction, covert self-talk) and subsequent performance.

Psychological Effects of Modeling

Although the role of modeling in children's motor skill development is pronounced, the motivational effects of modeling interventions have been less studied in the physical domain. Such psychological processes as self-efficacy, anxiety, and fear influence motivated behavior. Schunk and colleagues (Schunk, 1987; Schunk & Hanson, 1985, 1989; Schunk, Hanson, & Cox, 1987) have consistently shown that peer models enhance self-efficacy, desire to learn, and performance in the academic domain. The primary mechanism by which modeling influences psychological responses and motivated behavior is through characteristics of the model. Perceived model–observer similarity is perhaps the most important characteristic to consider in designing modeling interventions to modify psychological responses and subsequent motivation and performance.

Model–observer similarity refers to characteristics common to both the demonstrator and the learner, such as age, gender, race or ethnicity, and ability level. The reasoning behind the success of perceived model similarity lies in its effects on the observer's attention and motivation. A similar model should elicit in the observer undivided attention to information being conveyed and the desire to change one's self-efficacy, emotions, and behavior through the attitude "If he or she can do it, so can I!" Peer models, who are roughly equivalent in development to the observer and may be similar in other ways such as gender and competence level (Schunk, 1998), represent one form of model–observer similarity that carries tremendous potential for effecting psychological change and motivated behavior in the physical domain.

Peer Models

Schunk (1987, 1989, 1998) contended that peer models convey information and motivation to observers pertaining to learning strategies, self-regulation skills, outcome expectations, and self-efficacy. These psychological processes translate to motivated behavior and improved performance. For children, the advantages of peer models over adult models include observers' ability to identify better with skills and learning strategies and the tendency for peer models to focus on practical strategies that are more understandable to child learners. Peer models may be especially helpful when observers are uncertain about their capabilities to do the task, are unfamiliar with the skills, or have experienced difficulty or anxiety on previous performance attempts. A case study by Feltz (1980) supports these contentions in the physical domain. A peer model (similar age, gender, IQ) was used (in combination with performance assistance) to teach a 12-year-old boy with a cognitive disability a modified forward dive. The boy was motivated to learn the skill but exhibited anxiety toward any type of head-first dive. Only four 30-minute sessions with a peer model and physical assistance were needed for the boy to learn the dive, and a retention test three weeks later revealed that he could successfully execute the skill without fear.

Variations of peer modeling include peer mastery and peer coping models (Schunk, 1987, 1998). Mastery and coping models are similar to the correct and learning models discussed previously. Peer mastery models demonstrate flawless performance and verbalize confidence (i.e., "I can do this skill"), positive attitude (i.e., "This is fun"), high ability (i.e., "I'm good at this"), and low task difficulty (i.e., "This is pretty easy"). For activities in which observers have little or no anxiety, a peer mastery model is the logical choice for a demonstrator. However, when teaching high-avoidance skills (e.g., gymnastics, swimming) or ones in which the observer displays fear, low self-confidence, and high anxiety based on personal or vicarious experience, a peer coping model should result in more positive outcomes. Peer coping models are similar to observers because they initially demonstrate incorrect performance and verbalizations that resemble the same uncertainties or fears (e.g., "I can't do this," "I'm not very good at this," "This is tough to do," "I don't like doing this"). Over the course of repeated demonstrations, the peer coping model proceeds from negative self-statements and poor skill performance to coping statements and partially correct performance and then to positive self-statements and exemplary skill execution.

Schunk and colleagues (see Schunk, 1987, 1998) provided strong support for peer coping models as an intervention to enhance children's cognitive skill learning, self-efficacy, and academic performance. Peer coping models have also been effective in medical situations such as preoperative anxiety and recovery from surgery (Flint, 1991; Melamed & Siegel, 1975). Peer coping models can logically extend to sport environments where many skills may be perceived as dangerous or anxiety provoking. Besides obvious activities such as water and extreme sports, skills such as taking a charge in basketball, sliding into home plate, and diving for a volleyball may meet with hesitation by novice learners or observers experiencing prior difficulty. Evidence for the effect of peer models in general, and peer coping models specifically, in the physical domain is sparse. However, results from two studies encourage a more concerted effort to use peer coping models in many applied sport situations.

Lewis (1974) used peer modeling as an intervention for children showing avoidance of and anxiety about water activities. Children were assigned to one of these groups: a peer coping model plus participation, peer coping model only, participation only, or control conditions. The peer coping model consisted of three children similar to observers in age, race, and gender. At postintervention, the peer coping model plus participation group showed less avoidance behaviors and fear about swimming and greater swim skill improvement. These results were dormant for more than 20 years, until Weiss, McCullagh, Smith, and Berlant (1998) replicated and extended the study with young children who were fearful of and exhibited low self-confidence in water activities. Children viewed a peer mastery, peer coping, or no model (control) in combination with group swim instruction. Postintervention, the peer modeling groups (mastery and coping) showed stronger improvements in swimming skills, better self-efficacy, and less fear of swimming than did the control group. Peer coping participants were higher in self-efficacy than peer mastery participants. These results highlight the superiority of peer models in combination with swim lessons over swim lessons alone for improved performance and psychological responses and of peer coping models for maximizing self-efficacy.

Recently, attention has been directed toward peer-assisted learning techniques (see Topping & Ehly, 1998). *Peer-assisted learning* is defined as the acquisition of knowledge, skills, attitudes, and social behaviors through active helping and supporting among status equals. By helping others learn, it follows that "helpers" also learn themselves. Peer-assisted learning methods include peer tutoring, counseling, education, modeling, and monitoring. By far, peer modeling is the least investigated area in a variety of educational domains, including sport. Based on the robust evidence from academic and medical settings, peer modeling can be advocated as a viable method for modifying children's motor skills and psychological responses.

Applications to Sport Injury

The psychological outcomes accompanying sport injury have been well documented in the sport psychology literature (see Brewer, 1998). Many sport psychology consultants and researchers are interested in interventions that can facilitate physical and psychological rehabilitation. Applied articles suggest that modeling in the form of live or videotaped models (e.g., athletes who experienced the same injury or surgery as the target athlete) may be an effective technique in the rehabilitation process (Flint, 1999; Weiss & Troxel, 1986). In a data-base study, Gould, Udry, Bridges, and Beck (1997) elicited the coping strategies used by injured elite skiers and found that 10% of the responses related to seeking out and using social resources. One of the key strategies was the use of other injured athletes as models for enhancing motivation as well as for learning effective recovering strategies.

Flint (1991) conducted an extensive study examining the effectiveness of a modeling intervention on psychological responses to sport injury. Female basketball players who had undergone anterior cruciate ligament surgery were assigned to either an experimental or a control group. The experimental-group participants watched a videotape of multiple coping models that were similar in age, playing position, and type of injury. The models were interviewed at various stages in rehabilitation, and one model was shown postsurgery, at complete recovery, and returning to competition. The control group did not view the videotape. Results revealed that modeling-group participants perceived themselves to be similar to one or more of the models, adopted strategies conveyed by the models, and showed a trend toward higher self-efficacy and perceived athletic competence in relation to the control group.

Flint (1999) suggested that modeling may be an effective intervention in rehabilitation for two primary reasons. First, the video is a tool that can be used on repeated occasions and with numerous individuals to provide information to injured athletes. Second, seeing similar others rehabilitate can help reduce anxiety and increase self-efficacy.

Intervention Possibilities for Makaila, Harrison, and Felicia

Makaila

Slumps, or declines in performance, are a major concern for athletes and their coaches. Also of concern is Makaila's hesitation about an upcoming competition that is essential for her success. After discussing the situation with both the coach and the athlete, the sport psychology consultant developed some self-modeling videos. The self-modeling videos were used to solve the performance slump as well as to help Makaila overcome her concerns about her nemesis competitor.

First, it was necessary to develop a library of videos of both Makaila and her competitor (taken at local meets when they were not in the same competition). Second, Makaila and her coach were shown the videos, and shots that were especially successful were singled out. By editing the video, a highlight video was made showing Makaila shooting progressively better shots over trials or scoring her personal best. (Because of the separation between the archer and the target, it is possible to alter the outcome on video.) Once Makaila became accustomed to seeing herself shoot successfully, a video was produced of her shooting against her competitor. Simulating the competition as much as possible (e.g., shooting alternately, announcing scores) also contributed to the success of the modeling intervention.

Harrison

Harrison's avoidance of water activities had nothing to do with his competencies; he still knew how to execute the strokes. But proximity to others in the pool (simulating his traumatic experience) and the tension he felt in the water were more than enough to keep him away. Harrison's fear and low self-efficacy led to avoidance behaviors during swimming period at summer camp (i.e., not putting on a swimsuit; feigned illness) that further exacerbated the situation (i.e., isolation from peers, skills falling further behind).

One day, Harrison's teacher introduced him to Peter, who was a year older and in another class. The teacher explained that Peter did not like swimming until last year, when he found that it could be fun and a source of making friends. The reason Peter did not like swimming was that he saw another boy drown in a lake near his home and was frightened by this. Last year Peter was in a class with another boy who had finally shaken off his own fears through one-on-one instruction and use of performance aids (e.g., flotation devices). This boy shared with Peter many ways of doing the skills in a fun way (e.g., blowing bubbles, prone floating). Peter was more than willing to show Harrison some of these skills and share ways in which he dealt with his own anxiety in the water (e.g., verbalizing statements such as "I remind myself I'm in shallow water," "The water feels good when you can do the skills"). Harrison was transferred to Peter's swimming class where Peter served as a peer coping model, and the teacher taught him skills in a developmentally appropriate manner. Harrison returned to his own class a couple of weeks later and gradually immersed himself into the group.

Felicia

Felicia's negative thoughts and emotions are common among injured athletes who are not accustomed to being inactive and uninvolved in team practices and competitions. Unknowingly, teammates and coaches may neglect or be insensitive toward injured athletes. The athlete may feel as if she is alone and that nobody understands what she is going through. Fortunately for Felicia, the athletic trainers at her institution value the role that sport psychology consultants can play in such a situation.

The athletic trainer and sport psychology consultant introduced Felicia to Yolanda, a member of the soccer team who had just returned after a season off for anterior cruciate ligament surgery and rehabilitation. Yolanda empathized with Felicia and also actively informed and motivated her concerning anticipated physical landmarks and emotional setbacks. Yolanda's role as a peer coping model was supplemented by Felicia's attendance at an injured-athlete support group organized by the athletic trainer and the sport psychology consultant. The weekly meeting gave Felicia an opportunity to meet and observe several peer models who varied in gender, sport, and skill level. Together, they explored a multitude of coping strategies and provided each other critical social support.

Exhibit 7.1

Tips for Using Modeling as a Psychological Method

1. Remember that attention, retention, production, and motivation are essential factors in modeling. Therefore, select and implement methods that maximize observers' selective attention and active rehearsal of demonstrated actions so they are motivated and able to emulate modeled behaviors.
2. Observer attention and motivation can be addressed by carefully considering the type of model that may be most appropriate to the situation. Such decisions will entail whether to use a learning or correct model, coping or mastery model, and peer or self-model.
3. To ensure that observers remember the key aspects of demonstrations, ask them to recall salient behaviors or to recognize them among several alternatives. Observers may also be asked to use a remembering technique (e.g., self-talk, encoding, labeling) as they view the modeled actions.
4. Videotape is the most practical and effective way to induce a psychological modeling procedure. Observers are able to view selected episodes of behaviors that may be repeated over time and in the convenience of several venues (e.g., clinician's office, at home).
5. Providing feedback to the observer during or after demonstrations may enhance the effectiveness of the modeling technique. The feedback may impart information (e.g., focus attention to a particular aspect of the modeled action) or serve to motivate the observer (e.g., communicate progress in relation to past performance).
6. Overt modeling strategies may be interchanged with covert modeling or imagery procedures. Because modeling and imagery share many common cognitive mechanisms, the same physical and psychological effects may be achieved when individuals observe similar models or themselves on video, or imagine similar others or themselves.

Conclusion

Modeling interventions are highly effective as a means of modifying skills, psychological responses, and behaviors in physical activity contexts. Theory, research, and applications provide convincing reasons for absolving modeling of its label as "the forgotten psychological method in sport psychology." Learning models, self-observation techniques, covert models (imagery), peer models, and coping models are just a few of the many interventions available that can be used with both children and adults in practice, competition, and rehabilitation situations. In Exhibit 7.1 several helpful tips are given for implementing modeling as a psychological method in a sport psychology practice. We hope readers are more strongly convinced of the practicality of modeling as one of several methods that can be effectively used to influence psychological and behavioral change in students, athletes, and clients in a variety of sport and physical activity settings.

References

Balf, T. (1996). Think like a winner. *Self, 18*, 116–119.

Bandura, A. (1977a). Self-efficacy: Toward a unifying theory of behavioral change. *Psychological Review, 84*, 191–215.

Bandura, A. (1977b). *Social learning theory.* Englewood Cliffs, NJ: Prentice-Hall.

Bandura, A. (1986). *Social foundations of thought and action: A social cognitive theory.* Englewood Cliffs, NJ: Prentice-Hall.

Bandura, A. (1997). *Self-efficacy: The exercise of control.* New York: W. H. Freeman.

Bouffard, M., & Dunn, J. G. H. (1993). Children's self-regulated learning of movement sequences. *Research Quarterly for Exercise and Sport, 64*, 393–403.

Brewer, B. W. (1998). Introduction to the special issue: Theoretical, empirical, and applied issues in the psychology of sport injury. *Journal of Applied Sport Psychology, 10*, 1–4.

Dowrick, P. W. (1999). A review of self-modeling and related interventions. *Applied and Preventive Psychology, 8*, 23–39.

Evangelista, B. (2000, March 30). Instant replay. *San Francisco Chronicle,* pp. B1, B3.

Feltz, D. L. (1980). Teaching a high-avoidance motor task to a retarded child through participant modeling. *Education and Training of the Mentally Retarded, 15*, 152–155.

Feltz, D. L., & Landers, D. M. (1983). The effects of mental practice on motor skill learning and performance: A meta-analysis. *Journal of Sport Psychology, 5*, 25–57.

Flint, F. A. (1991). *The psychological effects of modeling in athletic injury rehabilitation.* Unpublished doctoral dissertation, University of Oregon, Eugene.

Flint, F. A. (1999). Seeing helps believing: Modeling in injury rehabilitation. In D. Pargman (Ed.), *Psychological bases of sport injuries* (2nd ed., pp. 221–234). Morgantown, WV: Fitness Information Technology.

Franks, I. M., & Maile, L. J. (1991). The use of video in sport skill acquisition. In P. W. Dowrick (Ed.), *Practical guide to using video in the behavioral sciences* (pp. 231–243). New York: Wiley.

Gallagher, J. D., French, K. E., Thomas, K. T., & Thomas, J. R. (1996). Expertise in youth sport: Relations between knowledge and skill. In F. L. Smoll & R. E. Smith (Eds.), *Children and youth in sport: A biopsychosocial perspective* (pp. 338–358). Madison, WI: Brown & Benchmark.

Gould, D., Udry, E., Bridges, D., & Beck, L. (1997). Coping with season-ending injuries. *The Sport Psychologist, 11*, 379–399.

Halliwell, W. (1990). Providing sport psychology consultant services in professional hockey. *The Sport Psychologist, 4*, 369–377.

Hebert, E. P., & Landin, D. (1994). Effects of a learning model and augmented feedback in tennis skill acquisition. *Research Quarterly for Exercise and Sport, 65*, 250–257.

Lee, T. D., Swinnen, S. P., & Serrien, D. J. (1994). Cognitive effort and motor learning. *Quest, 46*, 328–344.

Lewis, S. (1974). A comparison of behavior therapy techniques in the reduction of fearful avoidance behavior. *Behavior Therapy, 5*, 648–655.

Livermore, B. (1996, July/August). Mind games. *Women's Sports and Fitness, 18*, 77–78, 108, 112.

Martin, K. A., Moritz, S. E., & Hall, C. R. (1999). Imagery use in sport: A literature review and applied model. *The Sport Psychologist, 13*, 245–268.

McCullagh, P. (1993). Modeling: Learning, developmental, and social psychological considerations. In R. N. Singer, M. Murphey, & L. K. Tennant (Eds.), *Handbook of research on sport psychology* (pp. 106–125). New York: Macmillan.

McCullagh, P., & Caird, J. K. (1990). Correct and learning models and the use of model knowledge of results in the acquisition and retention of a motor skill. *Journal of Human Movement Studies, 18*, 107–116.

McCullagh, P., & Ram, N. (2000). A comparison of imagery and modeling. *Journal of Sport and Exercise Psychology, 22*, S9.

McCullagh, P., Stiehl, J., & Weiss, M. R. (1990). Developmental modeling effects on the quantitative and qualitative aspects of motor performance. *Research Quarterly for Exercise and Sport, 61*, 344–350.

McCullagh, P., & Weiss, M. R. (2001). Modeling: Considerations for motor skill performance and psychological responses. In R. N. Singer, H. A. Hausenblas, & C. M. Janelle (Eds.), *Handbook of sport psychology* (pp. 205–238). New York: Wiley & Sons.

McCullagh, P., Weiss, M. R., & Ross, D. (1989). Modeling consideration in motor skill acquisition and performance: An integrated approach. In K. B. Pandolf (Ed.), *Exercise and sport sciences reviews* (pp. 475–513). Baltimore, MD: Williams & Wilkins.

McPherson, S. L. (1999). Expert–novice differences in performance skills and problem representations of youth and adults during tennis competition. *Research Quarterly for Exercise and Sport, 70*, 233–251.

Melamed, B. G., & Siegel, L. J. (1975). Reduction of anxiety in children facing hospitalization and surgery by use of filmed modeling. *Journal of Consulting and Clinical Psychology, 43*, 511–521.

Nevett, M. E., & French, K. E. (1997). The development of sport-specific planning, rehearsal, and updating of plans during defensive youth baseball game performance. *Research Quarterly for Exercise and Sport, 68*, 203–214.

Rejeski, W. J., & Sanford, B. (1984). Feminine-typed females: The role of affective schema in the perception of exercise intensity. *Journal of Sport Psychology, 6*, 197–207.

Rushall, B. S. (1988). Covert modeling as a procedure for altering an elite athlete's psychological state. *The Sport Psychologist, 2,* 131–140.

Schunk, D. H. (1987). Peer models and children's behavioral change. *Review of Educational Research, 57,* 149–174.

Schunk, D. H. (1989). Social cognitive theory and self-regulated learning. In B. J. Zimmerman & D. H. Schunk (Eds.), *Self-regulated learning and academic achievement: Theory, research, and practice* (pp. 83–110). New York: Springer-Verlag.

Schunk, D. H. (1998). Peer modeling. In K. Topping & S. Ehly (Eds.), *Peer-assisted learning* (pp. 185–202). Malwah, NJ: Erlbaum.

Schunk, D. H., & Hanson, A. R. (1985). Peer models: Influence on children's self-efficacy and achievement. *Journal of Educational Psychology, 77,* 313–322.

Schunk, D. H., & Hanson, A. R. (1989). Influence of peer-model attributes on children's beliefs and learning. *Journal of Educational Psychology, 81,* 431–434.

Schunk. D. H., Hanson, A. R., & Cox, P. D. (1987). Peer-model attributes and children's achievement behaviors. *Journal of Educational Psychology, 79,* 54–61.

Starek, J., & McCullagh, P. (1999). The effect of self-modeling on the performance of beginning swimmers. *The Sport Psychologist, 13,* 269–287.

Topping, K., & Ehly, S. (Eds.). (1998). *Peer-assisted learning.* Malwah, NJ: Erlbaum.

Weinberg, R. S., & Gould, D. (1999). *Foundations of sport and exercise psychology* (2nd ed). Champaign, IL: Human Kinetics.

Weiss, M. R. (1983). Modeling and motor performance: A developmental perspective. *Research Quarterly for Exercise and Sport, 54,* 190–197.

Weiss, M. R., Ebbeck, V., & Rose, D. J. (1992). "Show and tell" in the gymnasium revisited: Developmental differences in modeling and verbal rehearsal effects on motor skill learning and performance. *Research Quarterly for Exercise and Sport, 63,* 292–301.

Weiss, M. R., Ebbeck, V., & Wiese-Bjornstal, D. M. (1993). Developmental and psychological skills related to children's observational learning of physical skills. *Pediatric Exercise Science, 5,* 301–317.

Weiss, M. R., & Klint, K. A. (1987). "Show and tell" in the gymnasium: An investigation of developmental differences in modeling and verbal rehearsal of motor skills. *Research Quarterly for Exercise and Sport, 58,* 234–241.

Weiss, M. R., McCullagh, P., Smith, A. L., & Berlant, A. R. (1998). Observational learning and the fearful child: Influence of peer models on swimming skill performance and psychological responses. *Research Quarterly for Exercise and Sport, 69,* 380–394.

Weiss, M. R., & Troxel, R. K. (1986). Psychology of the injured athlete. *Athletic Training, 21,* 104–109, 154.

Wiese-Bjornstal, D. M., & Weiss, M. R. (1992). Modeling effects on children's form kinematics, performance outcome, and cognitive recognition of a sport skill: An integrated perspective. *Research Quarterly for Exercise and Sport, 63,* 67–75.

Williams, A. M., Davids, K., & Williams, J. G. (1999). *Visual perception and action in sport.* London: E & FN Spon.

8

Hypnosis in Sport and Exercise Psychology

William P. Morgan

I t is remarkable that hypnosis has not been used more frequently by workers in the field of sport and exercise psychology, because the difference between success and failure is often minuscule. Indeed, the difference between a gold medal in Olympic competition and failure to even qualify for the final event is sometimes less than a hundredth of a second. Hence, any intervention that might have the ability to enhance performance by even a small margin (e.g., 0.001%), providing it is legal, would have potential value.

The use of hypnosis has not been banned by the U.S. Olympic Committee or the International Olympic Committee, nor are there any regulations against the use of hypnosis by other sport governing bodies, such as the National Collegiate Athletic Association, or by professional organizations, such as the American Psychological Association (APA) and the American College of Sports Medicine. There are, however, many instances in which the use of hypnosis in the practice of sport psychology or sports medicine would be questionable from both an ethical and a moral standpoint and, although not in direct violation of existing rules and codes, such actions would potentially violate the "spirit" of the law. It is inappropriate, for example, to use drugs such as morphine or novocaine to manage an athlete's pain so that she or he might compete; hence, the use of hypnosis for the same purpose would be questionable. Adherence to the APA's (1992) ethical code of

This chapter is an expanded and updated version of "Hypnosis and Sport Psychology," originally published in 1993 in J. Rhue, S. J. Lynn, & I. Kirsch (Eds.), *The Handbook of Clinical Hypnosis* (pp. 649–670). Washington, DC: American Psychological Association.

conduct should be viewed as necessary but not sufficient in such a case. It is imperative that psychologists who elect to use hypnosis in the treatment of athletes also become familiar with established ethical and legal guidelines adopted by sport governing bodies and professional organizations.

Theoretical Formulations

The rationale for the clinical applications described in this chapter is based on theoretical formulations advanced by Hanin (1978) and Uneståhl (1981) and on the empirical case studies described by Johnson (1961a, 1961b). Although the theoretical views of Hanin and Uneståhl represent independent proposals, these formulations converge in terms of hypnotic application.

Hanin (1978) presented a theory of performance that maintains that each athlete possesses a "zone of optimal function," and this zone is based on the person's optimal state anxiety level in precompetitive settings. Hanin empirically demonstrated that athletes have their best performances when they fall within this zone, and he has operationalized the zone as a given point ±4 raw score units on the state anxiety scale developed by Spielberger (1983). Although Hanin's theory is based largely on work carried out with elite Soviet athletes and with the Russian translation of the State–Trait Anxiety Inventory (STAI; Spielberger, 1983), his research has been replicated with both elite and nonelite American athletes (Morgan & Ellickson, 1989; Raglin, Morgan, & Wise, 1990; Raglin & Morris, 1994; Raglin & Turner, 1992, 1993; Turner & Raglin, 1996; Wilson & Raglin, 1997). Overviews of this research can be found in Morgan (1997) and Raglin (1992).

The external validity of Hanin's model has been well established because it has been shown to predict performance in adolescent boys and girls and in college and elite athletes. The model also has been shown to work well in various sports such as distance running (Morgan, O'Connor, Ellickson, & Bradley, 1988; Morgan, O'Connor, Sparling, & Pate, 1987), swimming (Raglin et al., 1990), volleyball (Raglin & Morris, 1994), and track and field (Raglin & Turner, 1993; Wilson & Raglin, 1997). The theory incorporates retrospective recall of precompetitive state anxiety levels obtained in the nonhypnotic state. It does not mention hypnotic procedures, but the potential for hypnotic intervention is obvious.

The theoretical views of Unestähl (1981) are related to those of Hanin (1978), because both believe that athletes experience unique affective states when having peak performances. Unestähl has labeled this the "ideal performing state." Although the theoretical views of Unestähl are in agreement with those of Hanin with respect to the existence of an ideal or optimal affective state, these theories differ in one respect: Whereas Hanin believed that these states can be accurately recalled, Unestähl has emphasized that athletes often have selective or even total amnesia after perfect performance, which makes it difficult for them to describe or analyze the ideal performing state afterward. Therefore, Unesthal has used hypnosis in defining this state, and this theory has been used with several thousand Swedish athletes (Railo & Unestähl, 1979).

Research and Appraisal

Research involving hypnosis and sport and exercise psychology has been carried out almost exclusively with laboratory experimentation in which attempts have been made to elucidate the effectiveness of hypnotic suggestion on the transcendence of baseline measures of physical capacity. Two principal methodological problems associated with the published literature warrant mention. First, investigators have used laboratory tasks (e.g., grip strength and weight-holding endurance) under controlled conditions, and it is unlikely that this work is valid in terms of competition settings. In other words, the results of research involving simple motor tasks performed in a laboratory setting with nonathletes cannot be easily generalized to complex sport skills performed by athletes in emotionally charged competitive settings. Second, performances in the laboratory following hypnotic suggestion have been compared with control, or baseline, performances in which suggestion has not been used. This traditional research paradigm has been characterized by the confounding of state (hypnosis vs. control) and suggestion. With few exceptions, it has been difficult to delineate between the effects caused by hypnosis and those caused by suggestion, because hypnosis with suggestion has typically been compared with nonhypnotic interventions without suggestion. Furthermore, the influence of demand characteristics has been largely ignored in the research literature, and additional behavioral artifacts known to influence experimental outcomes have often been overlooked (Morgan, 1972a).

The first comprehensive review of this topic was by Hull (1933), who focused on hypnotic suggestibility and transcendence of voluntary capacity. Hull's principal conclusion was that existing evidence bearing on this question was contradictory. Furthermore, Hull explained that the equivocal nature of this experimentation was due to design flaws. Later reviews by Gorton (1959), Johnson (1961b), Weitzenhoffer (1953), Barber (1966), Morgan (1972b, 1980a, 1993), and Morgan and Brown (1983) were inconsistent regarding the ability of hypnotic suggestion to enhance physical performance.

Historically, the most critical review of research in this area was by Barber (1966), who concluded that hypnosis, without suggestions for enhanced performance, did not influence muscular strength or endurance. Furthermore, Barber reported that motivational suggestions are generally capable of augmenting muscular strength and endurance in both nonhypnotic and hypnotic conditions. Barber presented a compelling argument in that review and, in related writings, about the necessity of not confounding hypnosis and suggestion. Typical experimental paradigms have compared muscular performance following suggestions of enhanced or decreased capacity under hypnosis, with muscular performance following no suggestions under control or nonhypnotic conditions (e.g., Ikai & Steinhaus, 1961). Exceptions to this paradigm include one of the earliest findings, by Nicholson (1920), that suggestions given during hypnosis were much more effective than the same suggestions given without hypnosis. Another exception is the report by Eysenck (1941) that hypnosis per se resulted in facilitation of muscular endurance. However, evidence exists that suggestion without hypnosis can lead to enhanced muscular performance (Barber, 1966; Morgan, 1981, 1997). Therefore, it is imperative that experimental designs not confound suggestion and procedure.

The reviews by Barber (1966), Gorton (1959), Hull (1933), Johnson (1961b), and Weitzenhoffer (1953) dealt primarily with the influence of hypnotic suggestion on muscular strength and endurance. Later research focused on the extent to which the hypnotic suggestion of an altered work-load can influence the perception of effort (Morgan, 1994) and the extent to which perturbation of effort sense (i.e., perceived exertion) is associated with corresponding changes in metabolism. It has been reported, for example, that hypnotic suggestion can influence cardiac output, heart rate, blood pressure, forearm blood flow, respiratory rate, ventilatory minute volume, oxygen uptake, and carbon dioxide production, at rest and during exercise (Morgan, 1985).

It also has been shown that perception of effort can be systematically increased and decreased during exercise with hypnotic suggestion (Morgan, 1970, 1981; Morgan, Hirota, Weitz, & Balke, 1976; Morgan, Raven, Drinkwater, & Horvath, 1973). Furthermore, when exercise intensity is perceived as being more effortful, a corresponding elevation in physiological responses takes place even though the actual work-load remains unchanged.

More recent research has replicated and extended these research findings to include the assessment of regional cerebral blood flow (rCBF) following the hypnotic manipulation of effort sense during dynamic exercise (Williamson et al., 2001). This more recent work has shown that hypnotic suggestion of increased and decreased work-load is associated with cardiovascular responses and brain activation even though the exercise intensity has not actually changed. The suggestion of downhill cycling was associated with a decrease in perceived exertion and rCBF in the left insular cortex and anterior cingulate cortex, whereas perceived uphill exercise was associated with right insular activation and right thalamus activation. The work by Williamson et al. (2001) revealed there were no differences in rCBF for leg sensorimotor regions across conditions. These findings indicate that hypnotic suggestion of increased and decreased effort sense during constant load cycling is associated with differential activation in selected brain regions.

Another line of research has examined the study of imagery perspectives on the psychophysiological responses to imagined exercise under nonhypnotic conditions (Wang & Morgan, 1992). In this research, the metabolic, cardiovascular, and perceptual responses of 30 men and women were studied before, during, and after actual exercise, and these responses were compared with those observed following internal versus external imagery of exercise. The perception of effort was higher following the use of an internal compared with an external imagery perspective, and the internal imagery resulted in a significant increase in ventilatory minute volume that exceeded the control condition. However, both the internal and external imagery resulted in significant increases in systolic blood pressure, and these increases did not differ from those noted for the actual exercise condition. Both approaches were associated with psychophysiological responses, but the internal imagery perspective produced changes closer to those observed for actual exercise. Although this study did not include a hypnosis comparison group, it is apparent that changes often attributed to hypnosis can be produced under nonhypnotic conditions.

In an attempt to quantify the influence of imagined exercise on cardiovascular responses and rCBF, Williamson et al. (in press) recently evaluated brain activation during an actual and an imagined handgrip exercise under hypnosis. In this study, five high-hypnotizable people were compared with four low-hypnotizable people during 3 minutes of maximal voluntary contraction at 30% of maximal voluntary contraction. The results were compared with those obtained during the imagined handgrip exercise. Integrated electromyography was done in both forearms, ratings of perceived exertion were collected during the 3-minute period, heart rate and mean blood pressure were recorded, and rCBF was measured using single photo emission computed tomography (SPECT) and magnetic resonance imaging (MRI).

Both groups experienced significant increases in heart rate and mean blood pressure following three minutes of actual handgrip exercise, but only the high-hypnotizable group experienced significant cardiovascular increases during imagined exercise. Furthermore, the rating of perceived exertion was higher for the high-hypnotizable group during imagined exercise. The high-hypnotizable group also rated the imagined exercise as being more vivid. During imagined exercise, the low-hypnotizable group experienced lower activity in the anterior cingulate and insular cortices, which led Williamson et al. (in press) to conclude that cardiovascular responses during imagined exercise are influenced by the activation of these brain regions.

This particular study might explain some of the discrepancies in the literature involving exercise responses to hypnotic suggestion, because it appears that level of hypnotizability is a crucial moderator variable. At any rate, not only does this work by Williamson and colleagues indicate that hypnosis is effective in modifying the perception of effort, but it also indicates that the hypnotic perturbation of effort sense is associated with changes in cardiovascular function and brain activation. This finding is important because it has been recognized for some time that perception of effort plays an important role in physical performance (Morgan, 1997, 2001).

A summary of findings reported in earlier reviews by Morgan (1972b, 1980a, 1985, 1993, 1996) and Morgan and Brown (1983) and the principal findings from recent reports by Williamson et al. (2001) and Williamson et al. (in press) follow:

1. Although some investigators have reported that hypnosis per se has no influence on muscular strength and endurance, an equal number have found that hypnosis (without suggestion) can lead

to both increases and decreases in muscular performance. The evidence in this area is equivocal.

2. Hypnotic suggestions designed to enhance muscular performance have generally not been effective, whereas suggestions designed to impair strength and endurance have been consistently successful.

3. Individuals who are not accustomed to performing at maximal levels usually experience gains in muscular strength and endurance when administered *involving* suggestions in the hypnotic state. However, suggestions of a *noninvolving* nature are not effective when administered to individuals who are accustomed to performing at maximal levels.

4. Efforts to modify performance on various psychomotor tasks (e.g., choice reaction time) have effects similar to those observed in research involving muscular strength and endurance. That is, efforts to slow reaction time are usually effective, whereas attempts to speed reaction time are not.

5. Case studies involving efforts to enhance performance in athletes by means of hypnosis appear to be universally successful. However, this observation should probably be viewed with caution because therapists and journals are not known for emphasizing case material depicting failures.

6. Hypnotic suggestion of exercise in the nonexercise state is associated with increased heart rate, respiratory rate, ventilatory minute volume, oxygen uptake, carbon dioxide production, forearm blood flow, cardiac output, and brain activation as measured by rCBF. Recent work has shown that brain activation during imagined exercise is influenced by the individual's level of hypnotizability. These physiological changes often approximate responses noted during actual exercise conditions.

7. Perception of effort during exercise can be systematically increased and decreased with hypnotic suggestion even though the actual physical work-load is maintained at a constant level. Furthermore, alterations in effort sense are associated with significant changes in metabolic responses and brain activation as measured by SPECT and MRI.

8. There is evidence that imagined exercise under nonhypnotic conditions is associated with physiological changes that resemble those noted during actual exercise, and outcomes have been shown to be dependent on imagery perspective (i.e., internal

vs. external). Responses tend to be greater for internal (i.e., first-person) compared with external (i.e., third-person) imagery perspectives.

Qualifications of Practitioners

The question of who is qualified to use hypnosis has been discussed for many years, and the issue involves a rather complex matter. Hilgard (1979) offered an interesting perspective on this issue in stating that "lack of advanced degrees does not necessarily mean incompetence and society memberships do not guarantee competence either" (p. 5). Hilgard also has pointed out that broader professional training extending beyond hypnosis has various advantages, the principal one being "that the true professional will know much more that is relevant about personality and individual differences than is implied by hypnosis" (p. 5). This is an important point, because a person who lacks training in fields such as psychology or psychiatry can easily learn how to perform hypnotic inductions.

It is reasonable to expect that a person who uses hypnosis has advanced training in fields such as psychology or psychiatry, and it is equally reasonable to expect that such a person would hold membership in hypnosis organizations such as the Society for Clinical and Experimental Hypnosis, Division 30 (Psychological Hypnosis) of APA, or the American Society of Clinical Hypnosis. However, affiliation with such professional groups should be regarded as a *necessary*, rather than a *sufficient*, form of evidence for the reasons stated by Hilgard (1979).

There was a time when Division 30 of APA was regarded as a quasi-licensing group, because applicants for membership in the division were required to provide letters of recommendation, evidence of training in hypnosis, and documented evidence of experience in the use of hypnosis. Today, however, membership in Division 30 merely requires application and payment of dues. Membership in this division can no longer be viewed as a sign that a person has competence in the use of hypnosis. Because the leading scientific and professional societies have not historically licensed or certified individuals in the use of hypnosis, Levitt (1981) has proposed that certification by the American Board of Psychological Hypnosis is the only realistic testimony of a person's ability as a hypnotist.

It is difficult to answer the question of who is qualified to use hypnosis to everyone's satisfaction. However, it is possible to provide some guidelines and principles that can be used by workers in the field of sport and exercise psychology. All professional organizations concerned with the use of hypnosis make a clear distinction between its use in research and its use in clinical practice. Manipulation of an independent variable in an experimental setting with hypnotic suggestion is very different than using hypnotherapy in the treatment of clinical problems such as anxiety disorder or depression. In other words, although the use of hypnosis in research and clinical practice may have several procedural and methodological similarities in technical terms, these applications require different competencies.

It would seem reasonable to expect that workers in sport and exercise psychology who use hypnotic procedures as an experimental tool would possess an advanced degree with a primary focus in psychology, and these individuals should have affiliations with appropriate hypnosis organizations such as Division 30 of APA, the American Society of Clinical Hypnosis or the Society for Clinical and Experimental Hypnosis. Although affiliation with professional organizations does not ensure that individuals will stay within their areas of competence, such affiliations will enhance the likelihood that a hypnotist will comply with existing ethical codes. All 50 states and the District of Columbia have enacted laws regulating the practice of psychology, and certification laws regulate the use of the title "psychologist" and limit the scope of practice to those areas in which individuals have competence and training. Sport and exercise psychologists who use hypnosis for clinical purposes should have the appropriate certification or licensure. A long-standing principle in the area of hypnosis, and one that applies to both clinical and research applications, is that individuals not use hypnosis to perform manipulations or treatments that they are not qualified to perform without hypnosis.

It is imperative that sport and exercise psychologists who use hypnosis in their research and clinical practice be qualified to use this intervention. It is often maintained that sport and exercise psychologists are concerned only with performance enhancement, and therefore, it is not necessary that these providers have clinical competencies and skills. That is, because these individuals do not treat clinical problems such as depression or anxiety disorders, for example, it is not necessary for them to have clinical competencies. The fallacy of this argument has been addressed elsewhere by the author (Morgan, 1997), and some of the more obvious reasons why the performance versus skill enhancement argument lacks validity follow:

1. Extensive literature demonstrates that some athletes have psychological problems of a clinical nature when seeking support (Carmen, Zerman, & Blaine, 1968; Davie, 1958; Morgan, 1997; Pierce, 1969; Raglin, 2001; Vanek, 1970).

2. It has been reported by Meyers, Whelan, and Murphy (1996) that performance issues represented the presenting symptom in approximately 60% of the cases seen at the U.S. Olympic Training Center, but about 80% of these athletes had psychological problems other than performance issues in the final analysis. This would suggest that a subset of athletes seeking assistance involving performance problems potentially have psychological problems requiring treatment by a psychologist with clinical competence.

3. Results from the 1995 National College Health Risk Behavior Survey has revealed that approximately 11% of the college students in a nationally representative sample had engaged in suicidal behavior during the 12-month period preceding completion of the survey (Douglas et al., 1997). Suicidal behavior was operationalized as thoughts about, plans for, or attempted suicide during the previous 12 months.

Therefore, a conservative estimate of the number of athletes of college age who might manifest suicidal behavior during a given 12-month period would be approximately 10%, or 1 in 10. However, there is not agreement on the relationship between sport and physical activity on the one hand and suicidal ideation on the other in college students (Brown & Blanton, 1998; Simon & Powell, 1999; Unger, 1997). The assumption that sport and exercise psychologists work only with performance problems is not defensible, and it is important that individuals who use hypnosis when treating athletes have the necessary clinical competencies.

Clinical Applications

The cases described in this section were selected on the basis of the assumption that important information associated with athletic competition is sometimes repressed and that this information can be retrieved by means of hypnotic age regression. Also, it is assumed that efforts to retrieve this repressed material should be of a nondirective nature, and the decision to use this approach is based primarily on the clinical reports described by Johnson (1961a, 1961b). Furthermore, these applications are based on a multidisciplinary approach that includes medical, physiological, and psychological components. Hypnotic applications should not be attempted in sport settings unless it can be shown that pathology does not exist and that the requisite physiological capacity is present.

One of the most widely cited hypnosis cases in sport psychology was described in a report by Johnson (1961a), who successfully used hypnosis to treat a professional baseball player. The athlete's batting average normally exceeded .300. However, he had not had a hit for the last 20 times at bat, and neither he nor any of his coaches could detect any problems with his swing, stance, and so on. The player had become frustrated about his inability to return to his prior performance level, and he had requested hypnosis to resolve the problem.

Johnson (1961a) initially asked the player under hypnosis to explain the nature of his problem, and the player replied that he had no idea why he was in a slump. Johnson then told the player that he would gradually count from 1 to 10, and with each number, the player would become more and more aware of why he could no longer hit effectively. He also told the player that at the count of 10 he would have complete awareness of why he was in the slump. Johnson reported that at the count of 10 a look of incredulity came across the player's face, and he then proceeded to give a detailed analysis of his swing. This self-analysis under hypnosis included elaboration of specific problems that the player was unaware of in the nonhypnotic state. Johnson asked the player if he wished to have immediate, conscious recall of his analysis or have the information "just come to him gradually" over time. The player replied that he would prefer to have this information come back to him over time rather than all at once. The player's slump ended at once, and he went on to complete the season with an impressive batting average of .400.

This particular case is instructive in several ways, and sport psychologists who elect to use hypnosis in the treatment of such problems should first consider each of the following points. First, it is widely recognized that athletes in various sports often have spontaneous remission of problems (e.g., "slumps"), and it would be difficult to argue that a hypnotic intervention was responsible for the resolution of a given problem. Second, the information gained in the hypnoanalysis done by John-son (1961a) was not available under nonhypnotic conditions. Third, the player demonstrated unusual insight, according to Johnson, because he chose to have the wealth of biomechanical information return gradually. Once a complex motor skill has been learned, athletes are encouraged by coaches to "do it" rather than "think about it." In some ways, the situation is analogous to the problem of "paralysis through analysis," which occurred when the mythical frog asked the centipede, "Pray tell, which foot do you move first?" As the story goes, the centipede was unable to resume normal locomotion once the question was considered. Fourth, at the completion of the season, the player returned and thanked Johnson for the hypnoanalysis that led to his improved performance. The player was unable to accept the fact that he, not the hypnotist, had performed the analysis.

The efficacy of hypnosis in the treatment of pain has been widely documented. One comprehensive report on the use of hypnosis in the management of various problems in sports medicine was presented by Ryde (1964), who used hypnosis in 35 individual cases involving problems such as tennis elbow, shin splints, chronic Achilles tendon sprain, bruised heels, arch sprains, and other common ailments involving minor trauma. Hypnosis was so effective in the treatment of minor trauma resulting from injuries in sports that Ryde reported that he offers "to treat these disabilities initially by hypnosis and only proceed with conventional methods, should hypnosis fail or be refused" (p. 244). Although Ryde's report appears to support the value of hypnosis in the treatment of sports injuries, no evidence was presented to suggest that it is any more effective than a placebo. This is an important consideration because it is known that placebo treatments can be just as effective as morphine in the treatment of moderate pain in anxious patients (Morgan, 1972a). However, the use of hypnosis in the treatment of medical problems associated with sport injuries should be attempted only by or under the supervision of an appropriately trained physician.

Not much has been written about the use of psychodynamic approaches involving the use of hypnosis in sport and exercise psychology. However, in the review by Johnson (1961b), several case studies were summarized dealing with performance decrements in sports as a consequence of aggression blockage. In each case, hypnotic age regression was used in an effort to retrieve repressed material, which was followed by psychoanalytic interpretation and treatment. Also, post-hypnotic suggestion was used to resolve the aggression conflicts. In one case, for example, a cycle of aggression–guilt–aggression was identified, and this cycle was directly associated with performance. The athlete, baseball pitcher, performed well when characterized by aggressive affect, but his performance fell when he felt guilty and lacked aggression. This transitory affect was found to be governed by feelings of guilt associated with repressed childhood incidents of aggression. When the athlete felt guilty, his performance declined, and his performance improved as the guilt passed and he became aggressive. The therapy in this case focused on resolution of the repressed guilt. Once this was achieved, the aggression–guilt–aggression cycle was broken, and the pitcher's performance became more consistent. This general theme is repeated in related cases described by Johnson (1961b).

Hanin (1978) has shown that some athletes experience their best performances when precompetition anxiety is low, some when anxiety is high, and some when anxiety is intermediate. This theoretical view is supported by empirical research involving athletes from various sports (Morgan & Ellickson, 1989; Morgan et al., 1988; Morgan et al., 1987; Raglin, 1992; Raglin et al., 1990; Raglin & Morris, 1994; Raglin & Turner, 1992, 1993; Turner & Raglin, 1996). Therefore, it would be inappropriate to use psychological interventions designed either to reduce or increase anxiety in *groups* of athletes. In other words, not only would an intervention such as autogenic training, hypnosis, meditation, or progressive relaxation with athletes in a precompetitive setting be ineffective, it also would place many athletes outside of their individual zone of optimal anxiety (ZOA). In addition, some people experience increased anxiety, and panic episodes, during and following interventions designed to produce a state of relaxation (Borkovec et al., 1987; Heide & Borkovec, 1984). However, the mechanisms underlying this phenomenon, known as relaxation-induced anxiety (RIA), are not well understood.

In a Navy diving experiment (Mittleman, Doubt, & Gravitz, 1992), researchers found that the use of self-hypnosis to produce relaxation during immersion in cold water led to paradoxical effects. The people who effectively used self-hypnosis became relaxed and felt warm, but they also stopped shivering. Because shivering is a normal response and has the effect of producing heat, these individuals were at increased risk for developing hypothermia. Hence, relaxation could have the potential for impairing performance in some people, and another subset could be at risk from a health and safety standpoint. There also seems to be a tendency to think of many relaxation procedures as being innocuous, but there is evidence that procedures such as autogenic relaxation (Schultz Method; Schultz & Luthe, 1969) and quiet rest result in mood shifts that are comparable to those following hypnosis (Garvin, Trine, & Morgan, 2001).

Given the phenomenon of RIA described by Borkovec et al. (1987) and Heide and Borkovec (1984), it is somewhat surprising that responses of this nature are seldom reported in connection with routine hypnotic inductions, because many hypnotic procedures involve suggestions of relaxation. During the course of administering the Harvard Group Scale of Hypnotic Susceptibility (Shor & Orne, 1962) to more than 2,000 college students, the author has detected only one incident of RIA during routine debriefings conducted following this hypnotic induction. It is possible that volunteers for hypnosis demonstrations and research projects tend to have low anxiety, which might explain the apparent absence of RIA with "generic" hypnosis procedures. At any rate, relaxation procedures can result in anxiety and panic attacks in some individuals, and even when this does not occur, there is strong evidence that a significant number of people would experience performance decrements if they relaxed in precompetitive settings (Morgan, 1997; Raglin, 1992).

The concept of a ZOA for athletes is well established (Hanin, 1978; Morgan & Ellickson, 1989; Raglin, 1992), and it is imperative that efforts designed to manipulate precompetition anxiety (up or down) be carried out on an individual basis. The difficulty, of course, involves the determination of an athlete's ZOA. It would be necessary to evaluate an athlete's anxiety level before many competitions to arrive at his or her ZOA. Alternatively, one might use hypnotic age regression to ascertain anxiety levels before an athlete's best, usual, and worst performances. When the person's ZOA is determined, it would then be possible to strive, with autohypnosis or post-hypnotic suggestion, for precompetition anxiety that fell within the athlete's optimal range. Although this view is speculative, it is based on a sound theoretical rationale (Hanin, 1978) and on extensive empirical evidence of an indirect nature (Morgan, 1997; Raglin, 1992).

Despite the compelling support for the ZOA theory, sport psychologists are more likely to be consulted about problems involving elevations in precompetition anxiety. Indeed, athletes have been reported to be almost incapacitated before competition, and these anxiety attacks often prevent customary levels of performance. Although an equal number of athletes may experience inadequately low levels of anxiety, this problem tends to be less apparent. Naruse (1965) presented one of the best discussions of how hypnosis can be used with athletes in the precompetitive setting. Naruse labeled intense anxiety in the precompetitive setting as "stage fright" and summarized the use of (a) direct hypnotic suggestions, (b) post-hypnotically produced autohypnosis, and (c) self-hypnosis in conjunction with autogenic training and progressive relaxation in the treatment of anxiety states in athletes.

There are two important points to be made about Naruse's (1965) report. First, the athletes used in this study consisted of elite performers, and the results may not generalize to pre-elite or nonelite athletes. Second, the procedure used with a given athlete in Naruse's study was determined on an individual basis. The unique nature of the athlete's stage fright and the person's personality structure were considered together in deciding on the procedure to be used. This article could be particularly useful to hypnotherapists involved in the treatment of pre-competition anxiety in athletes competing at the national or the Olympic level.

Vanek (1970) emphasized that attempts to manipulate anxiety levels before competition must be pursued with caution and that the psychologist should have a complete appreciation for the athlete's psychodynamic nature. Furthermore, Vanek described the case of a heavyweight boxer who experienced an anxiety attack before an Olympic contest. The boxer's anxiety was controlled effectively with the administration of a nonhypnotic (i.e., autogenic method) procedure. The boxer then proceeded to lose his match to an opponent he had previously beaten. Vanek reported that follow-up study revealed that the boxer typically experienced anxiety attacks before important competitions, but he apparently performed well in this state. Anxiety reduction, in retrospect, was judged by Vanek to be contraindicated. This case serves to confirm the ZOA theory, and makes apparent that indiscriminant use of psychological procedures to relax athletes before competition is not appropriate.

Garver (1977) described a novel approach to the use of hypnotic control of arousal levels to enhance performance. This method requires that athletes establish a personal arousal scale ranging from 0 (the lowest possible level of arousal an athlete might experience) to 10 (the highest level) while in the hypnotic state. The athlete is moved up and down this arousal scale to have him or her experience how different arousal intensities feel. Furthermore, the athlete's optimal level of arousal is defined as the sensations associated with a score of 5 on the scale. An effort is made to have the athlete perceive this optimal intensity level and use it as a post-hypnotic cue during competition. Garver described cases of a gymnast and a golfer who experienced performance problems associated with elevated anxiety and anger, respectively. In these cases, post-hypnotic cues and cognitive rehearsal were used to produce preferred arousal levels, and this approach led to enhanced performance.

Case Material

The cases reviewed in this section involve athletes from the sports of distance running, baseball, and cycling. The overall approach used in these cases relied on insight training through hypnotic age regression. The hypnotic procedure can be viewed as nondirective, and it built on the earlier case reports of Johnson (1961a, 1961b). Also, the theoretical formulations of Hanin (1978) and Unestähl (1981) specified that optimal or ideal affective states characterize peak performance, and both theories maintain that information of this nature can be retrieved. Therefore, efforts were made in these cases to retrieve repressed material by means of hypnotic age regression. A multidisciplinary approach was used in each situation, and these case studies demonstrate that performance decrements in sports are sufficiently complex to rule out simplistic, unidimensional solutions.

In the first two cases, hypnosis was used to help a distance runner and baseball player gain insights about problems they were experiencing during competition. In the third case, it was decided that hypnosis was contraindicated. In all three cases, the athletes were patients under the care of a sports medicine physician who participated in the hypnoanalysis. The author assumed responsibility in these cases for the hypnotic inductions.

Case 1: Distance Runner

This case represents a common problem in which an athlete is no longer able to perform at his or her customary level. This type of situation is considerably different from the case in which an athlete is performing at a given level and wishes to enhance his or her performance. In particular, this case involved an athlete who previously performed at an elite level but was now unable to do so.

The case involved a 21-year-old distance runner who had previously established a school and conference record but was unable to replicate the performance. Indeed, the runner was not able to even complete many of his races, much less dominate a given competition. Problems of this nature are usually diagnosed in the field of sports medicine as "staleness," and the only effective treatment appears to be rest (Morgan, Brown, Raglin, O'Connor, & Ellickson, 1987). However, staleness was not the problem in this case. The runner's inability to perform at his previous level was judged by the coach to reflect inadequate motivation and unwillingness to tolerate the distress and discomfort associated with high-level performance. However, the athlete reported that he was "willing to do anything" to perform at his previous level, and he felt that his principal problem stemmed from inadequate coaching. Although both the athlete and the coach were interested in the restoration of the runner's previous performance ability, they were clearly at odds with one another. The conflict had reached the point where the two were unable to discuss the matter, and the runner had turned to his team physician for support. However, a thorough physical examination, including blood and urine chemistries routinely used in sports medicine, failed to reveal any medical problems.

The physician proposed that hypnosis be used to resolve this problem, and the athlete was eager to try such an approach. However, it seemed appropriate to first evaluate the runner's physical capacity to ensure that he was actually capable of performing at the desired level. It is well documented that aerobic power is an important factor in successful distance running. Therefore, the runner was administered a test of maximal aerobic power on a treadmill. This required that he run at a pace of 12 miles per hour on the treadmill, and the grade was increased by 2% every minute until he could no longer continue. This test revealed that he achieved a peak, or maximal, VO_2 of 70 ml/kg·min by the 5th minute of exercise, and his ability to uptake oxygen fell during the 6th minute. That is, a true physiological maximum, as opposed to a volitional or symptomatic maximum, was achieved. The value of 70 ml/kg·min is the average reported for elite distance runners; therefore, the runner was physiologically capable of achieving the desired performance level. However, calculations revealed that it would be necessary for him to average 96% of his maximum throughout an event to replicate his record performance. This could potentially be problematic because exercise metabolites such as lactic acid begin to accumulate and limit performance during prolonged exercise, at 60%

to 80% of maximum in most trained people. In other words, it would have been possible for this runner to perform at the desired level, but such an effort would be associated with considerable discomfort (i.e., pain).

The runner was observed to score within the normal range on anxiety, depression, and neuroticism as measured by the State–Trait Anxiety Inventory (STAI; Spielberger, 1983), Depression Adjective Checklist (DACL; Lubin, 1962), and the Eysenck Personality Inventory (EPI; Eysenck & Eysenck, 1963) respectively. He scored significantly higher than the population norms on extroversion, but this is a common finding for many athletes (Morgan, 1980b). He was found to be hypnotizable following preliminary induction and deepening sessions, and he was eager to pursue "insight training" through hypnosis and deep relaxation. The runner was viewed as a good candidate for hypnosis for the following reasons: (a) No medical contraindications were detected, (b) he possessed the necessary physiological capacity to achieve the desired goal, (c) there were no apparent psychological contraindications, and (d) he was able to enter into a deep trance.

Next, the athlete was age-regressed to the day of his championship performance, and he was instructed to describe the competition and any related events that he judged to be relevant. However, rather than telling him that "the race was about to begin" or instructing him in the customary "on your mark" command, he was asked to recall all events leading up to the race on that day. He was instructed,

> For example, try to remember how you felt when you awakened that morning; your breakfast or any foods or liquids you consumed; the temperature before and during the race; the nature and condition of the course; interactions with your coach, teammates, and opponents; your general frame of mind; and then proceed to the starting line *when you are ready.*

The athlete's team physician and the author had previously asked the runner whether it would be acceptable for either or both of them to ask questions during the session, and the athlete had no objections. The athlete had a somewhat serious or pensive look, but within a few minutes he began to smile and chuckle, saying that he had false-started. When asked why this was so amusing, he replied that it was "ridiculous, since there is no advantage to a fast start in a distance race." This event can be viewed as a critical incident because runners and swimmers will intentionally false start at times to reduce tension. Others will do this to upset or "unnerve" their opponents. At any rate, his facial expression became serious once again, and his motor behavior (e.g., grimacing and limb movements) suggested the race had begun. The verbatim narrative follows:

> The pace is really fast. I'm at the front of the pack. I don't think I can hold this pace much longer, but I feel pretty good. The pace is picking up. . . . I don't think I can hold it . . . my side is beginning to ache . . . I have had a pain in the side many times. It will go away if I continue to press. There . . . it feels good now. The pain is gone, but I'm having trouble breathing. I'm beginning to *suck air* . . . the pain is unbearable . . . I'm going to drop out of the race as soon as I find a soft spot. There's a soft, grassy spot up ahead . . . I'm going to stop and lay in the soft grassy spot . . . wait, I can't, three of my teammates are up on top of the next grade . . . they are yelling at me to *kick* . . . I can't let them down. I will keep going. I'm over the hill now . . . on level grade . . . it feels ok . . . I'm alright. There's another hill up ahead. I don't like hills . . . It is starting to hurt again . . . I can't keep this up . . . I'm going to find a soft spot again and stop. There's a spot ahead . . . I'm going to quit . . . I'm slowing down . . . this is it. Wait, there . . . I see a television set about ten feet off the ground at the top of the hill . . . hey, I'm on the TV, but this race isn't televised . . . but I can see myself clearly on the TV . . . I'm not here anymore . . . I'm on the TV. Now there's another TV, but to the right of the first one. My parents are on that TV, and they are watching me run this race on the other TV. I can't stop now. I can't let them down. Got to keep going. I'm not here . . . I'm on TV. It's starting to feel better. I feel like I'm in a vacuum now. I can't feel anything. My feet aren't hitting the ground anymore . . . I can't feel the wind hitting me. Hey, I'm a Yankee Clipper . . . I'm on the high seas . . . I'm flying . . . the sails are full . . . the wind is pushing me . . . I'm going to *blow out* . . . I'm going to *kick* . . . I don't feel pain anymore . . . This is going to be a PB, maybe a record, I'm flying now, there is no one in sight, this is my race, there's the tape, I'm almost there, the tape hit my chest, it feels weird . . . weird . . . weird . . . the tape feels weird . . . that's the end . . . the end . . . the end . . . the end.

The runner appeared to be deeply relaxed at this point, and he had previously agreed to answer any questions we might have following his recall of the race. He was asked, "You almost dropped out of the race twice. Why didn't you simply slow your pace? Would that not have been better than quitting?" The runner replied without any hesitation that "Oh, no, you really have to take pride in yourself to quit. You have to be a *real* man . . . it takes guts to quit. Anybody can continue and turn in a lousy performance. I have too much pride to do that. I would rather quit." Although this view can be judged as somewhat unusual, it is noteworthy that he had dropped out of more races than he had completed during the present season.

The runner was asked to clarify the meaning of selected terms or phrases he had used, and then he was asked the following question: "Would you like to have complete recall for all of this information, or would you prefer to forget about it, or perhaps, have it come back to you gradually?" The decision to ask this question was based on the earlier demonstration by Johnson (1961a) that athletes sometimes do not wish to become aware of repressed material in the post-hypnotic state. The decision to ask whether he would prefer that this information gradually return also was based on Johnson's case study, and it was intended to prevent the athlete from becoming overwhelmed or further confused as a result of this previously repressed material. At any rate, the runner responded that he would like to have complete recall following the session. Hence, no effort was made to produce post-hypnotic amnesia.

The runner also was asked in the hypnotic state whether he wished to continue with this program of insight training, and he replied that he would like to give this some thought. For this reason, post-hypnotic suggestions designed to ensure adherence to future hypnotic sessions were not administered. In other words, post-hypnotic suggestions designed to produce amnesia regarding the previously repressed material, and motivating instructions designed to ensure continuation, could have been, but were not, administered to the runner. This decision was based on the presumed efficacy of nondirected approaches in such cases, and on a priori contingency agreements with the runner. These agreements were of a generic nature, and they were decided on before intervention with hypnosis.

This case illustrates several points that practitioners in sport psychology or sports medicine should consider before using hypnosis with an athlete. First, it is important to obtain relevant information concerning an athlete's physiological, psychological, and medical state. Efforts to enhance physical performance with hypnosis should not be carried out within a unidimensional context. Second, the decision to proceed with hypnosis should be made only after ruling out obvious contraindications (i.e., pathophysiology and psychopathology). Third, peak performances involving the transcendence of usual performance levels can be associated with cognitive–perceptual processes of a remarkable nature. The record-setting performance of this athlete was found to be associated with considerable pain, but the sensation of pain had been repressed; that is, the runner was unaware of this pain experience in the nonhypnotic state. However, the cognitive–perceptual experience was "replayed" during hypnotic age regression, and the runner elected to have awareness of this experience in the post-hypnotic state. It is possible that conscious awareness of this previously repressed material may have provided the runner with insights he previously lacked.

Fourth, it is noteworthy that the athlete's record performance was characterized by the cognitive strategy of dissociation (Morgan, 1984, 1997, 2001). Runners who use this strategy attempt to ignore sensory input (e.g., muscle pain and breathing distress) by thinking about other activities (i.e., distraction). Other runners have reported that they initiate "out-of-body" experiences by entering the body's shadow cast on the ground in front of them. These cognitive strategies have been labeled as dissociation. Although this strategy can clearly facilitate endurance performance (Morgan, Horstman, Cymerman, & Stokes, 1983), it is not the preferred strategy of elite distance runners (Morgan & Pollock, 1977). Elite runners have been found to use the cognitive strategy of association, which is based on systematic monitoring of physical sensations rather than on ignoring them (Morgan, 2001; Morgan et al., 1987, 1988; Morgan & Pollock, 1977).

It is possible that this athlete could have been taught to use dissociation (Morgan, 1984), in either the hypnotic or the nonhypnotic state, to help him cope with the perception of pain during competition. Also, it is possible that such an approach would have led to enhanced performance, because (a) laboratory research has shown that such an approach is ergogenic (Morgan, 1972b; Morgan et al., 1983), and (b) the runner had experienced a form of dissociation during his record-setting performance. However, ignoring sensory input while performing at a high metabolic level in a sport contest is not without risk, and such an approach can lead to heatstroke, muscle sprains or strains, and stress fractures (Morgan, 1984). Cognitive strategies designed to minimize or eliminate the sensation of pain and discomfort during athletic competition and training should be used judiciously and with caution.

This runner subsequently elected to terminate insight training, and this decision was not congruent with his initial statement that he would do anything to return to his previous level of performance. Keep in mind that although he did possess the physiological capacity necessary to perform at a high level, to do so would have been associated with considerable pain. Also, despite the fact that his subsequent performance did not improve, our subjective impression was that he had "come to terms" with the situation. In a sense, then, he did not terminate the insight training we were providing, but rather, the insight he gained resolved the problem—at least from his perspective.

Case 2: Baseball Player

Hypnotic age regression was used to resolve a periodic problem experienced by a college baseball player who was an outfielder on a Division 1 team. The player was introduced to me by his team physician in the hope that hypnosis might be used to improve the player's batting performance. He was regarded as a strong hitter, with the exception that he would "bail out" of the batter's box at times when he was not in apparent danger of being hit by a pitched ball. He had been examined and treated by the team physician and found to be in good physical health, including unimpaired vision. The player was highly regarded by several professional baseball teams, and he stood a good chance of earning a professional contract following graduation in two months. He was highly motivated to solve his batting problem because several professional scouts had arranged visits to observe him play. The coach was somewhat frustrated about the situation, and his only approach had been to instruct the player to "hang in with the pitch." This instruction was of no help to the batter, and the exhortation seemed to exacerbate the problem.

The player was deeply concerned about the possibility that he would bail out of the batter's box during the forthcoming visits by pro scouts. Because he had a .315 batting average despite bailing out of the batter's box periodically, it was decided that he would be a possible candidate for hypnoanalysis. A battery of psychological questionnaires was administered, and he was found to score within the normal range on measures of state and trait anxiety (STAI; Spielberger, 1983); aggression (Thematic Apperception Test and a Sentence Completion Test; Murray, 1971); tension, depression, anger, vigor, and confusion (Profile of Mood States; McNair, Lorr, & Dropplemann, 1992); and neuroticism–stability and extroversion–introversion (EPI; Eysenck & Eysenck, 1963). Also, his lie score on the personality inventory was not remarkable. This screening was followed by administration of the Harvard (Shor & Orne, 1962) and Stanford C (Weitzenhoffer & Hilgard, 1962) scales of hypnotizability on separate days. He was quite responsive, scoring 9 on the Harvard Scale and 10 on the Stanford C Scale.

On the basis of the earlier example described by Johnson (1961a), he was initially age-regressed to a recent game in which the problem occurred, and he was asked to describe the situation. He had previously agreed that he did not object to the team physician or author asking him questions as the analysis proceeded. Although the author assumed responsibility for the hypnoinduction, it was agreed by the athlete, physician, and author that the physician would be responsible for the clinical dimensions of the process. The athlete was unable to provide any detail during this age regression that was not available previously in the non-hypnotic state. The author indicated that he would count from 1 to 10 and that the player would have recall for relevant information that was not previously available when the number 10 was reached. This, too, was based on the earlier approach successfully used by Johnson. At the count of 10, the athlete began to shake his head from side to side, and he apologized for not remembering additional material. He was assured that such a response was not unusual, and he was given post-hypnotic suggestions to the effect that he would feel relaxed and refreshed following the session. It also was emphasized that he would look forward to next week's session.

The player returned a week later, at which time a second age regression was used, but on this occasion, he was asked to go back in time and try to recall any events in his baseball career that were of particular importance to him. Within a brief period, he described an occasion during his first year at the university in which he was hit on the back as he turned in an attempt to avoid a pitched ball. He thought the ball was going to "break," but it did not, and as he turned away from the ball, his left scapula was hit and broken. It is remarkable that he had apparently repressed this event, because it was significant. He had never mentioned this incident to us during the non-hypnotic state. He then proceeded to describe a situation in high school when, as a pitcher, he had attempted to "dust off" a batter (i.e., throw at the batter rather than the plate) to distract the batter and increase his apprehension about succeeding pitches. Unfortunately, he hit the batter in the head (helmets were not worn at that time). Although the injury was not serious, the batter did not return to the game, and the athlete reported that he felt badly about the event.

It would have been possible to administer various post-hypnotic suggestions, but we decided against it for several reasons. The case resembled the one described by Johnson (1961b), discussed previously, in which a pitcher regularly went through an aggression–guilt–aggression cycle, with performance decrements during the guilt phase and enhanced performance during periods of aggression. In this case, the player may have been experiencing a fear– or guilt–repression cycle, presumably at an unconscious level, in which he felt the fear of being hit or the guilt associated with the injury of his opponent, and these states could have created sufficient psychomotor perturbation to provoke the present problem. In addition, these affective states may have been repressed periodically, during which time performance was increased. These explanations are purely speculative, and we elected not to build on these hypotheses. Also, we felt that it would be inappropriate to administer suggestions designed to restrain him in the batter's box, because of the potential for injury from a pitched ball. Rather, we elected to ask the batter whether he wanted to have conscious recall of this previously repressed material in the post-hypnotic state. He indicated that he would like to recall all of the information, and he was then given the same concluding suggestions administered in the previous session.

In the next and final session, the athlete was asked following the induction to once again go back in time and recall events in his baseball career that had particular meaning for him. He responded to this request by saying,

> Okay, but I want to tell you something first. I think I have solved my "bailing out" problem. I have been using a *closed* stance, and I crowd the plate as much as possible in order to "control" the plate and reduce the pitcher's strike zone. All good batters do this, but you always run the chance of being "beaned." Therefore, I'm changing to an *open* stance with my left foot dropped back so I will have a wide open view of all pitches. I'm a good enough hitter that I can do that without hurting my average.

Because the athlete seemed to have gained insight and resolved the problem, we elected not to proceed with further age regression. We talked with him briefly about his decision, and he was encouraged to review this plan with his coach. He was then given post-hypnotic suggestion so that he would feel relaxed, rested, and confident about his decision following the session. He also was encouraged to contact us if he had any further problems.

This case can be judged as representing a successful resolution of a presenting symptom, because the batter's performance improved. He was no longer plagued with the problem of bailing out, he completed the remainder of the season with a .515 average, and his overall average ranked near the top for all Division 1 players that year.

Case 3: Cyclist

A 27-year-old competitive cyclist approached the author with the request that hypnosis be used to resolve a problem he was experiencing with his training. He was unable to complete routine training rides of 50 to 75 km, and he was concerned that he would not be able to compete effectively in a forthcoming national race. He completed a standard battery of psychological questionnaires, and the results were remarkable in that he was found to be depressed and anxious. Because of the elevated scores on these measures, it was felt that his performance problem should not be addressed with hypnoanalysis. He was referred to a clinical psychologist for evaluation and possible treatment. Not only did this assessment reveal that he was clinically depressed, but it also showed that crisis intervention was warranted. Therefore, he was referred to an outpatient psychiatry clinic where he was treated for several months. Treatment consisted of time-limited psychotherapy in concert with antidepressant drug therapy.

During the course of his psychotherapy, he continued to visit our physiology-of-exercise laboratory, where he had previously completed a test of maximal aerobic power on the bicycle ergometer. This test revealed that he had a peak VO_2 max of 66 ml/kg·min. That is, maximal capacity was defined in terms of physiological capacity rather than a symptom-limited, or subjective, maximum. He was retested using the same protocol, and the test was performed by the same laboratory technician who performed the earlier assessment. The cyclist's maximal capacity had fallen to 53 ml/kg·min. Because a reduction of 20% in actual physiological capacity is both atypical and remarkable, the cyclist was retested a week later to confirm the test results. The second test yielded identical results, and these data served to confirm that the decision to use hypnosis in such a case was contraindicated. That is, he could no longer perform at his customary level, because he no longer had the physiological capacity to do so. The unexplained reduction in VO_2 max warranted further assessment, and he was referred for a complete physical examination, including routine blood and urine chemistries. All results were negative, with the exception that he seemed to have some suspicious chest sounds. For this reason, he was referred to the pulmonary function laboratory, where all test results were found to be negative.

The psychotherapy and drug therapy led to a reduction in this cyclist's anxiety and depression, and he was eventually able to resume customary levels of training. However, the 20% decrement in physical capacity was not restored, nor was he able to return to competitive cycling at the national level. The purpose of elaborating on this case study is threefold. First, the "motivational" problem was based on a profound and difficult to explain reduction in the cyclist's physiological capacity. Second, the use of hypnosis to treat this problem was contraindicated owing to the demonstration of both psychopathology (anxiety and depression) and pathophysiology (reduced VO_2 max). Third, it is apparent in retrospect, and on theoretical grounds, that a multidisciplinary approach to performance problems was, and is, the only defensible course of action.

Summary

Hypnosis has been used in the field of sport and exercise psychology for many years as a research tool to elucidate the mechanisms underlying physical performance. Also, numerous clinical applications have been designed to enhance performance in sport settings, and these interventions have been largely based on theoretical formulations as opposed to empirical research evidence. These clinical applications have generally been successful, but little attention has been paid to behavioral artifacts, such as expectancy effects, placebo effects, and demand characteristics. Furthermore, there is no evidence that effects obtained with these clinical applications exceed those achieved with the same or comparable approaches in the absence of hypnosis.

Efforts to enhance athletic performance by increasing or decreasing precompetitive anxiety have usually not been effective. This can be explained by the observation that most athletes perform best within a narrow ZOA. Hence, efforts to decrease or increase anxiety in athletes should be discouraged unless the athlete's ZOA is known. Note that hypnotic age regression offers considerable promise in defining a person's ZOA. Furthermore, once this zone has been established, it can be reproduced with various hypnotic procedures (e.g., autohypnosis and post-hypnotic suggestion).

An additional area in which hypnosis has proven to be effective in sport and exercise psychology involves the interpretation of decreased performance levels (i.e., slumps and failure) in previously successful people. Examples of nondirective hypnotic age regression are presented in this chapter, and these cases emphasize the importance of multidisciplinary approaches. Direct hypnotic suggestions of enhanced performance are not likely to be successful, but the hypnotic tool can be used effectively in several ways in sport and exercise psychology.

Perception of effort plays an important role in many sport and exercise settings, and hypnosis has been used effectively in a series of studies designed to better understand the nature of effort sense. This research has demonstrated that perceived exertion can be manipulated hypnotically in a systematic manner. This has been accomplished by maintaining exercise intensity at a constant power output (e.g., 100 watts) and suggesting that the work-load has increased or decreased. This perturbation of effort sense has been associated with various physiological changes in variables such as heart rate, blood pressure, ventilatory minute volume, and brain activation as measured by rCBF. Although the physiological changes have been more consistent and dramatic for suggestions of increased work-load, modifications have been noted for decreased effort sense as well. Related research involving the comparison of actual and imagined exercise has shown that cardiovascular changes and brain activation are similar in high—but not in low—hypnotizable individuals. It is concluded that hypnosis can be an effective tool in both the resolution of performance problems and the experimental study of perceived exertion during exercise.

References

American Psychological Association. (1992, December). Ethical principles of psychologists and code of conduct. *American Psychologist, 47,* 1597–1611.

Barber, T. X. (1966). The effects of hypnosis and suggestions on strength and endurance: A critical review of research studies. *British Journal of Social and Clinical Psychology, 5,* 42–50.

Borkovec, T. D., Mathews, A. M., Chambers, A., Ebrahimi, S., Lytle, R., & Nelson, R. (1987). The effects of relaxation training with cognitive or nondirective therapy and the role of relaxation-induced anxiety in the treatment of generalized anxiety. *Journal of Consulting and Clinical Psychology, 55,* 883–888.

Brown, D. R., & Blanton, C. J. (1998). Physical activity and suicide ideation/attempts among undergraduate college students [Abstract #1260]. *Medicine and Science in Sports and Exercise, 30*(Suppl.), 221.

Carmen, L. R., Zerman, J. L., & Blaine, G. B., Jr. (1968). Use of the Harvard psychiatric service by athletes and nonathletes. *Mental Hygiene, 52,* 134–137.

Davie, J. S. (1958). Who uses a college mental hygiene clinic? In B. M. Wedge (Ed.), *Psychosocial problems of college men* (pp. 140–149). New Haven, CT: Yale University Press.

Douglas, K. A., Collins, J. L., Warren, C., Kann, L., Gold, R., Clayton, S., Ross, J. G., & Kolbe, L. J. (1997). Results from the 1995 National College Health Risk Behavior Survey. *College Health, 46,* 55–66.

Eysenck, H. J. (1941). An experimental study of the improvement of mental and physical functions in the hypnotic state. *British Journal of Medical Psychology, 18*, 304–316.

Eysenck, H. J., & Eysenck, S. B. G. (1963). *Manual for the Eysenck personality inventory.* San Diego, CA: Educational and Industrial Testing Service.

Garver, R. B. (1977). The enhancement of human performance with hypnosis through neuromotor facilitation and control of arousal level. *American Journal of Clinical Hypnosis, 19*, 177–181.

Garvin, A. W., Trine, M. R., & Morgan, W. P. (2001). Affective and metabolic responses to hypnosis, autogenic relaxation, and quiet rest in the supine and seated positions. *International Journal of Clinical and Experimental Hypnosis, 49*, 5–18.

Gorton, B. E. (1959). Physiologic aspects of hypnosis. In J. M. Schneck (Ed.), *Hypnosis in modern medicine* (pp. 246–280). Springfield, IL: Charles C Thomas.

Hanin, Y. L. (1978). A study of anxiety in sports. In W. F. Straub (Ed.), *Sport psychology: An analysis of athlete behavior* (pp. 236–249). Ithaca, NY: Mouvement.

Heide, F. J., & Borkovec, T. D. (1984). Relaxation-induced anxiety: Mechanisms and theoretical implications. *Behavioral Research and Therapy, 22*, 1–12.

Hilgard, E. R. (1979, April). More about forensic hypnosis. *Division 30 Newsletter*, p. 5.

Hull, C. L. (1933). *Hypnosis and suggestibility.* New York: Appleton–Century–Crofts.

Ikai, M., & Steinhaus, A. H. (1961). Some factors modifying the expression of human strength. *Journal of Applied Psychology, 16*, 157–163.

Johnson, W. R. (1961a). Body movement awareness in the nonhypnotic and hypnotic states. *Research Quarterly, 32*, 263–264.

Johnson, W. R. (1961b). Hypnosis and muscular performance. *Journal of Sports Medicine and Physical Fitness, 1*, 71–79.

Levitt, E. E. (1981, August). Presidential address. *Division 30 Newsletter*, p. 2.

Lubin, B. (1962). *Manual for the depression adjective check lists.* San Diego, CA: Educational and Industrial Testing Service.

McNair, D. M., Lorr, M., & Dropplemann, L. F. (1992). *Profile of mood states manual.* San Diego, CA: Educational and Industrial Testing Service.

Meyers, A. W., Whelan, J. P., & Murphy, S. M. (1996). Cognitive–behavioral strategies in athletic performance enhancement. In M. Hersen, R. M. Eisler, & P. M. Miller (Eds.), *Progress in behavior modification* (Vol. 30, pp. 137–164). Pacific Grove, CA: Brooks/Cole.

Mittleman, K. D., Doubt, T. J., & Gravitz, M. A. (1992). Influence of self-induced hypnosis on thermal responses during immersion in 25° water. *Aviation, Space, and Environmental Medicine, 68*, 689–695.

Morgan, W. P. (1970). Oxygen uptake following hypnotic suggestion. In G. S. Kenyon (Ed.), *Contemporary psychology of sport* (pp. 283–286). Chicago: Athletic Institute.

Morgan, W. P. (1972a). Basic considerations. In W. P. Morgan (Ed.), *Ergogenic aids and muscular performance* (pp. 3–31). New York: Academic Press.

Morgan, W. P. (1972b). Hypnosis and muscular performance. In W. P. Morgan (Ed.), *Ergogenic aids and muscular performance* (pp. 193–233). New York: Academic Press.

Morgan, W. P. (1980a). Hypnosis and sports medicine. In G. D. Burrows & L. Dennerstein (Eds.), *Handbook of hypnosis and psychosomatic medicine* (pp. 359–375). Amsterdam, The Netherlands: Elsevier/North Holland Biomedical Press.

Morgan, W. P. (1980b). The trait psychology controversy. *Research Quarterly for Exercise and Sport, 51*, 50–76.

Morgan, W. P. (1981). Psychophysiology of self-awareness during vigorous physical activity. *Research Quarterly for Exercise and Sports, 52*, 385–427.

Morgan, W. P. (1984). Mind over matter. In W. F. Straub & J. M. Williams (Eds.), *Cognitive sport psychology* (pp. 311–316). Lansing, NY: Sport Science Associates.

Morgan, W. P. (1985). Psychogenic factors and exercise metabolism. *Medicine and Science in Sports and Exercise, 17,* 309–316.

Morgan, W. P. (1993). Hypnosis and sport psychology. In J. Rhue, S. J. Lynn, & I. Kirsch (Eds.), *Handbook of clinical hypnosis* (pp. 649–670). Washington DC: American Psychological Association.

Morgan, W. P. (1994). Psychological components of effort sense. *Medicine and Science in Sports and Exercise, 26,* 1071–1077.

Morgan, W. P. (1996). Hypnosis in sport and exercise psychology. In J. L. Van Raalte & B. W. Brewer (Eds.), *Exploring sport and exercise psychology* (pp. 107–130). Washington, DC: American Psychological Association.

Morgan, W. P. (1997). Mind games: The psychology of sport. In D. R. Lamb & R. Murray (Eds.), *Perspectives in exercise science and sports medicine (Vol. 10): Optimizing sport performance* (pp. 1–62). Carmel, IN: Cooper.

Morgan, W. P. (2001). Psychological factors associated with distance running and the marathon. In D. Tunstall Pedoe (Ed.), *Marathon medicine 2000* (pp. 293–310). London: Royal Society of Medicine.

Morgan, W. P., & Brown, D. R. (1983). Hypnosis. In M. L. Williams (Ed.), *Ergogenic aids and sports* (pp. 223–252). Champaign, IL: Human Kinetics.

Morgan, W. P., Brown, D. R., Raglin, J. S., O'Connor, P. J., & Ellickson, K. A. (1987). Psychological monitoring of overtraining and staleness. *British Journal of Sports Medicine, 21,* 107–114.

Morgan, W. P., & Ellickson, K. A. (1989). Health, anxiety, and physical exercise. In C. D. Spielberger & D. Hackbart (Eds.), *Anxiety in sports: An international perspective* (pp. 165–182). Washington, DC: Hemisphere.

Morgan, W. P., Hirota, K., Weitz, G. A., & Balke, B. (1976). Hypnotic perturbation of perceived exertion: Ventilatory consequences. *American Journal of Clinical Hypnosis, 18,* 182–190.

Morgan, W. P., Horstman, D. H., Cymerman, A., & Stokes, J. (1983). Facilitation of physical performance by means of a cognitive strategy. *Cognitive Therapy and Research, 7,* 251–264.

Morgan, W. P., O'Connor, P. J., Ellickson, K. A., & Bradley, P. W. (1988). Personality structure, mood states, and performance in elite male distance runners. *International Journal of Sport Psychology, 19,* 247–263.

Morgan, W. P., O'Connor, P. J., Sparling, B. P., & Pate, R. R. (1987). Psychological characterization of the elite female distance runner. *International Journal of Sports Medicine, 8,* 124–131.

Morgan, W. P., & Pollock, M. L. (1977). Psychologic characterization of the elite distance runner. *Annals of the New York Academy of Science, 301,* 382–403.

Morgan, W. P., Raven, P. B., Drinkwater, B. L., & Horvath, S. M. (1973). Perceptual and metabolic responsivity to standard bicycle ergometry following various hypnotic suggestions. *International Journal of Clinical and Experimental Hypnosis, 31,* 86–101.

Murray, H. A. (1971). *Thematic apperception test manual.* Cambridge, MA: Harvard University Press.

Naruse, G. (1965). The hypnotic treatment of stage fright in champion athletes. *International Journal of Clinical and Experimental Hypnosis, 13,* 63–70.

Nicholson, N. C. (1920). Notes on muscular work during hypnosis. *Johns Hopkins Hospital Bulletin, 31,* 89–91.

Pierce, R. A. (1969). Athletes in psychotherapy: How many, how come? *Journal of the American College Health Association, 17,* 244–249.

Raglin, J. S. (1992). Anxiety and sport performance. In J. O. Holloszy (Ed.), *Exercise and sport sciences reviews* (Vol. 20, pp. 243–274), Baltimore, MD: Williams & Wilkins.

Raglin, J. S. (2001). Psychological factors in sport performance: The mental health model revisited. *Sports Medicine, 31,* 875–890.

Raglin, J. S., Morgan, W. P., & Wise, K. (1990). Pre-competition anxiety in high school girl swimmers: A test of optimal function theory. *International Journal of Sports Medicine, 11,* 171–175.

Raglin, J. S., & Morris, M. J. (1994). Precompetition anxiety in women volleyball players: A test of ZOF theory in a team sport. *British Journal of Sports Medicine, 28,* 47–51.

Raglin, J. S., & Turner, P. E. (1992). Predicted, actual, and optimal precompetition anxiety in adolescent track and field athletes. *Scandinavian Journal of Exercise and Science in Sports, 2,* 148–152.

Raglin, J. S., & Turner, P. E. (1993). Anxiety and performance in track and field athletes: A comparison of the inverted-U hypothesis with zone of optimal function theory. *Personality and Individual Differences, 14,* 163–171.

Railo, W. S., & Unestàhl, L-E. V. (1979). The Scandinavian practice of sport psychology. In P. Klavora (Ed.), *Coach, athlete, and the sport psychologist* (pp. 248–271). Champaign, IL: Human Kinetics.

Ryde, D. (1964). A personal study of some uses of hypnosis in sports and sports injuries. *Journal of Sports Medicine and Physical Fitness, 4,* 241–246.

Schultz, J. H., & Luthe, W. (1969). *Autogenic therapy, Volume I: Autogenic methods.* New York: Grane & Stratton.

Shor, R. E., & Orne, E. C. (1962). *Harvard Group Scale of Hypnotic Susceptibility.* Palo Alto, CA: Consulting Psychologists Press.

Simon, T. R., & Powell, K. E. (1999). Involvement in physical activity and risk for nearly lethal suicide attempts. *Medicine & Science in Sports and Exercise, 31*(Suppl.), 85.

Spielberger, C. D. (1983). *Manual for the State–Trait Anxiety Inventory.* Palo Alto, CA: Consulting Psychologists Press.

Turner, P. E., & Raglin, J. S. (1996). Variability in precompetition anxiety and performance in collegiate track and field athletes. *Medicine and Science in Sports and Exercise, 28,* 378–385.

Unestàhl, L. E. (1981). *New paths of sport learning and excellence* [Monograph]. Orebro, Sweden: Orebro University, Department of Sport Psychology.

Unger, J. B. (1997). Physical activity, participation in team sports, and risk of suicidal behavior in adolescents. *American Journal of Health Promotion, 12,* 90–93.

Vanek, M. (1970). Psychological problems of superior athletes: Some experiences from the Olympic Games in Mexico City, 1968. In G. S. Kenyon (Ed.), *Contemporary psychology of sport* (pp. 183–185). Chicago: Athletic Institute.

Wang, Y., & Morgan, W. P. (1992). The effect of imagery perspectives on the psychophysiological responses to imagined exercise. *Behavioral Brain Research, 52,* 167–174.

Weitzenhoffer, A. M. (1953). *Hypnotism: An objective study in suggestibility.* New York: Wiley.

Weitzenhoffer, A. M., & Hilgard, E. R. (1962). *Stanford hypnotic susceptibility scale, Form C.* Palo Alto, CA: Consulting Psychologists Press.

Williamson, J. W., McColl, R., Mathews, D., Mitchell, J. H., Raven, P. B., & Morgan, W. P. (2001). Hypnotic manipulation of effort sense during dynamic exercise: Cardiovascular responses and brain activation. *Journal of Applied Physiology, 90,* 1392–1399.

Williamson, J. W., McColl, R., Mathews, D., Mitchell, J. H., Raven, P. B., & Morgan, W. P. (in press). Brain activation by central command during actual and imagined handgrip under hypnosis. *Journal of Applied Physiology.*

Wilson, G. S., & Raglin, J. S. (1997). Optimal and predicted anxiety in 9–12-year-old track and field athletes. *Scandinavian Journal of Medicine and Science in Sports, 7,* 253–258.

Part II

Promoting Well-Being

Exercise Initiation, Adoption, and Maintenance in Adults: Theoretical Models and Empirical Support

Bess H. Marcus, Beth C. Bock,
Bernardine M. Pinto, Melissa A. Napolitano,
and Matthew M. Clark

This chapter focuses on the promotion of exercise behavior in the general population. The health benefits of regular exercise are presented, followed by data on the prevalence of a sedentary lifestyle in the U.S. population. The lack of theory-driven interventions has been a limitation in exercise promotion efforts. We present a summary of useful theoretical models for exercise adoption and adherence. For practitioners, we provide information on exercise interventions based on some of these theories. Finally, we identify important issues that need to be addressed in exercise promotion.

Benefits of Exercise and Physical Activity

Physical activity and cardiorespiratory fitness have been shown to be associated with decreased morbidity and mortality in both men and women (Blair, Kohl, & Barlow, 1993; Blair, Powell, et al., 1993; Paffenbarger, Hyde, Wing, Lee, Jung, & Kambert, 1993). Research indicates that people who engage in almost no exercise have a greater risk for coronary heart disease compared with people who perform a moderate amount of exercise on a regular basis. The risk differentials are smaller when the moderately active are compared with the most active people (Lakka et al., 1994; Leon, Connett, Jacobs, & Rauramaa, 1987; Paffenbarger et al., 1993). Over the past 50 years, data on the primary preventive effects of physical activity suggest that active people are less likely to develop coronary heart disease than their inactive peers; when they do develop the disease, it occurs at a later age and tends to be less severe (Berlin & Colditz, 1990; Powell, Thompson, Caspersen, & Kendrick, 1987).

In addition to protection against coronary heart disease (Blair et al., 1989), increased activity appears to provide weight control benefits and protection against other diseases, such as colon cancer and non-insulin-dependent diabetes (U.S. Department of Health and Human Services [USDHHS], 1996). Regular physical activity helps to maintain healthy joints and may control symptoms of osteoarthritis. Similarly, weight-bearing physical activity seems to build bone mass in childhood and early adolescence and to maintain bone mass in adulthood (USDHHS, 1996). Considering secondary prevention, exercise also is recommended as an adjunctive treatment to diet for control of non-insulin-dependent diabetes and is a useful adjunct to dietary management for weight loss (USDHHS, 1996).

Apart from the promising improvements in health, exercise also has been shown to offer psychological benefits for adults, such as improvements in anxiety, depression, and self-concept (Blumenthal et al., 1999; Raglin, 1990). Although numerous studies have found this link between exercise and mental health, the internal and external validity of many of the studies are weak and plagued by problems in design and measurement of exercise (Dishman, 1998). Available evidence suggests that participation in physical activity, rather than increased cardiovascular fitness, may be accounting for better health and mood (see review by LaFontaine et al., 1992). In summary, exercise can help modify risk factors for chronic disease, assist in the treatment of some chronic diseases, and has been shown to be associated with mental health benefits.

Current Status of Exercise Participation

The U.S. Centers for Disease Control and Prevention (CDC) and the American College of Sports Medicine (ACSM; Pate et al., 1995) have recommended that every American adult do at least 30 minutes of moderate intensity physical activity (e.g., brisk walking, heavy yard work, or gardening) over the course of most, ideally all, days of the week. The

National Institutes of Health (NIH) Consensus Development Conference Statement on Physical Activity and Cardiovascular Health (1995) also made similar recommendations for children and adults to do at least 30 minutes per day of moderate-intensity physical activity. Responses to the 1990 National Health Interview Survey have shown that only 32% of U.S. adults meet these recommendations for their leisure-time physical activity (Jones et al., 1998). The groups least likely to meet recommendations included women (30% women vs. 34% men), racial and ethnic minorities (30% African American, 26% Hispanic vs. 33% White), people who are less educated (25% among those with <12 years' education vs. 37% with >12 years' education), and the elderly population (32% of those ages 65 years or older vs. 37% among those ages 18 to 24 years).

These estimates of physical inactivity persist across populations, locations, and environments. People with disabilities have been found to be more sedentary than their healthy counterparts (Taylor, Baranowski, & Young, 1998). Data from the Third National Health and Nutrition Examination Survey found that 29% of people with a chronic disease or risk factor reported no leisure-time physical activity compared with those who did not report a chronic disease or risk factor (Crespo, Keteyian, Snelling, Smith, & Andersen, 1999). Surprisingly, leisure-time physical activity has an inverse relationship with degree of urbanization, such that even when analyses are adjusted for age, education, and income, 37% of residents in rural areas reported no activity versus 27% in central metropolitan areas (Behavioral Risk Factor Surveillance System data, BRFSS; CDC, 1988, 1998). Furthermore, 50% of people who begin an exercise program (e.g., supervised, community-based) stop within six months (Dishman, 1988; USDHHS, 1996). Therefore, there is a great need for the development of effective interventions to promote physical activity adoption and maintenance.

When type of activity is examined, women tend to report lower participation in vigorous activity than men do (Hovell et al., 1989; Sallis et al., 1986; Sidney et al., 1991). In a community sample of California adults, Sallis and colleagues found that 5% of women adopted vigorous activity compared with 11% of men, but 34% of women adopted moderate intensity activity compared with 26% of men. Traditionally, assessments of physical activity were developed for male samples, and this bias may account partially for the gender differences favoring greater vigorous activity in men (Ainsworth, 2000; Young, Rohm, King, Oka, & Haskell, 1994). When light and moderate intensity activities are considered in the determination of regular leisure-time physical activity levels, the gender difference for physical activity participation diminishes or disappears. Besides showing a difference in intensity of exercise, women show a greater preference for aerobic dance and videotaped exercise programs than do men (Ainsworth, 2000; King, Taylor, Haskell, & De-Busk, 1990).

Although physical inactivity has been identified as a major risk factor for chronic disease, the adoption of an active lifestyle remains a major challenge to health educators, health promotion experts, and health care professionals. The higher prevalence of inactivity among the economically disadvantaged, racial and ethnic minorities, and women makes it clear that exercise promotion in these groups is a public health necessity that cannot be neglected.

Theoretical Models Used in Exercise Research

Psychological theories can significantly contribute to the knowledge base for guiding the development of new interventions to promote exercise adoption and maintenance. Researchers define their questions on the basis of their theoretical frame of reference (Dzewaltowski, 1994). In the past, many sport and exercise psychology researchers sought an "exercise personality" (Feltz, 1992). Researchers examined profiles of athletes based on standard personality profiles. These researchers generally lacked a theoretical rationale, and few conclusive results were drawn from using these atheoretical approaches (Feltz, 1992). More recently, researchers have examined cognitive and behavioral models in exercise research. In this section, we describe several useful psychological models of exercise adoption and maintenance.

The Health Belief Model

The health belief model was developed by Rosenstock (1974) and by Becker and Maiman (1975). This model proposes that the likelihood that a person will engage in preventive health behaviors (e.g., exercise) depends on two assessments: (a) an individual's perception of the severity of a potential illness and (b) his or her perceived susceptibility to that illness. The person then weighs the benefits against the costs related to taking action. If a person believes the potential illness is serious, that he or she is at risk, and that the pros of taking action outweigh the cons, he or she is likely to adopt the target health behavior.

Note that other factors such as demographic characteristics (e.g., age, ethnicity, gender), social psychological variables (e.g., social class, peer influence), and cues in the environment (e.g., media campaigns, physician counseling) also can influence these assessments. For example, a younger person may feel less vulnerable to the types of diseases linked to inactivity, such as cardiovascular disease (Blair et al., 1989), which tend to occur later in life. Interventions targeted to a younger audience should therefore focus on factors to which there may already be a perceived vulnerability (e.g., body image issues) or should target other aspects of the health belief equation.

Theory of Reasoned Action

The theory of reasoned action, developed by Ajzen and Fishbein (1980), has its foundation in the premise that people generally do those behaviors that they intend. Therefore, to predict whether people will exercise, one should ask whether they intend to exercise. According to this model, intentions are the product of people's attitudes toward a particular behavior and their perceptions of what is normative regarding the behavior (subjective norm). The subjective norm is a product of beliefs about others' opinions and the person's motivation to comply with others' opinions. Attitudes are determined by beliefs about the outcome of the behavior and the value placed on that outcome.

For example, Susan, a sedentary person, may believe that other people think she should exercise, and she may wish to do what others want her to do. This results in a positive subjective norm for exercising. In addition, Susan also may believe that she will lose weight and feel less tired if she exercises regularly (outcome beliefs). Because Susan values these results highly, a positive attitude toward exercise is formed. The combination of this subjective norm and attitude should create a positive intention for Susan to exercise.

Ajzen and Fishbein (1980) observed that the theory of reasoned action was particularly useful when predicting behaviors that were entirely subject to volitional control. However, most behaviors involve a degree of practical constraint and are not entirely subject to volitional control. For example, the adoption of exercise requires opportunities, resources, and skills that many people lack.

Theory of Planned Behavior

Subsequent to the development of the theory of reasoned action, Ajzen (1985) proposed that intention could not be the sole predictor of behavior in situations in which people's control over the behavior might be incomplete. The theory of planned behavior incorporates notions of the subjective norm and attitudes similar to the theory of reasoned action (Ajzen & Madden, 1986). However, in the theory of planned behavior, perceived behavioral control, that is, people's perception of their ability to perform the behavior, also will affect behavioral outcomes. The notion of perceived behavioral control in this model is similar to Bandura's (1986) construct of self-efficacy. The theory of planned behavior postulates that if people believe that they do not have the resources or opportunities to perform that behavior, attitudes and subjective norms may not be enough to influence the intention to perform a behavior.

Social Cognitive Theory

Social cognitive theory is an integration of operant conditioning, social learning theory, and cognitive psychology. Social cognitive theory proposes that personal, behavioral, and environmental factors operate as reciprocal interacting determinants of each other (Bandura, 1977, 1986). This model of reciprocal causality is termed *reciprocal determinism.* Bandura proposed that the environment affects behaviors, but behaviors also affect the environment. Personal factors, including cognitions, emotions, and physiology, also are important. Bandura (1977) was one of the first to state that learning may occur as a result of direct reinforcement of a behavior or as a result of observing the consequences that others experience. People learn through the consequences of their own behavior and by observation of others. Modeling is an efficient method of learning, and therefore, according to social cognitive theory, researchers should examine the role of modeling in exercise.

Two cognitive processes, outcome expectations and self-efficacy, have been identified as important components in social cognitive theory. *Outcome expectations* are beliefs about the effects of a behavior. People may expect to improve health status, receive social approval, or experience self-satisfaction as an outcome of exercising (Dzewaltowski, 1994). Outcomes can be classified as immediate benefits, such as a lower stress level, or as long-term benefits, such as improvements in body composition.

Self-efficacy is one's judgment of one's ability to successfully perform a behavior (Bandura, 1977, 1986). People's perception that they can perform a behavior successfully increases the likelihood that they will engage in the behavior. Self-efficacy is behavior specific. Therefore, self-efficacy for exercise is different from self-efficacy for smoking cessation or weight management. Self-efficacy judgments have been found to predict exercise level (Bock et al., 1997; Sullum, Clark, & King, 2000). A five-item self-efficacy measure for exercise includes negative affect, resisting relapse, and making time for exercise as situational factors (Marcus, Selby, Niaura, & Rossi, 1992). Participants in an exercise and diet program demonstrated improvement on this scale (Pinto, Clark, Cruess, Szymanski, & Pera, 1999). Results from a recent study of 174 older adults (mean age = 65.5 years) who engaged in either a walking or a strength and toning program indicated that for both groups, increases in self-esteem (i.e., perceptions of attractiveness, physical conditioning, and strength) were significantly related to increases in self-efficacy (McAuley, Blissmer, Katula, Duncan, & Mihalko, 2000).

Decision Theory

Decisional balance, which is based on the theoretical model of decision making developed by Janis and Mann (1977), is a person's perception and evaluation of the relative benefits (pros) and costs (cons) associated with exercise participation. These strategies have been adapted and applied to exercise adoption (Marcus, Rakowski, & Rossi, 1992) by using a questionnaire that assesses anticipated consequences of exercise participation in terms of gains and losses to self and others and approval or disapproval from the self and others. This procedure may promote an awareness of the benefits and costs of exercise participation that are salient to the person (Hoyt & Janis, 1975; Wankel, 1984).

Transtheoretical Model

The transtheoretical model incorporates aspects of social cognitive theory (e.g., self-efficacy) and decision theory. According to the transtheoretical model of behavior change, people progress through the following stages of change: (a) precontemplation, (b) contemplation, (c) preparation, (d) action, and (e) maintenance. Precontemplators do not exercise and do not intend to start in the next six months. Contemplators do not currently exercise but intend to start in the next six months. Those in preparation are exercising but not regularly (three or more times per week for 20 minutes or longer of vigorous-intensity activity or accumulating 30 or more minutes per day five or more days per week of moderate-intensity activity; ACSM, 1990; Pate et al., 1995). Action is the stage for people who exercise regularly but have done so for less than six months. Maintenance includes people who exercise regularly and have done so for six months or longer (Marcus, Rossi, Selby, Niaura, & Abrams, 1992).

Movement across the stages is thought to be cyclic, not linear, as many do not succeed in their efforts at establishing and maintaining lifestyle changes (Prochaska, DiClemente, & Norcross, 1992). Most intervention programs are designed for people in the action stage. However, most people are not in the action stage. Marcus and colleagues (Marcus, Rossi, et al., 1992), in a sample of 1,172 participants in a work site health promotion project, classified 24% in precontemplation, 33% in contemplation, 10% in preparation, 11% in action, and 22% in maintenance. This pattern of distribution is similar to the distribution of stages of change for other behaviors. Research has demonstrated that when a mismatch exists between stage of change and intervention strategy, attrition is high. Therefore, matching treatment strategies to a person's stage of change is one strategy to improve adherence and reduce attrition.

The stages of change document *when* people change, and the processes of change describe *how* people change. The processes of change questionnaire is a 40-item measure of these processes for exercise (Marcus, Rossi, et al., 1992); a sample item from each process is listed in Exhibit 9.1. Use of the specific processes of change depends on a person's stage of change. Processes are divided into two categories: cognitive and behavioral. The cognitive processes for exercise are consciousness raising, dramatic relief, environmental reevaluation, self-reevaluation, and social liberation. The behavioral processes for exercise are counterconditioning, helping relationships, reinforcement management, self-liberation, and stimulus control. Use of the cognitive processes tends to peak in the preparation stage and use of the behavioral processes tends to peak in the action stage. Change over time on the processes of change questionnaire has been shown to predict success in attaining and maintaining a program of regular physical activity (Dunn et al., 1997, 1999).

Also related to stage of change is the cost–benefit analysis or decisional balance, which was discussed in the decision theory section. When people are considering a lifestyle change, they weigh the benefits (pros) of that behavior against the costs (cons) of that behavior. In a

Exhibit 9.1

Exercise Processes of Change

Cognitive Processes

    Consciousness raising
- I recall information people have personally given me on the benefits of exercise.

    Dramatic relief
- Warnings about health hazards of inactivity move me emotionally.

    Environmental reevaluation
- I feel I would be a better role model for others if I exercised regularly.

    Self-reevaluation
- I am considering the idea that regular exercise would make me a healthier, happier person.

    Social liberation
- I find society changing in ways that make it easier for the exerciser.

Behavioral Processes

    Counterconditioning
- Instead of remaining inactive, I engage in some physical activity.

    Helping relationships
- I have someone on whom I can depend when I am having problems with exercising.

    Reinforcement management
- I reward myself when I exercise.

    Self-liberation
- I tell myself I am able to keep exercising if I want to.

    Stimulus control
- I put things around my home to remind me of exercising.

Note. Items from "The Stages and Processes of Exercise Adoption and Maintenance in a Worksite Sample," by B. H. Marcus, J. S. Rossi, V. C. Selby, R. S. Niaura, & D. B. Abrams, 1992, *Health Psychology, 11,* p. 389. Reprinted with permission.

study of 12 problem behaviors, researchers found that the cons are usually greater than the pros in the precontemplation and contemplation stages (Prochaska et al., 1994). Typically, the crossover occurs in the preparation stage, and the pros are greater than the cons in the action and maintenance stages (Prochaska et al., 1994). The 16-item decisional balance measure for exercise has 10 pros (e.g., "I would sleep more soundly if I exercised regularly") and 6 cons (e.g., "I would have less time for my family and friends if I exercised regularly"; Marcus, Rakowski, et al., 1992). Participants have demonstrated positive changes on this measure after 12 weeks of exercise (Pinto et al., 1999), and decisional balance for exercise is predictive of relapse following participation in a cardiac rehabilitation program (Bock et al., 1997).

Relapse Prevention Model

The problem of relapse is an important challenge in health behaviors (Brownell, Marlatt, Lichtenstein, & Wilson, 1986). Relapse rates in exercise programs are high. Approximately 50% of exercise program participants drop out during the first six months (Dishman, 1988; USDHHS, 1996). One community-based survey of 1,811 people found that 20% of the participants experienced at least two exercise relapses (i.e., stopping exercise for at least 3 months) and 21% experienced three or more relapses. Other research on relapse found that of 7,135 Young Men's Christian Association (YMCA) members, 81% had a lapse (i.e., not attending for at least 7 consecutive days) during the course of a year (J. M. Jakicic, Brown University, personal communication, July 18, 2000). According to Marcus, Dubbert, and colleagues (2000), little is known about how lapses affect long-term adherence to exercise programs. They suggest that the relapse prevention model, which has been applied to the exercise literature (Dubbert & Stetson, 1995; Simkin & Gross, 1994), can be a useful framework for understanding the process from lapse to relapse.

The goal of relapse prevention is to help people anticipate problems and cope effectively in high-risk situations. Despite the prevalence of relapse, researchers identified only a few factors that may contribute to relapse. Negative emotions, physiological factors, limited coping skills, limited social support, low motivation, high-risk situations, and stress all appear to predict relapse (Brownell et al., 1986; Kayman, Bruvold, & Stern, 1990).

The principles of the relapse prevention model include identifying high-risk situations for relapse (e.g., change in season, change in work hours, end of organized team) and related problem-solving solutions for these high-risk situations (e.g., "When it starts to snow, I'll shift from outdoor walks to walking in the mall," "I'll find other times for my aerobic classes," "When tennis season ends, I'll join a soccer club"; Dishman, 1991). When people do experience a lapse (i.e., a few days of not participating in their planned activity), they need to challenge the abstinence violation effect (AVE), which applies to a range of behaviors. Simply stated, the AVE is the belief that once one has slipped, one is doomed. Therefore, people who have lapsed may see themselves as failures and give up exercising. In areas in which total abstinence (or perfection) is not possible, such as in exercise, researchers have suggested that people have a planned lapse, in order to practice challenging the AVE. Our clinical experience and research findings (Marcus & Stanton, 1993), however, have not found a planned lapse to be beneficial. Therefore, future research is needed to better understand the AVE in exercise.

Self-Determination Theory

Self-determination theory focuses on social and environmental conditions that are related to self-motivation and psychological development (Ryan & Deci, 2000). This theory emphasizes that there are ways the social environment can optimize a person's development, performance, and well-being (Ryan & Deci, 2000). It is obvious that people are motivated by different types of factors; two of these factors are intrinsic and extrinsic motivation.

Intrinsic Motivation
One subtheory of self-determination theory is cognitive evaluation theory (Deci & Ryan, 1985). This theory focuses on specifying factors that explain variability in intrinsic motivation or on performing an activity for the inherent satisfaction of that activity (Ryan & Deci, 2000). Cognitive evaluation theory seeks to describe social and environmental factors related to intrinsic motivation across a range of behaviors and situations. Intrinsic motivation consists of the tendency to seek out new experiences and challenges, explore, learn, and develop one's capacities (Ryan & Deci, 2000). Deci and Ryan (1985) identified several factors that influence intrinsic motivation, including choice, opportunities for self-direction, activities that are of intrinsic interest, and opportunities to show both competence and autonomy.

Extrinsic Motivation
Another type of self-determined motivation is extrinsic motivation, or performing an activity for the purpose of some other separate outcome (e.g., an external reward, praise; Ryan & Deci, 2000). Among extrinsic forces, one important component is the social influence related to facilitating behavior change (Basic Behavioral Science Task Force of the

National Advisory Mental Health Council, 1996; Corrigan, Dell, Lewis, & Schmidt, 1980; McNeill & Stoltenberg, 1989). Social influence theoretical perspectives highlight the influence of interpersonal interactions on perceptions of control (Bond, 1982).

One study of intrinsic motivation and exercise found intrinsic motivation to be associated with attendance in an eight-week aerobic fitness program and in confidence toward continuing exercising after the end of the program (Oman & McAuley, 1993). Also, some research suggests that extrinsic factors peak during earlier stages of motivational readiness, whereas the presence of intrinsic factors (e.g., enjoyment) are essential to prompt progression and maintenance (Ingledew, Markland, & Medley, 1998).

Motivational Interviewing

Motivational interviewing is a clinical and theoretical approach that was developed in the addictions field to assist people in working through their ambivalence toward making behavior changes (Miller, 1983; Miller & Rollnick, 1991). This approach has recently been applied to different problem behaviors, including diet (Berg-Smith et al., 1999), diabetes (Smith, Heckemeyer, Kratt, & Mason, 1997), eating disorders (Treasure & Ward, 1997), and HIV risk reduction (Kalichman, Cherry, & Browne-Sperling, 1999). Miller and Rollnick (1991) stated that motivation is not a personality trait but rather a state or eagerness of readiness, similar to the transtheoretical model (Prochaska & DiClemente, 1983). The counselor's task in motivational interviewing is to assist people in finding, using, and adhering to specific behavior change strategies (Miller, 1985). Miller and Rollnick (1991) identified eight important building blocks that counselors can use to facilitate behavior change: (a) give advice, (b) remove barriers, (c) provide choice, (d) decrease desirability, (e) be empathetic, (f) provide feedback, (g) clarify goals, and (h) actively help.

One recent study (Hillsdon, Thorogood, White, Foster, & Diamond, 2000; M. Hillsdon, personal communication, August 22, 2000) investigated the effects of a structured, client-centered intervention based on motivational interviewing principles. This study compared the effectiveness of two communication styles (negotiation vs. direct advice) and a no-intervention control. Participants were 1,658 men and women, ages 45 to 64. At posttest, both communication groups significantly increased their level of physical activity ($p \leq .05$). The negotiation group increased their physical activity behavior 10% more than the control group. This study highlights some of the benefits of interventions based on motivational interviewing for improving physical activity behavior.

Conclusions About Models

Exercise researchers have used theoretical models to guide their investigations. However, numerous questions still need to be addressed. Most of the theoretical models that have been applied to exercise behavior were developed for and first applied to other behaviors. How exercise may differ from other behaviors is currently unclear. One problem is that most of the research has used populations with a middle to upper socioeconomic status, and it is unclear how these models apply to other demographic groups. Furthermore, research has examined only the application of each model to exercise and has yet to compare the different models (King et al., 1992).

Many of the models reviewed contain common theoretical elements or share similar constructs. The health belief model examines a person's perception of risks associated with a sedentary lifestyle and the perceived benefits of engaging in exercise. This appears similar to the comparisons made within social cognitive theory, which examines the interactions of social, exercise, and personal factors (e.g., beliefs, emotions, and physiology). Both intrinsic and extrinsic motivation also can be thought of in the context of other theories; for example, each might influence benefits and barriers toward being active (health belief model) and can be related to personal factors. Intrinsic motivation, particularly, has been shown to be related to aspects of social cognitive theory: People with high self-efficacy also have been found to be more intrinsically motivated to participate in physical activity compared with people with lower self-efficacy (McAuley, Wraith, & Duncan, 1991). In decision theory, these comparisons can be reduced to a simpler two-factor structure comparing the benefits to the costs of exercising. In addition, the theory of planned behavior incorporates people's beliefs about exercise and confidence in their ability to exercise. Another important model is the relapse prevention model, which focuses on cognitive processes that enhance (e.g., problem-solving strategies for high-risk situations) or prevent (e.g., the AVE) a long-term active lifestyle. The transtheoretical model of behavior change incorporates many components of the previously described models, including perceived benefits and costs, self-confidence, and strategies for change, into a model of a series of stages of change. Motivational interviewing also incorporates aspects of other theoretical models, including the transtheoretical model. Further research is needed to highlight differences between these models.

Intervention Applications of Models

One concept that has been popular for years in psychotherapy is that of "patient–treatment matching." This notion that treatments should be matched to the specific characteristics and needs of a patient also has gained popularity in smoking cessation and obesity treatments. However, this concept has been slow to reach the arena of exercise interventions, in part because sedentary lifestyles have only recently begun to receive national recognition as a significant public health problem (USDHHS, 1996; Fletcher et al., 1992; King et al., 1992; Pate et al., 1995). When one considers the large percentage of sedentary people in the population, the many health clubs and YMCA-type programs, and the high dropout rate from programmed exercise (Dishman, 1994; Dishman & Buckworth, 1996), the time seems right to consider patient treatment matching for the promotion of physical activity.

The underlying theme of the transtheoretical model is that people are at different levels of readiness to change their behavior; thus, interventions need to use differing strategies and techniques to bring about the desired change in behavior. Several studies illustrate the utility of this model for physical activity. The impetus for conducting these studies came from the lack of success prior interventions had in recruiting and retaining people who were sedentary but thinking about becoming active (contemplators).

The Imagine Action campaign was a community-wide program designed to increase participation in physical activity (Marcus, Banspach, et al., 1992). Participants were 610 adults who enrolled through their work sites (53%) or in response to posted or mass-circulated announcements in the community. Potential participants received a description of the program with a letter explaining that if they were inactive or having difficulty staying active, this was a program designed for them. People who responded provided information about their physical activity level, name, address, gender, and birth date and were given a free T-shirt for enrolling. On average, participants were 42 years old, and most (77%) were women. At baseline, 39% were in contemplation, 37% were in preparation, and 24% were in action.

A six-week intervention was delivered consisting of stage-matched self-help materials, a resource manual, and weekly "fun walks" and "activity nights." The content of the manuals was based on key issues in the exercise adherence literature and was informed by the transtheoretical model, social cognitive theory, and decision theory. The manual for contemplators, called "What's in It for You," included information on increasing lifestyle physical activity (e.g., taking the stairs instead of the elevator, parking the car at the end of the parking lot), considering the benefits (e.g., weight control) and barriers (e.g., takes too much time) of becoming more active, considering the social benefits of activity (e.g., meet people in a class, walk with significant other), and determining ways of rewarding oneself for increasing activity (e.g., buying flowers as a reward for increasing from one to two walks per week).

The manual for those in preparation was called "Ready for Action," because this group was participating in some activity, and the goal was 30 minutes of moderate activity daily or 20 minutes of vigorous activity three to five times per week (i.e., action). This manual focused on describing the barriers and benefits of physical activity, setting short- and long-term activity goals (e.g., walking for 30 minutes five times per week), rewarding oneself for activity, managing time to fit activity into a busy schedule (e.g., ride exercise bicycle or walk on treadmill while watching the news or other television), and providing details on developing a walking program.

The manual for those in action was called "Keeping It Going," because these people had been regularly active for only a short time; thus, they were at great risk for relapse to the preparation stage, in which they would exercise only occasionally. This manual focused on troubleshooting situations that might lead to relapse (e.g., illness, injury, boredom), goal setting, rewarding oneself (both internal rewards, e.g., praise, and external rewards, e.g., flowers), cross-training to prevent boredom, avoiding injury, and gaining social support (e.g., finding people to be active with or people supportive of one's active lifestyle).

The resource manual described a wide variety of free and low-cost light, moderate, and vigorous intensity physical activity options in the local community. These activities included fun walks and classes at local facilities, such as low-impact aerobics and volleyball for people who had never played.

Following the intervention, 30% of those in contemplation and

61% of those in preparation at baseline progressed to action, and an additional 31% who had been in contemplation progressed to preparation. Only 4% of those in preparation and 9% of those in action regressed. These findings demonstrate that a low-cost, relatively low-intensity intervention can produce significant improvement in stage of exercise adoption.

This study was not a controlled trial, however. Another study investigating the efficacy of a stage-matched physical activity intervention at the workplace was conducted using a randomized design (Marcus, Emmons, et al., 1998). In this study, employees were randomly assigned to a stage-matched self-help intervention or a standard care self-help intervention. The interventions consisted of print materials delivered at baseline and at one month.

At baseline, people in the stage-matched group received manuals specifically tailored to their stage of readiness for exercise. At one month, people received the manual matched to their stage plus the next manual in the series. The manual written for precontemplators was entitled "Do I Need This" and focused on increasing awareness of the benefits of activity and encouraging participants to think about the barriers that prevent them from being active. Specific suggestions for starting an exercise routine were not provided in this manual. The contemplator's manual, entitled "Try It You'll Like It," included a discussion of the reasons to stay inactive versus the reasons to become more active and ways to reward oneself and set realistic goals. For those in preparation, "I'm on My Way" reviewed the benefits of activity, goal setting, tips on safe and enjoyable activities, and obstacles to regular activity. "Keep It Going" provided information for those in action on topics such as the benefits of regular activity, staying motivated, rewarding oneself, enhancing confidence in being active, and overcoming obstacles. For those in maintenance, "I Won't Stop Now" emphasized the benefits of regular activity, avoiding injuries, goal setting, varying activities, rewarding oneself, and planning ahead. People in the standard care group received American Heart Association manuals ("Walking for a Healthy Heart," "Swimming for a Healthy Heart") because these are excellent and readily available and thus the best proxy of standard care. Comparison of the results from baseline to the three-month follow-up revealed that significantly more people in the stage-matched group demonstrated stage progression, whereas significantly more people in the standard care group displayed stage stability or stage regression.

A recent study expanded the application of stage-matched interventions by adding individualized components. This community-based study compared a standard intervention (American Heart Association manuals) with a stage-matched intervention that also provided individualized feedback to participants. A computer program was used to compare each participant's questionnaire responses with a stage-matched value contained in a normative database (comparing a person with an already established group norm). The goal was to provide tailored messages for each participant that gave comparisons between how other successful people did and how the participant was doing, as well as comparison between how the participant was doing currently, relative to how he or she was doing previously, in reaching exercise goals. Individualized feedback on motivation, cognitive and behavioral strategies, decisional balance, and self-efficacy were provided in printed reports at baseline and at 1, 3, and 6 months. Study results showed that those who received the individualized intervention were more likely to achieve recommended levels of physical activity and more likely to maintain that activity through a 12-month follow-up compared with participants given only standard physical activity promotion materials (Bock, Marcus, et al., 2001; Marcus, Bock, et al., 1998).

Future Directions

Previously, we highlighted issues that merit further investigation. However, some specific challenges confront both the clinician and the researcher working in the area of exercise promotion.

It is important that interventions be disseminated to the large population of sedentary people. Although practitioners can assist many people on a one-on-one or group basis, their reach remains limited. Therefore, the use of the telephone, mailed print materials, and newer technologies such as the Internet may be critical for the delivery of programs or as an adjunct to brief face-to-face contacts (see reviews by Marcus, Owen, Forsyth, Cavill, & Fridinger, 1998; Marcus, Nigg, Riebe, & Forsyth, 2000).

The CDC/ACSM recommendations (Pate et al., 1995) regarding accumulating moderate amounts of activity need to be used in exercise programs for individuals, groups, work sites, and communities. Many of the barriers to the initiation and early adoption of physical activity may no longer be as potent now that people have a variety of ways to get their "dose" of exercise. A recent clinical trial has demonstrated that a lifestyle-based program is as effective as a gym-based program in promoting short- (6-month) and long-term (24-month) physical activity and fitness (Dunn et al., 1999).

Physical activity opportunities and programs should be tailored to a person's level of readiness to consider, prepare for, initiate, and maintain increases in physical activity. Particularly, creative efforts are needed to establish programs that appeal to the large proportion in the population of sedentary and underactive people. Further tailoring of programs to meet the diverse needs of various racial, ethnic, and socioeconomic groups also is critical. In addition, it is important for research to be conducted to examine whether tailoring does add benefit, relative to the added cost, compared with targeted interventions. There is still much to learn in terms of which variables to use for tailoring (e.g., literacy level, setting of intervention, self-efficacy), how many variables to assess, and how the variables combine additively or synergistically to influence behavior change.

Many people prefer to exercise on their own or with friends, but not in a formal class-based program. However, these same people need guidance and support from professional and lay people to initiate and maintain an active lifestyle (see review by Dunn, Andersen, & Jakicic, 1998). Therefore, a need exists for instruction in how to be physically active on one's own in one's own home or community. This approach may be particularly desirable for older adults, parents of young children, and people who have difficulty with transportation because of disabilities, finances, or other reasons. A recent study has shown that telephone-based approaches are effective for increasing physical activity behavior in both the short and long term (King, Haskell, Young, Oka, & Stefanick, 1995).

Work site health promotion and educational programs can be successful because they can reach people who may not ordinarily seek out information or opportunities for being physically active. However, these programs could be enhanced by offering a variety of physical activities, maximizing convenience, permitting employees to exercise on company time, allowing flexible time schedules, and using incentives judiciously (see Dishman, Oldenberg, O'Neal, & Shepard, 1998, for review).

Summary

The studies reviewed in this chapter highlight the importance of including theoretical approaches and techniques in physical activity interventions to enhance success. However, many other opportunities remain for using these approaches, particularly in clinical and community populations. In addition, it is essential that future studies incorporate strong theoretical foundations and innovative interventions, such as tailoring programs to individual characteristics and finding avenues for reaching people who may not avail themselves of traditional programs. These approaches show great promise for continuing to target and modify the public health burden of physical inactivity.

References

Ainsworth, B. E. (2000). Issues in the assessment of physical activity in women. *Research Quarterly for Exercise and Sport, 71*, 37–42.

Ajzen, I. (1985). From intentions to actions: A theory of focus on these important subgroups. In J. Kuhl & J. Beckman (Eds.), *Action–control: From cognition to behavior* (pp. 11–39). Heidelberg, Germany: Springer.

Ajzen, I., & Fishbein, M. (1980). *Understanding attitudes and predicting social behavior.* Englewood Cliffs, NJ: Prentice-Hall.

Ajzen, I., & Madden, T. J. (1986). Prediction of goal-directed behavior: Attitudes, intentions, and perceived behavioral control. *Journal of Experimental Social Psychology, 22*, 453–474.

American College of Sports Medicine. (1990). Position statement on the recommended quantity and quality of exercise for developing and maintaining cardiorespiratory and muscular fitness in healthy adults. *Medicine and Science in Sports and Exercise, 22*, 265–274.

Bandura, A. (1977). Self-efficacy: Toward a unifying theory of behavior change. *Psychological Review, 84*, 191–215.

Bandura, A. (1986). *Social foundations of thought and action. A social cognitive theory.* Englewood Cliffs, NJ: Prentice-Hall.

Basic Behavioral Science Task Force of the National Advisory Mental Health Council. (1996). Basic behavioral science research for mental health. Social influence and social cognition. *American Psychologist, 51*, 478–484.

Becker, M. H., & Maiman, L. A. (1975). Sociobehavioral determinants of compliance with health care and medical care recommendations. *Medical Care, 13*, 10–24.

Berg-Smith, S. M., Stevens, V. J., Brown, K. M., Van-Horn, L., Gernhofer, N., Peters, E., Greenberg, R., Snetselaar, L., Ahrens, L., & Smith, K. (1999). A brief motivational intervention to improve dietary adherence in adolescents. *Health Education Research, 14*, 399–410.

Berlin, J. A., & Colditz, G. A. (1990). A meta-analysis of physical activity in the prevention of coronary heart disease. *American Journal of Epidemiology, 132*, 612–628.

Blair, S. N., Kohl, H. W., & Barlow, C. E. (1993). Physical activity, physical fitness and all-cause mortality in women: Do women need to be active? *Journal of the American College of Nutrition, 12*, 368–371.

Blair, S. N., Kohl, H. W., III, Paffenbarger, R. S., Jr., Clark, D. G., Cooper, K. H., & Gibbons, L. W. (1989). Physical fitness and all cause mortality: A prospective study of healthy men and women. *Journal of the American Medical Association, 262*, 2395–2401.

Blair, S. N., Powell, K. E., Bazzarre, T. L., Early, J. L., Epstein, L. H., Green, L. W.,

Harris, S. S., Haskell, W. L., King, A. C., Kaplan, J., Marcus, B., Paffenbarger, R. S., & Yeager, K. C. (1993). Physical inactivity, Workshop V. *Circulation, 88,* 1402–1405.

Blumenthal, J. A., Babyak, M. A., Moore, K. A., Craighead, W. E., Herman, S., Khatri, P., Waugh, R., Napolitano, M. A., Forman, L. M., Appelbaum, M., & Krishnan, K. R. (1999). Effects of exercise training on older patients with major depression. *Archives of Internal Medicine, 159,* 2349–2356.

Bock, B. C., Albrecht, A. E., Traficante, R. M., Clark, M. M., Pinto, B. M., Tilkemeier, P., & Marcus, B. H. (1997). Predictors of exercise adherence following participation in a cardiac rehabilitation program. *International Journal of Behavioral Medicine, 4,* 60–75.

Bock, B. C., Marcus, B. H., Pinto, B. M., & Forsyth, L. H. (2001). Maintenance of physical activity following an individualized motivationally tailored intervention. *Annals of Behavioral Medicine, 23,* 79–87.

Bond, C. F., Jr. (1982). Social facilitation: A self-presentation point of view. *Journal of Personality and Social Psychology, 42,* 1042–1050.

Brownell, K. D., Marlatt, G. A., Lichtenstein, E., & Wilson, G. T. (1986). Understanding and preventing relapse. *American Psychologist, 41,* 765–782.

Centers for Disease Control and Prevention. (1988). Behavior Risk Factor Surveillance System user's guide. Atlanta: Author.

Centers for Disease Control and Prevention. (1998). Self-reported physical inactivity by degree of urbanization—United States, 1996. *Mortality and Morbidity Weekly Reports, 47,* 1097–1100.

Corrigan, J. D., Dell, D. M., Lewis, K. N., & Schmidt, L. D. (1980). Counseling as a social influence process: A review. *Journal of Counseling Psychology Monograph, 27,* 395–441.

Crespo, C. J., Keteyian, S. J., Snelling, A., Smith, E., & Andersen, R. E. (1999). Prevalence of no leisure-time physical activity in persons with chronic disease. *Clinical Exercise Physiology, 1,* 68–73.

Deci, E. L., & Ryan, R. M. (1985). *Intrinsic motivation and self-determination in human behavior.* New York: Plenum.

Dishman, R. K. (1988). Overview. In R. Dishman (Ed.), *Exercise adherence* (pp. 1–9). Champaign, IL: Human Kinetics.

Dishman, R. K. (1991). Increasing and maintaining exercise and physical activity. *Behavior Therapy, 22,* 345–378.

Dishman, R. K. (1994). The measurement conundrum in exercise adherence research. *Medicine and Science in Sports and Exercise, 26,* 1382–1390.

Dishman, R. K. (1998). Physical activity and mental health. In *Encyclopedia of Mental Health.* New York: Academic Press.

Dishman, R., & Buckworth, J. (1996). Increasing physical activity: A quantitative synthesis *Medicine and Science in Sports and Exercise, 28,* 706–719.

Dishman, R. K., Oldenberg, B., O'Neal, H., & Shepard, R. J. (1998). Worksite physical activity interventions. *American Journal of Preventive Medicine, 15,* 344–361.

Dubbert, P. M., & Stetson, B. A. (1995). Exercise and physical activity. In A. J. Goreczny (Ed.), *Handbook of health and rehabilitation psychology* (pp. 255–274). New York: Plenum.

Dunn, A. L., Andersen, R. E., & Jakicic, J. M. (1998). Lifestyle physical activity interventions. History, short- and long-term effects and recommendations. *American Journal of Preventive Medicine, 15,* 398–412.

Dunn, A. L., Marcus, B. H., Kampert, J. B., Garcia, M. E., Kohl, H. W., III, & Blair,

S. N. (1997). Reduction in cardiovascular disease risk factors: 6-month results from Project Active. *Preventive Medicine, 26,* 883–892.

Dunn, A. L., Marcus, B. H., Kampert, J. B., Garcia, M. E., Kohl, H. W., III, & Blair, S. N. (1999). Comparison of lifestyle and structured interventions to increase physical activity and cardiorespiratory fitness: A randomized trial. *Journal of the American Medical Association, 281,* 327–334.

Dzewaltowski, D. A. (1994). Physical activity determinants: A social approach. *Medicine and Science in Sports and Exercise, 26,* 1395–1399.

Feltz, D. L. (1992). The nature of sport psychology. In T. S. Horn (Ed.), *Advances in sport psychology* (pp. 3–11). Champaign, IL: Human Kinetics.

Fletcher, G. F., Blair, S. N., Blumenthal, J., Caspersen, C., Chaitman, B., Epstein, S., Falls, H., Froelicher, E. S., Froelicher, V. F., & Pina, I. L. (1992). Statement on exercise: Benefits and recommendations for physical activity programs for all Americans: A statement for health professionals by the Committee on Exercise and Cardiac Rehabilitation of the Council on Clinical Cardiology, American Heart Association. *Circulation, 86,* 340–344.

Hillsdon, M., Thorogood, M., White, I., Foster, C., & Diamond, A. (2000). Brief negotiation vs. direct advice: A randomized controlled trial of physical activity promotion in primary care. *Medicine and Science in Sports and Exercise, 32,* S252.

Hovell, M. F., Sallis, J. F., Hofstetter, C. R., Spry, V. M., Faucher, P., & Casperson, C. J. (1989). Identifying correlates of walking for exercise: An epidemiologic prerequisite for physical activity promotion. *Preventive Medicine, 18,* 856–866.

Hoyt, M. F., & Janis, I. L. (1975). Increasing adherence to a stressful decision via a motivational balance-sheet procedure: A field experiment. *Journal of Personality and Social Psychology, 31,* 833–839.

Ingledew, D. K., Markland, D., & Medley, A. R. (1998). Exercise motives and stage of change. *Journal of Health Psychology, 3,* 477–489.

Janis, I. L., & Mann, L. (1977). *Decision making: A psychological analysis of conflict, choice and commitment.* New York: Free Press.

Jones, D. A., Ainsworth, B. E., Croft, J. B., Macera, C. A., Lloyd, E. E., & Yusuf, H. R. (1998). Moderate leisure-time physical activity. Who is meeting the public health recommendations? A national cross-sectional study. *Archives of Family Medicine, 7,* 285–289.

Kalichman, S. C., Cherry, C., & Browne-Sperling, F. (1999). Effectiveness of a video-based motivational skills-building HIV risk-reduction intervention for inner-city African American men. *Journal of Consulting and Clinical Psychology, 67,* 959–966.

Kayman, S., Bruvold, W., & Stern, J. S. (1990). Maintenance and relapse after weight loss in women: Behavioral aspects. *American Journal of Clinical Nutrition, 52,* 800–807.

King, A. C., Blair, S. N., Bild, D. E., Dishman, R. K., Dubbert, P. M., Marcus, B. H., Oldridge, N. B., Paffenbarger, R. S., Powell, K. E., & Yeager, K. K. (1992). Determinants of physical activity and interventions in adults. *Medicine and Science in Sports and Exercise, 24,* S221–S236.

King, A. C., Haskell, W. L., Young, D. R., Oka, R. K., & Stefanick, M. L. (1995). Long-term effects of varying intensities and formats of physical activity on participation rates, fitness, and lipoproteins in men and women aged 50 to 65 years. *Circulation, 9,* 2596–2604.

King, A. C., Taylor, C. B., Haskell, W. L., & DeBusk, R. F. (1990). Identifying strategies for increasing employee physical activity levels: Findings from the Stanford/Lockheed exercise survey. *Health Education Quarterly, 17,* 269–285.

LaFontaine, T. P., DiLorenzo, T. M., Frensch, P. A., Stucky-Ropp, R. C., Bargman,

E. P., & McDonald, D. G. (1992). Aerobic exercise and mood: A brief review, 1985–1990. *Sports Medicine, 13,* 160–170.

Lakka, T. A., Venalaninen, J. H., Rauramaa, R., Salonen, R., Tuomilehto, J., & Salonen, J. (1994). Relation of leisure-time physical activity and cardiorespiratory fitness to the risk of acute myocardial infarction in men. *New England Journal of Medicine, 330,* 1549–1554.

Leon, A. S., Connett, J., Jacobs, D. R., & Rauramaa, R. (1987). Leisure-time physical activity levels and risk for coronary heart disease and death: The Multiple Risk Factor Intervention Trial. *Journal of the American Medical Association, 258,* 2388–2395.

Marcus, B. H., Banspach, S. W., Lefebvre, R. C., Rossi, J. S., Carleton, R. A., & Abrams, D. B. (1992). Using the stages of change model to increase the adoption of physical activity among community participants. *American Journal of Health Promotion, 6,* 424–429.

Marcus, B. H., Bock, B. C., Pinto, B. M., Forsyth, L., Roberts, M., & Traficante, R. (1998). Efficacy of individualized, motivationally tailored physical activity intervention. *Annals of Behavioral Medicine, 20,* 174–180.

Marcus, B. H., Dubbert, P. M., Forsyth, L. H., McKenzie, T. L., Stone, E. J., Dunn, A. L., & Blair, S. N. (2000). Physical activity behavior change: Issues in adoption and maintenance. *Health Psychology, 19*(Suppl. 1), 32–41.

Marcus, B. H., Emmons, K. M., Simkin-Silverman, L. R., Linnan, L. A., Taylor, E. R., Bock, B. C., Roberts, M. B., Rossi, J. S., & Abrams, D. B. (1998). Evaluation of motivationally tailored vs. standard self-help physical activity interventions at the workplace. *American Journal of Health Promotion, 12,* 246–253.

Marcus, B. H., Nigg, C. R., Riebe, D., & Forsyth, L. H. (2000). Interactive communication strategies: Implications for population-based physical-activity promotion. *American Journal of Preventive Medicine, 19*(2), 121–126.

Marcus, B. H., Owen, N., Forsyth, L. H., Cavill, N. A., & Fridinger, F. (1998). Physical activity interventions using mass media, print media, and information technology. *American Journal of Preventive Medicine, 15,* 362–378.

Marcus, B. H., Rakowski, W., & Rossi, J. S. (1992). Assessing motivational readiness and decision-making for exercise. *Health Psychology, 11,* 257–261.

Marcus, B. H., Rossi, J. S., Selby, V. C., Niaura, R. S., & Abrams, D. B. (1992). The stages and processes of exercise adoption and maintenance in a worksite sample. *Health Psychology, 11,* 386–395.

Marcus, B. H., Selby, V. C., Niaura, R. S., & Rossi, J. S. (1992). Self-efficacy and the stages of exercise behavior change. *Research Quarterly for Exercise and Sport, 63,* 60–66.

Marcus, B. H., & Stanton, A. L. (1993). Evaluation of relapse prevention and reinforcement interventions to promote exercise adherence in sedentary females. *Research Quarterly for Exercise and Sport, 64,* 447–452.

McAuley, E., Blissmer, B., Katula, J., Duncan, T. E., & Mihalko, S. L. (2000). Physical activity, self-esteem, and self-efficacy relationships in older adults: A randomized controlled trial. *Annals of Behavioral Medicine, 22,* 131–139.

McAuley, E., Wraith, S., & Duncan, T. E. (1991). Self-efficacy, perceptions of success, and intrinsic motivation for exercise. *Journal of Applied Social Psychology, 21,* 139–155.

McNeill, B. W., & Stoltenberg, C. D. (1989). Reconceptualizing social influence in counseling: The elaboration likelihood model. *Journal of Counseling Psychology, 36,* 24–33.

Miller, W. R. (1983). Motivational interviewing with problem drinkers. *Behavioural Psychotherapy, 11*, 147–172.

Miller, W. R. (1985). Motivation for treatment: A review with special emphasis on alcoholism. *Psychological Bulletin, 98*, 84–107.

Miller, W. R., & Rollnick, S. (1991). *Motivational interviewing. Preparing people to change addictive behavior.* New York: Guilford.

National Institutes of Health. (1995). *Consensus development conference statement on physical activity and cardiovascular health.* Bethesda, MD: Author.

Oman, R. F., & McAuley, E. (1993). Intrinsic motivation and exercise behavior. *Journal of Health Education, 24*, 232–238.

Paffenbarger, R. S., Hyde, R. T., Wing, A. L., Lee, I. M., Jung, D. L., & Kambert, J. B. (1993). The association of changes in physical-activity level and other lifestyle characteristics with mortality among men. *New England Journal of Medicine, 328*, 538–545.

Pate, R. R., Pratt, M., Blair, S. N., Haskell, W. L., Macera, C. A., Bouchard, C., Buchner, D., Caspersen, C. J., Ettinger, W., Heath, G. W., King, A. C., Kriska, A., Leon, A. S., Marcus, B. H., Morris, J., Paffenbarger, R. S., Patrick, K., Pollock, M. L., Rippe, J. M., Sallis, J., & Wilmore, J. H. (1995). Physical activity and public health: A recommendation from the Centers for Disease Control and Prevention and the American College of Sports Medicine. *Journal of the American Medical Association, 273*, 402–407.

Pinto, B. M., Clark, M. M., Cruess, D. G., Szymanski, L., & Pera, V. (1999). Changes in self-efficacy and decisional balance for exercise among obese women in a weight management program. *Obesity Research, 7*(3), 288–292.

Powell, K. E., Thompson, P. D., Caspersen, C. J., & Kendrick, J. S. (1987). Physical activity and the incidence of coronary heart disease. *Annual Review of Public Health, 8*, 253–287.

Prochaska, J. O., & DiClemente, C. C. (1983). Stages and processes of self-change of smoking: Toward an integrative model of change. *Journal of Consulting and Clinical Psychology, 51*, 390–395.

Prochaska, J. O., DiClemente, C. C., & Norcross, J. C. (1992). In search of how people change. *American Psychologist, 47*, 1102–1114.

Prochaska, J. O., Velicer, W. F., Rossi, J. S., Goldstein, M. G., Marcus, B. H., Rakowski, W., Fiore, C., Harlow, L. L., Redding, C. A., Rosenbloom, D., & Rossi, S. R. (1994). Stages of change and decisional balance for twelve problem behaviors. *Health Psychology, 13*, 39–46.

Raglin, J. S. (1990). Exercise and mental health: Beneficial and detrimental effects. *Sports Medicine, 9*, 323–329.

Rosenstock, I. M. (1974). Historical origins of the health belief model. *Health Education Monographs, 2*, 328–335.

Ryan, R. M., & Deci, E. L. (2000). Self-determination theory and the facilitation of intrinsic motivation, social development, and well-being. *American Psychologist, 55*, 68–78.

Sallis, J. F., Haskell, W. L., Fortmann, S. P., Vranizan, K. M., Taylor, C. B., & Solomon, D. S. (1986). Predictors of adoption and maintenance of physical activity in a community sample. *Preventive Medicine, 15*, 331–341.

Sidney, S., Jacobs, D. R., Haskell, W. L., Armstrong, M. A., Dimicco, A., Oberman, A., Savage, P. J., Slattery, M. L., Sternfeld, B., & Van Horn, L. (1991). Comparison of two methods of assessing physical activity in the Coronary Artery Risk Development in Young Adults (CARDIA) Study. *American Journal of Epidemiology, 133*, 1231–1245.

Simkin, L. R., & Gross, A. M. (1994). Assessment of coping with high-risk situations for exercise relapse among healthy women. *Health Psychology, 13*, 274–277.

Smith, D. E., Heckemeyer, C. M., Kratt, P. P., & Mason, D. A. (1997). Motivational interviewing to improve adherence to a behavioral weight control program for older obese women with NIDDM: A pilot study. *Diabetes Care, 20*, 53–54.

Sullum, J., Clark, M. M., & King, T. K. (2000). Predictors of exercise relapse in a college population. *Journal of American College Health, 48*, 175–180.

Taylor, W. C., Baranowski, T., & Young, D. R. (1998). Physical activity interventions in low-income, ethnic minority, and populations with disability. *American Journal of Preventive Medicine, 15*, 334–343.

Treasure, J., & Ward, A. (1997). A practical guide to the use of motivational interviewing for anorexia nervosa. *European Eating Disorders Review, 5*, 102–114.

U.S. Department of Health and Human Services. (1996). *Physical activity and health: A report of the Surgeon-General.* Atlanta, GA: Author, Centers for Disease Control and Prevention, National Center for Chronic Disease Prevention and Health Promotion.

Wankel, L. M. (1984). Decision-making and social support strategies for increasing exercise involvement. *Journal of Cardiac Rehabilitation, 4*, 124–135.

Young, D. R., King, A. C., Oka, R. K., & Haskell, W. L. (1994). Are older women really less active than men? Findings from a community sample. *Medicine, Exercise, Nutrition and Health, 3*, 66–73.

Promotion of Physical Activity Through Community Development

David A. Dzewaltowski, Paul A. Estabrooks,
Nancy C. Gyurcsik, and Judy A. Johnston

Policymakers and scientists have recognized that daily physical activity is central to decreasing the risk for chronic disease and increasing quality of life (U.S. Department of Health and Human Services [USDHHS], 2000). The American College of Sports Medicine and the Centers of Disease Control and Prevention have recommended that every U.S. adult should accumulate 30 minutes or more of moderate-intensity physical activity on most, preferably all, days of the week (Pate et al., 1995). However, the majority of adults are not meeting this guideline. As a result, the promotion of physical activity has become a high public health priority.

This chapter describes a theory-based community development framework to guide health promotion initiatives. This framework directs practitioners and scientists to move the focus of physical activity promotion strategies from program delivery within a facility to community development. In addition to formal structured exercise settings, community development strategies include the use of schools, clubs, parks, homes, work sites, and senior centers.

Although policymakers, community members, practitioners, and scientists share a common interest in developing and maintaining a community that can be described as healthy, consistent problems have occurred in documenting success within an ecologically valid model. Recently, however, Abrams, Emmons, and Linnan (1997) have defined

Our team is supported by 1 RO1 HD37367-01 cofunded by the National Institute of Child Health and Human Development, the National Institute of Nursing Research, the Office of Disease Prevention, the National Institute of Allergy and Infectious Diseases, and the Office of Dietary Supplements.

a successful strategy to assess impact of public health interventions on populations. The common measurement of intervention efficiency combines both the effectiveness of the intervention (e.g., the efficacy of a randomized clinical trial) and the reach of that intervention into a defined population (Abrams et al., 1997). Hence, the community impact of any given public health initiative is the product of the intervention's efficacy and reach.

For example, Project Active, a clinic-based professionally staffed program, documented that intensive interventions delivered at a specialty clinic can be successful in increasing the physical activity of sedentary adults (e.g., Dunn et al., 1999). Although Project Active has demonstrated *efficacy* for improving individual physical activity and health risk, the strategy is likely to have low *reach* (i.e., the proportion reached relative to the entire target population of sedentary adults). It is unlikely that structured exercise classes or counseling by experts alone can reach a large percentage of the population, especially among individuals who lack motivation to change. Alternatively, mass marketing campaigns that promote physical activity through radio and television advertisements may have a large reach, but they may lack efficacy to change health behavior.

This chapter begins by outlining an ecologically informed, social cognitive theory-based model, the Healthy Places Framework. Basic research supporting components of the model are reviewed. Then preliminary evidence is presented for the framework. The chapter concludes with practical tips on implementing the Healthy Places Framework in community settings.

The Healthy Places Framework

The Healthy Places Framework includes three underlying strategies. The first strategy is to combine community networks (new or existing) and theory-based initiatives that target a place to enhance both the reach and the efficacy of initiatives, resulting in a large public health impact. The second strategy is to target leaders in the places where people live, learn, work, and play to make the public health impact self-sustaining over time. The third strategy is to sustain contact with a place over time to reach and build a defined population's capacity for a lifestyle of physical activity. To successfully implement the Healthy Places

Framework and to have public health impact, it is necessary for many leaders to have the skills and beliefs to lead the development of healthy places. This approach shifts the role and responsibility of the practicing expert (e.g., an exercise and sport psychologist) from a person who delivers interventions to a consultant who trains local leaders.

Healthy Places Ecological Model

The ecological model suggests that a broad group of people who maintain involvement in healthy environments influences physical activity and leadership behaviors (Brofenbrenner, 1999; Dzewaltowski, 1997; Sallis & Owen, 1997). The interaction of individuals within their social and physical environments—the ecological relationship—occurs in community places such as schools (out-of-school programs), homes, parks, clubs, senior centers, and places of worship. Barker (1968) completed extensive work on the ecological relationship and coined the term "behavior setting," the physical and social environment in which behaviors take place.

The public health challenge is to implement and evaluate strategies that target the development of behavior settings that contain critical elements to promote healthy individual and group behavior, which we call "healthy places." This is a difficult task because community strategies targeting the places where individuals live, learn, work, and play must be applied at multiple organizational levels to have adequate reach. For example, to reach all western Kansas afterschool programs in a cost-effective way, it is necessary to target regional and community systems that come in contact with the leaders of children on a daily basis. By defining levels of influence, ecological theory helps identify where to target strategies to promote change (Brofenbrenner, 1999; McLeroy, Bibeau, Steckler, & Glanz, 1988). Central to the ecological approach is reaching the leaders who make the day-to-day decisions that in aggregate determine the success or failure of an initiative. These leaders are the volunteers, teachers, coaches, and parents who can develop a healthy place.

Figure 10.1 provides a description of the multiple levels of environment that can be informed and monitored. It illustrates the implementation of the Healthy Places Framework with a middle school target audience and three targeted behavior settings (afterschool programs, school lunch, school classroom). By connecting individuals and groups across systems, the Healthy Places Ecological Model develops a leader

Figure 10.1

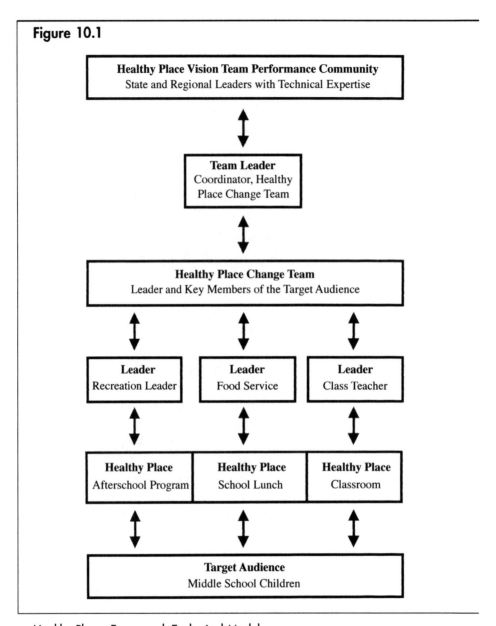

Healthy Places Framework Ecological Model.

community to facilitate the flow of knowledge to the individuals whose day-to-day behaviors affect the development of critical elements in environments that influence the target audience. Therefore, an expert or small team can obtain sustained influence, reach, and, ultimately impact, on a defined population by connecting individuals and groups and increasing the flow of knowledge to leaders who build healthy places.

Target Audience Level

Picture a healthy place where all people can live, learn, work, and play and be physically active? What do healthy places look like? The ecology of these places should have at least four critical elements: connection, autonomy, skill building, and healthy norms (CASH; Dzewaltowski, Johnston, Estabrooks, & Johannes, 2000). People need a place where they feel connected and have a sense of belonging. People who feel detached and isolated will neither enter nor return to participate (Catalano & Hawkins, 1996). People also need a place where they have control over their actions, or autonomy (Bandura, 1986; Deci & Ryan, 1985). Healthy places encourage people to make choices and learn from their successes and failures. People need a place where they can build skills and efficacy and demonstrate those skills (Bandura, 1986). Skills are important to long-term success, and success is about becoming competent at something that is positive and healthy. Furthermore, people need a place where the group norm is healthy behavior (Forsyth, 2000). All too often, people do not have the opportunity to be healthy, and places may not offer healthy examples or intentionally encourage healthy choices. Although the Healthy Places Framework presents these conceptual hypotheses in a novel manner, considerable research exists to support the influence of well-structured physical and social environments on individual capacity and healthy behavior (e.g., Bandura, 1986; Barker, 1968; Eccles & Roeser, 1999; Forsyth, 2000).

Change Team Level

At the change team level, the Healthy Places Framework focuses on critical elements of environments that are the antecedents of mediators of individual and group environmental change behavior. The team environment's influence on group mediators and behavior is best described by group dynamics literature. Group dynamics refers to the interactions and social environment associated with group membership (Carron & Hausenblas, 1998). The importance of group dynamics to healthy place development resides in its ability to identify: (a) the processes that mediate when groups excel at the tasks they attempt, and (b) group influences on members' self-conceptions (Forsyth, 2000).

When Do People Within Healthy Places Excel at the Tasks They Attempt?

Fundamentally, for a healthy place to be effective, it must exist. Thus, people must work together to create healthy places. Cohesion is essential. Cohesion has a further effect on the functioning of change teams over and above simply connecting its members together. Mullen and Copper (1994) performed a meta-analysis on the cohesion-performance relationship by using a wide range of work groups (e.g., sport, military, experimental). They found a consistent and significant, yet modest, relationship between cohesion and performance. To be consistent with the individual motivation literature, the Healthy Places Framework describes a behavior setting that includes opportunities for connection to allow for individual development of perceptions of cohesion.

Beyond cohesion, other group factors also affect performance. Although the literature is sparse, roles within the group should be related to productivity. Within a community team, three representations of member roles should be present—role choice (or acceptance if the role is assigned), role clarity, and role performance (Carron & Hausenblas, 1998). A community with the goal of improving activity will be most effective when the members have a choice in the roles they fulfill and are clear on the responsibilities related to those roles. In a team, if the members are excited (accepting) about their roles and have a clear understanding of the behaviors necessary to perform those roles, then overall group productivity will improve (Carron & Hausenblas, 1998). Again, to be consistent with individual literature, we describe places that include a critical level of individual choice as providing autonomy.

Group Influences on Members' Self-Conceptions

Although community strategies typically have expected group outcomes, these outcomes are ultimately realized through the individual behavior of members within the group. This does not mean that the group outcomes could be realized by individuals working in isolation, but rather, that a concentrated effort of member role fulfillment is necessary. Hence, individual self-conception relative to member roles is an important avenue of understanding for the change team. Indeed, membership in a group is hypothesized to result in an array of individual cognitive, affective, and motivational processes (Forsyth, 2000). Of the group variables, cohesion seems to have the greatest impact on individual self-conceptions. For example, in physical activity groups made up of older adults, those participants with higher perceptions of group cohesion around the task and social components of the environment were more likely to have better attitudes (outcome expectations) and control (self-efficacy) beliefs than those with lower perceptions of cohesion (Estabrooks & Carron, 1999a, 2000). Thus, consistent with the individual literature, it appears that providing the opportunity to participate in an environment that connects people, promotes individual autonomy, and helps build personal skills and efficacy leads to increased personal capacity for healthy place development.

Preliminary Evidence for the Healthy Places Framework

Connecting leaders through the ecological model and providing knowledge of the critical elements of healthy places are achieved through community team and leader development. Central to the success of communities building healthy places is the development of the group- and individual-level skills and efficacy of local professionals and volunteers to lead healthy community development efforts. Figure 10.1 illustrates the potential levels in the framework. It is possible to increase the number of levels at the top, alternating between leaders (individuals) and groups to increase the reach of the expert team. For example, in a Kansas-wide prevention initiative, a state-wide vision team trains regional leaders, who train community teams. From the community teams flow local leaders of healthy place change teams.

The Kansas Leadership to Encourage Activity and Nutrition (LEAN) School Health Project, which was initially developed in 1992, also has provided preliminary experiences and evidence for the Healthy Places Framework. Phase I of the project tested the framework in two communities in Kansas. The goal of Phase I was to reduce cardiovascular disease risk in elementary children by promoting nutrition and physical activity. Building on the experiences in Phase I, in 1996, a revised version of the framework was tested in Phase II in six communities. Again, the model was refined and is now being tested in Phase III in four communities.

The Phase I framework had three group goals: (a) modified school lunches to decrease fat content, (b) enhanced nutrition education, and (c) increased opportunities for physical activity. The central strategy was to develop a school and community partnership coalition that provided its members with opportunities for bonding, role choice and acceptance, and capacity development. A monitoring and feedback system was used by the coalition in Phase I to document the partnerships' activities and to track how the school and community became healthier by increasing opportunities for healthy choices (community changes). Graphing of community changes, services provided, and community actions permitted regular feedback on partnership leadership and staff. Feedback enabled the collaborators to detect and celebrate early successes and see increased group efficacy and cohesion. The data from these multiple case studies showed that environmental change-focused group and individual levels of community development can be effective in altering school and community environments to promote physical activity and healthy eating patterns (Harris, Andrews, Richter, Lewis, & James, 1997; Harris, Richter, Paine-Andrews, & Lewis, 1997; Harris, Richter, Schultz, & Johnston, 1998; Johnston, Marmet, Coen, Fawcett, & Harris, 1996).

The Phase II framework was modified to include less direct involvement by experts in the healthy place change team (and therefore, more involvement of local leadership) and was tested in six communities from 1996 through 1999. The multiple case study design tracked school changes in target grades each spring throughout the study period. Student cardiovascular endurance as well as upper-body and abdominal muscular strength and endurance showed significant improvement. Therefore, it appears that physical activity promotion efforts developed by school/community partnerships to meet the specific needs of the school and its community can affect student fitness (Noble et al., 2000).

The Kansas LEAN School Health Project (Phases I and II) showed that allowing local leaders and groups to craft the interventions to the local resources and cultures is very important with respect to institutionalization of programs. In the Kansas project, each school learned to develop, tailor, and manage their own interventions. From Phase II data, local leaders learned that coalitions (change teams) should focus on making small changes to build a sense of group efficacy. These small changes build relationships among key players and forge alliances among diverse groups. Coalitions that have attempted big changes early in the process often fail because the task is too difficult, which leads to a decrease in group efficacy and persistence in the face of difficulty.

Tips to Implement the Healthy Places Framework

The Healthy Places Framework creates a community of leaders whose goal is to develop places that provide four critical elements: connection, autonomy, skill building, and healthy norms. At the target audience level, the leader develops a social and physical environment that promotes healthy norms promoting physical activity. At the change team level, or at higher levels in the ecological model (Figure 10.1), the leader develops a social and physical environment (group) that promotes healthy norms building healthy places. Below are some steps or tips for the leaders of healthy place development efforts.

1. Connect People to Form Groups Targeting Healthy Place Development

If you always do what you have always done, you always get what you always got. If the formal, recognized leaders in the field of physical activity are the only ones brought together to plan, there will be little reach and innovation, and the needs of the target audience may not be met. When discussing intervention implications of group dynamics theory, it is important to ensure optimal member attributes and group resources. Connect with a wide variety of people. Invite people to the table who may have an interest in either physical activity or the targeted place. If you are working at the change team level, invite parents, grandparents, childcare providers, business people, and health care providers in addition to the parks and recreation staff, Little League coaches, and physical education teachers. Within schools, be sure that all student groups are represented, not just the athletes and National Honor Society members. Not only will you learn what people want, but you also will receive advice that will prevent mistakes. Community intervention is about developing leadership skills in a variety of people. Those same skills can be put to use throughout the community in several ways, but the first experience can be focused on physical activity.

2. Facilitate Connection and Autonomy Within Groups

Connection can be enhanced in several ways in a community team. Typically, a variety of team-building activities can connect people to provide opportunity for coalitions to become cohesive. These activities usually focus on providing the group with feelings of opportunities for connection and autonomy. Enhancing feelings of distinctiveness provides a sense of connection and can be achieved through several mechanisms. A common component of intervention includes providing the coalition and program with a distinctive name and logo (determined by coalition members). The name and logo can be used on letterhead, clothing, and posters advertising the program (Estabrooks & Carron,

1999b). The development of interaction and communication within the group also has been shown to improve connection (Hill & Estabrooks, 2000).

One strategy called "timeline" is a group facilitation process that aids the development of group connection by allowing a group to look at the stories that make up their past and to learn from that reflection (Clark & Heiny, 1997). The timeline reflects the thoughts, memories, and perceptions of group members and is not a history lesson based on "facts." The timeline is used to create a social connection among the group members and an understanding of the group vision. For example, in the middle school project mentioned in Figure 10.1, team leaders were asked to remember what physical activity environments were like when they were in middle school. On a large piece of paper, the group facilitator drew a timeline broken into segments, labeled 1960, 1970, 1980, and 1990. School leaders placed their names on the timeline when they were in middle school. They also drew a picture of a key personal event that reminded them of what physical activity environments were like during their middle school years. Group connection develops through the shared timeline experience and insight into personal past experiences, prepares people to participate in the cocreation of the future, brings a sense of shared identity by observing things in the past that are valued, and promotes discovery of the need to change.

3. Build Group Skill Building Around Strategic Planning

Although it is easier to implement and evaluate delivering a standardized program, environmental change is essential for long-term behavior change. This kind of change generally grows out of a recognition by several individuals that "things aren't quite right." This recognition must be followed by a vision of "how things should be." At the core of successful group functioning is the unity of the coalition around its primary outcome (i.e., vision and mission; Brawley, Carron, & Widmeyer, 1992). This point may seem intuitive; however, many groups form with a vague mission and never fully realize their reason for existence. Often, team outcomes can be identified early in the group's formation (within the first or second meeting). Autonomy as well as a clear vision and mission will support a community group and help it grow.

Two techniques that have been used to assist groups to identify primary outcomes are "listening sessions" and VMSOA (described below). A listening session is a simple and inexpensive way to engage a group in planning and defining outcomes. The group process begins with brainstorming answers to the following series of questions:

- If we get it right, what will it look like? (The most effective discussions remove funding for the project from the discussion.)
- Who will oppose us and why?
- What barriers are there that might make it difficult for us to achieve our dream?
- What are the experiences of this group or other groups in our community that we can learn from as we begin our work?
- Who else needs to be invited to join our group?

By answering these questions collectively, unity within the group will emerge around primary outcomes that are appropriate to the resources and makeup of the specific community.

Following the listening sessions, it is important to direct the activity of the group toward defining specific objectives to reach a desired outcome. VMSOA is a format, developed originally by the Kansas Health Foundation (2000) and modified here, that provides structure to the group planning process. The "V" is vision, a short and memorable description of an ideal condition the group is seeking. The "M" is the mission statement, what the group is trying to accomplish and why. The "S" is strategies, the broad approaches that the group will use to reach the desired outcome (e.g., targeting the development of places such as after-school programs to promote activity). The "O" is objectives, a statement of what and how much will be accomplished to build critical elements in healthy places, who will accomplish it, and by when. (There will be multiple objectives under each strategy.) The "A" is the timeline-based action steps that reflect the plan of work necessary to meet the objectives.

4. Facilitate Positive Group Norms Through Coalition Leadership

Researchers have reported that a group's cohesion interacts with the group's normative behaviors to determine productivity (Gammage, Carron, & Estabrooks, 2001). Group norms, once established, take a long time to change. As such, small assignments should be made for individual coalition members during any introductory meetings. Leaders should follow up with each individual in the group to ensure that assignments are done. Public description of the completion of assignments indicates to the group that the normative behavior is to complete assignments in a timely fashion. The follow-up by leaders can be reduced until it is no longer necessary and tasks are being completed because of participants adhering to group norms rather than responding to leader prompts.

5. Staff Roles Should Ebb and Flow From Facilitator to Adviser to Coach to Cheerleader

Community interventions must be designed and owned by the community group. For groups to be successful, all participants need experience in leadership, project coordination, and confidence in their ability to lead a diverse group. These growth experiences can be painful for the staff, but they are essential for the group to function effectively. The staff must be willing to support group members when they stumble while developing their leadership style, when they put the group's activities on the back burner so they can attend to other responsibilities, and when they change directions in the middle of a project. When these things happen, and they will, the staff must assist them in finding new direction or refining their leadership roles and responsibilities. It is appropriate for the staff to provide a menu of intervention options, to provide training as needed (and to accept the group's decisions about what they want to know and when they want to know it), to help articulate desired outcomes, to coach and encourage progress, and to celebrate successes.

6. Document Success

Groups involved in community intervention need information based on evaluation to inform their work. For example, they need to know how their group is functioning: Are the right people involved? Are their roles appropriate and comfortable? Do they have the skills they need to do the work or access to those who have the skills and can teach them? Do they have a vision of "What it will look like if we get it right"? And most important, Are they achieving their objectives? A group must be able to monitor its own development as a group and use that monitoring information to make decisions about how to proceed.

To assess if a given behavior setting is a healthy place, the Healthy Youth Places Evaluation (HYPE; Dzewaltowski et al., 2000) was developed. Based on the postulate that the development of the individual's capacity for health behavior and leadership is the result of sustained interaction in a healthy environment, the primary outcome of the HYPE is the total time youth spend in contact with the healthy place initiative. The impact can be documented as the product of the initiative's reach, frequency, and duration. Hence, a place can enhance its impact by increasing the duration or frequency of involvement of youth already participating in a healthy place or by increasing the participation of the number of youth. The HYPE also provides opportunity for the assessment of the presence (or absence) of the critical elements of a healthy place. That is, the quality of connection, autonomy, skill building, healthy norms, reach, and appeal can be documented. Exhibit 10.1 provides an outline of the steps necessary to complete the HYPE.

Exhibit 10.1

Steps Necessary to Complete the Healthy Youth Places Evaluation

Please follow all of the steps below, and complete the strategy sheets necessary to document activities in your school that target improving your students' fruit and vegetable consumption during school lunch and physical activity participation in the hours after school.

1. Target a place. Record that place.
2. State and document an objective that answers *one* of the following two questions:
   • How will we develop a healthy place?
   • How will we contact the participants and attract them to a place?
   • Record the start and end dates of the objective.
3. Document the frequency (contact periods per week), duration (length of contact periods), and reach (number of children contacted).
4. Identify and describe the targeted connection, autonomy, skill building, and healthy norms (CASH) processes of the objective. Then, do the following:
   • Describe how the objective affects CASH in the place.
   • Provide a rating of the quality of each of the processes (1 = *low*; 5 = *high*).
   • If a particular objective does not target these processes, leave the descriptions blank and record a "0" for the quality of each process.
5. Identify the targeted appeal processes of the objective. Then, do the following:
   • Describe how the objective affects task and social appeal of the place for the students.
   • Provide a rating of the quality of each of the processes (1 = *low*; 5 = *high*).
   • If a particular objective does not target these processes, leave the descriptions blank and record a "0" for the quality of each process.

Final Tip: Use the Targeted Process Questions from Steps 4 and 5 to assist you in identifying objectives that will create and draw your students to the healthy place.

Summary

The Healthy Places Framework directs practitioners and scientists to move the focus of physical activity promotion strategies from program delivery in a facility to community development. Healthy places are behavior settings at schools, clubs, parks, homes, work sites, and senior centers that give an adequate level of connection, autonomy, skill building, and healthy norms. Researchers and practitioners are encouraged to develop resources (intervention tools, measures) to support community development efforts that promote physical activity.

References

Abrams, D. B., Emmons, K. M., & Linnan, L. A. (1997). Health behavior and health education: The past, present, and future. In K. Glanz, F. M. Lewis, & B. K. Rimer (Eds.), *Health behavior and health education: Theory, research, and practice* (2nd ed., pp. 453–478). San Francisco, CA: Jossey-Bass.

Bandura, A. (1986). *Social foundations of thought and action: A social cognitive theory.* Englewood Cliffs, NJ: Prentice-Hall.

Barker, R. G. (1968). *Ecological psychology.* Stanford, CA: Stanford University Press.

Brawley, L. R., Carron, A. V., & Widmeyer, W. N. (1992). The nature of group goals in sport teams: A phenomenological analysis. *The Sport Psychologist, 6,* 323–333.

Brofenbrenner, U. (1999). Environments in developmental perspective: Theoretical and operational models. In S. L. Friedman & T. D. Wachs (Eds.), *Measuring environment across the life span: Emerging methods and concepts* (pp. 3–28). Washington, DC: American Psychological Association.

Carron, A. V., & Hausenblas, H. A. (1998). *Group dynamics in sport* (2nd ed.). Morgantown: Fitness Information Technology.

Catalano, R. F., & Hawkins, J. D. (1996). The social development model: A theory of antisocial behavior. In J. D. Hawkins (Ed.), *Delinquency and crime: Current theories.* New York: Cambridge University Press.

Clark, M. J., & Heiny, P. (1997). *Timeline: The complete guide to facilitation.* Richmond, IN: Contemporary Consulting.

Deci, E. L., & Ryan, R. M. (1985). *Intrinsic motivation and self-determination in human behavior.* New York: Plenum Press.

Dunn, A., Marcus, B., Kampert, J., Garcia, M., Kohl, H., & Blair, S. (1999). Comparison of lifestyle and structured interventions to increase physical activity and cardiorespiratory fitness. *Journal of the American Medical Association, 281,* 327–334.

Dzewaltowski, D. A. (1997). The ecology of physical activity and sport: Merging science and practice. *Journal of Applied Sport Psychology, 9,* 254–276.

Dzewaltowski, D. A., Johnston, J. A., Estabrooks, P. A., & Johannes, E. (2000, October). *Healthy places.* Paper presented at the Kansas State Research and Extension Annual Conference, Manhattan.

Eccles, J. S., & Roeser, R. W. (1999). School and community influences on human development. In M. H. Bornstein & M. E. Lamb (Eds.), *Developmental psychology: An advanced textbook.* Mahwah, NJ: Erlbaum.

Estabrooks, P. A., & Carron, A. V. (1999a). The influence of the group with elderly exercisers. *Small Group Research, 30,* 438–452.

Estabrooks, P. A., & Carron, A. V. (1999b). Group cohesion in older adult exercisers: Prediction and intervention effects. *Journal of Behavioral Medicine, 22,* 575–588.

Estabrooks, P. A., & Carron, A. V. (2000). Predicting scheduling self-efficacy in older adult exercisers: The role of task cohesion. *Journal of Aging and Physical Activity, 8,* 41–50.

Forsyth, D. R. (2000). One hundred years of groups research: Introduction to the Special Issue. *Group Dynamics: Theory, Research and Practice, 4,* 3–6.

Gammage, K. L., Carron, A. V., & Estabrooks, P. A. (2001). Team cohesion and individual productivity: The influence of the norm for productivity and personal identifiability. *Small Group Research, 32,* 3–18.

Harris, K. J., Andrews, A., Richter, K., Lewis, R. J., & James, V. (1997). Reducing elementary school children's risks for chronic diseases through school lunch modifications, nutrition education, and physical activity interventions. *Journal of Nutrition Education, 29,* 196–202.

Harris, K. J., Richter, K., Paine-Andrews, A., & Lewis, R. (1997). Community partnerships: Review of selected models and evaluation of two case studies. *Journal of Nutrition Education, 29,* 189–195.

Harris, K. J., Richter, K., Schultz, J., & Johnston, J. (1998). Formative, process, and intermediate outcome evaluation of a pilot school-based 5 a Day for Better Health project. *American Journal of Health Promotion, 12,* 378–381.

Hill, J. L., & Estabrooks, P. A. (2000, September). *The relationships between group interaction and cohesion in exercise classes for older adults.* Paper presented at the annual meeting of the Association for the Advancement of Applied Sport Psychology, Nashville, TN.

Johnston, J. A., Marmet, P. F., Coen, S., Fawcett, S. B., & Harris, K. J. (1996). Kansas LEAN: An effective coalition for nutrition education and dietary change. *Journal of Nutrition Education, 28,* 115–118.

Kansas Health Foundation. (2000). *VMSOA: An approach to strategic planning.* Wichita: Kansas Health Foundation.

McLeroy, K. R., Bibeau, D., Steckler, A., & Glanz, K. (1988). An ecological perspective on health promotion programs. *Health Education Quarterly, 15,* 351–377.

Mullen, B., & Copper, C. (1994). The relationship between group cohesiveness and performance: An integration. *Psychological Bulletin, 115,* 210–227.

Noble, J. M., Dzewaltowski, D. A., Roussos, S. T., Welk, G. J., Ryan, G. J., & Johnston, J. (2000, November). *Kansas LEAN school health project: Physical activity promotion component.* Paper presented at the annual meeting of the American Public Health Association, Boston, MA.

Pate, R. R., Pratt, M., Blair, S. N., Haskell, W. L., Macera, C. A., Bouchard, C., Buchner, D., Ettinger, W., Health, G. W., King, A. C., Kriska, A., Leon, A. S., Marcus, B. H., Morris, J., Paffenbarger, R. S., Patrick, K., Pollock, M. L., Rippe, J. M., Sallis, J., & Wilmore, J. H. (1995). Physical activity and public health: A recommendation from the Centers for Disease Control and Prevention and the American College of Sports Medicine. *Journal of the American Medical Association, 273,* 402–407.

Sallis, J. F., & Owen, N. (1997). Ecological models. In K. Glanz, F. M. Lewis, & B. K. Rimer (Eds.), *Health behavior and health education: Theory, research, and practice* (2nd ed., pp. 403–424). San Francisco, CA: Jossey-Bass.

U.S. Department of Health and Human Services. (2000). *Healthy People 2010: Understanding and improving health* (2nd ed.). Washington, DC: U.S. Government Printing Office.

Guidelines for Clinical Application of Exercise Therapy for Mental Health Case Studies

Wes Sime

Will is a 55-year-old marketing and sales executive. He is married with two preteen daughters and is at risk of losing both his job and his marriage. Lack of communication and frequent anger outbursts precipitate tension and conflict at home and at work. He has had great difficulty changing his hostile, reactive behavior even after numerous traditional counseling sessions that spanned four months. Finally facing a crisis at work that could cost him his job, Will agreed to walk while thinking through his history and talking about his options for the future. Walking casually made it easier to address the possible roots of his anger. Will's father, now deceased, was physically and emotionally abusive, but Will had always protected his father's image, refusing to acknowledge the hurt and anger that resulted from it. Walking side-by-side with the therapist and enjoying the scenery attenuated Will's resistance and allowed the therapist to penetrate the shield guarding Will's deep emotional trauma. Will had been advised to walk or exercise many times previously, but he just did not get around to it.

* * *

Bonnie is a 38-year-old public service employee. She has an excellent work record in spite of the fact that she is a victim of rape and childhood sexual abuse and has been diagnosed with posttraumatic stress disorder. She is married without children and is addicted to Internet relationships. She spends 4 to 6 hours per day in online "chat room" conversations and has difficulty with assertiveness because of low self-esteem. Bonnie is depressed and very anxious when interacting with people. She walks her dog somewhat regularly because she knows he needs exercise, but because the dog is tiny, she does not get much exercise herself. Bonnie has a treadmill in her house but finds it boring to use. She avoids unnecessary exercise but was willing to engage in "walk/talk" therapy after about six months of counseling, when her progress with the disorder came to a plateau. After a couple of walk/talk sessions, the counselor opted to increase intensity by climbing stairs in a five-story parking garage. It was an ideal exercise therapy challenge because the client was struggling with a weight problem and the additional effort seemed appropriate. The climbing was very slow, and Bonnie was encouraged to use a "rest step" common in mountain climbing. The exercise was stimulating but apparently too intense for Bonnie, because she stopped attending therapy. Six months later she returned to therapy for other reasons, but now is walking on her own three to four times per week for 30 to 40 minutes.

* * *

Amber is a 60-year-old executive secretary who is suffering from hypertension and a persistent anxiety disorder. She is a victim of child molestation, and when feeling self-conscious, she exhibits an inordinate flushing (reddening) of the neck that leaves her embarrassed and seeking isolation. After many years of therapy to confront the child molestation issues, Amber achieved only partial resolution of her symptoms. However, she discovered that the most effective element of the therapy she had experienced over the years was the combination of exercise and counseling. She found it easier to talk while walking and thus did not experience the flushing symptom. The greatest revelations about her traumatic history came to her either during or shortly after each of the exercise therapy sessions. Although her deepest anxiety triggers are still not fully resolved, the exercise gives her a very effective antidote that appears to be sufficient for her current needs. She exercises two to three times weekly on her own.

* * *

Donny is a 52-year-old retired Marine who is divorced from his wife. He had been verbally (and somewhat physically) abusive to his wife during the marriage and neglectful of his three adolescent children, who are now resisting court-ordered visitation. Communication between the two parents is hostile, and the effects spill over to the children. Negotiations regarding the custody, visitation, and supplemental medical expenses broke down because of the intense emotions felt by all parties. The therapist opted to visit with both parents about their respective complaints separately outside the traditional office setting, that is, while walking casually around the building. The outdoor temperature (about 50°F) seemed to cool the hostile emotions, and the walking allowed each of the clients to emote in a healthy way, separated from the target of their anger. The mediation was successful, in part, because the parents cooled off and dissipated their emotions with light exercise while problem solving in a rational manner. The children acquiesced to a healthy visitation arrangement that includes play and exercise with their father. The divorced parents are now able to resolve differences and prevent the heated emotional outbursts. "Cooling off" as a metaphor and walking as a way of working out problems served this client very well.

* * *

Matt is a 20-year-old college student who has a history of low self-esteem in spite of his outstanding academic ability and his talent for music. In his first serious romance with a young woman who appeared "needy," Matt was overwhelmed with compassion. He became emotionally dependent in the relationship and became seriously depressed when she pulled back in the relationship. It manifested in sleep disruption, irritability, and immobility. He was so obsessed with the thought of losing his good friend and first love that he could not get to sleep until 3–4 a.m. and then could not get up until midafternoon. Obviously he sacrificed his schoolwork, and eventually dropped out of school.

Matt had very little sport or exercise experience, but he did enjoy weight room workouts and extended bicycle trips with his brother. However, in the midst of his depression (during the winter), he could not get himself to engage in any physical activity. The therapist convinced Matt to try walking with him while counseling him about his academic future. Matt attempted to continue the activity by working out with his brother at home but ultimately failed. In consultation with his parents and the family physician, he was finally put on antidepressant medication. The exercise therapy was very effective in overcoming the depression temporarily, but during the winter season while under academic stress, pharmaceutical intervention was necessary to manage the ongoing crisis. One year later, Matt has only partially resolved the relationship problem and continues to struggle with depression and problems with sleep and academic performance. Occasional exercise experiences (e.g., four day skiing trip) provide dramatic mood elevation and abatement of symptoms, but the client is unable to maintain a regular schedule of activity in his home environment.

* * *

Waldo is a 55-year-old psychotherapist who has a long history of sport and recreational exercise. Waldo competed in sports that required intense training and experienced positive affect in the 24 to 48 hours following high-level aerobic and/or anaerobic activity. When discussing his exercise behavior with the therapist, Waldo acknowledged that he would sometimes avoid all activity and competition for 4 to 8 days at a time. As a result, he often succumbed to bad moods and relatively inefficient productivity. Waldo described his experiences with inadvertent exercise withdrawal as something that came upon him in such a gradual and insidious manner that it was almost beyond his awareness. As a result, he become much more empathic with his sedentary clients. Waldo told his therapist, "After a long period of lethargy when I finally get back to a regular habit of exercise, I wonder how I could have let myself get away from it that long (5–10 days). It feels so good after I workout once again, I must have been brain dead to have forgotten once again how important regular exercise is to me."

* * *

The psychological benefits of exercise are readily apparent to those who participate regularly. A growing body of scientific evidence shows that exercise is effective in both the treatment and prevention of various psychological disorders (Folkins & Sime, 1981; Petruzzello, Landers, & Salazar, 1993; Skrinar, Unger, Hutchinson, & Faigenbaum, 1992; Van Dixhoorn, Duivenvoorden, Pool, & Verhage, 1990). Thus, it is a concern that so few therapists are comfortable using exercise as therapy or feel competent or comfortable engaging in exercise or walk/talk therapy (McEntee & Halgin, 1996). The future holds some promise for expansion of these services as the concept of exercise therapy becomes more well known and understood.

The cases described previously are not fictitious examples. They are fairly typical clinical examples involving difficult situations in which exercise is a logical adjunctive treatment. These circumstances, and perhaps the personalities of the clients, however, are not all conducive to an easy course of therapy with either exercise or psychotherapy.

Physicians and mental health professionals often recommend exercise for their patients (Lehofer, Klebel, Gersdorf, & Zapotoczke, 1992). However, it should not be a surprise that when a therapist or a physician prescribes a treatment (like exercise) without providing either supervision or proper guidance, the patients either do not follow through at all or cannot maintain a regular program of exercise over the long term (Goldstein et al., 1999). It has been shown that intensive, sustained interventions are necessary even when exercise is prescribed by physicians, to achieve effective continuity in exercise among sedentary middle-aged and older adults. Success has been achieved in such programs when the activities are individually prescribed and motivationally tailored to the unique history and personal life experience of each participant (Marcus et al., 1998).

In some cases, prescribing exercise may be counterproductive (e.g., upon failure to achieve success in an exercise prescription, the client may feel more guilt, remorse, and a depressing sense of worthlessness than previously experienced). Therefore, it is critical for the therapist to understand the scientific and therapeutic bases for exercise and to approach the prescription process with knowledge derived from the success and failure of others as described herein. Furthermore, note that among the six clinical cases previously described, exercise therapy may be very difficult for some individuals and possibly even contraindicated for medical reasons or for personal preference based on negative experiences in previous years.

This chapter provides guidelines for the clinical application of exercise therapy for mental health. It discusses what exercise therapy is and how it has been used effectively. Theory and research explaining the relationship between exercise and mental health is presented. Also, specific information indicating for whom exercise therapy is effective is described. The chapter concludes with practical guidelines for clinical application of exercise therapy.

What Is Exercise Therapy and How Has It Been Used Effectively?

Providing a definition for exercise therapy requires a separation of the concepts of *exercise* and *therapy*. Traditional therapy involves a set of procedures aimed at facilitating return to normal functioning in a patient or client who has experienced some form of injury, temporary disorder, or permanent disability. Exercise consists of either passive or active muscle exertion involving small or large areas of body muscle mass sometimes taxing either the anaerobic and aerobic metabolism system or both. Exercise may be purely functional, in the form of daily activities of living such as walking, lifting, pushing, or climbing stairs. It also may include a wide variety of enjoyable, play-type, recreational or leisure activities in which the inherent satisfaction may be sufficient to maintain the behavior indefinitely. For example, activities such as hiking, biking, and cross-country skiing may create the opportunity to enjoy scenic vistas while enduring the physical challenge of both the exertion and the weather conditions, which have been shown to develop psychological hardiness (Dienstbier, 1991; Dienstbier, LaGuardia, & Wilcox, 1987; Rejeski, Thompson, Brubaker, & Miller, 1992).

How Exercise Therapy Is Different From Other Therapies: Active Versus Passive Therapy and Potency Versus Risk of Exercise

Exercise therapy is distinctly different from other forms of rehabilitation in which the active ingredient is a drug, a form of radiation therapy, or a palliative physical therapy intervention such as heat, stimulation, massage, and ultrasound. These are passive interventions; the client is merely a recipient in the process. By contrast, treatment applications using exercise for treatment of depression may make the client active in the process of therapy, as evidenced by effort, strain, pain, and increased metabolism (Johnston, Petlichkoff, & Hoeger, 1993). To follow the exercise prescription, the client must (a) overcome inertia to start motion; (b) make a choice of activity, including location and time; and (c) continue what some describe to be the effortful, sometimes painful, process of movement.

In the analysis of exercise therapy for mental health applications, it also is important to consider the potency versus risk dimensions. The active process of exercise therapy has the potential to be therapeutically potent, but there is also a certain degree of risk to the client, depending on the intensity and type of exercise chosen (aerobic, anaerobic, or leisure). However, other treatments, notably drug treatments, have greater potency as well as greater risk of side effects.

All therapy is fraught with similar problems of adherence, compliance, and recidivism. Because exercise incurs a certain degree of accommodation and strain or potential discomfort, it is not surprising that exercise programs in healthy as well as clinical populations show 50% losses after six months (Dishman, 1991, 1994). However, patient compliance with other psychological treatment (psychotherapy and drug therapy) can be equally compromised by client resistance to therapy or by the side effects of drug therapy (Martinsen & Stanghelle, 1997). Even exercise prescriptions given in physical therapy for rehabilitation of injury are poorly adhered to (Sluijs, Kok, & van der Zee, 1993). By following proper guidelines for clinical applications, it is possible to improve on the recidivism rate to achieve the desired psychological benefits. However, before outlining specific guidelines for setting up an exercise therapy program, it is important to present both the epidemiological and clinical literature supporting the association between exercise and mental health in prevention as well as treatment applications.

Theory and Research

Epidemiological Research on the Effects of Exercise

A significant association clearly exists between exercise and several psychological measures of mental health, based on research with large populations. In a psychosocial rehabilitation setting, a series of studies using intensive interview techniques were used to determine that level of fitness was inversely related to depression (Pelham, Campagna, Ritvo, & Birnie, 1993) and that depression is a common outcome following myocardial infarction (Frasure-Smith, Lesperance, & Talajic, 1993). Among both adolescents and middle-aged adults, exercise has been inversely related to anxiety, depression, hostility, and stress (Camacho, Roberts, Lazarus, Kaplan, & Cohen, 1991; Emery, Hauck, & Blumenthal, 1992; Norris, Carroll, & Cochrane, 1992; Rajala, Uusimaki, Keinanen-Kiukaanniemi, & Kivela, 1994; Ruuskanen & Parkatti, 1994; Weyerer, 1992). The influence of exercise habits on the incidence of depression rates, particularly, is noteworthy. Exercising clients are healthier and more stable, thus making it possible to reduce rate of suicide, which is the worst possible psychological outcome of depression (Paffenbarger, Lee, & Leung, 1994).

Clinical Effects of Exercise Therapy

Exercise therapy has been found to be effective with a broad spectrum of individuals. Institutionalized patients in Norway showed substantial improvements in mood and affect following an exercise program (Martinsen, 1993, 1994). Psychiatric patients randomly assigned to a running program were significantly less depressed than those assigned to non-running groups (Bosscher, 1993; Brown, Welsh, Labbe, Gitulli, & Kulkarni, 1992).

Others have found that the combination of exercise and talk therapy was more effective than an equivalent experience in cognitive therapy alone (i.e., the exercise was determined to be an essential element in the improvement of psychological functioning; McNeil, LeBlanc, &

Joyner, 1991; Sime, 1987). In a recent well-documented research report, modest exercise was shown to combat depression as effectively as antidepressants when maintained as a regular, ongoing life activity (Babyak et al., 2000). When the antidepressant was administered and the exercise was initiated, either alone or in combination, the reduction in depression was about the same. At the six-month follow-up, the benefits persisted, especially for members of the exercise group who maintained their habits. However, the long-term improvements in mood were significantly greater for the group doing exercise only, and the depression relapse rates were lower for the exercise-only group than for either the group taking antidepressants only or the group exercising and taking antidepressants. Ironically, it appears that the concurrent use of medication with exercise (Babyak et al., 2000; Martinsen & Stanghelle, 1997) may undermine the psychological benefits of exercise alone. Working hard to beat the depression with exercise may have longer lasting benefits than being medicated back to health.

In general, the psychiatric community has come to view exercise as a valuable adjunct to mental health therapy (Steptoe, Kearsley, & Walters, 1993), especially in the reduction of anxiety in nonclinical populations (Brown, Morgan, & Raglin, 1993) and in the treatment for depression (Lehofer et al., 1992). Several review articles (with meta-analyses) also support the effectiveness of exercise as a part of a comprehensive treatment program, although some compromises occur in experimental design and controlling for expectancy (Byrne & Byrne, 1993; Hinkle, 1992; North, McCullaugh, & Tran, 1990; Petruzzello, Landers, Hatfield, Kubitz, & Salazar, 1991; Rabins, 1992). In one very well controlled intervention study, a cognitive behavioral stress management program was initiated while clients were in the midst of a heavy training program (rowing) with very encouraging results (Perna, Antoni, Kumar, Cruess, & Schneiderman, 1998). A significant reduction in depression, fatigue, and cortisol together with an increase in adaptation to heavy training occurred among those getting psychological (cognitive–behavioral) intervention with exercise.

When Exercise Is Not an Effective Treatment

Although the benefits of exercise and stress management in the work site may not include improvements in mood state in spite of physiological changes in fitness levels (Gronningsaeter, Hyten, Skauli, & Christensen, 1992), exercise alone can serve a stress-buffering role, reducing anxiety (Fuchs & Hahn, 1992; Rejeski et al., 1992). When long-term habitual exercisers were compared with those who had recently embarked on an exercise program and those who were sedentary, the results showed that long-term exercisers reported less overall stress and more positive affect than the other two groups (Dua & Hargreaves, 1992). However, not all studies have found lower levels of negative affect or depression among community studies on previously sedentary participants (Szabo & Gauvin, 1992).

Note that among the studies reporting negative results on the effects of exercise intervention, multiple problems with design and experimental controls exist. Dishman (1994) noted that adherence of participants is frequently problematic in these poorly designed studies. Therefore, caution must be used in drawing conclusions from the accumulated data that are available. Clearly, however, there appears to be more potential benefit than risk associated with exercise therapy. Given the fact that ample evidence exists that supports the use of exercise for psychological benefit, the next step is for the therapist and the client to examine what possible mechanisms account for these benefits, thus addressing the logical question, Why does it work?

Physiological Basis for Why Exercise Is Beneficial for Mental Health

Several possible physiological mechanisms for the psychological benefits of exercise include thermogenic effects, endorphin release, and changes in several neurotransmitters and/or receptors in the autonomic nervous system (Hays, 1999; Johnsgaard, 1989; Leith & Taylor, 1990; Seraganian, 1993).

The Thermogenic Theory

It is of interest that exercise has been shown to increase heat tolerance and cold tolerance, thereby having an influence on emotional stability (Dienstbier et al., 1987). The elevation in core temperature during and after moderate-to-intense exercise is related to simultaneous decreases in muscle tension (deVries, Beckman, Huber, & Dieckmeir, 1968). This theory is supported by the fact that the physiological process of modulating core temperature is known to influence emotions substantially (Koltyn & Morgan, 1993). Reduction in gamma motor activity is a key physiological mechanism accounting for the reductions in muscle tension and state anxiety that occur following exercise and passive heating (Morgan, 1988). Temperature also may be related to changes in brain-wave laterality, thus linking exercise to mental health (Petruzzello et al.,

1993). Although temperature accounts for a small percentage of variance in anxiety and for changes in electroencephalogram laterality, electroencephalogram brainwave changes offer more direct benefits (Robbins, 2000). Although the thermogenic hypothesis appears to be related to a reduction in anxiety no data regarding effects on depression are available and there is no explanation for why the temperature change during exercise makes a difference.

The Endorphin "Exercise High" Theory

Another, more controversial, theory regarding exercise and mental health involves endorphins. Lobstein and Rasmussen (1991) found that endurance training changed resting plasma beta-endorphins and improved nonclinical depression in healthy middle-aged men. Daniels, Martin, and Carter (1992) used naltrexone, the opiate receptor antagonist, and a placebo in a randomized double-blind crossover design to demonstrate that high-intensity exercise reduced levels of depression. When naltrexone was given before exercise (to neutralize endorphins), there was no change in level of depression, thus supporting the endorphin effects. An increase in endorphin levels also is associated with a reduction in stress reactivity effects (McCubbin, Cheung, Montgomery, Bulbulian, & Wilson, 1992) and in sensitivity to pain (Haier, Quaid, & Mills, 1981). Although this theory is an interesting explanation for the psychological benefits of exercise, it is controversial because the measures are indirect and exact biochemical mechanism of impact is not yet clear.

Norepinephrine and Serotonin Theory

Deficiencies in norepinephrine and serotonin systems are associated with the onset of depression (Johnsgaard, 1989). Adaptive changes in serotonin receptor functioning appear to play an important role in mediating the action of various antidepressant medications (Dey, 1994; Dey, Singh, & Dey, 1992). Exercise increases the sensitivity of serotonin receptors, making these naturally produced chemicals more potent in the process of reducing depression. Because pharmaceutical treatments for depression also produce this neurotransmitter receptor effect, it is assumed that serotonin uptake is one of the more important mechanisms linking exercise to psychological benefits. Furthermore, it appears that the role of exercise in decreasing sympathetic and increasing parasympathetic activity also is associated with simultaneous improvement in emotional stability (Kubitz & Landers, 1993; Perna et al., 1998).

Type of Exercise and Dose–Response Effects on Mental Health

Aerobic activities such as running and swimming compare favorably with anaerobic exercise (strength training) in improving mental health (Berger & Owen, 1992; Folkins & Sime, 1981; Norvell & Belles, 1993). Benefits from weight training in reducing anxiety, depression, and hostility are surprisingly high. However, walking or running appears to be substantially advantageous for some populations, such as middle-aged or older depressed adults (Bosscher, 1993; McMurdo & Rennie, 1993). Some research advocates the benefits of one particular type of exercise or another. Overall, it is the personal preference and enjoyment of the activity that may be most important for mental health benefits rather than any single modality of exertion (Wankel, 1993).

Recently, great emphasis has been placed on discerning the level of intensity in combination with the type of exercise that might be optimal for achieving psychological benefits. Some studies have suggested that high-intensity aerobic activity is not necessary for achieving the mental health benefits of exercise (Blumenthal et al., 1991; Doyne, Schambless, & Beutler, 1983; Martinsen, 1993). When the effects of aerobic and nonaerobic exercise were compared among college students, both groups showed significant reduction in depression compared with a control group. Surprisingly, the nonaerobic group was superior to the aerobic group in self-concept enhancement (Stein & Motta, 1992). Similarly, in a comparison of high-intensity aerobic swimming with low-intensity yoga in college students, the yoga produced greater reductions in tension, fatigue, and anger (Berger & Owen, 1992).

Psychological Benefits and Mechanisms

It appears that a preponderance of the literature supports the use of exercise therapy with clinical populations, although a substantial number of patients (up to 50% or more) are not able or willing to continue exercise on a long-term basis (Dishman, 1991). Understanding the acute and long-term mechanism of the psychological benefits of exercise may serve to improve the efficacy of treatment (Van Dixhoorn et al., 1990). However, amidst the confusion of trying to isolate single mechanisms (physiological or cognitive), the most logical explanation for the effects of exercise may have been overlooked, that is, the "interaction effect." That some of the physiological theories may be interrelated or overlapping seems obvious perhaps. For example, temperature elevation may influence the release, synthesis, or uptake of certain brain monoamines (Morgan, 1988) or the endorphins and the monoamines may interact synergistically (Hamachek, 1987; Perna et al., 1998). Positive mood effects associated with exercise may also occur due to increased brain serotonin (Chaoulof, 1997).

Interactive cognitive effects also are likely. For example, exercise has been shown to produce a hardiness effect overlapping with feelings of self-worth mediated by social support (Oman & Haskel, 1993). It also is possible that both physiological and cognitive interactions are present, because exercise has been shown to develop overall hardiness by attenuating sympathetic nervous system responses (Dienstbier, 1991). Regardless of the exact mechanism or the statistical proof of the psychological benefits of exercise, the techniques applied in clinical exercise therapy need to be improved.

For Whom Is Exercise Therapy Appropriate?

Depression, Anxiety, and Low Self-Esteem (Body Image)

Clients with mild-to-moderate depression should be considered for treatment with exercise independently or conjointly with drug therapy. The evidence is clear that exercise can be therapeutically effective in this population, although many patients have difficulty overcoming the captivating inertia associated with depression. Exercise therapy also can be used for patients suffering from various forms of anxiety disorders (e.g., test anxiety, social phobia, panic attack). Many patients are plagued by a combination of depression and some form of anxiety. One interesting therapeutic approach has been used for high anxiety associated with snakes. As the client got closer to the snakes, she got more tense, anxious, and physiologically aroused. When exercise was introduced to move rapidly away from the snakes, the client learned that the exercise could be a more logical reason for her arousal, thus allowing for a cognitive behavioral treatment of the snake phobia to occur.

Those who suffer with low self-esteem also may benefit from an exercise program (Martin, Sinden, & Fleming, 2000). Especially those whose body image contributes to self-esteem problems should be considered for exercise therapy, because exercise habits have been shown to differentiate the effectiveness of weight-loss strategies (Schwartz, 1993). Both exercise and cognitive therapy are effective in improving overall body image. Caution is urged, however, regarding the use of exercise therapy for eating disorders, because depressive symptoms are prevalent in this population and exercise is overused by some bulimia patients in an effort to purge (Prussin & Harvey, 1991).

Special Populations in Need of Exercise Therapy

Three populations deserve special attention in regard to exercise therapy: young adults, older people, and those with disabilities. Given the developmental adaptations that young adults face, many are especially vulnerable to anxiety, depression, and low self-esteem. It has been shown that aerobic exercise (running) is an efficacious treatment with psychiatrically institutionalized (Brown et al., 1992) as well as outpatient (Norris et al., 1992) adolescents. Reductions were seen in depression, anxiety, hostility, confused thinking, and fatigue. Adolescents, as well as adults, with diagnoses of hyperactivity or attention deficit disorder also should be good candidates for exercise therapy (Shipman, 1984).

Older clients also can benefit greatly from exercise therapy; geriatric specialists have advocated and documented the benefits of physical activity, particularly for depression (Goldstein et al., 1999; Rooney, 1993). Another carefully controlled experimental study showed benefits for depression in a crossover design comparing older persons participating in high- versus low-intensity exercise: Both groups showed reduced psychiatric symptoms (McMurdo & Rennie, 1993).

People with disabilities also benefit psychologically from exercise programs (Shephard, 1991). Particularly, wheelchair-bound students who were able to exercise on an arm crank bicycle ergometer showed a significant decrease in anxiety (Brown et al., 1993). Confinement and loss of function easily precipitate depression. With the advent of road races featuring highly skilled wheel-chair athletes, a clear precedent has been set for creating more opportunities for house-bound paraplegics.

Having identified the populations that might benefit the most from exercise therapy, the practical applications of exercise therapy in a clinical setting are now considered.

Guidelines for the Clinical Application of Exercise Therapy

Therapists working with clients in the process of exercise therapy are advised to follow the general guidelines outlined in Exhibit 11.1 and detailed here:

1. *In taking the client's history, include questions about current exercise habits.* Find out what the client does regularly in work or leisure that

---

Exhibit 11.1

Guidelines for the Clinical Application of Exercise Therapy in Conjunction With Counseling or Psychotherapy

1. Explore the client's exercise history (good and bad experiences).
2. Engage in a walk/talk counseling session.
3. Explain the potential benefits of exercise.
4. Evaluate the impact of walk/talk therapy on catharsis and cognitive orientation.
5. Recognize differences in, age, gender, physical ability, preferences, and motivation.
6. Recommend desirable settings and comfortable clothing for exercise.
7. Make exercise practical and functional (e.g., commuting to work).
8. Include a variety of activities, from circuit training to social dance.
9. Prescribe duration, intensity, and frequency of exercise according to needs and limitations.
10. Evaluate the influence of family and friends (facilitate support).
11. Develop a self-behavior modification system to reinforce activity.
12. Develop a plan for recidivism and irregular patterns of activity.
13. Evaluate progress by using well-accepted, standardized psychological tests.
14. Follow ethical guidelines for professional practice.

---

might be conducive to the addition of more vigorous activity (e.g., if the job requires trips to different floors in the building, consider taking the stairs instead of the elevator). Then begin to explore past experiences (both good and bad outcomes) to identify opportunities for positive experiences with exercise. Previous research shows that finding "enjoyable" exercise is critical to the long-term continuity of an exercise program (Wankel, 1993). In Will's and Donny's cases described previously, both clients had extremely negative experiences with exercise in the past. Will had traumatic injuries from football that made vigorous movement painful, and Donny had aversive experiences with military exercise training. As a result, they were very resistant to exercise on their own. It took very strong urging to get them started in activity, which they eventually found to be beneficial.

2. During one of the early counseling sessions, suggest to the client that it might be interesting and enjoyable to continue talking while going for a walk in the nearby vicinity. For clients who are interested, this could occur in the hallway if there is not much traffic or on the sidewalks outside the building if the weather permits. The duration of this walk/talk might be 10 to 20 minutes depending on the condition of the client and on the attractiveness versus the distraction of the environment. If walking in this setting tends to facilitate the client's interaction, then continue as long as possible. However, if the walk in this setting tends to be intimidating to the client, then return to the counseling office after a short time. In Bonnie's case, she was willing to try exercise as long as it was a part of the counseling therapy. Will was desperate and viewed anything that took his mind off the risks of losing his job and family to be helpful. In addition, the exercise allowed him to be occupied with motoric actions that cleared his mind enough to be able to listen, undisturbed by his anxiety and worry and thus to be able to think clearly about the confrontational family (abusive father) issues brought up by the counselor.

3. *Explain to the client that the purpose of walk/talk therapy is to demonstrate the invigorating aspects of exercise and the refreshing aspects of recovery from exercise.* You also can give the client a brief explanation of the reasons (theories) underlying the potential benefits of exercise, noting the aesthetic and kinesthetic experiences associated with movement as well as the synergistic effects. The client should know, by first-hand observation, that the therapist uses exercise for preventive purposes in addition to the rehabilitative applications being prescribed. Bonnie's had no time for exercise as long as she was "addicted" to her Internet relationships. Only much later, when she began to realize how destructive the low-esteem outcomes of compulsive Internet communication were, did she finally gain some balance in her life (which then included more exercise on her treadmill at home).

4. *Use the walking experience as an opportunity for greater cognitive catharsis on the part of the client.* The exercise can be considered a catalyst to help clear the clutter and to free associate to achieve dreamlike thinking that is ordinarily ignored. In addition, it can be viewed as an opportunity for introspection and the creation of more lucid thinking. Be observant of how the client responds to this rationale and to the questions or comments he or she volunteers in the midst of walking conversation. For some clients, the side-by-side conversation (in contrast to face-to-face therapy) seems to elicit more candor; the movement, together with the informal nature of the activity, seems to break down barriers and to facilitate greater emotional release (Kendzierski & Johnson, 1993). This was a very important factor for the case of Amber, who was much less self-conscious about her flushing symptoms when she was walking side by side—precludes eye contact—with the therapist. Note

that the most intense exercise (e.g., marathon running) is, in fact, associated with much greater candor and catharsis and more dramatic changes in cognitive orientation than one would ordinarily see in walk/talk therapy (Acevedo, Dzewaltowski, Gill, & Noble, 1992). However, most therapists and most clients are not prepared for such vigorous activity during therapy.

5. *Recognize individual differences in ability and motivation.* Some clients may be unwilling to try this approach. Not every client is endowed with the burning desire to stay involved in exercise. Give examples of other persons who have overcome similar problems with exercise. Kenneth Cooper, the author of *Aerobics* (1968), tells the story of a man with heart disease who was so despondent that he wanted to die. Because his heart was weak, he logically thought the best way to commit suicide without embarrassing his family was to run around the block as fast as he could until he killed himself. After several futile attempts at causing a fatal heart attack in this manner, he discovered to his surprise that he began to feel better and eventually chose to live instead of to die.

6. *Encourage the client to walk near water, on beaches, over hills, through wooded areas, and down attractive streets to make exercise more pleasurable.* Suggest that in bad weather, the client exercise in enclosed stairways and malls and at home to eliminate excuses for not being active. Dealing with excuses is a critical issue (Kendzierski & Johnson, 1993). Encourage the client to obtain comfortable and attractive clothing (shorts, sweats, shoes) gradually as rewards or added incentives for the accomplishment of continuing the exercise program. Demonstrate to the client that wearing comfortable, casual clothing (e.g., bright-colored warm-ups) for work or leisure tends to make it feasible to include exercise as a natural part of daily activities of living, which can be important existentially (Fahlberg, Fahlberg, & Gates, 1992). In Waldo's case, he discovered a great deal of satisfaction (throughout his 35-year review of work vs. activity patterns) when he opted to commute one or both ways to work by bicycle. The savings in car expenses and bus and train fares was substantial, and the adventure of taking on the challenges of the environment and the elements to get to and from work brought twinges of nostalgia from his hard-working childhood roots on the farm.

7. *Consider options to make exercise functional, especially when the client cannot afford home exercise equipment and/or health club membership fees.* Cost-effective exercise options include commuting to and from work by walking, jogging, or biking; hiking to to a remote scenic area; or doing hard

physical work (e.g., shoveling snow or dirt, moving boxes, and lawn/ gardening work). Commuting exercise is perhaps the most functional because it can have the inherent rewards of saving money for bus fare, parking, and/or gas. In Matt's case, he (the depressed college student) discovered great satisfaction in commuting by bicycle even during inclement weather. If the commuting distance is not reasonable for biking or jogging, have the client compromise by getting a ride, taking a bus one way, or driving part way, thus saving on parking and avoiding traffic congestion.

8. Have clients consider a broad spectrum of activities: from some that involve socializing to others that involve the necessary conditioning to be able to enjoy a favored activity. For example, older, retired adults may choose to walk or climb stairs in order to be capable of maintaining the physical demands of social or square dancing. If a client complains that one form of exercise is uncomfortable, urge him or her to switch to other parallel activities. The multiple-station workout (e.g., stationary bicycle, rowing machine, minitramp, stair climber) is helpful to avoid boredom and local fatigue in one muscle area. During home exercise, suggest using radio, television, or tapes to relieve the boredom or as reinforcement for having started the exercise program for that day. Note that the music in aerobic dance or in recreational dancing may be an essential ingredient for motivating some clients. Waldo would often report that his ballroom dancing was great for exercise therapy because it also met his social needs. But for Amber, the dancing would have been too threatening as she struggled with self-conscious social phobia. Amber found it much more to her satisfaction to walk peacefully through the forest in parks and on nature trails.

9. Set the standards for duration, intensity, and frequency on the basis of level of conditioning, tolerance for discomfort, and length of time since beginning the exercise program. Set reasonable goals and be prepared to adjust the workload (i.e., to increase the duration, intensity, or total time of activity) as needed. If you are not trained or experienced in exercise physiology, it is advisable to seek the assistance of a local specialist who can supervise the ongoing prescription process. In Bonnie's case, she was not totally candid about her dislike of intense activity (climbing stairs), and she continued with the activity beyond her comfort zone. In spite of the fact that the practitioner (this author) has an exercise physiology background, the early signs of her growing discomfort with the more intense activity were missed. Above all, be aware of the risks of too much activity at one extreme and the lack of benefits with too little exercise at the other extreme.

10. Evaluate the influence of family and friends. If there is no support or a sense of disdain for exercise, the client will have a bigger hurdle to overcome in maintaining exercise. Initially, try to facilitate activities that bring the client into positive interaction with others while also gaining benefits from exercise. Also consider encouraging the client to exercise as a role model for his or her children or some other family member. Waldo discovered that he most enjoyed the long runs with a family member that allowed for comfortable conversation and commiseration about inclement weather or other unusually good or bad running conditions. Ultimately, his role modeling had an effect on the activity patterns of other family members, which was very reassuring to him.

11. Help the client develop self-behavior modification strategies to reinforce the activity. For example, the client might form a pact with you, whereby he or she will watch television only when exercising on a bicycle ergometer, minitramp, stair stepper, or treadmill. Alternatively, the client might agree to not watch more than one hour of television without engaging in at least 10 to 20 minutes of exercise. The TV becomes the reinforcer for the exercise behavior. Set up a log and a system of accountability for the client so they can review their progress in accomplishments (distance walked; consecutive days of exercise; change in mood, alertness, and fatigue; relief from joint or muscle pain). The system of record keeping can provide reinforcement for success in continuing the training regime and in discovering the correlation with psychological changes that might occur. Waldo was very conscientious about record keeping, but Bonnie could not find the time to do so, and failure to keep records added to her guilt feelings about not exercising enough.

12. Plan for the first bout of recidivism, and let the client know that it will happen sometime. Nearly everyone who engages in exercise also will experience periodic lapses from exercise due to job, family, illness, or injury. Planning ahead to accommodate serves to defuse the devastating effects of failure (i.e., guilt, remorse, low self-esteem). Help clients anticipate the problem, plan for the adjustment, and welcome the return to activity following a lapse. To prevent future relapse, seek to identify the client's immediate rewards for exercise, which may include (a) a break from the hassles of the day; (b) an opportunity to enjoy the outdoors; (c) a chance to talk with you, or with a friend, about problems;

(d) the refreshing sensation of the cool air or warm shower, depending on the existing weather conditions; and (e) a pleasant culinary satisfaction of a good meal or the fluid replacement with a favorite nonalcoholic drink after exercise.

13. Evaluate progress in mood state and overall state of "well being." One of several psychological tests for several of the important domains include (a) the Profile of Mood States (McNair, Lorr, & Droppleman, 1971), (b) the Beck Depression Inventory (Beck, Ward, Mendelson, Mock, & Erbaugh, 1961), (c) the State/Trait Anxiety Scale (Spielberger, 1983) before and after exercise, and (d) the Tennessee Self-Concept Scale (Fitts, 1964). It is also desirable to have the clinet keep a log of sleep habits and appetite control. It is possible that exercise is associated with more rapid sleep onset and more restful, night-long sleep patterns (Bliwise, King, Harris, & Haskell, 1992) and that healthy foods such as fruits and vegetables taste much better following a vigorous bout of exercise, a shower, and an extended recovery period. These aesthetic rewards of exercise can be very powerful immediate reinforcers. Plan to revise the exercise program on the basis of client feedback at 2- to 4-week intervals.

14. Follow ethical practices involving responsibility to and communication with other health care professionals. It is important to get medical approval for exercise and to establish regular communication with other health care professionals (e.g., primary physician, physical therapist, psychiatrist, social worker, counselor) regarding progress and concerns. Observe other ethical guidelines per medical or psychological licensing requirements. Maintain clearly established boundaries. For example, Amber had difficulty understanding that the walk/talk sessions constituted serious therapeutic interventions. She wanted to make the content of the conversations more informal and social. Obviously, some informal conversation will take place because of the circumstances (i.e., walking, change in scenery). Remember, as the therapist, your responsibility is to get the clients to start exercising and set well-founded goals, to participate with them on occasion during the counseling session while maintaining strict ethical boundaries, and to highlight the potential benefits of exercise to the client (Sime, 1987). You are not, however, personally responsible for clients' motivation or their personal social agenda. Be certain that you are able to articulate your purposes and your methods to the psychology licensing board should there be any question with a disgruntled client or a concerned community member.

Contraindications and Pitfalls To Be Avoided in Exercise Therapy

The areas of concern outlined in Exhibit 11.2 and detailed here should be seriously considered to avoid frustration and disappointment with difficult client problems and to aid in the prevention of unwarranted lawsuits:

1. Don't expect everyone to get benefits from exercise. Many very happy, healthy, functioning individuals with no mental health problems do not exercise in a manner that fits the definition of vigorous exercise, and some individuals seem to be allergic to activity and may never develop an appreciation for the benefits of exercise. Donny never started either a counseling or an exercise program. His physician could have made the exercise prescription obligatory for his personal well-being, but the risk of falling or having some other tragic outcome was too great given his attitude. A structured exercise program may be contra-indicated for this client, in part, because of his military background, which denigrated the positive qualities of hard work.

2. Do not expect the program to supersede other lifestyle patterns. Will is such a busy marketing and sales executive and has two young children at home that he could find little time for exercising. In addition, if he did not have a time conflict that prevented him from exer-cising, he would then often experience chronic knee pain (from old

---

Exhibit 11.2

Contraindicators and Pitfalls to Be Avoided in the Conduct of Exercise Therapy With Counseling or Psychotherapy

1. Don't expect all clients to be receptive to or enthusiastic about exercise as therapy.
2. Don't expect clients to make substantial changes in lifestyle to accommodate a structured exercise program.
3. Be aware that some clients may expect too much change in affect too soon following the onset of activity.
4. Be aware that some clients are prone to extreme behaviors (e.g., workaholic, alcoholic), thus, they may overdo exercise too.
5. Don't allow exercise therapy to be a substitute for counseling or psycho-therapy when it is indicated as the primary need.
6. Remember that exercise can create a potent risk in spite of the therapeutic intention (physical injury, misunderstanding clinical purpose).

football injuries), which discouraged him further. He is very quietly resistant to exercise.

3. Some clients may expect too much change in how they feel soon after onset of activity. Get them to appreciate the aesthetic aspects of the activity at the beginning and gradually increase the prescriptive work load to achieve a reasonable physiological training effect, which is especially important for treating depression. Be aware that the anti-anxiety effects of exercise last about two to four hours and the anti-depressant effects of exercise last about 12 to 24 hours. Therefore, for anxiety, you should recommend exercise (of shorter duration and lower intensity) at frequent intervals throughout the day. For depression, exercising daily but with somewhat greater intensity should be effective.

4. Some clients will take the exercise to extreme the same way that they have behaved with other life experiences (e.g., workaholic, alcoholic). Waldo was driven to work very long hours that, in some ways, mirrored his intense competitive physical activities. Other personality variables, such as the Type A behavior pattern, have been associated with overdoing it on the exercise prescription due to poor perception of appropriate exercise intensity (Hassm'en, Ståhl, & Borg, 1993). Be cautious in the use of exercise for clients with eating disorders. Exercise may produce more opiate-like endorphins than the client can handle, which can be addictive. Some people with bulimia use exercise as a means of purging, thus avoiding the need to deal with the cause of the depression (Prussin & Harvey, 1991). Even though the clients who exercise regularly have less depression, they still may be purging in addition to the exercise and therefore need careful psychological evaluation and therapy.

5. Do not let the exercise prescription preclude the need for traditional psychotherapy. Some clients tend to avoid the real problem, and exercise can be a risky substitute for "necessary" counseling about other issues not resolved by exercise (Sime, 1987). Remember that exercise, like medication, is generally a method of getting immediate (and temporary) symptom relief. As such, medication and exercise are similar in that they allow the person to get through a particularly difficult period of pain/discomfort (either physical or emotional), after which time, insight-oriented counseling may be needed for prevention of escalating problems.

6. Treatment with exercise can create a potential risk in spite of the therapeutic intention. Movement outdoors where automobile traffic

exists can be a problem if therapist and/or client are not totally aware of their surroundings. Parks and trails are not always easliy accessible from most clinical offices. In addition, a client could possibly use the exercise intervention as a way of avoiding emotional content rather than embracing it. Obviously, it is necessary to learn by trial and error as well as making adjustments with each client. Some clients may not recognize the professional boundaries of the client–therapist relationship. It is important to make sure that the exercise circumstances uphold professionalism in the form of clothing, behavior, physical contact, and transference.

Conclusion

In this chapter, exercise has been considered as a viable, adjunctive therapy in the treatment of a broad array of psychological disorders as well as other medical disorders with underlying psychological etiology. Evidence has been presented supporting the effectiveness of various modalities of exercise treatment among numerous divergent populations across a wide range of disorders. Although most of the evidence is positive in regard to exercise, the exact mechanism to account for the benefits of exercise (cognitively or physiologically) is not yet known. The dosage of exercise needed to achieve benefits may differ greatly across individuals, and the type of exercise prescribed should include personal preference tolerance levels and accessibility (opportunity to be active) as the primary determinants.

The benefits of exercise will occur only if clients find a way to become actively involved in vigorous motion as often as possible with as much enjoyment and satisfaction as possible. In addition, it seems desirable if some parts of an exercise program are functional, that is, the product of the activity is rewarding (e.g., commuting to work, chopping wood, dancing, hiking in a scenic area). Numerous guidelines, contraindications, and pitfalls have been provided. The exercise therapist is encouraged to be bold in the use of innovative strategies but cautious where there are extenuating circumstances that might be risky for the client.

References

Acevedo, E., Dzewaltowski, D., Gill, D., & Noble, J. (1992). Cognitive orientations of ultramarathoners. *The Sport Psychologist, 6,* 242–252.

Babyak, M., Blumenthal, J., Khatri, P., Doraiswamy, M., Moore, K., Craighead, W., Baldewicz, T., & Krishnan, K. (2000). Exercise treatment for major depression: Maintenance of therapeutic benefit at ten months. *Psychosomatic Medicine, 62,* 633–638.

Beck, A. T., Ward, C. H., Mendelson, M., Mock, J., & Erbaugh, J. (1961). An inventory for measuring depression. *Archives of General Psychiatry, 4,* 561–571.

Berger, B., & Owen, D. (1992). Mood alteration with yoga and swimming: Aerobic exercise may not be necessary. *Perceptual and Motor Skills, 75,* 1331–1343.

Bliwise, D., King, A., Harris, R., & Haskell, W. (1992). Prevalence of self-reported parsleep in a healthy population aged 50 to 65. *Social Science in Medicine, 34,* 49–55.

Blumenthal, J., Emery, C., Madden, D., Schmiebolk, S., Walsh-Riddle, M., George, L., McKee, D., Higginbothan, N., Cobb, F., & Coleman, R. (1991). Long-term effects of exercise on psychological functioning in older men and women. *Journal of Gerontology, 46,* 352–361.

Bosscher, R. J. (1993). Running and mixed physical exercises with depressed psychiatric patients: Exercise and psychological well being. *International Journal of Sport Psychology, 24,* 170–184.

Brown, D., Morgan, W., & Raglin, J. (1993). Effects of exercise and rest on the state anxiety and blood pressure of physically challenged college students. *Journal of Sports Medicine and Physical Fitness, 33,* 300–305.

Brown, S., Welsh, M., Labbe, E., Gitulli, W., & Kulkarni, P. (1992). Aerobic exercise and the psychological treatment of adolescents. *Perceptual and Motor Skills, 74,* 555–560.

Byrne, A., & Byrne, D. (1993). The effect of exercise on depression, anxiety and other mood states: A review. *Journal of Psychosomatic Research, 37,* 565–574.

Camacho, T. C., Roberts, R. E., Lazarus, N. B., Kaplan, G. A., & Cohen, R. D. (1991). Physical activity and depression: Evidence from the Alameda County study. *American Journal of Epidemiology, 134,* 220–231.

Chaoulof, F. (1997). Effects of acute physical exercise on central serotonergic systems. *Medicine and Science in Sports and Exercise, 29*(1), 58–62.

Cooper, K. H. (1968). *Aerobics.* New York: Evans.

Daniels, M., Martin, A., & Carter, J. (1992). Opiate receptor blockade by naltrexone and mood state after acute physical activity. *British Journal of Sports Medicine, 26,* 111–115.

deVries, H., Beckman, P., Huber, H., & Dieckmeir, L. (1968). Electromyographic evaluation of the effects of sauna on the neuromuscular system. *Journal of Sports Medicine and Physical Fitness, 8,* 61–69.

Dey, S. (1994). Physical exercise as novel anti-depressant agent: Possible role of serotonin receptor subtypes. *Psychological Behavior, 55,* 323–329.

Dey, S., Singh, R., & Dey, P. (1992). Exercise training: Significance of regional alterations in serotonin metabolism of rat brain in relation to anti-depressant effect of exercise. *Psychological Behavior, 52,* 1095–1099.

Dienstbier, R. (1991). Behavioral correlates of sympathoadrenal reactivity: The toughness model. *Medicine and Science in Sports and Exercise, 23,* 846–852.

Dienstbier, R. A., LaGuardia, R. L., & Wilcox, N. S. (1987). The tolerance of cold and heat: Beyond (cold hands–warm heart). *Motivation and Emotion, 11,* 269–295.

Dishman, R. K. (1991). Increasing and maintaining exercise and physical activity. *Behavior Therapy, 22,* 345–378.

Dishman, R. K. (1994). Prescribing exercise intensity for healthy adults using perceived exertion. *Medicine and Science in Sports and Exercise, 27,* 1087–1094.

Doyne, E., Schambless, D., & Beutler, L. (1983). Aerobic exercise as a treatment for depression in women. *Behavior Therapy, 41,* 434–440.

Dua, J., & Hargreaves, L. (1992). Effects of aerobic exercise on negative affect, positive affect, stress, and depression. *Perceptual and Motor Skills, 75,* 355–361.

Emery, C., Hauck, E., & Blumenthal, J. (1992). Exercise adherence and maintenance among older adults: One year follow-up study. *Psychology and Aging, 7,* 466–470.

Fahlberg, L. L., Fahlberg, L. A., & Gates, W. K. (1992). Exercise and existence: Exercise behavior from an existential–phenomenological perspective. *The Sport Psychologist, 6,* 172–191.

Fitts, W. H. (1964). *Tennessee Self-Concept Scale.* Nashville, TN: Counselor Recordings and Tests.

Folkins, C. H., & Sime, W. E. (1981). Physical fitness training and mental health. *American Psychologist, 36,* 373–389.

Frasure-Smith, N., Lesperance, F., & Talajic, M. (1993). Depression following myocardioinfarction: Impact on six-month survival. *Journal of American Medical Association, 270,* 1819–1825.

Fuchs, R., & Hahn, A. (1992). Physical exercise and anxiety as moderators of the stress–illness relationship. *Anxiety, Stress and Coping, 5,* 139–149.

Goldstein, M., Pinto, B., Marcus, B., Lyn, H., Jett, A., Rakowski, W., McDermott, S., Depew, J., Milan, F., Dube, C., & Tennstedt, F. (1999). Position based physical activity counseling for middle-aged and older adults: A randomized trial. *Annals of Behavioral Medicine, 21,* 40–47.

Gronningsaeter, H., Hyten, K., Skauli, G., & Christensen, C. (1992). Improved health and coping by physical exercise or cognitive behavioral stress management training in a work environment. *Psychology and Health, 7,* 147–163.

Haier, R. J., Quaid, B. A., & Mills, J. S. (1981). Naloxone alters pain perceptions after jogging. *Psychiatric Research, 5,* 231–232.

Hamachek, D. E. (1987). *Encounters with the self.* New York: Holt, Rinehart, & Winston.

Hassm'en, P., Stähl, R., & Borg, G. (1993). Psychophysiological responses to exercise in type A/B men. *Psychosomatic Medicine, 55,* 178–184.

Hays, K. F. (1999). *Working it out: Using exercise in psychotherapy.* Washington, DC: American Psychological Association.

Hinkle, J. (1992). Aerobic running behavior and psycho-teutices: Implications for sport counseling and psychology. *Journal of Sport Behavior, 15,* 163–177.

Johnsgaard, K. W. (1989). *The exercise prescription for depression and anxiety.* New York: Plenum.

Johnston, J. N. L., Petlichkoff, L. M., & Hoeger, W. W. K. (1993). Effects of aerobic and strength training exercise participation on depression [Abstract]. *Medicine and Science in Sports and Exercise, 25,* S135.

Kendzierski, D., & Johnson, W. (1993). Excuses, excuses, excuses: A cognitive behavioral approach to exercise implementation. *Journal of Sport and Exercise Psychology, 15,* 207–219.

Koltyn, K., & Morgan, W. P. (1993). The influence of wearing a wet suit on core temperature and anxiety responses during underwater exercise. *Medicine and Science in Sports and Exercise, 25,* S45.

Kubitz, K., & Landers, D. (1993). The effects of aerobic training on cardiovascular responses to mental stress: An examination of underlying mechanisms. *Journal of Sport and Exercise Psychology, 15,* 326–337.

Lehofer, M., Klebel, H., Gersdorf, C. H., & Zapotoczke, H. G. (1992). Running in motion therapy for depression. *Psychiatria–Danubina, 4,* 149–152.

Leith, L., & Taylor, A. (1990). Psychological aspects of exercise: A decade literature review. *Journal of Sport Behavior, 13,* 1–22.

Lobstein, D., & Rasmussen, C. (1991). Decreases in resting plasma beta-endorphine and depression scores after endurance training. *Journal of Sports Medicine and Physical Fitness, 31,* 543–551.

Marcus, B., Bock, B., Pinto, B., Forsyth, L., Roberts, M., & Traficante, R. (1998). Efficacy of an individualized, motivationally-tailored physical activity intervention. *Annals of Behavioral Medicine, 20,* 174–180.

Martin, K., Sinden, A., & Fleming, J. (2000). Inactivity may be hazardous to your image: The effects of exercise participation on impression formation. *Journal of Sport and Exercise Psychology, 22,* 283–291.

Martinsen, E. W. (1993). Therapeutic implications of exercise for clinically anxious and depressed patients: Exercise and psychological well being. *International Journal of Sport Psychology, 24,* 185–199.

Martinsen, E. (1994). Physical activity and depression: Clinical experience. *Acta Psychiatrica Scandanavia Supplement, 377,* 23–27.

Martinsen, E. W., & Stanghelle, J. K. (1997). Drug therapy and physical activity. In W. P. Morgan (Ed.), *Physical activity and mental health* (pp. 81–90). Washington, DC: Taylor & Francis.

McCubbin, J. A., Cheung, R., Montgomery, T. B., Bulbulian, R., & Wilson, J. F. (1992). Aerobic fitness and opiodergic inhibition of cardiovascular stress reactivity. *Psychophysiology, 19,* 687–697.

McEntee, D., & Halgin, R. (1996). Therapists' attitudes about addressing the world of exercise in psychotherapy. *Journal of Clinical Psychology, 52,* 48–60.

McMurdo, M., & Rennie, L. (1993). The controlled trial of exercise by residence of an old people's homes. *Age and Aging, 22*(1), 11–15.

McNair, D. M., Lorr, N., & Droppleman, L. F. (1971). *Manual for the Profile of Mood States.* San Diego: Educational and Industrial Testing Service.

McNeil, J., LeBlanc, E., & Joyner, M. (1991). The effect of exercise on depressive symptoms in the moderately depressed elderly. *Psychology and Aging, 6,* 487–488.

Morgan, W. P. (1988). Exercise and mental health. In R. K. Dishman (Ed.), *Exercise adherence: Its impact on public health* (pp. 9–121). Champaign, IL: Human Kinetics.

Norris, R., Carroll, D., & Cochrane, R. (1992). The effects of physical activity and exercise training on psychological stress and well-being in an adolescent population. *Journal of Psychosomatic Research, 36,* 55–65.

North, T. C., McCullaugh, P., & Tran, Z. V. (1990). Effective exercise on depression. *Exercise and Sports Sciences Review, 18,* 379–415.

Norvell, N., & Belles, D. (1993). Psychological and physical benefits of circuit weight training and law enforcement personnel. *Journal of Consulting and Clinical Psychology, 61,* 520–527.

Oman, R. F., & Haskel, W. L. (1993). The relationships among heartiness, efficacy, cognition, social support and exercise behavior [Abstract]. *Medicine and Science in Sports and Exercise, 25,* S135.

Paffenbarger, R., Jr., Lee, I., & Leung, R. (1994). Physical activity and personal characteristics associated with depression and suicide in American college men. *Acta Psychiatrica Scandanavia Supplement, 377,* 16–22.

Pelham, T. W., Campagna, P. D., Ritvo, P. G., & Birnie, W. A. (1993). The effects of exercise therapy on clients in a psychiatric rehabilitation program. *The Psychosocial Rehabilitation Journal, 16,* 75–84.

Perna, F., Antoni, M., Kumar, M., Cruess, D., & Schneiderman, N. (1998). Cognitive, cognitive–behavioral intervention effects on mood and cortisol during exercise training. *Annals of Behavioral Medicine, 20,* 92–98.

Petruzzello, S., Landers, D., Hatfield, P., Kubitz, K., & Salazar, W. (1991). A meta-analysis on the anxiety-reducing effects of acute and chronic exercise. Outcomes and mechanisms. *Sports Medicine, 11,* 143–182.

Petruzzello, S. J., Landers, D. M., & Salazar, W. (1993). Exercise and anxiety reduction: Examination of temperature as an explanation for effective change. *Journal of Sport and Exercise Psychology, 15,* 63–76.

Prussin, R., & Harvey, P. (1991). Depression, dietary restraint, and binge eating in female runners. *Addictive Behaviors, 16,* 295–301.

Rabins, P. (1992). Prevention of mental disorder in the elderly: Current perspective and future prospects. *Journal of the American Geriatrics Society, 70,* 727–733.

Rajala, U., Uusimaki, A., Keinanen-Kiukaanniemi, F., & Kivela, F. (1994). Prevalence of depression in a 55-year-old Finnish population. *Social Psychiatry and Psychiatric Epidemiology, 29,* 126–130.

Rejeski, W., Thompson, A., Brubaker, P., & Miller, H. (1992). Acute exercise: Buffering psychosocial stress responses in women. *Health Psychology, 11,* 355–362.

Robbins, J. (2000). *The symphony of the brain.* New York: Atlantic Monthly Press.

Rooney, E. M. (1993). Exercise for older patients: Why it's worth your effort. *Geriatrics, 48,* 68–77.

Ruuskanen, J., & Parkatti, T. (1994). Physical activity and related factors among nursing home residents. *Journal of the American Geriatric Society, 42,* 987–991.

Schwartz, F. (1993). Obesity in adult females: The relationship among personality characteristics, dieting, and weight. *AAOHN–J, 41,* 504–509.

Seraganian, P. (1993). Current status and future directions in the field of exercise psychology. In P. Seraganian (Ed.), *Exercise psychology: The influence of physical exercise on psychological processes* (pp. 383–390). New York: Wiley.

Shephard, R. (1991). Benefits of sports and physical activity for the disabled: Implications for the individual and for society. *Scandanavian Journal of Rehabilitation Medicine, 23*(2), 51–59.

Shipman, W. M. (1984). Emotional and behavioral effects of long-distance running on children. In M. Sachs & G. Buffone (Eds.), *Running as therapy: An integrated approach* (pp. 125–137). Lincoln: University of Nebraska Press.

Sime, W. E. (1987). Exercise in the prevention and treatment of depression. In W. P. Morgan & S. E. Goldston (Eds.), *Exercise and mental health* (pp. 145–152). Washington, DC: Hemisphere.

Skrinar, G., Unger, K., Hutchinson, D., & Faigenbaum, A. (1992). Effects of exercise training in young adults with psychiatric disabilities. *Canadian Journal of Rehabilitation, 5,* 151–157.

Sluijs, E., Kok, G., & van der Zee, J. J. (1993). Correlates of exercise compliance in physical therapy. *Physical Therapy, 73,* 41–53.

Spielberger, C. D. (1983). *Manual for the State–Trait Anxiety Inventory* (Form Y). Palo Alto, CA: Consulting Psychologists Press.

Stein, P., & Motta, R. (1992). Effects of aerobic and nonaerobic exercise on depression and self concept. *Perceptual and Motor Skills, 74,* 79–89.

Steptoe, A., Kearsley, M., & Walters, N. (1993). Acute mood responses to maximal and sub-maximal exercise in active and inactive men. *Psychology and Health, 8,* 89–99.

Szabo, A. & Gauvin, L. (1992). Reactivity to written mental arithmetic: Effects of exercise lay-off and habituation. *Physiological Behavior, 51,* 501–506.

Van Dixhoorn, J., Duivenvoorden, H., Pool, J., & Verhage, F. (1990). Psychic effects of physical training and relaxation therapy after myocardial infarction. *Journal of Psychosomatic Research 34*, 327–337.

Wankel, L. (1993). The importance of enjoyment to adherence and psychological benefits from physical activity. *International Journal of Sports Psychology, 24*, 151–169.

Weyerer, S. (1992). Physical inactivity and depression in the community. Evidence from the Upper Bavaria Field Study. *International Journal of Sports Medicine, 13*, 492–496.

12 Counseling Interventions in Applied Sport Psychology

Albert J. Petitpas

O ver the past two decades, there has been considerable debate over what types of interventions fall under the umbrella of sport psychology (e.g., Murphy, 1995, Silva, 1989). Much of this debate was fueled by the U.S. Olympic Committee's Advisory Board on Sport Psychology (1983), which issued a document defining three types of sport psychology activities: (a) clinical, (b) educational, and (c) research. Clinical interventions were described as those that help athletes who exhibited severe emotional problems such as depression, panic, and interpersonal conflicts. Educational interventions were said to focus on teaching psychological skills, such as relaxation, imagery, and attention control, that would enhance athletes' sport performance. Research was not seen as a form of intervention but as an important activity to enhance the work of both clinical and educational practitioners.

Although these guidelines were developed to show the range of activities deemed necessary for the provision of comprehensive sport psychology services to Olympic athletes, they inadvertently spawned several turf wars between professionals trained in psychology and those trained in the sport sciences. Surprisingly, statements about qualifications for practice and who can legally call themselves *sport psychologists* can still be found in sport psychology electronic media today (e.g., APA 47, http://www.psyc.unt.edu/apadiv47/listinfo.htm; SPORT PSY, http://listserv.temple.edu/archives/sportpsy.html).

Unfortunately, those professionals who come into sport psychology from counseling-based programs often find themselves classified as clinical specialists even though their primary orientation has much more in common with that of educational sport psychologists (Petitpas, Buntrock, Van Raalte, & Brewer, 1995; Petitpas, Danish, & Giges, 1999). This chapter examines counseling-based interventions with athletes; specifically, (a) a definition of counseling-based interventions is discussed, (b) the role of sport in human development is explored, (c) several examples of counseling strategies are outlined, and (d) suggestions for working with athletes from a counseling perspective is offered.

Defining Counseling Interventions

Although the differences between clinical and counseling psychology training have become less clear (Davis, Alcorn, Brooks, & Meara, 1992), traditional views suggest that counseling psychology is psychoeducational and developmental, whereas clinical approaches are more remedial and pathology oriented (Danish, Petitpas, & Hale, 1993). Unlike the clinical model's focus on illness, diagnosis, and therapy, counseling approaches emphasize enhancement and growth in normal populations.

Counseling psychologists have been described as *career development or life-work planning specialists, system change agents, psychoeducators,* and *primary prevention specialists* (Hansen, 1981). These work roles are consistent with Shertzer and Stone's (1966) definition of *counseling* as "an interaction process which facilitates meaningful understanding of self and environment and results in the establishment and/or clarification of goals and values for future behavior" (p. 26). For the purpose of this chapter, counseling interventions with athletes are those that focus on development, decision making, and life-work planning across the life span.

Recent trends show that many sport psychologists have changed their emphasis from a focus on improving sport skills to a broader concern for the impact of sport on human development and the use of sport to enhance personal competence (Danish et al., 1993; Murphy, 1995). Within this broader view of sport psychology, counseling interventions have been added to the traditional educational and clinical activities, resulting in a new model of sport psychology consultation. The first group of interventions in this model consists of the traditional educational sport performance enhancement skills, such as imagery, arousal regulation, and goal setting. The second group of interventions focuses on remediating various clinical problems such as eating disorders or adjustment reactions. The third group of interventions consists of counseling strategies that not only assist athletes through the use of various psychoeducational strategies but also use the sport experience as an opportunity to teach life skills and facilitate development as individuals progress through the life cycle.

Central to the counseling approach to sport psychology interventions is the relationship that is established between the practitioner and the athlete (Petitpas et al., 1999). This relationship can take the form of the working alliance described in traditional counselor training (Sexton & Whiston, 1994) and observed in one-on-one performance enhancement consultations or can be seen in interactions between caring adult mentors and young student–athletes (Petitpas & Champagne, 2000).

Sport and Human Development

If counseling interventions are based on developmental factors, then an understanding of the role of sport in human development is important in planning interventions for athletes. The legitimacy of sport as a cocurricular activity is based on the premise that sport participation prepares students for later adult roles. Sport teaches young people how to live by rules, work hard to achieve goals, and play and interact with others.

Over the years, the efficacy of sport as a vehicle to enhance development and "build character" has spawned considerable debate. Several authors have argued that the increased competitive nature of sport and the emphasis on winning can have a deleterious effect on the psychosocial development of youth-sport athletes (Ewing, Seefeldt, & Brown, 1996; Martens, 1986; Petitpas & Champagne, 2000). However, only a handful of empirical investigations have been reported, and these have questionable designs and inconsistent findings (Danish, Petitpas, & Hale, 1990).

Erikson's (1959) life-span developmental theory suggests that latency-aged children (6 to 10 years old) need to develop a sense of industry or be subject to feelings of inferiority. It has been argued that youth-sport involvement, unimpeded by an exclusive emphasis on winning, provides numerous opportunities for participants to acquire and master skills (Martens, 1983). Being a successful athlete, even at youth levels, is highly valued by children and adults and may result in increased feelings of self-efficacy and a sense of industry (Danish et al., 1993). If this is the case, then youth-sport participation can have a positive influence on children's psychosocial development. This notion has received some empirical support, as shown in Iso-Aloha and Hatfield's (1986) review of the youth-sport literature. They concluded that early participation in sport is correlated with positive psychosocial characteristics but cautioned that no direct causal relationships had been identified.

If sport is structured in a manner that allows young people to master skills and have fun, it is likely that they will continue to participate and accrue psychosocial benefits (Gould, 1987). Unfortunately, the nature of the sport system weeds out less physically gifted individuals at each progressive level of competition. The most gifted performers may continue to benefit from sport participation, whereas many others drop out or are deselected because of a lack of ability.

As children reach late adolescence, their primary developmental task shifts from an emphasis on developing a sense of industry to a need to establish a personal identity (Erikson, 1959). The quest for an identity involves two primary activities (Erikson, 1959; Marcia, Waterman, Matteson, Archer, & Orlofsky, 1993). First, individuals must engage in exploratory behavior by which they experiment with various adult roles. Second, these individuals must then make commitments to those ideological and occupational options that appear most consistent with their values, needs, interests, and skills.

Exploratory behavior has been identified as a critical activity for subsequent personal and career development (Jordaan, 1963; Super, 1957). Ironically, the same sport system that provides opportunities to enhance personal competence for youth-sport participants may preclude opportunities for exploratory behavior for college-age adults (Hurley & Cunningham, 1984). It has been suggested that the physical and time demands of intercollegiate sport participation, coupled with the restrictiveness of the sport environment, may discourage student–athletes from exploring nonsport roles or alternative identities (Chartrand & Lent, 1987; Nelson, 1983; Petitpas & Champagne, 1988). This may be particularly true for student–athletes who are Black (Leach & Conners, 1984; Sellers, 1993).

Although sport involvement is related to positive psychosocial factors for youth-sport participants, the same does not hold true for college athletes. In fact, several empirical investigations have shown that college student–athletes lag behind their age mates on several markers of psychosocial maturity (Blann, 1985; Good, Brewer, Petitpas, Van Raalte, & Mahar, 1993; Kennedy & Dimick, 1987; Murphy, Petitpas, & Brewer, 1996; Sowa & Gressard, 1983).

Danish (1983) has suggested that athletes may use selective optimization, a process in which athletes give exclusive attention to their sport at the expense of all other interests. This concept is closely linked to a developmental status called identity foreclosure (Marcia, 1966). Foreclosure occurs when individuals make commitments to roles without engaging in exploratory behavior. On the surface, identity-foreclosed individuals appear to be psychosocially mature (Marcia et al., 1993). They have low levels of anxiety and confusion, and are clearly committed to a role. However, this seemingly healthy presentation may mask a lack of self-awareness and a failure to develop adequate coping resources (Marcia et al., 1993; Petitpas, 1978). Problems associated with foreclosed commitments to sport roles are most likely to surface when the athletic identity is threatened (Baillie & Danish, 1992; Pearson & Petitpas, 1990).

Several studies have shown that the strength and exclusivity of an athletic identity is related to negative consequences when athletes disengage from sport roles because of retirement, injury, or the selection process (Brewer, 1993; Hinitz, 1988; Kleiber & Brock, 1992). Unfortunately, the sport system does little to assist athletes in preparing for threats to their identities and often promotes an attitude that only a 110% level of commitment to sport is acceptable (Danish et al., 1993).

Little has been written on the impact of athletic participation on later developmental tasks. Heyman (1987) suggested that athletes may not be experienced in developing meaningful interpersonal relationships and therefore may have difficulty resolving the "intimacy versus isolation" crisis of young adulthood. Although no empirical support exists for this notion with athlete samples, foreclosed men have been shown to engage in stereotyped or pseudo-intimate dating relationships (Marcia et al., 1993).

Most formal athletic careers end before individuals reach middle or later adulthood and are faced with the "generativity versus stagnation" crisis of this stage. Heyman (1987) suggested that retired athletes, who have not developed another source of meaning or enjoyment in life, would be prone to stagnation, but there is no empirical validation of this hypothesis. Assisting athletes in expanding their self-concepts and identities beyond athletics may be helpful in preparing for later adult transitions (Pearson & Petitpas, 1990).

On the basis of this developmental perspective, counseling interventions should, therefore, be geared toward creating an environment in which athletes can learn about themselves through exploratory behavior, develop coping skills, prepare for future events, and have fun. To accomplish these goals, counseling interventions need to target not only athletes, but all components of the athletic system, including coaches, parents, and athletic administrators.

Counseling-Based Interventions With Athletes

An examination of athletes' transitions provides a useful framework for understanding developmental processes that underlie counseling interventions with this population (Pearson & Petitpas, 1990). Athletes go through a series of normative transitions as they move through their athletic life cycle. For example, National Basketball Association (NBA) players typically progress from youth sports, to high school, to college, to the NBA, before they retire from sport. Each of these transitions can be anticipated and counseling services provided. In addition, athletes may also experience unexpected events (e.g., injury) or "nonevents" (e.g., not making the starting team) that may require attention (Danish et al., 1993; Pearson & Petitpas, 1990).

Although it may be possible to extrapolate from transitional theory and predict those athletes who might be most susceptible to problems during transitions, it is often difficult to convince at-risk athletes to participate in prevention programs (Pearson & Petitpas, 1990). Therefore, a well-designed counseling program should contain several types of interventions.

In designing counseling programs for athletes, it is helpful to link the timing of the transitional experience to an appropriate intervention (Danish et al., 1993). These interventions can occur before, during, or after a transition. Interventions that assist athletes in preparing for upcoming events by identifying transferable skills or developing new coping or life skills are called enhancement strategies. During a transition, interventions can buffer the impact of the transition by assisting athletes in mobilizing their personal and support resources. Other counseling-related strategies can be used to assist athletes in coping with the aftermath of a transition (Danish, Petitpas, & Hale, 1992). More information about other expected and unexpected transitions of athletes is available elsewhere (Baillie & Danish, 1992; Petitpas, Brewer, & Van Raalte, 1996; Taylor & Ogilvie, 1994).

To illustrate the link between developmental theory and counseling-based interventions, two approaches to service delivery were examined. First, a framework for assisting athletes in managing the psychological aspects often associated with a significant sport injury is presented. Second, "Play It Smart," a program that uses involvement with sport as a vehicle to teach life skills to disadvantaged youths, is described.

Counseling Athletes With Injuries

Incurring a physical injury can be a stressor for most individuals. For athletes, who derive significant portions of their self-worth from sports, a serious injury can be a threat to their basic identity (Brewer, Van Raalte, & Linder, 1993; Elkind, 1981; Little, 1969).

Several studies have shown a relationship between the strength and exclusivity of athletic identity and negative reactions in athletes who experience injury (Brewer, 1993; Kleiber & Brock, 1992). However, attempts to equate reactions to sport injury to stage models of grief and loss have received little empirical support (Brewer, 1994). It may be that severe injury presents a threat to the athletic identity, which causes emotional distress that continues until the individual believes that full recovery is possible. Two longitudinal studies revealed that athletes experienced mood disturbance following severe injury but that emotional distress diminished when athletes perceived they were making progress toward recovery (McDonald & Hardy, 1990; Smith, Scott, O'Fallon, & Young, 1990).

In planning counseling interventions for injured athletes, it is important to consider commitment to sport roles as one of several factors that can affect psychological adjustment. If this commitment suggests identity foreclosure, differentiating between situational and psychological types of foreclosure will facilitate treatment planning. As described by Henry and Renaud (1972), psychological foreclosure is an intrapsychic defense mechanism whereby individuals ward off threats to their self-worth by avoiding any situations that might challenge their identity. This contrasts markedly with situationally foreclosed individuals, whose commitment to an athletic identity is due to a lack of exposure to new options or possibilities, not because it is their main defensive structure. Many of these differences can be seen in the extended case study presented by Brewer and Petitpas (in press).

Other factors to be considered include coping skills, life stress, family life cycle dynamics, secondary gain, sources and types of support, the characteristics of the injury, and a range of situational variables (Hardy & Crace, 1993; Petitpas & Danish, 1995; Smith, Scott, & Wiese, 1990; Wiese-Bjornstal & Smith, 1993). The complexity of the sport injury situation requires counselors to put considerable time and energy into understanding athletes and their injury experience.

The goal in counseling athletes with injuries is to assist them in identifying and developing resources to more effectively cope with the injury process. Although several counseling models for athletes with injuries offer suggestions for *what* to do (e.g., Etzel & Ferrante, 1993; Smith et al., 1990; Wiese-Bjornstal & Smith, 1993), little attention has been given to *how* to intervene with injured athletes (Petitpas & Danish, 1995). Some guidelines are described next.

The first step in the counseling process with injured athletes is to build rapport and develop a working alliance. This is accomplished by using basic listening skills to learn what the injury means to the athlete. Many athletes display confusion, anxiety, and doubt during the initial period following a serious injury, so it is important to be patient and avoid the urge to offer a "quick fix." Some athletes may use potentially harmful strategies in coping with the injury (e.g., withdrawing from teammates or abusing alcohol). It is helpful to examine what these strategies are doing for the athlete and then explore other options that might give the athlete the same benefits without the potential costs. Premature confrontations may cause athletes to lose face and may jeopardize the therapeutic relationship (Brewer & Petitpas, in press; Petitpas & Danish, 1995).

The second step is to ensure that injured athletes are provided with specific information about the nature of the injury, the medical procedures to be used, any possible side effects, and the goals of rehabilitation (Danish, 1986). This type of information helps prepare injured athletes for possible plateaus or setbacks in rehabilitation and eliminates some of the potential "surprises" that could happen during rehabilitation.

The third step is to collaborate with injured athletes in identifying coping resources, which can help them feel more in control and more responsible for rehabilitation outcomes. Injured athletes' use of coping skills that they are already familiar with may help them feel more confident in their ability to influence their recovery. If injured athletes lack appropriate coping resources, counselors can teach them new skills (see Danish & Hale, 1981; Meichenbaum, 1985).

Once coping skills are identified or learned, the fourth step is for counselors and injured athletes to collaborate to develop goal ladders for the rehabilitation process and strategies to address any roadblocks to goal attainment. Counselors are also typically involved in working with injured athletes' support systems (e.g., family, sports medicine personnel, coaches) to ensure a good rehabilitation and smooth return to competition. A more detailed description of these suggested techniques is provided elsewhere (Petitpas & Danish, 1995).

Although these interventions take place after an injury has occurred, the focus of these counseling strategies should be on coping skills identification and acquisition, not pathology. In addition, it is the quality of the working alliance between the counselor and the athlete that facilitates skills acquisition and is often critical to treatment adherence and positive outcomes.

Play It Smart

Consistent with a counseling-based approach to sport psychology, Play It Smart is a school-based program created by the National Football Foundation (NFF, 1998) that seeks to use the sport experience as a vehicle to enhance the academic, athletic, career, and personal development of high school student–athletes. In this approach, sport participation provides an environment in which participants are exposed to caring adult mentors, have membership in a constructive group, and are given opportunities to test their abilities and to learn how to rely on others. The goal of the program is to demonstrate that the right kind of sport experiences can provide participants with opportunities to learn about themselves and to develop skills that will not only enhance their current athletic and academic performance but also better prepare them for productive futures.

The program is based on a life developmental framework that emphasizes continual growth and change (Danish et al., 1993). Participants are assisted in identifying their transferable skills and learning how to use these skills in academic preparation, in developing and maintaining productive relationships, and in gaining confidence in their abilities to function effectively in the world of work. Both individual and team goal setting are used to enable participants to measure progress, see possible futures, and gain the social support that is often required to form healthy habits and achieve life successes.

A two-year pilot program introduced student–athletes who were playing football in four inner-city high schools to the Play It Smart philosophy. These four schools were selected because they lacked many of the financial and support resources available in more affluent communities. The vast majority of the student–athletes were from minority racial or ethnic and economically disadvantaged backgrounds and lived in neighborhoods with high crime, gang involvement, and school dropout rates. As a group, they had lower grade point averages than their school peers, and few had any concrete post–high school plans.

The Play It Smart program was created to take advantage of the voluntary nature of sport participation and designed in accordance with knowledge gained from previous research and intervention efforts (Petitpas & Champagne, 2000). As such, it was important to strengthen the team identity as well as provide support and skills-building activities for individual participants within a constructive group. Consequently, it was necessary to understand the norms and belief system of each team and then to use the status of the coach to establish a group value system in which teamwork, sportsmanship, respect for rules, and community service were set as standards.

In addition to working directly with the head coaches and team leaders, Play It Smart provided each school with an "academic coach," who designed team-building and group activities (e.g., ropes courses and community service) to foster constructive group norms and pride in team membership. Activities were individualized for each school and took advantage of the collaborative efforts of the team leaders and the resources of the local community and area NFF chapter. Academic coaches are professionals who have training and experience in providing counseling and support services to student–athletes. They assisted the head coaches by facilitating communication and collaboration among school personnel, parents, community leaders, and students to create an expanded support system for the participants.

In addition to the group activities, academic coaches assisted student–athletes by helping them identify their values, needs, interests, and skills. As part of this process, specific academic, athletic, career, and community service goals were developed. The academic coach then monitored progress and provided the resources and support needed to overcome any roadblocks to goal attainment. In each case, the goal-setting program was linked to an individualized incentive plan that was based on the student–athlete's particular wish list. The incentive program was a reward for hitting goal targets and not a form of entitlement.

Student–athletes were also supported in securing leadership roles outside of sport to help them gain confidence in their abilities to transfer their athletic skills to other domains.

To measure progress, a series of outcome measures were assessed: (a) grade point averages, Scholastic Aptitude Test scores, and graduation rates; (b) involvement in community service activities; and (c) participation in educational and skills-building sessions that aimed to reduce the use of alcohol and other drugs. Academic coaches provided participants with ongoing feedback about the specific behaviors necessary to achieve their goals. For example, academic improvements typically require four specific behaviors: attend all classes, take organized notes, turn in assignments on time, and take tests on time. Coaches and team leaders then used their leadership status and the importance of sport participation to reinforce the desired behaviors.

Results from the two-year pilot program revealed that the participants' grade point averages increased from 2.16 to 2.54. This compares favorably to the general school average of 2.25. The average Scholastic Aptitude Test scores of participants was 829.86, compared with 801.67 for the general student population. Ninety-eight percent of the participants graduated from high school on schedule, and 83% of this group went on to higher education. In addition, participants engaged in 1,745 hours of community service.

The positive results from the four pilot schools opened the door for program expansion. Play It Smart expanded to 28 high schools across the United States. Academic coaches are now working with other sports teams to fulfill the NFF's commitment to expand Play It Smart to all athletes.

Special Considerations

Psychologists, who are accustomed to working with clients in clinical settings, often find that consultation work with athletes is different from their traditional practice (Danish et al., 1993). As described previously, the athletic system can be so narrowly focused that it becomes a closed system, in which nonparticipants are seen as outsiders. For example, athletes and coaches have reservations about working with "shrinks," whose lack of understanding of the sport environment can result in behaviors that are intrusive and potentially harmful to performance

(Orlick & Partington, 1987; Van Raalte, Brewer, Brewer, & Linder, 1992).

To gain access to the sport system, sport and exercise psychology consultants must demonstrate a general understanding of the sport environment and an appreciation for what athletes go through during practices and competitions (Danish et al., 1993). Psychology-trained consultants with a basic understanding of the sport sciences and experience as an athlete have clear advantages over their non-sport-oriented colleagues in gaining entry to the sports world. In lieu of this background, experience can be acquired by volunteering to coach youth sport teams or participating in personal fitness programs. It is critical to become familiar with the rules and language of sport. Even if they have many sport experiences, it is still necessary for sport and exercise psychologists to demonstrate their interest by attending practices and competitions.

Once sport and exercise psychology consultants gain entry into a sport system, they soon realize that boundaries are not as clearly defined as they are in traditional clinical practice. Contacts with clients are more extensive, and attendance at practices and games is often an expectation (Orlick & Partington, 1987). Although this extended contact is helpful in giving consultants opportunities to observe their clients perform, it is also very time consuming. In addition, consultants may be expected to travel with teams, have meals and share lodging with team members, and participate in team social functions. For psychologists, balancing relationship expectations with appropriate clinical boundaries is often a difficult challenge (Andersen, Van Raalte, & Brewer, in press).

Confidentiality is another common concern in working with athletes. Most often, the initial contact for consultation services will come from a coach, parent, or sport administrator who wants help for a team or an individual athlete. These individuals often assume that because they are responsible for these athletes, they should have access to records and be informed about what happens during counseling. It is important to address confidentiality and the nature of the counseling relationship before consultations begin. In cases in which a sport administrator hires a sport and exercise psychologist to work with a team, the sport and exercise psychologist must clearly define the nature of the consultation with the coach, as well as the sport administrator.

When working with high-visibility sports, it is common to have more exposure to the media. Sport and exercise psychology consultants in these situations are often under increased pressure to disclose information about athlete–clients. This is particularly the case when athletes identify the consultant with whom they work. Aggressive media personnel often assume that because athletes have publicly named their sport and exercise psychologists, confidentiality is no longer applicable.

Athletes have been shown to be highly influenced by the expectations of significant others, most particularly their coach (LeUnes & Nation, 1983). Consultants working with athletes must acknowledge this influence and work diligently to build a cooperative working relationship with the coach. Sport and exercise psychologists who claim credit for athlete–clients' successes will often create an adversarial relationship with coaches. The most effective consultants appear to be those who work through coaches and know when to assist and when to stay in the background (Orlick & Partington, 1987).

Athletes tend to be action oriented. Consultants who provide concrete information that is sport specific are likely to be more effective than those who use more abstract, insight-oriented interventions (Danish et al., 1993).

Conclusion

This chapter examined counseling interventions with athletes. Counseling-based approaches not only can be used to enhance sport performance but also can enhance athletes' abilities to transfer skills that they acquired through sport to other life domains. Sport and exercise psychologists who understand the unique world of sport are in a better position to gain access to consulting with this unique population.

References

Andersen, M. B., Van Raalte, J. L., & Brewer, B. W. (in press). Sport psychology service delivery: Staying ethical while keeping loose. *Professional Psychology: Research and Practice.*

Baillie, P. H. F., & Danish, S. J. (1992). Understanding the career transition of athletes. *The Sport Psychologist, 6,* 77–98.

Blann, W. (1985). Intercollegiate athletic competition and students' educational and career plans. *Journal of College Student Personnel, 26,* 115–118.

Brewer, B. W. (1993). Self-identity and specific vulnerability to depressed mood. *Journal of Personality, 61,* 343–364.

Brewer, B. W. (1994). Review and critique of models of psychological adjustment to athletic injury. *Journal of Applied Sport Psychology, 6,* 87–100.

Brewer, B. W., & Petitpas, A. J. (in press). Returning to self: The anxieties of coming back after injury. In M. B. Andersen (Ed.), *Doing sport psychology: Process and practice.* Champaign, IL: Human Kinetics.

Brewer, B. W., Van Raalte, J. L., & Linder, D. E. (1993). Athletic identity: Hercules' muscles or Achilles heel? *International Journal of Sport Psychology, 24,* 237–254.

Chartrand, J., & Lent, R. (1987). Sports counseling: Enhancing the development of the student–athlete. *Journal of Counseling and Development, 66,* 164–167.

Danish, S. J. (1983). Musings about personal competence: The contributions of sport, health, and fitness. *American Journal of Community Psychology, 11,* 221–240.

Danish, S. J. (1986). Psychological aspects in the care and treatment of injured athletes. In P. E. Vinger & E. F. Hoerner (Eds.), *Sports injuries: The unthwarted epidemic* (2nd ed., pp. 345–353). Boston: John Wright.

Danish, S. J., & Hale, B. D. (1981). Toward an understanding of the practice of sport psychology. *Journal of Sport Psychology, 3,* 90–99.

Danish, S. J., Petitpas, A. J., & Hale, B. D. (1990). Sport as a context for developing competence. In T. Gullotta, G. Adams, & R. Montemayor (Eds.), *Developing social competency in adolescence* (Vol. 3, pp. 169–194). Newbury Park, CA: Sage.

Danish, S. J., Petitpas, A. J., & Hale, B. D. (1992). A developmental–educational intervention model of sport psychology. *The Sport Psychologist, 6,* 403–415.

Danish, S. J., Petitpas, A. J., & Hale, B. D. (1993). Life development interventions for athletes: Life skills through sports. *The Counseling Psychologist, 21,* 352–385.

Davis, K. L., Alcorn, J. D., Brooks, L., & Meara, N. M. (1992). Crystal ball gazing: Training and accreditation in 2000 A.D. *The Counseling Psychologist, 20,* 352–371.

Elkind, D. (1981). *The hurried child.* Reading, MA: Addison Wesley.

Erikson, E. H. (1959). Identity and the life cycle. *Psychological Issues, 1,* 1–171.

Etzel, E. F., & Ferrante, A. P. (1993). Providing psychological assistance to injured and disabled college student–athletes. In D. Pargman (Ed.), *Psychological bases of sport injuries* (pp. 265–283). Morgantown, WV: Fitness Information Technology.

Ewing, M. E., Seefeldt, V. D., & Brown, T. P. (1996). Role of organized sport in the education and health of American children and youth. In A. Poinsett (Ed.), *The role of sports in youth development* (pp. 1–157). New York: Carnegie Corporation.

Good, A. J., Brewer, B. W., Petitpas, A. J., Van Raalte, J. L., & Mahar, M. T. (1993). Identity foreclosure, athletic identity, and college sport participation. *The Academic Athletic Journal, 8,* 1–12.

Gould, D. (1987). Promoting positive sport experiences in children. In J. R. May & M. J. Askens (Eds.), *Sport psychology: The psychological health of the athlete* (pp. 77–98). New York: PMA.

Hansen, F. K. (1981). Primary prevention and counseling psychology: Rhetoric or reality? *The Counseling Psychologist, 9,* 57–60.

Hardy, C. J., & Crace, R. K. (1993). The dimensions of social support when dealing with sport injuries. In D. Pargman (Ed.), *Psychological bases of sport injuries* (pp. 121–144). Morgantown, WV: Fitness Information Technology.

Henry, M., & Renaud, H. (1972). Examined and unexamined lives. *Research Reporter, 7,* 5.

Heyman, S. R. (1987). Counseling and psychotherapy with athletes: Special considerations. In J. R. May & M. J. Asken (Eds.), *Sport psychology: The psychological health of the athlete* (pp. 135–156). New York: PMA.

Hinitz, D. R. (1988). *Role theory and the retirement of collegiate gymnasts.* Unpublished doctoral dissertation, University of Nevada, Reno.

Hurley, R. B., & Cunningham, R. L. (1984). Providing academic and psychological services for the college athlete. In A. Shriberg & F. R. Brodzinski (Eds.), *Rethink-*

ing services for college athletes (New Directions for Student Services, No. 28, pp. 51–58). San Francisco: Jossey-Bass.

Iso-Aloha, S., & Hatfield, B. (1986). *Psychology of sports: A social psychological approach.* Dubuque, IA: William C. Brown.

Jordaan, J. P. (1963). Exploratory behavior: The formulation of self and occupational concepts. In D. E. Super, R. Starishevsky, N. Matlin, & J. P. Jordaan (Eds.), *Career development: Self-concept theory* (pp. 46–57). New York: CEEB Research Monographs.

Kennedy, S. R., & Dimick, K. M. (1987). Career maturity and professional expectations of college football and basketball players. *Journal of College Student Personnel, 28,* 293–297.

Kleiber, D. A., & Brock, S. C. (1992). The effect of career-ending injuries on the subsequent well-being of elite college athletes. *Sociology of Sport Journal, 9,* 70–75.

Leach, B., & Conners, B. (1984). Pygmalion on the gridiron: The Black student–athlete at the White university. In A. Shriberg & F. R. Brodzinski (Eds.), *Rethinking services for college athletes* (New Directions for Student Services, No. 28, pp. 31–49). San Francisco: Jossey-Bass.

LeUnes, A., & Nation, J. R. (1983). Saturday's heroes: A psychological portrait of college football players. *Journal of Sport Behavior, 5,* 139–149.

Little, J. C. (1969). The athletic neurosis: A deprivation crisis. *Acta Psychiatrica Scandinavia, 45,* 187–197.

Marcia, J. E. (1966). Development and validation of ego-identity status. *Journal of Personality and Social Psychology, 3,* 551–558.

Marcia, J. E., Waterman, A. S., Matteson, D. R., Archer, S. L., & Orlofsky, J. L. (1993). *Ego identity: A handbook for psychosocial research.* New York: Springer-Verlag.

Martens, R. (1986). Youth sports in the USA. In M. R. Weiss & D. Gould (Eds.), *Sport for children and youths* (pp. 27–33). Champaign, IL: Human Kinetics.

Martens, R. (1983). Coaching to enhance self-worth. In T. Orlick, J. Partington, & J. Salmela (Eds.), *Mental training for coaches and athletes.* Ottawa: Coaching Association of Canada.

McDonald, S. A., & Hardy, C. J. (1990). Affective response patterns of the injured athlete: An exploratory analysis. *The Sport Psychologist, 4,* 261–274.

Meichenbaum, D. (1985). *Stress inoculation training.* Elmford, NY: Pergamon Press.

Murphy, G. M., Petitpas, A. J., & Brewer, B. W. (1996). Identity foreclosure, athletic identity, and career maturity in intercollegiate athletes. *The Sport Psychologist, 10,* 239–246.

Murphy, S. (Ed.). (1995). *Sport psychology interventions.* Champaign, IL: Human Kinetics.

National Football Foundation. (1998). *Play it smart: Training manual.* Morristown, NJ: Author.

Nelson, E. S. (1983). How the myth of the dumb jock becomes fact: A developmental view for counselors. *Counseling and Values, 27,* 176–185.

Orlick, T., & Partington, J. (1987). The sport psychology consultant: Analysis of critical components as viewed by Canadian Olympic athletes. *The Sport Psychologist, 1,* 4–17.

Pearson, R., & Petitpas, A. (1990). Transitions of athletes: Developmental and preventive perspectives. *Journal of Counseling and Development, 69,* 7–10.

Petitpas, A. (1978). Identity foreclosure: A unique challenge. *Personnel and Guidance Journal, 56,* 558–561.

Petitpas, A. J., Brewer, B. W., & Van Raalte, J. L. (1996). Transitions of student–athletes: Theoretical, empirical, and practical perspectives. In E. F. Etzel, A. P. Ferrante,

& J. W. Pinkney (Eds.), *Counseling college student–athletes: Issues and interventions* (2nd ed.; pp. 137–156). Morgantown, WV: Fitness Information Technology.

Petitpas, A. J., Buntrock, C. L., Van Raalte, J. L., & Brewer, B. W. (1995). Counseling athletes: A new specialty in counselor education. *Counselor Education and Supervision, 34,* 212–219.

Petitpas, A., & Champagne, D. E. (1988). Developmental programming for intercollegiate athletes. *Journal of College Student Development, 29,* 454–460.

Petitpas, A., & Champagne, D. (2000). Sport and social competence. In S. J. Danish & T. P. Gullotta (Eds.), *Developing competent youth and strong communities through after-school programming* (pp. 115–137). Washington, DC: CWLA Press.

Petitpas, A., & Danish, S. (1995). Psychological care for injured athletes. In S. Murphy (Ed.), *Sport psychology interventions* (pp. 255–282). Champaign, IL: Human Kinetics.

Petitpas, A. J., Danish, S. J., & Giges, B. (1999). The sport psychologist–athlete relationship: Implications for training. *The Sport Psychologist, 13,* 344–357.

Sellers, R. M. (1993). Black student–athletes: Reaping the benefits or recovering from the exploitation. In D. D. Brooks & R. C. Althouse (Eds.), *Racism in college athletics: The African-American athlete's experience* (pp. 143–174). Morgantown, WV: Fitness Information Technology.

Sexton, T. L., & Whiston, S. C. (1994). The status of the counseling relationship: An empirical review, theoretical implications, and research directions. *The Counseling Psychologist, 22,* 6–78.

Shertzer, B., & Stone, S. (1966). *Fundamentals of counseling.* Boston: Houghton Mifflin.

Silva, J. M. III. (1989). Toward the professionalization of sport psychology. *The Sport Psychologist, 3,* 265–273.

Smith, A. M., Scott, S. G., O'Fallon, W. M., & Young, M. L. (1990). Emotional responses of athletes to injury. *Mayo Clinic Proceedings, 65,* 38–50.

Smith, A. M., Scott, S. G., & Wiese, D. M. (1990). The psychological effects of sports injuries: Coping. *Sports Medicine, 9,* 352–369.

Sowa, C. J., & Gressard, C. F. (1983). Athletic participation: Its relationship to student development. *Journal of College Student Personnel, 24,* 236–239.

Super, D. E. (1957). *The psychology of careers.* New York: Harper & Row.

Taylor, J., & Ogilvie, B. C. (1994). A conceptual model of adaptation to retirement among athletes. *Journal of Applied Sport Psychology, 6,* 1–20.

U.S. Olympic Committee. (1983). USOC establishes guidelines for sport psychology services. *Journal of Sport Psychology, 5,* 4–7.

Van Raalte, J. L., Brewer, B. W., Brewer, D. D., & Linder, D. E. (1992). NCAA Division II college football players' perceptions of an athlete who consults a sport psychologist. *Journal of Sport and Exercise Psychology, 14,* 273–282.

Wiese-Bjornstal, D. M., & Smith, A. M. (1993). Counseling strategies for enhanced recovery of injured athletes within a team approach. In D. Pargman (Ed.), *Psychological bases of sport injuries* (pp. 149–182). Morgantown, WV: Fitness Information Technology.

Teaching Life Skills Through Sport: Community-Based Programs to Enhance Adolescent Development

**Steven J. Danish, Robert J. Fazio,
Valerie C. Nellen, and Susanna S. Owens**

We consider sport psychology to be the use of sport to enhance competence and promote development throughout the life span (Danish, Petitpas, & Hale, 1993). Given this definition, sport psychologists are as concerned about "life" development as they are about athletic development. Sport is so closely tied to other life domains that the value of sport psychology interventions extends well beyond the domain of sport, serving as a metaphor for a variety of life situations (Danish et al., 1993). By emphasizing the promotion of life development, sport psychology interventions can provide a real life test of what Seligman and Csikszentmihalyi (2000) referred to as "positive psychology."

This chapter describes a community-based intervention using sport as a means of teaching life skills to adolescents. We begin with a definition of adolescence and a discussion of how life experiences influence adolescent behavior and of the value of sport in adolescence. We then address the particular characteristics of sport and their relationship to life skills. Following this, the Sports United to Promote Education and Recreation (SUPER), a program designed to teach sport and life skills, is described and several sport-related examples are given. The value and rationale of implementing these sport-based interventions in the community is then introduced. We then outline a process whereby the reader can develop, implement, and evaluate a sport-based, community-oriented, life-skills program.

A Perspective on Adolescence and Adolescent Development

We begin by defining adolescence, because our perspective on this period of the life span has influenced the intervention program we developed. The decision as to what kind of intervention to develop is based in large measure on one's understanding of individual development and societal functioning. This understanding enables one to have the ability to differentiate normative, dysfunctional, and optimal development of a target population and thus to discriminate normal from abnormal behavior (Baltes & Danish, 1980; Danish, 1990).

What constitutes adolescence has become increasingly confusing. For many, adolescence is considered simply the period between childhood and adulthood. However, the difficult question to answer has always been, When is that? Generally, adolescence has been divided into three periods: early (ages 11–14), middle (ages 15–18), and late (ages 18–21; Steinberg, 1993). Rather than use age as the variable for determining these boundaries, in this chapter, adolescence is considered a time when an individual is faced with an increasingly complex set of new roles and also needs to reject or modify previously held roles.

Havighurst (1953) proposed that particular developmental tasks are associated with each phase of the life span. Among the tasks identified for adolescence and expanded on by Chickering (1969) were achieving competence, managing emotions, becoming autonomous, establishing relationships, developing more mature interpersonal relationships, clarifying purpose, and developing integrity. The focus, then, during adolescence is on broadening one's horizons.

Hill (1983) organized his perspective of adolescence around three components: the fundamental changes associated with adolescence, the contexts of adolescence, and the psychosocial developments of adolescence. Some of the fundamental changes are the onset of puberty (biological), the beginning of detachment from parents and the attainment of a separate identity (emotional), the development of advanced reasoning (cognitive), a focus on peer as opposed to parental relations (interpersonal), and a transition to adult work and family roles (social). The four main contexts that affect the development of adolescents are families, peer groups, schools, and work and leisure groups. In addition, five major psychosocial issues accompany adolescent development: identity, autonomy, intimacy, sexuality, and achievement (Steinberg, 1993).

The intervention described here is directed at teaching life skills to adolescents ages 10–16. Because of the changes these adolescents are undergoing, developing an effective intervention provides several unique challenges. An adolescent's well-being can be viewed as encompassing four domains of health: physical, psychological, social, and personal. Within each of these domains, adolescents may engage in health-compromising behaviors (Jessor, 1982), that is, behaviors that threaten the well-being of the individual; or in health-enhancing behaviors, that is, behaviors that improve an individual's well-being (Perry & Jessor, 1985).

Unfortunately, so much energy is directed toward eliminating health-compromising behaviors while health-enhancing behaviors are virtually ignored. In other words, the focus is on prevention—prevention of drug and alcohol abuse, violent and delinquent behaviors, out-of-wedlock pregnancies and sexually transmitted diseases, and dropping out of school. What is clear is that these prevention programs, regardless of how effective they are, will never totally eliminate youths' involvement in health-compromising behaviors. Too often, these programs teach only partial mediators of the desired outcome. For example, teaching violence prevention is more than teaching self-control and conflict resolution. An adolescent's decision to commit a violent act may be caused by a lack of future orientation, the inability to forgive, or some intrapsychic problem (Danish, 2000).

We believe that many adolescents will be able to avoid unhealthy behaviors if they learn healthy options—the life skills associated with future success. For this reason, we focus on what is needed to become a "successful" adolescent and emphasize the positive side: the learning of health-enhancing behaviors. The core of our interventions is teaching "what to say yes to" rather than "just say no."

To help teach adolescents how to succeed, it is necessary to operationalize success. The definition of success will vary across different individuals. However, in general terms, we view a successful adolescent as one who has attained the life skills necessary for effective functioning in the family, school, and community. The Task Force on Education of Young Adolescents (1989) described the five desired outcomes, or characteristics, for every young adolescent as the ability to (a) process information from multiple sources and communicate clearly; (b) be en route to a lifetime of meaningful work by learning how to learn and therefore being able to adapt to different educational and working environments; (c) be a good citizen by participating in community activities and feeling concern for, and connection to, the well-being of others; (d) be a caring and ethical individual by acting on one's convictions about right and wrong; and (e) be a healthy person. Another way to conceptualize success is to adopt the components of psychosocial competence identified by Bloom (2000): play well, think well, work well, love well, and serve well. The concept "be well" also could be added to Bloom's list. Our rationale, then, is to teach adolescents how to think about and develop confidence about their future, as well as to acquire a sense of personal control over themselves and their environment so that they can make better decisions and ultimately become better citizens.

The Rationale for Sport-Based Programming for Adolescents

Understanding adolescent development and the life events that they experience provides an indication of why the use of an ecological intervention such as sport has value when targeting these youth. Sport has the participation level necessary for practitioners to reach many, if not most, of the youth in a given community. The demographics are undeniable—only family, school, and television involve children's and adolescents' time more than sport (Institute for Social Research, 1985). Ewing, Seefeldt, and Brown (1996) estimated that 48,374,000 children in the 5–17 age range participate in sports. Twenty-two million, or 45%, of children and youth are involved in community-based sports organizations such as Little League Baseball and Pop Warner Football. Almost 2.5 million, or 5%, pay to participate in sports activities such as ice skating and swimming; 14.5 million, or 30%, participate in recreational sports programs; 451,000 participate in intramural sports in middle, junior, and senior high school; and 12% play interscholastic sports. By far, the largest number of youth participate in non-school-based programs. In the past five years, a significant increase in participation in youth sports leagues has occurred (Edmundson, 2000).

The qualities intrinsic to participation in sport make it an excellent metaphor for many elements that one would wish to teach in an intervention. For many adolescents, as their interest and involvement in sport increase, so does their concern about their performance and competency. Sport then becomes a readily accessible metaphor and example of personal competence and, as a result, an effective analogy for teaching skills for successful living. All skills regardless of their purpose require practice to master. Basic goal-setting skills can enhance sport performance by clarifying an athlete's training and competition objectives.

Furthermore, goal setting can help athletes gain self-efficacy and competence as they master progressive steps in reaching goals.

It is this connection between sport skills and skills for successful living that makes most coaches, athletes, and sport administrators believe that participation in sport can have a beneficial effect on the psychosocial development of participants far beyond the immediacy of what is learned on the field or in the pool. It is generally believed that what is learned in sport is directly transferable to the classroom and the boardroom. For example, Kleiber and Roberts (1981) observed that sport has been advocated as "a forum for learning responsibility, conformity, subordination to the greater good, persistence, delay of gratification, and even a degree of risk taking" (p. 114). Kleiber (1983) also suggested that "the sporting contest itself is a deliberately structured test of strength, courage, endurance, and self-control—attributes that may seem elusive to the developing adolescent" (p. 87).

A review of the research on the effects of sport on development concluded that sport can have a positive impact on youth development (Danish, Petitpas, & Hale, 1990). Danish and colleagues also concluded that to fully understand the role played by sport in the development of adolescents, it is preferable to examine the topic across the life span rather than to focus on a single specific developmental period.

Most of the research about the value of sport on adolescents has focused on the impact of sport on the development of identity and feelings of competence among youth (Danish, 1983; Danish, Kleiber, & Hall, 1987; Danish et al., 1990; Kleiber & Kirshnit, 1991). Sport is an arena in which the adolescent searches for personal identity and dreams about what he or she might become. This identity, a product of past experiences and the feedback of significant others, is defined by Waterman (1985) as "a self-definition comprised of those goals, values and beliefs which a person finds personally expressive and to which he or she is unequivocally committed" (p. 6). For most adolescent athletes, sport is an area in which they can clearly define themselves, a welcome respite from the confusion usually associated with being "no longer a child, but not yet an adult."

Sport has the potential to enhance development and to enable people to enjoy themselves in the process. However, enhancing development is not an unplanned outcome of sports participation. It occurs when athletes compete against themselves, and more specifically, against their own potential and goals. As Danish noted, "When knowing oneself becomes as important as proving oneself, sport becomes an essential element in personal growth and self expression'' (cited in Athletic Footwear Association, 1990, p. 6).

Sport-Related Life Skills for Adolescents

To use sport to promote personal growth, it must be recognized that the activity is a metaphor for enhancing competence, not an end in itself. In other words, the lasting value of a sport experience lies in the application of the principles learned through participation to other areas. Of the millions of youth who play sports, only a tiny fraction of a percentage will parlay those activities directly into a career. For the rest, growing up means further defining their identity, discovering other skills and interests and, it is our hope, applying some of the valuable principles learned during sport participation to their adult pursuits. These transferable behaviors and attitudes are called *life skills.*

Life skills enable individuals to succeed in the environments in which they live. Examples of these environments include families, schools, workplaces, neighborhoods, and communities. Life skills are both behavioral (e.g., effective communication with peers and adults) and cognitive (e.g., effective decision making). As people age, the number of environments in which they must be successful increases. Environments vary from individual to individual, just as the definition of what it means to succeed differs across individuals and across environments.

Individuals in the same environment are likely to be dissimilar from each other as a result of the life skills they have already mastered, their other resources, and their opportunities, real or perceived. For this reason, those who teach life skills must be sensitive to developmental, environmental, and individual differences, and the possibility that the life skills needed may not be the same for individuals of different ages, ethnic and racial groups, or economic status (Danish, 1995).

Although it is necessary to be sensitive to individual differences, it also is important to recognize that individuals can often effectively apply life skills learned in one environment to other environments. Sport is a particularly appropriate environment to learn skills that can be transferred to other environments. First, physical skills are similar to life skills in the way they are learned, that is, through demonstration and practice (Danish & Hale, 1981). Second, many of the skills learned in sport—including performing under pressure, solving problems, meeting deadlines and challenges, setting goals, communicating, handling both success and failure, working with a team and within a system, and receiving feedback and benefiting from it—are transferable to other life domains.

In transferring skills from one domain to another, it is important to recognize that abilities acquired in one area do not automatically transfer to another area. Understanding what is necessary for skills to be transferable and learning to transfer them are critical life skills in themselves (Danish, Petitpas, & Hale, 1992). To this end, those running programs that use sport as their metaphor need to be aware of this, and to realize that the teaching of skills must be accompanied by explanations of how and why these skills will be useful later in life and in other domains.

To be able to transfer skills, adolescents must first believe that they have skills and qualities that are of value in other settings. Individuals of all ages often do not recognize that many of the skills they have acquired to excel in one domain such as sport are transferable to other life areas. Petitpas, Danish, McKelvain, and Murphy (1992) found that elite athletes had several insecurities and doubts about their ability to embark on new careers. Generally, these athletes felt that they possessed only sport-related skills and lacked the skills to succeed in a new career. These athletes, who had demonstrated the ability to learn one set of skills to an elite level and were not able to transfer them to another setting, provide an object lesson for the importance of ensuring that adolescents learn about transferable skills.

Second, adolescents participating in sports must learn that they possess both physical and cognitive skills. There is more to sport than just throwing a ball or running fast. Athletes plan, set goals, make decisions, seek out instruction, and manage their arousal levels as a routine part of their athletic participation. Some of these same skills are necessary for success in other domains. Without these cognitive skills, it is unlikely that an individual can succeed in any domain. When adolescents are able to recognize that the cognitive skills they have are critical to their success in sport, they improve their performance in sport and can transfer these skills to other domains.

Third, adolescents must know how physical and cognitive skills were learned and in what context they were learned. Both types of skills are learned in the same fashion. Skills can be acquired through both formal instruction and trial and error. When learned through formal instruction, the skill is named and described, and a rationale for its use is given. The skill is demonstrated so the individual can observe the correct and incorrect use of the skill. Then the individual is given numerous opportunities to practice the skill under supervision to ensure continuous feedback. Adolescents learn skills through trial and error by practicing skills they observe, for example, at the playground or on television. They attempt to imitate these skills on their own, and with continual trial and error, they acquire their own version of the skill.

Fourth, adolescents must understand the rationale for learning the skill for sport and nonsport environments and must be willing to try to use the skill in a nonsport setting. Adolescents may lack confidence in their ability to apply skills in nonsport settings. They may fear failure or "looking bad." They also may lack understanding of the new setting, and this fear of the unknown may add to their hesitancy in attempting to apply the skill.

Fifth, some adolescents have so much of their personal identity tied up in sport that they have little motivation to explore nonsport roles (Petitpas & Champagne, 1988). They view themselves as successful athletes, not successful people. This mind-set can rob them of their confidence and prevent them from exploring nonsport roles. If they do not think they can be successful in other settings, they may choose not to explore other options.

For many, interest and involvement in sport increases during adolescence, as does the concern about performance and competency. Sport then becomes a readily accessible metaphor and an example of personal competence and, as a result, an effective analogy for teaching life skills. Through programs such as SUPER, adolescents can master and refine basic skill-building by learning how to break objectives into smaller steps, focus on features that are under their control, and build on personal strengths.

The SUPER Program

SUPER is a sports-based program that takes advantage of the clearly defined, contingency-dependent, closed environment of sport and uses it as a training ground for life. Participants are taught to use a variety of skills, some physical and some mental, to improve their athletic performance and to recognize situations both in and out of sports requiring these skills and then to apply them in sport and nonsport settings.

The goals of the SUPER program are for each participant to leave the program with the understanding that (a) there is a relationship between performance excellence in sport and personal excellence in life, (b) mental skills can enhance both sport performance and personal performance, and (c) there are effective and accessible student–athlete role models. The skills taught in the different SUPER programs vary depending on the sport and the environment within which the program is taught. However, some of the basic skills taught include identifying sport dreams, turning dreams into goals, setting reachable goals, developing plans to reach goals, identifying and overcoming goal roadblocks, coaching oneself by managing emotions, believing in oneself, and developing a support team.

In most SUPER programs, older student–athletes are chosen to teach the program to younger adolescents. When peers teach other peers, they become part of what Seidman and Rappaport (1974) called an "educational pyramid." Such a pyramid starts with the staff of the Life Skills Center at Virginia Commonwealth University, which develops the intervention and then trains and teaches the SUPER student–athlete leaders how to implement the intervention. The SUPER leaders then teach SUPER programs to the target audience, the younger peers. Training time for the leaders ranges between 10 and 20 hours. The ultimate goal is to extend the pyramid by training on-site, community professionals how to select and train SUPER leaders.

This implementation strategy has several advantages. First, by using older peers, there is a potential for choosing natural, indigenous leaders to serve as role models. Successful high school students serve as concrete images of what younger adolescents can become. Because these high school students have grown up in the same neighborhoods, attended the same schools, and confronted similar roadblocks, they serve as important role models; thus, they are in an ideal position to be effective teachers (Danish, 1997). Second, there has been an increasing awareness of the mutual benefits to the peer leaders and to the younger students. Riessman (1976) identified what he called the "helper therapy principle." He noted that the "helper" gained a sense of power, control, and being needed through the helping process. More recently, Hogan (2000) found that peer leaders reported that teaching a health-oriented life skills program improved their perception of their leadership skills. They also improved their understanding of what is required to set and attain goals. This finding by Hogan is consistent with the beliefs held by educational psychologists, who have long concluded that teaching is one of the best ways of learning. Peer teaching, then, provides the peer teacher with benefits of both a psychological and content nature. By teaching others how to succeed, the peer teacher's ability to succeed is enhanced.

SUPER leaders are involved in three sets of activities with their younger peers. They teach sport skills related to specific sports, coach them to improve their sport performance, and teach them life skills. To assist leaders in the teaching and coaching of sport skills, Life Skills Center staff teach them how skills are learned; how to teach sport skills to athletes who are less able and experienced; and how to use the Sport Observation System, an instrument to observe how others play sports. The leaders are told that when they instruct, demonstrate, and conduct practices they should focus on *how* the youths are participating as well as on *how well* they are performing and participating. Understanding "how" provides information on the mental skills that youths use in dealing with coaching and teaching and may be indicative of how they will respond to other forms of instruction, such as school and job training. Observing how participants react refers to the answers to questions such as the following:

- Are they attentive when given instructions or observing demonstration?
- Do they become frustrated with themselves when they cannot perform the activity to their expectations, and does this frustration impede or enhance later efforts?
- Are they first to initiate questions when they do not understand something being taught, or do they wait quietly for someone else to talk first?
- Are they first to initiate conversation with group members, or do they wait for someone else to talk to them first?
- How do they react when they have a good performance or a bad performance?
- How do they react when others have a good performance or a bad performance?
- How do they react when someone gives them praise or criticism?
- Do they give up when they cannot do as well as they would like or as well as others, or do they continue to practice in a determined manner to learn the skill?
- Do they compete or cooperate with the other youth?

We ask the SUPER leaders to speak to participants about what they have observed. They are asked to explain to the participants what they have learned by observing their activities and help them explore what this means to them. We expect that the leaders will spend at least a few minutes with each adolescent to discuss the "hows" of his or her performance (separate from the "how wells") during each session of the sport clinics.

Community-Based Examples of the SUPER Program

The SUPER Basketball Program

In 1998 and 1999, the Virginia Commonwealth University (VCU) women's basketball team taught life and basketball skills as part of a service-learning course to 80 middle school girls. About half the girls came from underserved areas within the community. Once per week for 12 weeks, students came after school to participate in the program. Students were placed in teams of approximately 10 girls. Two varsity student–athletes served as their coaches. During the 90-minute sessions, three stations were set up: basketball fundamentals, basketball games, and life skills. In preparation for teaching SUPER, the student–athletes were taught the skills they would teach and were asked to apply them to their own basketball and school. They were then taught how to teach the skills and to use the Sport Observation System. A "report card" was given to each participant at the end of the clinic. The report card provided feedback on the "how" and "how well" for each participant.

About a third of the girls chose to return the second year, and several have started attending the VCU women's games regularly. Women team members have been invited to dinners, plays, and graduations.

The First Tee

The First Tee was launched in November 1997 as an initiative of the World Golf Foundation. The mission of The First Tee is to create affordable and accessible golf facilities, primarily for youth. The vision is for a diversity of youth to have a place to learn and play golf and to enrich their lives by the lessons taught through golf. The target group is young people ages 7–18. A national teaching and certification program with a life skills component has been developed.

A First Tee National Youth Golf and Leadership Academy was held at Kansas State University. A total of 119 youth, ages 14–17, from 22 states attended. During this week-long program, the developers of the academy hoped to have an effect on the personal values (e.g., concern with the welfare of others), emotional intelligence (e.g., empathy, effective interpersonal skills), and leadership ability (e.g., helping others set goals and develop plans to reach these goals) of participants. Each participant completed a pre- and postsurvey to measure the amount of change that occurred on several of the instruments.

The academy seemed to have a positive impact on the participants. Many reported positive changes, which were associated with specific leadership and life skills that the participants formally learned and practiced during the week. They felt more competent to lead others and to set and achieve their goals. However, there was also a change in values and attitudes measures, which was surprising, because attitudes and values are resistant to change and are more likely to evolve over time and through experience. For example, participants reported that they felt more concern for others, felt that they better understood the importance of effective communication, and felt more able to act responsibly. Thus, it appears that teaching life skills through golf may be an effective primer for continued growth, both in skills and values.

The NFL/NFF Coaching Academy

A different but essential aspect of adolescent development is the importance of adults as positive role models and teachers. Lessons learned from parents, mentors, and coaches often prove to be valuable later in life. Successful athletes at all levels tell inspirational stories about how their high school or youth coaches were the greatest influences on their lives. The National Football League (NFL) and National Football Foundation (NFF) wanted to enhance the contributions coaches who work with youth could make to the development of their players. The two organizations joined forces to develop a coaching academy for coaches who work with youth.

The NFL/NFF Coaching Academy was designed to teach high school and youth coaches how to develop a coaching philosophy consistent with adolescent development, best teach football skills, develop a system for organizing a team, and incorporate life skills into their coaching style. The expectation was that more effective coaches would inspire their athletes to learn life lessons as they became more skilled at football.

The Community as a Setting for Sport-Based Interventions

We believe that the most effective way to implement sport-based life skills programs such as SUPER is through the community. As defined by *The Random House Dictionary of the English Language* (1966), a *community* is "a social group sharing common characteristics or interests and perceived or perceiving itself as distinct in some respect from the larger society within which it exists" (p. 298).

The rationale for this belief is based on several factors. First, as Eitzen (1984) noted,

> Sport is such a pervasive activity in contemporary America that to ignore it is to overlook one of the most significant aspects of society. It is a social phenomenon which extends into education, politics, economics, art, the mass media, and even international diplomatic relations. Involvement in sport, either as a participant or in more indirect ways, is almost considered a public duty by many Americans. (p. 9)

Second, involvement in sport is a community activity. Although individual athletes compete in sport, it is generally a group activity played with or against others and often viewed by interested fans and spectators. Third, participation in sport creates and defines new and unique communities (e.g., master's-level participants in such sports as swimming and track) and generates identification with community, professional, college, and high school teams.

Rappaport (1977) delineated several models for the delivery of mental health services. He identified two factors that constitute his model: a conceptual component and a style of delivery. An intervention can be based on several possible conceptual components. Our framework is a cognitive–behavioral one in which life skills are taught to enable youths to learn health-enhancing behaviors, to assist them in developing resources and resiliency to overcome the effects of past health-compromising behaviors, or to prevent them from engaging in health-compromising behaviors. However, it is the style of delivery that is often overlooked and is so critical. Rappaport identified two styles: a waiting-mode and a seeking-mode. We have adopted a seeking-mode for the purpose of teaching life skills because we are trying to reach adolescents in their everyday environments and with an educational rather than a clinically oriented approach.

Developing and Evaluating Community-Based Programs

Effective community-based sport programming requires careful design, implementation, and evaluation. Although the specifics of the programs vary, seven essential steps should be followed in developing all programs (for a more complete discussion of this process, see Danish, 1990).

Step 1: Determine the Objectives of the Intervention

The goals of the intervention should be based on a needs assessment. Needs can be determined by surveying the community and ascertaining community members' expressed needs, either through a demographic study of the community or by reviewing research reports and literature on the community. Often, both of these procedures are used.

In developing our sport-related life skills program for adolescents, we found a need to help youths develop more optimism about their future, to reduce their involvement in behaviors that compromise health, and to help them understand that skills learned and applied in sport can be transferred from sport to other life domains. Our goals, then, were to teach sport skills and life skills related to sport. In identifying goals, the question asked was: For what purpose is the program being developed?

Step 2: Determine the Targets of the Intervention

When designing interventions, the questions of *who*, *where*, and *when* are critical. Rappaport (1977) identified six potential targets for interventions: the individual, group, organization, institution, community, or society. In the SUPER programs, intervention is at the individual level, using a group format. The focus is on individuals because we believe that adolescents must be taught new skills before an intervention at a larger level is tried.

A separate target issue relates to the timing of the intervention. Danish and colleagues (1993) developed a set of categories related to the timing of intervention. Their system related the timing of the intervention to the experiencing of critical life events (Danish, Smyer, & Nowak, 1980). Interventions occurring before an event are *enhancement* strategies; those occurring during an event are *supportive* strategies; and once an event has occurred, interventions are considered *counseling* strategies. From the life development intervention perspective developed by Danish and colleagues (1992, 1993, 1995), the SUPER programs are enhancement strategies.

Step 3: Develop the Technology to Be Used in Implementing the Intervention

Implementation involves assessing both what the intervention is and how it is delivered. What is delivered should be closely related to the goals of the intervention. In the case of SUPER, we have identified specific life and sport skills to teach, especially ones that transfer from one setting or domain to another.

Unfortunately, how the intervention is implemented is often overlooked or taken for granted. It is in the development of technology to be used in program implementation that the program developer becomes an instructional technologist. For example, a program curriculum must be developed, printed, and made available for dissemination. Programs that depend exclusively on the charisma of the leader are less likely to be successful and clearly cannot be replicated. An operations manual describing how to train staff as well as design, implement, and evaluate the program is also very useful. In addition, issues such as how to disseminate the program from one site to another and how to work with various organizations to implement the intervention should be included.

Step 4: Determine the Most Effective Means of Carrying Out the Intervention

It is critical when deciding where to deliver the intervention that a credible local person assists in developing contacts and serves as a champion for the program. Discussions about implementing the program should be organized so that people in the community believe that the program is being done *with* them not *to* or *for* them. One way to ensure this atmosphere is to hire staff who are or have been employed in the setting and are indigenous to the community where the program is to be implemented. For example, in one of our programs taught in conjunction with the schools, we arranged with Richmond City Public Schools to pay for a teacher to be on loan to the Life Skills Center. This arrangement has helped us better understand the school environment.

As a result, we have been able to minimize the disruption to the schools in terms of how we implement the program and how intrusive we are when we evaluate.

Step 5: Determine the Reasons Why Evaluation Is Done

Evaluation serves three purposes. The first purpose is to prove that the intervention was effective, valuable, and/or did what it was intended to do. In an age of accountability, decisionmakers and funding sources want this kind of evidence as a means of determining whether a program should be continued. Too often, this kind of evaluation is confused with research. Evaluators must be sensitive to the needs and expectations of those wanting the evaluation and provide it in a format that meets these needs. The second purpose is to improve the intervention. The emphasis is on gathering information and making judgments to change any aspect of the intervention in order to better it. The first two purposes should be interactive. The third purpose is to advance scientific knowledge. Interventions serve a knowledge application as well as a knowledge generation role (Danish, 1990).

Step 6: Determine the Type of Evaluation to Be Conducted and the Most Effective Means of Carrying It Out

For evaluation to be effective, it must become a part of the development of the intervention, not a process applied after its implementation. There are two types of evaluation: process, or formative, evaluation, and outcome, or summative, evaluation (Scriven, 1980). Although the goals of the two types of evaluations are different, they are generally interrelated in that they occur at the same time. Process evaluations are conducted for several reasons, including monitoring the progress of the intervention to determine how it is being received, to assess the cost-effectiveness of the activity, and to assist in making replication possible. The overall question being asked in the process evaluation is whether the target population learned what was taught; and if so, why; and if not, why not (Danish, 1990)? The failure of the target population to learn what was taught may have nothing to do with the goals of the intervention but with the process of the implementation. Problems can stem from the participants, the instructors, the topic area, and the setting (Meyer, Nicholson, Danish, Fries, & Polk, 2000).

Researchers often confine themselves to outcome evaluations, determining whether the intervention goal was attained. However, unless careful attention is paid to how the intervention is implemented, we cannot be certain what was implemented and how well it was done. Consequently, we are unable to assess whether the outcomes are a result of our efforts. When careful monitoring of an intervention does take place, it helps the researcher delineate the strengths and weaknesses of the intervention and how it may be improved.

Step 7: Develop Intervention Programs That Can Be Disseminated at More Than One Site

Interventions are often developed and implemented for one site. However, one test of the effectiveness of a program is how well it can be disseminated to more than one site. If a program cannot be implemented at more than one site, the intervention, regardless of how effective it is in the original site, has limited utility. A program should have some or all of the following characteristics (Danish, 2000):

- *Modular.* The program should have multicomponents based on modules that can be used independently.
- *Flexible.* Although any program must have a core, or essence, that must be taught, it should be sufficiently flexible so it can be customized to the audience.
- *Cost and time efficient.* Keeping youth interested is critical. Therefore, programs that are time modular to fit time constraints should be developed. It is easier to expand a program once participants are committed, as opposed to shortening it.
- *Multimedia training and program materials.* Delivering the training and developing program materials in multiple formats, including manuals, hand outs, and videos is essential.
- *Consistent.* In determining critical elements for a program, there must be a consistency of viewpoint and philosophy.
- *Teachable/learnable.* Different people at different times in different settings must be able to teach the program, and participants must be able to learn it in the same versatile fashion. This is especially important if community ownership of the program is to be achieved.
- *Transportable/replicable.* The program must be transportable across communities and organizations and replicable within various activities, settings, and neighborhoods.
- *Scale-able.* The program must be sufficiently robust, so it can be applied in communities with different levels of resources.

- *"Evalua-able."* The program must contain multiple levels of assessment and evaluation, many of which can be embedded in the delivery of the program.

Conclusion

In this chapter, we described a community-based intervention that uses sport as a means of teaching life skills to adolescents. We also presented a rationale for such a program based on an understanding of developmental issues faced by adolescents, their commitment to sport, and the value of using the community as a setting to deliver such an intervention. Further, we have outlined a process that can be used by others to develop, implement, and evaluate a sport-based, community-oriented, life skills program.

Psychologists have few opportunities to observe adolescents who are intent on optimizing their development in any area and assist them in this process. Because of the importance of sport for youths, psychologists are in a unique position to help them enhance their sport performance and, at the same time, teach them how to transfer skills learned in sport to other life domains. Moreover, programs such as the ones described enable psychologists interested in sport to combine some of their vocational and avocational interests—something psychologists rarely have the opportunity to do.

References

Athletic Footwear Association. (1990). *American youth and sports participation.* Unpublished manuscript. North Palm Beach, FL.

Baltes, P. B., & Danish, S. J. (1980). Intervention in life-span development and aging: Issues and concepts. In R. R. Turner & H. W. Reese (Eds.), *Life-span developmental psychology: Intervention* (pp. 49–78). New York: Academic Press.

Bloom, M. (2000). The uses of theory in primary prevention practice: Evolving thoughts on sports and after-school activities as influences of social competence. In S. J. Danish & T. Gullotta (Eds.), *Developing competent youth and strong communities through after-school programming* (pp. 17–66). Washington, DC: CWLA Press.

Chickering, A. W. (1969). *Education and identity.* San Francisco: Jossey-Bass.

Danish, S. J. (2000). Youth and community development: How after-school programming can make a difference. In S. J. Danish & T. Gullotta (Eds.), *Developing competent youth and strong communities through after-school programming* (pp. 275–302). Washington, DC: CWLA Press.

Danish, S. (1997). Going for the goal: A life skills program for adolescents. In T. Gullotta & G. Albee (Eds.), *Primary prevention works* (pp. 291–312). Newbury Park: Sage.

Danish, S. (1995). Reflections on the status and future of community psychology. *Community Psychologist, 28,* 16–18.

Danish, S. J. (1990). Ethical considerations in the design, implementation and evaluation of developmental interventions. In C. B. Fisher & W. W. Tryon (Eds.), *Ethics in applied developmental psychology: Emerging issues in an emerging field* (Vol. 4, pp. 93–112). New York: Ablex.

Danish, S. J. (1983). Musing about personal competence: The contributions of sport, health, and fitness. *American Journal of Community Psychology, 11,* 221–240.

Danish, S. J., & Hale, B. D. (1981). Toward an understanding of the practice of sport psychology. *Journal of Sport Psychology, 3,* 90–99.

Danish, S., Kleiber, D., & Hall, H. (1987). Developmental intervention and motivation enhancement in the context of sport. In *Advances in motivation and achievement: Enhancing motivation* (Vol. 5, pp. 211–238). Greenwich, CT: JAI Press.

Danish, S., Petitpas, A., & Hale, B. (1995). Psychological interventions with athletes: A life development model. In S. Murphy (Ed.), *Clinical sport psychology* (pp. 19–38). Champaign, IL: Human Kinetics.

Danish, S. J., Petitpas, A. J., & Hale, B. D. (1993). Life development intervention for athletes: Life skills through sports. *The Counseling Psychologist, 21,* 352–385.

Danish, S., Petitpas, A., & Hale, B. (1992). A developmental–educational intervention model of sport psychology. *The Sport Psychologist, 6,* 403–415.

Danish, S. J., Petitpas, A. J., & Hale, B. D. (1990). Sport as a context for developing competence. In T. Gullotta, G. Adams, & R. Monteymar (Eds.), *Developing social competency in adolescence* (Vol. 3, pp. 169–194). Newbury Park: Sage.

Danish, S., Smyer, M. A., & Nowak, C. A. (1980). Developmental intervention: Enhancing life-event processes. In P. B. Baltes & O. G. Brim, Jr. (Eds.), *Life-span development and behavior* (Vol. 3, pp. 339–366). New York: Academic Press.

Edmundson, K. (2000). Issues in after-school youth development programming. In S. J. Danish & T. Gullotta (Eds.), *Developing competent youth and strong communities through after-school programming* (pp. 217–238). Washington, DC: CWLA Press.

Eitzen, D. S. (1984). *Sport in contemporary society.* New York: St. Martin Press.

Ewing, M., Seefeldt, V., & Brown, T. (1996). *The role of organized sport in the education and health of American children and youth.* Unpublished manuscript.

Havighurst, R. J. (1953). *Human development and education.* New York: Longmans.

Hill, J. (1983). Early adolescence: A research agenda. *Journal of Early Adolescence, 3,* 1–21.

Hogan, C. (2000). *The impact of a peer-led program on the peer leaders' leadership-related skills.* Unpublished master's thesis, Virginia Commonwealth University, Richmond, VA.

Institute for Social Research. (1985). *Time, goods and well-being.* Ann Arbor: University of Michigan Press.

Jessor, R. (1982). Critical issues in research on adolescent health promotion. In T. J. Coates, A. C. Peterson, & C. Perry (Eds.), *Promoting adolescent health: A dialogue on research and practice* (pp. 447–465). New York: Academic Press.

Kleiber, D. A. (1983). Sport and human development: A dialectical interpretation. *Journal of Humanistic Psychology, 23,* 76–95.

Kleiber, D. A., & Kirshnit, C. E. (1991). Sport involvement and identity formation. In L. Diamant (Ed.), *Mind–body maturity: Psychological approaches to sports, exercise, and fitness* (pp. 193–211). New York: Hemisphere.

Kleiber, D. A., & Roberts, G. C. (1981). The effects of sport experience in the development of social character: An exploratory investigation. *Journal of Sport Psychology, 3,* 114–122.

Meyer, A., Nicholson, R., Danish, S., Fries, E., & Polk, V. (2000). A model to measure peer-led programs in rural middle schools: Implementation of a sixth-grade Goals for Health program. *Journal of Educational and Psychological Consultation, 11*(2), 223–252.

Perry, C., & Jessor, R. (1985). The concept of health promotion and the prevention of adolescent drug abuse. *Health Education Quarterly, 12*(2), 169–184.

Petitpas, A. L., & Champagne, D. E. (1988). Developmental programming for intercollegiate athletes. *Journal of College Student Development, 29*(5), 454–460.

Petitpas, A., Danish, S., McKelvain, R., & Murphy, S. (1992). A career assistance program for elite athletes. *Journal of Counseling and Development, 70,* 383–386.

Rappaport, J. (1977). *Community psychology: Values, research and action.* New York: Holt.

Riessman, F. (1976). How does self-help work? *Social Policy, 7,* 41–45.

Scriven, M. (1980). *The logic of evaluation.* Inverness, CA: Edgepress.

Seidman, E., & Rappaport, J. (1974). The educational pyramid: A paradigm for training, research, and manpower utilization in community psychology. *American Journal of Community Psychology, 2,* 119–130.

Seligman, M., & Csikszentmihalyi, M. (2000). Positive psychology. *American Psychologist, 55,* 5–14.

Steinberg, L. (1993). *Adolescence* (3rd ed.). New York: McGraw-Hill.

Task Force on Education of Young Adolescents. (1989). *Turning points: Preparing American youth for the 21st century.* New York: Carnegie Corporation.

The Random House Dictionary of the English Language. (1966). New York: Random House, Inc.

Waterman, A. S. (1985). *Identity in adolescence: Processes and contents.* San Francisco: Jossey-Bass.

Part III

Clinical Issues

Assessment in Sport and Exercise Psychology

Sean C. McCann, Douglas P. Jowdy, and
Judy L. Van Raalte

The role of assessment in the history and practice of sport psychology differs from other psychology disciplines because of the unique gestation of the field as a subdiscipline of physical education rather than psychology. Traditionally in psychology, assessment has been the foundation and launching pad for the growth of several applied fields. The development of tools to assess intellectual ability, aptitude, school achievement, job skills, psychopathology, and personality has resulted in new areas of applied work for psychologists. Advances in assessment allowed psychologists to be taken seriously as "scientists," and the development of specialized knowledge in assessment enhanced the effectiveness and credibility of applied psychologists.

Assessment has not held a preeminent role in the field of sport psychology because of several factors. First, the start of sport psychology as a subdiscipline of physical education, rather than assessment-dominated psychology, is one obvious factor. Second, the timing of academic and applied growth in sport psychology coincided with controversy over the role of assessment in mainstream psychology (Fisher, 1984). Third, participants and practitioners in the field sport psychology (see McCullagh & Noble, chapter 7, this volume) have diverse backgrounds in training, resulting in divergent views on assessment. Fourth, the environment of sport, particularly elite sport, creates many ethical and practical hurdles for assessment efforts by sport psychologists.

Despite the idiosyncratic development of assessment in sport psychology, assessment has played a critical role in the history of the field and remains an important issue for current and future development.

This chapter briefly reviews the history of assessment in sport psychology, describes current issues faced by practitioners, and provides practical tips for the use of assessment in applied sport psychology.

Assessment and Sport Psychology: Historical Context

A boom in applied sport psychology in the 1960s and 1970s coincided with growth and controversy in the area of assessment in psychology. Although the relatively new field of applied sport psychology was evolving, the area of personality assessment in psychology was under siege by behavioral psychologists. Behaviorists were decrying the "trait-based philosophy" underlying many personality tests of the time, saying that this approach underestimated the role of environment and learning in "personality" as measured by expressed behavior (Mischel, 1968). During the 1970s frequent calls were made for the elimination of personality testing and trait concepts in psychology (Anastasi, 1988; Peterson, 1992).

Meanwhile, in sport psychology, more than 1000 studies assessing personality in sport were published in the late 1960s and 1970s (Fisher, 1984). Most prominently, the Athletic Motivation Inventory (AMI; Tutko, Lyon, & Ogilvie, 1969), which was designed to measure critical mental characteristics of elite athletes, generated extensive interest in sport psychology among college and professional teams (Williams, 1986). Eventually, the AMI became embroiled in both a psychometric and a professional controversy, and the National Football League (NFL) players association lobbied to have "psychological tests" banned from use in the NFL (Nideffer, 1981). Today, the NFL and some NFL teams perform psychological testing before the annual draft and before the athletes are members of the Players Union.

With the practical challenge to the legitimacy of psychological testing for selection of professional athletes coming on the heels of a general movement in psychology away from trait-oriented personality measures, interest in assessment in applied sport psychology slowed (Silva, 1984). A few researchers continued the focus on assessment and test development (e.g., Mahoney, Gabriel, & Perkins, 1987; Martens, Vealey, & Burton 1990; Morgan 1980; Nideffer, 1981, 1987, 1990; Smith, Smoll, Schutz, & Ptacek, 1995). For the most part, however, academics in kinesiology and psychology did not publish systematic lines of sport psychology assessment research that took assessment devices through the long and arduous process of test development and establishment of reliability as well as content, construct, and criterion-related validity. Instead, they focused on new, unexplored areas as the sport psychology assessment boom of the 1960s and 1970s went bust.

The utility of sport psychology assessment tools has suffered from the lack of a strong academic base. As Marsh (1998) described the situation, "the quality of assessments in early sport/exercise work was weak (p. xv)." Without reliable and valid assessments to use, individual researchers created ad hoc instruments to measure athletes in a variety of areas (Marsh, 1998). Other researchers used "established" measures from other psychology disciplines without establishing their validity with a sport population or developing sport-specific measures (Silva, 1984). Furthermore, practitioners without "gold standard" assessment tools were left to their own devices, resulting in some questionable and some downright unethical practices that still occur today in sport psychology. Although some of these practices have been motivated by financial self-interest, many of these anecdotal "horror stories" derive from the lack of a strong assessment foundation for the field.

Two texts have helped strengthen the foundation of sport psychology assessment. In 1990, Ostrow published the *Directory of Psychological Tests in the Sport and Exercise Sciences*, which catalogued 175 instruments used in research and practice in sport psychology. A second edition, published in 1996, listed 314 sport psychology tests. In 1998, Duda edited the first text on assessment in sport psychology, *Advances in Sport and Exercise Psychology Measurement*, which is required reading for anyone wishing to go beyond the overview presented in this chapter (see Exhibit 14.1).

Current Assessment Methods in Sport Psychology

Several assessment methods are available to applied sport psychologists working in the field. These include, but are not limited to, the interview, behavioral observation, coach reports, videotape review, and testing. Ideally, several methods are used to develop a full understanding of athlete–clients and their unique situations. Before a particular assessment approach is selected, it is important to identify the client, to clarify the referral question (which helps determine the best choice of assess-

Exhibit 14.1

Common Uses of Assessment in Applied Sport Psychology

1. Establish a baseline of mental skills as part of an intake or in a group setting.
   Common assessment techniques:
   • Interview, with or without an intake form with checklist
   • Multiple Scale Assessment Device (e.g., ACSI–28, TOPS)

2. Monitor overtraining as part of a team's effort to peak for key events.
   Common assessment techniques:
   • Regular meetings with athletes and/or coach
   • Repeated written assessment tool (POMS, Rest–Q)

3. Determine the role of anxiety in an athlete's performance.
   Common assessment techniques:
   • Clinical interview to rule out anxiety disorder
   • Behavioral observation in practice and competition
   • Review of competition videotape with athlete
   • Regular meetings with athlete that include athlete self-report
   • Anxiety Measurement Scales (Spielberger State–Trait Anxiety Inventory; CSAI–2)

4. Assessment as part of "team-building" intervention
   Common assessment techniques:
   • Interview with coaches
   • Group and/or individual interview with athletes
   • Team-building exercise and debriefing
   • Personality and/or interaction measures (e.g., MBTI, FIRO–B, TAIS)

5. Clinical assessment as part of applied work with an athlete
   Common assessment techniques:
   • Clinical interview
   • Potential referral to psychiatrist to determine appropriateness of medications
   • Psychodiagnostic assessment tools (e.g., MMPI–2, BDI, EDI)
   • Ongoing treatment sessions

6. Neuropsychology testing (often used in the National Hockey League and the NFL, per their concussion protocols)
   Common assessment techniques:
   • Clinical interview
   • Baseline testing (e.g., brief neuropsychological screening)
   • Brief mental status exam (in the field)
   • Follow-up testing (postconcussion)
   • Full neuropsychological testing (e.g., Halstead–Reitan Neuropsychological Battery, Luria–Nebraska)

Exhibit 14.2

Guidelines for Sport Psychological Testing

1. Identify the client.
2. Clarify the referral questions. Indicate the limits of ability to answer the question.
3. Consider all the potential assessment methods.
4. Determine the potential costs and benefits of using testing (e.g., time, money, change of role for consultant).
5. Consider a referral to someone else for assessment (e.g., a psychiatrist concerning the suitability of medication or someone with more assessment expertise).
6. Clarify *in writing* who will have access to test results. Make sure this is clearly understood by all concerned parties.
7. Given the decision to use testing, select tests with strong psychometric properties.
8. Be familiar with the administration, scoring, and interpretation of tests.
9. Provide feedback as soon as possible. If written reports are provided, maintain security of these test reports.

---

ment methods), to determine the manner of assessment, to consider confidentiality concerns, and to determine the manner in which feedback will be provided to the athlete (see Exhibit 14.2). Each of these issues is discussed subsequently in more detail.

Who Is the Client?

In sport settings, identifying the client is not always a simple task. A coach may request and pay for testing to assess current levels of team cohesion. The sport psychologist might be asked to provide feedback to the coach and athletes on cohesion in an effort to improve team dynamics. It also is possible that the coach may be interested in identifying athletes who are disrupting cohesion. In this situation, the coach is clearly a client, paying the sport psychologist for assistance with cohesion concerns. The athletes, however, also may be considered clients. They are providing personal information about themselves and also expect to see changes in cohesion. Clarifying issues of confidentiality (subsequently discussed in more detail) and having athletes and coaches complete an informed consent form (see Exhibit 14.3) can help prevent misunderstandings and conflicts around these issues.

Exhibit 14.3

Sample Informed Consent Form

Consent for Sport Psychology Assessment

I hereby give my permission for sport psychology assessment for the purpose of research and for individual feedback. I understand that the confidentiality of all assessments will be strictly safeguarded. None of my individual data will be released to anyone other than me. I understand that my individual data may be used as part of a database for research, but individual assessment data will never be revealed.

I give my permission with full knowledge that access to sport psychology services is not contingent upon my granting of this permission. I also understand that if I feel at all uncomfortable at any time while being assessed, I can ask that the assessment be stopped.

_____
Signature

_____
Print Name

_____   _____
Date   Sport Psychology Consultant

What Is the Referral Question?

In many clinical settings, psychologists are often asked to provide an assessment because other professionals are "stumped" by an individual client or are having problems working effectively with the client. Getting a clear understanding of the situation is necessary before testing is conducted. The same approach applies to sport. A coach may refer an athlete who "has trouble learning," and suggest that the athlete be tested for a learning disability. If the real issue is that the coach "teaches" by screaming and humiliating his athletes, who then shut out the coach's ideas, then this type of testing is not warranted. Clarifying the referral question allows sport psychologists to avoid "fishing trips" in which questions are asked or tests are administered without a clear understanding of the situation, a process that can aggravate athletes and reduce a sport psychologist's future effectiveness.

Athlete Selection

In some cases, the referral question is clear. Coaches or administrators are interested in learning which athletes will be the most effective performers. Several authors in the field of sport psychology have strongly questioned the appropriateness of using psychological or "personality" testing to help a team or coach select athletes (Gill, 2000; Singer, 1988; Vealey & Garner-Holman, 1998). These criticisms are based on both the lack of evidence that assessment devices are effective for this purpose and the concerns engendered by the use of the AMI and other assessments in athlete selection in professional settings. Indeed, even the authors of a measure shown to predict future baseball success have strongly recommended that the measure not be used for selection purposes (Smith & Christensen, 1995). As they note, an athlete's awareness of the test's use for selection creates a response bias for social desirability (e.g., faking good, lying) that invalidates the test's predictive ability. Thus, the ideal of an assessment tool for athlete selection has not yet been met.

Before all hope of creating sport selection instruments is thrown out, it is important to note that selection testing with reliable and valid tests is a common practice in academic settings in the United States, as reflected by the role of SAT and GRE testing in undergraduate and graduate school admissions, respectively. Psychologists are frequently employed to perform selection testing in such settings as police departments (Heil & Henschen, 1996). With further efforts, it may be possible to develop appropriate instruments for sport selection. For now, however, the use of psychological assessment to select athletes is an endeavor fraught with peril, given the limits of assessment tools. The peril is, of course, greatest for the test taker, whose entire professional career may be altered or ended by a decision based on a psychological assessment.

Performance Enhancement

In the area of performance enhancement, mental-skills profiling has received a great deal of attention (see Murphy & Tammen, 1998, for a review). For athletes interested in this area, the referral questions are generally one of the following: "What are the mental skills of a champion?" or "Do I have those skills and to what degree?" Years of descriptive and exploratory research have helped to identify the mental skills of successful athletes. Although no single mental-skills measurement tool has emerged as an essential part of a performance enhancement program, the Athletic Coping Skills Inventory–28 (ACSI-28; Smith et al., 1995) and the Test of Performance Strategies (TOPS; Thomas, Murphy, & Hardy, 1999) show promise.

These two measures are examples of multiple-factor scales attempting to categorize the essential mental skills of athletes. These scales can be used for a variety of purposes, including (a) quickly assessing an individual's mental-skill use, (b) developing a baseline of mental-skill use before an intervention, and (c) serving as a starting point for a discussion of mental skills with an athlete.

Determining the Manner of Assessment

Most often, assessment begins with an interview. The great advantage of an interview format is the ability to probe deeply into specific issues. The interview suffers, however, from being time-intensive and notoriously prone to interviewer bias (Meehl, 1954). Applied sport psychologists also gather information via behavioral observation, by attending practices and competitions. This "face time" is invaluable if assessment is part of an ongoing intervention, but it is time-intensive and some athletes and coaches feel awkward being watched, especially if the psychologist is busily scribbling notes. Coach reports about sport-related issues are nearly always invaluable, although coaches often ask for advice in the early part of assessment before enough information has been gathered. Other assessment tools might include viewing videotapes of competition and practice, usually in the company of the coach or athlete to determine key sport behaviors, and formal written testing in both group and individual settings. Testing might be particularly useful for shy athletes who are uncomfortable talking about themselves and for large groups of athletes when a lot of information must be gathered in a short period of time. For all types of testing, several special considerations (subsequently described in more detail) should be taken into account when working with teams and athletes.

Issues to Consider When Using Testing With Teams and Athletes

The Role of the Sport Psychologist

Applied sport psychology consultants who are called on to administer tests may find themselves in a dual role: that of examiner and that of consultant. Although this can sometimes be a useful mechanism for enhancing a consulting relationship, occasionally, the assessment role can create a distance between the athlete and the psychologist, espe-

cially when an athlete feels "exposed" by an assessment of clinical issues. In these situations, it is appropriate to refer athletes to another
qualified practitioner (see Andersen & Van Raalte, chapter 16, this volume, for more on referral).

Confidentiality

Issues of confidentiality are particularly important in the highly publicized world of sport. The *Denver Post* recently printed stories by sports
staff comparing the specific intelligence test scores of various NFL players
who took the Wonderlic Intelligence Test at the NFL combine (Saunders,
2000; Wonderlic, 1983)). These data were released because athletes who
were hoping to join, but were not yet members of the NFL Players Union,
had signed a consent form releasing all data collected about them (e.g.,
vertical leap, percentage of body fat, intelligence test scores).

The code of ethics of the American Psychological Association (APA,
1992) explicitly protects the confidentiality of psychologist–client relationships. With a few exceptions, this confidential relationship also is
legally protected. Sport's prominence in society, however, makes everyone in sport a potential news story, and every piece of information
about an athlete that is not specifically protected may appear on the
nightly news. These sport environment realities mean that the athlete–
client's right to confidentiality is one of the most challenging ethical
(and practical) considerations for a sport psychologist considering the
use of an assessment tool.

Explicitly protecting confidentiality with an informed consent form
signed by all individuals being assessed is the most efficient way for a
practitioner to establish the confidentiality of test scores (see Exhibit
14.2). It is simplest if only the athlete who takes the test is allowed to
see the results, but often, coaches will want results to "help understand
the athlete better," or "to help choose my team." Although one of these
requests may seem benign and another less so, both requests pose the
same confidentiality-based ethical issue for the practitioner. Many sport
psychology consultants have become embroiled in conflict with coaches
looking for confidential information ("I know this stuff is confidential,
but ..."), often leading to the dismissal of the consultant, who had
mistakenly assumed the coach understood that individual test data
could not be shared. Clarifying who will see the results of any assessment
before conducting the assessment is always the best way to proceed.

Test User Qualifications

Who is qualified to conduct psychological assessment? The simple answer is that "it depends." Some of the variables to consider include (a) the type of test, (b) formal training in assessment, and (c) clinical implications of a test result.

Type of Test

Thousands of psychological assessment tools have been developed. To determine who can administer which tests, the APA (1954) created a three-level test classification system. Level A tests can be administered and scored by anyone who understands the instrument and the purpose for testing. Level B tests such as the Fundamental Interpersonal Relations Orientation-Behavior Scales (FIRO–B; Schutz & Wood, 1985) or Myers–Briggs Type Indicator (MBTI; Briggs & Myers, 1962) require some psychology coursework and knowledge of psychometrics and test construction as well as an understanding of the particular test. Level C tests (e.g., intelligence tests, psychodiagnostic tests, neuropsychology tests) require national or state certification or professional licensure (see Zizzi, Zaichkowsky, & Perna, chapter 22, this volume, for additional information about professional credentials) as well as knowledge of the particular test.

The strength of the APA's classification system is that it formalizes the notion that assessment devices differ in their potential impact on clients. In particular, the system suggests that giving individual feedback on some assessment devices is a form of professional practice and should be as carefully regulated as "therapy."

Formal Training in Assessment

Although the APA's three-level classification system uses graduate degrees and licensure status to determine the qualifications of a potential user of a test, degree status is not enough to ensure competence in assessment. Many neuropsychology and forensic assessment devices require test-specific coursework and a certification procedure before allowing a practitioner to use the instrument. Parallels exist in the sport environment. A PhD in clinical psychology or exercise science is no substitute for formal supervised training and supervised use of assessment tools and techniques in sport psychology. Expertise in assessment comes with time, practice, and familiarity with an assessment device.

Clinical Implications of a Test

One obvious situation in which test administration should be carefully supervised is the use of psychodiagnostic assessment devices such as the Beck Depression Inventory (Beck, Ward, Mendelson, Mock, & Erbaugh, 1961), the Eating Disorder Inventory (EDI; Garner, Olmstead, & Polivy, 1984), or the Minnesota Multiphasic Personality Inventory–2 (MMPI-2; Hathaway & McKinley, 1989). Whether these scales are used as part of a research protocol (e.g., assessing the rate of eating disorders in a sport or the impact of exercise on mood) or in individual work with an athlete, taking a test that may highlight difficult emotional terrain can have a powerful impact. Test takers should be provided with individual feedback on the measures by someone with experience in treating clinical issues.

Proprietary Tests

The dark underside of athlete testing involves individuals and businesses selling tests purported to "tell teams things that no other test can." These tests are not published or subjected to peer review. They typically are presented without explanation of underlying theory, reliability, or validity. Unfortunately, "secret" assessment techniques are somewhat like snake oil. They are sold to decision makers in professional and collegiate teams via broad generalizations, a willingness to promise anything, and slick marketing. The sense of getting something "new and exclusive" has special cachet in the competitive world of sport. When coaches approach a sport psychologist, asking for an opinion about amazing claims from someone with an "exclusive" technique, one good response is to use a medical analogy. If your star athlete needs an anterior cruciate ligament (ACL) operation, do you go to a doctor who has an "exclusive technique," never reviewed by other physicians or scientists, or do you go to the best traditional knee surgeon with a proven track record and a great reputation among other surgeons? The willingness of coaches to take a chance in sport psychology assessment is a reflection of the lack of proven success in this arena, along with the disconnection between this critical applied area and the academic base of the field.

Limits of a Test

Unfortunately, no assessment device created in psychology has had a unanimous stamp of approval. For example, even the widely used

Wechsler intelligence scales (e.g., the *Wechsler Adult Intelligence Scale–Revised,* WAIS–R; Wechsler, 1981) have been periodically criticized for ethnic bias, lack of up-to-date norms, and theoretical limitations in understanding intelligence (Kaufman, 1985). These criticisms have not prevented widespread use of assessment devices in several areas, but broad acceptance of a test comes only with vigorous research, debate about test limitations, and subsequent improvements in the reliability and validity of tests. Additional research on the devices used by sport psychologists in their practices is needed. Most sport assessment devices do not meet the highest standards of test reliability and validity. Given this state of affairs, it is critical that practitioners in sport psychology are aware of the limits of any test that they are considering and weigh these limits when deciding whether formal assessment will add value to an intervention.

Test Feedback

Older elite athletes report with surprising frequency that "someone gave our team a test," but that person provided no follow-up on the results of testing. Although lack of follow-up may not seem to be a critical issue, psychologists have a legal and an ethical obligation to give feedback on test results to all clients or research participants (APA, 1992). When talking with athletes or coaches about test results, it is important to avoid the use of psychological jargon and to explain the importance of results with language and examples that are familiar (e.g., examples from the athlete's sport). Allow athletes to ask questions and arrange for a possible follow-up meeting for further questions at a later date. Restating confidentiality guidelines with athletes also is useful (e.g., with whom and under what circumstances information will be shared). Failure to provide comprehensive feedback can leave athletes and coaches unwilling to work with sport psychologists because "they took a lot of our time, collected a bunch of data, and we never got to see any results."

Summary

Despite a zealous, early pursuit of the ideal sport personality in the 1960s and 1970s, assessment is a generally underdeveloped area in sport psychology. A great number of assessment tools have been developed over the past 35 years; however, few of these tests have been used in more than a handful of sport psychology research studies. Recently, researchers have noted the critical need for theory-driven, reliable, and valid instruments, as well as the unacceptability of using hastily constructed "one-shot" assessment tools (Marsh, 1998). Although the first complete text on sport psychology assessment (Duda, 1998) bodes well for the future of test development, much work remains to be done in this critical area.

Without proven "off-the-shelf" assessment tools, some sport psychologists do no formal assessment, whereas others have created their own "tests" without thorough studies of what the test actually measures. Practical and ethical concerns unique to the environment of sport make sport psychology assessment a potential minefield for the applied sport psychologist. Perhaps the greatest concern for the field of sport psychology assessment is the lack of discussion of effective and ethical assessment practices. For sport psychology assessment to continue to mature as a subfield of sport psychology, the much discussed and rarely seen scientist-practitioner will need to bridge the gap. Practitioners must do a better job of documenting their assessment practices, and scientists must continue to push the development of psychometrically sound assessment tools that have real utility in the world of sport.

References

American Psychological Association. (1954). *Technical recommendations for psychological tests and diagnostic techniques*. Washington, DC: Author.

American Psychological Association. (1992). Ethical principles and code of conduct. *American Psychologist, 47*, 1597–1611.

Anastasi, A. (1988). *Psychological testing*. New York: Macmillan.

Beck, A. T., Ward, C. H., Mendelson, M., Mock, J., & Erbaugh, J. K. (1961). An inventory for measuring depression. *Archives of General Psychiatry, 4*, 561–571.

Briggs, K. C., & Myers, I. B. (1962). *Myers–Briggs Type Indicator*. Consulting Psychologists Press: San Francisco, CA.

Duda, J. L. (Ed.). (1998). *Advances in sport and exercise psychology measurement*. Morgantown, WV: Fitness Information Technology.

Fisher, A. C. (1984). New directions in sport personality research. In. J. M. Silva & R. Weinberg (Eds.), *Psychological foundations of sport* (pp. 70–80). Champaign, IL: Human Kinetics.

Garner, D. M., Olmstead, M. P., & Polivy, J. (1984). *Eating disorder inventory*. Lutz, FL: Psychological Assessment Resources.

Gill, D. L. (2000). *Psychological dynamics of sport and exercise*. Champaign, IL: Human Kinetics.

Hathaway, S. R., & McKinley, S. C. (1989). *Minnesota Multiphasic Personality Inventory–2* [Manual]. Minneapolis: University of Minnesota Press.

Heil, J., & Henschen, K. (1996). Assessment in sport and exercise psychology. In J. Van Raalte & B. Brewer (Eds.), *Exploring sport and exercise psychology* (pp. 229–255). Washington, DC: American Psychological Association.

Kaufman, A. S. (1985). Review of the Wecshler Adult Intelligence Scale–Revised. In J. M. Mitchell (Ed.), *The Ninth Mental Measurements Yearbook* (pp. 1699–1703). Lincoln: University of Nebraska Press.

Mahoney, M. J., Gabriel, T. J., & Perkins, T. S. (1987). Psychological skills and exceptional athletic performance. *The Sport Psychologist, 1,* 181–199.

Marsh, H. (1998). Foreword. In J. L. Duda (Ed.), *Advances in sport and exercise psychology assessment* (pp. xv–xix). Morgantown, WV: Fitness Information Technology.

Martens, R., Vealey, R. S., & Burton, D. (1990). *Competitive anxiety in sport.* Champaign, IL: Human Kinetics.

Meehl, P. (1954). *Clinical versus statistical prediction.* Minneapolis: University of Minnesota Press.

Mischel, W. (1968). *Personality and assessment.* New York: Wiley.

Morgan, W. P. (1980). The trait psychology controversy. *Research Quarterly for Exercise and Sport, 51,* 50–76.

Murphy, S. M., & Tammen, V. (1998). Searching for mental skills. In J. L. Duda (Ed.), *Advances in sport and exercise psychology measurement* (pp. 195–209). Mogantown, WV: Fitness Information Technology.

Nideffer, R. M. (1981). *The ethics and practice of applied sport psychology.* Ithaca, NY: Mouvement.

Nideffer, R. M. (1987). Issues in the use of psychological tests in applied settings. *The Sport Psychologist, 1,* 18–28.

Nideffer, R. M. (1990). Use of the Test of Attentional and Interpersonal Style (TAIS) in sport. *The Sport Psychologist, 4,* 285–300.

Ostrow, A. C. (1990). *Directory of psychological tests in the sport and exercise sciences.* Morgantown, WV: Fitness Information Technology.

Peterson, C. (1992). *Personality.* New York: Harcourt, Brace, Jovanovich.

Saunders P. (2000). Wonderlic key evaluator for Broncos. *Denver Post.Com*

Schutz, W. C., & Wood, M. (1985). *FIRO–B Scales.* San Francisco, CA: Consulting Psychologists Press.

Silva, J. (1984). Personality and sport performance: Controversy and challenge. In J. Silva & R. Weinberg (Eds.), *Psychological foundations of sport* (pp. 59–69). Champaign, IL: Human Kinetics.

Singer, R. N. (1988). Psychological testing: What value to coaches and athletes? *International Journal of Sport Psychology, 19,* 87–106.

Smith, R. E., & Christensen, D. S. (1995). Psychological skills as predictors of performance and survival in professional baseball. *Journal of Sport and Exercise Psychology, 17,* 399–415.

Smith, R. E., Smoll, F. L., Schutz, R. W., & Ptacek, J. T. (1995). Development and validation of a multidimensional measure of sport-specific psychological skills: The Athletic Coping Skills Inventory–28. *Journal of Sport and Exercise Psychology, 17,* 379–398.

Thomas, P. R., Murphy, S. M., & Hardy, L. (1999). Test of performance strategies: Development and preliminary validation of a comprehensive measure of athletes' psychological skills. *Journal of Sports Sciences, 17,* 1–15.

Tutko, T. A., Lyon, L. P., & Ogilvie, B. C. (1969). *Athletic Motivation Inventory.* San Jose, CA: Institute for the Study of Athletic Motivation.

Vealey, R. M., & Garner-Holman, M. (1998). Applied sport psychology. In J. L. Duda (Ed.), *Advances in sport and exercise psychology measurement* (pp. 433–446). Morgantown, WV: Fitness Information Technology.

Wechsler, D. (1981). *Wechsler Adult Intelligence Scale–Revised.* San Antonio: Psychological Corporation.

Williams, J. (1986). *Applied sport psychology.* Palo Alto, CA: Mayfield.

Wonderlic, E. F. (1983). *Wonderlic Personnel Test.* E. F. Wonderlic & Associates: Northfield, IL.

Psychopathology in Sport and Exercise

Britton W. Brewer and Trent A. Petrie

At first glance, it may seem unusual to discuss psychopathology in association with sport and exercise. After all, there is evidence that "success in sport is inversely correlated with psychopathology" (Morgan, 1985, p. 71), and exercise has been used therapeutically for depression and other disorders (for a review, see McCullagh & Weiss, chapter 7, this volume). Nevertheless, because sport and exercise participants, as human beings, may be susceptible to psychopathology, examination of psychopathology in the context of sport and exercise is warranted (Heyman, 1986). Indeed, factors associated with sport and exercise participation contact may foster the development and maintenance of mental health concerns (Auerbach, 1994; Beisser, 1977; Heyman, 1986; Ogilvie & Tutko, 1971). For example, the rough physical contact and emphasis on physical appearance characteristics of some sports may contribute to the occurrence of cognitive impairments (Matser, Kessels, Jordan, Lezak, & Troost, 1998) and eating disorders (Petrie, 1993), respectively, among athletes. For some disorders (e.g., developmental coordination disorder, bulimia nervosa), pathological symptoms may include sport and exercise behaviors, such as poor sport performance and excessive exercise (American Psychiatric Association, 2000).

Case studies and anecdotal reports have documented the occurrence of a wide variety of mental disorders in sport and exercise participants (Beisser, 1977; Ogilvie & Tutko, 1966). Examples of disorders experienced by top-level athletes include bipolar disorder ("Yancey Dead," 1994), major depression (Fish, 2000), obsessive compulsive disorder ("Malarchuk Discloses," 1992), panic disorder (Hales, 1993), seasonal affective disorder (Rosen, Smokler, Carrier, Shafer, & McKeag, 1996), schizoaffective disorder ("Maine Issue," 1997), and Tourette's syndrome (Page, 1990). In nationwide surveys of clinical and counseling psychologists (Petrie & Diehl, 1995; Petrie, Diehl, & Watkins, 1995), the primary areas of psychopathology addressed in individual therapy with athlete–clients were reported to be anxiety/stress, depressive disorders, eating disorders, and substance-related disorders.

Athletes and exercisers experience a wide range of psychopathological conditions. For those interested in working in sport and exercise settings, a basic understanding and knowledge of psychopathology is both necessary and consistent with Association for the Advancement of Applied Sport Psychology (1991) certification criteria. The main purposes of this chapter are to highlight areas of psychopathology particularly relevant to sport and exercise, to review empirical research on the epidemiology of psychopathology in sport and exercise populations, and to provide recommendations for diagnosis and treatment of psychopathology in the context of sport and exercise.

Psychopathology Relevant to Sport and Exercise

Although sport and exercise participants may experience a variety of mental disorders, some disorders are especially pertinent to physical activity contexts. In this section, we discuss the epidemiology and treatment issues associated with eating disorders, substance-related disorders, psychological factors affecting physical condition (i.e., psychosocial antecedents of athletic injury), and adjustment reactions (e.g., to sport injury). In addition, we highlight other disorders and subclinical syndromes (i.e., conditions in which impairment of behavioral, cognitive, or affective functioning is evident, but insufficient to satisfy diagnostic criteria) that may be associated with sport and exercise participation but have been investigated less thoroughly.

Eating Disorders

For girls in late adolescence and women in early adulthood, approximately 0.5 to 1.0% and 1.0 to 3.0% meet diagnostic criteria for anorexia nervosa and bulimia nervosa, respectively (American Psychiatric Association, 2000). Male prevalence rates are believed to be one-tenth of female rates. For athletes, prevalence rates of eating disorders have varied considerably because of differences in the instrumentation and diagnostic criteria used. However, when more stringent inclusion criteria are applied, prevalence rates tend to approximate those found in the general population (e.g., Petrie & Stoever, 1993).

The prevalence of subclinical disorders (also referred to as "disordered eating"), however, is considerably higher than diagnosable disorders (Beals & Manore, 1994; Thompson & Sherman, 1999) and appears to be even larger than rates reported among nonathletes. In their meta-analysis, Hausenblas and Carron (1999) found that male athletes had higher scores on bulimic, anorexic, and drive for thinness indices than nonathletes, whereas female athletes reported more anorexic and bulimic symptoms than nonathletes (effect sizes were significantly greater than zero in all analyses). Furthermore, male and female athletes who competed in aesthetic sports (e.g., figure skating) consistently had the highest scores on the disordered eating indices.

Female athletes with disordered eating also may develop amenorrhea and osteoporosis—a cluster of events referred to as the "female athlete triad." Although no firm prevalence data are available, up to 66% of female athletes may be amenorrheic compared with just 2 to 5% of nonathletes (Sanborn, Horea, Siemers, & Dieringer, 2000). These data, combined with the high levels of disordered eating that have been found (e.g., Petrie, 1993), suggest that many female athletes may eventually develop osteoporosis, which can result in increased bone fractures, increased skeletal fragility, and permanent bone loss (Sanborn et al., 2000). Epidemiological research is needed to document more fully the extent to which athletes across competitive levels experience disordered eating, amenorrhea, and osteoporosis.

In addition to family, biological, personality, and genetic factors, Thompson and Sherman (1999) have identified four unique aspects of the sport environment that need to be considered in relation to the development of disordered eating in athletes. First, athletes are under increasing pressure to lose weight in the hopes of improving performance, an erroneous belief that is held by a majority of coaches (Griffin & Harris, 1996). Second, health status has become secondary to weight loss and performance. Coaches may encourage athletes to diet excessively, substantially increase training load, or engage in other pathogenic weight loss techniques to achieve a performance ideal (Swoap & Murphy, 1995). Such an approach sends a strong message to athletes that they are valued primarily for their performances, even at the expense of their health. Third, common stereotypes exist about athletes' size and shape. Gymnasts should be "tiny," runners "lanky," and football players "big." When athletes do not conform to these images, they may stand out among their teammates and experience incredible pressure to achieve unrealistic and unhealthy body weights and shapes. Fourth, athletes are reinforced for displaying certain characteristics or traits, such as exercising excessively, denying pain or discomfort, complying completely with requests, and pursuing perfection, that may in reality be symptoms of disordered eating.

Because of these unique pressures, special consideration needs to be given to prevent eating disorders among athletes. Thompson and Sherman (1999) argued that the sport culture, with its emphasis on weight loss and body size, must be changed if eating disorders are to be decreased. They argued for the following changes: (a) deemphasizing weight as a salient factor ("don't diet"); (b) eliminating weighing athletes in front of one another (and only weighing athletes when medically necessary); (c) eliminating unhealthy but commonly accepted cultural standards, such as "cutting weight" in wrestling; (d) treating each athlete as an individual and developing individualized training regimens that are based on health, not weight; and (e) controlling the competitiveness that exists on sport teams regarding weight loss or body size changes. Undoubtedly, to make such changes, coaches must play an active role. They, more than anyone else, have the power and influence to shape the environment, making it either conducive to health or focused primarily on winning at all costs. The scope of this chapter does not allow for a more detailed discussion of treatment issues, thus we strongly encourage readers to consider existing sources, such as Thompson and Sherman (1993) and Petrie and Sherman (1999, 2000) before undertaking such work.

Substance-Related Disorders

Although sport and exercise may connote images of clean living, health, and well-being, drug use by athletes is a serious concern. The highly publicized substance-related problems of well-known athletes, such as tennis player Jennifer Capriati, golfer John Daly, baseball player Daryl Strawberry, and soccer player Diego Maradona, provide vivid examples of the potential consequences of drug use. The issue of substance use is more complicated for sport and exercise participants than for other individuals because athletes may use drugs for both "recreational" and performance enhancement purposes (Anshel, 1993, 1998). In addition to the legal and health (physical and mental) ramifications of drug use experienced by the general population, competitive athletes may have their eligibility to participate in sport restricted, because many substances have been banned by most major sport governing bodies (Chappel, 1987). The disqualification of athletes competing in recent Olympics and Tour de France competitions for using performance-enhancing drugs bears witness to the potential negative sport-related consequences of substance use.

Research has indicated that the prevalence of alcohol use for athletes, at least at the high school and college levels, is greater than that for nonathletes (Eccles & Barber, 1999; Leichliter, Meilman, Presley, & Cashin, 1998; Rainey, McKeown, Sargent, & Valois, 1996). Although athletes may curb their use of recreational drugs during the competitive season (Selby, Weinstein, & Bird, 1990), they still binge drink and become drunk more often than nonathletes (Rainey et al., 1996; Wechsler, Davenport, Dowdall, Grossman, & Zanakos, 1997). Alcohol and marijuana are the primary substances used recreationally by athletes (Selby et al., 1990; Spence & Gauvin, 1996). In terms of anabolic steroids, which are used to increase muscular size and strength, a conservative prevalence estimate of 2.9% has been obtained for anabolic steroid use by high school seniors (National Institute on Drug Abuse, 2000), with the prevalence three to five times higher for male athletes than for female athletes (Gaa, Griffith, Cahill, & Tuttle, 1994; Kersey, 1996; Middleman & DuRant, 1996). Athletes also may use other banned substances to reduce pain (e.g., morphine), to increase energy and arousal (e.g., amphetamines), to promote relaxation or reduce arousal (e.g., beta-blockers), or to control weight (e.g., diuretics; Anshel, 1993, 1998).

In summarizing the empirical and theoretical literature, Anshel (1993, 1998) identified physical, psychological, and social factors that increase the use of recreational and performance enhancement drugs. Physical factors include performance enhancement (e.g., heightened alertness, relaxation) and coping with pain and injury. Psychological factors include perfectionism, low self-confidence, and reduction of (or distraction from) unpleasant emotions (e.g., anxiety), boredom (e.g., during the off season), and personal problems. Social factors include peer pressure and experimentation. These reasons parallel explanations for drug use by members of the general population but take into account unique aspects of the sport environment.

Strategies for preventing drug use in sport have focused on deterrence (e.g., drug testing), education, coping skills training, and peer support (Anshel, 1993, 1998). Although comprehensive substance abuse prevention programs for athletes have been implemented (e.g., Goldberg et al., 1996; Grossman & Smiley, 1999), less well-developed programs suffer from several limitations, including a reliance on one-time lectures and a lack of follow-up (Petitpas & Van Raalte, 1992). Treatment for athletes with an identified substance-related disorder is likely to involve outpatient or inpatient modalities, depending on the severity of the problem (Carr & Murphy, 1995; Stainback, 1997). Although it is clear that scare tactics alone are not effective (Goldberg, Bents, Bosworth, Trevisan, & Elliot, 1991), intervention evaluation studies conducted with athletes are scarce and currently there is no empirical basis for recommending the use of one particular type of intervention over another (Anshel, 1993, 1998).

Psychological Factors Affecting Medical Condition

Because psychosocial factors such as coping resources, life stress, and social support may influence the occurrence of sport injury (Williams & Andersen, 1998), it can be argued that the psychosocial antecedents of sport injury constitute "psychological factors affecting medical condition" (American Psychiatric Association, 2000, p. 731). Research investigating the relationship of psychological variables to sport injury has been conducted primarily with high school and college football players and has focused mainly on life stress as a predictor of injury, although other sports and predictor variables have been considered (for a review, see Williams & Andersen, 1998). Empirical findings have provided consistent support for a theoretical model in which life stress and other psychosocial factors (e.g., coping resources, personality) exert direct and moderated effects on the occurrence of sport injury (Williams & Andersen, 1998), which has been estimated at 3 million to 5 million injuries per year in the United States (Kraus & Conroy, 1984).

Although theory suggests that interventions aimed at changing cognitive appraisals of potentially stressful events and modifying physiological and attentional responses to stress might be effective in reducing vulnerability to sport injury (Williams & Andersen, 1998), little controlled research has been conducted in this area (for a review, see Cupal, 1998). In a promising demonstration of the influence of psychological intervention on the occurrence of sport injury, Kerr and Goss

(1996) reported a high-medium effect for a stress management program on the reduction of injury in a sample of elite gymnasts.

Adjustment Reactions

During the course of their involvement in sport and exercise, participants may experience several personally challenging transitions to which they must adjust (Pearson & Petitpas, 1990). For example, competitive athletes face the prospects of deselection (i.e., being cut from the team) and sport career termination, and both competitive athletes and exercisers may become injured. Psychological adjustment injury is a topic of growing interest among researchers, who have examined the prevalence and correlates of postinjury emotional disturbance.

An estimated 5 to 24% of athletes report clinically meaningful levels of psychological distress, at least in the short term (i.e., 1 to 2 months), following injury (for a review, see Brewer, 2001). Research findings support a conceptualization in which personal and situational variables interact to influence cognitive, emotional, and behavioral responses to injury (Brewer, 2001). Thus, characteristics of the person (e.g., age, personality, psychological investment in sport) and the situation (e.g., injury severity, injury duration, life stress, social support) affect how the individual appraises the injury, reacts emotionally, and responds behaviorally. Managing affective responses to injury may be critical to the physical rehabilitation of injured athletes, because postinjury emotional disturbance has been associated with poor adherence to sport injury rehabilitation regimens (Brickner, 1997; Daly, Brewer, Van Raalte, Petitpas, & Sklar, 1995) and poor rehabilitation outcome following sport injury (Brewer et al., 2000).

A variety of psychological treatments have been advocated for athletes with injuries, ranging from relaxation and imagery to counseling and psychotherapy (for reviews, see Heil, 1993; Petitpas & Danish, 1995). Research has documented the beneficial effects of biofeedback, imagery, relaxation, and other cognitive–behavioral procedures on outcomes such as pain, reinjury anxiety, and physical rehabilitation parameters (for a review, see Cupal, 1998). Regardless of the particular intervention selected, which, of course, depends on the nature of the client's concerns and resources, it is important to build rapport, educate injured athletes about their injury, help injured athletes to develop coping skills, provide injured athletes with opportunities to practice their newly acquired coping skills, and evaluate the effectiveness of the intervention (Petitpas & Danish, 1995).

Various Disorders and Subclinical Syndromes

Dose–Response Reactions

Sport and exercise participants engage in physical activity presumably to prepare for competition or to enhance their fitness and well-being. Sometimes, however, the amount, or dose, of physical training can be excessive and counterproductive. Competitive athletes who engage in high-volume training regimens are at risk for developing staleness, a condition characterized by diminished performance and a variety of symptoms, including disturbances in mood, sleep, and appetite (for a review, see Raglin, 1993). Because the symptoms of staleness may mimic those of depressive disorders and chronic fatigue syndrome, careful evaluation is needed to rule out alternative causes of the symptoms (Puffer & McShane, 1991). At present, rest is the sole accepted treatment for staleness, although adjunctive psychological and medical care may also be appropriate (Raglin, 1993).

Although many individuals struggle to establish a regular exercise habit, some exercisers and recreational athletes have the opposite problem in that they become "dependent" on their involvement in physical activity and persist in their participation past the point at which physical and mental health benefits are gained. Characteristics of exercise dependence, which has been studied most extensively in association with running, include prioritizing exercise over other important activities and relationships, engaging in exercise despite the presence of exercise-related physical health problems (e.g., injury, pain), and experiencing withdrawal symptoms (e.g., mood disturbance) when restricted from participation in physical activity (Adams & Kirkby, 1998). Comorbidity with eating disorders (de Coverley Veale, 1987) and general psychopathology (White-Welkley, Higbie, Fried, Koenig, & Price, 1998) are strong possibilities among individuals with exercise dependence. Although little information is available on treatment of exercise dependence, Morrow (1988) developed a cognitive–behavioral intervention for exercise dependence in which clients are reinforced for gradually relinquishing exercise time to other activities after being assessed and trained in coping skills.

Anxiety Reactions

Anxiety is a central aspect of sport participation (Hackfort & Spielberger, 1989), with some athletes experiencing precompetitive anxiety to an extent that it interferes with performance (for a review, see Gould, Damarjian, & Greenleaf, chapter 4, this volume). For the most part, the anxiety associated with sport involvement, even when it has an adverse effect on performance, is subclinical and can be addressed through performance enhancement interventions. In rare cases, however, the level of anxiety experienced is more severe and warrants clinical attention (e.g., Farkas, 1989; Friedberg, 1987). Silva (1994) identified a sport-specific condition in which anxiety is "isolated on an *element* of a total performance" (p. 104). As examples of this condition, termed "sport performance phobia," Silva cited the behavior of a tennis player who was afraid to come to the net and a baseball catcher who developed an inability to throw the ball back to the pitcher despite being able to throw the ball to second base. Phobias and other extreme anxiety reactions should be addressed by sport and exercise psychology practitioners with clinical training.

Another sport- and exercise-related phenomenon with an anxiety component is muscle dysmorphia, a variant of body dysmorphic disorder. Muscle dysmorphia is found primarily in men and involves (a) a pathological preoccupation with one's body (viewing it as insufficiently lean, muscular, and large); (b) obsessive–compulsive involvement with dieting, weightlifting, and related activities; and (c) severe impairment of social and occupational functioning (e.g., giving up other activities to workout) (Pope, Gruber, Choi, Olivardia, & Phillips, 1997). Although no epidemiological prevalence studies have been conducted, Pope and colleagues argued that many individuals suffer from muscle dysmorphia, particularly weightlifters and body builders.

Personality Disorders

Several forces in competitive sport may contribute to the development and maintenance of personality disorders in athletes. For example, the coddling and adulation received by gifted athletes may help to foster narcissistic personality disorder (Andersen, Denson, Brewer, & Van Raalte, 1994; House, 1989). Similarly, reinforcement of qualities such as toughness and aggressiveness in the sport environment may increase the likelihood of problem behavior among athletes with antisocial personality disorder (Andersen et al., 1994). Another factor that may exacerbate or contribute to the development of personality disorders in athletes is the dysfunctional, performance-contingent social support that athletes receive in many circumstances (House, 1989). Although no empirical investigations have been done on the prevalence and treatment of personality disorders in athletic populations, anecdotal evidence suggests that athletes with personality disorders may not respond well to performance enhancement interventions and likely require clinical attention (Andersen et al., 1994).

Pathological Gambling

Along with substance abuse and violence, gambling is an athlete behavior that has received considerable media attention. Baseball player and manager Pete Rose and football player Art Schlichter are among the individuals whose gambling activities have been widely publicized. Only recently has athlete gambling behavior become a topic of interest to researchers. Although definitive epidemiological studies using rigorous diagnostic criteria for pathological gambling among athletes have yet to be conducted, early prevalence estimates suggest that (a) the vast majority (72%) of athletes in National Collegiate Athletic Association (NCAA) Division I football and basketball programs engage in some form of gambling (e.g., casino gambling, slot machines, playing cards for money, betting on sports) while in college (Cross & Vollano, 1999); (b) approximately one-quarter of NCAA Division I football players bet on college sporting events (Cullen & Latessa, 1996); and (c) the extent of gambling behavior, as assessed by the South Oaks Gambling Screen, is at a problematic or pathological level for a considerable percentage (12% for males and 3% for females) of American intercollegiate athletes (Weinstock, Whelan, & Meyers, 2000). Because pathological gambling can exact tolls on the personal adjustment and sport participation eligibility of athletes as well as adversely affect the integrity of sport, further research is needed to identify the prevalence, causes, and concomitants of and optimal treatments for pathological gambling among athletes.

Recommendations for Diagnosis and Treatment

For sport and exercise participants with diagnosable psychopathology, appropriate treatment can improve their quality of life and enhance their sport or exercise. In the absence of empirical data suggesting otherwise, diagnosis and treatment of psychopathology in sport and exercise participants should be the same as with nonparticipants. Circumstances specific to sport and exercise, however, should be taken into consideration. Accordingly, the following recommendations for diagnosis and treatment of psychopathology in the context of sport and exercise are offered:

1. Practitioners should recognize that some athletes' attitudes and behaviors that may appear to be pathological actually have adaptive value in sport and may be considered "normal" in the sport subculture. For example, detachment and lack of social conformity might assist ultramarathon runners in training and competition, which can be solitary activities (Folkins & Wieselberg-Bell, 1981). Thus, practitioners need to carefully monitor their own attitudes and reactions to ensure that labeling and bias do not occur. In addition, they may need to educate themselves about the general sport culture as well as specific competitive or exercise milieus before working with athletes and exercisers.

2. Practitioners should be sensitive to forces outside of the individual that may be particularly influential in producing apparently pathological behavior. For example, the constant scrutiny faced by athletes both on and off the field may produce feelings of paranoia and anxiety (House, 1989). Likewise, a variety of sport-induced stressors such as pressure from coaches, restriction of social interaction, travel, and pain or injury (Petrie et al., 1997; Wrisberg, Johnson, & Brooks, 1997) may adversely affect athletes' mental state. Furthermore, characteristics such as aggressiveness and single-minded devotion to sport may be reinforced by coaches and teammates (Heyman, 1986). Thus, it is important to consider both the athlete and the athletic environment when assessing the behavior of sport and exercise participants (Miller, Vaughn, & Miller, 1990). Personal and situational factors should be assessed thoroughly before concluding that a problem resides within the individual.

3. Practitioners should be aware that athletes in particular may be reluctant to seek psychological treatment. Research has shown that college student–athletes underutilize university mental health services relative to college student–nonathletes (e.g., Bergandi & Wittig, 1984; Carmen, Zerman, & Blaine, 1968). Athletes may be hesitant to seek counseling for several reasons, including personal attributes (e.g., self-reliance), limited time, closed/protected sport environments, high visibility as an athlete, and potential loss of status/negative evaluation by others (Ferrante, Etzel, & Lantz, 1996). Although athletes may be receptive to working with a sport psychologist for performance enhancement (Van Raalte, Brewer, Brewer, & Linder, 1992) and have expectations about counseling similar to those of nonath-

letes (Miller & Moore, 1993), the idea of consulting a mental health practitioner for psychotherapy may be met with resistance. Because entering treatment for psychopathology may have negative ramifications for athletes' sport participation, they may be especially concerned about confidentiality. Practitioners should be attuned to this possibility and should make every effort to alleviate athlete–clients' concerns.

4. Practitioners should recognize that although sport may seem to be "just a game," many athletes are heavily invested in sport as a source of self-identity and self-worth (Brewer, Van Raalte, & Linder, 1993). Strong self-identification with sport involvement may benefit athletes in terms of developing a sense of self and enhancing motivation for training and competition, but it may leave athletes vulnerable to psychological distress when they experience transitions such as deselection, injury, and sport career termination (Brewer, 1993; Pearson & Petitpas, 1990). In extreme cases, threats to athletic self-identity may precipitate suicide (Petitpas & Danish, 1995; Smith & Milliner, 1994). Accordingly, the high degree of self-investment in sport participation possessed by some athletes should be acknowledged by practitioners and not dismissed as preoccupation with a frivolous activity. Furthermore, during transitional times when athletic identity is disrupted, practitioners may work with athletes to establish support networks among friends and teammates and to develop other roles (e.g., student, worker, romantic partner) with which the athletes may also identify.

5. Practitioners should be aware that although many athletic organizations may not ordinarily be receptive to psychological interventions, psychologists may be sought in crisis situations such as a player death or a suicide attempt/threat (Vernacchia, Reardon, & Templin, 1997). In such situations, sport psychologists with crisis intervention skills can provide counseling and consultation to help athletes, coaches, and administrators deal with the immediate and long-term consequences of the crisis (Heil, 1993) and perhaps increase receptiveness to additional assistance in the future.

6. In keeping with ethical guidelines, practitioners should provide referrals for their sport and exercise participant–clients who have presenting problems that are outside the practitioner's realm of competence. Referral is clearly needed when a client's

problem is centered on a technical aspect of sport performance or when a client requests a performance enhancement intervention and the practitioner lacks sport- or exercise-specific knowledge. Referral also may be necessary when a client presents with psychopathology for which the clinically oriented practitioner has not received training or where supervision or consultation is not available. Thus, during the intake and early sessions, practitioners must thoroughly assess all areas of the athlete's life and functioning to determine the extent to which the problem is clinical in nature or performance-related (Taylor & Schneider, 1992). For a review of referral processes in sport and exercise psychology, see Petitpas, chapter 12, this volume.

Summary

In this chapter, we reviewed the major categories of psychopathology that have been identified and studied with sport and exercise participants. In addition, we provided recommendations for treatment and prevention as warranted by current research. Several points become clear from this review. First, athletes do experience psychopathology, such as eating disorders and substance abuse, at rates equal to and sometimes greater than the general population. Second, psychopathology specific to or exacerbated by sport or exercise involvement also exists. Third, research examining psychopathology in sport and exercise participants has been lacking, thus comments concerning this area still are tentative. Epidemiological, longitudinal, and well-controlled studies need to be conducted to expand the knowledge base. Fourth, when treating athletes with psychopathology, it is essential that circumstances specific to sport and exercise be taken into consideration.

References

Adams, J., & Kirkby, R. J. (1998). Exercise dependence: A review of its manifestation, theory and measurement. *Sports Medicine, Training and Rehabilitation, 8,* 265–276.

American Psychiatric Association. (2000). *Diagnostic and statistical manual of mental disorders* (4th ed., text rev.). Washington, DC: Author.

Andersen, M. B., Denson, E. L., Brewer, B. W., & Van Raalte, J. L. (1994). Disorders of personality and mood in athletes: Recognition and referral. *Journal of Applied Sport Psychology, 6,* 168–184.

Anshel, M. H. (1993). Psychology of drug use in sport. In R. N. Singer, M. Murphey,

& L. K. Tennant (Eds.), *Handbook of research in sport psychology* (pp. 851–876). New York: Macmillan.

Anshel, M. H. (1998). Drug abuse in sport: Causes and cures. In J. M. Williams (Ed.), *Applied sport psychology: Personal growth to peak performance* (3rd ed., pp. 372–397). Mountain View, CA: Mayfield.

Association for the Advancement of Applied Sport Psychology. (1991). Questions regarding certification. *Association for the Advancement of Applied Sport Psychology Newsletter, 6*(3), 3–4.

Auerbach, J. (1994). *Psychopathology in the world of men's sports*. Unpublished doctoral dissertation, Widener University, Chester, PA.

Beals, K., & Manore, M. (1994). The prevalence and consequences of subclinical eating disorders in female athletes. *International Journal of Sport Nutrition, 4*, 175–195.

Beisser, A. R. (1977). *The madness in sports* (2nd ed.). Bowie, MD: Charles Press.

Bergandi, T., & Wittig, A. (1984). Availability of and attitudes toward counseling services for the collegiate athlete. *Journal of College Student Personnel, 25*, 557–558.

Brewer, B. W. (1993). Self-identity and specific vulnerability to depressed mood. *Journal of Personality, 61*, 343–364.

Brewer, B. W. (2001). Psychology of sport injury rehabilitation. In R. N. Singer, H. A. Hausenblas, & C. M. Janelle (Eds.), *Handbook of research in sport psychology* (2nd ed., pp. 787–809). New York: Wiley.

Brewer, B. W., Van Raalte, J. L., Cornelius, A. E., Petitpas, A. J., Sklar, J. H., Pohlman, M. H., Krushell, R. J., & Ditmar, T. D. (2000). Psychological factors, rehabilitation adherence, and rehabilitation outcome following anterior cruciate ligament reconstruction. *Rehabilitation Psychology, 45*, 20–37.

Brewer, B. W., Van Raalte, J. L., & Linder, D. E. (1993). Athletic identity: Hercules' muscles or Achilles heel? *International Journal of Sport Psychology, 24*, 237–254.

Brickner, J. C. (1997). *Mood states and compliance of patients with orthopedic rehabilitation*. Unpublished master's thesis, Springfield College, Springfield, MA.

Carmen, L., Zerman, J., & Blaine, G. (1968). Use of Harvard psychiatric service by athletes and nonathletes. *Mental Hygiene, 52*, 134–137.

Carr, C. M., & Murphy, S. M. (1995). Alcohol and drugs in sport. In S. M. Murphy (Ed.), *Sport psychology interventions* (pp. 283–306). Champaign, IL: Human Kinetics.

Chappel, J. N. (1987). Drug use and abuse in the athlete. In J. R. May & M. J. Asken (Eds.), *Sport psychology: The psychological health of the athlete* (pp. 187–212). New York: PMA.

Cross, M. E., & Vollano, A. G. (1999). *The extent and nature of gambling among college student athletes*. Ann Arbor: University of Michigan, Department of Athletics.

Cullen, F. T., & Latessa, E. J. (1996). *The extent and sources of NCAA rule infractions: A national self-report study of student–athletes*. Cincinnati, OH: University of Cincinnati, Division of Criminal Justice.

Cupal, D. D. (1998). Psychological interventions in sport injury prevention and rehabilitation. *Journal of Applied Sport Psychology, 10*, 103–123.

Daly, J. M., Brewer, B. W., Van Raalte, J. L., Petitpas, A. J., & Sklar, J. H. (1995). Cognitive appraisal, emotional adjustment, and adherence to sport injury rehabilitation. *Journal of Sport Rehabilitation, 4*, 23–30.

de Coverley Veale, D. M. W. (1987). Exercise dependence. *British Journal of Addiction, 82*, 735–740.

Eccles, J. S., & Barber, B. L. (1999). Student council, volunteering, basketball, or marching band: What kind of extracurricular involvement matters? *Journal of Adolescent Research, 14*, 10–43.

Farkas, G. (1989). Exposure and response prevention in the treatment of an okeanophobic triathlete. *The Sport Psychologist, 3,* 189–195.

Ferrante, A. P., Etzel, E., & Lantz, C. (1996). Counseling college student–athletes: The problem, the need. In E. Etzel, A. P. Ferrante, & J. W. Pinkney (Eds.), *Counseling college student athletes: Issues and interventions* (2nd ed., pp. 3–26). Morgantown, WV: Fitness Information Technology.

Fish, M. (2000). Extra hurdles to clear. *Track & Field News, 53*(11), 36.

Folkins, C. H., & Wieselberg-Bell, N. (1981). A personality profile of ultramarathon runners: A little deviance may go a long way. *Journal of Sport Behavior, 4,* 119–127.

Friedberg, F. (1987). Coping skills treatment of situational vomiting: A case study. *Journal of Cognitive Psychotherapy: An International Quarterly, 1,* 183–188.

Gaa, G. L., Griffith, E. H., Cahill, B. R., & Tuttle, L. D. (1994). Prevalence of anabolic steroid use among Illinois high school students. *Journal of Athletic Training, 29,* 216–222.

Goldberg, L., Bents, R., Bosworth, E., Trevisan, L., & Elliot, D. L. (1991). Anabolic steroid education and adolescents: Do scare tactics work? *Pediatrics, 87,* 283–286.

Goldberg, L., Elliot, D., Clarke, G. N., MacKinnon, D. P., Moe, E., Zoref, L., Green, C., Wolf, S. L., Greffrath, E., Miller, D. J., & Lapin, A. (1996). Effects of a multidimensional anabolic steroid prevention intervention: The adolescents training and learning to avoid steroids (ATLAS) program. *Journal of the American Medical Association, 276,* 1555–1562.

Griffin, J., & Harris, M. B. (1996). Coaches' attitudes, knowledge, experiences, and recommendations regarding weight control. *The Sport Psychologist, 10,* 180–194.

Grossman, S. J., & Smiley, E. B. (1999). APPLE: Description and evaluation of a substance abuse education and prevention program for collegiate athletics. *Journal of Primary Prevention, 20,* 51–59.

Hackfort, D., & Spielberger, C. D. (Eds.). (1989). *Anxiety in sports: An international perspective.* New York: Hemispere.

Hales, D. (1993, December 19). When panic strikes. *Parade Magazine,* pp. 12–13.

Hausenblas, H., & Carron, A. (1999). Eating disorder indices and athletes: An integration. *Journal of Sport and Exercise Psychology, 21,* 230–258.

Heil, J. (1993). *Psychology of sport injury.* Champaign, IL: Human Kinetics.

Heyman, S. R. (1986). Psychological problem patterns found with athletes. *The Clinical Psychologist, 39,* 68–71.

House, T. (1989). *The jock's itch: The fast-track private world of the professional ballplayer.* Chicago: Contemporary Books.

Kerr, G., & Goss, J. (1996). The effects of a stress management program on injuries and stress levels. *Journal of Applied Sport Psychology, 8,* 109–117.

Kersey, R. D. (1996). Anabolic–androgenic steroid use among California community college student–athletes. *Journal of Athletic Training, 31,* 237–241.

Kraus, J. F., & Conroy, C. (1984). Mortality and morbidity from injuries in sports and recreation. *Annual Review of Public Health, 5,* 163–192.

Leichliter, J. S., Meilman, P. W., Presley, C. A., & Cashin, J. R. (1998). Alcohol use and related consequences among students with varying levels of involvement in college athletics. *Journal of American College Health, 46,* 257–262.

Maine issue is health. (1997, August 20). *Union–News,* p. D16.

Malarchuk discloses an anxiety disorder. (1992, March 12). *The Boston Globe,* p. 68.

Matser, J. T., Kessels, A. G. H., Jordan, B. D., Lezak, M. D., & Troost, J. (1998). Chronic traumatic brain injury in professional soccer players. *Neurology, 51,* 791–796.

Middleman, A. B., & DuRant, R. H. (1996). Anabolic steroid use and associated health risk behaviors. *Sports Medicine, 21,* 251–255.

Miller, M. J., & Moore, K. K. (1993). Athletes' and nonathletes' expectations about counseling. *Journal of College Student Development, 34,* 267–269.

Miller, T. W., Vaughn, M. P., & Miller, J. M. (1990). Clinical issues and treatment strategies in stress-oriented athletes. *Sports Medicine, 9,* 370–379.

Morgan, W. P. (1985). Selected psychological factors limiting performance: A mental health model. In D. H. Clarke & H. M. Eckert (Eds.), *Limits of human performance* (pp. 70–80). Champaign, IL: Human Kinetics.

Morrow, J. (1988, October). *A cognitive–behavioral interaction for reducing exercise addiction.* Paper presented at the annual meeting of the Association for the Advancement of Applied Sport Psychology, Nashua, NH.

National Institute on Drug Abuse. (2000). *Anabolic steroid abuse.* Bethesda, MD: National Institutes of Health.

Ogilvie, B. C., & Tutko, T. A. (1966). *Problem athletes and how to handle them.* London: Pelham.

Ogilvie, B. C., & Tutko, T. A. (1971). Sport: If you want to build character, try something else. *Psychology Today, 5*(10), 61–63.

Page, P. (1990). Tourette syndrome in athletics: A case study and review. *Athletic Training, 25,* 254–259.

Pearson, R. E., & Petitpas, A. J. (1990). Transitions of athletes: Pitfalls and prevention. *Journal of Counseling and Development, 69,* 7–10.

Petitpas, A., & Danish, S. J. (1995). Caring for injured athletes. In S. M. Murphy (Ed.), *Sport psychology interventions* (pp. 255–281). Champaign, IL: Human Kinetics.

Petitpas, A. J., & Van Raalte, J. L. (1992, Spring). Planning alcohol education programs for intercollegiate student–athletes. *The Academic Athletic Journal,* pp. 12–25.

Petrie, T. A. (1993). Disordered eating in female collegiate gymnasts: Prevalence and personality/attitudinal correlates. *Journal of Sport and Exercise Psychology, 15,* 424–436.

Petrie, T. A., & Diehl, N. S. (1995). Sport psychology in the profession of psychology. *Professional Psychology: Research and Practice, 26,* 288–291.

Petrie, T. A., Diehl, N. S., & Watkins, C. E., Jr. (1995). Sport psychology: An emerging domain in the counseling psychology profession? *The Counseling Psychologist, 23,* 535–545.

Petrie, T. A., Falkstein, D. L., Varnado, J. L., Austin, L. J., Harmison, R. J., Jenkins, M., & Harvey, P. (1997). The occurrence of negative life events in male and female college-student athletes. *Journal of Applied Sport Psychology, 9*(Suppl.), S144.

Petrie, T. A., & Sherman, R. (1999). Recognizing and treating athletes with eating disorders. In R. Ray & D. Wiese-Bjornstal (Eds.), *Counseling in sports medicine* (pp. 205–226). Champaign, IL: Human Kinetics.

Petrie, T. A., & Sherman, R. (2000). Counseling athletes with eating disorders: A case example. In M. B. Andersen (Ed.), *Doing sport psychology* (pp. 121–138). Champaign, IL: Human Kinetics.

Petrie, T., & Stoever, S. (1993). The incidence of bulimia nervosa and pathogenic weight control behaviors in female collegiate gymnasts. *Research Quarterly for Exercise and Sport, 64,* 238–241.

Pope, H. G., Gruber, A. J., Choi, P., Olivardia, R., & Phillips, K. A. (1997). Muscle dysmorphia: An underrecognized form of body dysmorphic disorder. *Psychosomatics, 38,* 548–557.

Puffer, J. C., & McShane, J. M. (1991). Depression and chronic fatigue in the college student–athlete. *Primary Care, 18,* 297–308.

Raglin, J. S. (1993). Overtraining and staleness: Psychometric monitoring of endurance athletes. In R. N. Singer, M. Murphey, & L. K. Tennant (Eds.), *Handbook of research in sport psychology* (pp. 840–850). New York: Macmillan.

Rainey, C. J., McKeown, R. E., Sargent, R. G., & Valois, R. F. (1996). Patterns of tobacco and alcohol use among sedentary, exercising, nonathletic, and athletic youth. *Journal of School Health, 66*, 27–32.

Rosen, L. W., Smokler, C., Carrier, D., Shafer, C. L., & McKeag, D. B. (1996). Seasonal mood disturbances in collegiate hockey players. *Journal of Athletic Training, 31*, 225–228.

Sanborn, C., Horea, M., Siemers, B., & Dieringer, K. (2000). Disordered eating and the female athlete triad. *Clinics in Sport Medicine, 19*, 199–213.

Selby, R., Weinstein, H. M, & Bird, T. 3. (1990). The health of university athletes: Attitudes, behaviors, and stressors. *Journal of American College Health, 39*, 11–18.

Silva, J. M., III. (1994). Sport performance phobias. *International Journal of Sport Psychology, 25*, 100–118.

Smith, A. M., & Milliner, E. K. (1994). Injured athletes and the risk of suicide. *Journal of Athletic Training, 29*, 337–341.

Spence, J. C., & Gauvin, L. (1996). Drug and alcohol use by Canadian university athletes: A national survey. *Journal of Drug Addiction, 26*, 275–287.

Stainback, R. D. (1997). *Alcohol and sport*. Champaign, IL: Human Kinetics.

Swoap, R. A., & Murphy, S. M. (1995). Eating disorders and weight management in athletes. In S. M. Murphy (Ed.), *Sport psychology interventions* (pp. 307–329). Champaign, IL: Human Kinetics.

Taylor, J., & Schneider, B. A. (1992). The sport–clinical intake protocol: A comprehensive interviewing instrument for applied sport psychology. *Professional Psychology: Research and Practice, 23*, 318–325.

Thompson, R., & Sherman R. T. (1999). Athletes, athletic performance, and eating disorders: Healthier alternatives. *Journal of Social Issues, 55*, 317–337.

Thompson, R. A., & Sherman, R. (1993). *Helping athletes with eating disorders*. Champaign, IL: Human Kinetics.

Van Raalte, J. L., Brewer, B. W., Brewer, D. D., & Linder, D. E. (1992). NCAA Division II college football players' perceptions of an athlete who consults a sport psychologist. *Journal of Sport and Exercise Psychology, 14*, 273–282.

Vernacchia, R. A., Reardon, J. P., & Templin, D. P. (1997). Sudden death in sport: Managing the aftermath. *The Sport Psychologist, 11*, 223–235.

Wechsler, H., Davenport, A. E., Dowdall, G. W., Grossman, S. J., & Zanakos, S. I. (1997). Binge drinking, tobacco, and illicit drug use and involvement in college athletics: A survey of students at 140 American colleges. *Journal of American College Health, 45*, 195–200.

Weinstock, J., Whelan, J. P., & Meyers, A. W. (2000, June). *Gambling among collegiate athletes and non-athletes: Is there much action off the field?* Paper presented at the 11th International Conference on Gambling and Risk Taking, Las Vegas, NV.

White-Welkley, J. E., Higbie, E. J., Fried, A. L., Koenig, L. J., & Price, L. R. (1998). Exercise patterns, injury incidence, eating habits, aerobic fitness and psychopathology among non-competitive females [Abstract]. *Medicine and Science in Sports and Exercise, 30*(Suppl.), S118.

Williams, J. M., & Andersen, M. B. (1998). Psychosocial antecedents of sport injury: Review and critique of the stress and injury model. *Journal of Applied Sport Psychology, 10*, 5–25.

Wrisberg, C. A., Johnson, M. S., & Brooks, G. (1997). The life experience of collegiate athletes: A phenomenological investigation [Abstract]. *Journal of Applied Sport Psychology, 9*(Suppl.), S76.

Yancey dead at 56. (1994, August 27). *The Union–News*, pp. 23–24.

Referral Processes in Sport Psychology

Judy L. Van Raalte and Mark B. Andersen

Malika began working with a sport psychologist because she lacked confidence during competitions and was often worried. As the consultation progressed, Malika learned ways to control her anxiety and bolster her confidence in her sport. She told the sport psychologist that she was able to manage her emotions in her sport but was now feeling worried because she was losing a lot of money betting on professional sports. Gambling had been a problem in high school, and it was getting out of control again.

* * *

Although Al sometimes seemed "different," he was an integral member of his team throughout the year. He wanted to improve in his sport and gladly put in extra hours training and working with a sport psychologist. At the team fundraiser, Al started acting strange again. He was rude to some of the people who were contributing to the team. The next week, Al was found wandering around barefoot in a nearby town. He was disheveled and seemed to be disoriented.

* * *

Chris was a team leader who took advantage of an opportunity to meet with a sport psychologist to discuss various issues. Chris told the sport psychologist that chronic knee pain kept her from performing in a relaxed manner. Chris asked the sport psychologist for performance enhancement suggestions that would allow her to compete and block out the pain.

Athletes begin working with sport psychologists for a variety of reasons. As described in these cases, consultation often begins with a focus on performance enhancement. Athletes may contact a sport psychology consultant or be referred to one for other problems as well (e.g., coach/teammate conflicts, career issues, injury). Over the course of consultation, the sport psychologist may come to believe that issues other than performance enhancement (e.g., gambling, psychopathology, physical injury) are of central concern to the athlete. When these issues are outside the sport psychologist's areas of expertise, or when the sport psychologist feels frustrated and is not making progress with a client, a referral may be in order (Bobele & Conran, 1988).

The issue of referral in sport psychology service delivery has received increasing attention in recent years. This change may be due to the incorporation of clinical and counseling models of service delivery into mainstream sport and exercise psychology (e.g., Balague, 1999; Lesyk, 1998; Petitpas, Danish, & Giges, 1999; Poczwardowski, Sherman, & Henschen, 1998) as well as to greater awareness of the fact that referral is such a delicate and potentially risky process (Andersen, 2001; Petrie & Sherman, 2000).

The structure of the referral can set the stage for the quality and efficacy of the therapeutic relationship that follows (Bobele & Conran, 1988). For athletes, referrals are complicated by the stigma associated with mental problems and the derogation of those who seek help from mental health practitioners. Research has indicated that male college students and older male sports fans derogate an athlete who consults a sport psychologist or a psychiatrist relative to an athlete who attempts to resolve the same problem by working with his coach (Linder, Brewer, Van Raalte, & DeLange, 1991). Although college athletes do not derogate a fellow athlete who consults a sport psychologist, they do have a negative regard for an athlete who consults a psychiatrist (Van Raalte, Brewer, Brewer, & Linder, 1992). Thus, fear of derogation may leave athletes hesitant to accept referrals to mental health professionals.

This chapter addresses some of the complexities of the referral process in sport psychology. First, some of the typical problems requiring referral in sport psychology settings are presented. Second, referral networks are described. Third, "dos" and "don'ts" for the referral of athletes are provided.

Typical Problems Requiring Referral

Athletes, in general, probably exhibit a smaller range and frequency of mental disorders than are found in the population at large. Severe pathology among athletes may be rare because of a natural selection process. For example, maintaining an athlete's schedule and regimen is generally more than a severely depressed person or a person with borderline personality can handle for any significant length of time. The good mental health of athletes (Morgan, 1985) may also be due in part to their involvement in regular exercise. Various forms of physical activity have been found to be effective in treating depression and other psychological disorders (e g , Martinsen, 1990; Sachs & Buffone, 1984). Nevertheless, problems requiring referral do occur in the athletic population (Andersen, Denson, Brewer, & Van Raalte, 1994; Brewer & Petrie, chapter 15, this volume). Depending on the specific knowledge and competencies of the sport psychologist, a variety of psychological problems may be detected that require referral. Some of the more common physical concerns, interpersonal and intrapersonal issues, and psychopathology that a sport psychologist might encounter, and make referrals for, are detailed next.

Physical Issues

Sport psychologists should make every effort to gain knowledge of the technical and physical aspects of sport and exercise activities. Such knowledge helps sport psychologists recognize when a problem is more physical than psychological and make appropriate referrals to coaches and sports medicine personnel. Knowledge of the technical aspects of the sport helps the sport psychologist better judge when an athlete's problems need the attention of the coach more than that of the sport psychologist. An example from our case books illustrates this point. A beginning 110-meter hurdler was seeing a sport psychologist and starting work on imaging her event. Upon asking the athlete about the quality, viewpoint, and pace of the hurdling images, the psychologist learned that she was "watching" each hurdle as her leg went over it. The sport psychologist was fairly sure her eyes should have been focused farther down the track and not on the hurdle that was being passed. Because this visual focus question was a coaching point outside of the sport psychologist's area of competence, it was suggested that the athlete discuss ideal focus techniques with her coach. This discussion resulted in improved hurdling for the athlete, enhanced the athlete's relationship with her coach, and gave the coach a favorable impression of the sport psychologist. Sport psychologists who interfere in the technical area of athletes' sport performances and cross the line into coaching may not last in the field.

Sport psychologists working in competitive sport may encounter athletes who are encouraged to "play through the pain." In some cases, athletes may be sent to a sport psychologist because they are not "tough" enough. That is, the coach may believe that athletes are "wimping out" or that psychological factors are causing recurrent injuries. Before working with an athlete on specific techniques (e.g., pain management, concentration), the sport psychologist should refer the athlete to a sports medicine provider to make sure that additional athletic involvement will not cause physical damage. This referral itself can pose problems. The coach should be informed of any referral to sports medicine personnel so that the coach does not feel left out of important athlete-related decisions. However, the sport psychologist cannot ethically reveal that a referral has been made without the express consent of the athlete. Referral for a thorough check-out framed as "just covering all the bases" may prove effective in putting both the athlete and coach at ease.

As relationships between sport psychologists and athletes develop, athletes may begin to feel comfortable voicing dissatisfaction with training schedules and techniques. Athletes may discuss technical problems with their training that they believe are contributing to poor performances. Naturally, athletes should talk to their coaches about technical issues, but some athletes are uncomfortable around their coaches and are fearful of coach reactions. Sport psychologists can help athletes develop strategies to facilitate dialogue. Although encouraging athletes to talk to their coaches is not a referral in the strict sense, it is directing athletes to the appropriate person (see Smith & Smoll, chapter 17, this volume).

Personal and Interpersonal Issues

Helping athletes cope with interpersonal issues may be within sport psychologists' realm of expertise, depending on their training. For those trained in exercise science or research psychology, or for those hired to work in performance enhancement only, the structure of the consultation setting necessitates referral for interpersonal concerns. For example, if sport psychologists are hired primarily to provide performance enhancement services, they may decide to refer athletes to other practitioners for longer term consultation on interpersonal issues such as aggression and sexual issues.

Aggression is an accepted part of the athletic culture (Heyman &

Andersen, 1998). In some cases, however, athletes' aggression may become problematic. Difficulties can arise when athletes are so aggressive that they are unable to compete within the rules and are extremely aggressive off the field. For athletes who have been using alcohol, steroids, or other illegal drugs, the situation becomes even more complicated. A sport psychologist may have success helping athletes manage their aggression if the athletes have a history of reasonable anger and aggression control. Athletes with more problematic histories may require more extensive treatment and may be good candidates for referral (Heyman & Andersen, 1998).

The sexual activities of athletes are often considered newsworthy, although little research has been conducted on the actual sexual behavior of athletes (Heyman & Andersen, 1998). Like the rest of the population, athletes confront several issues concerning relationships, sexuality, and gender roles. Sport psychologists working primarily in the performance enhancement area still may come across sexuality issues with their athlete–clients. It is common for an athlete after a month or two of building up trust with a sport psychologist to then reveal some very personal information. In some cases, sexuality issues may be part of that information. In most cases, being a gay, lesbian, or bisexual athlete is not the problem. Many of the problems these athletes face have to do with homophobia in sport and society. Sport psychologists not familiar or comfortable with sexual orientation and sexual identity issues need to refer the athlete to a professional who is knowledgeable about these concerns (see also Andersen, Butki, & Heyman, 1997; Griffin, 1998).

Psychopathology

Sport psychologists also must be familiar with the symptoms associated with psychopathology to be able to appropriately treat or refer athletes (Andersen et al., 1994). Brewer and Petrie (chapter 15, this volume) provide a discussion of some of the more common disorders that sport psychologists may encounter (e.g., adjustment reactions, anxiety disorders, eating disorders, pathological gambling, and personality disorders).

Knowing What We Know

A central issue in deciding whether or not to make a referral is the determination of the limits of one's competence. Competence is not defined by degree titles, departmental affiliates, or even licensure; competence is an issue of knowledge and skills. As Giges (in Simons & Andersen, 1995) aptly stated,

> What we know and what we do, need not be limited by what we call ourselves. Is helping someone learn a new behavior, change a belief, or change thinking considered education, counselling or therapy? I believe it is a part of each and all three, therefore, it can be done by an educator, counselor, or therapist who has acquired the necessary knowledge, skill, and experience to do so. (p. 466)

How can one determine the limits of one's own competency? Even careful self-assessment can have limited utility, because blind spots in knowledge and training are, by definition, difficult to see. The answer to the question is supervision (see Andersen, Van Raalte, & Brewer, 2000; Andersen, Van Raalte, & Harris, 2000; Van Raalte & Andersen, 2000). The first objective of supervision is the care and welfare of the athlete–client. The second objective, however, is the development of the sport psychologist as a competent practitioner. Through the help of a supervisor, sport psychologists can explore what they know and what they do not know in order to understand their boundaries of competence. Armed with such knowledge, decisions about whether to refer become easier to make.

Supervision can also serve a third, educational function. An athlete's problem may be just beyond the competence of a sport psychologist. With proper supervision and study, however, the practitioner may proceed with treating the athlete. This process of learning through supervision and study facilitates professional growth. Supervision is not only for neophyte practitioners; it is a career-long process. Even seasoned practitioners can learn and expand their boundaries of competence through supervisory consultation with colleagues.

Referral Networks

Having gathered information about the typical problems that may require referral, and knowing the limits of one's competence, it is incumbent on the sport psychologist to develop an appropriate referral network. A sport psychology referral network is a group of people with expertise in a variety of areas to whom athletes can be referred. Ideally, the professionals in the referral network have knowledge of sports and experience working with athletes. At the least, they should be interested in learning about sport and exercise and open to working with an athletic population.

Establishing a referral network takes time and motivation. First, appropriate professionals in the local area should be identified (Andersen, 2001). These professionals can include coaches, exercise physiologists, sports medicine experts, physical therapists, athletic trainers, psychologists, psychiatrists, and social workers. Selecting both male and female professionals of various theoretical orientations and professional backgrounds can be useful. Second, an effort should be made to develop a relationship with these professionals. Meeting for lunch and talking on a regular basis can facilitate the "getting to know each other" process. Referrals are often smoother and more comfortable if sport psychologists know the professionals to whom they are referring their athlete–clients and have asked them how they would like athletes to be referred (Bobele & Conran, 1988). Athletes seem to find this "team approach," in which various sport professionals work together, to be appealing (Andersen, 1992). Third, the referral network should be evaluated and modified on an ongoing basis to provide the best service for athletes. Having a broad group of practitioners available allows the sport psychologist to have some flexibility in this process.

When developing a referral network, sport psychologists should keep in mind some of the specific concerns that athletes may have. Athletes generally have limited time because of the demands of training and work or school. Many athletes have limited funds. Thus, it is useful to select local practitioners, at least some of whom provide services on a sliding-scale basis. For student–athletes attending colleges or universities, free on-campus services are usually available. Developing a relationship with these providers increases the likelihood that athletes will follow through on the referrals made.

The Referral Process

There is no one way to make the perfect referral. Nevertheless, the following "dos" about the referral process may be useful for sport psychology practitioners (also see Exhibit 16.1):

- Do prepare athletes for the referral. This preparation should begin at the first meeting with the athlete. Athletes should be informed that during the course of their work with the sport psychologist, referral to other practitioners is possible. Because

---

Exhibit 16.1

Tips for Making Good Referrals

1. Assess the timing of the referral. Athlete–sport psychologist rapport makes the referral process smoother.
2. Explain why you are making the referral (Bobele & Conran, 1988).
3. Describe to athletes what is generally involved in working with a mental health (or other) practitioner (Heil, 1993).
4. Be sensitive to athlete concerns in the referral process.
5. Get written consent from athletes to share information with the referral source if necessary.
6. Give athletes the necessary information to schedule an appointment or schedule an appointment at the time that the referral is made.
7. If athletes decide not to follow through, discuss alternate strategies. Do not hesitate to reintroduce the idea of referral (Heil, 1993).

---

a lot of information is covered in the initial session, many psychologists (Strein & Hershenson, 1991) and sport psychologists have developed written handouts reiterating important details about the consultation process for athletes to read and take with them.

If it becomes evident that the athlete should be referred, do explain to the athlete why the referral is being made (Bobele & Conran, 1988; Heil, 1993). Athletes may be more receptive to the referral if it is explained in terms of their sport, using performance enhancement terms rather than in terms of pathology-based language. If appropriate referral networks have been cultivated, it also is possible for sport psychologists to match athletes with compatible, competent practitioners.

• Do describe to athletes what is generally involved in working with the practitioner to whom they are being referred (Heil, 1993). This is particularly important for athletes who are being referred to mental health practitioners. Although athletes do not seem to differ from nonathletes in their expectations about counseling (Miller & Moore, 1993), misconceptions about mental health treatments clearly exist. It is acceptable to tell athletes about various forms of payment available (e.g., insurance, sliding scale, pro bono), but the practitioner should set the specific fee (Bobele & Conran, 1988).
• Do present referrals in a manner that allows athletes to maintain their dignity and save face (Brewer, Petitpas, & Van Raalte, 1999).

Some athletes consider referrals to be extremely embarrassing, an indication that that they are serious "head cases." Special attention to athlete concerns can help athletes feel supported and make it more likely that they will pursue referrals.

- Do be sensitive to the concerns and fears of the athlete during the referral process. Athletes may be afraid that if they pursue the referral, the practitioner may take away what made them "great" performers (Heyman & Andersen, 1998). Focusing on athletes' return to competition if athletes want to return is also important (Bobele & Conran, 1988).

- Do carefully assess the timing of the referral. A solid relationship helps the referral process proceed more smoothly.

- Do contact and confidentially discuss the referring issue with a skilled colleague. With supervision and guidance, it may be possible to work with the athlete on an issue that is just beyond your current level of comfort and/or competence. Reassess regularly with this supervisor, and refer the athlete if necessary.

- Do get written consent to share information about the athlete with the practitioner to whom the referral is being made, if necessary (Strein & Hershenson, 1991). Information is appropriately shared on a "need to know" basis. Athletes who are aware of exactly what information will be provided may be more comfortable with the referral.

- Do facilitate follow through on the referral. Refer "in" as much as possible. That is, bring in the practitioner to work together with the athlete and the sport psychologist (Andersen, 1992). This team approach has the advantage of being convenient for the athlete and alleviating some athlete concerns about rejection and fears that if they pursue the referral, they will be abandoned by their sport psychologist (for an example of an athlete resistant to talking to someone else and the referral process, see Andersen, 2000). When referring in is not feasible, give athletes the information needed for them to schedule an appointment with the practitioner. Some athletes may prefer to have the sport psychologist help them schedule the first appointment when the referral is made.

- Do assess the effectiveness of the referral process. Sport psychologists may want to schedule follow-up meetings to see how the referral worked. If the athlete decides not to follow through on the referral, the sport psychologist should then discuss alternate strategies for dealing with the problem (Heil, 1993). Sport psychologists should not hesitate to reintroduce the idea of referral at a later date (Heil, 1993).

There are several don'ts for the referral process. Although this list is not exhaustive, avoiding these pitfalls may help referrals go more smoothly (also see Exhibit 16.2):

- Don't wait for the perfect moment to refer. The perfect moment may never come to pass. If the athlete decides not to follow up on the referral, you can refer again in the future.
- Don't oversimplify the situation and tell the athlete that the problem will be easily fixed if the athlete pursues the referral (Bobele & Conran, 1988). Although it is important to sound positive and confident about the skills of the practitioner, creating false expectations will make it more difficult for the practitioner to work effectively.
- Don't disguise the expertise and/or function of the practitioner (Bobele & Conran, 1988). Particularly if the athlete is hesitant to pursue the referral, it may be tempting to omit some of the details of the practitioner's expertise. Failure to reveal relevant information, however, violates trust and can make it difficult for the practitioner to work effectively with the athlete.
- Don't use referral follow through as a condition for a favorable report to the coach or a prerequisite to avoid negative consequences (Bobele & Conran, 1988). Coaches may want to support the referral by punishing athletes who do not comply, but placing these additional conditions on the referral process can make it

Exhibit 16.2

Referral Don'ts

1. Don't wait for the "perfect" moment for a referral. It may never come.
2. Don't oversimplify the situation and say that the problem is minor and will easily be fixed (Bobele & Conran, 1988).
3. Don't disguise the expertise and/or function of the practitioner to whom the athlete is being referred (Bobele & Conran, 1988).
4. Don't use referral follow through as a condition for a favorable report to the coach or a prerequisite to avoid negative consequences (Bobele & Conran, 1988).
5. Don't violate athlete confidentiality by telling others about the referral.
6. Don't undermine the treatment of the referral source.

impossible for the practitioner to work effectively with the athlete.

- Don't violate confidentiality. Some athletes are referred to sport psychologists by significant others (e.g., coach, parent, dean) with an interest in the outcome of the athletes' consultation. When making new referrals for these athletes, don't inform these others of the referral process unless this has been agreed to by the athlete in writing. It may be useful to teach these significant others about sport psychologists' responsibility to protect athletes' confidentiality when the initial referral is accepted (Heyman & Andersen, 1998). Information about confidentiality vis-a-vis these other interested parties should also be provided to athletes (McGrath, 1990).

- Don't undermine the treatment of the practitioner to whom the athlete is referred. When a referral is made for a specific problem, the sport psychologist should make an effort to focus on other issues to minimize the risk of athletes' confusion (American Psychological Association, 1992). If the athlete requires medical treatment, the sport psychologist can work as part of the sports medicine team, helping the athlete with psychological issues (Heil, 1993).

Conclusion

Referral comes in many varieties. For referrals that primarily have to do with the athlete's body (e.g., massage, sports medicine, nutrition), it is wise for athletes to keep the coach informed. For referrals that have a psychological or psychiatric nature (e.g., anxiety, depression, eating disorders), the specifics of the problem may dictate what the athlete chooses to reveal to the coach.

Some referrals, such as sending an athlete to a sport nutritionist to learn how to eat correctly during heavy training, are relatively easy. Referring an athlete to a psychiatrist because it appears medication could be of some benefit requires a delicate touch. Much of appropriate referral focuses on issues of competence. Routinely assessing one's own skills, participating in ongoing supervision, and continuing to develop referral networks to cover areas of athlete concerns are important steps to take.

References

American Psychological Association. (1992). Ethical principles of psychologists and code of conduct. *American Psychologist, 47*, 1597–1611.

Andersen, M. B. (1992). Sport psychology and procrustean categories: An appeal for synthesis and expansion of service. *Association for the Advancement of Applied Sport Psychology Newsletter, 7*(3), 8–9.

Andersen, M. B. (2000). *Doing sport psychology*. Champaign, IL: Human Kinetics.

Andersen, M. B. (2001). When to refer athletes for counseling or psychotherapy. In J. M. Williams (Ed.), *Applied sport psychology: Personal growth to peak performance* (4th ed., pp. 401–415). Mountain View, CA: Mayfield.

Andersen, M. B., Butki, B. D., & Heyman, S. R. (1997). Homophobia and sport experience: A survey of college students. *Academic Athletic Journal, 12*(1), 27–38.

Andersen, M. B., Denson, E. L., Brewer, B. W., & Van Raalte, J. L. (1994). Disorders of personality and mood in athletes: Recognition and referral. *Journal of Applied Sport Psychology, 6*, 168–184.

Andersen, M. B., Van Raalte, J. L., & Brewer, B. W. (2000). When applied sport psychology consultants and graduate students are impaired: Ethical and legal issues in training and supervision. *Journal of Applied Sport Psychology, 12*, 134–150.

Andersen, M. B., Van Raalte, J. L., & Harris, G. (2000). Supervision II: A case study. In M. B. Andersen (Ed.), *Doing sport psychology* (pp. 167–180). Champaign, IL: Human Kinetics.

Balague, G. (1999). Understanding identity, value, and meaning when working with elite athletes. *The Sport Psychologist, 13*, 89–98.

Bobele, M., & Conran, T. J. (1988). Referrals for family therapy: Pitfalls and guidelines. *Elementary School Guidance, 22*, 192–198.

Brewer, B. W., Petitpas, A. J., & Van Raalte, J. L. (1999). Referral of injured athletes for counselling and psychotherapy. In R. Ray & D. M. Wiese-Bjornstal (Eds.), *Counseling in sports medicine* (pp. 127–141). Champaign, IL: Human Kinetics.

Griffin, P. (1998). *Strong women, deep closets: Lesbians and homophobia in sport*. Champaign, IL: Human Kinetics.

Heil, J. (1993). *Psychology of sport injury*. Champaign, IL: Human Kinetics.

Heyman, S. R., & Andersen, M. B. (1998). When to refer athletes for counseling or psychotherapy. In J. M. Williams (Ed.). *Applied sport psychology: Personal growth to peak performance*. (3rd ed., pp. 359–371). Mountain View, CA: Mayfield.

Lesyk, J. L. (1998). *Developing sport psychology within your clinical practice: A practical guide for mental health professionals*. San Francisco: Jossey-Bass.

Linder, D. E., Brewer, B. W., Van Raalte, J. L., & DeLange, N. (1991). A negative halo for athletes who consult sport psychologists: Replication and extension. *Journal of Sport and Exercise Psychology, 13*, 133–148.

Martinsen, E. (1990). Benefits of exercise for the treatment of depression. *Sports Medicine, 9*, 380–389.

McGrath, R. J. (1990). Assessment of sexual aggressors. *Journal of Interpersonal Violence, 5*, 507–519.

Miller, M. J., & Moore, K. K. (1993). Athletes' and nonathletes' expectations about counseling. *Journal of College Student Development, 34*, 267–270.

Morgan, W. P. (1985). Selected psychological factors limiting performance: A mental health model. In D. J. Clark & H. M. Eckert (Eds.), *Limits of human performance* (pp. 70–80). Champaign, IL: Human Kinetics.

Petitpas, A. J., Danish, S. J., & Giges, B. (1999). The sport psychologist-athlete relationship: Implications for training. *The Sport Psychologist, 13*, 344–357.

Petrie, T. A., & Sherman, R. T. (2000). Counseling athletes with eating disorders: A case example. In M. B. Andersen (Ed.), *Doing sport psychology* (pp. 121–137). Champaign, IL: Human Kinetics.

Poczwardowski, A., Sherman, C. P., & Henschen, K. P. (1998). A sport psychology service delivery heuristic: Building on theory and practice. *The Sport Psychologist, 12,* 345–356.

Sachs, M. L., & Buffone, G. W. (Eds.). (1984). *Running as therapy: An integrated approach.* Lincoln: University of Nebraska Press.

Simons, J. P., & Andersen, M. B. (1995). The development of consulting practice in applied sport psychology: Some personal perspectives. *The Sport Psychologist, 9,* 449–468.

Strein, W., & Hershenson, D. B. (1991). Confidentiality in nondyadic counseling situations. *Journal of Counseling & Development, 69,* 312–316.

Van Raalte, J. L., & Andersen, M. B. (2000). Supervision I: From models to doing. In M. B. Andersen (Ed.), *Doing sport psychology* (pp. 153–165). Champaign, IL: Human Kinetics.

Van Raalte, J. L., Brewer, B. W., Brewer, D. D., & Linder, D. E. (1992). NCAA Division II college football players' perceptions of an athlete who consults a sport psychologist. *Journal of Sport and Exercise Psychology, 14,* 273–282.

Part IV

Working With
Specific Populations

Youth Sports as a Behavior Setting for Psychosocial Interventions

Ronald E. Smith and Frank L. Smoll

Athletic competition for children is a firmly established part of American society. Today in the United States, approximately 41 million youngsters between the ages of 6 and 18 participate in non-school sport programs (e.g., Little League Baseball, Pop Warner Football, Boys and Girls Clubs), and 6 to 7 million more participate in school-sponsored programs (Ewing & Seefeldt, 2002). Sport scientists and popular writers have noted that the sport environment provides socialization opportunities and places adaptive demands on participants that parallel those of other important life settings (Martens, 1978; Michener, 1976; Smoll & Smith, 2002a). For this reason, organized athletic experiences are regarded as potentially important in child and adolescent development.

Although youth sports are firmly entrenched in the U.S. social and cultural milieu, concerns about their desirability have been expressed for some time. Those who favor youth sports emphasize that many aspects of the experience contribute to personal development. Proponents generally view youth sports as miniature life situations in which participants can learn to cope with several of the important realities of life. Within sport, youngsters can compete and cooperate with others, learn risk taking and self-control, and deal with success and failure. Important attitudes are formed about achievement, authority, moral standards, and persistence in the face of adversity (Weiss, in press). In addition, advocates point out, lifelong patterns of physical activity that promote health and fitness can be initiated through involvement in youth sports.

Critics counter with claims that excessive physical and psychological demands are placed on young people and that programs exist primarily for the self-serving needs of coaches and parents. Sometimes, moral principles are compromised at the altar of winning (Shields, Brede-meier, & Power, 2002). Many critics suggest that children and youths would benefit far more if adults simply left them alone to participate in their own games and activities.

A realistic appraisal of youth sports indicates that participation does not automatically result in beneficial or detrimental effects. We believe that the sport environment affords a strong potential for achieving desirable objectives. The question is not whether youth sports should continue to exist, for they are here to stay. The real issue is how the programs can be structured effectively and conducted in ways that ensure attainment of positive outcomes.

Research on Youth Sports

Sport consultants who choose to work in the arena of youth sports should be aware of the complex physical, psychological, and sociological phenomena that affect the developing child. Since the mid-1970s, the scientific community has increasingly studied the impact of the complex social network comprising coaches, parents, and peers. The accumulation of empirical evidence has resulted in a body of knowledge that spans several disciplinary areas, including psychology, sociology, and the sport sciences.

Personality Development and Sport Participation

Research on the psychological consequences of sport participation for personality development has centered on several variables of interest, most notably, self-concept and performance anxiety. Sport experiences can have an important role in the development of self-concept and can affect a child's self-esteem as well (Horn & Hasbrook, 1987; Smoll, Smith, Barnett, & Everett, 1993). Scanlan (1996) noted that youth sport participation occurs during a period when children have limited information about their competencies. They derive such information from both social and nonsocial sources, and this input helps form their self-concept and their evaluative responses to it (i.e., their self-esteem).

Three separate social evaluation processes—comparative appraisal, reflected appraisal, and direct feedback—provide important information that is incorporated into the developing self-concept (Harter, 1978; Masters, 1972). Children compare their abilities with those of their peers; they make inferences about themselves based on the meanings they infer from the reactions of others; and they receive direct feedback from "experts," such as parents, teachers, and coaches. Moreover, physical skills are highly valued throughout childhood, particularly by boys, and they are important determinants of peer acceptance (Chase & Dummer, 1992). Thus, it is clear why sport experiences can have an important impact on the developing self-concept. Sports provide many opportunities for social comparison, and athletes receive a good deal of direct and indirect feedback from peers, parents, and coaches. The reactions of a high-status adult such as a coach can make a strong impression on a child. The information received by the child in the course of sport participation can therefore contribute to either a positive or a negative self-concept, with resulting high or low self-esteem. Given this fact, the prospect of intervening in the sport system in such a way as to facilitate positive self-concept development is an exciting one.

Performance anxiety also has received a good deal of empirical attention (Smith, Smoll, & Passer, 2002). This form of anxiety involves high levels of somatic arousal, worry about the consequences of performing poorly, and concentration disruption caused mainly by cognitive interference (Smith, Smoll, & Schutz, 1990). In many ways, performance anxiety is the athlete's worst enemy, because fear of failure has been shown to interfere with performance, decrease enjoyment of sport participation, and promote avoidance of or withdrawal from sport participation (Gould & Dieffenbach, in press; Smith & Smoll, 1990b). In one study, more than half of a sample of 8- and 9-year-old sport nonparticipants indicated that they would like to compete but were fearful of performing poorly or failing to make a team (Orlick & Botterill, 1975). Brustad (1993, in press) reviewed several studies that indicate that parents and coaches can be potent sources of anxiety for child athletes, particularly when the perceived demands and expectations of these significant adults severely tax the self-perceived abilities of the athlete. Concern about negative evaluations from parents and coaches (and peers) is the primary source of worry (Brustad, 1988). Such worries are undoubtedly augmented by the fact that failure in sport occurs in a public context for all to see. Predictably, antecedents of performance anxiety include a history of being punished and criticized for achievement failures (Smith & Smoll, 1990b).

In recent years, increasing concern has arisen about the causal role of stress in high levels of burnout and attrition in youth sports (Biddle, in press; Gould, Tuffey, Udry, & Loehr, 1996). Some studies have found annual dropout rates (defined as total withdrawal from sport participation) of about 30% to 40% (e.g., Barnett, Smoll, & Smith, 1992; Gould, 1987). Follow-up data collected from such athletes reveal that many of them choose to discontinue participation because pressures to win have taken the fun out of the sport and engendered high levels of performance anxiety. Exposure to continuous psychological stress is viewed as a contributor to burnout, which also may prompt withdrawal from sport activities that at one time were highly enjoyable for the athlete (Gould et al., 1996; Smith, 1986a). Because of the negative effects of stress and anxiety on performance, participation, and enjoyment in sport, attempts to minimize their development within youth sports should be a high-priority goal (Biddle, in press).

Coaches, Parents, and Athletes

The coach–parent–athlete triad has been referred to as the "athletic triangle" (Smith, Smoll, & Smith, 1989). The members of this social system interact with one another in complex ways, and the nature of those interactions can have significant consequences for the psychological development of the child. The coach–athlete relationship influences the child during important developmental periods, and the nature of the interpersonal transactions between coach and athlete has been shown to affect such variables as enjoyment of the activity, attraction toward coach and teammates, self-esteem, performance anxiety, team cohesion, and sport attrition (Fisher, Mancini, Hirsch, Proulx, & Staurowsky, 1982; Smoll & Smith, 2002b; Westre & Weiss, 1991).

Parental influences on children's socialization in sport and on psychosocial consequences once involved also have been documented (Brustad & Partridge, 2002; Greendorfer, Lewko, & Rosengren, 2002). Although there is a paucity of research on observed parental behaviors and their consequences, the negative impact they can have on child athletes is all too obvious. Parental misbehavior at competitive events has become such a problem that in some programs, parents are barred from attending games. Other programs have resorted to scheduling games in the morning or afternoon so that parents cannot easily attend.

If the quality of supervision is a critical issue in youth sports, so is the manner in which some misguided parents can undermine the laudable goals of youth sport programs and thereby detract from the benefits that athletic experiences should provide for children. Assisting parents in assuring that sports will be a positive influence on their relationship with their child is a worthy target for sport psychology intervention.

The young athlete is a third point of intervention in the athletic triangle. Psychology has developed an impressive and effective arsenal of techniques to enhance human performance and well-being. The fact that children engage in youth sports during a formative period of their lives provides a window of opportunity for sport psychology interventions designed to foster the personal development of the athlete and to facilitate the development of life skills that generalize from sports to other areas of life.

The following sections provide practical guidelines for practitioners who wish to work in the area of youth sports. It will become readily apparent that some promising and empirically validated intervention strategies already exist but also that there is great opportunity for innovative approaches to enhancing the youth sport environment.

Coach-Based Interventions

Most athletes have their first sport experiences in programs staffed by volunteer coaches. Although many of these coaches are fairly well versed in the technical aspects of the sport, they rarely have had any formal training in creating a healthy psychological environment for youngsters. Moreover, through the mass media, these coaches are frequently exposed to college or professional coaches who model aggressive behaviors and a "winning is everything" philosophy that is inappropriate in a recreational and skills development context. Because the vast majority of youth coaches have desirable motives for coaching (Martens & Gould, 1979; Smith, Smoll, & Curtis, 1978), one can assume that their limitations result primarily from a lack of information on how to create a supportive interpersonal climate. Several educational programs have been developed for the purpose of positively affecting coaching practices, thereby increasing the likelihood that youngsters will have positive sport experiences.

Four training programs currently available in the United States include curricular components designed to influence the manner in which volunteer coaches interact with young athletes. The American Coaching Effectiveness Program (ACEP; Martens, 1987a), Coach Effectiveness Training (CET; Smoll & Smith, 2001), the National Youth Sport Coaches Association program (NYSCA; Brown & Butterfield, 1992), and the Program for Athletic Coaches' Education (PACE; Seefeldt & Brown, 1992) have been administered to many thousands of youth coaches. The national coaching associations of Australia and Canada also have developed formal programs that provide training in sport psychology and other areas, such as sport pedagogy (teaching sport skills and strategies), sport physiology (conditioning, weight training, and nutrition), and sports medicine (injury prevention, care, and rehabilitation).

Weiss and Hayashi (1996) noted that ACEP, NYSCA, and PACE "have provided coaching workshops to thousands of individuals involved in community-based and school-sponsored sports, but evaluation research is essential to determine the effectiveness of these training programs on increasing sport science knowledge and applications" (p. 53). Unfortunately, CET is the only program that has been subjected to systematic evaluation to determine its influence on coaches' behaviors and the effects of such behaviors on youngsters' psychosocial development (Brown & Butterfield, 1992). We present CET as an illustration of an empirical approach to the development and evaluation of intervention strategies in the youth sport setting. Specifically, overviews of (a) the development of CET, (b) the content of CET and procedures for its implementation, and (c) empirical studies used to assess the efficacy of CET are provided.

Developing a Coach Training Program

A crucial first step in developing a training program is to determine what is to be presented. In this regard, our work was guided by a fundamental assumption that a training program should be based on scientific evidence rather than on intuition and what we "know" on the basis of informal observation (Smith & Smoll, 1997). An empirical foundation for coaching guidelines not only enhances the validity and potential value of the program, but it also increases its credibility in the eyes of consumers.

Theoretical Model and Research Paradigm

In the early 1970s, recognition of the potential impact of youth coaches on athletes' psychological welfare prompted several scientific questions. For example, what do coaches do, and how frequently do they engage in such behaviors as encouragement, punishment, instruction, and organization? What are the psychological dimensions that underlie such behaviors? How are observable coaching behaviors related to children's reactions to their organized athletic experiences? Answers to such questions are not only a first step in describing the behavioral ecology of one aspect of the youth sport setting, but they also provide an empirical basis for the development of psychologically oriented intervention programs.

To begin to answer such questions, a systematic program of research was carried out over several years. The project was guided by a mediational model of coach–athlete interactions, the basic elements of which are represented as follows:

Coach behaviors → Athlete perception and recall → Athletes' evaluative reactions.

This model stipulates that the ultimate effects of coaching behaviors are mediated by the meaning that athletes attribute to them. In other words, what athletes remember about their coaches' behaviors and how they interpret these actions affect the way that athletes evaluate their sport experiences. Furthermore, a complex of cognitive and affective processes is involved at this mediational level. The athletes' perceptions and reactions are likely to be affected not only by the coaches' behaviors but also by other factors, such as the athlete's age; what he or she expects of coaches (i.e., normative beliefs and expectations); and certain personality variables, including self-esteem and anxiety. In recognition of this, the basic three-element model has been expanded to reflect these factors (Smoll & Smith, 1989). The expanded model specifies several situational factors and coach and athlete characteristics that could influence coach behaviors and the perceptions and reactions of athletes to them. Using this model as a starting point, we sought to determine how observed coaching behaviors, athletes' perception and recall of the coach's behaviors, and athlete attitudes are related to one another. We also explored the manner in which athlete and coach characteristics might affect these relations.

Measurement of Coaching Behaviors

To measure leadership behaviors, we developed the Coaching Behavior Assessment System (CBAS) to permit the direct observation and coding of coaches' actions during practices and games (Smith, Smoll, & Hunt,

1977). The CBAS contains 12 categories divided into two major classes of behaviors. *Reactive* (elicited) behaviors are responses to immediately preceding athlete or team behaviors, whereas *spontaneous* (emitted) behaviors are initiated by the coach and are not a response to a discernible preceding event. Reactive behaviors are responses to desirable performance or effort (reinforcement, nonreinforcement), mistakes and errors (mistake-contingent encouragement, mistake-contingent technical instruction, punishment, punitive technical instruction, ignoring mistakes), or misbehaviors on the part of athletes (keeping control). The spontaneous class includes general technical instruction, general encouragement, organization, and general communication. The system thus involves basic interactions between the situation and the coach's behavior. Use of the CBAS in observing and coding coaching behaviors in a variety of sports indicates that the scoring system is sufficiently comprehensive to incorporate the majority of overt leader behaviors, that high interrater reliability can be obtained, and that individual differences in behavioral patterns can be discerned (Chaumeton & Duda, 1988; Cruz et al., 1987; Horn, 1984, 1985; Jones, Housner, & Kornspan, 1997; Krane, Eklund, & McDermott, 1991; Rejeski, Darracott, & Hutslar, 1979; Sherman & Hassan, 1986; Smith, Zane, Smoll, & Coppel, 1983; Wandzilak, Ansorge, & Potter, 1988).

Coach Behaviors and Children's Evaluative Reactions

Following development of the CBAS, a field study was conducted to establish relationships between coach behaviors and several athlete variables specified in the conceptual model (Smith et al., 1978). Observed behaviors of 51 baseball coaches during 202 complete games were coded, and 542 children who played for the coaches were interviewed and administered questionnaires after the season ended.

At the level of overt behavior, three independent behavioral dimensions were identified through factor analysis: supportiveness (comprised of reinforcement and mistake-contingent encouragement), instructiveness (general technical instruction and mistake-contingent technical instruction vs. general communication and general encouragement), and punitiveness (punishment and punitive technical instruction vs. organizational behaviors). Relationships between coach scores on these behavioral dimensions and player measures indicated that players responded most favorably to coaches who engaged in higher percentages of supportive and instructional behaviors. Players on teams whose coaches created a supportive environment also liked their teammates more.

A somewhat surprising finding was that the team's won-lost record was essentially unrelated to how well the players liked the coach and how much they wanted to play for the coach in the future. However, players on winning teams felt that their parents liked the coach more and that the coach liked them more than did players on losing teams. Apparently, winning made little difference to the children, but they knew that it was important to the adults. It is worth noting, however, that winning assumed greater importance after age 12, although it continued to be a less important attitudinal determinant than coach behaviors.

Another important issue concerns the degree of accuracy with which coaches perceive their own behaviors. Correlations between CBAS-observed behaviors and coaches' ratings of how frequently they performed the behaviors were generally low and nonsignificant. The only significant correlation occurred for punishment. Children's ratings on the same perceived behavior scales correlated much more highly with CBAS measures than did the coaches' ratings. It thus appears that coaches have limited awareness of how frequently they engage in particular forms of behavior and that athletes are more accurate perceivers of actual coach behaviors.

Furthermore, analysis of the children's attraction responses toward the coaches revealed a significant interaction between coach supportiveness (the tendency to reinforce desirable performance and effort and to respond to mistakes with encouragement) and athletes' level of self-esteem (Smith & Smoll, 1990a). Specifically, children with low self-esteem were especially responsive to variations in supportiveness in a manner consistent with a self-enhancement model of self-esteem (Shrauger, 1975; Swann, 1990; Tesser, 1988). This finding is consistent with the results of other studies that, collectively, suggest that self-enhancement motivation causes people who are low in self-esteem to be especially responsive to variations in supportiveness because of their greater need for positive feedback from others (Brown, Collins, & Schmidt, 1988; Dittes, 1959; Tesser & Campbell, 1983).

Assessing the Efficacy of CET

Sweeping conclusions are often drawn about the efficacy of intervention programs in the absence of anything approximating acceptable scientific evidence. We therefore felt it was important not only to develop an empirical foundation for CET but also to measure its effects on coaches and the young people who play for them.

We focused on five important outcome questions in our program evaluation studies. First, does the CET program affect the behaviors of the trained coaches in a manner consistent with the behavioral guidelines? Second, because the program is designed to help coaches create an environment that increases children's positive reactions to coach, teammates, and their sport experience, how does the program affect children's reactions to their athletic experience? Third, does exposure to a positive interpersonal environment created by trained coaches result in an increase in general self-esteem, particularly among children with low self-esteem? Fourth, does CET training help reduce performance anxiety among young athletes? Fifth, do positive changes in the first four outcomes increase the likelihood that young athletes will choose to return to the sport program?

Positive outcomes regarding all five of these questions have been established in a series of studies in which experimental groups of youth baseball coaches exposed to the CET program were compared with untreated, control groups of coaches. Coaches exposed to CET differed in both observed behaviors and in athlete-perceived behaviors in a manner consistent with the behavioral guidelines. Experimental-group coaches were more reinforcing, were more encouraging, gave more technical instruction, and were less punitive and controlling than control-group coaches. In turn, the athletes who played for the trained coaches indicated that they enjoyed their experience more and liked their coach and teammates more. They also demonstrated significant increases in general self-esteem and significant decreases in performance anxiety over the course of the season (Smith, Smoll, & Barnett, 1995; Smith, Smoll, & Curtis, 1979; Smoll et al., 1993).

Further, a study of attrition showed a dropout rate of 26% among children who played for control-group coaches, a figure that is consistent with previous reports of attrition in youth sport programs (Gould, 1987). In contrast, only 5% of the children who played for CET-trained coaches failed to return to the program the next season (Barnett et al., 1992). These positive psychosocial outcomes are all the more noteworthy in light of the fact that experimental and control groups have not differed in average won-lost percentages in any of the studies.

Conducting a CET Clinic

CET Principles

A set of five core principles underlie the behavioral coaching guidelines of the CET program (Smith & Smoll, 2002). A most important first principle is that winning is defined not in terms of won–lost records but instead in terms of giving maximum effort and making improvement. The explicit and primary focus is on having fun, deriving satisfaction from being on the team, learning sport skills, and developing increased self-esteem. This philosophy is designed to maximize young athletes' enjoyment of sport and their chances of deriving the benefits of participation, partly as a result of combating competitive anxiety (Smoll & Smith, 1990). The focus on controllable effort rather than uncontrollable outcome also promotes separation of the athlete's feelings of self-worth from the game outcome, which serves to help overcome fear of failure.

The second principle emphasizes a "positive approach" to coaching. In such an approach, coach–athlete interactions are characterized by the liberal use of positive reinforcement, encouragement, and sound technical instruction that help create high levels of interpersonal attraction between coaches and athletes. Punitive behaviors are strongly discouraged, because they have been shown to create a negative team climate and to promote fear of failure. Reinforcement should not be restricted to the learning and performance of sport skills. Rather, it should be liberally applied to strengthen desirable psychosocial behaviors (e.g., teamwork, leadership, sportsmanship). Coaches are urged to reinforce effort as much as they do results. This guideline has direct relevance to developing a healthy philosophy of winning and a reduction in performance anxiety.

CET includes several positive-approach guidelines pertaining to the appropriate use of technical instruction. For example, when giving instruction, coaches are encouraged to emphasize the good outcomes that will happen if athletes execute correctly rather than focusing on the negative outcomes that will occur if they do not. This approach motivates athletes to create desirable outcomes (i.e., develop a positive achievement orientation) rather than building fear of making mistakes.

The third principle is to establish norms that emphasize athletes' mutual obligations to help and support one another. Such norms increase social support and attraction among teammates, thereby enhancing cohesion and commitment to the team. Such norms are most likely to develop when coaches (a) model supportive behaviors and (b) reinforce athlete behaviors that promote team unity. Coaches also learn how to develop a "we're in this together" group norm. This norm can play an important role in building team cohesion among teammates, particularly if the coach frequently reinforces relevant bench behaviors of attention and mutual supportiveness.

A fourth principle is that compliance with team roles and responsibilities is most effectively achieved by involving athletes in decisions regarding team rules and reinforcing compliance with them rather than by using punitive measures to punish noncompliance. We believe that coaches should recognize that youngsters want clearly defined limits and structure.

The positive approach also applies to promoting compliance with team rules. One of the most effective ways of eliminating negative behaviors (and avoiding the negative side effects of punishment) is to strengthen incompatible positive behaviors. Thus, coaches are encouraged not to take rule compliance for granted but instead to acknowledge instances of compliance with the rules. By using positive reinforcement to strengthen desirable behaviors, coaches can often avoid having to deal with misbehaviors on the part of athletes. In addition, coaches are urged to obtain behavioral feedback and to engage in self-monitoring to increase awareness of their own behaviors and to encourage compliance with the positive-approach guidelines.

CET Procedures

In a CET workshop, which lasts approximately 2.5 hours, behavioral guidelines are presented both verbally and in written materials (a printed outline and a 24-page manual) given to the coaches. The manual (Smoll & Smith, 1997) supplements the guidelines with concrete suggestions for communicating effectively with young athletes, gaining their respect, and effectively relating to their parents. The importance of sensitivity and being responsive to individual differences among athletes also is stressed. The written materials serve to (a) organize the workshop, (b) facilitate coaches' understanding of the information, (c) eliminate the need for coaches to take notes, and (d) give coaches a tangible resource to which they can refer in the future. Also, visual aids, such as content slides and cartoons illustrating important points, are used to facilitate ease of comprehension and retention and to add to the organizational quality of the session.

Not only do we believe in the importance of establishing an empirical foundation for training guidelines, but also we feel that the ability to present supportive data increases the credibility of the guidelines for the coaches. Therefore, CET workshops include a description of the development and testing of the program. Using lay terms and avoiding scientific jargon, we describe the 12 coaching behaviors studied and the manner in which these behaviors were related to athletes' reactions to their sport experience (see Smith & Smoll, 1991, for a summary of this work). This information sets the stage for the presentation of coaching guidelines.

In introducing coaching guidelines, we emphasize that they should not be viewed as a "magic formula" and that mere knowledge of the principles is not sufficient. We stress that the challenge is not so much in learning the principles—they are relatively simple. Rather, the challenge is for the coach to integrate the guidelines into his or her own coaching style.

The most basic objectives of CET are to communicate coaching principles in a manner that is comprehended easily and to maximize the likelihood that coaches will adopt the information. As part of our approach to creating a positive learning environment, coaches are encouraged to share their own experiences and associated practical knowledge with the group. CET workshops are thus conducted with an interactive format in which coaches are treated as an integral part of the session rather than as an audience. The open atmosphere for exchange promotes active versus passive learning, and the dialogue enhances the participants' interest and involvement in the learning process.

The instructional procedures described contain many verbal modeling cues that essentially tell coaches what to do. To supplement the didactic verbal and written materials, coaching guidelines are transmitted through behavioral modeling cues (i.e., actual demonstrations showing coaches how to behave in desirable ways). In CET, such cues are presented by a live model (the trainer) and by symbolic models (coach cartoons). In addition, modeling is frequently used in conjunction with role playing of positive behaviors. Coaches are kept actively involved in the training process by presenting critical situations and asking them to role play appropriate ways of responding. This form of behavioral rehearsal has great promise in enhancing acquisition of desired behaviors, in providing the opportunity to practice the behaviors, and in establishing an increased level of participant involvement during the workshops.

One of the striking findings from the initial research was that coaches had limited awareness of how often they behaved in various ways (Smith et al., 1978). Thus, an important component of a training program should be an attempt to increase coaches' awareness of what they are doing and their motivation to comply with behavioral guidelines. In CET, coaches are taught the use of two proven behavioral change techniques, namely, behavioral feedback (Edelstein & Eisler, 1976; McFall & Twentyman, 1973) and self-monitoring (Kanfer & Gaelick-Buys, 1991; Kazdin, 1974; McFall, 1977). To obtain feedback, coaches are encouraged to work with their assistants as a team and share descriptions of each other's behaviors. They can discuss alternate ways of dealing with difficult situations and athletes and prepare themselves for dealing with similar situations in the future. Other potential feedback procedures include coaches soliciting input from athletes and league committees.

Self-monitoring (observing and recording one's own behavior) has the potential for increasing coaches' awareness of their own behavioral patterns and encouraging their compliance with the guidelines. This method of self-regulation has proven to be effective in a variety of intervention contexts (see Kanfer & Gaelick-Buys, 1991; Kazdin, 1974; McFall, 1977). Because of the impracticality of having coaches monitor and record their own behavior during practices or games, CET coaches are given a brief self-monitoring form that they are encouraged to complete immediately after practices and games (see Smoll & Smith, 2001). On the form, they indicate approximately what percentage of the time they engaged in the recommended behaviors in relevant situations. For example, coaches are asked, "Approximately what percentage of the times they occurred did you respond to mistakes/errors with encouragement?" Self-monitoring is restricted to desired behaviors in light of evidence that tracking of undesired behaviors can be detrimental to effective self-regulation (Cavior & Marabotto, 1976; Gottman & McFall, 1972; Kirschenbaum & Karoly, 1977). Coaches are encouraged to engage in self-monitoring on a regular basis to achieve optimal results.

CET also includes discussion of coach–parent relationships and provides instructions for organizing and conducting a sport orientation meeting with parents. Some purposes of the meeting are to inform parents about their responsibilities for contributing to the success of the sport program and to guide them toward working cooperatively with the coach (see Smoll, 2001).

Parent-Based Interventions

Mass media reports abound concerning parental influences that can potentially undermine the best-intentioned youth sport program. We hear on an increasingly frequent basis about parents engaging in objectionable and, at times, criminally violent actions toward coaches, young athletes, and sport officials. Consider the following examples:

- In Massachusetts, a man died after he was beaten unconscious by another parent who was upset about rough play in their sons' hockey game. The assailant was charged with manslaughter.
- National Guard troops on hurricane duty in Alabama were diverted to a Tinymite football game after a full-scale riot broke out between parents of opposing teams. Videotapes showed adults striking children and attacking one another.
- In California, a man was sentenced to 45 days in jail for beating a coach who took his 11-year-old son out of a youth baseball game. "How dare you make my son a three-inning player," the parent said as he attacked the coach.
- A New Mexico dentist sharpened the face mask of his son's football helmet so he could slash opposing players. Five opponents and an official were hurt.

Fortunately, such incidents are not the norm. Yet, in their own dramatic fashion, they illustrate pervasive problems that have caused some programs to take steps to protect the welfare of youth sport participants, coaches, and officials. The importance of parents in the youth sport experience cannot be overemphasized. Research has shown that parents play an important role in the socialization of children into sports and influence the psychosocial outcomes of sport experiences, including self-concept development and enjoyment of the activity (see Brustad, 1993; Brustad & Partridge, 2002; Coté, 1999; Greendorfer et al., 2002). Thus, parents are an appropriate focus of intervention.

Several books have been written for youth sport parents (e.g., Fine & Sachs, 1997; Murphy, 1999; Smith et al., 1989; Smoll & Smith, 1999; Wolff, 1997). Workshops for parents similar to those developed for coaches can be another vehicle for reaching parents and influencing the ways in which they interact with their child athlete.

We have developed a set of guidelines for parents that parallel those emphasized in CET (Smoll & Smith, 1999), and we also have provided coaches with guidelines for conducting a workshop with parents of the athletes they are coaching (Smoll, 2001). However, in contrast to the empirical base for CET, no outcome data are available for assessing the efficacy of the parent program. Nonetheless, several issues can be covered by a sport psychologist in a workshop for parents.

Developmental vs. Professional Models of Sport

A fundamental issue is the distinction between youth and professional models of sport. Youth sports are intended to provide an educational medium for the development of desirable physical and psychosocial characteristics. The sport environment is viewed as a microcosm of society in which children can learn to cope with realities they will face in later life. Thus, athletics provide a developmental setting within which an educational process can occur. Professional sports are an explicit commercial enterprise. Their goals, simply stated, are to entertain and, ultimately, to make money. Financial success is of primary importance and depends heavily on a product orientation, namely, winning. Is this wrong? Certainly not! The professional sports world is a part of the entertainment industry, and as such, it is enormously valued in society.

What, then, is the problem? Most of the negative consequences of youth sports occur when adults erroneously impose a professional model on what should be a recreational and educational experience for youngsters. When excessive emphasis is placed on winning, it is easy to lose sight of the needs and interests of the young athlete.

Objectives of Youth Sports

There are many benefits of participating in youth sports. Some are physical, such as acquiring sport skills and increasing health and fitness. Others are psychological, such as developing leadership skills, self-discipline, respect for authority, competitiveness, cooperativeness, sportsmanship, and self-confidence. Youth sports are also an important social activity in which children can make new friends and acquaintances and become part of an ever-expanding social network. Furthermore, the involvement of parents in the athletic enterprise can serve to bring families closer together and strengthen family unity. In addition, of course, youth sports are (or should be) just plain fun.

The basic right of the young athlete to have fun participating in sports should not be neglected. One of the quickest ways to reduce fun is for adults to begin treating children as if they were professional athletes. Coaches and parents need to keep in mind that young athletes are not miniature adults. They are children, and they have the right to play as children. Youth sports are first and foremost a play activity, and youngsters deserve to enjoy sports in their own way. In essence, it is important that programs remain child-centered and do not become adult-dominated.

What About Winning?

The common notion in sports equates success with victory. However, with a winning is everything philosophy, young athletes may lose opportunities to develop their skills, to enjoy participation, and to grow socially and emotionally. Well-informed parents realize that success is not equivalent to winning games and that failure is not the same as losing. Rather, the most important kind of success comes from striving to win and giving maximum effort. The only thing athletes can control is the amount of effort they give. They have incomplete control over the outcome that is achieved. Athletes at all levels of competition should be taught that they are never "losers" if they give maximum effort in striving for excellence. This philosophy of success is relevant to parents and coaches. In fact, it may be more important for parents to understand its meaning. They can apply it to many areas of their child's life in addition to athletics.

When Is Winning out of Perspective?

Martens (1978) suggested that winning is out of perspective (a) when a display of comradeship with an opponent is considered a sign of weakness or when laughter is judged to be a lack of competitiveness; (b) when a coach instructs athletes in strategies designed to take unfair advantage of an opponent; (c) when youngsters are given drugs, coaxed to cheat, and intimidated to excel; and (d) when winning the game becomes more important than winning friends, respect, self-confidence, skill, health, and self-worth. When winning is kept in perspective, the child comes first and winning is second (Martens & Seefeldt, 1979). In this case, rather than focusing on a won–lost record, the most important sport product is the quality of the experience provided for young athletes.

What About the Objectives That Young Athletes Seek to Achieve?

A survey of more than 100,000 youth sport participants in Michigan indicated that young athletes most often participated in organized sports for the following reasons: (a) to have fun, (b) to improve their skills and learn new skills, (c) to be with their friends or make new friends, and (d) to succeed or win (Universities Study Committee, 1978). In a report based on data derived from a national survey of approximately 8,000 boys and girls, these same items were included in lists of the 10 most frequently selected reasons why youngsters play non-school and interscholastic sports (Seefeldt, Ewing, & Walk, 1992). These goals should be communicated to parents, and parents should be cautioned that none of these outcomes is achieved automatically through participation in sports. Coaches, parents, and sport administrators should work as a team to reduce chances of misunderstanding and problems and to help children attain these objectives. In this regard, parents should be encouraged to view their involvement in youth sports as an integral part of their child-rearing responsibilities.

Parent Responsibilities and Challenges

When a child enters a sport program, parents automatically take on some obligations. Some parents do not realize this at first and are surprised to find what is expected of them. Others never realize their responsibilities and miss opportunities to help their children grow through sports, or they may actually do things that interfere with their children's development.

To begin, parents must realize that children have a right to choose not to participate (Martens & Seefeldt, 1979). Although parents might choose to encourage participation, children should not be pressured, intimidated, or bribed into playing. In fulfilling their responsibility, parents should counsel their children, giving consideration to the sport selected and the level of competition at which the children want to play. And, of course, parents should respect their children's decisions.

Parents can enjoy their children's participation more if they acquire an understanding and appreciation of the sport. This includes knowledge of basic rules, skills, and strategies. Coaches can serve as valuable resources by answering parents' questions and by referring parents to a local library or a bookstore for educational materials (i.e., books and videos). In addition, coaches should devote part of an early season practice to a lecture or demonstration of the fundamentals of the sport, and parents having little background in the sport should be encouraged to attend this session.

Reversed-Dependency Phenomenon

Parents often assume an extremely active role in youth sports, and in some instances, their influence becomes an important source of children's stress (Brustad, 1993, Brustad & Partridge, 2002; Passer, 1984; Scanlan, 1986; Smith, 1986a,b; Smoll & Smith, 1990). What might constitute the underlying basis of parent-induced stress? One factor is referred to as the reversed-dependency phenomenon. All parents identify with their children to some extent and thus want them to do well. Unfortunately, in some cases, the degree of identification becomes excessive, and the child becomes an extension of the parent. When this happens, parents begin to define their own self-worth in terms of the success of their son or daughter. The father who is a "frustrated jock" may seek to experience the success he never knew as an athlete through his child. Or the parent who was a star may be resentful and rejecting if the child does not attain similar achievements. Some parents thus become "winners" or "losers" through their children, and the pressure placed on the children to excel can be extreme. A child *must* succeed or the parent's self-image is threatened. Much more is at stake than a mere game, and the child of such a parent carries a heavy burden. When parental love and approval depend on adequacy of performance, sports are bound to be stressful (see Smith et al., 1989; Smoll & Smith, 1990; Smoll & Smith, 1999).

Youth sport consultants may be able to counteract this tendency by explaining the identification process to parents. They can tell parents that if they place excessive pressure on children, they can decrease the potential that sports can have for enjoyment and personal growth. A key to reducing parent-produced stress is to impress on parents that youth sport programs are for young athletes and that children are *not* adults. Parents must acknowledge the right of each child to develop athletic potential in an atmosphere that emphasizes participation, personal growth, and fun.

Commitments and Affirmations

To contribute to the success of a sport program, parents must be willing and able to commit themselves in many ways. The following questions serve as thought-provoking reminders of the scope of parents' responsibilities, questions to which parents must honestly answer "yes" (Smoll & Smith, 1999, pp. 12–13):

- *Can the parents share their son or daughter?* This requires putting the child in the coach's charge and trusting him or her to guide the sport experience. It involves accepting the coach's authority and the fact that the coach may gain some of the admiration and affection that the child once directed solely at the parents. This commitment does not mean that parents cannot have input, but the coach is the boss. If parents are going to undermine the coach's leadership, it is best for all concerned not to have their child join the program.

- *Can the parents accept their child's disappointments?* Every child athlete experiences "the thrill of victory and the agony of defeat" as part of the competition process. In addition to enjoying triumphs, parents are called on to support their children when they are disappointed and hurt. This may mean not being embarrassed, ashamed, or angry when their son or daughter cries after losing a contest. When an apparent disappointment occurs, parents should be able to help their children learn from the experience. By doing this without denying the validity of their feelings, parents can help their children see the positive side of the situation and thus change their children's disappointment into self-acceptance.

- *Can the parents show their child self-control?* Parents should be reminded that they are important role models for their children's behavior. It is not surprising that parents who lose control of themselves often have children who are prone to emotional outbursts and poor self-discipline. Coaches can hardly be expected to teach sportsmanship and self-control to youngsters whose parents obviously lack these qualities.

- *Can the parents give their child some time?* Parents need to decide how much time can be devoted to their children's sport activities. Conflicts arise when parents are very busy, yet also want to encourage their children. To avoid this, the best advice coaches can give parents is to deal honestly with the time commitment issue and not promise more time than they can actually deliver. Coaches should recommend that parents ask their children about their sport experiences and make every effort to watch some of their contests.

- *Can the parents let their child make his or her own decisions?* Accepting responsibility for one's own behavior and decisions is an essential part of growing up. Coaches should encourage parents to offer suggestions and guidance about sports, but ultimately, within reasonable limits, they should let the child go his or her own way. All parents have ambitions for their child, but they must accept the fact that they cannot dominate their child's life. Sports can offer an introduction to the major parental challenge of letting go.

Conduct at Sports Events

The most noticeable parent problem is misbehavior at games. As part of their responsibilities, parents should watch their children compete in sports. But their behavior must meet acceptable standards. In addition to acknowledging some obviously inappropriate actions (e.g., using profanity, drinking alcohol, throwing objects), the following rules for parental behavior ("dos" and "don'ts") are recommended (Smoll & Smith, 1999, p. 27):

1. Don't interfere with your child's coach; be willing to relinquish the responsibility for your child to the coach for the duration of the practice or contest.
2. Don't shout instructions or criticisms to the children.
3. Do remain in the spectator area during the event.
4. Don't make abusive comments to athletes, parents, officials, or coaches of either team.
5. Do express interest, encouragement, and support to your child.
6. Do lend a hand when a coach or official asks for help.

Good sportsmanship among spectators is a goal worth reaching. Parents have the obligation not only to control their own behavior, but also to remind others, if necessary. When parents misbehave, it is the duty of other parents and league administrators to step in and correct the situation. The golden rule for all spectators is that nothing in their actions should interfere with any child's enjoyment of the sport.

Athlete-Based Interventions

The third point in the athletic triangle is the young athlete. Several intervention programs directed at athletes have been developed. Some of these interventions involve the application of psychological principles to enhance sport performance. Others are directed at psychosocial outcomes.

Performance Enhancement Interventions

Notable among the performance enhancement interventions is "behavioral coaching" (Martin & Hyrcaiko, 1983), which involves teaching coaches to apply operant techniques, such as analysis and behavioral assessment of skill components, videotaped feedback, response-contingent reinforcement of response execution, the use of shaping procedures, self-monitoring and behavioral graphing of the skill acquisition process, and the systematic application of modeling procedures. More than a dozen studies have shown that operant techniques can be highly effective in facilitating skill acquisition and enhancing performance in a variety of sports and age levels (see Lee, 1993; Martin, 1992; and Smith, Smoll, & Christensen, 1996, for reviews). Sport consultants who are conversant with the application of operant principles will find an eager audience of coaches who wish to be trained in these powerful performance enhancement techniques.

Imagery-based performance enhancement techniques also have been applied to child athlete populations. For example, a study by Zhang, Ma, Orlick, and Zitzelberger (1992) tested the efficacy of a mental-imagery program designed to increase the performance of promising Chinese table tennis players between ages 7 and 10. The children were divided into three groups. Those in the first condition received a comprehensive 22-week mental training program, which included relaxation, video observation, and mental-imagery sessions. A second treatment group received only the video observation component of the training. The third group was a no-treatment control condition. Results indicated that compared with the other two groups, the children who received the full mental-training package significantly improved both the accuracy and technical quality of their table tennis forehand attack.

Because sport psychology consultants are often not available to work with young athletes, one potential training medium is the coach. Several useful psychological skills, such as goal setting, relaxation training, and imagery could easily be adopted by youth sport coaches who receive instruction in how to apply these techniques to their athletes. Materials are available to guide coaches who wish to teach their athletes performance enhancement skills of this nature (e.g., Loehr & Striegel, 1994; Martens, 1987b; Smith & Smoll, 2002; Vernacchia, McGuire, & Cook, 1996). Their efficacy as instructional materials and as methods for improving athletes' sport performance remain to be established, however. A more recent survey of junior tennis coaches revealed they had great interest in being able to impart psychological skills to their athletes, but they failed to do so because of a self-perceived lack of competence (Gould, Damarjian, & Medbery, 1999). Clearly, there is an opportunity for sport psychologists to offer coaches training in this area, then to evaluate the effects of the instruction on coaches and their athletes.

Sportsmanship and Moral Development

Although it is frequently asserted that sports build sportsmanship and character, research on moral reasoning and behavior suggests a less optimistic view. For example, recent research indicates that the sanctioning of aggressive and competitive behavior in sport may have negative consequences on moral development (Bredemeier, in press; Bredemeier & Shields, 1987; Shields et al., 2002). Using measurement tools derived from Haan's (1978) structural–developmental model of morality, researchers have found that child and adolescent athletes exhibit lower levels of moral reasoning than do nonathletes and show greater acceptance of aggression in sports (Bredemeier & Shields, 1984). Whether sport participation contributes to lower levels of moral reasoning or whether children who are lower in moral development are more likely to be drawn to sport is a question as yet unanswered. Nevertheless, these findings are provocative in pointing to sport as a potentially important arena for moral development.

Paralleling the results of the leadership and coaching research described previously, there are indications that psychological intervention may have salutary effects on moral development. Several studies have shown that explicit attention to moral training in sport and physical activity settings can promote significant advances in the moral reasoning maturity of children (Bredemeier, Weiss, Shields, & Shewchuk, 1986; Romance, Weiss, & Bockoven, 1986). In one study (Bredemeier et al., 1986), children participating in a summer sports camp were exposed to one of two 6-week moral education programs derived from different theoretical approaches to moral development. In the first program, based on a social learning model emphasizing the learning of moral principles through modeling and vicarious and direct reinforcement, adult leaders described to the children how they themselves thought about and responded to moral issues involving themes of fairness, sharing, verbal and physical aggression, and distributive and retributive justice. They also acknowledged and reinforced instances of verbal and nonverbal moral behavior performed by the children. In the second program, based on structural developmental theory, instructors used dialogue aimed at resolving interpersonal disruptions and conflicts among the children as a vehicle for promoting moral growth. Children in a control condition participated in the normal camp program.

In a pre–post design, moral reasoning maturity was assessed by means of the Piagetian Intentionality Task and a measure of children's understanding of fairness, or distributive justice. On both measures, the social learning and the structural developmental conditions yielded significant positive changes in moral reasoning, but they did not differ from one another. Children in the control group exhibited no significant changes in their moral reasoning.

Many important issues concerning moral education in sports remain to be studied. One important question involves the effects of interventions not only on moral reasoning, but also on behavior. Another involves the extent to which moral principles learned in sports generalize to other life settings. Sports would appear to be a two-edged sword as far as moral development is concerned, and it is important to identify the factors that promote positive and negative outcomes. The very act of sportsmanship implies the exercise of moral decision making, and sport is a setting in which, potentially, children can be guided through dealing with moral dilemmas.

Life Skills Interventions

Another approach has been training children in skills that not only enhance their sport performance but that also extend as life skills to other areas of the child's life, such as academics and social interactions. For example, Orlick and McCaffrey (1991) described a psychological skills program for elementary school children that includes training in relaxation, imagery, focusing, and refocusing. Another promising program featuring goal-setting procedures has been developed by Danish and colleagues (1992). In both programs, the skills training is adapted to the child's level. For example, relaxation training is carried out while comparing tense muscles to uncooked spaghetti and relaxed muscles to limp, cooked spaghetti (Orlick & McCaffrey, 1991). Likewise, goal-setting training is embellished with exciting imagery and games (Danish et al., 1992).

Although the effects of these school-based programs await soundly designed evaluation studies, this approach seems to hold considerable promise for promoting the development of important psychological skills. Such training could easily be applied to child athletes as well, with the inclusion of generalization training to facilitate transfer of sport skills to other life areas. Such training might be particularly useful in working with high-risk inner-city youths, who are typically resistant to life skills programs implemented within the school setting. Such young-sters might be more enthusiastic about a program designed and con-ducted within the realm of sport.

Conclusion

Sport psychology interventions are a promising development that can enhance the well-being and psychosocial development of children. This area constitutes an exciting arena for both psychological research and intervention. The researcher can discover the principles that govern the youth sport social system and that make a difference in the well-being of its members. Similarly, practitioners are in a position to apply the principles and procedures of sport psychology in a manner that can better the lives of many young athletes, their coaches, and their parents.

We presented CET as an example of a scientifically developed pro-gram. CET has proven to be an economical and effective program that alters coaching behaviors in a desirable fashion and thereby has positive psychosocial effects on the children who play for trained coaches. All five classes of outcome variables—coaching behaviors, children's atti-tudes, self-esteem, performance anxiety, and attrition—have been sig-nificantly influenced by the training program. Nonetheless, several im-portant research questions remain. For example, dismantling studies are needed to assess the relative contributions of the various com-ponents of the training program, which included didactic instruc-tion, modeling and role playing of desired behaviors, training in self-monitoring of coaching behaviors, and behavioral feedback. Such research could help to establish the necessary and sufficient compo-nents of an effective program and could facilitate the development of improved training programs.

Likewise, little is known about the efficacy of parent interventions. Do the parent guidelines influence parents in desirable ways? Do they have salutary consequences on nonsport-related areas of the parent–child relationship? If efficacious, does it matter if the guidelines are presented by a coach or by a sport consultant? These are empirical questions that have not yet been addressed. Clearly, more data are needed on the effects of both coach- and parent-directed interventions.

A promising development is the application of psychological skills training programs to young athletes (e.g., Gould, 2002; Orlick & Mc-Caffrey, 1991; Zhang et al., 1992). Preliminary results suggest that training in such skills as relaxation, mental rehearsal, and goal setting can be of value to children. These skills can be readily taught in a sport setting, and appropriate generalization training should permit transfer to other life areas as well. Psychological skills training in sport contexts may be especially valuable for high-risk children who do not respond positively to life skills training carried out in academic settings.

Children's sports is an area that invites the attention of both researchers and practitioners. Many important empirical questions remain to be addressed, and the skillful application of psychological principles and intervention procedures can have a salutary impact on sport participants during a period of development when important foundations for later life are being established.

References

Barnett, N. P., Smoll, F. L., & Smith, R. E. (1992). Effects of enhancing coach–athlete relationships on youth sport attrition. *The Sport Psychologist, 6*, 111–127.

Biddle, S. (in press). Attrition and dissatisfaction in youth sports. In R. M. Malina & M. A. Clark (Eds.), *Youth sports in the 21st century: Organized sport in the lives of children and adolescents.* Champaign, IL: Sagamore.

Bredemeier, B. J. L. (in press). Moral community and youth sport in the new millenium. In R. M. Malina & M. A. Clark (Eds.), *Youth sports in the 21st century: Organized sport in the lives of children and adolescents.* Champaign, IL: Sagamore.

Bredemeier, B. J., & Shields, D. (1984). The utility of moral stage analysis in the understanding of athletic aggression. *Sociology of Sport Journal, 1*, 138–149.

Bredemeier, B. J., & Shields, D. (1987). Moral growth through physical activity: A structural/developmental approach. In D. Gould & M. R. Weiss (Eds.), *Advances in pediatric sport sciences: Vol. 2. Behavioral issues* (pp. 143–165). Champaign, IL: Human Kinetics.

Bredemeier, B. J., Weiss, M. R., Shields, D., & Shewchuk, R. M. (1986). Promoting moral growth in a summer sport camp: The implementation of theoretically grounded instructional strategies. *Journal of Moral Education, 15*, 212–220.

Brown, B. R., & Butterfield, S. A. (1992). Coaches: A missing link in the health care system. *American Journal of Diseases in Childhood, 146*, 211–217.

Brown, J. D., Collins, R. L., & Schmidt, G. W. (1988). Self-esteem and direct versus indirect forms of self-reinforcement. *Journal of Personality and Social Psychology, 55*, 445–453.

Brustad, R. J. (1988). Affective outcomes in competitive youth sport: The influence of intrapersonal and socialization factors. *Journal of Sport and Exercise Psychology, 10*, 307–321.

Brustad, R. J. (1993). Youth in sport: Psychological considerations. In R. N. Singer, M. Murphy, & L. K. Tennant (Eds.), *Handbook of research on sport psychology* (pp. 695–717). New York: Macmillan.

Brustad, R. J. (in press). Parental roles and involvement in youth sports: Psychological outcomes for children. In R. M. Malina & M. A. Clark (Eds.), *Youth sports in the 21st century: Organized sport in the lives of children and adolescents.* Champaign, IL: Sagamore.

Brustad, R. J., & Partridge, J. A. (2002). Parental and peer influence on children's psychosocial development through sport. In F. L. Smoll & R. E. Smith (Eds.), *Children and youth in sport: A biopsychosocial perspective* (2nd ed., pp. 187–210). Dubuque, IA: Kendall/Hunt.

Cavior, N., & Marabotto, C. M. (1976). Monitoring verbal behaviors in a dyadic interaction. *Journal of Consulting and Clinical Psychology, 44*, 68–76.

Chase, M. A., & Dummer, G. M. (1992). The role of sports as a social status determinant for children. *Research Quarterly for Exercise and Sport, 63*, 418–424.

Chaumeton, N. R., & Duda, J. L. (1988). Is it how you play the game or whether you win or lose? The effect of competitive level and situation on coaching behaviors. *Journal of Sport Behavior, 11*, 157–173.

Coté, J. (1999). The influence of the family in the development of talent in sport. *The Sport Psychologist, 13*, 395–417.

Cruz, J., Bou, A., Fernandez, J. M., Martin, M., Monras, J., Monfort, N., & Ruiz, A. (1987). Avaluacio conductual de les interaccions entre entrenadors i jugadors de basquet escolar. *Apunts Medicina de L'esport, 24*, 89–98.

Danish, S. J., Mash, J. M., Howard, C. W., Curl, S. J., Meyer, A. L., Owens, S., & Kendall, K. (1992). *Going for the goal: Leader manual* (5th ed.). Richmond: Virginia Commonwealth University.

Dittes, J. E. (1959). Attractiveness of group as a function of self-esteem and acceptance by group. *Journal of Abnormal and Social Psychology, 59*, 77–82.

Edelstein, B. A., & Eisler, R. M. (1976). Effects of modeling and modeling with instructions and feedback on the behavioral components of social skills. *Behavior Therapy, 7*, 382–389.

Ewing, M. E., & Seefeldt, V. (2002). Patterns of participation and attrition in American agency-sponsored youth sports. In F. L. Smoll & R. E. Smith (Eds.), *Children and youth in sport: A biopsychosocial perspective* (2nd ed., pp. 39–66). Dubuque, IA: Kendall/Hunt.

Fine, A. H., & Sachs, M. L. (1997). *The total sports experience for kids: A parents' guide to success in youth sports.* South Bend, IN: Diamond Communications.

Fisher, A. C., Mancini, V. H., Hirsch, R. L., Proulx, T. J., & Staurowsky, E. J. (1982). Coach–athlete interactions and team climate. *Journal of Sport Psychology, 4*, 388–404.

Gottman, J. M., & McFall, R. M. (1972). Self-monitoring effects in a program for potential high school dropouts: A time series analysis. *Journal of Consulting and Clinical Psychology, 39*, 273–281.

Gould, D. (1987). Understanding attrition in children's sport. In D. Gould & M. R. Weiss (Eds.), *Advances in pediatric sport sciences* (pp. 61–85). Champaign, IL: Human Kinetics.

Gould, D. (2002). Sport psychology: Future directions in youth sport research. In F. L. Smoll & R. E. Smith (Eds.), *Children and youth in sport: A biopsychosocial perspective* (2nd ed., pp. 565–589). Dubuque, IA: Kendall/Hunt.

Gould, D., & Dieffenbach, K. (in press). Psychological issues in youth sports: Competitive anxiety, overtraining, and burnout. In R. M. Malina & M. A. Clark (Eds.),

Youth sports in the 21st century: Organized sport in the lives of children and adolescents. Champaign, IL: Sagamore.

Gould, D., Damarjian, N., & Medbery, R. (1999). An examination of mental skills training in junior tennis coaches. *The Sport Psychologist, 13*, 127–143.

Gould, D., Tuffey, S., Udry, E., & Loehr, J. (1996). Burnout in competitive junior tennis players: II. A qualitative analysis. *The Sport Psychologist, 10*, 341–366.

Greendorfer, S. L., Lewko, J. H., & Rosengren, K. S. (2002). Family and gender-based influences in sport socialization of children and adolescents. In F. L. Smoll & R. E. Smith (Eds.), *Children and youth in sport: A biopsychosocial perspective* (2nd ed., pp. 153–186). Dubuque, IA: Kendall/Hunt.

Haan, N. (1978). Two moralities in action contexts: Relationship to thought, ego regulation, and development. *Journal of Personality and Social Psychology, 36*, 286–305.

Harter, S. (1978). Effectance motivation reconsidered. *Human Development, 21*, 34–64.

Horn, T. S. (1984). Expectancy effects in the interscholastic athletic setting: Methodological considerations. *Journal of Sport Psychology, 6*, 60–76.

Horn, T. S. (1985). Coaches' feedback and changes in children's perceptions of their physical competence. *Journal of Educational Psychology, 77*, 174–186.

Horn, T., & Hasbrook, C. (1987). Psychological characteristics and the criteria children use for self-evaluation. *Journal of Sport Psychology, 9*, 208–221.

Jones, D. F., Housner, L. D., & Kornspan, A. S. (1997). Interactive decision making and behavior of experienced and inexperienced basketball coaches during practices. *Journal of Teaching in Physical Education, 16*, 454–468.

Kanfer, F. H., & Gaelick-Buys, L. (1991). Self-management methods. In F. H. Kanfer & A. P. Goldstein (Eds.), *Helping people change: A textbook of methods* (4th ed., pp. 305–360). New York: Pergamon.

Kazdin, A. E. (1974). Self-monitoring and behavior change. In M. J. Mahoney & C. E. Thoresen (Eds.), *Self-control: Power to the person* (pp. 218–246). Monterey, CA: Brooks/Cole.

Kirschenbaum, D. S., & Karoly, P. (1977). When self-regulation fails: Tests of some preliminary hypotheses. *Journal of Consulting and Clinical Psychology, 45*, 1116–1125.

Krane, V., Eklund, R., & McDermott, M. (1991). Collaborative action research and behavioral coaching intervention: A case study. In W. K. Simpson, A. LeUnes, & J. S. Picou (Eds.), *The applied research in coaching and athletics annual 1991* (pp. 119–147). Boston: American Press.

Lee, C. (1993). Operant strategies in sport and exercise. *International Journal of Sport Psychology, 24*, 306–325.

Loehr, J. E., & Striegel, D. A. (1994). *The USTA sport psychology guidebook for coaches.* White Plains, NY: U.S. Tennis Association.

Martens, R. (1978). *Joy and sadness in children's sports.* Champaign, IL: Human Kinetics.

Martens, R. (1987a). *American coaching effectiveness program: Level 1 instructor guide* (2nd ed.). Champaign, IL: Human Kinetics.

Martens, R. (1987b). *Coaches' guide to sport psychology.* Champaign, IL: Human Kinetics.

Martens, R., & Gould, D. (1979). Why do adults volunteer to coach children's sports? In G. C. Roberts & K. M. Newell (Eds.), *Psychology of motor behavior and sport—1978* (pp. 79–89). Champaign, IL: Human Kinetics.

Martens, R., & Seefeldt, V. (1979). *Guidelines for children's sports.* Reston, VA: American Alliance for Health, Physical Education, Recreation, and Dance.

Martin, G. L. (1992). Applied behavior analysis in sport and physical education. In R. P. West & J. Hammerlynck (Eds.), *Designs for excellence in education: The legacy of B. F. Skinner* (pp. 223–257). Longmont, CO: Sopris West.

Martin, G. L., & Hyrcaiko, D. (Eds.). (1983). *Behavior modification and coaching: Principles, procedures, and research.* Springfield, IL: Charles C Thomas.

Masters, J. C. (1972). Social comparison in young children. In W. W. Hartup (Ed.), *The young child* (pp. 320–339). Washington, DC: National Association for Education of Young Children.

McFall, R. M. (1977). Parameters of self-monitoring. In R. B. Stuart (Ed.), *Behavioral self-management: Strategies, techniques and outcomes* (pp. 196–214). New York: Brunner/Mazel.

McFall, R. M., & Twentyman, C. T. (1973). Four experiments on the relative contributions of rehearsal, modeling, and coaching to assertion training. *Journal of Abnormal Psychology, 81,* 199–218.

Michener, J. A. (1976). *Sports in America.* New York: Random House.

Murphy, S. (1999). *The cheers and the tears: A healthy alternative to the dark side of youth sports today.* San Francisco: Jossey-Bass.

Orlick, T., & Botterill, C. (1975). *Every kid can win.* Chicago: Nelson-Hall.

Orlick, T., & McCaffrey, N. (1991). Mental training with children for sport and life. *The Sport Psychologist, 5,* 322–334.

Passer, M. W. (1984). Competitive trait anxiety in children and adolescents: Mediating cognitions, developmental antecedents and consequences. In J. M. Silva & R. S. Weinberg (Eds.), *Psychological foundations of sport and exercise* (pp. 130–144). Champaign, IL: Human Kinetics.

Rejeski, W., Darracott, C., & Hutslar, S. (1979). Pygmalion in youth sport: A field study. *Journal of Sport Psychology, 1,* 311–319.

Romance, T. J., Weiss, M. R., & Bockoven, R. (1986). A program to promote moral development through elementary school physical education. *Journal of Teaching in Physical Education, 5,* 126–136.

Scanlan, T. K. (1986). Competitive stress in children. In M. R. Weiss & D. Gould (Eds.), *Sport for children and youths* (pp. 113–118). Champaign, IL: Human Kinetics.

Scanlan, T. K. (1996). Social evaluation and the competition process: A developmental perspective. In F. L. Smoll & R. E. Smith (Eds.), *Children and youth in sport: A biopsychosocial perspective* (pp. 298–308). Boston: McGraw-Hill.

Seefeldt, V., & Brown, E. W. (Eds.). (1992). *Program for athletic coaches' education.* Carmel, IN: Cooper.

Seefeldt, V., Ewing, M. E., & Walk, S. (1992). *Overview of youth sport programs in the United States.* Washington, DC: Carnegie Council on Adolescent Development.

Sherman, M. A., & Hassan, J. S. (1986). Behavioral studies of youth sport coaches. In M. Pieron & G. Graham (Eds.), *The 1984 Olympic Scientific Congress proceedings: Vol. 6. Sport pedagogy* (pp. 103–108). Champaign, IL: Human Kinetics.

Shields, D. L., Bredemeier, B. L., & Power, F. C. (2002). Character development in children's sport. In F. L. Smoll & R. E. Smith (Eds.), *Children and youth in sport: A biopsychosocial perspective* (2nd ed., pp. 537–559). Dubuque, IA: Kendall/Hunt.

Shrauger, J. S. (1975). Responses to evaluation as a function of initial self-perceptions. *Psychological Bulletin, 82,* 581–596.

Smith, R. E. (1986a). Toward a cognitive-affective model of athletic burnout. *Journal of Sport Psychology, 8,* 36–50.

Smith, R. E. (1986b). A component analysis of athletic stress. In M. Weiss & D. Gould (Eds.), *Sport psychology for children and youths* (pp. 107–112). Champaign, IL: Human Kinetics.

Smith, R. E., & Smoll, F. L. (1990a). Self-esteem and children's reactions to youth sport coaching behaviors: A field study of self-enhancement processes. *Developmental Psychology, 26,* 987–993.

Smith, R. E., & Smoll, F. L. (1990b). Sport performance anxiety. In H. Leitenberg (Ed.), *Handbook of social and evaluation anxiety* (pp. 417–454). New York: Plenum.

Smith, R. E., & Smoll, F. L. (1991). Behavioral research and intervention in youth sports. *Behavior Therapy, 22,* 329–344.

Smith, R. E., & Smoll, F. L. (1997). Coaching the coaches: Youth sports as a scientific and applied behavioral setting. *Current Directions in Psychological Science, 6,* 16–21.

Smith, R. E., & Smoll, F. L. (2002). *Way to go, coach: A scientifically-proven approach to coaching effectiveness* (2nd ed.). Portola Valley, CA: Warde.

Smith, R. E., Smoll, F. L., & Barnett, N. (1995). Reduction of children's sport performance anxiety through social support and stress-reduction training for coaches. *Journal of Applied Developmental Psychology, 16,* 125–142.

Smith, R. E., Smoll, F. L., & Christensen, D. S. (1996). Behavioral assessment and interventions in youth sports: A review. *Behavior Modification, 20,* 3–44.

Smith, R. E., Smoll, F. L., & Curtis, B. (1978). Coaching behaviors in Little League Baseball. In F. L. Smoll & R. E. Smith (Eds.), *Psychological perspectives in youth sports* (pp. 173–201). Washington, DC: Hemisphere.

Smith, R. E., Smoll, F. L., & Curtis, B. (1979). Coach Effectiveness Training: A cognitive–behavioral approach to enhancing relationship skills in youth sport coaches. *Journal of Sport Psychology, 1,* 59–75.

Smith, R. E., Smoll, F. L., & Hunt, E. B. (1977). A system for the behavioral assessment of athletic coaches. *Research Quarterly, 48,* 401–407.

Smith, R. E., Smoll, F. L., & Passer, M. W. (2002). Competitive anxiety: Sources, consequences, and intervention strategies. In F. L. Smoll & R. E. Smith (Eds.), *Children and youth in sport: A biopsychosocial perspective* (2nd ed., 501–536). Dubuque, IA: Kendall/Hunt.

Smith, R. E., Smoll, F. L., & Schutz, R. W. (1990). Measurement and correlates of sport-specific cognitive and somatic trait anxiety: The Sport Anxiety Scale. *Anxiety Research, 2,* 263–280.

Smith, R. E., Smoll, F. L., & Smith, N. J. (1989). *Parents' complete guide to youth sports.* Reston, VA: American Alliance for Health, Physical Education, Recreation, and Dance.

Smith, R. E., Zane, N. W. S., Smoll, F. L., & Coppel, D. B. (1983). Behavioral assessment in youth sports: Coaching behaviors and children's attitudes. *Medicine and Science in Sports and Exercise, 15,* 208–214.

Smoll, F. L. (2001). Coach–parent relationships in youth sports: Increasing harmony and minimizing hassle. In J. M. Williams (Ed.), *Applied sport psychology: Personal growth to peak performance* (4th ed., pp. 150–161). Mountain View, CA: Mayfield.

Smoll, F. L., & Smith, R. E. (1989). Leadership behaviors in sport: A theoretical model and research paradigm. *Journal of Applied Social Psychology, 19,* 1522–1551.

Smoll, F. L., & Smith, R. E. (1990). Psychology of the young athlete: Stress-related maladies and remedial approaches. *Pediatric Clinics of North America, 37,* 1021–1046.

Smoll, F. L., & Smith, R. E. (1997). *Coaches who never lose: Making sure athletes win, no matter what the score.* Portola Valley, CA: Warde.

Smoll, F. L., & Smith, R. E. (1999). *Sports and your child: A 50-minute guide for parents.* Portola Valley, CA: Warde.

Smoll, F. L., & Smith, R. E. (2001). Conducting sport psychology training programs for coaches: Cognitive–behavioral principles and techniques. In J. M. Williams (Ed.), *Applied sport psychology: Personal growth to peak performance* (4th ed., pp. 150–161). Mountain View, CA: Mayfield.

Smoll, F. L., & Smith, R. E. (Eds.). (2002a). *Children and youth in sport: A biopsychosocial perspective* (2nd. ed). Dubuque, IA: Kendall/Hunt.

Smoll, F. L., & Smith, R. E. (2002b). Coaching behavior research and intervention in youth sports. In F. L. Smoll & R. E. Smith (Eds.), *Children and youth in sport: A biopsychosocial perspective* (2nd ed., pp. 211–233). Dubuque, IA: Kendall/Hunt.

Smoll, F. L., Smith, R. E., Barnett, N. P., & Everett, J. J. (1993). Enhancement of children's self-esteem through social support training for youth sport coaches. *Journal of Applied Psychology, 78,* 602–610.

Swann, W. B., Jr. (1990). To be known or to be adored? The interplay of self-enhancement and self-verification. In R. M. Sorrentino & E. T. Higgins (Eds.), *Handbook of motivation and cognition: Foundations of social behavior* (Vol. 2, pp. 69–92). Orlando, FL: Academic Press.

Tesser, A. (1988). Toward a self-evaluative maintenance model of social behavior. In L. Berkowitz (Ed.), *Advances in experimental social psychology* (Vol. 21, pp. 69–92). San Diego, CA: Academic Press.

Tesser, A., & Campbell, J. (1983). Self-definition and self-evaluation maintenance. In J. Suls & A. G. Greenwald (Eds.), *Psychological perspectives on the self* (Vol. 2, pp. 1–31). Hillsdale, NJ: Erlbaum.

Universities Study Committee. (1978). *Joint legislative study on youth programs: Phase III. Agency sponsored sports.* East Lansing: Michigan Institute for the Study of Youth Sports.

Vernacchia, R., McGuire, R., & Cook, D. (1996). *Coaching mental excellence: It does matter whether you win or lose.* Portola Valley, CA: Warde.

Wandzilak, T., Ansorge, C. J., & Potter, G. (1988). Comparison between selected practice and game behaviors of youth soccer coaches. *Journal of Sport Behavior, 11,* 78–88.

Weiss, M. R. (in press). Social influences on children's psychosocial development in youth sports. In R. M. Malina & M. A Clark (Eds.), *Youth sports in the 21st century: Organized sport in the lives of children and adolescents.* Champaign, IL: Sagamore.

Weiss, M. R., & Hayashi, C. T. (1996). The United States. In P. De Knop, L-M. Engstrom, B. Skirstad, & M. R. Weiss (Eds.), *Worldwide trends in youth sport* (pp. 43–57). Champaign, IL: Human Kinetics.

Westre, K., & Weiss, M. (1991). The relationship between perceived coaching behaviors and group cohesion in high school football teams. *The Sport Psychologist, 5,* 41–54.

Wolff, R. (1997). *Good sports: The concerned parent's guide to competitive youth sports.* Champaign, IL: Sagamore.

Zhang, L., Ma, Q., Orlick, T., &, Zitzelberger, L. (1992). The effect of mental-imagery training on performance enhancement with 7–10-year-old children. *The Sport Psychologist, 6,* 230–241.

18

Helping College Student–Athletes In and Out of Sport

Mark B. Andersen

Jonathan was a freshman basketball player at a National Collegiate Athletic Association (NCAA) Division I school (highest level of university competition in the United States) who was on a full scholarship. He referred himself to a sport psychologist after some group presentations on mental training. He wanted to work on staying focused during games. As is often the case, the presenting concern was only the surface of Jonathan's performance and personal issues. As consultation progressed, it became apparent that one of the sources of his lack of focus during games was his anxiety about others judging him and his coach possibly rethinking whether he deserved to keep his scholarship. His family was not well off, and they could not afford to send him to college, so his scholarship was a central concern. He was not well prepared academically for university and struggled through his classes. He, thus, had two major performance concerns: his behavior on the court and in the classroom.

Jonathan began to develop some somatic symptoms (e.g., gastrointestinal distress) and started to lose weight. He was slim to begin with and could not afford to lose muscle mass. His coaches had him on a weight-training program to increase strength and agility, but he was not making much progress. All of the anxieties and pressures on Jonathan to perform on the court were having exactly the effect that might endanger what he feared most: losing his scholarship. He eventually confided to the psychologist that he had considered taking steroids in order to bulk up and show his coaches that he was trying hard. He also told the psychologist that he was so desperate to do well in the classroom that he was thinking of buying some term papers in order to get more than passing grades. Jonathan's case illustrates the high-pressure environment university athletes can find themselves in and what costs are involved in big-time college sports.

Jonathan was so worried about his scholarship that he was contemplating actions, that, if discovered, would place his funding in serious jeopardy. The sport psychologist was employed by the intercollegiate athletics department and had an uneasy time reconciling professional standards with the administration's need to know about infractions of NCAA regulations. For example, if Jonathan revealed he was taking steroids, the psychologist was supposed to inform the athletic director, but informing the athletic director would be a breach of confidentiality. After consulting with colleagues, the psychologist told Jonathan to not inform the psychologist if he took steroids.

For weeks the psychologist and Jonathan worked on managing his anxieties. His constant negative thinking and worry about the future were addressed through cognitive restructuring. They also worked on somatic relaxation techniques that he could use at home (e.g., autogenic training) and on the court (e.g., breathing exercises). The relaxation techniques seemed to be helpful for his somatic symptoms (e.g., intermittent diarrhea), and he stopped losing weight. As he got his thoughts under control, he found he could focus more on the court. Probably the intervention that eased Jonathan's anxiety most was teaching him productive study habits. The psychologist and Jonathan spent a great deal of time helping Jonathan manage his time better and teaching him how to study more efficiently.

Jonathan did make it through his freshman year with his scholarship intact. He developed sound study habits and was able to get acceptable grades. His anxieties, however, did not completely disappear, but they were under better control, and not controlling him.

For many student–athletes, starting college brings about substantial psychosocial change and adjustment (Finch & Gould, 1996). The demands placed on student–athletes (e.g., academic pressures, sport performance, training, travel) usually exceed the demands experienced by nonathlete students. Student–athletes face a variety of developmental issues and have several special pressures, including maintaining academic eligibility and staying in compliance with the myriad regulations of the NCAA (2000). This chapter describes student–athletes in general, discusses some of the important developmental issues that affect them, identifies special pressures that college student–athletes are under, describes common clinical concerns of student–athletes, and provides some practical information about the NCAA and intercollegiate athletics for practitioners interested in working with this population.

Varieties of Student–Athletes

Student–athletes, like everyone else, come in a variety of shapes, sizes, talents, and commitments. Demographic variables of student–athletes (e.g., gender, division status, scholarship) may have a great effect on some of the problems and issues they confront.

NCAA Division I athletic programs are usually the largest and best funded. Many of the student–athletes receive full or partial scholarships. Division I programs also have regional, and often national, visibility. Athletes in these programs face a great deal of public scrutiny. These universities usually have high-power programs, and some of the issues student–athletes may bring to the sport psychologist include worries over maintaining scholarships, pressure from coaches, and exposure in the media. Division I schools are often "pressure cookers" for athletes, especially in the revenue sports of football, basketball, and baseball. Many schools also specialize in one or two nonrevenue sports (e.g., swimming at Stanford University and the University of Texas), and pressures on athletes in those sports can be substantial.

NCAA Division II student–athletes may not experience the national exposure and pressure of Division I athletes, but local and state-wide attention are still there. Division II schools offer scholarships to student–athletes but on a more limited basis than Division I schools do.

NCAA Division III schools offer no athletic scholarships and usually do not receive the great attention and pressures of Division I and II programs. Media attention, however, at the local level may be extensive. Although sport psychologists will not encounter anxieties about athletic scholarships, the Division III athlete may still feel substantial pressures from the team, their families and friends, the coach, and the local press.

A distinction in intercollegiate athletics that is probably more important than the NCAA Division I, II, and III designations is the difference between revenue and nonrevenue sports. The revenue sports are usually football and men's basketball, with baseball a distant third. There are a few exceptions, but it is usually these programs that get the most attention, acknowledgment, and money. Athletes and coaches in nonrevenue sports may feel resentment toward football and basketball for "hogging" the attention and money. Poor relationships between those who participate in revenue and nonrevenue sports are not helped when coaches in revenue sports remind those affiliated with other sports that it is the football and basketball programs that support the rest of the sports. This claim is a commonly held belief, even by coaches and athletes, but in a vast majority of cases, football and basketball programs operate in the red and are themselves a drain on university resources (Sperber, 1990).

Another important distinction in intercollegiate athletics is between men's and women's sports. Even though Title IX is more than 20 years old, female athletes and women's programs, with some exceptions, are still second-class entities. Title IX helped increase the number of collegiate teams for women in the United States, but it also brought with it many men to coach those new teams. Communication problems between coaches and athletes occur in all types of coaching situations, but the potential for difficulties between female athletes and male coaches may be a bit greater than same-sex coaching relationships.

Community college and junior college athletes form another variety of athletes that sport psychologists may serve. Often high school athletes with academic difficulties, financial concerns, or athletic deficiencies (e.g., size, strength, speed) will go to a community or junior college, play their sports, hone their skills, and shore up their academic records. Some of these athletes, after two years, apply to NCAA Division I, II, or III institutions. The transfer to a four-year school may not be an easy one. Transferring from a community or junior college to a four-year school brings up issues of transitions in student–athletes' lives, and these concerns and other developmental landmarks are covered in the following section.

Developmental Issues

Intercollegiate athletes usually range in age from 17 to 23 years. In Eriksonian terms, the developmental tasks they face concern identity and establishing intimate relationships (Erikson, 1968). In Erikson's formulations, student–athletes are in the process of forming pictures of who they are (i.e., ego-identity) and also may be well on their way to making intimate lifelong links with others. The flip side of these challenges is that student–athletes may not develop strong identities (i.e., role confusion) or may develop self-images that have "expiration dates," that is, their identities as athletes will expire long before they reach the ends of their lives. Student athletes may also, in their struggles with establishing intimacy, end up in the usually unhappy state of isolation. The developmental issues that follow are presented in this Eriksonian framework.

Transition

The first potentially difficult period is the transition into college. High school student–athletes may have some of their first experiences in the realm of ethics and sport (e.g., inducements, promises, cash; see Davenport, 1985; Lapchick, 1989). Also, many athletes go from being a star player on their high school teams to being just another member of the team in college. An athlete's identity may take a blow when the high school thinking was "I am a great ballplayer" and the college reality is that "there's a bunch of players way better than I am here." Learning such lessons may be particularly difficult for athletes who have moved away from their homes for the first time and are in new environments (Pearson & Petitpas, 1990).

Sometimes the move to college is also a cultural transition. For example, a Northeast urban student may have some adjustment problems if he or she accepts a scholarship at a rural university in the Southwest. The move to college can make some athletes feel like strangers in a strange land. Again, self-concept and identity may suffer in a foreign environment.

The overidentification with the athlete role may lead to maladaptive thinking and behavior. Many athletes in revenue sports come to college with the plan of going on to a career in professional sport. The painful reality is that few athletes even get a tryout with a professional team and that pro careers are extremely short (in the National Football League, the average career is less than four years). This thinking about and planning for pro careers can lead to neglect of other career options and academics. For students who end their college careers with little career planning, poor academic records, and no professional sport opportunities, the transition out of sport can be traumatic. For athletes who sustain career-ending injuries, the sudden loss of dreams and identity can leave them susceptible to severe adjustment problems and possibly depression (Brewer, 1993; Kleiber & Brock, 1992).

Sport psychologists working with collegiate athletes might want to assess identification with the athlete role, especially in athletes who are juniors and seniors, because for many, their careers will soon come to an end. Ideally, career planning should start for collegiate athletes in their first year and continue throughout college (see Grove, Lavallee, & Gordon, 1997; Lavallee & Andersen, 2000; Perna, Ahlgren, & Zaichkowsky, 1996; Perna, Zaichkowsky, & Bockneck, 1996; Petitpas, Brewer, & Van Raalte, 1996; Price & Andersen, 2000). Career counseling is available at most universities, but usually such services do not have a delivery agreement in place for intercollegiate athletics (see Coleman & Barker, 1991; Petitpas, Danish, McKelvain, & Murphy, 1992; Petitpas, Champaign, Chartrand, Danish, & Murphy, 1997; Wittmer, Bostic, Phillips, & Waters, 1981, for discussions of career counseling for student–athletes). Many academic athletic advisers, however, do a good job of guiding athletes in their exploration of alternate career tracks. Exploration and identity development are critical tasks of late adolescence and early adulthood, and college provides many avenues (and pressures) for exploration and experimentation.

Substance Use and Abuse

In Eriksonian terms, one of the reasons that student–athletes may fall into chronic use and abuse of alcohol and drugs is to self-medicate for the pain and confusion that come from unsuccessfully meeting the challenges of intimacy and identity. Alcohol use may also stem from the adoption of a negative identity such as the "beer-drinking jock." For many, college is a continuation of the exploration and experimentation that began in high school (or even earlier). College, however, may offer a greater variety of experiences and relationships along with greater freedom to pursue those experiences. Student–athletes differ little from students in general in the area of substance use and abuse (Damm & Murray, 1996).

Where student–athletes differ from the general student population is that they take drug tests occasionally, a process that is, at best, embarrassing, and at worst, dehumanizing. Many universities, in compliance with NCAA directives, have initiated drug education and substance abuse prevention programs. Unfortunately, many of these programs are one-time affairs with a primary prevention approach (Tricker & Cook, 1989) and probably have little effect on student patterns of drug and alcohol use. For college populations, secondary and tertiary prevention and care programs seem more appropriate because attitudes and experiences with drugs and alcohol usually have their roots in high school and middle school (Damm & Murray, 1996; Marcello, Danish, & Stolberg, 1989; Tricker, Cook, & McGuire, 1989). Sport psychologists who wish to offer services in the area of substance abuse education and prevention aimed at college populations might wish to consult Petitpas and Van Raalte (1992) for some guidelines on designing programs better suited to the needs of university student–athletes.

In addition, student–athletes differ from the general student population when it comes to the legal (and media) ramifications of drug and alcohol use. A college student, in most universities, if caught smoking marijuana or being drunk and disorderly, will probably garner a mention on the back page of the local paper's police report. If the infraction did not occur on university property, it probably will not come to the attention of university officials. An intercollegiate athlete arrested for drug possession or public drunkenness, no matter where it occurs, will make at least the sporting page and possibly, depending on the athlete's status, even the front page of the newspaper. When it comes to legal and "moral" behavior, many student–athletes live under extremely close scrutiny.

Sexuality

The use of alcohol is part of many student–athletes' experiences in college, as is the exploration of sexuality and intimate behavior. College is a time for developing relationships, sexual and otherwise, and sexuality is closely tied to the developmental challenge of intimacy versus isolation. There is a vast literature on the sexuality and sexual behavior of college-age populations. In general, there is little reason to suspect that the issues of sexuality and sexual behavior among college student–athletes differ significantly from the college population as a whole. In a few areas, such as living up to stereotypes of sexual athleticism and hypervirility and dealing with expectations about sexual orientation (e.g., females in "masculine" sports, males in "expressive" sports), student–athletes may have special concerns. The reader should consult Cogan and Petrie, chapter 20, this volume for a review of sexual orientation issues in sport, and see Andersen, Butki, and Heyman (1997) for a discussion of homophobia in college sports. College sports are strong bastions of heterosexism, and gay or lesbian athletes may actually have a more difficult time than their similarly oriented nonathlete peers on campus. Because of fears about being "outed" and the repercussions (e.g., being dropped from the team, getting less playing time, verbal and physical abuse), gay and lesbian athletes may struggle with both identity and intimacy more than their straight teammates.

Little specific literature exists on college athletes and sexual behavior. Some recent studies, however, have revealed that compared with student–nonathletes, student–athletes reported having significantly more sexual partners in a year's time (Butki, Andersen, & Heyman, 1996; Heyman, Varra, & Keahey, 1993). Both athletes and nonathletes also reported low frequencies of condom use. More partners and low condom use suggest that many athletes, and college students in general, are involved in risky sexual behavior. Offering psychoeducational programs on responsible sexual behavior might be another way sport psychologists can assist athletic departments in better caring for their athletes.

The Eriksonian Challenges Revisited

As previously mentioned, the psychosocial developmental challenges of the college athlete are to establish an identity and form intimate relationships. Erikson's stages of ego-identity versus role confusion and intimacy versus isolation describe sources of struggle for many athletes in college. University athletic administrations may claim to strive to develop the whole person in their athletes, but the environment usually sends a different message. Athletes often live in athletic dorms, have social support systems that are primarily composed of other athletes, and are exposed to an organization that can foster an "us versus them" ("them" being the rest of the university population) viewpoint. Sport psychologists can be helpful in an athlete's struggle to form an identity, but the obstacles that are in place for such development are substantial.

Establishing intimate relationships is the job of young adulthood and is strongly tied to identity. We often develop our identities with the assistance of intimate others. In some collegiate sporting environments, the cult of masculinity is pervasive (e.g., football, basketball). The attitudes behind that cult (e.g., male entitlement, viewing women as objects of gratification) work against the establishment of intimacy. The locker-room, fraternity-house mentality that often is propagated from the athletics administration through the coaches to the athletes poses serious challenges to those struggling with intimacy. The world of the collegiate athlete can sometimes be inimical to the establishment of strong multifaceted identities and healthy, satisfying intimate relationships.

Special Pressures on Student–Athletes

The life of a student–athlete, when school is in session, is often a series of attempts to get caught up. It is the rare student–athlete who is well ahead in his or her studies. A certain standard of academic performance is necessary in order to maintain athletic eligibility. The pressures and demands of both academic and sport performance often leave little time for student–athletes to engage in common student activities such as play and socializing. The following sections discuss some of the special pressures on student–athletes.

Academic Performance

By their junior year, student–athletes must have earned at least a 2.0 overall grade point average and have passed at least 24 semester units a year in order to maintain eligibility. (NCAA rules are constantly changing; see the latest NCAA regulations for a complete discussion of academc eligibility rules.) At some universities, student–athletes who do not have a certain grade point average must attend study hall or see tutors. A student–athlete's day might run something like this: classes, 9:00 a.m. to 1:00 p.m.; lunch, 1:30 p.m.; practice, 2:30 to 5:30 p.m.; dinner, 6:00 p.m.; study hall, 7:00 to 10:00 p.m.; and then maybe some more studying at home later. Time for scheduling extra activities (including sport psychology consultation) is limited.

Jonathan, in the opening case example, had many anxieties about his academic performance, primarily because he was ill-prepared for university work. Athlete anxieties about academic performance, scholarships, and eligibility may consume a substantial portion of the athlete's resources and may actually bring about academic probation. Managing anxieties about academic performance is a common issue for sport psychologists and athletes to confront in university settings.

Time Management

Organizing student–athletes' time is often not a problem. Much of their time is already scheduled. Pinkney (1996) made the wise suggestion that some common time management techniques are just not appropriate for many student–athletes. For example, do not ask student–athletes to find more time in the day or set aside more time to get things done. They do not have "extra" time. In a true sense, they already have great time management skills. They get to practice on time; they use their time effectively in the pool or in the weight room. Time management for student–athletes should not focus on finding more time, but on using available time more effectively and efficiently. In Jonathan's case, the sport psychologist was helpful, not so much in finding more time for him, rather in teaching study skills that helped Jonathan derive more benefit from the time he did have to pursue his studies.

Managing study time is a good starting point for teaching student–

athletes how to use their time more efficiently. Pinkney (1996) suggested a variety of techniques such as flash cards; short bouts of studying during the day between classes; and transferring time management skills learned in sport to the academic realm, such as reframing the academic environment into a long series of competitions (e.g., tests, papers). The transfer of sport training can also play a role in common student study and performance problems such as test anxiety.

Test Anxiety

A sport psychologist working with athletes on performance issues is likely to introduce relaxation and imagery techniques. Thus, when it comes to dealing with test anxiety, the student–athlete already has the basic tools for systematic desensitization. Coupling imagery and relaxation with more efficient study skills may help raise the comfort level of the student in the classroom. For Jonathan, the skills he learned for handling on-court anxieties were transferred to the classroom.

One major problem student–athletes face involves missing classes and tests because of travel and competition commitments. This scheduling issue remains a thorny problem. Many university professors are more than willing to let student–athletes take tests at different times, especially if student–athletes notify them in advance. Some professors, however, are rigidly attached to their own schedules, which leave student–athletes in "damned if you do, damned if you don't" situations. A sport psychologist speaking to a stubborn professor on behalf of a student–athlete needs great tact and advanced negotiating skills in order not to alienate the professor and make the matter worse.

Academic performance is the student–athlete's responsibility, and making up missed class time and tests is part of being a student–athlete. The sport psychologist, however, can help the student–athlete by occasionally checking on how things are going and suggesting various strategies for making up for time missed (e.g., arranging for another student to record the lecture, getting lecture notes from others). The sport psychologist must remember that academic progress and eligibility fall in the realm of responsibility of the academic athletic advisers and the NCAA eligibility coordinator. Making sure that all parties involved in the academic progress of student–athletes know what each other are doing will help obviate the potential for conflicting suggestions that could arise when all parties are not well informed.

Sport Injury

Connecting with student–athletes through the sports medicine unit may be one of the best routes a sport psychologist wishing to work with student–athletes can take. Establishing good rapport with sports medicine personnel and working in the training room can help the sport psychologist ease into helping student–athletes with the often difficult physical and psychological demands of the rehabilitation process. Sport psychologists, unfamiliar with general rehabilitation psychology, may wish first to do some homework in this field to gain knowledge about helping athletes with rehabilitation (e.g., Kolt, 2000; Tunick, Etzel, Leard, & Lerner, 1996; Wiese & Weiss, 1987) and working with sports medicine organizations (e.g., Andersen & Brewer, 1995). Sport injury is a challenge for many athletes on several levels. An injury brings up questions of athletic scholarships (they may be taken away), friendships (teammates may become more distant), and self-esteem (identity issues). One positive note about injuries is that athletes are often particularly willing to meet with a sport psychologist because they have extra time and also may have bouts of depressed mood. Injury can be a catalyst for seeking service.

Dealing With the Media

Student–athletes, especially those in highly visible sports, often interact with the media. Many NCAA Division I schools actually require some of their athletes to attend seminars on how to communicate with the press. The sport psychologist may be able to offer services and viewpoints that help the athlete keep the media attention in perspective (e.g., how to keep cool in interview situations, how to keep one's head from getting too big with all the attention). The suggestions offered by Baillie and Ogilvie, chapter 19, this volume, about elite athletes dealing with the media, are relevant to collegiate athletes.

In addition, major athletic events at universities often provide opportunities for the press to bring up sport psychology and sport psychologists. These opportunities contain good news and bad news. The good news is that sport psychology gets some air time, and such exposure may help increase the acceptance of sport psychology among the sporting community and the general public. The bad news is that the media portrayals of sport psychology and sport psychologists are often slanted or misrepresentative of how the majority of sport psychologists at universities operate. A major error by the media (and by some athletes) is to attribute athletes' success to their interactions with sport psychologists. This error can lead to resentment on the part of athletes who should be recognized for their performances. Excessive media attention also challenges sport psychologists attempting to maintain appropriate confidentiality boundaries. It is recommended that sport psychologists remain in the background as much as possible and inform athletes that that is where they want to remain.

Common Clinical Issues With Collegiate Athletes

Collegiate athletes are, in general, a healthy group, but they are also subject to many of the same mental and social problems of their non-athlete peers. In some instances, student–athletes may actually be more at risk of developing mental and behavioral problems than other students (e.g., eating disorders, adjustment disorders). Following are some of the common clinical concerns that may occur in the student–athlete population.

Depression

Depression is the "common cold" of mental disorders, and athletes may become depressed for a variety of reasons. For example, although Jonathan, from the previously described case study, was not diagnosed with depression, his response to his pressure-filled environment could easily have been manifested in depressive symptoms. Brewer (1993) found that athletes who identified with the athlete role were more likely to experience depressed mood when confronted with injury, and Hinkle (1996) described depression among student–athletes (see also a case study of an athlete with depression in Cogan, 2000). The pressures to perform athletically and scholastically often place student–athletes under great stress, and sometimes the response to that stress is to shut down.

Adjustment Disorders

Jonathan could be described as having an adjustment disorder with anxiety and somatic symptoms. He was trying to adjust to being a first-year student, to the academic demands, to a new coach, and to the pressures to perform. His task was a formidable one. Student–athletes, and especially those in transition into or out of university, can be at risk of developing adjustment disorders. In Jonathan's case, the disorder was accompanied by anxiety and physical distress. Adjustment disorders may also be associated with depressed mood, acting out, agitation, and substance abuse. Each of these maladaptive responses represents a destructive method of trying to cope with the overwhelming situation of being in a new and demanding environment. For a case study of serious adjustment problems coupled with grief and depressed mood, see Barney and Andersen (2000).

Eating Disorders

Athletes in some sports, especially those sports that emphasize appearance (e.g., diving, gymnastics) or have weight classes (e.g., wrestling), may be at greater risk of developing eating disorders. In recent years, interest has increased in eating disorders among student–athletes. This interest has developed not only because of an increased concern for the health and welfare of athletes, but also because of litigation brought against intercollegiate athletics departments by athletes who have developed eating disorders as a result of pressures in their sports. The etiology and treatment of eating disorders are beyond the scope of this chapter, but many useful resources are available to sport psychologists (e.g., Black & Burckes-Miller, 1988; Borgen & Corbin, 1987; Parker, Lambert, & Burlington, 1994; Petrie, 1993; Rosen & Hough, 1988; Thompson & Sherman, 1993). For a description of the diagnosis and cognitive–behavioral treatment of an athlete with an eating disorder, see Petrie and Sherman (2000).

The Practitioner and the NCAA

Knowing the Rules

The NCAA has a Byzantine set of ever-changing rules and regulations concerning what one can and cannot do for athletes. The sport psychologist needs to become familiar with these rules to avoid putting the athlete or the team in jeopardy of NCAA violations (NCAA, 2000). Depending on the NCAA rule infraction, the consequences can range from a warning to the loss of the student's eligibility to the whole team being placed on probation or worse.

Current NCAA regulations have been interpreted as stating that psychological consultation should occur only in a group or classroom-like setting or in the sport psychologist's office. The minute sport psychologists go out on the playing field to work with athletes (e.g., helping athletes with some on-site self-talk strategies), they are considered extra coaches. If the team has the maximum number of coaches allowed by the NCAA, then the sport psychologist has just placed the team in violation. If the team has fewer coaches than the maximum allowed, doing on-site interventions might not pose a problem. The NCAA has no regulations about a sport psychologist attending and observing practices.

Regarding the services offered by the sport psychologist, a wise tack would involve a "whole-person" approach (Carr & Baumann, 1996; Chartrand & Lent, 1987; Denson, 1996; Etzel, Ferrante, & Pinkney, 1996; Greenspan & Andersen, 1995; Petitpas & Champagne, 1988). If a coach or administrator employs a sport psychologist for the sole purpose of making more points or winning more games, the NCAA is likely to take a very dim view of this practice and consider it a type of exploitation.

Sport psychologists may do group psychoeducational sessions with the whole team, but the coach needs to include that time in the weekly allotment of hours for practice and team meetings (i.e., 20 hours, as stated by NCAA regulations). If sport psychologists work for the intercollegiate athletics department or the university, they may not buy anything for the athlete, not even a hamburger, and they may not phone prospects unless it is counted as an official call. This latter prohibition speaks to the area of recruitment. Although a sport psychologist may be involved with the recruitment process, that role should be limited. The NCAA rules for recruiting are strict. The level of recruitment involvement that seems best and safest would be for the sport psychologist to meet with interested prospective student–athletes when they make their campus visit. Deeper involvement than that, and forays into the selection of recruits, should be avoided.

If a student–athlete initiates individual meetings with a sport psychologist, those meetings do not count toward the NCAA's 20 hours of "athletically related activities." Therefore, there is no limit to performance counseling, or any counseling for that matter, as long as the student–athlete initiates the counseling session. As stated previously, sport psychologists need to be familiar with the current NCAA regulations and should get to know their institution's NCAA compliance coordinator, who can help clear up any doubts or misunderstandings sport psychologists may have about service delivery and NCAA regulations. For the latest update on NCAA rules concerning eligibility, enforcement, SAT/ACT scores, and considerations for athletes with learning disabilities, refer to the NCAA's Web site at http://www.ncaa.org.

Who Works With College Student–Athletes

At a medium-sized or large university, student–athletes may have access to a variety of sources that provide psychological and other one-on-one services. At smaller colleges, the range of such services may be limited. Many departments and campus organizations may offer services (of a psychological, academic, or counseling nature) to athletes *if* the athlete is the one who initiates contact. University personnel who work with student–athletes may include academic athletic advisers, tutors, counseling center staff, academic department staff (e.g., exercise science professors), and university job placement staff.

For those who have little or no contact with intercollegiate sport (e.g., private practitioners, academics) and wish to establish a relationship with athletes and coaches, there are a couple of paths to take. The first path leads to the academic athletic counselors. These individuals counsel athletes on academic matters, eligibility, registration, and so forth. They are intimately familiar with the factors that influence academic success for student–athletes (see Lapchick, 1989). Many academic athletic counselors also help athletes with their concerns about sport performance and life in general. These people are often overworked, and many would welcome having a good referral for athletes who want to work on performance enhancement or other personal issues. Forming a liaison with academic athletic counselors is probably one of the smarter moves a university counseling center psychologist (or any other practitioner) could make.

A second path for developing a relationship with intercollegiate athletics involves connections with the sports medicine unit. Recent studies (Francis, Andersen, & Maley, 2000) have found that athletic trainers and sport physical therapists would like to see more training in psychology and more psychological services in sports medicine settings. It appears that many athletic trainers would welcome contact with sport psychologists, especially those with experience and knowledge of psychological processes in injury rehabilitation. One caveat: Sports medicine units in intercollegiate athletics departments often have convoluted structures (Andersen & Brewer, 1995), and thorough familiarity with the structure and reporting lines of such organizations may help avoid unintentional faux pas when offering services.

Working in Intercollegiate Athletics

Intercollegiate athletic departments can assume, especially at large universities, very complex organizational structures. Unless a sport psychologist was a college athlete, an intercollegiate athletics department can be somewhat bewildering. To understand athletics departments better, the sport psychologist should keep in mind that, at least at the NCAA Division I level, intercollegiate athletics is in the entertainment business with an entertainment product to sell (often a football or basketball team). Different pressures come to bear on administrators, coaches, and athletes than what happens "across the street" at the university, where teaching and research receive the most attention.

Large universities may have a chief athletic director and several associate and assistant athletic directors to cover areas such as marketing, sports information, contest management, student support services, and so forth. The athletic administrators with whom a sport psychologist should probably make connections are the ones responsible for sports medicine units and student services. The sport psychologist may enter at any level of the complex intercollegiate athletic structure. Whenever sport psychologists enter the system, the assistant athletic director or other administrator responsible for the "area of service" (e.g., sports medicine) in which the sport psychologist is working needs to be advised that the sport psychologist is on board. Entering into the system without checking in with the "top brass" may set off the organizational immune system and get the sport psychologist hastily removed.

An administrator, a coach, or a team member may seek out services. These various service seekers present a challenge to the sport psychologist, who must remain clear on who the client is. Who receives service and who pays for it in college athletics are usually not the same person. If administrators allocate money for services for an athlete, then they may want some information about what that money is buying and how the services are going. Do not assume that administrators, coaches, or athletes know the subtleties of confidentiality, protection, and privilege. Plan on doing some pre-emptive education about psychologists' ethical codes for coaches, administrators, and athletes alike.

Boundaries

Sport psychologists often have boundaries that differ from more traditional clinical or counseling psychology boundaries (Andersen, Van Raalte, & Brewer, 2001). Sport psychologists may attend practices and competitions and even travel to away games and meets. This rather "familiar" behavior may pose some problems. Sport psychologists might want to clarify their boundaries to themselves and their clients. Some sport psychologists travel with the team, eat with the team, and even work out with the team. The rationale behind this behavior involves getting the sport psychologist to be accepted as one of the team or coaching staff. Although the intentions seem good, the results of such familiar behavior pose problems of potential dual relationships (Ellickson & Brown, 1990).

Travel with the team can provide rich information about team dynamics and performance at different venues. It has some pitfalls, however, and can lead to role confusion. Recommendations for team travel might include separate travel for the sport psychologist. One would not want to be seated next to a client for a 5-hour plane flight. Rooming with coaches or athletes sets up more boundary issues, so lodging arrangements should allow the sport psychologist some distance. Such an arrangement also allows athletes to talk with the sport psychologist in private without interruptions.

Large NCAA Division I universities may send sport psychologists, and more often, academic athletic counselors, to away games and meets. Sport psychologists, especially those outside the intercollegiate athletics department, usually have to supply their own transportation and lodging if they wish to observe the team at an away event. Although NCAA Division I universities are the ones most likely to have funds to pay for a sport psychologist's travel and services, institutions at other NCAA divisional levels may also request psychological services at away competitions.

Conclusion

This chapter has not covered all of the potential services sport psychologists can offer to collegiate athletes nor touched on even the majority of college athlete concerns. The problems of athletes in college cover much the same territory of athletes in general. For example, issues of prejudice and discrimination also confront minority athletes through their careers and beyond (see Cogan & Petrie, chapter 20, this volume; Parham, 1996; Sellers & Damas, 1996). This chapter has focused on the unique and most salient points of service delivery with collegiate student–athletes.

Intercollegiate athletics offers a potentially vast market for sport psychologists, but even today, it is still rather closed and guarded. Sport psychologists may find many difficulties "breaking into the market." The good news is that more and more athletics departments and universities are paying closer attention to the health and welfare of athletes in and out of sport, and sport psychologists will continue to play a role in providing services for college student–athletes.

References

Andersen, M. B., & Brewer, B. W. (1995). Organizational and psychological consultation in collegiate sports medicine groups. *Journal of American College Health, 44,* 63–69.

Andersen, M. B., Butki, B. D., & Heyman, S. R. (1997). Homophobia and sport experience: A survey of college students. *Academic Athletic Journal, 12*(1), 27–38.

Andersen, M. B., Van Raalte, J. L., & Brewer, B. W. (2001). Sport psychology service delivery: Staying ethical while keeping loose. *Professional Psychology: Research and Practice, 32,* 12–18.

Barney, S. T., & Andersen, M. B. (2000). Looking for help, grieving love lost: The case of C. In M. B. Andersen (Ed.), *Doing sport psychology* (pp. 139–150). Champaign, IL: Human Kinetics.

Black, D. R., & Burckes-Miller, M. E. (1988). Male and female college athletes: Use of anorexia nervosa and bulimia nervosa weight loss methods. *Research Quarterly for Exercise and Sport, 59,* 252–256.

Borgen, J. S., & Corbin, C. B. (1987). Eating disorders among female athletes. *The Physician and Sportsmedicine, 15*(2), 89–95.

Brewer, B. W. (1993). Self-identity and specific vulnerability to depressed mood. *Journal of Personality, 61,* 343–364.

Butki, B. D., Andersen, M. B., & Heyman, S. R. (1996). Knowledge of AIDS and risky sexual behaviors among athletes. *Academic Athletic Journal, 11*(1), 29–36.

Carr, C., & Bauman, N. J. (1996). Life skills for collegiate student–athletes. In E. F. Etzel, A. P. Ferrante, & J. W. Pinkney (Eds.), *Counseling college student athletes: Issues and interventions* (2nd ed., pp. 281–308). Morgantown, WV: Fitness Information Technology.

Chartrand, J. M., & Lent, R. W. (1987). Sports counseling: Enhancing the development of the student–athlete. *Journal of Counseling and Development, 66,* 164–167.

Cogan, K. D. (2000). The sadness in sport: Working with a depressed and suicidal athlete. In M. B. Andersen (Ed.), *Doing sport psychology* (pp. 107–119). Champaign, IL: Human Kinetics.

Coleman, V. D., & Barker, S. A. (1991, Spring). A model of career development for student–athletes. *Academic Athletic Journal, 6,* 33–40.

Damm, J., & Murray, P. (1996). Alcohol and other drug use among college student–

athletes. In E. F. Etzel, A. P. Ferrante, & J. W. Pinkney (Eds.), *Counseling college student athletes: Issues and interventions* (2nd ed., pp. 185–220). Morgantown, WV: Fitness Information Technology.

Davenport, J. (1985). From crew to commercialism: The paradox of sport in higher education. In D. Chu, J. O. Segrave, & B. J. Becker (Eds.), *Sport and higher education* (pp. 5–16). Champaign, IL: Human Kinetics.

Denson, E. L. (1996). An intergrative model of academic and personal support services for student–athletes. In E. F. Etzel, A. P. Ferrante, & J. W. Pinkney (Eds.), *Counseling college student athletes: Issues and interventions* (2nd ed., pp. 247–281). Morgantown, WV: Fitness Information Technology.

Ellickson, K. A., & Brown, D. R. (1990). Ethical considerations in dual relationships: The sport psychologist–coach. *Journal of Applied Sport Psychology, 2,* 186–190.

Erikson, E. H. (1968). *Identity: Youth and crisis.* New York: Norton.

Etzel, E. F., Ferrante, A. P., & Pinkney, J. W. (Eds.). (1996). *Counseling college student athletes: Issues and interventions* (2nd ed.). Morgantown, WV: Fitness Information Technology.

Finch, L., & Gould, D. (1996). Understanding and intervening with the student–athlete-to-be. In E. F. Etzel, A. P. Ferrante, & J. W. Pinkney (Eds.), *Counseling college student athletes: Issues and interventions* (2nd ed., pp. 223–246). Morgantown, WV: Fitness Information Technology.

Francis, S. F., Andersen, M. B., & Maley, P. (2000). Physiotherapists' and male professional athletes' views on psychological skills for rehabilitation. *Journal of Science and Medicine in Sport, 3,* 17–29.

Greenspan, M., & Andersen, M. B. (1995). Providing psychological services to student athletes: A developmental psychology approach. In S. M. Murphy (Ed.), *Sport psychology interventions* (pp. 177–191). Champaign, IL: Human Kinetics.

Grove, J. R., Lavallee, D., & Gordon, S. (1997). Coping with retirement from sport: The influence of athletic identity. *Journal of Applied Sport Psychology, 9,* 191–203.

Heyman, S. R., Varra, E. M., & Keahey, J. (1993, August). Comparison of high school varsity athletes and non-varsity students on measures of homophobia, sexual activity, and knowledge about AIDS. In S. R. Heyman (Chair), *Homophobia in sport: Confronting the fear.* Symposium conducted at the annual meeting of the American Psychological Association, Toronto, Ontario, Canada.

Hinkle, J. S. (1996). Depression, adjustment disorder, generalized anxiety, and substance abuse: An overview for sport professionals working with college student athletes. In E. F. Etzel, A. P. Ferrante, & J. W. Pinkney (Eds.), *Counseling college student athletes: Issues and interventions* (2nd ed., pp. 109–136). Morgantown, WV: Fitness Information Technology.

Kleiber, D. A., & Brock, S. C. (1992). The effect of career-ending injuries on the subsequent well-being of elite college athletes. *Sociology of Sport Journal, 9,* 70–75.

Kolt, G. S. (2000). Doing sport psychology with injured athletes. In M. B. Andersen (Ed.), *Doing sport psychology* (pp. 223–236). Champaign, IL: Human Kinetics.

Lapchick, R. E. (1989). The high school student–athlete: Root of the ethical issues in college sport. In R. E. Lapchick & J. B. Slaughter (Eds.), *The rules of the game.* New York: Macmillan.

Lavallee, D., & Andersen, M. B. (2000). Leaving sport: Easing career transitions. In M. B. Andersen (Ed.), *Doing sport psychology* (pp. 249–260). Champaign, IL: Human Kinetics.

Marcello, R. J., Danish, S. J., & Stolberg, A. L. (1989). An evaluation of strategies developed to prevent substance abuse among student–athletes. *The Sport Psychologist, 3,* 196–211.

National Collegiate Athletic Association. (2000). *2000–01 NCAA guide for the college-bound student–athlete.* Available at http://www.ncaa.org.

Parham, W. D. (1996). Diversity within intercollegiate athletics: Current profile and welcomed opportunities. In E. F. Etzel, A. P. Ferrante, & J. W. Pinkney (Eds.), *Counseling college student athletes: Issues and interventions* (2nd ed., pp. 27–54). Morgantown, WV: Fitness Information Technology.

Parker, R. M., Lambert, M. J., & Burlington, G. M. (1994). Pathological features of female runners presenting with pathological weight control behaviors. *Journal of Sport and Exercise Psychology, 16,* 119–134.

Pearson, R. E., & Petitpas, A. J. (1990). Transitions of athletes: Developmental and preventive perspectives. *Journal of Counseling and Development, 69,* 7–10.

Perna, F. M., Ahlgren, R. L., & Zaichkowsky, L. (1996). The influence of career planning, race, and athletic injury on life satisfaction among recently retired collegiate male athletes. *The Sport Psychologist, 13,* 144–156.

Perna, F. M., Zaichkowsky, L., & Bockneck, G. (1996). The association of mentoring with psychological development among male athletes at termination of college career. *Journal of Applied Sport Psychology, 8,* 76–88.

Petitpas, A., Champaign, D., Chartrand, J., Danish, S., & Murphy, S. (1997). *Athlete's guide to career planning.* Champaign, IL: Human Kinetics.

Petitpas, A. J., Brewer, B. W., & Van Raalte, J. L. (1996). Transitions of the student–athlete: Theoretical, empirical, and practical perspectives. In E. F. Etzel, A. P. Ferrante, & J. W. Pinkney (Eds.), *Counseling college student athletes: Issues and interventions* (2nd ed., pp. 137–156). Morgantown, WV: Fitness Information Technology.

Petitpas, A. J., & Champagne, D. (1988). Developmental programming for intercollegiate athletes. *Journal of College Student Development, 29,* 454–460.

Petitpas, A. J., Danish, S., McKelvain, R., & Murphy, S. (1992). A career assistance program for elite athletes. *Journal of Counseling and Development, 71,* 383–386.

Petitpas, A. J., & Van Raalte, J. L. (1992, Spring). Planning alcohol education programs for intercollegiate student–athletes. *Academic Athletic Journal, 7,* 12–25.

Petrie, T. A. (1993). Disordered eating in female collegiate gymnasts: Prevalence and personality/attitudinal correlates. *Journal of Sport and Exercise Psychology, 15,* 424–436.

Petrie, T. A., & Sherman, R. T. (2000). Counseling athletes with eating disorders: A case example. In M. B. Andersen (Ed.), *Doing sport psychology* (pp. 121–138). Champaign, IL: Human Kinetics.

Pinkney, J. W. (1996). Coaching student–athletes toward academic success. In E. F. Etzel, A. P. Ferrante, & J. W. Pinkney (Eds.), *Counseling college student athletes: Issues and interventions* (2nd ed., pp. 309–332). Morgantown, WV: Fitness Information Technology.

Price, F. L., & Andersen, M. B. (2000). Into the maelstrom: A five-year relationship from college ball to the NFL. In M. B. Andersen (Ed.), *Doing sport psychology* (pp. 193–206). Champaign, IL: Human Kinetics.

Rosen, L., & Hough, D. (1988). Pathogenic weight control behaviors of female college gymnasts. *The Physician and Sportsmedicine, 16*(9), 141–144.

Sellers, R. M., & Damas, A. (1996). The African-American student–athlete experience. In E. F. Etzel, A. P. Ferrante, & J. W. Pinkney (Eds.), *Counseling college student athletes: Issues and interventions* (2nd ed., pp. 55–76). Morgantown, WV: Fitness Information Technology.

Sperber, M. (1990). *College sports, Inc.: The athletic department vs. the university.* New York: Holt, Henry, & Co.

Thompson, R. A., & Sherman, R. (1993). *Helping athletes with eating disorders*. Champaign, IL: Human Kinetics.

Tricker, R., & Cook, D. L. (1989). The current status of drug intervention and prevention in college athletic programs. *Journal of Alcohol and Drug Education, 34*(2), 38–45.

Tricker, R., Cook, D. L., & McGuire, R. (1989). Issues related to drug use in college athletics: Athletes at risk. *The Sport Psychologist, 3*, 155–165.

Tunick, R., Etzel, E., Leard, J., & Lerner, B. (1996). Counseling injured and disabled student athletes: A guide for understanding and intervention. In E. F. Etzel, A. P. Ferrante, & J. W. Pinkney (Eds.), *Counseling college student athletes: Issues and interventions* (2nd ed., pp. 157–184). Morgantown, WV: Fitness Information Technology.

Wiese, D. M., & Weiss, M. R. (1987). Psychological rehabilitation and physical injury: Implications for the sportsmedicine team. *The Sport Psychologist, 1*, 318–330.

Wittmer, J., Bostic, D., Phillips, T., & Waters, W. (1981). The personal, academic, and career problems of college student athletes: Some possible questions. *Personnel and Guidance Journal, 60*, 52–55.

Working With Elite Athletes

Patrick H. F. Baillie and Bruce C. Ogilvie

If applied sport psychology has an area of glamour, it likely rests in the realm of providing services to elite athletes. We define "elite athletes" as those whose pursuit of excellence in sport has led to their participation and success in competition at the Olympic or professional level. Unfortunately, among some practitioners, there is a tendency to promote themselves based on the number of medals or championship teams with which they have been associated. More appropriately, working with elite athletes should be seen as an opportunity to work with talented and dedicated clients, athletes who have reached the pinnacle of their sport.

Work with elite athletes brings into play special challenges for the sport psychologist. It is more than an extension of services offered to amateur sports clubs and other competitors. Travel schedules can disrupt the regularity of involvement. The media may look to the sport psychologist for that extra insight or news tip. Administrative structures may become increasingly burdensome. Substance abuse issues may put the sport psychologist in an ethical or even a legal dilemma. At times, when consultation fails to lead to effective changes in service delivery, one side or the other may choose to abruptly terminate the consultation process.

This chapter addresses some of these unique issues, including gaining entry and acceptance with Olympic and professional athletes, recognizing differences between work with teams and work with individu-

The authors thank Ken Ravizza and Hap Davis, who provided commentary and suggestions on earlier drafts of this chapter.

als, coping with the distractions and obligations that face athletes and sport psychologists at this level of competition, and evaluating the on-going effectiveness of consultation, for both the client and the practitioner. Although there is no doubt that special pleasures may come from working with elite athletes, there also are specific perils about which a prepared consultant must be aware.

The Starting Point: Gaining Entry With Elite Athletes

The value of first impressions has seldom been denied, and the image that sport psychologists present at their first meeting with elite athletes often will characterize the nature and duration of the professional relationship. Honesty, genuineness, and the ability to earn athletes' trust are frequently mentioned as essential elements on which practitioners build their reputation (Ravizza, 1988).

Strategies for Access and Acceptance by Professional and Olympic Athletes

It is essential for sport psychology consultants to use a variety of methods to gain access to and acceptance by professional and Olympic athletes (see Exhibit 19.1). Many athletes and coaches realize the importance of sport psychology, but their enthusiasm for working with a mental training consultant may be restrained. Coaches, for example, may feel that sport psychology techniques such as goal setting, focus control, and avoidance of burnout are basic skills that fall under the coach's purview. Athletes may believe that consultation with a sport psychologist is an admission of weakness. Other significant barriers to the involvement of a sport psychologist are negative connotations associated with the image of a "shrink" (Linder, Brewer, Van Raalte, & De Lange, 1991; Van Raalte, Brewer, & Linder, 1992), lack of sport-specific knowledge by the practitioner, and inadequate experience in the elite sport environment (Ravizza, 1988). Ravizza recommended using terms such as mental training or mental toughness instead of sport psychology, because athletes are likely to be more comfortable with these alternatives. For athletes referred to a sport psychologist, feelings of paranoia are not uncommon (Ogilvie, 1979). Supervised experience with amateur sports clubs or with college teams provides the practitioner with exposure to the sport and to introductory administrative issues. As the past several

---

Exhibit 19.1

Strategies for Access to and Acceptance by Professional and Olympic Athletes

1. Gain experience working with athletes in a variety of settings, including schools and universities, local sports clubs, development teams, and other amateur organizations.
2. Develop name recognition by volunteering with sports teams, presenting at coaching clinics, working with individual athletes, making cold calls to sports organizations and following up with written materials, and giving public presentations or lectures to other interested audiences.
3. Accurately assess the needs of athletes, rather than imposing any sort of predetermined program developed elsewhere. Assessment includes identification of the athletes' strengths, requirements, experiences with applied sport psychology, and interests in performance enhancement and mental training.
4. Be sensitive to the needs of athletes, be flexible in scheduling, provide support for the athletes, and provide clear strategies with a positive focus.
5. Use language that is appropriate to the sport setting, emphasizing plain language, direct communication, and simple ideas instead of psychological jargon. Knowledge and use of terms related to player positions, game rules, and sport strategies assist in the development of early rapport.

---

years have shown, with huge athlete contracts, cuts to Olympic program funding, and strikes or lockouts in each of the four major professional team sports, elite athletics is business-driven, and sport psychologists often need to immediately prove to be worth their fees. On-the-job training is almost nonexistent.

Sport psychology positions working with elite athletes are rare and are almost never advertised. In North America, there are perhaps 50 practitioners working with professional sports teams and an approximately equal number involved with Olympic athletes. For a handful of skilled practitioners, years of experience and a track record of proficiency may lead to unsolicited offers of employment. For slightly more, presentations to coaching conferences, publications in popular magazines or books, and involvement with development teams serve to provide name recognition when approaching teams or National Governing Bodies (NGB), the organizations that allocate funding and determine policy for Olympic sports. Experience, in short, helps, but "cold calls" and other sales techniques are required before novice practitioners are able to get their foot in the door. Experience with a single team member, collegiality with an administrator, or a willingness to start with volunteer services have proven to be useful approaches.

Understanding athletes' motivations and commitment is an important step in earning their respect and trust. As a result, Ravizza (1988), Orlick (1989), and some of the contributors to a special edition of *The Sport Psychologist* (i.e., Botterill, 1990; Ravizza, 1990) recommended that the consultation process begin with a detailed assessment of the athlete's or team's needs, rather than the imposition of a packaged program. Orlick stated, "I never begin an individual consultation session with a preconceived notion of what a particular high performance athlete might want or need. Each one has different needs, and these needs differ at various times in his or her career" (pp. 358–359). Orlick described beginning an assessment by discussing the athlete's goals, his or her experiences with mental preparation, and the athlete's identification of mental tasks that require focused work. Ravizza added that the practitioner also must determine how to integrate mental skills training into the coach's schedule, to minimize disruption. Coaches are likely to be more comfortable with a consultant who provides assurances that sport psychology interventions are intended to complement the coach's role, and not to impinge on typical coaching domains such as skill acquisition, game strategy, and roster decisions.

Athletes also may need sport psychologists to be sensitive to scheduling issues. Given the pressures and commitments of elite-level athletic competition, several authors (e.g., Botterill, 1990; Halliwell, 1990) have suggested that time with family is important for the athlete and that sport psychology interventions offered on road trips, when "down time" is more common, may be more well-received. Other dimensions of access will likely reflect the practitioner's own values, such as being in the locker room before games, on the field during practices, or in a conveniently located arena office. Preferences vary: "I have found that I can be most effective by keeping a low profile and being available on planes, buses, or in my hotel room. An open-door policy based upon a genuine interest in each player has proven to be the most effective approach for me" (Ogilvie, 1979, p. 51).

Personality also may play a central role in determining the goodness-of-fit between an athlete or team and a practitioner. Orlick and Partington (1987) surveyed 75 Canadian Olympic athletes and found that sport psychology consultants were given positive evaluations when they were accessible, applied, flexible, seen to have something concrete to offer, and willing to provide athlete-specific input. Negative evaluations were found with consultants who lacked sensitivity, failed to provide sufficient feedback, and had poor application of psychology to sport, and whose interpersonal styles were described, among other adjectives, as wimpy or domineering. Orlick and Partington concluded, "As a result of this study, . . . we have become acutely aware of the importance of having people with the right kind of personal qualities enter the field" (pp. 16–17). Gould, Murphy, Tammen, and May (1991) found that effectiveness of the consultant was highly correlated with his or her fitting in with the team, drawing on the athletes' strengths, being trustworthy, having a positive focus, and providing clear strategies.

Effectiveness also may be improved by consultants making modifications to their use of language. For those practicing from a clinical perspective, diagnostic labels and psychological terms offer efficient professional communication but are likely to be met with negative connotations among coaches and athletes. Even nonclinical terms such as "sensitive," "loner," and "having an edge" come with different meanings in the sport context. Evaluative language when used by the practitioner, particularly, may interfere with the development of a trusting relationship with the athlete. Experience with professional and Olympic sports quickly focuses the consultant's vocabulary on words and phrases that provide specific direction and clarity for the athlete. Through this sort of adjustment, consultants begin to develop rapport with their clients, enhancing trust and commitment.

Negotiating and Detailing the Terms of Consultation

Multiple models of service delivery exist within applied sport psychology. These varying models may be related to the practitioner's self-perceived competencies or may reflect coaching philosophies and team needs. Murphy (1988), for example, compared medical, consultation, and educational models in applied sport psychology and recommended a consultation-type model drawn from a base in industrial–organizational psychology. Neff (1990) described a wide-ranging employee assistance program with a professional sports organization, including personal counseling and testing. Ravizza (1990) presented an educational model that consists of information, practice, and support for the athlete, similar to Rotella (1990), who argued for a role in performance enhancement only, avoiding counseling areas and any part in player selection. Dorfman (1990) offered a combined clinical/educational approach with personal and family counseling, referrals for drug rehabilitation, financial advice, and academic assistance.

The issue of philosophy of service delivery must be clarified before a contract between practitioner and client can be formalized. Recommendations regarding the content of the contract are presented in Exhibit 19.2. Essential elements include financial terms, clarification of access, clarification of role, and details of the referral process. Specific services to be provided will vary, as will the amount of time to be provided by the practitioner, the term of the contract, and, accordingly, the level of compensation. Contracts based on a barter system are not uncommon, for example, providing season tickets to the consultant, but barter should be avoided when it is clinically contraindicated or exploitative. The sport psychologist may be well-advised to review the relevant literature on the impact of remuneration on therapeutic outcome (e.g., Cerney, 1990; Yoken & Berman, 1987) before making a quick agreement with this type of payment. In short, the value that the team or athlete writes into the practitioner's contract is an early reflection of the importance or relevance that the client gives to mental training and is a comment on the perceived worth of sport psychology services.

We have found that proper orientation to sport psychology programs is essential for consultation work with teams. Meetings with the coaching staff, team members, and the team athletic trainer and physician may each serve to introduce your services as a sport psychologist.

The primary goal of the meeting with the coaches is to have them

Exhibit 19.2

Recommendations for the Content of Contract for Sport Psychology Services With Elite Athletes

1. Financial Terms
   - Determine an appropriate level of compensation for services rendered.
   - Attempt to avoid contracts based on barter, particularly with individual athletes.
   - Specify the time period during which the contract is in effect.
   - Identify escape clauses through which either side may prematurely terminate services, with associated periods of notification.
2. Contract for Sufficient Orientation
   - Present orientation workshops for the entire coaching staff.
   - Schedule individual meetings with each athlete.
3. Professional Issues
   - Detail professional boundaries.
   - Describe specific competencies.
   - Explain referral process.

see the sport psychologist as a contributor to their personal goals, while, at the same time, respecting the individual needs of the players. With team members, the focus shifts to describing sport psychology strategies and interventions, detailing the nature of privileged communication, and explaining that all psychological insights—be they from testing, interviews, or coaches—are designed to enhance the athlete's performance. In some cases, you may choose to offer appropriate readings, give practical examples of interventions, and inform players that you can contribute most when they seek your services on the basis of their particular concerns. The central theme is that your services will be tailored to the needs of the individual athlete.

In addition, with the team physician and athletic trainer, the initial meeting serves to establish open communication that will assist in integration of later programs for injury recovery, substance abuse, eating disorders, and other elements of physical conditioning that the sport psychologist feels competent to address. An ongoing collaborative effort is needed to effectively address each of these topics.

The orientation process can be facilitated by clear delineation of the specific role of the sport psychologist. Professional boundaries relating to test materials, the voluntary nature of athlete involvement, and the referral process should be stipulated at the outset. Clarify, with the contract holder, the nature of your feedback regarding his or her influence on the team and team performance. Ensure that all services are delivered within the ethical framework of your field. When the sport psychologist has authority for referrals to outside services, such as substance abuse programs, the contract also should identify at least one individual with whom the sport psychologist shares a privileged relationship should subsequent referrals require that level of professional protection.

The contract is one place to begin to clarify issues around competencies of the sport psychologist. In their study of 19 sport psychology consultants, Partington and Orlick (1991) found a common core of services. "The eight most frequently mentioned services in descending order included focus and refocus control, activation and anxiety control, competition planning, monitoring and evaluation, imagery, precompetition planning, goal-setting, and interpersonal communication" (p. 186). Gould and colleagues (1991) found that coaches and athletes were most interested in imagery and visualization techniques, concentration and attention training, stress management, relaxation, self-talk strategies, and regulation of arousal. Career transition planning, eating disorders, substance abuse concerns, and personal development were rated as less important.

Inevitably, crisis management occasions arise when consultants are asked, with little warning, to aid in the resolution of problems of an extremely complex nature. It is imperative that consultants define their roles. Although it may be ideal to refer or to take the time to discuss options with colleagues, the reality is that circumstances often conspire to limit flexibility. For example, when a star athlete is traded or hurt, a press release may actually precede any discussion with other team members. Should the sport psychologist hold a team meeting or hope to chat with each athlete before the day is through? Perhaps the sport psychologist might even be asked to break the news of a trade to an athlete, a decision that will affect future relationships with team members, who may believe that the sport psychologist was part of the trade decision. These types of requests are more likely to arise in situations in which the practitioner either has opted to provide comprehensive counseling services or has failed to specify the exact nature of the mental training program.

Many potential problems can be avoided by developing and using an appropriate contract, such as that shown in Exhibit 19.3. At every opportunity, sport psychology consultants should clarify that their work should be evaluated on the basis of improved use of mental skills strategies by the athlete or other parameters, but not on the basis of winning or losing by the athlete or team. Although your ethical and moral stance may be that of separating your services from that of producing winners, you will find that managers, coaches, and parents will continue to evaluate the practitioner, and sport psychology, in terms of contributions to this end. When financial pressures increase for the athlete or team as a result of losing competitions and losing fans or sponsors, sport psychologists are likely to learn quickly their true significance to the organization.

With an employee assistance program as the model of service, sport psychology consultants need to clarify the referral procedures and payment of costs associated with outside services (e.g., substance abuse programs, family counseling, and financial management). Because confidentiality issues may limit the ability of practitioners to make referrals consultants must state up front under what circumstance they can make independent decisions to make a referral and to spend a significant amount of a team's or an NGB's money (e.g., without a previously agreed-upon procedure, the sport psychologist may be put in a position

Exhibit 19.3

Sample Contract for the Provision of Sport Psychology Services

1. This agreement is between [the sport psychologist(s)] and [the client(s)] for the provision of sport psychology services by [the sport psychologist(s)] with [the client(s)].

2. The agreement covers the period between [the present date or the first day of the season] and [one year less a day from the present date or the last possible day of competition]. Either party may terminate services at any time on written notice [one month] prior to the termination.

3. Areas in which [the sport psychologist] is competent to provide service include: (add or delete as applicable) goal setting, stress management, substance abuse counseling, focus control, psychometric assessment, marital or couples counseling, imagery, precompetition and competition planning, crisis management, interpersonal communication, self-talk strategies, and regulation of arousal. [Data collection for research by the sport psychologist, assessments of draft prospects, and] other services will be negotiated separately.

4. Required services outside of these areas of competence will be accessed through referrals at the discretion of [the sport psychologist], wherever possible in consultation with [the client]. Costs associated with additional treatment resources will be paid by [the client]. Such services may include substance abuse treatment, family or marital counseling, or career transition programs.

5.* Fees for the provision of sport psychology services by [the sport psychologist] will be in the amount of $[   ], to be paid in [   ] equal installments, on [date(s)] by [the client].

6. The nature and content of all services provided by [the sport psychologist] to an individual athlete are privileged, and will not be disclosed by [the sport psychologist] to anyone without the written consent of the athlete. The nature and content or services provided to the team as a whole also are privileged, and will not be disclosed outside of the team by [the sport psychologist] without the written consent of [the head coach].

7. (When working with a team or NGB) [The sport psychologist] will consult [every two weeks] with [the head coach] to discuss issues of team cohesion, communication, and mental focus, and other topics as determined by mutual concern.

8. At a time agreed on by the parties, [the sport psychologist] will hold an introductory meeting with [the athlete(s)] to outline expectations for the provision of sport psychology services. This meeting is to describe the training and background of [the sport psychologist], services to be offered, relevant readings, ethical standards, and scheduling, and to answer questions from [the athlete(s)]. Meetings with each individual athlete will be arranged at times of mutual convenience.

continued

Exhibit 19.3, cont.

9. At a time agreed on by the parties, [the sport psychologist] will meet separately with the coaching staff, the medical staff, and any other team personnel as appropriate, to describe the training and background of [the sport psychologist], services to be offered, procedures for interdisciplinary consultation, relevant readings, ethical standards, and scheduling, and to answer questions from each of these groups.

10. Any modifications to this agreement must be made by mutual consent of the parties.

Dated [date] at [city] ,

Signed [the sport psychologist] [name of the sport psychologist, printed]

[the athlete or head coach] [name of the signatory/client, printed]

*Fees may cover all or part of the services to be provided. If the fees cover preseason training and regular contact during the season, but not crisis management issues or other circumstances such as attendance at nonlocal competitions, additional fees should be specified in the contract. An informal survey by the authors suggests that, at time of publication, fees for a season of service to a professional team range from barter for a pair of season tickets to more than $50,000.

of having to disclose personal information about an athlete before the team or NGB will authorize funds for other treatment). In addition, consultants must take into account how referrals will affect training and travel schedules, should the needs of the athlete include comprehensive treatment alternatives.

Knowing Your Client: A Comparison Between Working With Teams and Working With Individuals

The single most important ethical issue faced by sport psychologists working with elite athletes is clarification of exactly "who is the client?" Is the practitioner's primary allegiance to the athlete, coach, general manager, or NGB? The nature of this element of the relationship must be clarified during initial negotiations, but it also requires careful monitoring throughout the term of the contract.

Respecting Boundaries Among Administrators, Coaches, and Athletes

Although many authors have commented on their preference for work with individual athletes rather than with a team as a group (e.g., Dorfman, 1990; Ravizza, 1990), clarification of primary allegiance and ethical issues has been less widely discussed. When it has been discussed, the results have often been fractious. On one hand, many practitioners are licensed or chartered psychologists and function within the professional framework provided by the standards of the American Psychological Association (APA). On the other hand, people with a sport science background, who clearly may have much to offer a prospective client, may have a different perspective on interventions and ethics. As one example, APA ethics prohibit the therapist from involvement in a second, nontherapeutic role—if it is potentially exploitative—with the client (e.g., providing a student with treatment services while instructing him or her in a required university course). However, dual relationships such as that of off-campus employer and sport psychologist or coach and sport psychologist depend on the personal ethics of those practitioners not covered under the aegis of APA (Burke & Johnson, 1992; Ellickson & Brown, 1990; Petitpas, Brewer, Rivera, & Van Raalte, 1994). In such a circumstance, boundary issues between the service provider and the athlete become even more salient. The sport psychologist must be mindful of engaging in any activity that compromises his or her therapeutic relationship with the athlete, for example, by, asking the "employee" during a therapy session to work an extra shift or by raising sport psychology issues with the athlete in a nonconfidential setting.

Working with individual athletes may result in a reduction of several extraneous factors that can disrupt the therapist–athlete relationship. When golf or tennis professionals, for example, seek service, responsibility is usually restricted to the clients and their agents. There are notable occasions where sponsors or parents have, by the nature of their relationship to the athlete, influenced the implementation of mental skills training programs. Ideally, the practitioner–athlete relationship is based totally on collaborative efforts. When service is extended to an entire team or NGB, functioning within established ethical guidelines becomes a continuous challenge. Coaches and administrators, understandably seeking accountability from the sport psychologist, may ask what specific services are being provided to a given athlete, including the content and frequency of sessions. Coaches who use the sport psychologist as a sounding board may disclose pending personnel decisions that affect an individual athlete but that the sport psychologist is not allowed to disclose to that athlete. When the trade or cut then comes, some athletes may question the allegiances of the sport psychologist.

In working with teams, sports psychologists must obtain the approval of the coach before they can develop rapport with the team and implement a program. As a result, some practitioners view an allegiance to the coach as being a prerequisite to work with sports teams (Ogilvie, 1979; Ravizza, 1990). Others find this relationship troubling, or at least limiting in perspective: "If a sport psychology consultant failed to deal with problems identified by athletes, and only dealt with those viewed as real by the coach, he or she would turn away from everything we have learned about high quality consulting from athletes and coaches" (Partington & Orlick, 1987b, p. 101). In any event, the nature of the relationship must be clear for all participants. A coach may feel that the sport psychology consultant is stepping into traditional coaching territory, such as enhancing team motivation or getting the athlete more focused, and, therefore, expect the practitioner's allegiance. The athlete, by contrast, is a high functioning individual for whom the acknowledgement of a need for psychological help can be such a violation of his or her self-concept that any suggestion of collusion between the coach and the consultant may obstruct the athlete's openness. The balance between allegiance and ethics becomes all the more precarious.

In working with teams, the sport psychology consultant may find varying levels of acceptance among the athletes. Issues such as race, history with other consultants, overall trust, and personal motivation influence the comfort of athletes in seeking mental skills training. Ravizza (1988) suggested that three groups may arise, "In general, I find that about one third of the athletes on a team are very receptive to the program in the beginning, one third will seek it out when they are struggling, and one third are not receptive" (p. 249). Put simply, not all members of a team will feel comfortable in accessing offered sport psychology services. Practitioners must identify whether they need to address this reluctance, or allow for a more gradual building of acceptance by the team. Goodness-of-fit applies to the whole team and the sport psychologist, not necessarily each team member.

Maintaining Confidentiality

One of the most potentially lethal issues facing the sport psychology consultant relates to information gained through work with an individual athlete and about which the coach or administrator seeks disclosure. The most acute focus of this issue occurs when the sport psychologist becomes involved in personnel decisions. If assessment of potential draft choices is one of the services being provided, team members may question the allegiance of the practitioner, perhaps fearing that confidential information will be passed along to management. Whenever possible, the practitioner should revert to an educational role and explain the nature of privileged communication to both the athletes and their coach. Primary emphasis on the relationship with the coach does not have to mean a flow of confidential material or the coach's expectation of such communication if the coach understands that privilege is necessary for consultants to maximize their effectiveness.

Beyond the coach, additional questions of allegiance arise when sport psychologists begin, as they must, to interact with administrators. Throughout the hierarchy of the team or NGB, each individual has a private agenda. These agendas reflect the various administrative roles played by each member within the organization. Professional survival often depends on one's skill in identifying each agenda and then deciding on an appropriate course of behavior. Consultants are ultimately involved with athletes in whom the team or NGB has made great financial investments. Protection of the capital investment is a primary concern. If a sport psychologist works with an athlete on sensitive issues such as substance abuse, the situation can become difficult. One sport psychologist worked in a professional sport with a substance abuse policy that provided for fines "of any team official knowing of a player's drug use and not reporting such use." To respect confidentiality, the contract stated that the team would pay any fines levied against the consultant.

Distractions and Obligations: Factors That May Impair Peak Performance for Elite Athletes

Competition at the Olympic or professional level may offer athletes the ultimate showcase for their talents. Also, it is likely to bring into play new time demands; new sources of competitive stress; and other challenges such as dealing with the media, life on the road, and heightened pressure, either self-imposed or external, for consistent excellence. For the sport psychology consultant, these issues must be addressed in order to assist athletes in maintaining focus during training and competitions.

However, the disturbances also interfere with athletes' time, and may, therefore, impinge on access and the availability of suitable consultation sessions.

Coping With Travel, Outside Employment, and Other Distractions

At multisport competitions such as the Olympic Games, the Pan-American Games, or the World University Games, athletes are often faced with significant disruptions to training schedules; crowded accommodations; time spent traveling to and from practice venues; and hours spent waiting, eating, making travel arrangements; and trying to find an e-mail connection to home. Greenleaf (1999) found that Olympic athletes responded best to these negative distractions when a plan had been prepared, addressing, for example, how to access friends and family and how and when to interact with media. In short, when the athlete had a sense of control amidst changes that sometimes included working with different coaches, such preparation seemed to help. As Canadian diver Eryn Bulmer recently stated, "Whoever can ignore the distractions the best is going to perform the best. I've learned how to compete under pressure and how to block those things out" (Jones, 2000). Giges and Petitpas (2000) offered a framework for brief contact interventions in the field, describing them as time-limited, action-oriented, and present-focused.

Most professional sports teams spend half of their season on the road. For golfers, bowlers, and tennis players, among others, the entire season may be spent traveling. Unless well-sponsored, Olympic athletes may need to balance training and competition with the demands of earning a living outside of sport. These and other factors not only conspire against the best performances of the athletes, but also affect the delivery of sport psychology services.

Michelle Mullen, a professional bowler interviewed by Gould and Finch (1990), described life on tour as being extremely stressful as a result of struggling to make a living and to maintain a healthy perspective on the role of sport:

> You must be able to keep your bowling in the right regard and not let it become your total life. Sometimes the tour can become so all consuming, and in many ways it has to be. However, you must remember that it's just part of your life and not necessarily the total essence of it. (p. 422)

Discussing possible research areas for sport psychology, Mullen noted:

> Interesting things to study have to do with lifestyle and getting an understanding for the stressful lifestyle. It's different in every sport for different reasons. Finances have a lot to do with it, depending on what you're competing for. Understanding what kind of roller coaster it is as a professional athlete, especially the uncertainty. . . . dealing with different issues like that, the stress levels are underestimated by far. (p. 426)

Gould and Finch also commented that "the ability to compete effectively on television while audiences of millions may watch is a stress source that may be more prevalent in the professional rather than the amateur ranks" (p. 427). Attention to these sorts of stresses is necessary to optimize performance.

Botterill (1990) described the importance of spouses, families, and friends in the life of the professional athlete; therefore, when serving as sport psychology consultant, he offers his services to these people. Botterill also has noted the difficulty of scheduling interventions. "Road trips often contain unique challenges to work through and players can be more receptive to spending additional time on things on the road. Professional players spend so much time away from home they are often well advised to maximize time with their families when at home" (p. 366). A broader analysis of the scheduling of interventions suggests that team meetings or coach referrals after a home practice are likely to be met with annoyance and disinterest from team members. Athletes, as noted previously, like a consultant to be available, but flexible. When a program truly is supported by the coaching staff, mental training exercises may replace some or all of the allotted practice time. Other times for less intrusive interventions include while traveling (e.g., at or on the way to airports, bus stations, or hotels) and during meals. Sport psychologists should discuss the issue of scheduling as part of the introductory stage of the consultation. Sensitivity to scheduling, so as to avoid adding to the demands on the athlete, is likely to be favorably received.

Dealing With the Media

Just as professional sport is a business, so is the media's function in covering it. For this reason, both the athlete and the sport psychologist must learn how to handle inquiries from reporters. Exposure on television or in print may improve the marketability of both athlete and consultant, but an ongoing relationship with the media also increases the risk of making a potentially damaging off-the-cuff comment (never "off the record"—reporters are always researching, even if not actually quoting). The simple fact that an athlete is seeing the "shrink" may become a story.

Most elite sport organizations employ public relations staff who can provide excellent counsel regarding media contacts. Reporters gain access to the athletes only at limited times, although they may freely editorialize about issues that, when read or seen by athletes, can interfere with their training and competitive focus. Among the worst mistakes that an athlete might make are comments that suggest dissension among team members or that insult their opponent, thereby offering a grudge motivation to the other. Athletes are, therefore, well-advised to make comments that describe personal disappointment only (e.g., "I felt that I didn't play up to my potential this evening") or that offer positive reflections on team members (e.g., "Mike played hard today, and we capitalized on the opportunities he created") or the competition (e.g., "State played well, so we had to beat a good team"). Generally, athletes should remember that members of the media are dependent on the quotes they receive from their subjects. If an athlete has nothing to say, then he or she will not be quoted. The reporter will have to look elsewhere but ultimately will find and file a story. Conversely, complete avoidance of the media has worked only for the rare athlete and is likely to hamper the athlete in developing community involvement and potential revenues from endorsements. Careful management of media interactions, then, becomes an asset.

The same concerns may be raised for the sport psychology consultant. Directing media to the press officer is often the safest way to avoid an errant comment. When the practitioner becomes the focus of a story, extreme caution must be exercised by the team and by the consultant. Although the original story may be a favorable account of the sport psychologist's activities, competing media sources are likely to reframe the idea in order to boost their own sales. A broad educational role, for example describing the purpose and techniques of applied sport psychology in performance enhancement, is perhaps the best subject for media interactions. Discussing team dynamics, coaching styles, and athlete preparedness may lead to a quick end to the consultant relationship with the sports organization.

Win or Lose, the Season Ends: Reflecting on the Consultation and Planning for the Future

After each involvement with elite athletes, it is important that practitioners evaluate the consultation process, including self-assessment, and elicit feedback from athletes, coaches, and administrators. Such a procedure is likely to provide valuable insights that can prepare consultants for future opportunities or for marketing themselves in another setting. The Consultant Evaluation Form developed by Partington and Orlick (1987a) may be a useful tool for this evaluation process.

Assessing the Effectiveness of the Consultation

In a study of consultants, administrators, coaches, and athletes, Gould and colleagues (1991) used the Consultant Evaluation Form to assess the characteristics of effective services provided to 25 NGBs. A similar process was used by Orlick and Partington (1987), with both studies providing a practical basis for comparing the results of self-evaluation. Ultimately, the goodness of fit with the organization and the use of the sport psychology consultant by the athlete are the measures of overall effectiveness. Shortcomings, however, may be the result of various elements that are beyond the control of the practitioner. Athletes, for example, may fear their coach; hence, they may fear the sport psychologist whose allegiance has been demanded by the coach. Beginning a consultation in a crisis management mode also is likely to influence its positive utility. The length of the relationship with an athlete or team may influence effectiveness. "Establishing initial rapport with coaches takes time. Yet the pressure on coaches of elite teams is for quick results," wrote Ravizza (1988, p. 247), contrasted with the opinion expressed by Orlick (1989), "In my best or most effective consulting situations I have enough time to make a difference, which means multiple contacts at the individual level. . . . Usually it takes about 3 years of ongoing work before things really come together mentally for highly committed athletes" (p. 363).

The evaluation process should include an assessment of the contracting body as well to determine what changes might enhance the implementation of consulting services in the future, even if these are with other athletes, teams, and coaches. For example, the following questions may need to be answered: Were adequate facilities made available to the consultant? What support did the coach provide for learning and practice of mental skills strategies? Could the issue of confidentiality and privilege have been better introduced or explained? Was enough time made available for consultations? Were team meetings (if any) appropriately scheduled and attended? This type of evaluation also is useful *during* the consultation process.

Contending With the End of a Relationship and Marketing Yourself Again

Athletes retire or are traded; coaches resign or are fired; and teams shift priorities or look for scapegoats in seasons of underachievement. For these and other reasons, the job of sport psychology consultant may come to an abrupt end. On occasion, consultants may make decisions to fire themselves.

Whether the practitioner's relationship continues with a team or NGB after significant personnel changes depends on the consultant's ability to market services to the new power brokers. When possible and appropriate, an introduction to the new coach, for example, is best made by the general manager or other team official, and done privately, with discussion about the effectiveness of the previous consultation. Sometimes, of course, the departure of a coach or general manager spells the beginning of a major house cleaning that is likely to include the sport psychologist. "The sign that you should take your Rorschach cards and run will be when you go to the box office for your free tickets to the game and find that the attendant has forgotten your name" (Ogilvie, 1979, p. 55).

The end of a consulting relationship also offers an appropriate opportunity for self-evaluation. Before marketing in search of a new contract, it may be helpful to reflect on success (or failure) in achieving the objectives of the previous consultation. Even if won–lost ratios and excellence in competition have not changed, more internal variables may be analyzed. These variables include, among others, the athletes' knowledge of sport psychology strategies, effective use of techniques, rapport between the athlete(s) and the sport psychologist, utilization of the sport psychologist, team cohesion, and athletic skill development. Between contracts is also a good time to consider necessary changes in service delivery, such as accessibility and availability of the consultant, communication with coaches, team versus individual sessions, and the model of consultation.

Letters of introduction or reference may be a suitable way to mark the end of a positive consultation process, while laying the foundation for the next contract. Testimonials, although now acceptable under APA ethical standards (APA, 1992), draw a range of responses from practitioners. Loehr (1990), for example, described negotiating endorsements by athlete–clients in lieu of financial remuneration. Because of the issues of confidentiality and barter raised by this approach, it is widely discouraged. Written evaluations by coaches and NGBs, instead of from athletes themselves, may be a more acceptable method for presenting documentation of previous experiences and accomplishments to potential clients. Cold calls, submission of proposals, and all the other procedures used previously should be used to search for another position.

No doubt, the end of a consultation may begin a trying time for the sport psychologist. There may be financial implications, and feelings of loss. Trying to find the next job can be just as difficult as trying to find the first. Even a positive reputation as a sport psychologist will not easily create a new elite- or professional-level position. As a result, the process of marketing, gaining access, and establishing the trust and respect of athletes and coaches begins again.

Summary

This chapter has provided a perspective on the role of the sport psychologist working with Olympic and professional athletes. Although this level of competition offers athletes the pinnacle of sport excellence, it also introduces new challenges for the provision of mental training or broader psychological interventions. Practitioners intending to work at this level must first gain experience in other sport settings to clarify, for themselves, issues such as the model of service delivery, negotiation of contracts, guarantees regarding confidentiality, and the scope of skills and programs they are competent to offer.

The difficulties of gaining access, earning the trust of athletes and coaches, providing effective service, and evaluating the usefulness of the consultation may make the provision of sport psychology with elite athletes a demanding and, at times, perilous process. As Ravizza (1990) wrote, "In every situation there is an ideal way to do your job, and then there is reality" (p. 331). In their profiles of 10 leading sport psychologists, Straub and Hinman (1992) cited the opinion of Tara Scanlan that "sport psychology is not for the faint hearted. She advises prospective sport psychologists to seriously assess the strength of their 'pioneering spirit.' Sport psychologists, Scanlan continues, often have to travel uncharted routes, and they should make sure they can handle the challenges" (p. 307).

The interested reader should study additional perspectives on consultation with elite athletes, such as those offered in *The Sport Psychologist*. We recommend supervised experience in beginning all levels of involvement, and we encourage the development and maintenance of a network of colleagues and mentors. Furthermore, we promote the attendance and contributions of consultants working in elite sport at conferences and in other forums that allow for the exchange of ideas or concerns and for the improvement of sport psychology techniques to be used with Olympic and professional athletes and teams.

References

American Psychological Association. (1992). Ethical principles of psychologists and code of conduct. *American Psychologist, 47,* 1597–1611.

Botterill, C. (1990). Sport psychology and professional hockey. *The Sport Psychologist, 4,* 358–368.

Burke, K. L., & Johnson, J. J. (1992). The sport psychologist–coach dual role position: A rebuttal to Ellickson and Brown (1990). *Journal of Applied Sport Psychology, 4,* 51–55.

Cerney, M. S. (1990). Reduced fee or free psychotherapy: Uncovering the hidden issues. *Psychotherapy Patient, 7,* 53–65.

Dorfman, H. A. (1990). Reflections on providing personal and performance enhancement consulting services in professional baseball. *The Sport Psychologist, 4,* 341–346.

Ellickson, K. A., & Brown, D. R. (1990). Ethical considerations in dual relationships: The sport psychologist–coach. *Journal of Applied Sport Psychology, 2,* 186–190.

Giges, B., & Petitpas, A. (2000). Brief contact interventions in sport psychology. *The Sport Psychologist, 14,* 176–187.

Gould, D., & Finch, L. (1990). Sport psychology and the professional bowler: The case of Michelle Mullen. *The Sport Psychologist, 4,* 418–430.

Gould, D., Murphy, S., Tammen, V., & May, J. (1991). An evaluation of U.S. Olympic sport psychology consultant effectiveness. *The Sport Psychologist, 5,* 111–127.

Greenleaf, C. A. (1999, August). Individual interviews with 1998 Nagano Olympic athletes. In D. Gould (Chair), *Factors influencing 1998 U.S. Olympic athlete and coach performance,* symposium conducted at the annual meeting of the American Psychological Association, Boston.

Halliwell, W. (1990). Providing sport psychology consulting services in professional hockey. *The Sport Psychologist, 4,* 369–377.

Jones, T. (2000, September 14). Calmer waters: Bulmer a veteran in the Olympic battle of nerves. *Calgary Sun,* p. 8.

Linder, D. E., Brewer, B. W., Van Raalte, J. L., & De Lange, N. (1991). A negative halo for athletes who consult sport psychologists: Replication and extension. *Journal of Sport and Exercise Psychology, 13,* 133–148.

Loehr, J. (1990). Providing sport psychology consulting services to professional tennis players. *The Sport Psychologist, 4,* 400–408.

Murphy, S. M. (1988). The on-site provision of sport psychology services at the 1987 U.S. Olympic Festival. *The Sport Psychologist, 2,* 337–350.

Neff, F. (1990). Delivering sport psychology services to a professional sport organization. *The Sport Psychologist, 4,* 378–385.

Ogilvie, B. (1979). The sport psychologist and his professional credibility. In P. Klavora & J. V. Daniel (Eds.), *Coach, athlete and the sport psychologist* (pp. 44–55). Champaign, IL: Human Kinetics.

Orlick, T. (1989). Reflections on sportpsych consulting with individual and team sport athletes at Summer and Winter Olympic Games. *The Sport Psychologist, 3,* 358–365.

Orlick, T., & Partington, J. (1987). The sport psychology consultant: Analysis of critical components as viewed by Canadian Olympic athletes. *The Sport Psychologist, 1,* 4–17.

Partington, J., & Orlick, T. (1987a). The Sport Psychology Consultant Evaluation Form. *The Sport Psychologist, 1,* 309–317.

Partington, J., & Orlick, T. (1987b). The sport psychology consultant: Olympic coaches' views. *The Sport Psychologist, 1,* 95–102.

Partington, J., & Orlick, T. (1991). An analysis of Olympic sport psychology consultants' best-ever consulting experiences. *The Sport Psychologist, 5,* 183–193.

Petitpas, A. J., Brewer, B. W., Rivera, P. M., & Van Raalte, J. L. (1994). Ethical beliefs and behaviors in applied sport psychology: The AAASP ethics survey. *Journal of Applied Sport Psychology, 6,* 135–151.

Ravizza, K. (1988). Gaining entry with athletic personnel for season-long consulting. *The Sport Psychologist, 2,* 243–254.

Ravizza, K. (1990). Sportpsych consultation issues in professional baseball. *The Sport Psychologist, 4,* 330–340.

Rotella, R. J. (1990). Providing sport psychology consulting services to professional athletes. *The Sport Psychologist, 4,* 409–417.

Straub, W. F., & Hinman, D. A. (1992). Profiles and professional perspectives of 10 leading sport psychologists. *The Sport Psychologist, 6,* 297–312.

Van Raalte, J. L., Brewer, D. D., & Linder, D. E. (1992). NCAA division II college football players' perceptions of an athlete who consults a sport psychologist. *Journal of Sport and Exercise Psychology, 14,* 273–282.

Yoken, C., & Berman, J. S. (1987). Third-party payment and the outcome of psychotherapy. *Journal of Consulting and Clinical Psychology, 55,* 571–576.

20 Diversity in Sport

Karen D. Cogan and Trent A. Petrie

If the mental health profession is to receive acceptance from racial/ethnic minority groups, it must demonstrate, in no uncertain terms, its good faith and ability to contribute to the betterment of a group's quality of life. (Sue & Sue, 1999, p. 24)

Despite a long-held belief within the field of counseling psychology concerning the importance of understanding and appreciating individual differences, constructive change in how many mental health professionals work with issues of diversity, at the individual and community level, has been slow in coming. For example, many graduate training programs operate from a predominantly Western orientation, in which learning about issues of diversity and multiculturalism are peripheral, and some mental health professionals hold to a worldview that considers minorities to be inherently pathological (Sue & Sue, 1999). Furthermore, because of inadequate training of mental health professionals, minority clients may be in therapy with therapists who lack the basic competencies for working ethically and effectively with diverse populations (Sue, Arredondo, & McDavis, 1992). Clearly, psychology and other mental health professions continue to face the challenge of how to adequately address the needs of minority populations.

Unfortunately, the field of sport and exercise psychology has fared no better with respect to diversity issues. Despite the inclusion of awareness of individual differences in Principle D, Respect for People's Rights and Dignity in the Association for the Advancement of Applied Sport Psychology's (AAASP, 1994) ethical principles, little attention has been paid to multiculturalism in sport and exercise psychology research, theory, and practice (Duda & Allison, 1990). Even the most current applied sport psychology textbooks (e.g., Andersen, 2000; Williams, 2001) fail to adequately address this issue.

This chapter directs attention to the important topic of diversity within sport by addressing four specific areas of individual differences: gender, race/ethnicity, sexual orientation, and physical disabilities. The purpose is to present information on the general and specific issues related to athletes from these four groups. Specifically, the chapter gives (a) a brief description of each group's involvement in sport, (b) an overview of empirical research covering the current status of each group, and (c) a summary of practical suggestions for how professionals might work more effectively with athletes from each group. To accomplish these goals, we have drawn from general psychology, sport psychology, and sport sociology literatures.

Gender

The Population

Since the early 1970s, women's and girls' participation in sport has increased dramatically as a result of new opportunities, legislative changes demanding equal treatment (Title IX), and greater publicity for female athletes (Coakley, 1998). The 1996 Atlanta Olympics was a breakthrough for American women, with gold medals captured in five team sports, including soccer, gymnastics, basketball, softball, and synchronized swimming. At the 2000 Sydney Olympics, approximately 4400 women (38% of competitors) participated, which was an increase from the 3513 women (34.1% of competitors) who participated in 1996 (Harasta, 2000).

Historically, though, sport psychology research has focused on male athletes' experiences, limiting the generalizability of findings. Fortunately, current research and scholarship are addressing gender issues more and more (e.g. Duda, 1991; Gill, 1994; Krane, 1994; Marsh, 1998), beginning the process of delineating how women's sport experiences differ from men's. Because of the relative lack of information on women in sport, we focus primarily on women's sport experiences in this section. We do so, recognizing that there are considerable within-group differences for men and women (Eccles, Barber, Jozefowecz, Malenchuk, & Vida, 1999).

Current Status

Any exploration of men's and women's sport experiences must consider the influence of societal factors. A primary factor, socialization, is defined as "the process whereby individuals learn the skills, values, norms, and behaviors enabling them to function competently in many different social roles within their group or culture" (Weiss & Glenn, 1992, p. 140). Historically and currently, society communicates through many outlets (e.g., school, family, television) the gender roles children are expected to adopt. In North America, boys usually are taught to be competitive, active, and independent, characteristics that are congruent with the general sport environment (Oglesby, 1983). Girls, however, are expected to be nurturing, kind, cooperative, and even passive (Ortner, 1974). Although females may view the general sport environment as inconsistent with their gender identity, certain sports, such as gymnastics and figure skating, may fit this female gender profile better than others (Csizma, Wittig, & Schurr, 1988).

During childhood, the groundwork is laid for future sport participation. In their model of activity choice, Eccles and colleagues (1983) proposed that gender role stereotypes and the beliefs and behaviors of significant socializing agents mediate expectancies and activity choices. These mediators can easily influence children's self-concepts, self-perceptions, perceived values of various activities, and performance expectations. Studying kindergartners through seventh graders, Eccles and Herold (1991) found that girls express more negative assessments of their general athletic ability than do boys, which appears to be more of a consequence of gender role socialization than of natural differences in sports aptitude.

In early adolescence, research has consistently found that European American girls' general self-esteem drops dramatically (American Association of University Women, 1990; Gilligan, 1990; Orenstein, 1994). African American girls' self-esteem, however, was higher than that of European-American girls and African American boys, suggesting that cultural factors may play a role in maintaining girls' self-esteem during adolescence (Eccles et al., 1999). With regard to sport-specific self-esteem, longitudinal studies of adolescents have shown that girls generally rate their sports abilities lower than boys do (Wigfield, Eccles, MacIver, Reuman, & Midgley, 1991). Girls also learn that general achievement and femininity are incompatible and thus they need to make a choice between the two (Eccles et al., 1999; Hyde, 1992). This conflict can create ambivalence and anxiety when a young woman is faced with a competitive or achievement-oriented environment (Eccles et al., 1999). Such a pervasive and limiting message may discourage some talented young athletes from persisting in sport (Allison, 1991).

Interestingly, however, both female and male adolescent elite athletes, and males in general, have systematically higher physical self-concepts than nonathletes and females (Marsh, 1998). The cause of this higher self-regard among adolescent female athletes is unknown, although participation in an elite sport environment may serve to protect them from the generally deleterious effects of society by offering opportunities to develop instrumental qualities.

During the traditional college years (ages 18 to 22), issues of separation and individuation arise for both men and women. College can be a stressful time, as students cope with increasing independence and financial responsibility, exposure to drugs and alcohol, identity development, and romantic and peer relationships. Parham (1993) argued that college student–athletes face additional challenges, such as balancing academics and athletics, isolation from the mainstream campus community, coping with athletic successes and failures, maintaining elite physical conditioning, and ending an athletic career, that make the resolution of these "normal" developmental tasks even more difficult. In addressing gender-specific stressors, Parham noted that female athletes often struggle with eating disorders or weight management issues, participating in sports with traditionally smaller budgets, and the societal biases concerning women's participation in sport. (See Cogan & Petrie, 1996, for a more thorough review of the effects of clinical issues; e.g., eating disorders and sexual abuse on women's sport experiences and performances.)

Concerning role conflict, which refers to the conflict between a woman's femininity (e.g., submissiveness, grace, beauty) and attributes needed to succeed in her sport (e.g., strength, achievement, aggressiveness), Allison (1991) suggested that it is a nonissue for women athletes. In fact, by focusing on this topic, sport psychologists are missing the "real" issue, which is the societal belief that women are supposed to experience such conflict. Female athletes, for the most part, seem comfortable with their roles. Thus, changes need to occur in society's attitudes toward women's participation in sport and not in the athletes themselves.

Another societal issue concerns negative stereotypes of female sport participants. Females who participate in sports such as basketball (Pedersen & Kono, 1990; Snyder & Spreitzer, 1983), softball, and track and field (Snyder & Spreitzer, 1983) may be stigmatized, viewed as unfeminine, and questioned about their sexual orientation (Krane, 1996; Snyder & Spreitzer, 1983). Some sports, however, such as gymnastics, tennis (Pedersen & Kono, 1990; Snyder & Spreitzer, 1983), and swimming (Snyder & Spreitzer, 1983), are considered more gender appropriate. Women who participate in such sports are chosen more often as a dating partner by men and as a best friend by women than those who participate in less gender-appropriate sports (Kane, 1988). Thus, society's biases can add an extra burden for women who participate in some sports.

Although women currently have more opportunities than ever to participate in sport at the collegiate and professional level (Coakley, 1998), they have fewer professional sport or coaching options compared with men (e.g., Acosta & Carpenter, 1992). Thus, from a career perspective, women continue to experience sport involvement differently than men. The upside is that women may harbor fewer unrealistic expectations about making a career out of sport and place more emphasis on obtaining an education (Meyer, 1990).

Intervention Strategies

Working With Women Athletes

Guidelines for working competently with women have been suggested for psychologists (American Psychological Association, 1975; Fitzgerald & Nutt, 1986) and can be applied to working with female athletes. First, sport psychology consultants must have some knowledge of how men's and women's socialization and sport experiences differ because of gender. Second, sport psychology consultants must be sensitive to circumstances in which a woman would work best with a female or a male counselor and make referrals as needed. With some issues such as sexual abuse or eating disorders, a female athlete might feel more comfortable working with a female consultant. However, some female athletes may relate better to or be more comfortable consulting with a male consultant. In the end, the sport psychology consultant must respect an athlete's wishes and assist her in determining who might best meet her needs. Third, sport psychology consultants should seek supervision or consultation with colleagues knowledgeable in this area if they are facing situations or issues about which they are unclear.

Female Sport Psychologists Working With Male Athletes

Female sport psychology consultants working with male athletes may face a variety of stereotypes because of their gender (Petrie, Cogan, Van Raalte, & Brewer, 1996). Athletes or coaches may question female consultants' competence, acceptability, and trustworthiness, citing the impression that women like to "gossip" and will not honor confidentiality, the possibility of attraction and transference, the view that women will be manipulative to get athletes to comply, and the perception that women are less knowledgeable about sport than men (Yambor & Connelly, 1991). Because sport remains primarily a male domain (Coakley, 1998), it is important for female consultants to recognize that these misperceptions exist and can interfere with their work with athletes and sport teams. It is useful to address the issues proactively at the beginning of consultation, exploring any concerns the male athlete or coach has about a female consultant's potential effectiveness.

Race, Ethnicity, and Athletes of Color

The Population

It is hard to imagine watching a televised sporting event—football, baseball, basketball, track and field, boxing—without seeing an athlete of color. These images suggest that athletes of color participate in all sports at high levels. Or do they? Outside of certain sports, such as professional and college football and baseball and professional basketball, where African Americans may be overrepresented, rates of participation among athletes of color are low. In fact, in most sports at most competitive levels, athletes of color, including African Americans, Latinos, Asian Americans, and Native Americans, are underrepresented or even nonexistent (Coakley, 1998).

There are many reasons for this underrepresentation in sport, including a long history of discrimination, denial of opportunities, stereotypes, immigration patterns of certain racial or ethnic groups, and inconsistencies among expectations in sport and cultural value systems (Coakley, 1998). Even today, in some sporting contexts, teams may appear segregated by race or ethnicity (e.g., Harris, 1994), and individuals of color are denied opportunities to advance in management positions (Coakley, 1998). Clearly, changes must occur within the structure of sport organizations and among coaches' belief systems if individuals of color are to gain the same access and opportunity to sport that is found in White middle- and upper-income communities.

Current Status

In 1990, Duda and Allison reviewed the sport and exercise psychology literature and found that researchers rarely addressed athletes of color, at either a conceptual or descriptive level. This analysis was presented as a wake-up call to the field, providing direction for how to examine the influences of cultural factors in sport and exercise. Since that time, research with athletes of color has increased, examining topics such as attributional style (Morgan, Griffin, & Heyward, 1996), goal orientation and achievement motivation (Gano-Overway, 1995; Hayashi, 1996), self-fulfilling prophecy (Solomon et al., 1996), social support (Harris, 1994), and ethnic identity (Hall, 1996), to name a few. Despite this needed increase, the picture of racial and ethnic minorities' athletic experience is only slightly more clear, with most available information pertaining to the experiences of African American athletes.

African American athletes are highly represented in certain sports, such as football, basketball, and track and field, but not so in others, such as soccer, softball, and equestrian. Many theories have been proposed to explain these differential patterns of sport participation among African American athletes (and other athletes of color), ranging from genetic explanations that have not been supported (e.g., Davis, 1990) to sociocultural factors that have proven more useful. Genetic and biological explanations, which were often based in a racist ideology, viewed African Americans as intellectually inferior to Whites, a way of thinking Coakley (1998) referred to as "race-logic." Such racism has been used to justify all forms of discrimination, ranging from athletes banned from professional sports or from certain athletic venues (e.g., golf courses) to racial and ethnic minorities not being given opportunities in coaching and management. Despite these obstacles, athletes of color have added to the development of sport and have begun to gain opportunities in coaching and athletic administration (e.g., Frank Robinson, Isaiah Thomas, Dennis Green).

From a sociological perspective, patterns of sport participation have been explained through the different social opportunities, motivations (e.g., financial), and community support that exist for racial and ethnic minorities. For example, African American children may have more opportunities to participate in certain sports, such as basketball and track and field, because of the low cost of equipment and the availability of places to train and compete. Furthermore, with many African American role models being athletes, African American boys may view athletic fame as the best way to escape poverty and attain financial security (Curry & Jiobu, 1984). Young African American athletes also may receive high levels of support from community members and coaches to pursue specific sports, such as basketball, which may encourage their current involvement and maintain their college and professional sport aspirations (Harris, 1994).

Unfortunately, the racism and discrimination that African American male athletes have faced throughout their lives can persist into college (Anshel, 1990; Parham, 1993). These athletes may have to deal with individuals, such as professors, coaches, and peers, who have little understanding of their culture (Anshel, 1990; Parham, 1993), coaches who are too authoritarian (Anshel & Sailes, 1990), and assumptions that they are in college only because of affirmative action (Scales, 1991) or an athletic scholarship. Such experiences can contribute to the general feelings of mistrust that African American male athletes report (Anshel & Sailes, 1990; Sellers & Damas, 1996) and leave them less willing to seek assistance from sport psychologists than their White counterparts (Martin, Wrisberg, Beitel, & Lounsbury, 1997; Sellers & Damas, 1996). Even so, African American male athletes report getting along well with their teammates and being generally satisfied with their college experience, including academics and athletics (Sellers, Kuperminc, & Damas, 1997).

Recent research has focused on the experiences of African American female athletes as well (Howard-Hamilton, 1993; Sellers et al., 1997; Stratta, 1995). Although these athletes may face psychological, societal, and cultural barriers to sport participation like their male counterparts, in college they experience little to no racial isolation or discrimination and almost never feel alienated or abused (Sellers et al., 1997). Furthermore, they reported few academic difficulties, such as having to repeat a class or being placed on probation, and felt that their involvement in athletics contributed to their personal development (e.g., learn social skills, be more assertive). Overall, African American female athletes were satisfied with their college experiences, including their academic and athletic performances.

Although the research discussed in this section provides some basic information about African American athletes, clearly more is needed to fully understand their experiences in sport and those of other racial and ethnic groups. It has been more than a decade since Duda and Allison (1990) made their call for greater inclusion of cross-cultural studies in sport and exercise psychology. Unfortunately, substantial attention still needs to be paid to this important issue.

Intervention Strategies

To be effective in multicultural contexts, sport psychology consultants must realize that their work (and athletes' reactions to this work) is influenced by larger social–political factors in our society (Sue & Sue, 1999). As such, consultants must deal with the racism that exists on personal and institutional levels and develop specialized knowledge and skills. Consistent with these statements, we offer the following suggestions for working more competently with athletes of color. In doing so, we freely acknowledge that consultants also must seek other sources of information, supervision, and continued education if they want to work effectively in multicultural contexts.

Acknowledge Biases and Racism

All individuals have biases and racial attitudes, which are products of growing up in a racist society. In the United States, this has been evident in the police bias charges from New York to California. Become aware of your own racial attitudes and biases and then work to limit their negative influence. Be willing to develop new and broader assumptions about human behavior (Sue & Sue, 1999), extending beyond the traditional Western views that permeate graduate psychology training. If you are White, recognize the privileges that you have and how these play a role (albeit unconscious at times) in interracial relationships (McIntosh, 1986).

Recognize Within-Group Differences

Do not assume that all the members of any racial or ethnic group are the same or that all athletes of color experience their race or ethnicity in the same manner. For example, the broad category of "Asian Americans" is made up of people from the following nationalities: Chinese, Japanese, Korean, Vietnamese, Thai, Hmong, Cambodian, Filipino, and East Indian, to name just a few. Clearly, tremendous variation exists within racial and ethnic minority groups, some of which may be due to acculturation (Atkinson, Morten, & Sue, 1993), racial identity development (e.g., Helms, 1995), or ethnic group affiliation. To understand an athlete solely (or even primarily) through the prism of his or her racial or ethnic group is to do that individual a disservice. Race or ethnicity is but one factor to consider when trying to understand an individual's worldview (Speight, Myers, Cox, & Highlen, 1991).

Develop Multicultural Skills and Knowledge

In addition to understanding within-group differences, consultants need to develop counseling skills, interventions, and knowledge that are multiculturally sensitive and to take into account the social, environmental, and cultural factors that broadly influence athletes of color (Sue & Sue, 1999). Learning about different worldviews, models of acculturation and racial identity, cultural mistrust, communication styles, family systems, non-Western or indigenous healing methods, and the histories and values of each specific racial or ethnic group will be an important first step in developing a multicultural knowledge base.

Address Societal Racism and Promote Institutional Change

This strategy involves the consultant moving beyond the role of individual change agent to confront problems at a societal and institutional level. Being an advocate for an oppressed group may be the most effective role for the sport psychology consultant depending on the circumstances (Atkinson, Thompson, & Grant, 1993). If consultants who have credibility and influence do not work to make changes in racist and discriminatory institutional policy and social practices, then athletes of color will continue to be oppressed by these powerful forces. Such advocacy can be as simple as providing diversity training to coaches and athletic department officials or as complex as helping sport organizations change policies regarding the recruitment and hiring of racial/ethnic minorities. If sport psychologists truly believe in the importance of developing positive, supportive sport environments for *all* athletes, then they must be willing to step forward to confront the racist and discriminatory practices, whether overt or subtle, that occur around them.

Sexual Orientation: Gay, Lesbian, and Bisexual (GLB) Athletes

The Population

Research using probability sampling methods indicates that 1.4% of women and 2.8% of men in the United States self-identify as homosexual. When actual same-gender sexual behaviors are considered, prevalence rates are slightly higher, ranging from 1.3% to 4.1% for women and from 2.7% to 4.9% for men (Laumann, Gagnon, Michael, & Michaels, 1994). In sport, researchers (e.g., Griffin, 1994; Heyman, 1986) have suggested that there is a higher percentage of lesbians than in the general population, although the exact percentage is unclear. Unfortunately, even less information has been published about gay and bisexual athletes. As Krane (personal communication, August 30, 2000) noted, it may be virtually impossible to determine accurate prevalence rates because most athletes are not open about their sexual orientation.

In the current status section, the primary focus is on the experiences of lesbian athletes because more research has been conducted in that area. In the intervention section, however, we offer general comments about working with GLB athletes as a group. In taking this approach, we do recognize that differences may exist among these three groups of athletes.

Current Status

Because of general societal homonegativity and heterosexual biases, a GLB athlete is likely to deal with the same issues that any other GLB individual would encounter (Cogan & Petrie, 1996). Such issues include but are not limited to (a) the need to conceal sexual orientation; (b) difficulty trusting others; (c) overt and subtle pressure from society, self, family, and or friends to change sexual orientation; (d) reconciliation of religious beliefs that may not condone a GLB lifestyle; and (e) a general assumption of a heterosexual life. Although a positive support system and strong self-identity can provide some protection (Krane, 1996), as a result of these pressures, GLB individuals may experience depression, anger, isolation, shame, anxiety, and confusion, and for athletes, poor sport performance.

GLB athletes also likely experience stressors that are unique to the sport environment (Krane, 1996, 1997; Lenskyj, 1991; Rotella & Murray, 1991), such as avoiding success for fear of being "outed" by the media, losing endorsement contracts because of their sexual orientation, and being encouraged (subtly and overtly) to leave the team or their sport. In addition, athletes have been passed over in selection processes because they have the appearance of being a lesbian, and coaches have not been hired because of a lesbian label (Wellman & Blinde, 1997).

For lesbian athletes, homonegativity and heterosexual bias are experienced not only from the broader society, but also from the sport environment. Negative stereotypes, in the forms of labeling, vulgarities, and derogatory media depictions, likely affect all lesbian athletes to some degree (Krane, 1996). In fact, Krane (1997) argued that the sport environment, in its current masculine form, is hostile toward lesbian athletes. She found that lesbian college athletes experience three major forms of homonegativism: (a) pressure to adhere to a feminine gender role and image (e.g., athletes may be dismissed from the team if they "look" too masculine), (b) labeling female athletes as lesbian as a way of stigmatizing them (e.g., athletes being assumed that they are lesbian because they are part of a specific team or teammates gossiping about other teammates or coaches), and (c) pressure to distance oneself from the lesbian label (e.g., making fun of other lesbians or not speaking out against homonegative or derogatory comments; Krane, 1997). Although Krane's (1996, 1997) theoretical model and research focused on the experiences of lesbian athletes, one can see how the previously stated components of homonegativism could apply to gay and bisexual athletes as well. Clearly, more research and scholarly discussion are needed to "transform the silence" (Vealey, 1997) surrounding GLB athletes. Through such a dialogue, sexual orientation may become a nonissue or simply a part of one's identity, and not the accusation, label, vulgarity, or stigma it currently is for so many athletes.

Intervention Strategies

Although not an exhaustive list, in this section we provide strategies for assisting GLB athletes at the individual and societal level.

Gain Self-Awareness

Sport psychology consultants who work with GLB athletes must be comfortable with their own and others' same-gender attractions. If the consultant is struggling with the acceptability of these feelings, supervision or a referral is in order.

Be Aware That Sexual Orientation Is Not Always an Issue

Do not assume that an athlete's sexual orientation is the primary reason for seeking assistance. Like any other athlete, GLB athletes will seek assistance from a sport psychology consultant for issues that are not directly linked to their sexual orientation. It is important to be open to discussing sexual orientation, but realize that GLB athletes may only want to focus on developing specific mental skills to enhance their performance.

Be Open and Supportive When Sexual Orientation Is an Issue

For athletes, sexual orientation may be a concern for several reasons. First, the athlete may be in the early stages of sexual identity development and may be confused about his or her feelings or behaviors. In such situations, normalizing their confusion and feelings and educating them on the process of developing a healthy sexual identity is in order. In addition, consultants can help GLB athletes develop a positive support system (Clark, 1987) to counter the sense of aloneness and isolation from teammates. To accomplish this goal, consultants need to be aware of available community resources and knowledgeable about GLB athlete role models (e.g., Martina Navratilova, Greg Louganis) and sport competitions, such as the Gay Games (Krane & Waldron, 2000).

Second, athletes may be in the process of making decisions regarding "coming out" to friends, family, teammates, and coaches. Such disclosure should always be the individual's decision, and the athlete should never be pressured to do so. If the athlete chooses to come out, it will be important to offer support, encouragement, patience, and understanding. Furthermore, the athlete might role play coming out with the consultant to become more comfortable with the process and to better anticipate reactions from others.

Third, because of homonegative team or athletic department environments, GLB athletes may feel pressure to "go along" with the negativity or face ridicule and isolation if they speak out against it. Thus, GLB athletes may seek counseling concerning how to cope with this situation. If that is the case, the consultant can support the athlete in his or her decision making, which may range from doing nothing to directly confronting the offending individuals to leaving the environment altogether. If the athlete chooses to confront the homonegativity, consultants may help him or her by role playing different approaches and discussing possible reactions.

Become an Advocate

As an advocate, sport psychology consultants can speak out against discrimination and prejudice (Krane, 1996) and educate those in positions of authority, such as coaches and athletic administrators, about the toxic effects of homonegativity and heterosexual bias. Although such an approach may have negative repercussions, such as being labeled "gay" and denigrated as a result, sport psychology professionals have an ethical and moral responsibility to make sport a positive environment for *all* participants. To limit such potential negative consequences and help their message be received, sport psychology professionals should be open, positive, and nonevaluative in their educational efforts.

Disabled Athletes

The Population

Athletes with disabilities, including, but not limited to, blindness, deafness, cerebral palsy, spinal cord injuries, and amputations, compete in local, regional, and national competitions in most sports (Asken, 1989). In the United States, several organized sport programs exist for persons with disabilities. For instance, at the international level, disabled athletes can compete in the Paralympics, which is an elite-level competition that parallels the Olympics. In fact, in the year 2000, approximately 4000 athletes with disabilities competed in the Sydney Paralympics, and in 2002, approximately 500 are expected to participate in the Salt Lake City Paralympic Games (Paralympic Games, n.d.). With so many athletes competing in national and international competitions, this is not a population that can be easily ignored by sport psychology consultants.

Although people with disabilities can partake in physical activity on a variety of levels, the information in this section focuses on competitive athletes with disabilities. Since 1986, the U.S. Olympic Festival has offered opportunities for athletes with disabilities to compete (Paciorek, Jones, & Tetreault, 1991), as have the Olympics for the Physically Disabled, the Special Olympics, and the Paralympics. In addition, the U.S. Olympic Committee has made a commitment to athletes with disabilities by acting as the National Paralympic Committee (NPC) for the United States. The United States is one of the few countries in which the Olympic and Paralympic committees are the same.

Current Status

Most research in this area has focused on comparing athletes with disabilities to those without disabilities on a variety of indicators. In general, this research has shown that the two groups of athletes, across sports such as marathon running, track and field, swimming, weightlifting, and table tennis, are similar to one another in terms of their mood states and psychological health (Henschen, Horvat, & Roswal,

1992; Horvat, French, & Henschen, 1986; Horvat, Roswal, & Henschen, 1991; Horvat, Roswal, Jacobs, & Gaunt, 1989) and their commitment to sport (Fung, 1992). Furthermore, Clark and Sachs (1991) found that the psychological skills of deaf athletes were more similar to than different from nonhearing impaired athletes. Likewise, athletes with disabilities have been found to be just as goal-oriented as able-bodied athletes (Martin, 1999).

Other research has focused on sport injury and sport transitions. Unfortunately, athletes with disabilities tend to lose more training time as a result of injury than do athletes without disabilities (Davis & Ferrara, 1995). This may be because many injuries (e.g., pressure sores) and illnesses (e.g., bladder infections) are directly related to the disability itself. Research on the transition out of sports (Martin, 1999), for example, due to injury, suggests that life transition models are applicable to the study of sport disengagement for athletes with disabilities as well. Factors associated with transitions out of sport include self-identity, postcareer planning, sport goal achievement, voluntary withdrawal, and social support (Martin, 1999). Clearly, the research suggests that although it is necessary to be cognizant of the athletes' disability and physical limitations, those athletes are likely to have many of the same psychological needs and abilities as their counterparts without disabilities.

Intervention Strategies

Historically, athletes with disabilities have been underserved by sport psychology consultants (Martin, 1999). Recently, however, consultants have acknowledged the importance of psychological skills training for this population (Hanrahan, 1998; Martin, 1999). In addition, because athletes with disabilities are generally very receptive to sport psychology interventions (Martin, 1999), sport psychology consultants may find working with these athletes a winning situation for all involved.

To be effective when working with athletes with disabilities, sport psychology consultants must recognize the unique needs of this population and have special knowledge in the following areas (Asken, 1991):

- the psychology of physical disability and the physical and psychological trauma these athletes may have experienced;
- the physiological and medical considerations unique to the disability that can influence future injury and performance;
- the complexities in motivation to compete, which range from the

usual desires for challenge and/or fitness to denial of the physical disability;

- performance problems, such as anxiety, that result from limitations associated with the disability;
- the varied organizational structure of wheelchair and competitive disabled sport (e.g., restricted funding and financial rewards so athletes may have mixed priorities with job demands, limited training time and facilities, and dealing with several sports at a time); and
- the social environment, such as physical and social barriers (e.g., the disability may get a negative reaction from the community and the individual may be stigmatized).

Although standard interventions may need to be adapted to fit the unique needs of the disability, athletes with disabilities can benefit from a wide range of performance enhancement skills, such as arousal control, attention and concentration, goal setting, self-talk, negative thought stopping, interpersonal and assertiveness skills training, confidence enhancement, imagery, and precompetition preparation (Asken, 1989; Hanrahan, 1998; Martin, 1999). Furthermore, Martin has suggested that sport psychology consultants work to create an environment that emphasizes the whole person and in which mental skills are taught so that they can be easily transferred to other life areas.

Conclusion

As illustrated in this chapter, issues of diversity have been overlooked in the sport and exercise psychology literature. Clearly, a need exists for additional research to help sport psychology consultants better understand diverse individuals' sport and exercise experiences and to help guide interventions. Our hope is that a decade from now, Duda and Allison's (1990) call for change is no longer applicable.

It is important for sport psychology consultants to become familiar with the general issues and characteristics that are known about minority groups. However, we caution consultants on using general information as the primary criterion for guiding assessment and interventions. Instead, we encourage sport psychology professionals to approach athletes from these groups as individuals, recognizing that culture or group membership is but one important factor that defines each person. As Sue and Sue (1990) noted, generalizations are a necessary part of human interaction, but they need to be applied tentatively and one must always be open to individual differences.

References

Acosta, R., & Carpenter, L. (1992). As the years go by: Coaching opportunities in the 1990s. *Journal of Physical Education, Recreation, and Dance, 63,* 36–41.

Allison, M. T. (1991). Role conflict and the female athlete: Preoccupation with little grounding. *Journal of Applied Sport Psychology, 3,* 49–60.

American Association of University Women. (1990). *Shortchanging girls, shortchanging America: Full data report.* Washington, DC: Author.

American Psychological Association. (1975). Report on the task force on sex bias and sex-role stereotyping in psychotherapeutic practice. *American Psychologist, 30,* 1169–1175.

Andersen, M. B. (Ed.). (2000). *Doing sport psychology.* Champaign, IL: Human Kinetics.

Anshel, M. H. (1990). Perceptions of Black intercollegiate football players: Implications for the sport psychology consultant. *The Sport Psychologist, 4,* 235–248.

Anshel, M. H., & Sailes, G. (1990). Discrepant attitudes of intercollegiate team athletes as a function of race. *Journal of Sport Behavior, 13,* 68–77.

Asken, M. J. (1989). Sport psychology and the physically disabled athletes: Interview with Michael D. Goodling, OTR/L. *The Sport Psychologist, 3,* 166–176.

Asken, M. J. (1991). The challenge of the physically challenged: Delivering sport psychology services to physically disabled athletes. *The Sport Psychologist, 5,* 370–381.

Association for the Advancement of Applied Sport Psychology. (1994). *Ethical principles of the Association for the Advancement of Applied Sport Psychology.* [Brochure]. Boise, ID: Author.

Atkinson, D. R., Morten, G., & Sue, D. W. (1993). *Counseling American minorities: A cross-cultural perspective.* Dubuque, IA: Brown & Benchmark.

Atkinson, D. R., Thompson, C., & Grant, S. (1993). A three-dimensional model for counseling racial/ethnic minorities. *The Counseling Psychologist, 21,* 257–277.

Clark, D. (1987). *The new loving someone gay.* Berkeley, CA: Celestial Arts.

Clark, R. A., & Sachs, M. (1991). Challenges and opportunities in psychological skills training in deaf athletes. *The Sport Psychologist, 5,* 392–398.

Coakley, J. (1998). *Sport in society: Issues & controversies.* Boston, MA: McGraw-Hill.

Cogan, K. D., & Petrie, T. A. (1996). Counseling women college student–athletes. In E. Etzel, A. Ferrante, & J. Pinkney (Eds.), *Counseling college student athletes* (pp. 77–106). Morgantown, WV: Fitness Information Technology.

Csizma, K. A., Wittig, A. F., & Schurr, K. T. (1988). Sport stereotypes and gender. *Journal of Sport and Exercise Psychology, 10,* 62–74.

Curry, T. J., & Jiobu, R. M. (1984). *Sports: A social perspective.* Englewood Cliffs, NJ: Prentice-Hall.

Davis, L. (1990). The articulation of difference: White preoccupation with the question of racially linked genetic differences among athletes. *Sociology of Sport Journal, 7,* 179–187.

Davis, R. W., & Ferrara, M. S. (1995). Sports medicine and athletes with disabilities. In K. P. DePauw & S. J. Gavron (Eds.), *Disability and sport* (pp. 133–149). Champaign, IL: Human Kinetics.

Duda, J. L. (1991). Editorial comment. *Journal of Applied Sport Psychology, 3,* 1–6.

Duda, J., & Allison, M. (1990). Cross-cultural analysis in exercise and sport psychology: A void in the field. *Journal of Sport and Exercise Psychology, 12,* 114–131.

Eccles (Parsons), J., Adler, T. F., Futterman, R., Goff, S. B., Kaczala, C. M., Meece, J. L., & Midgley, C. (1983). Expectations, values and academic behaviors. In J. T. Spence (Ed.), *Achievement and achievement motivation* (pp. 75–146). San Francisco: W. H. Freeman.

Eccles, J., Barber, B., Jozefowecz, D., Malenchuk, O., & Vida, M. (1999). Self-evaluations of competence, task values, and self-esteem. In N. G. Johnson, M. C. Roberts, & J. Worell (Eds.), *Beyond appearance: A new look at adolescent girls* (pp. 53–83). Washington, DC: American Psychological Association.

Eccles, J. S., & Herold, R. D. (1991). Gender differences in sport involvement: Applying the Eccles' expectancy-value model. *Journal of Applied Sport Psychology, 3,* 7–35.

Fitzgerald, L. F., & Nutt, R. (1986). The Division 17 principles concerning the counseling/psychotherapy of women: Rationale and implementation. *The Counseling Psychologist, 14,* 180–216.

Fung, L. (1992). Commitment to training among wheelchair marathon athletes. *International Journal of Sport Psychology, 21,* 138–146.

Gano-Overway, L. (1995). *Goal perspectives and their relationships to beliefs, affective responses and coping strategies among African and Anglo American athletes.* Unpublished master's thesis, Purdue University, West Lafayette, IN.

Gill, D. L. (1994). A feminist perspective on sport psychology practice. *The Sport Psychologist, 8,* 411–426.

Gilligan, C. (1990). *Making connections: The relational world of adolescent girls at the Emma Willard School.* Cambridge, MA: Harvard University Press.

Griffin, P. (1994). Homophobia in sport: Addressing the needs of lesbian and gay high school athletes. *The High School Journal, 77,* 80–87.

Hall, R. (1996). *Ethnic identity and cross racial experiences of college athletes.* Unpublished master's thesis, Temple University, Philadelphia.

Hanrahan, S. J. (1998). Practical considerations for working with athletes with disabilities. *The Sport Psychologist, 12,* 346–357.

Harasta, C. (2000, August 27). Women of the world. *Dallas Morning News,* pp. 1J, 10J.

Harris, O. (1994). Race, sport, and social support. *Sociology of Sport Journal, 11,* 40–50.

Hayashi, C. (1996). Achievement motivation among Anglo-American and Hawaiian male physical activity participants: Individual differences and social contextual factors. *Journal of Sport and Exercise Psychology, 18,* 194–215.

Helms, J. (1995). An update of Helms's White and people of color racial identity models. In J. G. Ponterotto, J. M. Casas, L. A. Suzuki, & C. M. Alexander (Eds.), *Handbook of multicultural counseling* (pp. 181–198). Thousand Oaks, CA: Sage.

Henschen, K., Horvat, M., & Roswal, G. (1992). Psychological profiles of the United States wheelchair basketball team. *International Journal of Sport Psychology, 23,* 128–137.

Heyman, S. R. (1986). Psychological problem patterns found with athletes. *The Clinical Psychologist, 39,* 68–71.

Horvat, M., French, R., & Henschen, K. (1986). A comparison of the psychological characteristics of male and female able-bodied and wheelchair athletes. *Paraplegia, 24,* 115–122.

Horvat, M., Roswal, G., & Henschen, K. (1991). In the field: Psychological profiles of disabled male athletes before and after competition. *Clinical Kinesiology, 45,* 14–18.

Horvat, M., Roswal, G., Jacobs, D., & Gaunt, S. (1989). Selected psychological comparisons of able-bodied and disabled athletes. *The Physical Educator, 45,* 202–208.

Howard-Hamilton, M. (1993). African-American female athletes: Issues and implications for educators. *NASPA Journal, 30,* 153–159.

Hyde, J. S. (1992). *Half the human experience: The psychology of women* (2nd ed.). Lexington, MA: D.C. Heath.

Kane, M. J. (1988). The female athletic role as a status determinant within the social systems of high school adolescents. *Adolescence, 23,* 253–264.

Krane, V. (1994). A feminist perspective on contemporary sport psychology practice. *The Sport Psychologist, 8,* 393–410.

Krane, V. (1996). Lesbians in sport: Toward acknowledgment, understanding, and theory. *Journal of Sport and Exercise Psychology, 18,* 237–246.

Krane, V. (1997). Homonegativism experienced by lesbian collegiate athletes. *Women in Sports and Physical Education Journal, 6,* 141–163.

Krane, V., & Waldron, J. (2000). The Gay Games: Creating our own sport culture. In K. Schafer & S. Smith (Eds.), *The Olympics at the millennium: Power, politics, and the Olympic games* (pp. 147–164). Piscataway, NJ: Rutgers University Press.

Laumann, E., Gagnon, J., Michael, R., & Michaels, S. (1994). *The social organization of sexuality: Sexual practices in the United States.* Chicago: University of Chicago Press.

Lenskyj, H. (1991). Combating homophobia in sport and physical education. *Sociology of Sport Journal, 8,* 61–69.

Marsh, H. W. (1998). Age and gender effects in physical self-concepts for adolescent elite athletes and nonathletes: A multicohort–multioccasion design. *Journal of Sport and Exercise Psychology, 20,* 237–259.

Martin, J. (1999). A personal development model of sport psychology for athletes with disabilities. *Journal of Applied Sport Psychology, 11,* 181–193.

McIntosh, P. (1986). *White privilege and male privilege: A personal account of coming to see correspondence through work in women's studies.* Working paper No. 189, Wellesley College, MA, Center for Research on Women. Available as EDRS document ED 335 262.

Morgan, L., Griffin, J., & Heyward, V. (1996). Ethnicity, gender, and experience effects on attributional dimensions. *The Sport Psychologist, 10,* 4–16.

Oglesby, C. A. (1983). Interactions between gender identity and sport. In J. M. Silva & R. S. Weinberg (Eds.), *Psychological foundations of sport* (pp. 387–399). Champaign, IL: Human Kinetics.

Orenstein, P. (1994). *School girls: Young women, self-esteem, and the confidence gap.* New York: Anchor Books.

Ortner, S. (1974). Is female to male as nature is to culture? In M. Rosaldo & L. Lamphere (Eds.), *Woman, culture and society* (pp. 67–87). Stanford, CA: Stanford University Press.

Paciorek, M. J., Jones, J., & Tetreault, P. (1991). Disabled athlete participation at the 1990 U.S. Olympic Festival. *Palaestra, 7,* 18–25.

Paralympic Games (n.d.). Retrieved January 8, 2001, from http://www.paralympic.org/

Parham, W. D. (1993). The intercollegiate athlete: A 1990's profile. *The Counseling Psychologist, 21,* 411–429.

Pedersen, D. M., & Kono, D. M. (1990). Perceived effects on femininity of the participation of women in sport. *Perceptual and Motor Skills, 71,* 783–792.

Petrie, T. A., Cogan, K. D., Van Raalte, J. L., & Brewer, B. W. (1996). Gender and the evaluation of sport psychology consultants. *The Sport Psychologist, 10,* 132–139.

Rotella, R., & Murray, M. (1991). Homophobia, the world of sport, and sport psychology consulting. *The Sport Psychologist, 5,* 355–364.

Scales, J. (1991). African American student-athletes: An example of minority exploitation in collegiate athletics. In E. Etzel, A. P. Ferrante, & J. Pinkney (Eds.), *Counseling College student-athletes: Issues and interventions* (pp. 71–99). Morgantown, WV: Fitness Information Technology.

Sellers, R., & Damas, A. (1996). The African American student athlete experience. In E. Etzel, A. P. Ferrante, & J. Pinkney (Eds.), *Counseling college student athletes: Issues and interventions* (pp. 55–76). Morgantown, WV: Fitness Information Technology.

Sellers, R., Kuperminc, G., & Damas, A. (1997). The college life experiences of African American women athletes. *American Journal of Community Psychology, 25,* 699–720.

Solomon, G., Wiegardt, P., Yusuf, F., Kosmitzki, C., Williams, J., Stevens, C., & Wayda, V. (1996). Expectancies and ethnicity: The self-fulfilling prophecy in college basketball. *Journal of Sport and Exercise Psychology, 18,* 83–88.

Snyder, E. E., & Spreitzer, E. (1983). Change and variation in the social acceptance of female participation in sports. *Journal of Sport Behavior, 6,* 3–8.

Speight, S. L., Myers, L. J., Cox, C. I., & Highlen, P. (1991). A redefinition of multicultural counseling. *Journal of Counseling and Development, 70,* 29–36.

Stratta, T. (1995). Cultural inclusiveness in sport—Recommendations from African American women college athletes. *Journal of Physical Education, Recreation and Dance, 66*(7), 52–56.

Sue, D. W., Arredondo, P., & McDavis, R. J. (1992). Multicultural competencies/standards: A call to the profession. *Journal of Counseling and Development, 70,* 477–486.

Sue, D. W., & Sue, D. (1990). *Counseling the culturally different: Theory and practice.* New York: Wiley.

Sue, D. W., & Sue, D. (1999). *Counseling the culturally different: Theory and practice* (3rd ed.). New York: Wiley.

Vealey, R. (1997). Transforming the silence on lesbians in sport: Suggested directions for theory and research in sport psychology. *Women in Sports and Physical Activity Journal, 6,* 61–107.

Weiss, M. R., & Glenn, S. D. (1992). Psychological development and female sport participation: An interactional perspective. *Quest, 44,* 138–157.

Wellman, S., & Blinde, E. (1997). Homophobia in women's intercollegiate basketball: Views of women coaches regarding coaching careers and recruitment of athletes. *Women in Sports and Physical Activity Journal, 6,* 165–188.

Wigfield, A., Eccles, J. S., MacIver, D., Reuman, D. A., & Midgley, C. M. (1991). Transitions at early adolescence: Changes in children's domain-specific self-perceptions and general self-esteem across the transition to junior high school. *Developmental Psychology, 27,* 552–565.

Williams, J. (2001). *Applied sport psychology: Personal growth to peak performance* (5th ed.). Mountain View, CA: Mayfield.

Yambor, J., & Connelly, D. (1991). Issues confronting female sport psychology consultants working with male students athletes. *The Sport Psychologist, 5,* 304–312.

Part V

Professional Issues

21 Education for Becoming a Sport Psychologist

Penny McCullagh and John M. Noble

In 1925, an early leader in applied sport psychology, Coleman Griffith, stated, "Although a great many men have hitherto used the words *psychology* and *athletics* in the same sentence, no one has, until the present, undertaken a thorough survey of all that might be done in the field" (p. 193, italics added). Griffith then suggested that psychologists could contribute to the sport field in three ways. One way was to demonstrate to young coaches the psychological principles practiced by experienced coaches. The second was to apply principles discovered in the laboratory to sport, and the third was for psychologists to expose coaches to a scientific approach to use in their coaching techniques. Thus, the interdisciplinary nature of psychology and physical activity has a well-established legacy. This chapter highlights the educational and career paths available to aspiring sport and exercise psychologists.

Adequately defining the term *sport psychologist* is challenging. Because the term *psychologist* is restricted by laws in each state and typically refers only to an individual schooled in mainstream psychology, an individual with a training emphasis in sport and exercise should not technically be called a "psychologist." For simplification, we use "sport psychologist" in a broad sense to refer to an individual working from either a research or applied perspective in the area of human movement. The *sport* component of the term also causes confusion because work is often conducted outside of the sport setting. It must be emphasized that sport psychology extends well beyond the sport environment and includes exercise, rehabilitation, and other domains in which basic movement skills are of importance (Rejeski & Brawley, 1988).

Potential graduate students often ask where sport psychologists are best trained: in a psychology department or in a program emphasizing the exercise sciences? Although it is true that sport psychologists typically receive their degrees from either a psychology department or a kinesiology/physical education department, directing students toward a particular department depends on a variety of issues, most notably, specific career goals and interests.

Training in Kinesiology

Although many might think that the field of sport psychology has emerged only in the past decade or two, this view is refuted by the previous Griffith (1925) quote. Furthermore, as early as the 1960s, sport psychology classes were being offered in numerous physical education programs across the country, and numerous sport psychology textbooks became available (e.g., Cratty, 1968; Lawther, 1972; Martens, 1975; Morgan, 1970; Singer, 1975). Many early sport psychology classes focused on the application of psychological principles to teaching and coaching. As physical education departments moved from a teacher preparation focus to a research focus, the role of sport psychology within these departments also changed. During this period, many departments of physical education selected other names, such as *exercise science, movement science, sport science,* and *kinesiology,* to reflect this research emphasis and a move away from a sole emphasis on physical education teaching. For the purposes of this chapter, "kinesiology" refers to the broad realm of movement-oriented fields of study.

The majority of academics involved in sport psychology during the 1950s, 1960s, and 1970s were working in kinesiology departments. These were the people most instrumental in the establishment of academic societies and scholarly conferences devoted to sport psychology. The International Society of Sport Psychology first met in Rome in 1965, and the North American Society for the Psychology of Sport and Physical Activity was organized in 1967. The *International Journal of Sport Psychology* was established in 1970 and the *Journal of Sport Psychology* in 1979. These organizations and journals were devoted to the development of a knowledge base in sport psychology and the dissemination of that information, and they continue to serve that role today (see Exhibits 21.1, 21.2, and 21.3 for a listing of organizations and journals).

Exhibit 21.1

Professional Organizations Dealing Totally or Partially With Sport and Exercise Psychology

- American Alliance for Health, Physical Education, Recreation and Dance (www.aahperd.org)
  This is a very large organization with one small section, the Sport Psychology Academy, devoted to sport psychology.
- American College of Sports Medicine (www.acsm.org)
  This organization is a very large society that focuses on numerous subdisciplines, including exercise physiology, biomechanics, sport psychology, fitness, and wellness.
- American Psychological Association (www.apa.org)
  This is a very large organization with one section devoted completely to sport psychology, Division 47 (Exercise and Sport Psychology).
- Association for the Advancement of Applied Sport Psychology (www.aaasponline.org)
  This society is devoted entirely to sport psychology.
- Canadian Society for Psychomotor Learning and Sport Psychology (www.scapps.org)
  This organization focuses on motor learning/control, motor development, and sport psychology.
- International Society for Sport Psychology (www.phyed.duth.gr/sportpsy/)
  This international society focuses on motor learning, development, and sport psychology.
- North American Society for the Psychology of Sport and Physical Activity (www.naspspa.org)
  This organization focuses on motor learning/control, sport psychology, and motor development.

Undergraduate Programs

Before specific training in sport psychology, students at the undergraduate level typically receive a broad-based education in kinesiology that can range from biologically based fields to behavioral and social sciences to the humanities. Basic courses at the undergraduate level usually include exercise physiology, biomechanics, motor learning and control, sport sociology, and sport and exercise psychology. Some universities also include courses in the history and philosophy of sport. Many of these courses have prerequisites in the parent disciplines of psychology, biology, chemistry, physics, and sociology. Depending on the academic focus of the kinesiology department, many programs offer specialized tracks that prepare students for professional careers. For

---

Exhibit 21.2

Journals Dealing Primarily With Sport and Exercise Psychology Issues

- *International Journal of Sport Psychology*
  Official publication of the International Society of Sport Psychology. Publisher: Pozzi, Rome, Italy. Begun in 1970.
- *Journal of Applied Sport Psychology*
  Official publication of the Association for the Advancement of Applied Sport Psychology. Publisher: Taylor & Francis, Philadelphia, PA. Begun in 1989.
- *Journal of Sport and Exercise Psychology*
  Official publication of the North American Society for the Psychology of Sport and Physical Activity. Publisher: Human Kinetics, Champaign, IL. Begun in 1979.
- *Journal of Sport Behavior*
  Publisher: United States Sport Academy, Mobile, AL. Begun in 1978.
- *The Sport Psychologist*
  Official publication of the International Society of Sport Psychology. Publisher: Human Kinetics, Champaign, IL. Begun in 1987.

Note. An excellent electronic resource for accessing these journals is Sport Discus. Most university libraries have this as a resource on their electronic database.

example, programs may prepare students for athletic training, fitness management, coaching, teaching physical education, or sport administration. Other programs are not professional-based but provide a liberal arts degree that may lead to graduate training in such medically related fields as physical therapy, physician assistant, occupational therapy, nursing, and medicine or to further research within the field of kinesiology. Regardless of the focus of the program, most departments offer an undergraduate course in sport psychology that may be titled "Psychology of Physical Activity," "Sport and Exercise Psychology," or "Psychological Basis of Human Movement."

Questions frequently arise about the rationale for taking movement-related courses in areas beyond the psychology of sport and exercise. This may be best explained by briefly describing each area and its importance to the sport psychologist. First, *exercise physiology* is the study of the body's function during exercise (Brooks, Fahey, & White, 1996). Although the topics covered in any one course may vary, several issues are especially relevant for individuals interested in sport and exercise psychology, including body composition, nutrition, training in

Exhibit 21.3

Journals Dealing Regularly With Sport and Exercise Psychology Issues

- *Medicine and Science in Sport and Exercise*
  Official journal of the American College of Sports Medicine. Publisher: ACSM, Madison, WI. Begun in 1969.
- *Pediatric Exercise Science*
  Official journal of the North American Society of Podiatric Exercise Science. Publisher: Human Kinetics, Champaign, IL. Begun in 1989.
- *Research Quarterly for Exercise and Sport*
  Official publication of the Research Consortium of the American Alliance for Health, Physical Education, Recreation and Dance. Publisher: AAHPERD, Washington, DC. Begun in 1930.

altitude or other environmental conditions, fatigue, sex differences, and special populations.

Second, *biomechanics* is "concerned with the internal and external sources acting on a human body and the effects produced by these forces" (Hay, 1985, p. xv). Determining what is mechanically unsound about a particular movement pattern is primarily the domain of coaches and biomechanists, but it is important for the aspiring sport psychologist to be schooled in these basic principles.

Third, many undergraduate courses in motor learning and control examine the processes underlying the principles of skilled learning and performance in teaching, coaching, and rehabilitation settings. Information processing and attention, the role of feedback in motor skills learning, strategies for designing effective practice sessions, and the assessment of motor memory are central issues to this field (see Schmidt & Lee, 2000).

In contrast to exercise physiology, biomechanics, and motor learning and control, sport sociology focuses on a macroscopic level on specific categories, or groups, of people. Sport sociologists examine the connection between sports and other spheres of social life, including family, education, social class, ethnicity, disability, economy, and religion (Coakley, 2001). Other topics of interest include socialization factors, drug use, aggression, and media or political issues.

Typical sport and exercise psychology classes within kinesiology departments focus on the research and application of psychological principles in movement, sport, and exercise settings. Specifically, these courses focus on antecedent variables that may predispose an individual to engage in physical activity or on the consequences of participation in physical activity on a host of psychological characteristics. Basic topics covered may include anxiety and arousal effects on physical activity, attention, motivation, gender differences, aggression, group dynamics, modeling, socialization, and exercise adherence. Application of mental imagery, goal setting, and relaxation skills to physical activity settings are also likely to be included, and numerous textbooks that address these and other topics are available.

Although these courses may cover the basics, numerous other classes could add to an individual's movement-based education. Courses in sports medicine, sport history and philosophy, and sport nutrition, as well as classes that focus on the teaching of sport skills, may be useful to the sport psychologist. Taking courses in these specialty areas by no means makes one an expert. However, it should provide the consultant or researcher increased knowledge to allow better communication with athletes, clients, coaches, and study participants.

Graduate Programs

At the graduate level, training in sport and exercise psychology becomes more specialized. The *Directory of Graduate Programs in Applied Sport Psychology* (Sachs, Burke, & Schrader, 2000) lists more than 100 programs. For the most part, these programs are housed in kinesiology departments. If you intend to search for these programs through Web-based university home pages, the programs may be difficult to find. First, one does not receive a PhD in sport psychology; one receives a PhD in kinesiology (or physical education, exercise science, or human performance), with a specialization in sport psychology. Second, the departments may be housed in a variety of colleges, ranging from schools of education to colleges of arts and sciences or health and human services.

Typically, students complete a master's degree before being selected for a PhD program. To gain admission to a master's program, students generally must provide evidence that they have completed prerequisites in kinesiology-based courses. If students come from another discipline, such as psychology, they may need to complete these courses as part of their graduate training.

The breadth of course offerings in graduate programs and the focus of programs are diverse. Programs tend to take either a basic research approach to the topic of sport and exercise psychology, an applied approach in which emphasis is on interventions to enhance performance, or some combination of research and practice. Prospective students should carefully weigh the pros and cons of each approach and how each will enhance their respective needs.

Individuals are advised to carefully examine the *Directory of Graduate Programs in Applied Sport Psychology,* as well as *The World Sport Psychology Sourcebook* (Salmela, 1992), for more information on specific programs. The *Graduate Training and Career Possibilities in Exercise and Sport Psychology* brochure (American Psychological Association [APA], 1994; www.psych.unt.edu/apadiv47/careers.htm) is also a useful source of information.

A typical sport psychology graduate program (master's or PhD) in a kinesiology department includes courses in research methods and statistics, motor behavior (motor development, motor learning and control), and other advanced courses (biomechanics, exercise physiology, sport sociology). These programs will likely require supportive courses outside the discipline in sociology, psychology, educational psychology, or perhaps anthropology. At the graduate level, students typically enroll in two or more sport psychology courses that focus on such topics as applied issues in sport psychology, youth sport, social psychological aspects of physical activity, psychophysiological approaches, or exercise motivation. Depending on the focus of the program, students could also engage in internships working in sport or exercise settings under the supervision of an adviser.

One basic purpose of most graduate programs in kinesiology departments is to conduct research. Much of this research may be applied research, and many programs offer opportunities to practice sport psychology consulting. At the PhD level, students may become involved with various aspects of their adviser's research program before moving on to more independent experiences. Training students to conduct presentable and publishable research in an ethical fashion is an important concern within such graduate programs. The adviser's primary role is to mentor students for a future career. A survey of 175 sport psychology graduate students indicated that approximately half were pleased with the current level of training in research and writing and in ethical standards for publications and presentations (Butki & Andersen, 1994). However, the other half expressed that their training on these topics was either fair or poor, suggesting the need for improved training. The topic of ethical considerations across a wide variety of academic settings, including human and animal research, teaching, and advising, is an important one and was addressed by The Academy of Kinesiology and Physical Education, and an entire issue of *Quest* (Thomas & Gill, 1993) was devoted to these topics.

The Association for the Advancement of Applied Sport Psychology (AAASP) has developed competencies in 12 areas for individuals who desire to become certified consultants (see Zizzi, Zaichkowsky, & Perna, chapter 22, in this volume, devoted to certification). Van Raalte, Brown, Brewer, Avondoglio, Hartmann, and Scherzer (2000) did an online survey of 79 graduate programs to determine whether universities offered coursework that met the AAASP standards. The majority of programs they studied were housed in kinesiology departments. Only 25% of the schools offered coursework that fulfilled all 12 specified content areas. They did identify some limitations in their data collection procedures; nonetheless, they noted that students interested in becoming AAASP certified would have to be alert to the course offerings available at their universities and to the AAASP certification requirements.

Training in Psychology

Undergraduate Programs

Most psychology departments are housed in a college of arts and sciences and provide students with a liberal-arts undergraduate degree. The purpose of a psychology degree is to achieve a broad understanding of the content, concepts, and research methods of contemporary psychology. *Psychology*, recognized as a fairly young science, has been defined as "the scientific study of behavior and mental processes" (Atkinson, Atkinson, Smith, & Hilgard, 1987, p. 13). Psychologists can serve a variety of functions, and an array of coursework is necessary to adequately encompass the field. For example, subdisciplines within psychology include biological, neuro-, developmental, social, cognitive, organizational, and clinical, to name just a few.

Typically, undergraduate students take coursework across this entire spectrum of psychology. Of course, the emphasis and course offerings vary depending on the expertise of faculty members at any particular college or university. The emphasis in psychology departments typically does not address human movement issues, particularly sport and exercise. An article in the APA's *Monitor* in 1982 recognized the huge potential for sport and exercise psychology and suggested it would move from the "back stairs to the center court." However, a survey of psychology department chairs revealed that only 15% of 102 respondents offered an undergraduate course in sport psychology (LeUnes & Hayward, 1990). The majority of such courses are offered in kinesiology departments. Recently, an increasing number of psychologists have examined exercise-related issues from a social or health psychology perspective.

Graduate Programs

Graduate students in psychology departments focus on any one of the previously mentioned specialization areas. Very few psychology departments offer specialties in sport psychology, and students are likely to get experience in sport psychology only if particular faculty members have these interests. Springfield College in Massachusetts has offered a unique program in its psychology department since 1982. Students are able to combine their interests in counseling with sport psychology and gain a master's degree in psychology with an emphasis in athletic counseling. Springfield College does not offer a doctorate in psychology, however. Most graduate students in psychology departments who are interested in sport psychology choose to earn a PhD or PsyD in clinical or counseling psychology. The PhD is generally a research-oriented degree, whereas the PsyD is designed for individuals who want to engage in applied practice and has less emphasis on research. Entrance to clinical and counseling psychology programs is extremely competitive. Many programs have several hundred applicants for only five or six positions.

Clinical psychology is the "application of psychological principles to the diagnosis and treatment of emotional and behavioral problems" (Atkinson et al., 1987, p. 15). Clinical psychologists typically work with people with mental illness, personality disorders, criminal behavior, drug addiction, eating disorders, or other behavior problems. Clinical psychologists work in mental hospitals, juvenile courts, mental health clinics, prisons, medical schools, or private practice. Recently, some private schools such as the Argosy University have initiated MA and PsyD clinical degrees that offer specializations in sport psychology.

Counseling psychologists often deal with less serious problems and help individuals with social adjustments or vocational issues. Although some psychology faculty members may have interests in sport and exercise psychology (LeUnes & Hayward, 1990), it is clearly not the main focus of most programs. A survey of counseling psychology programs (Petrie & Watkins, 1994) found that only 7.5% of the programs offered courses in sport psychology. Students may choose clinical or counseling psychology as a first option, because in these programs they are trained to help a wide range of people, their services are reimbursable, and they are eligible to be licensed. If a student wants to pursue a counseling or clinical degree and apply some of their knowledge to athletes, he or she should carefully discuss these options with faculty advisers before choosing a program. Once they select a program, students must obtain sufficient knowledge in the kinesiological sciences to facilitate this application. To obtain further information about graduate training in psychology, consult *The Complete Guide to Graduate School Admission: Psychology, Counseling, and Related Professional Fields* (Keith-Spiegel & Wiederman, 2000).

What options do individuals have if they already have been trained in clinical or counseling psychology and want to make a transition and include sport psychology as part of their practice? Some psychologists have chosen to complete AAASP certification requirements. This typically requires the completion of additional courses in kinesiology and participation in supervised practice with sport, exercise, or rehabilitation clients. With increasing Internet sources available, some of these courses can now be completed online. Some believe that this process is rather cumbersome for practicing psychologists, and the Executive Board of Division 47 of the APA is investigating some alternatives to assist psychologists in gaining competencies in the field of sport and exercise psychology.

Practicing Sport Psychology

Faculty members receive innumerable queries from students interested in sport psychology programs. Most students, having reviewed the *Directory of Graduate Programs,* are well-prepared with questions about the research versus applied nature of the programs. We have found the differentiation troublesome and emphasize the need to clarify some terminology.

It is meaningful to make a distinction between applied research and practice (McCullagh, 1998). *Applied research* attempts to either develop theory or find solutions to immediate problems in sport psychology. A majority of research, including much of our own, falls into this category. We prefer to use the term *practice* to refer to the use of interventions in sport psychology, or what Andersen (2000) has called "doing sport psychology." Thus, if a person simply asks whether a program is applied, it is not clear whether they mean applied research or practice.

Graduate training in the practice of sport psychology varies widely, depending on the type of program and the faculty involved. Waite and Pettit (1993) surveyed doctoral graduates in sport psychology from 1984 to 1989. On the basis of responses from program directors, they identified 55 graduates, 34 of whom returned surveys. Almost all the students had graduated from kinesiology programs. Although many identified their program emphasis as applied sport psychology, 44% said they had not received practical experiences with athletes, and many were concerned about this deficit in their training.

Andersen, Williams, Aldridge, and Taylor (1997) conducted a more extensive study of sport psychology graduates from 1989 to 1994. They received surveys from 162 master's program graduates and 92 doctoral graduates. Of the master's students, 66% had completed an internship with athletes. Of those who reported consulting with athletes as a career goal, 21% had no practicum experience. For doctoral candidates, there was a difference in experience for those in kinesiology compared with psychology programs. For kinesiology students, 63% had a practicum with athletes, whereas 75% of the psychology students had this experience. It was found that psychology students received an average of 379 client contact hours with athletes, whereas kinesiology students received only 226 hours. To be considered for AAASP certification, individuals need 400 hours of contact. Andersen and colleagues noted that practical experience had increased since the last survey and also that not all students want practical experience, so assessing mean data may be inappropriate.

Because many graduate students and professionals are interested in practice, some concerns about the level of supervision of practical experiences in sport psychology have been raised (Andersen, 1994). Helping professionals (athletic trainers, clinical psychologists) typically have well-documented procedures for supervision. However, sport psychology has only recently begun to address this issue. Petitpas, Brewer, Rivera, and Van Raalte (1994) conducted an ethics survey and found that only 6% of the respondents had formal coursework in supervision. In a follow-up study directly related to supervision, Andersen, Van

Raalte, and Brewer (1994) found that of those individuals who were supervising trainees, 56% had never received supervision of their own work. Van Raalte and Andersen (2000) reiterated that supervision is necessary to ensure the well-being of the client and serves as a professional development tool for practitioners. They offered several models of supervision that could be used to guide supervisory practice.

Another recent concern regarding the practice of sport psychology is that of impairment (Andersen, Van Raalte, & Brewer, 2000). The issue of impairment has been examined in the mainstream counseling and clinical psychology literature for several years. *Impairment* refers to a service provider whose own personal problems or characteristics have a detrimental effect on practice. Andersen and colleagues (2000) suggested that it may be time to examine this issue among sport psychology professionals to ensure the well-being of sport psychologists, student trainees, and clients receiving sport psychology services.

Employment Opportunities

Employment opportunities differ for students from kinesiology and students from counseling and clinical psychology. The primary employment opportunity for individuals trained in kinesiological psychology at the PhD level is an academic position (Andersen et al., 1997; Waite & Pettit, 1993). This academic position may or may not involve opportunities to work with individuals in performance enhancement settings. The primary responsibilities of academicians are research, teaching, and service, and the relative importance of these responsibilities varies. For example, some departments may view delivery of sport and exercise psychology services as a viable role that contributes to tenure and promotion, whereas other universities place heavy emphasis on data-based research published in refereed journals. Most academic positions require teaching in sport and exercise psychology, and many include teaching in other related fields (e.g., statistics, motor learning).

Examination of the characteristics of individuals publishing in sport and exercise psychology journals indicates a shift from the early to latter 1980s. In the first six years of its existence (1979–1985), 65% of the *Journal of Sport and Exercise Psychology* (renamed from the *Journal of Sport Psychology*) authors were from kinesiology/physical education departments and 21% were from psychology or clinical programs (Landers, Boutcher, & Wang, 1986). From 1985 to 1990, 54% of papers came from kinesiology/physical education departments, 29% from psychology, and 18% from other areas (sociology, medicine, business, counseling; Gill, 1992). These trends may be indicative of the growing interest in sport psychology in mainstream psychology. Most of the academic jobs with an emphasis in sport psychology, however, are in kinesiology departments rather than in psychology departments.

Academic applied sport psychology professors may do practical work with the athletic teams on campus or may provide information to youth sport leagues or professional teams. Consultation with sports medicine or physical therapy clinics is also a potential means of providing services. Because individuals trained in kinesiological psychology are not qualified to deal with clinical issues (e.g., eating disorders, depression), their primary role is one of education or performance enhancement. Unfortunately, providing such services is not necessarily a financially lucrative route (Andersen et al., 1997).

Although an academic career is probably the most prevalent one for individuals trained in kinesiology, alternative possibilities exist and are dependent on the specific training and creativity of those individuals. These alternatives include jobs in coaching, corporate fitness, consulting on psychological performance issues in business, and rehabilitation and other allied health fields. The U.S. Olympic Committee and some universities have hired sport psychologists to work with their athletes on a full-time basis, but very few of these positions exist.

Limited employment possibilities exist for individuals who complete their graduate training in sport psychology before obtaining the PhD. For example, a master's degree in clinical or counseling psychology (with coursework in kinesiology) or a master's degree in kinesiology (with coursework in psychology) might prepare a person to work in academic advising, health promotion, or coaching. A person with a master's degree may not be a "psychologist" in most states, nor will he or she have the necessary credentials to obtain the status of "certified consultant" by AAASP (see Zizzi, Zaichkowsky, & Perna, chapter 22, this volume). Thus, although not exactly becoming a "sport psychologist," one may obtain employment with a master's degree in the psychological aspects of human movement. In a few states, master's-level professionals with clinical or counseling training may be certified and deliver reimbursable services.

Career options for individuals in psychology are diverse. In one excellent resource (Sternberg, 1997), especially for students or individuals changing careers, psychologists from numerous career paths—including school psychology, private practice, counseling and clinical psychology, academia, and health psychology—provide insights on their careers. Also, the APA provides excellent information about employment opportunities on its Web page (www.apa.org). Other online sources of employment information for careers in sport and exercise psychology are included in Exhibit 21.4.

Integration

For a person to be well-equipped to deal with sport and exercise psychology issues, he or she must have training in both psychology and kinesiology. Depending on the career path chosen, the emphasis from these disciplines will vary. People interested in applying interventions (whether they come from a psychological or kinesiological background) need to understand the research process to evaluate the effectiveness of the interventions. For example, individuals wanting to help athletes cope with stress must have sufficient psychological knowledge about coping behaviors and sources of stress as well as knowledge about the particular sport they are dealing with. Likewise, researchers must understand and help impart the practical applications of the knowledge they generate. Thus, although it is not necessary to obtain a degree from both psychology and kinesiology departments, it is imperative to receive adequate training in both areas to fulfill the likely requirements of future employment in sport and exercise psychology (Petitpas et al., 1994; Taylor, 1991; Van Raalte et al., 2000).

Exhibit 21.4

Online Sources for Employment Opportunities Related to Sport and Exercise Psychology

- Association for the Advancement of Applied Sport Psychology (www.aaasponline.org)
- Chronicle of Higher Education (www.chronicle.merit.edu)
- Human Kinetics Publishers (www.hkusa.com)
- National Association for Physical Education in Higher Education (www.napehe.org)
- National Collegiate Athletic Association (www.ncaa.org)
- North American Society for Psychology of Sport and Physical Activity (www.naspspa.org)

Figure 21.1 provides a taxonomy for the education and roles of individuals trained in the different disciplines and with different interests. Sage advice would be to carefully determine where one wants to fall in this taxonomy and follow the appropriate educational route to achieve that goal. Although these appear to be four mutually exclusive categories, anyone operating within the field of sport and exercise psychology should have knowledge of the other quadrants. Also note that the same general issue might be examined from the perspective of any particular quadrant. For example, psychological factors associated with sport and exercise injury are currently a hot topic in the field and may fall within any of these categories.

Current Issues

Several significant issues currently hover over the field of sport psychology. Some of these issues have been discussed and debated for several years, whereas others have surfaced only recently. These professional issues include certification as a sport psychologist, the realm of sport psychology, ethical principles involved in the practice of applied sport psychology, and defining the field. Many of these issues became prevalent in the late 1970s and 1980s with the publication of new journals devoted to the psychology of sport and physical activity (see, e.g., Danish & Hale, 1981, 1982; Dishman, 1983; Harrison & Feltz, 1979; Heyman, 1982; Nideffer, DuFresne, Nesvig, & Selder, 1980). Developing issues of concern to the field are debated in any number of journals and newsletters and at annual conventions.

A recent concern that has been raised but not adequately addressed is multicultural training for sport psychology consultants. Martens, Mobley, and Zizzi (2000) made a strong case for including such training in sport psychology graduate programs. Also, Silva, Conroy, and Zizzi (1999) argued that accreditation of sport psychology programs is critical for enhancing and maintaining the field. Others (e.g., Hale & Danish, 1999) convincingly argued that other options for the development of the field provide a more balanced approach.

Conclusion

Many options are available for pursuing educational goals related to the field of exercise and sport psychology. Some of the major decisions are

Figure 21.1

ACADEMIC TRAINING AREA

PRIMARY INTEREST AREA	Kinesiology		Psychology	
	Employment Opportunities	Typical Issues	Employment Opportunities	Typical Issues
Research	1. Academic 2. Medical Setting	1. Theory testing 2. Scale development 3. Data collection w/ scientific methods 4. Data analysis 5. Publication 6. Undergraduate/ graduate teaching 7. Training graduate students	1. Academic 2. Clinical institution 3. Medical Setting	1. Theory testing 2. Scale development 3. Data collection w/ scientific methods 4. Data analysis 5. Publication 6. Undergraduate/ graduate teaching 7. Intervention testing 8. Training doctoral students
Practice	1. Part-time academic 2. Allied health field 3. Coaching clinics 4. Life skills training for student athletes	1. Consultation/athletes 2. Consultation/coaches 3. Consultation on issues related to performance enhancement: - anxiety reduction - goal setting - attentional focus - preperformance plans	1. Academic (part- or full-time) 2. Private practice 3. Hospital 4. Clinic 5. Law enforcement 6. Social services 7. Life skills training for student athletes	1. Individual differences accounting for per- formance 2. Individualized counseling in sport or nonsport settings: - family problems - marital problems - eating disorders - anxiety disorders

Employment areas and typical issues of sport psychologists with varied academic training.

made early in one's education; therefore, individuals are advised to talk to both students and professionals in the field; read published materials regarding career options; and investigate, or perhaps even join, professional societies. Interdisciplinary work divided between a psychology and a kinesiology program is ideal but is not readily available at many institutions. Before applying to graduate school, it is important to spend time carefully examining the requirements of the program and discussing career goals with faculty advisers and current students in a variety of programs. Because the field is relatively young and continually developing, in a sense, all professionals are in continuing training to enhance their skills.

References

American Psychological Association. (1994). *Graduate training and career possibilities in exercise and sport psychology* [Brochure]. Washington, DC: Author.

Andersen, M. B. (1994). Ethical considerations in the supervision of applied sport psychology graduate students. *Journal of Applied Sport Psychology, 6,* 152–167.

Andersen, M. B. (Ed.). (2000). *Doing sport psychology.* Champaign, IL: Human Kinetics.

Andersen, M. B., Van Raalte, J. L., & Brewer, B. W. (1994). Assessing the skills of sport psychology supervisors. *The Sport Psychologist, 8,* 238–247.

Andersen, M. B., Van Raalte, J. L., & Brewer, B. W. (2000). When sport psychology consultants and graduate students are impaired: Ethical and legal issues in training and supervision. *Journal of Applied Sport Psychology, 12,* 134–150.

Andersen, M. B., Williams, J. M., Aldridge, T., & Taylor, J. (1997). Tracking the training and careers of advanced degree programs in sport psychology, 1989 to 1994. *The Sport Psychologist, 11,* 326–344.

Atkinson, R. L., Atkinson, R. C., Smith, E. E., & Hilgard, E. R. (1987). *Introduction to psychology* (9th ed.). New York: Harcourt, Brace, Jovanovich.

Brooks, G. A., Fahey, T. D., & White, T. P. (1996). *Exercise physiology: Human bioenergetics and its applications* (2nd ed.). New York: Macmillan.

Butki, B. D., & Andersen, M. B. (1994). Mentoring in sport psychology: Students' perceptions of training in publications and presentation guidelines. *The Sport Psychologist, 8,* 143–148.

Coakley, J. J. (2001). *Sport in society: Issues and controversies* (7th ed.). Boston: McGraw-Hill.

Cratty, B. J. (1968). *Psychology and physical activity.* Englewood Cliffs, NJ: Prentice-Hall.

Danish, S. J., & Hale, B. D. (1981). Toward an understanding of the practice of sport psychology. *Journal of Sport Psychology, 3,* 90–99.

Danish, S. J., & Hale, B. D. (1982). Further considerations on the practice of sport psychology. *Journal of Sport Psychology, 4,* 10–12.

Dishman, R. K. (1983). Identity crisis in North American sport psychology: Academics in professional issues. *Journal of Sport Psychology, 5,* 123–134.

Gill, D. L. (1992). Status of the *Journal of Sport and Exercise Psychology,* 1985–1990. *Journal of Sport and Exercise Psychology, 14,* 1–12.

Griffith, C. R. (1925). Psychology and its relation to athletic competition. *American Physical Education Review, 30,* 193–199.

Hale, B. D., & Danish, S. J. (1999). Putting the accreditation cart before the AAASP horse: A reply to Silva, Controy and Zizzi. *Journal of Applied Sport Psychology, 11,* 321–328.

Harrison, R. P., & Feltz, D. L. (1979). The professionalization of sport psychology: Legal considerations. *Journal of Sport Psychology, 1,* 182–190.

Hay, J. G. (1985). *The biomechanics of sports techniques* (3rd ed.). Englewood Cliffs, NJ: Prentice-Hall.

Heyman, S. R. (1982). A reaction to Danish and Hale: A minority report. *Journal of Sport Psychology, 4,* 7–9.

Keith-Spiegel, P., & Wiederman, M. W. (2000). *The complete guide to graduate school admission: Psychology, counseling and related professions.* Mahwah, NJ: Erlbaum.

Landers, D. M., Boutcher, S. H., & Wang, M. Q. (1986). The history and status of the *Journal of Sport Psychology*: 1979–1985. *Journal of Sport Psychology, 8,* 149–163.

Lawther, J. D. (1972). *Sport psychology.* Englewood Cliffs, NJ: Prentice-Hall.

LeUnes, A. D., & Hayward, S. A. (1990). Sport psychology as viewed by chairpersons of APA-approved clinical psychology programs. *The Sport Psychologist, 4,* 18–24.

Martens, R. (1975). *Social psychology and physical activity.* New York: Harper & Row.

Martens, M. P., Mobley, M., & Zizzi. S. J. (2000). Multicultural training in applied sport psychology. *The Sport Psychologist, 14,* 81–97.

McCullagh, P. (1998). What is the applied in applied sport psychology? The role of integration. *Journal of Applied Sport Psychology, 10,* S1–S10.

Morgan, W. P. (Ed.). (1970). *Contemporary readings in sport psychology.* Springfield, IL: Charles C Thomas.

Nideffer, R. M., DuFresne, P., Nesvig, D., & Selder, D. (1980). The future of applied sport psychology. *Journal of Sport Psychology, 2,* 170–174.

Petitpas, A. J., Brewer, B. W., Rivera, P. M., & Van Raalte, J. L. (1994). Ethical beliefs and behaviors in applied sport psychology. The AAASP ethics survey. *Journal of Applied Sport Psychology, 6,* 135–151.

Petrie, T. A., & Watkins, C. E., Jr. (1994). A survey of counseling psychology programs and exercise/sport science departments: Sport psychology issues and training. *The Sport Psychologist, 8,* 28–36.

Rejeski, W. R., & Brawley, L. R. (1988). Defining the boundaries of sport psychology. *The Sport Psychologist, 2,* 231–242.

Sachs, M. L., Burke, K. L., & Schrader, D. C. (2000). *Directory of graduate programs in applied sport psychology* (6th ed.). Morgantown, WV: Fitness Information Technology.

Salmela, J. H. (1992). *The world sport psychology sourcebook.* Champaign, IL: Human Kinetics.

Schmidt, R. A., & Lee, T. (2000). *Motor control and learning* (3rd ed.). Champaign, IL: Human Kinetics.

Silva, J. M., Conroy, D. E., & Zizzi, S. J. (1999). Critical issues confronting the advancement of applied sport psychology. *Journal of Applied Sport Psychology, 11,* 298–320.

Singer, R. N. (1975). *Myths and truths in sport psychology.* New York: Harper & Row.

Sternberg, R. J. (Ed.). (1997). *Career paths in psychology: Where your degree can take you.* Washington, DC: American Psychological Association.

Taylor, J. (1991). Career direction, development, and opportunities in applied sport psychology. *The Sport Psychologist, 5,* 266–280.

Thomas, J. R., & Gill, D. L. (1993). The Academy papers: Ethics in the study of physical activity [Special issue]. *Quest, 45.*

Van Raalte, J. L., & Andersen, M. B. (2000). Supervision I: From models to doing. In M. B. Andersen (Ed.), *Doing sport psychology* (pp. 153–165). Champaign, IL: Human Kinetics.

Van Raalte, J. L., Brown, T. D., Brewer, B. W., Avondoglio, J. B., Hartmann, W. M., & Scherzer, C. B. (2000). An on-line survey of graduate course offerings satisfying AAASP certification criteria. *The Sport Psychologist, 14,* 98–104.

Waite, B. T., & Pettit, M. E. (1993). Experiences of graduates from doctoral programs in sport psychology. *Journal of Applied Sport Psychology, 5,* 234–250.

Certification in Sport and Exercise Psychology

Samuel Zizzi, Leonard Zaichkowsky, and Frank M. Perna

Sport and exercise psychology is a multidisciplinary profession. Scientists, educators, and practitioners of sport and exercise psychology share a common interest, but most have received their primary training from an array of general fields spanning psychology, sport science, and medicine that include subspecialties such as clinical and counseling psychology, exercise physiology, and biomechanics, to name but a few of the possibilities other than a distinct sport and exercise psychology track. A leading sport and exercise psychology organization, the Association for the Advancement of Applied Sport Psychology (AAASP, 2000), lists about equal distributions of members trained in psychology specialties or in one of the sport sciences.

Similar to other applied disciplines in an early stage of development, sport and exercise psychology faced the task of generating a mutually accepted mode of professional training, code of practice, and espoused core knowledge base. Perhaps no other area in an applied profession generates as much attention and controversy as codifying standards for professional preparation and practice because the practice of a profession serves as the primary interface of the field with the general public and encompasses both legal and professional issues (see Brooks & Gerstein, 1990, on the credentialing of counselors; see Cummings, 1990; Fretz & Mills, 1980, on credentialing of professional psychologists). Fairly or unfairly, the general public views the educational background and professional behavior of those who practice as the model for the field. The field of sport and exercise psychology is no exception. Issues surrounding the provision of sport and exercise psychology services have generated considerable debate about whether services should be provided (Kirschenbaum, 1994; Morgan, 1988), how individuals should be trained, and who should provide those services (Anshel, 1992, 1994; Danish & Hale, 1981; Dishman, 1983; Gardner, 1991; Harrison & Feltz, 1979; Heyman, 1993; May, 1993; Monahan, 1987; Silva, 1989; Zaichkowsky, 1993; Zaichkowsky & Perna, 1992).

Certification is a function of a professional organization that attempts to codify a common standard of preparation and practice. At a beginning stage, these standards must serve the dual purpose of recognizing the experience of members currently in the field as well as setting guidelines for those newer members who wish to pursue sport and exercise psychology. This chapter (a) defines terminology associated with certification, which has been at the root of much controversy; (b) provides a brief history of international certification; (c) provides a rationale for the existence of the certification process; (d) presents AAASP certification criteria; (e) outlines and responds to criticisms that have been levied against certification and the associated criteria in sport and exercise psychology; and (f) explores future improvements in certification that could further develop the field.

Defining Certification and Related Terms

Clearly, there is a need to clarify the terminology associated with the credentialing process in general and in sport and exercise psychology in particular. For instance, confusion exists regarding statutory versus nonstatutory designations and regarding certification versus licensure.

- *Credentialing.* This is a broad, generic term that is commonly defined as a process of giving a title or claim of competence. Credentialing includes statutory designations that are protected by law and enacted by a legislative body, as well as nonstatutory designations, such as recognition by organizations and registries, that are not protected by law. In the mental health field, credentialing appears to take five basic forms: association membership, accreditation of educational and training programs, certification by a nongovernmental agency, government licensure, and registration on an official roster (Anchor, 1988).

- *Certification.* This is generally a nonstatutory designation granted by an organization rather than by a legislative body. However, some states use the label in reference to statutory designations (e.g., certified teacher, certified psychologist). Certification is usually a transitional designation that may serve as a preliminary step toward statutory standards for that profession (Smith, 1986). The National Coaching Certification Program in Canada and AAASP certification are examples of nonstatutory certification, whereas public school certification and certified mental health counselors are examples of statutory certification.

- *Registry.* This term is generally a nonstatutory designation indicating "that an individual has been publicly identified as meeting qualifications as specified by the organization and is eligible for formal listing" (Smith, 1986, p. 13). The National Registry of Health Service Providers in Psychology, the Canadian Mental Training Registry (Canadian Association of Sport Sciences, 1994), and the U.S. Olympic Committee (USOC, 1983) Sport Psychology Registry are examples of registries.
- *Licensure.* This is a statutory process and is the most restrictive of all these terms. The statutory designation of licensure indicates a state or provincial process that is designed to regulate professional conduct within a particular field. At times, a state may adopt a professional organization's admission standards or code of ethics, and it may even relegate the monitoring of the field to a professional board of the organization. However, the state legislature retains legal authority and determines the professional organization's involvement. Licensure as a psychologist is an example of a statutory process that protects the use of the title (i.e., psychologist) and scope of practice (e.g., psychological test interpretation).
- *Psychologist.* This title is restricted in many states and provinces in the United States and Canada. Use is generally restricted to those who are licensed or certified to offer services to the public. Psychologists generally have a doctoral degree in counseling or clinical psychology. Exceptions to this restricted use of title include individuals who teach and conduct research in psychology and individuals from selected states and provinces that recognize master's-level psychologists.
- *Counselor.* This is a term that appears to apply to literally a cast of thousands. Any person who is helping another is in fact offering counseling services. For instance, there are academic counselors, drug and alcohol counselors, career counselors, marriage counselors, and so forth. In many cases, little or no training is

provided for these "lay" counselors; however, in other cases, counselors undergo rigorous training, making them eligible for statutory designation such as "licensed mental health counselor" or "licensed counseling practitioner."

- *Accredited or approved program.* These terms generally refer to an educational, training, or service program that has met certain standards that may or may not be related to certification or licensure. Accreditation is usually the result of a review of relevant documentation (of curriculum and practicum offerings) and a site visit by a team of reviewers from the accreditation agency. The American Psychological Association (APA) has an accreditation program that approves training programs in counseling, school, and clinical psychology. It should be emphasized, however, that by participating in an APA-approved program, one does not automatically become licensed to practice psychology. This point is particularly confusing to aspiring young professionals, because they may be unaware of the fact that licensing is a state function and not a function of APA. Typically, state licensing boards require applicants to complete a standardized exam and a set number of clinical hours (usually 2,000 hours), along with graduation from a doctoral-level program.

A Brief History of Sport Psychology Certification

The question of who is qualified to be a "sport psychologist" has been an issue ever since the field of sport psychology expanded from being primarily a topic for research and teaching in universities to providing "professional services" to athletes and coaches. Several position papers have been written on the topic, beginning in the late 1970s (Harrison & Feltz, 1979) and continuing to the present (Anshel, 1992; Danish & Hale, 1981; Dishman, 1983; Nideffer, Feltz, & Salmela, 1982; Silva, Conroy, & Zizzi, 1999; Zaichkowsky & Perna, 1992).

The USOC initiated the first systematic attempt in North America to credential sport and exercise psychologists. In the early 1980s, the USOC chose to improve the provision of sport science services to athletes. The USOC Sports Medicine Council was comfortable with identifying qualified biomechanists and exercise physiologists but thought that the standards for quality control in sport psychology were "elusive." In August 1982, the USOC brought together 12 individuals with established expertise and experience with the differing orientations of sport psychology to develop an approach to standards and identify organizational and referral processes and relationships. Guidelines proposed by this committee were subsequently published (USOC, 1983). The main recommendation made by the committee was that a sport psychology registry be established that would include the names of qualified workers in three separate categories of sport psychology: (a) clinical/counseling sport psychologists, (b) educational sport psychologists, and (c) research sport psychologists. The committee provided criteria for the three categories (USOC, 1983) and invited sport psychologists to apply for membership in the registry. From 1983 to 1995, a total of 67 sport psychologists were listed on the USOC registry.

In 1989, after several years of committee deliberations, AAASP approved a certification program. The AAASP Executive Board, Certification Committee, and Fellows focused particular attention on matters pertaining to role definition (i.e., what can "sport and exercise psychologists" do?) and title (i.e., what is the most appropriate legally acceptable title for members working in sport and exercise psychology?). Numerous experts in law and psychology were consulted regarding the issue of title. After extensive deliberation, it was concluded that if AAASP certified individuals as "sport psychologists," the association might be in violation of state and provincial laws. Because of this legal issue, AAASP Fellows voted to use the title "Certified Consultant, AAASP" rather than a title supported by many members—"certified sport psychologist." The criteria for AAASP certification are presented in Exhibit 22.1. A total of 143 AAASP members have been certified through 2000. In 1995, the USOC and AAASP formed a certification partnership (AAASP, 1995). All AAASP-certified consultants who are also members of APA are considered to have met the criteria for acceptance to the registry.

International Developments in Sport and Exercise Psychology Certification

Canada

In 1987, under the leadership of Dr. Murray Smith, Canada instituted the Canadian Registry for Sport Behavioral Professionals. This national registry was a part of the Canadian Association of Sport Sciences (CASS)

Exhibit 22.1

Criteria for AAASP Certification

1. Completion of a doctoral degree from an institution of higher education accredited by one of the regional accrediting bodies recognized by the Council of Postsecondary Accreditation. In Canada, an institution of higher education must be recognized as a member in good standing of the Association of Universities and Colleges of Canada. Programs leading to a doctoral degree must include the equivalent of three full-time academic years of graduate study, two years of which are at the institution from which the doctoral degree is granted and one year of which is in full-time residence at the institution from which the doctoral degree is granted.

2. Four hundred hours of supervised experience with a qualified person (i.e., one who has an appropriate background in applied sport psychology), during which the individual receives training in the use of sport psychology principles and techniques (e.g., supervised practicums in applied sport psychology in which the recipients of the assessments and interventions are participants in physical activity, exercise, or sport).[a]

3. Knowledge of professional ethics and standards. This requirement can be met by taking one course on these topics or by taking several courses in which these topics comprise parts of the courses or by completing other comparable experiences.

4. Knowledge of the sport psychology subdisciplines of intervention/performance enhancement, health/exercise psychology, and social psychology as evidenced by three courses or two courses and one independent study in sport psychology (two of these courses must be taken at the graduate level).

5. Knowledge of the biomechanical and/or physiological bases of sport (e.g., kinesiology, biomechanics, exercise physiology).

6. Knowledge of the historical, philosophical, social behavior, or motor behavior bases of sport (e.g., motor learning/control, motor development, issues in sport/physical education, sociology of sport history, and philosophy of sport/physical education).

7. Knowledge of psychopathology and its assessment (e.g., abnormal psychology, psychopathology).

8. Training designed to foster basic skills in counseling (e.g., graduate coursework on basic intervention techniques in counseling, supervised practica in counseling, clinical psychology, or industrial/organizational psychology).[a]

9. Knowledge of skills and techniques within sport or exercise (e.g., skills and techniques courses, clinics, formal coaching experiences, or organized participation in sport or exercise).

10. Knowledge and skills in research design, statistics, and psychological assessment.[a] At least two of the following four criteria must be met through educational experiences that focus on general psychological principles (rather than sport-specific ones).

continued

Exhibit 22.1, cont.

11. Knowledge of the biological bases of behavior (e.g., biomechanics/kinesiology, comparative psychology, exercise physiology, neuropsychology, physiological psychology, psychopharmacology, sensation).
12. Knowledge of the cognitive-affective bases of behavior (e.g., cognition, emotion, learning, memory, motivation, motor development, motor learning/control, perception, thinking).
13. Knowledge of the social bases of behavior (e.g., cultural/ethnic and group processes, gender roles in sport, organization and system theory, social psychology, sociology of sport).
14. Knowledge of individual behavior (e.g., developmental psychology, exercise behavior, health psychology, individual differences, personality theory).

*Graduate-level work only.

and was designed to provide a list of names of providers who were qualified to provide professional services to the sport community, including athletes, coaches, parents, teams, administrators, agencies, and sport governing bodies. The registry was similar to the USOC registry in that it listed qualified professionals in three categories: (a) licensed psychologists, (b) sport educators or counselors, and (c) sport researchers. For a variety of reasons, this version of the registry ceased to function and was replaced by the Canadian Mental Training Registry (CMTR) in 1994.

The CMTR, which lists 26 active members (Coaching Association of Canada, 1999), states two purposes: (a) to identify people in Canada who may be able to assist athletes and coaches with mental training and performance enhancement and (b) to promote the continued development of effective mental training services for athletes and coaches in Canada. The Registry Review Committee is a subcommittee of the High Performance Sport Committee (HPSC) of the Canadian Society for Exercise Physiology. The HPSC identified the following areas of preparation and experience as important applied sport psychology training: (a) academic training that generates an appropriate knowledge base with respect to mental links to excellence, applied mental training consulting, and applied sport sciences; (b) demonstrated personal experience in sport as a participant/athlete/performer or teacher/coach; (c) mental training supervised internship or demonstrated experience in mental training consulting; and (d) favorable client evaluations (CASS,

1994). The CMTR review committee indicates that most registrants acquire a master's or doctoral degree with specialization in sport psychology or mental training, as well as participate in a supervised internship with athletes and coaches. The recommended length for an internship is 30 weeks of supervised consulting experience.

In addition, the CMTR is careful to state what registrants do not do. Mental training consultants do not "conduct psychometric testing for the purpose of diagnosing or treating psychiatric disorders; nor do they provide psychotherapy, prescribe drugs, deal with deep-seated personality disorders or mental illness" (CASS, 1994, p. 4). The treatment of patients with mental disorders clearly falls outside the scope of ongoing mental training consulting work with athletes or others pursuing excellence. This is a distinctly different role from the mental strengthening role that mental training consultants engage in with athletes and coaches.

Australia

Like their colleagues in North America, Australians have struggled with the question of who can be a sport psychologist. Jeffrey Bond was appointed as the first "applied" sport psychologist at the Australian Institute of Sport in 1982. Since then, educational programs as well as opportunities in the field of sport and exercise psychology have grown at a rapid rate. After many years of debate regarding credentialing of sport psychologists, the Australians have determined that, to be called a sport psychologist, one needs to be a full member in the Australian Psychological Society (APS) and accepted as a member of the Board of Sport Psychologists. The board has been sanctioned by and held directly accountable to the APS. As such, sport and exercise psychology is closely linked to the profession of psychology (Chairperson's Report, 1993).

In Australia, psychologists do not have to complete a doctoral degree to call themselves psychologists. Individuals can provide psychological services to the public if they are full members of APS. The criteria for full membership, in the absence of a graduate psychology degree from a certified APS university program, include a record of research publications, letters of endorsement from current APS members, and successful completion of supervised field experience. Recent changes within APS require future psychologists to have six years of university training plus two years of supervised clinical experience. Several universities have recently instituted master's degree programs in psychology in sport psychology to provide the type of interdisciplinary training that is needed for preparing professionals with a specialization in sport and exercise psychology.

United Kingdom

The British Association of Sport and Exercise Sciences (BASES) has accreditation criteria for sport and exercise scientists (psychology section) that are designed to outline and regulate the standards for professionals in the sport and exercise sciences (BASES, 1994). Accreditation is available in two categories: (a) research accreditation (i.e., carrying out research in sport and exercise science) and (b) support accreditation (i.e., providing appropriate guidance and service to client groups). To be accredited as a "researcher," one has to make presentations and publish articles on sport and exercise psychology. For "support accreditation," a candidate must submit a portfolio that demonstrates involvement in the scientific study of sport and exercise and the ability to transpose relevant scientific knowledge into effective work in the field with clients. The accreditation process also requires supervised experience to be accredited as a sport and exercise psychologist. BASES does not require a specific number of hours of supervision for accreditation, but applicants must submit three nonconsecutive annual reports of supervised experience in a period of six years.

Benefits of Certification

In every instance in which certification has been instituted, the sponsoring organization has written about the benefits of certification. The statement issued by AAASP captures much of what other organizations have said

> Because the Association for the Advancement of Applied Sport Psychology (AAASP) and its membership are committed to the promotion of applied sport psychology, its members strive to maintain high standards of professional conduct while rendering consulting service, conducting research, and training others. AAASP has made a commitment to promoting excellence in sport psychology by instituting a certification program. (AAASP, 1991, p. 5)

This was followed by a statement of the benefits of a certification program, including accountability and professionalism, recognition, credibility, professional preparation, and public awareness. In addition to these, another benefit to certification not listed by the AAASP but stated by Smith (1987) in the Canadian registry document is that of "proactive self-determination." There is clearly an advantage to having the sport and exercise psychology profession proactively define education/training, roles, ethical standards, and so forth, rather than having external professional organizations define conditions in possibly unacceptable ways.

Accountability and Professionalism

The primary objective of a certification program is to provide a standard by which sport administrators, coaches, psychologists, other health care professionals, the media, and the public accept as reliable evidence that an individual has attained specified professional competency. In this way, AAASP is assuming accountability for high standards of performance in sport and exercise psychology. Certification also attests to the professionalism of the individual, thereby serving to protect the public interest.

Recognition

Individuals certified as consultants are listed in a registry of accredited specialists. They are recognized for having fulfilled prescribed standards of performance and conduct. This registry is made available to all amateur and professional sport organizations as well as other professional groups. In this way, certification provides a vehicle for identifying qualified practitioners.

Credibility

The certification process affords credibility because certification procedures for identifying qualified professionals are rigorous and based on peer review. The public can be assured that sport and exercise psychology is maintaining high standards of performance because of the recertification procedure, which requires the continuing education of consultants.

Professional Preparation

By specifying what is considered to be appropriate preparation of professionals, the AAASP certification process provides colleges and universities with guidelines regarding programs, courses, and practicum experiences in the field of sport and exercise psychology.

Public Awareness

Certification serves to raise awareness and understanding about sport and exercise psychology for all members of the sport community as well as the public at large.

Criticisms of AAASP Certification

Considering that sport and exercise psychology and AAASP are relative newcomers as an applied science and professional organization, it is not surprising that the organization's attempt to codify guidelines for professional practice has been met with both favorable and unfavorable reactions. It is our position that division in opinion is not only understandable but also desirable. In this section, a rationale for AAASP certification is presented, and the major criticisms levied against it are addressed. See Anshel (1992, 1994) and Zaichkowsky and Perna (1992) for a full discussion of these issues.

In brief, Anshel (1992, 1994) has suggested that vague language permeates the certification guidelines. He has also asserted that the process and criteria associated with AAASP certification are flawed with respect to three primary areas: (a) Certification is overexclusionary; (b) the criteria are discriminatory toward individuals trained in the sport sciences; and, perhaps most important, (c) certification in sport and exercise psychology has greater potential for harm than for good.

Generic and Specific Language

Some of the AAASP guidelines clearly identify many specific behaviors, whereas other guidelines describe the practice of sport and exercise psychology in generic terms. Guidelines specifically address required preparatory coursework, educational degrees, and field experiences, as well as identify professional behaviors that are outside the scope of practice for AAASP-certified consultants. Although it is true that some guidelines are left to interpretation, this is the case for most professional codes of conduct. Broad language is necessary because guidelines attempt to convey heuristics to govern practice rather than concretely specify a wide array of behaviors constituting either wrongful or desirable practice. This type of language provides a document with longevity and sensitivity to the organization membership's views that may change as a function of new information such as legal statutes and public feedback. The Constitution of the United States is based on the same principle that provides citizens with both the specific letter of the law and an opportunity for an interpretative review of the spirit of the law. Similarly, AAASP certification guidelines allow professional peers to determine whether adherence to the spirit of the guidelines is followed and whether a particular guideline is appropriate.

Overexclusionary

Anshel (1994) stated that AAASP certification "fails to recognize the expertise of individuals who meet many, but not all, of the criteria for certification" (p. 345). Anshel presented the scenario of an émigré to the United States who had been recognized by his or her country as a sport psychologist and the case of a licensed, but not AAASP-certified, U.S. psychologist who provides clinical services to athletes with eating disorders as examples of competent individuals who would be excluded from AAASP certification or precluded from providing clinical services.

When the AAASP certification process was in the early stages, certification guidelines stated that current professionals desiring certification were not expected to meet all of the stated educational criteria, particularly if they could document applied experience or expertise by training, research, or continuing education. A five-year grandparenting provision was instituted specifically to recognize such individuals and to serve as an appeals process that provided a forum for professionals to state their case. No statement in AAASP certification guidelines should be construed to preclude professionals from practicing within a protected scope of practice in their recognized areas of expertise. Grandparenting is no longer in effect and, as such, all applicants must now meet the minimum requirements in all areas to achieve certification.

Returning to the first scenario, a sport psychologist from a country other than the United States would be eligible for AAASP certification; however, the burden of proof would lie with the individual seeking certification, regardless of his or her country of origin. In addition, AAASP certification does not require U.S. citizenship. In the case of the psychologist, AAASP certification guidelines do not govern the practice of professionals other than certified consultants. Furthermore, although statutes from state to state may vary, the use of psychological methods and testing to diagnose and treat psychological disorders; disorders of habit or conduct; and psychological aspects accompanying physical illness, injury, or disability are but a few of the functions protected by law. Therefore, psychologists could not be preempted from providing services that are within their legal scope of practice and areas of expertise even if their clients were athletes. It is important to note, however, that licensure as a psychologist is not sufficient to qualify for AAASP-certified consultant status.

Discriminatory Against the Sport Sciences

A major criticism of AAASP certification suggests that biased representation of the certification committee existed and that the ensuing guidelines favor individuals with psychology over sport science backgrounds. However, no data support this view. During the development of AAASP certification standards, experts from psychology, sport science, and the legal and medical disciplines as well as the AAASP membership contributed input at the inception of proposed guidelines and in ensuing years. In addition, an empirical analysis comparing the educational backgrounds of applicants accepted or rejected for AAASP-certified consultant status revealed that significantly more individuals with sport science training than individuals with psychology training achieved certification (Zaichkowsky & Perna, 1992). In recent years, this gap has narrowed, although sport science professionals achieving certification still outnumber psychology professionals achieving certification (AAASP, 2000; D. Burton, Chair of Certification Committee, University of Idaho, personal communication, September 26, 2000).

Potential for Harm

It has been suggested that credentialing an individual as a certified consultant may diminish rather than promote quality service. This criticism is based largely on the premise that certification may create the illusion of sanctioning fraudulent practice (Anshel, 1992; Zaichkowsky & Perna, 1992). Fraudulent practices in sport and exercise psychology primarily include practitioners who misrepresent the efficacy of sport and exercise psychology interventions and those who engage in practice without proper training. Although it is true that certified consultants who make fraudulent claims, misapply techniques, and generally practice outside of their area of expertise would likely damage the field of sport and exercise psychology, no evidence exists to suggest that certification promotes this occurrence. More arguments can be made supporting the opposite view—that certification likely minimizes unethical practice.

An ample knowledge base exists supporting the efficacy of many interventions used in the provision of sport and exercise psychology services (Druckman & Bjork, 1991; Greenspan & Feltz, 1989; Kendall, Hrycaiko, Martin, & Kendall, 1990; Meyers, Schleser, & Okwumabua, 1982; Meyers, Whelan, & Murphy, 1996; Zaichkowsky & Fuchs, 1988). The coursework and supervised practica required for certification are intended to document that applicants for certification are not only exposed to these techniques but also demonstrate proficient skill and judgment in their application. Present AAASP-certified consultants, similar to other applied professionals, are encouraged to regularly apprise themselves of new developments through journals, conferences, workshops, and consultation. To maintain certified status, consultants are also required to complete continuing education credits to keep abreast of new information and applications within the field.

It is true that certification, similar to all credentialing processes, can only minimally define competent practice. Whether consultants seek to adjust their practice as new evidence accumulates or engage in consultation and referral where appropriate is not an issue of certification but rather an issue of professional integrity. However, we contend that certification standards serve to promote competent practice by providing a structure and training guidelines for students and professionals seeking to expand their practice.

A related criticism that often arises concerns the belief that licensed mental health practitioners without requisite experience in the practice of sport and exercise psychology, specifically psychologists, would be eligible for AAASP-certified consultant status. This is simply not the case. Nor is it appropriate to assume that a psychologist, without demonstrated expertise, may opt to advertise and practice as a sport and exercise psychologist without the potential for censure. Although state statutes typically protect the title of psychologist and permutations thereof, state regulatory boards prohibit psychologists and other mental health professionals from practicing and advertising in areas outside of their expertise. Professionals may be reported to their respective certifying or licensing boards for practicing outside of their area of expertise. Therefore, although AAASP has no legal jurisdiction over professionals who practice unethically, having publicly stated AAASP certification criteria, individuals and sport and exercise psychology organizations are in a better position to curtail practice that is detrimental to the field of sport psychology.

It is our view that certification, as designed by AAASP, provides the public with standard criteria that certified consultants have met and a means by which certified and noncertified professionals can be compared. With time, professional sport and exercise psychology organizations and the public will decide whether distinction by AAASP certification is important. In the interim, the public is protected, to the greatest extent possible, from fraud. However, as is the case with credentialing in other professional fields, certification does not, and never was intended to, guarantee expertise or personal integrity. All professional organizations contain some individuals who have engaged in unethical, and at times criminal, conduct. To allege that certification promotes inappropriate behavior detrimental to the field is unsubstantiated. On the contrary, to dispense with certification and let "the market" determine quality, as has been suggested (Anshel, 1992), would likely be a professional disaster.

Future Developments in AAASP Certification

For certification credentialing to significantly improve the quality of training and services provided within applied sport psychology, it must be supported by a large number of professionals within the field. Currently, there are approximately 570 professional members of AAASP, which includes 295 trained in psychology, 247 trained in the sport sciences, and 28 trained in other disciplines (AAASP, 2000). Yet, there are only 143 certified consultants, which represents just 25% of the professional membership. Furthermore, based on the most recent statistics from the certification committee, AAASP certifies an average of only 9 to 10 new consultants per year, which will not substantially increase the certified consultant pool in years to come.

The following section addresses several alternative approaches to meeting AAASP certification that, if adopted, would provide a more flexible model of credentialing while maintaining the standard of training. The overall goal of these alternative approaches would not be to simply increase the *quantity* of certified consultants but rather to facilitate the application process to allow for *qualified* consultants to become certified more efficiently.

Meeting the Practicum Hours Requirements

Many applicants struggle to meet the 400 supervised hours working in sport and exercise settings, and this struggle includes candidates from both sport science and psychology backgrounds. One key issue involves acquiring qualified supervision for applied work with sport and exercise clients. To provide support for those seeking certification, AAASP may need to establish a clearinghouse, wherein certified consultants could offer supervision by telephone and e-mail to those consultants who are unable to acquire personal supervision in their geographic area. This indirect supervision model may be effective in encouraging applicants to complete their hours and would establish a more direct mentoring relationship beyond the boundaries of graduate programs.

Aside from supervision issues, students also often struggle to get diversity of experience across sport and exercise settings. To ensure comprehensive training, opportunities need to be developed within graduate programs to ensure that students have access to high school and college athletes, youth sport participants, adult and older adult exercisers and, possibly, populations with chronic diseases (e.g., diabetes, heart disease). For instance, some sport psychology or counseling programs have already developed relationships with other academic units (e.g., community medicine, exercise physiology) to provide practicum opportunities for their students. It would be useful for AAASP to establish a formal outlet for communicating new and creative practicum opportunities to all applied sport psychology programs. This outlet could come in the form of a committee within AAASP charged with collecting and disseminating ideas for applied experiences or in the form of a Web site focused on applied experience within graduate programs. Not only would the development of new applied opportunities increase the likelihood that students could meet the minimum hour requirements for AAASP certification, it would also allow them to gain experience in providing sport psychology interventions to several different populations.

Meeting the Coursework Requirements

In addition to their struggles with practicum hours, students preparing to apply for AAASP certification often have difficulty in meeting all of the 12 curriculum areas as well. According to the current certification committee chair, students from sport science backgrounds have the most difficulty with ethics courses, a graduate counseling class, and various psychology classes in the last four areas (Areas 11–14 in Exhibit 22.1). Those with a psychology background also have difficulty, but these applicants struggle to fill the three sport psychology courses and the sport science courses such as biomechanics, motor learning, and exercise physiology (D. Burton, personal communication, September 26, 2000). Two general approaches may help students get the courses they need for certification.

The first approach involves encouraging programs to develop coursework that mirrors the requirements for AAASP certification. This coursework would be especially beneficial to students with a sport psychology specialization at the graduate level. A recent study of online course catalogs revealed that the majority of graduate programs in sport psychology are not offering the necessary courses for students interested in pursuing AAASP certification (Van Raalte et al., 2000). Some authors have argued that certification will not be able to sustain itself in the future without the support of quality graduate training programs (Silva et al., 1999). Thus, in addition to support from AAASP members, certification also needs the support of sport psychology graduate programs to help produce a greater number of consultants who have the requisite training to become certified consultants.

Second, on an institutional level, and regardless of programmatic change (which can be slow and costly), the minimal involvement for faculty advisers and department chairs interacting with sport psychology students should include teaching students about the requirements of certification early in their careers and considering the 12 coursework components of AAASP certification when developing plans of study with their students. Then, if the program or department does not offer a particular class, students can proactively seek out their remaining requirements in other departments before graduation.

Another idea related to curriculum improvements is the possibility of meeting some of the coursework requirements for certification through continuing education workshops or Web-based courses. These options may be particularly appealing to those individuals who have already completed a degree and are working in the field. The current inflexibility of AAASP certification coursework criteria may have deterred these applicants from becoming certified consultants. Internet-based and workshop-centered training methods could create a more efficient model through which professionals who are lacking only a few classes or competencies could be eligible for certification.

Summary

In this chapter, we attempted to educate the readers about certification in sport and exercise psychology. We defined nomenclature associated with certification, emphasized legal issues concerned with the title *psychologist*, and presented arguments for and against the process. Important papers associated with certification are referenced. We also provided a brief history of certification of sport and exercise psychologists in the United States, Canada, Australia, and the United Kingdom. Emphasis was placed on the certification process used by AAASP. Future directions and improvements in AAASP certification were explored.

References

Anchor, K. N. (1988). Professional regulation in the U.S.: Task force on issues and problems in current credentialing practices. *Medical Psychotherapy: An International Journal, 1*, 173–180.

Anshel, M. H. (1992). The case against the certification of sport psychologists: In search of the phantom expert. *The Sport Psychologist, 6*, 265–286.

Anshel, M. H. (1994). *Sport psychology: From theory to practice.* Scottsdale, AZ: Gorsuch, Scarisbrick.

Association for the Advancement of Applied Sport Psychology. (1995). A New USOC-AAASP Partnership. *AAASP Newsletter, 10*(3), 9.

Association for the Advancement of Applied Sport Psychology. (2000). 1999 membership report. *AAASP Newsletter, 15*(2), 43.

British Association of Sport and Exercise Sciences. (1994). *Accreditation criteria for sport and exercise scientists—Psychology section.* Unpublished manuscript.

Brooks, D. K., & Gerstein, L. H. (1990). Counselor credentialing and interprofessional collaboration. *Journal of Counseling & Development, 68*, 476–490.

Canadian Association of Sport Sciences. (1994). *Canadian Mental Training Registry.* [Brochure]. Gloucester, Ontario, Canada: Author.

Chairperson's report. (1993). *Australian Sport Psychology Association Bulletin, 2*, 4–6.

Coaching Association of Canada. (1999). *Canadian Mental Training Registry.* Retrieved from http://www.coach.ca/cmtr/home.htm.

Cummings, N. A. (1990). The credentialing of professional psychologists and its implication for the other mental health disciplines. *Journal of Counseling & Development, 68*, 485–490.

Danish, S. J., & Hale, B. D. (1981). Toward an understanding of the practice of sport psychology. *Journal of Sport Psychology, 3*, 90–99.

Dishman, R. K. (1983). Identity crisis in North American sport psychology. *Journal of Sport Psychology, 5*, 123–134.

Druckman, D., & Bjork, R. A. (1991). *In the mind's eye: Enhancing human performance.* Washington, DC: National Academy Press.

Fretz, B. R., & Mills, D. H. (1980). *Licensing and certification of psychologists and counselors: A guide to current policies, procedures and legislation.* San Francisco: Jossey-Bass.

Gardner, F. L. (1991). Professionalization of sport psychology: A reply to Silva. *The Sport Psychologist, 5*, 55–60.

Greenspan, M. J., & Feltz, D. L. (1989). Psychological interventions with athletes in competitive situations: A review. *The Sport Psychologist, 3,* 219–236.

Harrison, R. P., & Feltz, D. L. (1979). The professionalization of sport psychology: Legal considerations. *Journal of Sport Psychology, 1,* 182–190.

Heyman, S. (1993, August). *The need to go slowly: Educational and ethical issues in proposed sport psychology certification.* Paper presented at the annual meeting of the American Psychological Association, Toronto, Ontario, Canada.

Kendall, G., Hrycaiko, D., Martin, G. L., & Kendall, T. (1990). The effects of imagery rehearsal, relaxation and self-talk package on basketball game performance. *Journal of Sport and Exercise Psychology, 12,* 157–166.

Kirschenbaum, D. S. (1994, August). *Helping athletes improve sport performance—Best guesses.* Division 47 Presidential Address at the annual meeting of the American Psychological Association, Los Angeles, CA.

May, J. (1993, August). *Issues concerning certification of sport psychologists.* Paper presented at the annual meeting of the American Psychological Association, Toronto, Ontario, Canada.

Meyers, A. W., Schleser, R., & Okwumabua, T. M. (1982). A cognitive–behavioral intervention for improving basketball performance. *Research Quarterly for Exercise and Sport, 53,* 344–347.

Meyers, A. W., Whelan, J. P., & Murphy, S. M. (1996). Cognitive–behavioral strategies in athletic performance enhancement. In M. Hersen, R. M. Eisler, & P. M. Miller (Eds.), *Progress in behavior modification: Vol. 30* (pp. 137–164). Pacific Grove, CA: Brooks Cole.

Monahan, T. (1987). Sport psychology: A crisis identity? *The Physician and Sportsmedicine, 15,* 203–212.

Morgan, W. P. (1988). Sport psychology in its own context: A recommendation for the future. In J. S. Skinner, C. B. Corbin, D. M. Landers, P. E. Martin, & C. L. Wells (Eds.), *Future directions in exercise and sport science* (pp. 97–110). Champaign, IL: Human Kinetics.

Nideffer, R. M., Feltz, D., & Salmela, J. (1982). A rebuttal to Danish and Hale: A committee report. *Journal of Sport Psychology, 2,* 2–4.

Silva, J. M. (1989). Toward the professionalization of sport psychology. *The Sport Psychologist, 3,* 265–273.

Silva, J. M., Conroy, D. C., & Zizzi, S. J. (1999). Critical issues confronting the advancement of applied sport psychology. *Journal of Applied Sport Psychology, 11,* 298–320.

Smith, M. F. R. (1986, October). *Background to the proposal for a Canadian registry for sport psychology.* Paper presented at the annual meeting of the Canadian Association of Sport Science, Ottawa, Ontario, Canada.

Smith, M. F. R. (1987). *Canadian Association of Sport Sciences: Registry for Sport Behavioral Professionals.* Unpublished manuscript.

U.S. Olympic Committee. (1983). U.S. Olympic Committee establishes guidelines for sport psychology services. *Journal of Sport Psychology, 5,* 4–7.

Van Raalte, J. L., Brown, T. D., Brewer, B. W., Avondoglio, J. B., Hartmann, W. M., & Scherzer, C. (2000). An on-line survey of graduate course offerings satisfying AAASP certification criteria. *The Sport Psychologist, 14,* 98–104.

Zaichkowsky, L. D. (1993, August). *Certification program of AAASP.* Paper presented at the annual meeting of the American Psychological Association, Toronto, Ontario, Canada.

Zaichkowsky, L. D., & Fuchs, C. Z. (1988). Biofeedback applications in exercise and athletic performance. In K. Pandolf (Ed.), *Exercise and sport science reviews* (pp. 381–421). New York: Macmillan.

Zaichkowsky, L. D., & Perna, F. M. (1992). Certification of consultants in sport psychology: A rebuttal to Anshel. *The Sport Psychologist, 6,* 287–296.

Incorporating Sport and Exercise Psychology Into Clinical Practice

Kate F. Hays and Robert J. Smith

The emerging field of sport and exercise psychology offers considerable potential and promise for individuals considering a career in psychology (American Psychological Association [APA], 1994). Graduate and postgraduate training opportunities in sport psychology are increasingly expanding (Sachs, Burke, & Schrader, 2000). For established practitioners, the route to sport and exercise psychology may be somewhat different. This chapter addresses questions such as, How can sport and exercise psychology be used in clinical practice? What skills are needed? What practice opportunities exist for sport and exercise psychology practitioners? How is a sport and exercise psychology practice created? What business issues are most salient? What practitioner concerns need to be addressed?

Current Public and Professional Climate

The field of sport and exercise psychology holds considerable appeal for both the public and practitioners. Several factors contribute to its emergence as a field in which special skills and knowledge can be developed. American culture values both exercise (i.e., fitness) and sport (i.e., competition). Furthermore, changes in health care practice and funding mean that practitioners are being challenged to adapt and innovate. Market pressures for diversification, cost-effectiveness, and specialization (cf. Psychotherapy Finances, 1997) can all be met through sport and exercise psychology.

A general sense of well-being or quality of life is theorized as being composed of three major constructs: the absence of negative affect, the presence of positive affect, and high levels of life satisfaction (Diener, 1994; Mroczek & Kolarz, 1998). At least in attitude, if not in actuality, people are developing a holistic perspective. They recognize that exercise, health, and wellness contribute to an enhanced quality of life (Berger & Motl, 2001).

For psychologists, this is a time of economic, entrepreneurial, and practice flux. As psychology and mental health practice become increasingly positioned within the spectrum of health care (Yenney & APA Practice Directorate, 1994), sport and exercise psychology, with its focus on the interaction of mind and body, fits naturally within this general framework.

A consensus poll of therapists suggested that therapies of the future will be those that are brief, directive, present-centered, and problem-focused (Norcross, Alford, & DeMichele, 1992). These characteristics are descriptive of the practice of sport and exercise psychology (Hays, 1995a). Increasingly, cost-effectiveness and practice efficiency have become driving forces for practitioners (Austad & Hoyt, 1992). The impact of managed mental health care and brief treatment methods have, if anything, accelerated this trend.

Specialization is important for both one's business and professional identity. Finding a niche is a constructive way to become "identifiable," distinct from the competition (Edwards, Edwards, & Douglas, 1998). Furthermore, sport and exercise psychology practitioners may prevent their own burnout or ameliorate the effects of vicarious traumatization by focusing on either healthier populations or the healthier aspects of people's lives (Pearlman, 1995; Seligman & Csikszentmihalyi, 2000).

The field of sport and exercise psychology has increasingly been of interest to psychologists and, in particular, to psychologists in independent practice. More than half the members of the Association for the Advancement of Applied Sport Psychology (AAASP, 2000) identify themselves as psychologists. The majority of members of the Division of Exercise and Sport Psychology (Division 47), one of the newest divisions of the APA, describe themselves as providing mental health services, and two-fifths list themselves as employed full-time in independent practice (APA, 1998a).

Practice Opportunities in Sport

The practitioner may engage in sport and exercise psychology in three somewhat distinct ways: focusing on the mind-to-body aspect (i.e., the use of mental techniques within sports), focusing on the body-to-mind aspect (i.e., the positive impact of exercise on mental health), and practicing psychotherapy with athletes.

Mind-to-Body: Peak Performance Training

Peak performance, or psychological skills training (PST), is based on the assumption that aspects of thoughts and feelings can inhibit effectiveness and that use of mental skills can enhance optimal performance. Considerable research, especially with competitive athletes, suggests that educational psychological skills intervention improves competitive performance (see meta-analyses by Greenspan & Feltz, 1989; Meyers, Whelan, & Murphy, 1995). PST programs typically include training in relaxation, imagery, goal setting, concentration, and cognitive self-management.

The cognitive–behavioral techniques that form the "canon" of PST (Andersen, 2000b) are consonant with a specific, goal-focused, time-limited frame that can result in marked behavior change. These techniques are most effective when individually prescribed rather than packaged or presented only en masse (Meyers et al., 1995). As with any other techniques, they must be understood and practiced correctly for maximum impact. For the clinician, PST can also function as a diagnostic tool: If the performance enhancement intervention is rapidly effective, there may not be an underlying pathology. To the extent that a person does not respond easily to PST, additional issues may need to be addressed (Hays, 1995a; May, 1986).

Practitioners may offer PST to athletes of varying ages, sports, and skill levels in several individual or group settings. Increasingly, information concerning the practical aspects of such training, the most popular and most popularized aspect of sport psychology, is becoming available to interested practitioners (see, e.g., Andersen, 2000a; Cogan, 1998; Lesyk, 1998; Petrie, 1998; Simons & Andersen, 1995; Wildenhaus, 1997). The establishment of a full-time practice with a performance enhancement focus may take considerable time and work. Most practitioners augment their PST work with other forms of service, whether academic or clinical (Meyers, Coleman, Whelan, & Mehlenbeck, 2001). Although some practitioners develop solo practices, they could often be more effective if they worked within a multidisciplinary establishment, such as a sports medicine facility (Petitpas, 1998), medical organization (Heil, 1993), or university health setting (Pargman, 1999).

> Six years after establishing an independent practice, and having done considerable marketing (workshops, articles, radio and TV appearances, and systematic networking), a clinical and sport psychologist was invited to relocate his entire practice to a new fitness facility that also serves as the training site for a national professional team. After moving, referrals came from physicians, physical therapists, and other allied health professionals, augmented by staff and members of the health facility. Because the psychologist did not need to make large upfront investments in marketing expenses, it was possible to quickly develop a profitable practice. In synergistic fashion, the health facility benefited in terms of rental income, cross-referrals, and public relations.

Body-to-Mind: Exercise and Mental Health

As noted in Chapter 11, this volume, there is a positive connection between physical and mental functioning. Moderate exercise performed regularly (e.g., aerobic exercise performed three times a week for one half hour at a time) has profound effects not only on the cardiovascular system but also on mood and sense of well-being (Berger & Motl, 2000; Kirkcaldy & Shephard, 1990; Morgan, 1985a). Research suggests that exercise is associated with a reduction in depression and the amelioration of anxiety (e.g., Martinsen & Morgan, 1997; Raglin, 1997). Furthermore, exercise appears to result in improvements in self-esteem, mastery, body image, and socialization, all contributory to improvements in mental and emotional functioning (Boutcher, 1993; Sonstroem, 1997). Although only minimal research in this arena has been conducted among people with severe mental illness, exercise appears to have a salutary effect with this population as well (Auchus, 1993; Skrinar, Unger, Hutchinson, & Faigenbaum, 1992). Detailed descriptions of the use of exercise with various clinical populations form the basis of some recent books on the mental benefits of physical activity (Hays, 1999; Leith, 1994).

Exercise has multiple potential uses in the psychotherapy setting (Hays, 1993). It may be prescribed as a form of therapy, encouraged as adjunctive to psychotherapy, or used as the medium in which therapy is conducted (Hays, 1995b). The therapist's engagement with the client in relation to exercise may include consultation, modeling, or participation. The client's level of involvement in sport or exercise may range from the sedentary nonathlete to the competitive or professional athlete.

> A clinical and sport psychologist with knowledge of current research on the mental benefits of physical activity began systematically incorporating support for physical activity as part of treatment recommendations to outpatient clients. By addressing issues of motivation and adherence with clients and assisting clients in appreciating the "affective beneficence" (Morgan, 1985a) of exercise, many clients used individualized exercise plans to good effect. Selectively, the therapist used the exercise setting (walking or running) as the medium in which to conduct therapy. When the therapist relocated, this treatment emphasis was easily incorporated in the new environment.

Psychotherapy With Athletes

In an early prospective study, Pierce (1969) found college athletes less likely than other students to seek psychotherapy. Athletes may also tend to be mentally healthier than the general population; however, they may exhibit fairly severe psychopathology by the time they seek services (Morgan, 1985b).

Typical presenting problems include anxiety, depression, eating disorders, substance abuse, fears of success or failure, and relationship and motivational concerns, suggesting that a substantial overlap exists between athletic and nonathletic clinical populations (Mahoney & Suinn, 1986). The athlete seeking psychotherapy may be more comfortable working with a therapist knowledgeable about sport and respectful of its role in the athlete's life (Cogan, 1998). Psychotherapists should be sensitive to the client in context: respecting the client's identification as an athlete, taking seriously the client's engagement in competitive sport, and recognizing the legitimacy of time constraints created by competitive schedules (Van Raalte, 1998).

In reality, the distinction between PST and counseling or psychotherapy may be arbitrary at times. In the only large-scale survey of its kind, Meyers and colleagues (1995) found that even though the initial focus of services at the U.S. Olympic Training Center concerned performance, 85% of all cases seen by the sport psychology staff involved personal counseling with athletes. Detailed case descriptions of this combination of PST and psychotherapy or counseling provide interesting examples of flexible adaptation (see, e.g., Andersen, 2000a; Cogan, 1998; Petrie, 1998).

> An elite tennis player sought assistance from a clinical and sport psychologist to resolve anger and distrust of her father, who had been an abusive coach to her throughout her childhood and adolescence. Although her father was no longer part of her life on the tennis circuit, she felt that her past experiences with him were still restricting her full enjoyment of her sport and optimal performance. Short-term, but intense, psychotherapy, conducted during the off-season, was designed to assist her in addressing the impact of her history on her current sense of self. As an athlete, she was extremely disciplined, used to being coached, and willing to do self-examining "homework" between sessions. The tennis player proved to be adept at working through complex family interaction patterns and learning to interact with her parents in a markedly more constructive and adult fashion. She shifted with ease into occasional consultation with the psychologist regarding self-confidence, concentration, and competition.

The Business of Practice in Exercise and Sport Psychology

Integrating sport and exercise psychology into clinical practice raises several issues that can be subsumed under three central self-assessment questions: (a) Where am I now—that is, what is my level of interest, skills, and knowledge? (b) Where do I want to be—that is, what are my goals? and (c) How do I get there—or, in business terms, how do I market this practice? Careful consideration of these questions will facilitate the integration of sport and exercise consultation into a practice.

Interest, Skills, and Knowledge Development

Interest Level

Hill (1960) proposed that people ask themselves what they are willing to give up to achieve their goals. Researchers in the area of self-regulation (Karoly & Kanfer, 1982; Kirschenbaum, 1992) have agreed that persistence underlies the success of any program of change. Strong motivation is vital when incorporating sport and exercise psychology into applied practice. The level of commitment one has to this field relates strongly to the quality of subsequent experiences.

There are potential intrinsic motives, such as intellectual stimulation or personal growth, and extrinsic reasons, including financial reward, visibility, or special perks, for entering a new field. Some evidence suggests that people pursuing goals for money or fame are less persistent than those with more personal investment (Kirschenbaum, 1992). When reviewing reasons for becoming a sport and exercise consultant, it is useful to recognize that relatively few professionals in this field report significant external incentives such as lucrative contracts with professional sports teams (APA, 1994; Meyers et al., 2001).

Relevant Skills and Knowledge Development

Sport and exercise psychology consultants need to have knowledge in both psychological and sport sciences (APA, 1998b; Ethical Standards, n.d.). The relative balance of knowledge and skills in counseling or therapy compared with motor learning or kinesiology depends on the practitioners' professional and practice goals, including types of work settings, clientele, and practice focus (Simons & Andersen, 1995).

Psychological skills training typically involves such cognitive techniques as arousal regulation, mental imagery, goal setting, and attentional control (Weinberg & Gould, 1995; Williams, 1998;). In addition, psychologists who understand the theory and practice of organizational development, hypnosis, or systemic perspectives may bring a solid foundation on which to base work with athletes and coaches. Other important aspects of the consultative process may include clinical assessment, teaching skills, and knowledge of how people behave in family and other group systems.

Beyond general psychological skills, sport and exercise psychologists must have specialized knowledge. Sport sciences—exercise physiology, biomechanics, and motor learning—provide consultants with important knowledge about physiological contributions to athletic performance. Formal training is also needed in the area of nutrition and performance-enhancing drugs. Knowledge of sport-specific terminologies, rules, assessment, and intervention techniques is also essential (Gould & Damarjian, 1998).

Sport and exercise psychologists with firsthand experience of specific sport or exercise skills are at an advantage when consulting. It is also possible to gain experience and learn more about a sport through reading; observation; and discussion with athletes, coaches, and others who are knowledgeable about that sport. Athletes generally are less concerned that a consultant has specific knowledge of their sport than that the consultant is open to learning the common terms used and willing to help them achieve their goals (Gould & Damarjian, 1998; Parham &

Singer, 1994; Van Raalte, 1998). Perhaps this reflects athletes' appreciation for the practical reality that even experienced sport and exercise psychologists cannot possibly have firsthand expertise in all sports.

Although sport experience is important, too much investment in a specific sport can potentially interfere with a consultant's effectiveness. If a consultant swam competitively throughout college, for example, advanced knowledge of the sport might make it harder to avoid giving advice on physical skills when working with swimmers. This situation can cause conflicts with coaches, who perceive the role of a sport psychologist to be strictly that of a mental skills consultant (May, 1986; Yambor, 1997).

No matter how much knowledge sport psychology consultants have, they must be able to communicate their findings and recommendations in lay terms. Consultants should speak with athletes and coaches appropriately, using proper terminology (Eklund, 1993). In addition, consultants who let go of clinical language and formality will communicate better with their clients and be rewarded with better results (Gould & Damarjian, 1998; Van Raalte, 1998).

These skill areas require a significant investment of time and resources. Aspiring sport and exercise psychology consultants can gain knowledge and experience by (a) reading some of the introductory texts on sport psychology (e.g., Horn, 1992; Weinberg & Gould, 1995; Williams, 1998), (b) pursuing continuing education offerings at conferences and seminars (e.g., APA regularly offers an all-day sport psychology workshop at its annual convention, and AAASP offers several continuing education workshops at its conference), (c) obtaining a comprehensive list of graduate programs in sport psychology training (e.g., Sachs et al., 2000), (d) attending practices and competitive events to learn more about specific sports, and (e) finding a mentor.

Goal Development

In *The Seven Habits of Highly Effective People,* Covey (1989) advised people pursuing a goal to "begin with the end in mind" (p. 97). If one begins with the goal of incorporating sport and exercise psychology into clinical practice, what would an ideal sport and exercise psychology practice look like? From a business perspective, important areas to address include the product, that is, the services to be offered; the target market, or type of clientele; and financial and practical integration of sport psychology into general clinical practice.

Product

The services provided by sport and exercise psychologists vary greatly. As illustrated previously, they may include individual performance counseling, adjustment counseling or psychotherapy, seminars and workshops, and team consultation (Lesyk, 1998). In a survey of sports medicine physicians, Brewer, Van Raalte, and Linder (1991) found that the five most common reasons for which physicians referred athletes to sport psychologists were depression, stress or anxiety, substance abuse, family adjustment issues, and pain.

Determining one's focus is key to the development of any business (Edwards et al., 1998), and sport psychology is no exception (Lesyk, 1998). Increasingly, it is recognized that developing a particular niche makes business, economic, practice, and personal sense (Dean, 2000; Edwards & Edwards, 1996; Foster, 1999; Haber, Rodino, & Lipner, 2001; Hays, 1995a). A niche is the intersection of one's "compelling desires" (the aspects of life that are of most interest to the person); personal resources, including background and training, experiences, and contacts; and opportunities (Edwards & Edwards, 1996). A niche needs to be narrow enough to distinguish the practitioner from the competition but large enough to sustain sufficient business. One needs to be competent and find the niche enjoyable (Edwards & Edwards, 1996). Part of niche development involves finding out what services local sport and exercise psychologists provide, as well as how they get paid. Generally, the likelihood of success as a consultant increases by offering what competitors do not. If other sport and exercise psychology consultants work only with athletes and coaches, for example, there may be a market for specializing in services to athlete families.

As in a general practice, there should be limitations to the types of service offered to clients. In addition to the ethical issue of practicing within one's areas of competence, a lack of focus can interfere with effective practice. Trying to be all things to all people usually results in being spread too thin, causing all one's work to suffer. Potential clients become confused (Edwards et al., 1998). Thus, it is wise to identify two or three areas of concentration and refer clients needing other services to colleagues who can better meet those needs.

Target Market

Taylor (1994) noted that training and experience with specific presenting problems, intervention skills, and client populations should guide the decision about whom to serve. Within the boundaries of one's competence, it is useful to identify both the most and the least desirable types of consultation.

The search for a target market can begin with a written description of an ideal client referral. Demographic variables include age group; gender; race or ethnicity; sports ability level; type of sport; referral source; and whether the client is a team, an individual athlete, a coach, a parent, an official, or an administrator (Taylor, 1994). The type of work settings preferred (e.g., professional sports, business, school, fitness or country clubs) also helps shape the target market and sources of referrals.

A critical task in practice development involves conducting a needs analysis of the target market. It makes no sense to offer a service if prospective clients fail to see a need for it. Important information can be gathered by hiring a marketing consultant or conducting surveys oneself, such as asking numerous prospective clients or referral sources what they would want. Athletes, coaches, doctors, athletic trainers, or sports agents can be asked questions such as, Would you ever seek or refer someone for consultation with a sport and exercise psychologist, and why? If so, how much would you (or others) be willing to pay for this service? What are the top five psychological factors affecting your (or your athletes') game, ranked in order? Do you think sport and exercise psychologists can serve an important role in resolving some of these problems and, if so, how?

Financial Goals and Practice Balance

During a presentation to a summer basketball clinic, one of the authors asked the group what they thought a sport psychologist offers to athletes. A 12-year-old boy stood up confidently and said, "That's when you get paid a million dollars to have some athlete sit on your couch and talk about their problems." Although it was a naive and bald statement, it reflected a belief, perhaps shared by many practitioners as well as the general public, that sport and exercise psychology is a readily lucrative field. Some individuals do indeed make a good living as sport and exercise psychology consultants, but the vast majority supplement their income from sport and exercise psychology with general clinical work or academic positions (APA, 1994; Meyers et al., 2001).

One may address particular sport groups or target particular types of issues, for example, injured athletes, athletes with eating disorders, the challenges of retirement, or parents of young athletes (Lesyk, 1998). Different segments of the sport and exercise psychology market offer varying levels of financial remuneration. Professional athletes and coaches certainly provide one market. Among amateur enthusiasts, many golfers, tennis players, figure skaters, rowers, marksmen, polo players, and equestrians are more affluent; college athletes tend to have fewer resources to spend on mental training.

Although pro bono work does not add directly to the income stream, it does provide sport and exercise psychology services to athletes who might benefit from them. Besides being a good deed, offering free workshops and consultations to specific people or groups often leads to other paying opportunities. Careful attention to the ratio of pro bono services that can be provided is an important aspect of realistic financial planning.

Typically, sport and exercise psychology work develops slowly enough that the desirable balance between consultations within sport and other work can emerge (Lesyk, 1998). Nevertheless, it is useful to consider how much time to invest in general practice maintenance (including marketing efforts) while concurrently pursuing sport psychology opportunities. In fact, we recommend continued attention to the "bread-and-butter" business, phasing in sport and exercise psychology marketing and networking gradually. This approach allows for a smoother transition.

Marketing

Few psychologists enter the field with an entrepreneurial focus, and fewer still obtain graduate training in this important aspect of practice (Haber et al., 2001). An initial phase of the shift toward a sport and exercise psychology practice may involve coming to terms with being in business. This is especially true at the point where one needs to sell, or market, oneself and one's product.

Indirect marketing, including word-of-mouth referral and public presentations, can be effective. Although word-of-mouth methods (such as satisfied clients) may feel more comfortable to the practitioner, they may be a slow way to build up a practice (Kelly-Jones, 1999). Public presentations directed at a target audience may result in direct self-referrals or lead to future paid speaking engagements, at the same time yielding income from the presentation itself. Clinicians uncomfortable with public speaking can develop these skills either through formal means, such as local meetings of Toastmasters or public-speaking courses (Carnegie, 1966, 1994), or through informal methods, such as practicing with friends.

Systematic networking with coaches, athletic directors, athletic trainers, fitness instructors, sports medicine personnel, sport–exercise scientists, nutritionists, and sports agents is reciprocally important: Not only are these professionals potential referral sources, they also can form the basis of one's own referral network. Networking can both benefit clients and increase one's credibility. The ideal mindset one should have when networking is, "How can I present myself as a useful resource to this referral source?" (Stephens, 1996; video).

Such networking functions best if it is tied intentionally to one's goals and target market and if these contacts are developed over time and include follow-up contact. After identifying potential referral sources in the local area, it is useful to develop a variety of ways to educate these sources about services available. Networking and marketing methods include introductory letters with enclosures such as brochures, topical newspaper or magazine articles, association newsletters, or workshop flyers; follow-up phone calls; meeting with prospective referral sources; offering free training workshops; carrying business cards and keeping extra supplies in the car or office in case someone offers to distribute them to prospective clients; and maintaining a file with names of sports contacts.

Direct marketing, such as advertising and direct mail, is a focused action that directly sells a product or service. Some mass marketing, including generic advertising, may be necessary. However, marketing that addresses one's communications to a specific group of potential clients, whether sport groups or ones defined by a common issue, is generally more cost-effective (Lesyk, 1998). Moreover, marketing experts note that even among target populations, a business must cultivate trust and rapport through its marketing efforts (Godin, 1999). Otherwise, in this day of information overload, mailings and announcements will likely be overlooked, at best. At worst, the notice may be seen as another form of "spam," and the marketing effort can backfire.

Although professionals tend to present themselves in terms of their credentials and services, one of the basic principles of marketing suggests that it is essential to focus instead on the benefits that will be derived from such services (Heller, 1997). A "capability sheet" can be developed for each of one's target markets (e.g., parents of underachieving teenagers, injured athletes, corporate wellness programs). A sample of a capability sheet is shown in Exhibit 23.1.

Exhibit 23.1

Sample Capability Letter

Dear _____:

Thank you for inquiring about my background and services. Below you will find a summary of the type of work that I do, as well as some problem areas I address with individuals, families, and organizations. In addition, you will find a brief description of my credentials and how to contact me.

Although much of my work involves face-to-face consultations with private clients, I also serve as a consultant and trainer for companies of all sizes (from start-ups to Fortune 500). Below are some of the most frequent issues which I address:

Performance enhancement	Weight loss
Group/team effectiveness	Low self-confidence
Leadership	Injury/illness recovery
Career transition	Managing anxiety/stress
Conflict/negotiation skills	Problem solving

I am licensed as a Psychologist in Massachusetts, a Consultant certified by the Association for the Advancement of Applied Sport Psychology, a former college basketball player and high school coach, and a Black Belt Instructor in Kenpo Style Karate.

My offices are conveniently located at the downtown fitness center—the training site for a professional sport team. Come to the reception desk, and they will direct you to the first floor of the office facility. For counseling services, I accept many local and national insurance plans (please inquire before the first appointment). For more information or to make an appointment, please call my secretary to arrange a convenient time to meet.

I look forward to the possibility of our working together.

Sincerely,

Robert J. Smith, PhD

Developing Professional Supports

Solo practitioners know all too well that consultants can experience a sense of isolation. Therefore, nurturing connections with professionals from sport and exercise psychology and other related fields is critical. A professional support network can be developed by (a) identifying colleagues who can provide supervision or consultation services, whether face-to-face or at a distance; (b) creating prospective informal networks or legal partnerships with other sport and exercise psychologists, sports medicine professionals, fitness professionals, or sports agents; (c) identifying professionals in other fields who can provide guidance in setting up a practice, such as attorneys, certified public accountants, marketing consultants, and public relations consultants; and (d) joining local and national sport and exercise psychology associations for continuing education, referrals, credentialing, electronic resources, and visibility. At a national level, involvement in APA's Division of Exercise and Sport Psychology and AAASP offer practitioners support, education, and the opportunity to assist in shaping the field.

Practitioner Issues

Despite the promise presented by the inclusion of sport and exercise psychology in one's practice, several issues need to be addressed. Salient concerns include coping with becoming a novice again, suffering setbacks, scheduling, managing diagnostic concerns, and dealing with ethical issues.

Humility, Ambiguity, and Hubris

Expanding one's practice into an unfamiliar area involves the acquisition of new information and skills, as well as their integration into existing knowledge and practice. The seasoned practitioner may experience discomfort in being placed in the position of learner once again. Yet, acknowledging ignorance can assist in lowering the barriers so that learning can occur, whether through reading, coursework, or supervised practice. An attitude of humility, openness, and curiosity makes this process not only more interesting but also more effective (Leonard, 1992).

Because of the emergent status of the field, different training models and expectations, and the general flux of practice at the present time, sport psychology does not automatically provide a clearly defined, comfortable niche. Whether new to the field or seasoned, practitioners are therefore likely to encounter a series of dead-ends and opportunities that do not quite work out. In assessing rejections, it is important to differentiate between situations in which a sport and exercise psychologist is undertrained or inappropriate from instances in which others (e.g., coaches and athletic staff or sports medicine personnel) need education concerning the field's potential value to them. When starting commercial enterprises, it is considered preferable to be the second person bringing a new product or service to an area. Sport psychology practice is still developing, however. Depending on the target population and location, it may be necessary to create a market before fulfilling that market's needs, that is, educate potential clients to the scope, value, and need for such services.

Practical Concerns

Working with amateur and professional athletes may require some flexibility and variation in scheduling, depending on the particular sport and the nature and length of the contact with the athlete. Some sports are seasonal, and an athlete may not see the relevance of contact during the off-season. Some athletes may require intensive work before important events. Sport teams may expect the sport and exercise psychologist to travel with them (Gould & Damarjian, 1998; Van Raalte, 1998). The psychologist who has other clients or contracts needs to develop backup services to ensure sufficient and appropriate coverage when necessary. If sport and exercise psychology obligations occur at predictable times, it may be helpful to print a schedule beforehand, so that other clients know these plans well in advance. When clinicians take vacations, it is important to pay attention to clients' subjective experience of such absences.

Involvement in seasonal sports can create a "boom-or-bust" cycle. There are various ways to handle this problem. One is to become involved with athletes whose sports have different seasons; another is to adapt other aspects of the overall practice to these demands. Even in the face of high demand at the peak of season, it is important to set aside regular time for planning and marketing, as well as for other practice management functions.

Few psychologists receive training in the establishment of formal business relationships with individuals and organizations. Many organizations will not purchase services from a consultant without engaging in the process of a formal proposal and contract. Exhibit 23.2 shows a sample proposal, using the hypothetical example of an organization concerned about conflict between coaches and players.

Psychopathology and Diagnosis

The clinical practitioner working in sport and exercise psychology often operates on the cusp of the wellness–illness continuum. Clients may

Exhibit 23.2

Sample Contract Proposal

Proposal for [Team Name] Intervention

Situation Summary

[Team name] is a franchise that generates over $100 million in annual revenues. [Coach's name] serves as the head coach and is involved in planning, recruiting, and daily operations. His main assistant is [person's name], who has been with the team for nearly 4 years. Two players who contribute strongly to the team's success—[persons' names]—have apparently been involved in a series of conflicts with [Head Coach], which have consumed a considerable amount of everyone's time and energy. The players are both under long-term contracts.

[Head Coach and Assistant Coach] were interviewed separately to assess

- the nature and sources of the conflicts between [Head Coach and players' names],
- the "costs" of this problem to the organization,
- how people have responded to prior efforts to resolve the issues, and
- what might happen if nothing were done to address this issue.

Several factors seem to have contributed to the current situation:

- [Player 1's name]'s style of expressing and processing emotions, along with his expectations for his relationship with [Head Coach] at the outset (e.g., friend vs. colleague);
- [Head Coach]'s style of addressing problems only indirectly;
- [Assistant Coach]'s being "caught in the middle," failing to represent a "unified front" with his boss;
- Leadership's admission that they have not intervened more directly/decisively at earlier stages of this development, hoping that the problem would "work itself out."

It seems clear that these struggles have hurt the team's ability to function optimally and that tension in the organization is unlikely to subside without direct intervention. If the situation is not resolved it would probably lead to a poor season, the firing of [Head Coach], and the trading of one or both of these key team members. This could cost the organization considerably in terms of lost revenues, morale, resources, and time spent replacing these people.

Intervention

Given the sensitivity and volatility of the present situation, introducing an outside consultant to the team would be more distracting than helpful. Instead, it is proposed that a strategy be devised among the consultant, [Head Coach and Assistant Coach] during a regular series of planning meetings. [Head Coach and Assistant Coach] would then follow the steps developed in these meetings. [Consultant] may become more directly involved with face-to-face individual or team meetings at a later time if deemed necessary and appropriate.

continued

Exhibit 23.2, cont.

Objectives

The following goals would serve as early (within 1 month) and longer-term (3–6 months) indicators of the success of the proposed intervention:

- The team's goals will be reviewed to re-establish a shared vision for everyone's role on the team (individual and team needs to be articulated, integrated);
- Guidelines will be established to ensure that the safety and courtesy of each involved person will be observed in the organization (specific training for this to be provided by [Consultant]);
- Individual/team/staff meeting (run by [Head Coach]) agenda and protocols will be reviewed, and suggestions will be made by [Consultant];
- [Head and Assistant Coaches] will be trained on other effective leadership skills by [Consultant].

Joint Responsibilities

The success of this intervention hinges on the cooperation and coordination of the efforts of [Consultant, Coaches] and the other members of the [Team's name] organization. We will need to continue regular assessment of the effectiveness of the strategies outlined in this intervention, and new needs may arise as we work toward reaching the stated objectives. We must therefore be ready and willing to redirect our efforts accordingly.

Terms and Conditions

Fees are structured by the project rather than by units of time. This allows members of the [Team name] to use [Consultant] without concern that a "meter is running."

This intervention will likely take around 3 months to achieve a lasting result. Anticipated time frame is from [Suggested timeline]. There are some urgent concerns to be addressed, and some longer standing problems that have contributed to the kinds of relationship issues that have surfaced in your organization. The following options can be discussed when we meet on [Day, date, time]:

- *Option 1*—Weekly planning meetings/phone consults with [Key Personnel, Consultant] to address the above-cited issues. This option will provide [Team name] personnel with face-to-face meetings or phone consultations to tackle concerns relevant to achieving the desired results. In-person meetings will be held at [Designated] office. Fee: $2,500.
- *Option 2*—Unlimited planning meetings/phone consults with [Consultant] to address the above-cited issues. These will likely take place more often (e.g., multiple contacts per week) initially and then reduce in frequency over time, but this option gives personnel the flexibility to utilize [Consultant] on an as-needed basis. Face-to-face meetings will be held at [Designated] office. Fee: $5,000.

continued

Exhibit 23.2, cont.

- *Option 3*—Unlimited meetings/consults (as described in Option 2), plus on-site consultations and training (e.g., communication/teamwork training program, 1:1 meetings/consults with players and staff) as needed. Fee: $7,500.

Fees are payable in two installments—50% at the beginning and the remainder at the end of the project. A 10% discount is offered to clients who pay the full fee at the beginning. Any reasonable expenses will be billed at the end of each month. The acceptance of these terms forms an agreement between [Company name] and [Consultant]. The project is payable as described and is noncancellable. You may, however, choose to postpone or delay any part of the work in progress without penalty.

[Consultant signature, date]   [Company authorized signature, date]

---

not be seeking psychotherapy and may not have definable psychopathology. Although therapeutic, the services provided may not be psychotherapy. In addition, it has been suggested that pathologizing normative experiences may have demoralizing effects on clients (Danish, Petitpas, & Hale, 1993). The practitioner accustomed to diagnosis and third-party billing thus confronts both ethical and legal dilemmas in considering the source of payment for services, particularly with individuals. False diagnosis for the purpose of reimbursement is both unethical and illegal; however, when the consultation involves more than PST, diagnostic criteria for reimbursement may be met. It is prudent to consider sources of reimbursement as one aspect of one's overall business plan. It is also important to review payment options with the contracting party.

Ethical Concerns for Practitioners

Boundary Issues

Concerns about boundaries, present for all sport and exercise psychologists (see chapter 24, this volume), take on particular significance for the practitioner entering this field (Andersen, 1994; Hays, 1995a; Sachs, 1993; Taylor, 1994). As one's practice shifts toward consultation, it is important to note changes in the relationship between psychologist and client and how these changes are understood and monitored. The potential for increased engagement with the client when one is outside the office setting increases the possibility for loss of traditional structures and for a more casual relationship. Exercising with clients, observing them on the playing field (whether in practice or competition), traveling with a team, and working with high-profile clients involve changes from the standard therapist–patient 50-minute hour (Meyers, 1997). Sport and exercise psychologists need to monitor possible shifts in role relationships, levels of self-disclosure, and power and gender imbalances (Hays, 1995b). It is vital to have an ongoing way to review these questions, whether through reflection, supervision, or consultation (Andersen, Van Raalte, & Brewer, 2001).

Sport Psychology as a "Title"

The professionalization of applied sport psychology has brought increased attention to the complex issues surrounding the use of the title *sport psychologist*. The title *psychologist* is restricted by states to those so certified or licensed. Beyond this restriction, psychologists are additionally bound by ethics to practice within their level of competence (APA, 1992). By virtue of specialized education, training, and experience in exercise and sport, however, it becomes appropriate for psychologists to claim this title (APA, 1998b). Without additional clinical, counseling, or psychotherapy training, those with training only in sport science should not maintain an independent counseling or psychotherapy practice (for additional discussion, see chapter 24, this volume).

Confidentiality

Confidentiality issues are reflected in many aspects of exercise and sport psychology. Psychologists are obligated not to disclose information concerning clients unless that privilege is waived by clients (APA, 1992). In contrast, coaches are routinely quoted in the press discussing their players. Does psychologists' commitment to confidentiality change when they work in the arena of sport and exercise psychology? The temptation of disclosure to the media becomes increasingly seductive the more important or famous the client is (Lesyk, 1998; Van Raalte, 1998). As in other contractual or consultative contexts, there is the common ethical dilemma of disclosure if hired by a team administrator to work with individuals who are members of the team. It is important to discuss and specify, possibly in writing, how this will be handled before the work begins.

Further confidentiality issues can arise as a function of the entrepreneurial nature of sport psychology and the high public visibility of some athletes. For example, client endorsements and the public identification of those clients presents a marketing or ethical dilemma. At present, no standard exists, and practitioners handle these issues in markedly different ways. There is a wide range of practice, from offering services in exchange for endorsements to insisting that athletes not indicate that they are working with a sport psychologist (Botterill, Rotella, Loehr, Ravizza, & Halliwell, 1993). We would err on the side of caution and respect for privacy. Even if clients waive their rights to confidentiality, such decisions may reflect the power differential between the sport and exercise psychologist and the client rather than a freely accepted agreement. In addition, placing the client in a position of endorsing one's services in essence creates a dual relationship in which the client serves as the psychologist's marketing agent. Therefore, the sport and exercise psychologist should weigh carefully the implications and effects of any decision that does not fully protect the client's identity.

Conclusion

The opportunities to include sport and exercise psychology in clinical practice are rich and varied. The professional who is retooling combines the inquiry of the scientist with the practitioner's attention to individual differences. Practice opportunities range from prevention and performance enhancement to psychotherapy and remedial treatment.

The business of learning and developing a new practice in sport and exercise psychology involves an assessment of both current practice and future goals. Various potential problem areas also require careful consideration and proactive planning.

It cannot be overemphasized that, for one's own protection as well as growth in regard to all of these issues, it is helpful to have informal or formal networks of colleagues with whom to consult. To the extent that one's education in this field has been "on-the-job training," it is even more important to develop viable ways of anticipating and addressing troublesome issues before they arise.

References

American Psychological Association. (1992). Ethical principles of psychologists and code of conduct. *American Psychologist, 47,* 1597–1611.

American Psychological Association. (1994). *Graduate training and career possibilities in exercise and sport psychology.* Washington, DC: Author.

American Psychological Association. (1998a). *Employment characteristics of Division 47 members: 1998* (Report prepared by American Psychological Association Research Office). Washington, DC: Author.

American Psychological Association. (1998b). *How can a psychologist become a sport psychologist?* Washington, DC: Author.

Andersen, M. B. (1994). Ethical considerations in the supervision of applied sport psychology graduate students. *Journal of Applied Sport Psychology, 6,* 152–167.

Andersen, M. B. (Ed.). (2000a). *Doing sport psychology: Process and practice.* Champaign, IL: Human Kinetics.

Andersen, M. B. (2000b). Introduction. In M. B. Andersen (Ed.), *Doing sport psychology: Process and practice* (pp. xiii–xvii). Champaign, IL: Human Kinetics.

Andersen, M. B., Van Raalte, J. L., & Brewer, B. W. (2001). Sport psychology service delivery: Staying ethical while keeping loose. *Professional Psychology: Research & Practice, 32,* 12–18.

Association for the Advancement of Applied Sport Psychology. (2000). 1999 Membership report. *AAASP Newsletter, 15*(2), 43.

Auchus, M. P. (1993). Therapeutic aspects of a weight lifting program with seriously psychiatrically disabled outpatients. *The Psychotherapy Bulletin, 28,* 30–31, 34–36.

Austad, C. S., & Hoyt, M. F. (1992). The managed care movement and the future of psychotherapy. *Psychotherapy, 29,* 109–118.

Berger, B. G., & Motl, R. W. (2000). Exercise and mood: A selective review and synthesis of research employing the profile of mood states. *Journal of Applied Sport Psychology, 12,* 69–92.

Berger, B. G., & Motl, R. W. (2001). Physical activity and the quality of life. In R. N. Singer, H. A. Hausenblas, & C. M. Janelle (Eds.), *Handbook of research on sport psychology* (2nd ed., pp. 636–671). New York: Wiley.

Botterill, C., Rotella, R., Loehr, J., Ravizza, K., & Halliwell, W. (1993, October). *Issues and implications in professional sport consulting.* Symposium conducted at the annual meeting of the Association for the Advancement of Applied Sport Psychology, Montreal, Quebec, Canada.

Boutcher, S. (1993). Emotion and aerobic exercise. In R. N. Singer, M. Murphey, & L. K. Tennant (Eds.), *Handbook of research on sport psychology* (pp. 799–814). New York: Macmillan.

Brewer, B. W., Van Raalte, J. L., & Linder, D. E. (1991). Role of the sport psychologist in treating injured athletes: A survey of sports medicine providers. *Journal of Applied Sport Psychology, 3,* 183–190.

Carnegie, D. (1966). *The quick and easy way to effective speaking.* New York: Dale Carnegie & Associates.

Carnegie, D. (1994). *The Dale Carnegie course* [Manual]. New York: Dale Carnegie & Associates.

Cogan, K. D. (1998). Putting the "clinical" into sport psychology consulting. In K. F. Hays (Ed.), *Integrating exercise, sports, movement, and mind: Therapeutic unity* (pp. 131–143). Binghamton, NY: Haworth.

Covey, S. R. (1989). *The seven habits of highly effective people.* New York: Fireside/Simon & Schuster.

Danish, S. J., Petitpas, A. J., & Hale, B. D. (1993). Life development intervention for athletes: Life skills through sports. *The Counseling Psychologist, 21,* 352–385.

Dean, B. (2000). Niche criteria for a successful coaching practice. *The Independent Practitioner, 20,* 112–114.

Diener, E. (1994). Assessing subjective well-being: Progress and opportunities. *Social Indicators Research, 31,* 103–157.

Edwards, P., & Edwards, S. (1996). *Finding your perfect work.* New York: Tarcher.

Edwards, P., Edwards, S., & Douglas, L. C. (1998). *Getting business to come to you.* New York: Tarcher.

Eklund, R. (1993). Considerations for gaining entry to conduct sport psychology field research. *The Sport Psychologist, 7,* 232–243.

Ethical Standards. (n.d.). Retrieved February 11, 2002, from http://www.aasponline.org/ethics.html

Foster, S. (1999). Creating a theme-based practice specialization outside of managed care. *The Independent Practitioner, 19,* 118–121.

Godin, S. (1999). *Permission marketing.* New York: Simon & Schuster.

Gould, D., & Damarjian, N. (1998). Insights into effective sport psychology consulting. In K. F. Hays (Ed.), *Integrating exercise, sports, movement, and mind: Therapeutic unity* (pp. 111–130). Binghamton, NY: Haworth.

Greenspan, M. J., & Feltz, D. F. (1989). Psychological interventions with athletes in competition: A review. *The Sport Psychologist, 3,* 219–236.

Haber, S., Rodino, E., & Lipner, I. (2001). *Saying good-bye to managed care: Building an independent psychotherapy practice.* New York: Springer.

Hays, K. F. (1993). The use of exercise in therapy. In L. VandeCreek, S. Knapp, & T. L. Jackson (Eds.), *Innovations in clinical practice: A source book, 12* (pp. 155–168). Sarasota, FL: Professional Resource Press.

Hays, K. F. (1995a). Putting sport psychology into (your) practice. *Professional Psychology: Research & Practice, 26,* 33–40.

Hays, K. F. (1995b). Running therapy: Special characteristics and therapeutic issues of concern. *Psychotherapy, 31,* 725–734.

Hays, K. F. (1999). *Working it out: Using exercise in psychotherapy.* Washington, DC: American Psychological Association.

Heil, J. (1993). *Psychology of sport injury.* Champaign, IL: Human Kinetics.

Heller, K. (1997). *Strategic marketing: How to achieve independence and prosperity in your mental health practice.* Sarasota, FL: Professional Resource Press.

Hill, N. (1960). *Think and grow rich.* New York: Fawcett Crest.

Horn, T. (Ed.). (1992). *Advances in sport psychology.* Champaign, IL: Human Kinetics.

Karoly, P., & Kanfer, F. H. (1982). *Self-management and behavior change: From theory to practice.* New York: Pergamon.

Kelly-Jones, L. (1999). *Promote your practice exclusively to a fee-for-service clientele.* Morgan Hill, CA: Grow Publications.

Kirkcaldy, B. D., & Shephard, R. J. (1990). Therapeutic implications of exercise. *International Journal of Sport Psychology, 21,* 165–184.

Kirschenbaum, D. S. (1992). Elements of effective weight control programs: Implications for exercise and sport psychology. *Journal of Applied Sport Psychology, 4,* 77–93.

Leith, L. M. (1994). *Foundations of exercise and mental health.* Morgantown, WV: Fitness Information Technology.

Leonard, G. (1992). *Mastery: The keys to success and long-term fulfillment.* New York: Penguin.

Lesyk, J. J. (1998). *Developing sport psychology within your clinical practice: A practical guide for mental health professionals.* San Francisco: Jossey-Bass.

Mahoney, M. J., & Suinn, R. M. (1986). History and overview of modern sport psychology. *The Clinical Psychologist, 39,* 64–68.

Martinsen, E. W., & Morgan, W. P. (1997). Antidepressant effects of physical activity.

In W. P. Morgan (Ed.), *Physical activity and mental health* (pp. 93–106). Washington, DC: Taylor & Francis.

May, J. R. (1986). Sport psychology: Should psychologists become involved? *The Clinical Psychologist, 39,* 77–81.

Meyers, A. W. (1997). Sport psychology service to United States Olympic Festival: An experiential account. *The Sport Psychologist, 11,* 454–468.

Meyers, A. W., Coleman, J., Whelan, J., & Mehlenbeck, R. (2001). Examining careers in sport psychology: Who is working and who is making money? *Professional Psychology: Research & Practice, 32,* 5–11.

Meyers, A. W., Whelan, J. P., & Murphy, S. (1995). Cognitive behavioral strategies in athletic performance enhancement. In M. Hersen, R. M. Eisler, & P. M. Miller (Eds.), *Progress in behavior modification* (pp. 137–164). Pacific Grove, CA: Brooks/Cole.

Morgan, W. P. (1985a). Affective beneficence of vigorous physical activity. *Medicine and Science in Sports and Exercise, 17,* 94–100.

Morgan, W. P. (1985b). Selected psychological factors limiting performance: A mental health model. In D. H. Clarke & H. M. Eckert (Eds.), *Limits of human performance* (pp. 70–80). Champaign, IL: Human Kinetics.

Mroczek, D. K., & Kolarz, C. M. (1998). The effect of age on positive and negative affect: A developmental perspective on happiness. *Journal of Personality and Social Psychology, 75,* 1333–1349.

Norcross, J. C., Alford, B. A., & DeMichele, J. T. (1992). The future of psychotherapy: Delphi data and concluding observations. *Psychotherapy, 29,* 150–158.

Pargman, D. (Ed.). (1999). *Psychological bases of sport injuries* (2nd ed.). Morgantown, WV: Fitness Information Technology.

Parham, W. D., & Singer, R. N. (1994, August). *A discussion with elite coaches and athletes.* Discussion conducted at the annual meeting of the American Psychological Association, Los Angeles.

Pearlman, L.A. (1995). Self-care for trauma therapists: Ameliorating vicarious traumatization. In B. H. Stamm (Ed.), *Secondary traumatic stress: Self-care issues for clinicians, researchers, and educators* (pp. 51–64). Lutherville, MD: Sidran Press.

Petitpas, A. (1998). Practical considerations in providing psychological services to sports medicine clinics. *Journal of Applied Sport Psychology, 10,* 157–167.

Petrie, T. A. (1998). Anxiety management and the elite athlete: A case study. In K. F. Hays (Ed.), *Integrating exercise, sports, movement, and mind: Therapeutic unity* (pp. 161–173). Binghamton, NY: Haworth.

Pierce, R. A. (1969). Athletes in psychotherapy: How many, how come? *Journal of the American College Health Association, 17,* 244–249.

Psychotherapy Finances. (1997). 10 ideas to help you stay in independent practice, Vol. 23(11), Issue 283.

Raglin, J. S. (1997). Anxiolytic effects of physical activity. In W. P. Morgan (Ed.), *Physical activity and mental health* (pp. 107–126). Washington, DC: Taylor & Francis.

Sachs, M. L. (1993). Professional ethics in sport psychology. In R. N. Singer, M. Murphey, & L. K. Tennant (Eds.), *Handbook of research on sport psychology* (pp. 921–932). New York: Macmillan.

Sachs, M. L., Burke, K. L., & Schrader, D. (2000). *Directory of graduate programs in applied sport psychology* (5th ed.). Morgantown, WV: Fitness Information Technology.

Seligman, M., & Csikszentmihalyi, M. (2000). Positive psychology: An introduction. *American Psychologist, 55,* 5–14.

Simons, J. P., & Andersen, M. B. (1995). The development of consulting practice in applied sport psychology: Some personal perspectives. *The Sport Psychologist, 9,* 449–468.

Skrinar, G. S., Unger, K. V., Hutchinson, D. S., & Faigenbaum, A. D. (1992). Effects of exercise training in young adults with psychiatric disabilities. *Canadian Journal of Rehabilitation, 5,* 151–157.

Sonstroem, R. J. (1997). Physical activity and self-esteem. In W. P. Morgan (Ed.), *Physical activity and mental health* (pp. 127–143). Washington, DC: Taylor & Francis.

Stephens, N. (1996). *Five alive: Networking for sales results* [Video Series]. Carlisle, MA: NetWorks.

Taylor, J. (1994). Examining the boundaries of sport science and psychology trained practitioners in applied sport psychology: Title usage and area of competence. *Journal of Applied Sport Psychology, 6,* 185–195.

Van Raalte, J. L. (1998). Working in competitive sport: What coaches and athletes want psychologists to know. In K. F. Hays (Ed.), *Integrating exercise, sports, movement, and mind* (pp. 101–110). Binghamton, NY: Haworth.

Weinberg, R. S., & Gould, D. (1995). *Foundations of sport and exercise psychology.* Champaign, IL: Human Kinetics.

Wildenhaus, K. J. (1997). Sport psychology services in a clinical practice. In L. VandeCreek, S. Knapp, & T. L. Jackson (Eds.), *Innovations in clinical practice: A source book, 15* (pp. 365–383). Sarasota, FL: Professional Resource Press.

Williams, J. M. (1998). *Applied sport psychology* (3rd ed.). Mountain View, CA: Mayfield.

Yambor, J. (1997, September). Lessons learned the hard way in sport psychology consulting. *Journal of Applied Sport Psychology, 8*(Suppl.), S174.

Yenney, S. L., & American Psychological Association Practice Directorate. (1994). *Business strategies for a caring profession.* Washington, DC: American Psychological Association.

24 Ethics in Sport and Exercise Psychology

James P. Whelan, Andrew W. Meyers, and T. David Elkins

One might surmise that a discussion about ethical issues in sport and exercise psychology would be straightforward and simple. Sport and exercise psychology professionals appear to participate in the same range of activities and services as their peers in the other areas of psychology (Cox, Qiu, & Liu, 1993; Singer, 1993). Some of these professionals hold academic positions that enable them to teach, conduct research, and mentor, whereas others focus on the application of scientific knowledge about human behavior (e.g., Smith, 1989), providing evaluations and interventions. Still others focus on educational training and other types of consultation. As with other psychology professionals, there is a clear concern for the quality of services delivered and for the general well-being of individuals and groups with whom these professionals work (e.g., Taylor, 1994; Weinberg, 1989). Logically, then, a discussion about ethical issues could focus on the American Psychological Association's (APA) ethics code (APA, 1992) as applied to sport and exercise settings. (Alternatively, this discussion could center on the Canadian Psychological Association's Ethics code. For those interested in this code or a comparison between the APA and this code, see Canadian Psychological Association, 1991, and Sinclair, 1996.)

Unfortunately, such discussions have been neither straightforward nor simple. One complication has been that the creation of unique ethics guidelines is seen as central to the professional autonomy of sport and exercise psychology. Zeigler (1987), for example, argued that an ethics code designed specifically for sport and exercise psychology is a "vital aspect of the overall professionalization of the field" (p. 138).

Adoption of the APA ethics code would be inconsistent with the goal of public recognition of sport psychology as a unique profession. Successful professionalization, it follows, requires a profession-specific ethics code. Furthermore, the application of the APA ethics code can lead to conflicts among sport and exercise professionals, involving issues such as boundaries of practice, title usage, and academic identity of sport psychology (Brown, 1982; May, 1986; Nideffer, 1981; Rejeski & Brawley, 1988; Taylor, 1994). Many competent exercise and sport scientists who are the backbone of this profession were not trained in psychology departments. These scientists become understandably bothered by laws governing the provision of psychological services that restrict the application of their science (Silva, 1989).

A related complication to these ethics discussions concerns whether sport and exercise psychology services are unique and require unique ethical standards (e.g., Petitpas, Brewer, Rivera, & Van Raalte, 1994; Sachs, 1993; Singer, 1993; Whelan, 1993; Willis & Campbell, 1992). Clearly, there are similarities and differences between sport and exercise services and traditional psychological services. Sport and exercise psychology services may be delivered in the context of therapy or counseling (Whelan, Meyers, & Donovan, 1995). However, performance enhancement and psychological skill consultation are not necessarily therapy and not necessarily clinical (Singer, 1993). Application of the 1992 APA ethics code to similar behaviors in different contexts can be confusing. Indeed, the ethics code has been criticized for being too focused on clinical service delivery. In addition, it fails to provide specific guidance for some applied sport and exercise psychology situations (e.g., Petitpas et al., 1994; Sachs, 1993; Singer, 1993; Willis & Campbell, 1992). The APA ethics code seems to lack the specificity to be practical and interpretable to those providing services in sport and exercise settings.

Furthermore, the pending revisions to the APA ethics code mean that no discussion of ethics can be uncomplicated. APA's Ethics Code Task Force anticipates possible adoption of the next revision of the code in 2002 (Clay, 2000; Martin, 1999). The extent of the pending revisions is unclear; more than several hundred critical incidents and more than 600 comments were collected mid-year 2000. Under consideration are issues related to sexual relationships, informed consent requirements, protecting graduate students, avoiding harm in group therapy, and possibly implications for services delivered by e-mail or the Internet.

Although we would like to say that the discussion that follows will remove these complications and proceed with a straightforward and simple presentation about how to be an ethical sport and exercise psychologist, unfortunately, we cannot. We can put aside discussion of the role of an ethics code in the professionalization of sport psychology and the conflicts about professional organization and identity. These issues are important, but they are not really about ethics or ethical obligation. They need to be considered elsewhere. The complications related to the frustrations of not having specific ethical rules that anticipate unique and specific sport and exercise psychology situations or dilemmas, however, cannot be eradicated. Being prepared for future changes to the ethics code as psychological services continue to develop and evolve cannot be avoided. Ambiguity, uncertainty, and uniqueness seem to be part of each complex ethical situation faced by sport and exercise psychology professionals (Windt, Appleby, Battin, Francis, & Landesman, 1989). It would be impossible to have ethical standards or rules for every situation (Koocher & Keith-Spiegel, 1998). Professionals, therefore, need to understand how to use the ethics code to guide decisions about right and wrong actions (Windt et al., 1989). The foundation for this emphasis is the shared sense of values and responsibilities that is part of the role of the sport and exercise psychology professional, regardless of training background or credentials.

Our discussion begins with a declaration about the purpose of professional ethics and a brief history of the APA ethics code. This history concludes with a summary of the criticisms of the 1992 version of the code. Next, an exploration of two primary traditions in ethical theory of right and wrong is provided, with details about the major premises of these theories. The focus then turns to pragmatics of applying these ideas. Specifically, the applications of ethical reasoning to the issues and areas of practical concern to those working in exercise and sport settings are addressed. Using a survey of dilemmas and controversial behaviors found in these settings (Petitpas et al., 1994), we consider how professionals can approach problematic situations ethically in an a priori manner.

Purpose of Professional Ethics Codes

Questions about ethical conduct permeate our culture. One need only pick up a newsmagazine or newspaper or spend a few evenings watching television to find aggressive inquiries into the ethics of politicians, lawyers, physicians, psychologists, and a variety of other professionals. Our society, with good reason, has become less trusting and more cynical about the judgments of its professionals and experts. In turn, this mistrust and cynicism has led to decreased tolerance for professional misbehavior and increased demands for ethical reform (Windt, 1989; Krause, 1996). It is expected that the professional can judge between right and wrong and should behave in accordance with what is right. Partly as a consequence of this cultural mistrust, the study of ethics and the development of written codes of ethics in the social science and helping professions has absorbed much energy and generated a great deal of debate in recent years (Ellickson & Brown, 1990; Windt et al., 1989). This activity in the realm of ethics reflects the concern felt by many that ethics codes need to address the cultural concerns and fears articulated by society.

To address these concerns, a profession and its members must attend to both the privileges and the responsibilities of professional status (Koocher & Keith-Spiegel, 1998; Pryzwansky & Wendt, 1999; Windt, 1989). Privileges derive from society's agreement to designate a group of trained individuals as possessing specialized knowledge and holding the power implicit in this knowledge. The profession's responsibilities result from society's expectation that the profession will regulate itself to "do no harm" and will govern itself to ensure the dignity and welfare of individuals and the public. The profession also agrees to ensure the quality of its interactions with society. To maintain this status, professional organizations must develop and enforce guidelines that regulate their members' professional conduct. In other words, professional groups must demonstrate to society that they hold themselves accountable for their professional conduct (Pryzwansky & Wendt, 1999). Ethical principles, which go above and beyond personal ethics, are one such set of self-regulatory guidelines. These principles, written as an ethics code, guide professionals to act responsibly as they use the privileges granted by society. A profession's inability to regulate itself violates the public's trust and causes cultural and societal cynicism toward the profession.

Before turning to the APA code, it is important to differentiate professional ethics from personal morals and from legal regulation. It is not unreasonable that professional ethics decision making is often influenced by these other guidelines. Each of these guidelines is important for how we decide between what is right and wrong in a particular situation. Our personal morals, like our professional ethics, are based on important core values and specific rules we have for reaching decisions about our personal behavior. However, personal morals are personal; they typically develop from our own cultural context, religious education, and personal experiences (Midgley, 1993). These morals define our personal integrity. However, professional ethics is a collective agreement among the members of a profession about how the professional behaves when in the professional role. Personal morals and professional ethics are not likely to conflict, although the two might not always be in complete agreement. A thorough understanding of professional ethics and a separate awareness of personal value systems help prepare the professional for conflicts between the professional and the personal.

Equally common is the blending of ethical considerations and legal responsibilities in a specific situation (Pryzwansky & Wendt, 1999). Indeed, ethical and legal issues are frequently combined to help professionals manage the risks of independent professional practice (e.g., Koocher & Keith-Spiegel, 1998; Pettifor, 1996; Reaves, 1996). It is not uncommon for ethics to be part of licensing laws for psychologists. The standards of the APA ethics code have been adopted by 49 of the 50 state licensing boards to regulate professional conduct (Bass et al., 1996). However, a foundation and reason for an ethical decision can be different from the reason for a legal decision. For example, legal informed consent is a signed document. Ethical informed consent is the knowledge that the consenting individual understands what and why he or she is agreeing to something. We advise that the professional engaged in the ethical decision-making process have a separate understanding of the moral, ethical, and legal issues before choosing how to act.

The APA Ethics Code

Psychology as a field has a long and successful history of acting responsibly and proactively on issues of ethical conduct. The APA first adopted an ethics code in 1953 (APA, 1953), which was fairly early in the history of the profession. This first ethics code was developed by polling members for specific vignettes that related to ethical situations. The response was so great that the code was unwieldy because of its size (Canter, Bennett, Jones, & Nagy, 1994). The code has been revised seven times in the ensuing years to meet the needs of the profession and to fulfill obligations to society. The code thus has become a living document; as psychology has changed, the code has changed with it (Pope & Vetter, 1992).

The current code (APA, 1992) consists of six general principles: competence, integrity, professional and scientific responsibility, respect for people's rights and dignity, concern for others' welfare, and social responsibility. Under each of these principles are specific standards, or practical applications of the general principles. These standards are generally thought of as rules of ethical behavior. The primary goal of the code has always been to respect the dignity of the individual and to guarantee the welfare of the consumer and the profession (Canter et al., 1994). This foundational goal of the code can be conceptualized in general terms as "do no harm," and it serves to inform the six general principles. The general principles then become specific in the form of the standards, the discrete rules and regulations that result from the application of the general principles to real-life situations. The entire model can be conceptualized as a triangle: At the widest point on the bottom are the specific standards, or the individual rules that make the ethics code enforceable; these are seen as flowing logically from the general principles, which constitute the next tier. These general principles are derived from the top point, which is the foundational goal of the ethics code, respect for human beings.

The code has not been without criticism. The 1992 version is generally seen as a great improvement over previous renditions (Bersoff, 1994). However, the current code has been criticized for being too concerned with protecting the profession rather than the public (Bersoff, 1994), indifferent to the concerns of diverse groups (Payton, 1994), equivocal about multiple relationships (Sonne, 1994), and, in general, vague (Vasquez, 1994). These criticisms seem to occur because of two problems inherent in the nature of the ethics code. First, it seeks to address a wide range of activities, thus necessitating a cursory treatment of each. Second, it fails to anticipate the unique and specific situations in which psychologists find themselves.

In addition, an omission in the APA ethics code is guidance on ethical decision making. A thorough familiarity with this standard of conduct assists professionals in how to manage their professional conduct (for a detailed commentary on the APA ethics code, see Canter et al., 1994). Unfortunately, the code does not deal adequately with many of the possible contradictions that can arise. At such times, the professional is advised to be prepared with a strategy to effectively solve conflicts. It is not the intent of this chapter to consider various ethical decision-making models. The reader who needs assistance on this topic is encouraged to consider one of the many references to a detailed discussion of how to make ethically informed decisions (e.g., Hass & Malouf, 1995; Kitchner, 1984; Koocher & Keith-Spiegel, 1998; Nagle, 1987).

A study of the philosophy of ethics may help to clarify these concerns regarding specific ethics codes and the omission of how to make ethical decisions. Although a thorough understanding of philosophy of ethics is not a prerequisite for further discussion of ethics codes, a brief treatment of the philosophy of ethics will aid the professional in understanding the foundations of ethics and in applying ethics in difficult situations.

Philosophy of Ethics in the History of Psychology

The philosophical study of ethics involves the inquiry into the principles and presuppositions that operate in moral judgments. It has been traditionally concerned with the study of what is good and bad, what is right and wrong, and the values that define a "good life." Ethical codes, therefore, are an attempt to put into practice this good life. Codes of ethics may exist for many different populations and diverse situations: Different cultures, religions, and professions may have very different codes of ethics. The one common factor underlying different codes, however, is their definitional acceptance of ethical codes as "moral guides to self regulation" (O'Donohue & Mangold, 1996; Windt, 1989). Thus, the function of ethics in general and professional ethical codes in particular is to define right and wrong behavior for a given population, especially as that population interacts with other populations.

Philosophy of ethics must be theory-driven. In other words, one cannot make a determination of what is right and wrong behavior on the basis of personal whims. If that was the case, then ethics and, by implication, professional codes of ethics, would merely be the fickle voice of the majority. Codes of ethics cannot exist without some sort of theory behind them, informing them, grounding them, and providing for their application. This does not mean, however, that codes of ethics are vastly different from ordinary morality. Indeed, professional codes of ethics do not have a "hierarchy of values" different from ordinary morality (O'Donohue & Mangold, 1996, p. 394).

In the history of philosophy, many distinct sources for ethics and ethics codes exist. From the Judeo–Christian ethic to Aristotle to Nietzsche, philosophies of ethics have abounded. However, the works of the deontologists and the consequentialists have been described as particularly influential in the field of psychology and especially on the APA ethics code (O'Donohue & Mangold, 1996). The following sections present a brief description of these competing ethical philosophies.

Consequentialists

The consequentialist school of philosophy argues that actions are ethical or not on the basis of their consequences. Behaviors are not determined in an a priori manner to be ethical or not. We can determine whether an action is ethical only by making judgments after the behavior occurs. It is the end that is important, not the means by which one arrives at the end. To be ethical, an individual must follow specific rules that make an attempt to guarantee that the consequences of actions will be ethical. A representative of this school was John Stuart Mill, whose contribution to ethical philosophy is known as utilitarianism (Mill, 1861/1979). Although the utilitarian principle has been stated in many ways, it can be summarized in the well-known statement, "the greatest good for the greatest number." Mill assumed that human beings do not desire only lofty things such as virtue and duty, nor only desire base things, such as wealth. What human beings desire is happiness, and when things such as virtue and wealth make them happy, they seek them. The goal of morality, then, becomes one of maximizing happiness, that is, when the greatest number of people are happy.

In creating moral and ethical codes, the necessity of maximizing pleasure for the majority of human beings is paramount. The way to maximize this happiness is by ensuring that the rules that are developed for that purpose are followed. If it can be shown that a particular action produces the greatest good for the greatest number, then people should engage in that action. Ethics codes are rules based on past experiences.

Deontologists

In contrast to consequentialism, the deontological viewpoint holds that before any discussion of ethics and ethics codes can take place, a philosophical foundation must be established. The deontological view argues that ethics need to be founded on firm and lasting principles that can be applied to many different situations. These principles are, in a sense, immutable; otherwise, ethics would exist merely by the will of the majority. The deontologists argue that the whole point of discussions about ethics is to center on the ideal. Ethics is concerned with what should be, not with what is; therefore, what needs to be established is the ideal, or what ought to be. The ideal is encapsulated in principles, which are not specific but can be applied to many different areas. For example, philosophers of this school would prefer to have general principles, such as "respect other people," than to have a litany of specific rules that apply this principle in many different areas. The problem becomes one of deciding which principles to emphasize.

An example of a philosopher from the deontological school was Immanuel Kant. Kant argued that morality entails duty to one's conscience. He stated that rationality exists in every human and that reason is capable of generating the possibilities of future experiences. People can think ahead in time and judge whether an action will be ethical or not on the basis of past experiences. Morality, therefore, is a duty to the future possibilities of experience and is based on the general principle of respect for other human beings.

In *Grounding for the Metaphysics of Morals,* Kant (1785/1977) described the categorical imperative, which has several qualifications and conditions. It states that a moral action is one that dictates universality and consistency. Stated differently, a moral action must be able to be applied to all human beings and must involve no contradictions. The categorical imperative is then used to test whether actions are moral or not. In other words, one could test a maxim (e.g., I will borrow money and never repay it) by thinking, "If everyone were to do this, could they continue to do it forever?" In this example, everyone could of course engage in this behavior, but everyone could not continue to engage in it forever; it would become a self-destructive action. Out of this example comes one of the underlying principles in discussions such as this one: respect for human beings. Actions that are destructive to human beings are not moral because they cannot be universalized. The work of Kant provides philosophical justification for the grounding of morals and a framework from which specific moral maxims can be generated for novel situations that have never been questioned before.

Integrating Philosophy and Ethics

The philosophers Mill and Kant and the views that they espouse can be argued to have a unique relationship to the APA ethics code. Kant would argue for the general principles; with his emphasis on duty to conscience and the use of reason to test all possible actions, his view of ethics points to the understanding and documentation of general principles, or general plans of action, that would guide future tests of actions for ethicality. His philosophy allows no room for particular rules; it is a dynamic system that is constantly capable of evaluating every single possible action that can be thought of at any moment.

The philosophy of Mill addresses the problem from a very different direction. His philosophy points to the necessity of specific codes and standards that deal with specific situations. Only by dealing with the specific contingencies of the environment and behavior can the happiness and the good of the greatest number be ensured. Only by looking to past experiences can rules be generated that will cover future experiences. Mill would make no provisions for general principles that inform ethics in a global sense; rather, his framework demands the specific and works toward spelling out exactly what contributes to the greatest good for the greatest number. Thus, the work of the consequentialists can be seen as arguing for the creation of specific rules, or standards, that govern behavior.

It can be argued that the APA ethics code (1992) operates according to both of these assumptions. The code is functionally a mixture of the different philosophical frameworks epitomized by Kant and Mill. From the deontologists, the code derives its six general principles, all of which operate as ethical maxims capable of being universalized and consistent without resorting to individual rules for specific cases. These principles are designed to be portable, in a sense; they transcend specific situations and therefore are capable of influencing a wide range of behaviors. Likewise, the code follows the consequentialists, with its standards. These are specific rules that are thought to flow out of the general principles and that apply to specific situations within the field of psychology. The problem with attempting to create an exhaustive list is that one cannot anticipate every problematic circumstance. Undoubtedly, the standards as they are currently written do not represent all of the possible rules that a psychologist would need to follow to behave ethically. However, the code claims to be "enforceable," and ethics codes can be enforceable only if specific rules are spelled out. The question of other rules that also are enforceable but have not yet been codified naturally arises. The code recognizes this dilemma and provides for the creation of additional rules: "The Ethical Standards are not exhaustive. The fact that a given conduct is not specifically addressed by the Ethics Code does not mean that it is necessarily ethical or unethical" (APA, 1992, p. 1598).

This dynamic model of ethics, in which standards often fail to fit perfectly and principles give guidance across context areas, may make some people uncomfortable. People seem naturally to desire specificity and ease of applicability, which a list of rules seemingly provides. However, codes of ethics are moving away from the conception of a mere list of rules and toward a dynamic model of ethics, one that treats ethics in a thematic sense by emphasizing general principles. The Association for the Advancement of Applied Sport Psychology (AAASP) is considering adopting this type of model. In the AAASP model, the general principles are listed and then provision is made for future clarification of these principles as the field develops. This flexibility is particularly appropriate for professionals who are working in a new field but attempting to develop and adhere to specific statements.

Ethical Philosophy Applied to Sport and Exercise Psychology

Sport and exercise psychologists frequently encounter ethically challenging situations. Consider the following situation. "Dr. Bob" has a PhD in counseling psychology with a background in exercise and sport sciences. He accepted a split position funded by a university counseling center and the university's athletic department. His charge in the new position included sport psychology and personal counseling services to the university's sports teams and the individual student–athletes. While moving into his office, Dr. Bob received a call from the head coach for one of the women's sports teams. The coach reported that her team really needed a psychologist. She requested mental skills training for her team, assistance with a couple of "head cases," and information about the psychology of coaching and feedback about her coaching. The coaching issue centered on more effective communication between her and the team. The coach said that several players seemed to be insulted and discouraged by her feedback. Because the coach worked with a sport psychologist as an athlete, she was very responsive to Dr. Bob's clarifications about confidentiality and his role with the coach and team. Dr. Bob was confident that he and the coach had a clear understanding of his role with her and her team.

Through the early fall, Dr. Bob's efforts appeared to pay off. The coach was initially receptive during the preseason consultation meetings about communication with her team. Unfortunately, the pressure of conference play precipitated a return to what, for the sake of simplicity, could be labeled as an authoritarian and condescending style of coaching. The team benefited from the psychological skills training meetings and appeared to be mastering some basic psychological skills related to performance preparation. Several of the team members had confidentially contacted Dr. Bob with concerns about their relationship with the coach. He assured each of these women that their meetings were confidential and that the coach understood each athlete's right to confidentiality. An added bonus was that the coach had mentioned to the athletic director and other coaches that "sport psychology" was okay.

At the end of a successful season for this team, Dr. Bob's experience was drastically altered. One-third of the squad, including many of the starters, requested to meet with Dr. Bob as a group. They each reported feeling abused by the coach, and with their parents' support, they wanted to seek a release from the team. They wanted to know how to get this release. The women and their parents considered calling the university president to secure their release. Several described specific incidents in which the coach's behavior could be viewed as psychologically abusive. Dr. Bob had neither witnessed nor heard of these incidents before.

Instantly, Dr. Bob found himself in an ethical dilemma. He had a fiduciary relationship with both the coach and the team members. The seriousness of the conflict between these two parties meant that he was in a position to fail the trust of one of these relationships. In fact, his fiduciary responsibilities were threatened by his simply listening to the team members and engaging them in a discussion of their options. A further complication was that this scenario could jeopardize his job and the degree to which the athletic department and the student–athletes had access to a sport psychologist. Although Dr. Bob had educated all parties involved about his ethical responsibilities, he was not ready for the specifics of this situation. However, Dr. Bob cannot be blamed. There are no specific rules concerning a situation like this one. A simple answer stating what is the right action to take does not exist for such circumstances.

Unpredictable and complicated situations such as this occur for professionals working in clinical psychology (Pope, Tabachnick, & Keith-Spiegel, 1987; Pope & Vasquez, 1991; Pope & Vetter, 1992), sport psychology (Petitpas et al., 1994; Sachs, 1993; Whelan, 1993), and other public service areas (Bayles, 1981; Windt et al., 1989). These situations challenge the professional's knowledge of the meaning and the application of ethics codes. They call for psychologists to identify and clarify their personal values and their professional and institutional guidelines.

Responses to a sample of situations like this were elicited in a national survey of the beliefs and behaviors of psychologists and sport scientists interested in the application of psychology to exercise and sport settings (Petitpas et al., 1994). Petitpas and colleagues mailed questionnaires to 508 student and professional members of AAASP. Respondents were provided with 47 ethical situations and asked to report their own behavior and their belief about the ethicality of the choices. This survey also requested a brief description of difficult ethical situations experienced by members. Of the 165 members who returned the survey, approximately half of the respondents identified themselves as psychologists, with most of the other half self-identified as exercise scientists. It is interesting that more than 90% of the respondents reported that they engage in sport psychology services less than 17 hours per week and 70% less than 5 hours per week. Therefore, individuals in this sample, representing the two major traditions within sport psychology, were only minimally engaged in applied sport psychology services. Meyers, Coleman, Whelan, and Mehlenbeck (2001) recently replicated this finding with a larger sample of sport and exercise psychology professionals.

As for the ethical issues in practice, the central findings of the survey by Petitpas and colleagues (1994) replicated the work of Pope and colleagues (1987), with most of these professionals reporting that they behave in accordance with their beliefs about ethics. There were only minor differences between members identified as psychologists and those identified as sport and exercise scientists in terms of ethical beliefs and behaviors. Of the 47 ethical situations, respondents found 8 to be difficult ethical judgments and 24 to be controversial behaviors. Difficult ethical judgments were defined as situations for which more than 25% of the respondents indicated that they were unsure whether the behavior was ethical. The 8 difficult ethical situations can be classified into three general categories (see Exhibit 24.1). Controversial behaviors were items for which the opinions of the respondents were significantly diverse. The behaviors that were rated as controversial can be classified into four general categories that are consistent with the APA ethics code (APA, 1992): (a) issues of confidentiality, (b) conflicts between personal and professional ethics, (c) dual-role relationships, and (d) self-presentation and advertising (see Exhibit 24.2).

Exhibit 24.1

Behaviors Identified as Difficult Judgments

Conflict with confidentiality:
  Reporting recruiting violations to appropriate officials
  Reporting an athlete's gambling activity
  Reporting an athlete who acknowledged committing rape in the past
Conflict between personal values and professional ethics:
  Consulting with athletes in a sport that you find morally objectionable (e.g., boxing)
  Working with an athlete who uses steroids
  Refusing to continue consulting with a client after you discover that he or she is involved in illegal activity
Conflict with dual relationships:
  Socializing with clients (e.g., partying with the team)
  Allowing out-of-town clients to reside in your home while services are being provided

---

Issues of confidentiality are frequently encountered by professionals working in sport and exercise psychology, as in the following hypothetical example. A PhD psychologist is contracted by a major university to work with an athlete who reports "anxiety." Before beginning the consultation, the professional is instructed about National Collegiate Athletic Association rules and regulations that specifically state the professional cannot attend practices or performance situations because that professional would be considered part of the coaching staff. Over the course of consultation, this issue becomes problematic for the professional, who knows that effective treatment for anxiety should involve on-site exposure to anxiety-eliciting stimuli by the athlete and behavior monitoring of the athlete by the professional. Also, after one month of consultation, the coaching staff, who claims that the athlete has signed a consent waiver, approaches the professional with questions about what happened during the consultation process. This, too, is problematic, because the professional has discovered information relating to the anxiety of the athlete that might result in the athlete losing eligibility. What can the professional do? The ethics code is not particularly clear at this point. The professional's primary responsibility is to the athlete; behaving ethically involves being true to the foundational principle of doing no harm to the athlete. Therefore, the professional should not divulge information concerning the athlete without the athlete's permission. The professional should contact the athlete, discuss what is to be re-

Exhibit 24.2

Behaviors Identified as Controversial

Conflict with confidentiality:
  Reporting recruiting violations to appropriate official
  Reporting an athlete who uses cocaine
  Reporting an athlete who uses steroids
  Reporting abusive coaching practices
  Reporting an athlete's gambling activity
  Reporting an athlete who committed burglary
  Reporting an athlete who acknowledged committing rape in the past
Conflict between personal values and professional ethics:
  Working with an athlete whose sexual or religious practices you oppose
  Consulting with athletes in a sport that you find morally objectionable (e.g., boxing)
  Working with an athlete who uses steroids
  Refusing to continue consulting with a client after you discover that he or she is involved in illegal activity
Conflict with dual relationships:
  Accepting goods or services in exchange for sport psychology consultation
  Serving concurrently as coach and sport psychologist for a team
  Serving concurrently as college instructor and psychologist for a student–athlete
  Being sexually attracted to a client
  Becoming sexually involved with a client *after* discontinuing a professional relationship
  Entering into a business relationship with a client
Conflict with self-presentation or advertising:
  Publicly claiming to be a sport psychologist
  Advertising sport psychology services
  Including athlete testimonials in advertising
  Using institutional affiliation to recruit private clients

vealed, and proceed from there. This is an example in which issues of confidentiality become clouded; even though the professional is under contract by the university, the professional's primary fiduciary responsibility lies with the athlete.

Conflicts between personal and professional ethics frequently occur to those who work in sport and exercise psychology (Appleby, 1989). It is always recommended that ethical issues be clearly defined and clarified before one enters into a formal consultation (Dougherty, 1990). Although this advice is helpful, it is not always possible to follow. Often, issues arise during the consultation process that were not foreseeable from the outset and involve conflicts between personal and professional ethics. Returning to the previous example, suppose that during the consultation process, the professional discovers that one of the sources of anxiety that the athlete is experiencing is the athlete's frequent use of illegal drugs. The professional may be personally against the use of drugs but must take into account, first and foremost, the obligation to professional ethics. What should the professional do? The professional may feel that it would benefit the athlete in the long run to enter a drug rehabilitation program, but the athlete does not want to do this. Here, the professional's obligation involves acting in the athlete's best interest as far as sport and exercise performance is concerned, in line with the professional's original contract with the university. Again, the specific rules are not clear, but the professional is aided by an understanding of the philosophy of ethics and complying with general principles.

Dual-role relationships in sport and exercise psychology are especially problematic. Sometimes, professionals may find that the relationship boundary between themselves and the client becomes clouded. In the previous example, if the professional chooses to use on-site exposure by attending practices and games, the role of the professional changes slightly. The professional is now part of the coaching staff and hence may be viewed by the athlete as less objective. Likewise, the visual intimacy that a locker room affords can be problematic for the professional and may lead to feelings of decreased objectivity by both the professional and the athlete (Sachs, 1993). Dual-role relationships open the possibility of distorting the professional relationship, creating conflicts of interest, and undermining the fiduciary nature of the consultation process (Pope & Vazquez, 1991; Sonne, 1994). For the professional, the difficulty lies in avoiding dual-role relationships; however, no rules exist that clearly delineate all possible dual-role relationships. The professional must operate from general principles, with a view toward clearly defining future dual-role relationships.

With regard to *self-presentation and advertising,* the APA ethics code frequently finds itself at odds with the rules and regulations of the Federal Trade Commission (Koocher, 1994). The basic rule applied by the ethics code is that advertising by a professional is wrong; however, the Federal Trade Commission has in the past investigated whether this prohibition is correct (Koocher, 1994). To return to the previous example, after a period of time, the athlete with whom the professional has worked shows no signs of anxiety, is playing in top form, and credits the professional for the comeback. The athlete has an upcoming television interview and has told the professional that he plans to mention the professional's name on the air. What should the professional do? Although the professional had not actively sought out this endorsement from the athlete, it is not something that the professional can easily reject. It could mean many more referrals in the future for other athletic consultations. However, the professional knows that advertising is not encouraged in the ethics code. In this case, the professional again should remember the general principles, which state that the primary goal of consultation is to benefit the athlete, not the professional.

Furthermore, telehealth (Stamm, 1998) is an increasingly important issue that did not arise in this survey and is not mentioned specifically in the APA ethics code. Nickelson (1998) defined telehealth "as the use of telecommunications and information technology to provide access to health assessment, diagnosis, intervention, consultation, supervision, education, and information across distance" (p. 527), meaning that activities that traditionally would take place face-to-face between the professional and the client would be done using the telephone or Internet technology. The application of this technology to sport and exercise psychology work is particularly intriguing. For example, a traveling athlete or coach can establish and maintain communication with the sport psychology professional.

The technological developments in telehealth are occurring more quickly than ethical guidance or regulation can accommodate them (Jerome & Zaylor, 2000). Critical questions about provider competence, confidentiality, and consumer protection need to be carefully considered before professionals utilize these technologies. The APA Ethics Committee (1997) has issued a statement that stressed the relevance of the ethics code to psychologists engaged in telehealth. Specifically, the committee warned that psychologists are required to work within the bounds of their competence. The statement also details that sections of the 1992 ethics code may be particularly relevant to telehealth activities, such as assessment (section 2.01 to 2.10), therapy (section 4.01 to 4.09), and several of the general standards. To date, no statement indicates that the next revision of the ethics code will include a section on using technology. A growing number of professionals believe that such guidance is needed (e.g., Humphreys, Winzelberg, & Klaw, 2000; Jerome & Zaylor, 2000; Stamm, 1998). As one might imagine, the addition of telehealth makes possible a virtually endless number of difficult situations.

Conclusion

An ethics code is a helpful tool in guiding behavior. It is especially helpful for a profession that, in part, fulfills its societal contract by providing for the regulation of its members' behavior. But ethics codes change as the profession changes in its relation to society. Furthermore, as developing fields emerge, ethical situations are encountered that an existing ethics code may not adequately address. Although sport and exercise psychology is by definition a branch of psychology, the professionals who practice it often encounter unique ethical situations that are difficult and controversial. It is clear from the examination of difficult and controversial situations that behaving ethically does not involve simply following the rules of the ethics code. Understanding the philosophy of ethics guides the professional toward ethical behavior. The ultimate goal would naturally be the creation of standards that clearly delineate ethical behavior; however, the creation of standards is an ongoing process. The professional is aided, therefore, by an understanding of the foundational principle and the general principles of an ethics code until such time as specific standards are created that address the particular situations of concern to the professional.

References

American Psychological Association. (1953). *Ethical standards of psychologists.* Washington, DC: Author.

American Psychological Association. (1992). Ethical principles of psychologists and code of conduct. *American Psychologist, 47,* 1597–1611.

American Psychological Association Ethics Committee. (1997). *Services by telephone, teleconferencing, and internet* [Online]. Washington, DC: Author. Retrieved from http://www.apa.org/ethics/stmnt01.html. Accessed December 2000.

Appleby, P. C. (1989). Personal, professional, and institutional obligations. In P. Y. Windt, P. C. Appleby, M. P. Battin, L. P. Francis, & B. M. Landesman (Eds.), *Ethical issues in the professions* (pp. 229–255). Englewood Cliffs, NJ: Prentice-Hall.

Bass, L. J., DeMars, S. T., Ogloff, J. R., Peterson, C., Pettifor, J. L., Reaves, R. P., et al. (1996). *Professional conduct and discipline in psychology.* Washington, DC: American Psychological Association and Association of State and Provincial Boards of Psychology.

Bayles, M. D. (1981). *Professional ethics.* Belmont, CA: Wadsworth.

Bersoff, D. N. (1994). Explicit ambiguity: The 1992 ethics code as an oxymoron. *Professional Psychology: Research and Practice, 25,* 382–387.

Brown, J. (1982). Are sport psychologists really psychologists? *Journal of Sport Psychology, 4,* 13–18.

Canadian Psychological Association. (1991). *Canadian ethics code for psychologists, revised.* Ottawa, ON: Author.

Canter, M. B., Bennett, B. E., Jones, S. E., & Nagy, T. F. (1994). *Ethics for psychologists:*

A commentary on the APA Ethics Code. Washington, DC: American Psychological Association.

Clay, R. A. (2000). APA task force considers changes to proposed ethics code. *APA Monitor, 31*(7), 86–87.

Cox, R. H., Qiu, Y., & Liu, Z. (1993). Overview of sport psychology. In R. N. Singer, M. Murphey, & Tennant, L. K. (Eds.), *Handbook of research on sport psychology* (pp. 3–31). New York: Macmillan.

Dougherty, A. M. (1990). *Consultation: Practice and perspectives.* Pacific Grove, CA: Brooks/Cole.

Ellickson, K. A., & Brown, D. R. (1990). Ethical considerations in dual relationships: The sport psychologist–coach. *Journal of Applied Sport Psychology, 2,* 186–190.

Hass, I. J., & Malouf, J. L. (1995). *Keeping up the good work: A practitioner's guide to mental health ethics* (2nd ed.). Sarasota, FL: Professional Resources Exchange.

Humphreys, K., Winzelberg, A., & Klaw, E. (2000). Psychologists' ethical responsibilities in Internet-based groups: Issues, strategies, and a call for dialogue. *Professional Psychology: Research and Practice, 31,* 493–496.

Jerome, L. W., & Zaylor, C. (2000). Cyberspace: Creating a therapeutic environment for telehealth applications. *Professional Psychology: Research and Practice, 31,* 478–483.

Kant, I. (1785/1977). Grounding for the metaphysics of morals. In S. M. Cahn (Ed.), *Classics of Western Philosophy* (pp. 925–976). Indianapolis, IN: Hackett.

Kitchner, K. S. (1984). Intuition, critical evaluation and ethical principles: The foundation for ethical decisions in counseling psychology. *The Counseling Psychologist, 12,* 43–55.

Koocher, G. P. (1994). The commerce of professional psychology and the new ethics code. *Professional Psychology: Research and Practice, 25,* 355–361.

Koocher, G. P., & Keith-Spiegel, P. (1998). *Ethics in psychology: Professional standards and cases* (2nd ed.). New York: Oxford.

Krause, E. A. (1996). *Death of the guilds: Professionals, states and the advance of capitalism, 1930 to the present.* New Haven, CT: Yale

Martin, S. (1999). Revision of the ethics code calls for stronger former client sex rules. *APA Monitor, 30*(7), 44.

May, J. (1986). Sport psychology: Should psychologists become involved? *The Clinical Psychologist, 39,* 77–81.

Meyers, A. W., Coleman, J. K., Whelan, J. P., & Mehlenbeck, R. S. (2001). Examining the career contributions of sport psychology work: Who is working and who is making money? *Professional Psychology: Research and Practice, 32,* 5–11.

Midgley, M. (1993). The origins of ethics. In P. Singer (Ed.), *A companion to ethics* (pp. 3–13). Cambridge, MA: Blackwell.

Mill, J. S. (1861/1979). Utilitarianism. In G. Sher (Ed.), *John Stuart Mill: Utilitarianism* (pp. 1–63). Indianapolis, IN: Hackett.

Nagle, R. J. (1987). Ethics training in school psychology. *Professional School Psychology, 2,* 163–171.

Nickelson, D. W. (1998). Telehealth and the evolving health care system: Strategic opportunities for professional psychology. *Professional Psychology: Research and Practice, 29,* 527–535.

Nideffer, R. (1981). *The ethics and practice of applied sport psychology.* Ithaca, NY: Movement.

O'Donohue, W., & Mangold, R. (1996). A critical examination of the ethical principles of psychologists and code of conduct. In W. O'Donohue & R. F. Kitchener (Eds.), *The philosophy of psychology.* New York: Allyn & Bacon.

Payton, C. R. (1994). Implications of the 1992 ethics code for diverse groups. *Professional Psychology: Research and Practice, 25,* 317–320.

Petitpas, A., Brewer, B., Rivera, P., & Van Raalte, J. (1994). Ethical beliefs and behaviors in applied sport psychology: The AAASP ethics survey. *Journal of Applied Sport Psychology, 6,* 135–151.

Pettifor, J. L. (1996). Maintaining professional conduct in daily practice. In L. J. Bass, S. T. DeMars, J. R. Ogloff, C. Peterson, J. L. Pettifor, R. P. Reaves, et al. (Eds.), *Professional conduct and discipline in psychology* (pp. 91–100). Washington, DC: American Psychological Association and Association of State and Provincial Boards of Psychology.

Pope, K. S., Tabachnick, B. G., & Keith-Spiegel, P. (1987). Ethics of practice: The beliefs and behaviors of psychologists as therapists. *American Psychologist, 42,* 993–1006.

Pope, K. S., & Vasquez, M. J. T. (1991). *Ethics in psychotherapy and counseling: A practical guide for psychologists.* San Francisco: Jossey-Bass.

Pope, K. S., & Vetter, V. A. (1992). Ethical dilemmas encountered by members of the American Psychological Association. *American Psychologist, 47,* 397–411.

Pryzwansky, W. B., & Wendt, R. N. (1999). *Professional and ethical issues in psychology.* New York: Norton.

Reaves, R. P. (1996). Enforcement of codes of conduct by regulatory boards and professional associations. In L. J. Bass, S. T. DeMars, J. R. Ogloff, C. Peterson, J. L. Pettifor, R. P. Reaves, et al. (Eds.), *Professional conduct and discipline in psychology* (pp. 101–108). Washington, DC: American Psychological Association and Association of State and Provincial Boards of Psychology.

Rejeski, W. J., & Brawley, L. (1988). Defining the boundaries of sport psychology. *The Sport Psychologist, 2,* 231–242.

Sachs, M. (1993). Professional ethics in sport psychology. In R. N. Singer, M. Murphey, & L. K. Tennant (Eds.), *Handbook of research on sport psychology* (pp. 921–932). New York: Macmillan.

Silva, J. (1989). Toward the professionalization of sport psychology. *The Sport Psychologist, 3,* 265–273.

Sinclair, C. (1996). A comparison of codes of professional conduct and ethics. In L. J. Bass, et al. (Eds.). *Professional conduct and discipline in psychology* (pp. 53–70). Washington, DC: American Psychological Association and Association of State and Provincial Boards of Psychology.

Singer, R. N. (1993). Ethical issues in clinical services. *Quest, 45,* 88–145.

Smith, R. E. (1989). Applied sport psychology in an age of accountability. *Journal of Applied Sport Psychology, 1,* 166–180.

Sonne, J. L. (1994). Multiple relationships: Does the new ethics code answer the right questions? *Professional Psychology: Research and Practice, 25,* 336–343.

Stamm, H. (1998). Clinical applications of telehealth in mental health care. *Professional Psychology: Research and Practice, 29,* 536–542.

Taylor, J. (1994). Examining the boundaries of sport science and psychology trained practitioners in applied sport psychology: Title usage and area of competence. *Journal of Applied Sport Psychology, 6,* 185–195.

Vasquez, M. J. (1994). Implications of the 1992 ethics code for the practice of individual therapy. *Professional Psychology: Research and Practice, 25,* 321–328.

Weinberg, R. S. (1989). Applied sport psychology: Issues and challenges. *Journal of Applied Sport Psychology, 1,* 181–195.

Whelan, J. P. (1993, Summer). Considering ethics. *AAASP Newsletter,* pp. 24, 27.

Whelan, J. P., Meyers, A. W., & Donovan, C. (1995). Interventions with competitive recreational athletes. In S. Murphy (Ed.), *Sport psychology interventions* (pp. 71–116). Champaign, IL: Human Kinetics.

Willis, J., & Campbell, L. (1992). Counseling in the fitness profession. In J. Willis & L. Campbell (Eds.), *Exercise psychology* (pp. 147–171). Champaign, IL: Human Kinetics.

Windt, P. Y. (1989). Professions and professional ethics: The theoretical background. In P. Y. Windt, P. C. Appleby, M. P. Battin, L. P. Francis, & B. M. Landesman (Eds.), *Ethical issues in the professions* (pp. 1–24). Englewood Cliffs, NJ: Prentice-Hall.

Windt, P. Y., Appleby, P. C., Battin, M. P., Francis, L. P., & Landesman, B. M. (Eds.). (1989). *Ethical issues in the professions*. Englewood Cliffs, NJ: Prentice-Hall.

Zeigler, E. F. (1987). Rational and suggested dimensions for a ethics code for sport psychologists. *The Sport Psychologist, 1,* 138–150.

25

Sport and Exercise Psychology: A Positive Force in the New Millennium

Robert N. Singer and Kevin L. Burke

Seligman and Csikszentmihalyi (2000) recently described the field of psychology as one that has focused too much on the negative (pathology). They called for more focus on "positive psychology," which is concerned with the "positive features that make life worth living" (p. 5). Exercise and sport psychologists are associated with many situations that are beneficial to humans, and that provide the foundation for interesting research and practical applications related to the positive side of life's pursuits. Sport and exercise have been an integral part of society that has allowed for opportunities of self-exploration, self-fulfillment, self-assessment, self-regulation, and satisfaction. They bring challenges and enjoyment to our lives as well as contribute to our quality of life. Within sport and exercise psychology, however, much more can be learned about how individuals and groups have positive experiences.

This chapter begins with a discussion of the uniqueness of sport and exercise psychology and suggestions for a more prominent influence of the field in society. Commentary on specializing within sport and exercise psychology is followed by a discussion of emerging opportunities for services and activities. A brief description of research directions also is presented.

A Unique Sport Science

Sport and exercise psychology has its roots in both psychology and kinesiology (previously physical education) and is somewhat unique as a sport science. A commonality among the sport sciences includes the intent to contribute to the understanding and maximizing of human performance and achievement—to help athletes be the best they can be. Although this goal will continue to be a major focal point, sport and exercise psychology can and should be more concerned with the well-being of athletes, not only their achievements.

This unique personal contribution is especially valuable in high-level sport, where the pressure to win is intense. Any advantages over opponents, through potentially useful products or approaches to training and competition, are eagerly sought. Sport science and medical breakthroughs are becoming increasingly available for this purpose. However, sport and exercise psychology can represent something more compelling to athletes. An athlete's personal and social development, responsibilities, decision-making skills, rights, and happiness should be addressed. Of the cadre of specialists enlisted to ensure the competitive edge of athletes and teams, the sport psychologist might be the only one who may clearly assume the designated role of a support person, caring more than most others about an athlete's personal development and fulfillment (Burke, 1999). Sport psychologists can help athletes at all levels of competition to place sport in perspective, as one aspect of their lives. It is hoped that this function increases in subsequent years.

Sport and exercise psychology is more directly in tune with the welfare of people when considering exercise and health for the general population than when concerned with the small number of elite athletes. Specialists with a focus on the lifestyles and well-being of individuals help them to become involved with and committed to meaningful physical activity and nutritional programs, which can result in invaluable benefits throughout their lives. These efforts may serve society in a more beneficial fashion than solely trying to help athletes win contests.

A Multidisciplinary Field

On the basis of current sport and exercise psychology courses offered in universities (Petrie & Watkins, 1994), employment possibilities, and academic specializations within departments in North American universities, it has been shown that sport and exercise psychology is most likely to be housed in departments of kinesiology or exercise and sport science or departments with a similar title, rather than in psychology departments. See, for example, the *Directory of Graduate Programs in Applied Sport Psychology* (Sachs, Burke, & Schrader, 2001). Furthermore, LeUnes and Hayward (1990) noted that according to clinical psychology program chairpersons, sport psychology is not a significant curricular component in major psychology departments. Course offerings in sport psychology in psychology or counseling departments are rare. Due to the expected growth in collaboration between academic departments and the anticipated increased interest in and acceptance of sport psychology by psychologists as a viable field of study and practice, we believe that more faculty members in psychology departments will be receptive to courses and programs housed in their departments. Furthermore, more psychology professionals will expand their practices to include sport and exercise psychology. More opportunities for psychology professionals to respecialize (as is offered by schools of professional psychology), as well as expanded opportunities to obtain certification, will emerge as a result of this growing interest.

Although some territorial conflict between psychologists and kinesiologists has occurred and continues to occur (Taylor, 1994), psychology and kinesiology departments are expected to collaborate increasingly with regard to the academic preparation of future exercise and sport psychologists. The future may see the development of graduate programs on the same campus (not necessarily competing with each other for the same students) offering specialized tracts in sport and exercise psychology. For example, a psychology department may offer a clinical sport psychology specialization, a kinesiology department an educational sport psychology specialization, and either department an exercise psychology specialization. Ideally, both departments would complement each other in offering beneficial experiences to students. For those students primarily concerned with the applied aspects of sport and exercise psychology, more practical field experiences and internships (Waite & Pettit, 1993) should become available. Although some graduate programs currently do offer applied experiences, students at more universities will expect and request these types of learning experiences and opportunities.

Sport and exercise psychology scholars and students interested in pursuing research will collaborate more with scientists with different specializations on various research endeavors, thereby enriching the knowledge base of sport and exercise psychology. It appears that this base crosses over other areas dealing with human potential, achievement, and fulfillment; yet unique considerations are present as well.

Good science leads to respectability and identity of a discipline. Future students and would-be sport and exercise psychologists need to appreciate this observation.

Exercise and sport psychologists will need to analyze and understand their capabilities and limitations more effectively than has been the case, on occasion. That is, they need to know what they can do and what they cannot or should not do. The *Ethical Principles and Standards of the Association for the Advancement of Applied Sport Psychology* (Sachs, Burke, & Schrader, 2001) requires this understanding of all sport psychologists, and the American Psychological Association's (APA's) *Ethical Principles of Psychologists and Code of Conduct* (APA, 1992) requires this of all psychologists. The validity, acceptability, and respectability of the profession are at stake. As has been heatedly debated in the past by kinesiologists and psychologists concerning boundaries or territories (Taylor, 1994), the importance of realizing one's limitations of knowledge and practice is perhaps of greater importance than recognizing what one can do well. Furthermore, whether one receives a doctorate in psychology or one in kinesiology should determine in part the type of services that can be rendered.

Development of Specializations

Historically, the sport and exercise psychology field has been called sport psychology. The focus was exclusively on sport performance. In more recent years, health and well-being through regular participation in vigorous physical activity programs have become of increasing interest to consumers, researchers, and practitioners. We expect sport and exercise psychology to splinter into two separate, distinct fields (i.e., sport psychology and exercise psychology). However, it is imperative that professionals in both specializations commit to open communication and remain collegial with each other. Singer (1995) has proposed that the commonality of interests between and among exercise and sport psychologists is in human achievement and welfare through the medium of movement. Sport, physical activity, exercise, recreation, and play are representative of this medium.

Sport and exercise psychologists are becoming more specialized, and the trend will continue. Expertise is function-specific. Areas of specialization expected to grow include the following:

- Youth sport (development considerations, motivational factors, optimal learning periods, ideal experiences).
- Group dynamics (morale, productivity, leadership, cohesiveness).
- Learning and expertise (learning processes, practice conditions and simulations, demands of events, expert systems).
- Counseling (coping with problems and maladaptive behaviors, substance abuse, depression, injury, severe anxiety).
- Performance enhancement (mental preparation routines, intervention techniques, motivation, self-regulation approaches).
- Well-being (motivational factors and psychological benefits related to exercise programs).
- Health promotion (understanding and contributing to healthy lifestyles and enhancing one's quality of life).

The body of knowledge in these areas has been increasing steadily in recent years, owing to the scholarly efforts of exercise and sport psychologists around the world. Such research developments stimulated the need to unify the body of knowledge, which led to the publication of the first *Handbook of Research on Sport Psychology* (Singer, Murphey, & Tennant, 1993). Research advancements during the last decade of the 20th century suggested the need for a second edition of this book (Singer, Hausenblas, & Janelle, 2001).

One of the more appealing newer areas of specialty in sport and exercise psychology, as demonstrated by student interest and potential occupations, is health promotion. Understanding and contributing to healthy lifestyles and enhancing one's quality of life concern many exercise and sport psychologists. Well-prepared exercise psychologists will play more of a major role in this area in the future. The challenge is in not only determining ways to encourage more people to be involved in regular programs of physical activity, but also educating the general public about the valuable education, research, and services for promoting healthy lifestyle choices that exercise psychologists can provide. In the future, it may become commonplace for a physician to refer obese and sedentary clients to an exercise psychologist to provide an exercise adherence and motivation program. Psychological as well as physiological benefits will be demonstrated. Health and fitness club administrators also will turn to qualified exercise psychologists for the same reasons, but these services will be primarily related to client motivation, enthusiasm, enjoyment, and adherence to exercise programs.

Career Choices

Although an undergraduate course in sport psychology has become commonplace at colleges and universities, specializations in sport and exercise psychology usually begin at the master's and doctoral levels. There is concern in higher education about the overproduction of graduates with doctoral degrees in virtually every field. Many graduates have difficulty locating positions in their specialization and are considered to be fortunate to obtain any kind of employment. Perhaps pressure will be put on graduate school faculties to think through the dilemma carefully and to reduce the size of their programs or promote further diversification of job opportunities for their graduates, especially for those who wish to gain meaningful employment after earning a master's degree. One possible boost to the careers of those who earn a master's degree would be eligibility for a level of certification. Since 1992, the Association for the Advancement of Applied Sport Psychology (AAASP) has permitted only those with a doctoral degree to become a "Certified Consultant, AAASP." The intention is to help practitioners be more positively viewed by the public and confidently selected by potential clients. We predict that possibly AAASP and Division 47 (Exercise and Sport Psychology) of the APA may eventually create master's level certification standards (although historically the APA has maintained that the doctorate is the terminal degree for psychologists). This "stamp of approval" by one or both of these major sport psychology associations may help to create more opportunities but certainly with restrictions for those with a master's degree versus a doctoral degree.

Perhaps other sport and exercise psychology organizations will be involved in this process by either becoming a part of the certification process or supporting and endorsing a common certification method. If this happens, the master's degree in sport and exercise psychology might be more valued than it is now. One future trend expected is that coaches who have traditionally earned their master's degrees in physical education will instead opt for a master's degree in sport psychology (as well as in other sport sciences, e.g., biomechanics, sports medicine, and sport management) because of the obvious beneficial practical applications to coaching (Buceta, 1993; Burke & Johnson, 1992).

The number of sport psychologists consulting with athletes and teams has increased in recent years, but much of the consulting is done on an irregular basis. This subjective appraisal is based on presentations and commentaries made at various sport psychology conferences. If sport psychologists currently are effective in producing favorable outcomes, even on a part-time basis, more opportunities will arise for sport psychologists in the future. But those interested in sport and exercise psychology should not be naive about their chances for employment in this capacity. Furthermore, when positions open in athletic programs for sport psychologists, direct performance enhancement may be of low priority. For example, a university athletic department may hire a sport psychologist as a counselor–adviser to help student–athletes make responsible decisions about their lifestyles and university education and remain academically eligible to compete. When a professional sports team searches for a sport psychologist, the major concern may be with substance abuse education and other factors related to the private lives of athletes.

Performance enhancement—helping athletes by using intervention techniques, education, and self-regulation strategies—is at a modest stage of understanding and application in sport programs. Sport psychologists who are convincing communicators are making breakthroughs, creating a niche for themselves. Professional education, experience, and the ability to market oneself are critical considerations. As sport continues to grow as an entertainment medium, sport psychologists are likely to be involved in more clearly defined roles. If visibility of sport psychologists in the media grows and the report of their involvement is favorable, recreational athletes and exercise participants will become more interested in availing themselves of similar services.

Emerging Opportunities

The career paths of exercise and sport psychologists are varied, which can make the field seem confusing and unstable. This variety also may be interpreted optimistically as opportunities. Many opportunities exist to conduct research, to provide services to various constituencies, and to be involved in interesting and challenging activities. Sport psychologists also have opportunities to be educators. One of the most interesting facets of the near future will be the role of the Internet and the Web on sport and exercise psychology. Beyond the teaching of sport and exercise psychology courses on the Web, many sport psychology Web sites (e.g., www.aaasponline.org, www.aheadinthegame.com) are already making an impact. Sport psychology advice and information have been shared over the Internet over the past decade (Burke, 1994). Is it possible that some individuals will be able to make a living or substantially increase their base income performing consultations over the Internet? As sport and exercise psychology professionals learn more about consumer preferences for receiving sport and exercise psychology education and services, these and other consulting opportunities should continue to develop.

Professional Activities and Service

To keep abreast of the latest information and activities in sport and exercise psychology and to help shape the future, exercise and sport psychologists will have the opportunity to be directly active in Division 47 (Exercise and Sport Psychology) in APA, AAASP, the North American Society for the Psychology of Sport and Physical Activity (NASPSPA), the International Society of Sport Psychology (ISSP), the European Society of Sport Psychology (Fédération Européan de Psychologie du Sport et Activité Corporelle), the Canadian Society for Psychomotor Learning and Sport Psychology, and the Asian South Pacific Association of Sport Psychology. Other more broad-based organizations, such as the American College of Sport Medicine, also may be of interest. Involvement in professional organizations includes participating in conferences with opportunities to learn about the latest research and professional and practical directions and serving on committees, task forces, or in executive positions. All of these optional commitments present unique ways of having a long-standing and far-reaching impact on the field. Also, just as some of the previously mentioned organizations were "born" from the earlier ones, it will be interesting to see whether any other more specialized organizations develop to serve the interests of those connected to sport and exercise psychology. Possibly an association will emerge that focuses exclusively on exercise psychology, thereby holding its own annual conference and publishing its own journal of exercise psychology.

International Trends

International interactions among sport and exercise psychologists have come a long way since the formation of the ISSP in 1965 under the insightful vision and dedicated efforts of Ferruccio Antonelli. ISSP sponsored the first World Congress of Sport Psychology in Rome that year. Congresses have been continued every four years in different countries.

In addition, ISSP encouraged the development of continental sport psychology societies (NASPSPA and the European Society of Sport Psychology in 1967) and subsequent societies in various countries (Lidor, Morris, Bardaxoglou, & Becker, 2001). Likewise, with increasing frequency, various conferences are held throughout the world, with sport and exercise psychologists from all countries encouraged to participate. Each year seems to bring about more opportunities for collaborating, sharing ideas, and learning about "happenings." This is true not only for sport psychology conferences, but also for the increasing number of sports medicine and sport science conferences.

Such activities and opportunities will be even more valued in the future as forums and mediums to be enlightened and stimulated; to speak and to be heard; to make new friendships; and to understand scientific, professional, educational, cultural, and practical perspectives in other countries are provided. Political, educational, and economic barriers among countries are being reduced rapidly, thereby encouraging the exchange of ideas. Through greater future international collaboration, mutual understandings will be improved. They will lead to enhanced developments everywhere in establishing sport and exercise psychology as a scientifically based specialization associated with generating a significant body of knowledge, preparing students with legitimate credentials, and offering appropriate services.

Recognition and Respectability

An athlete's skills take many years of dedicated training and practice to hone. Similarly, this should be the case for the services that are offered to them and others. Sport and exercise psychologists must proceed carefully, yet vigorously, to attain acceptance and identity. The dangers are clear when inexperienced sport psychologists, for example, try to start at the top with professional or Olympic athletes. The excitement surrounding the emergence of sport and exercise psychology has led to unfortunate consequences on occasion. Individuals with inadequate academic preparation in psychology and kinesiology, as well as limited experiences in sport settings, will, as others do now, promise services that are not professionally and scientifically acceptable. Professionally competent exercise and sport psychologists will need to establish stronger standards and guidelines for the field.

The Significance of Research and a Body of Knowledge

The field will continually need the formulation and advancement of a scholarly body of knowledge. The 1970s and early 1980s witnessed the generation of lines of research, usually laboratory-centered and experimental in nature, to establish the credibility and acceptability of sport and exercise psychology within university settings. More practical research and the increased use of qualitative and descriptive methodologies are becoming more evident in recently published research journals. Applied research will continue to be in vogue. A goal for many contemporary scholars is to conduct research in ecologically valid settings to have a more direct impact on the potential and practical concerns of the consumers of the information (Singer, 1989).

The critical point will be the need for sport and exercise psychology to continue to be anchored in a legitimate body of knowledge. Both applied and basic research are necessary and have different primary missions. It is important that research advance the body of knowledge and provide identity for sport and exercise psychology as well as a suitable and defensible basis for services rendered. Those who practice sport and exercise psychology should be well versed in the values, methods, and outcomes of scientific research, as Howell (1992) suggested for psychology in general. A solid scientific base provides credibility in the minds of fellow scholars in other specializations as well as the general public. The body of knowledge associated with sport and exercise psychology must continue to grow in the future, with researchers attempting to address significant questions and issues, and practicing specialists being aware of developments in the field.

Research Themes

Regardless of their occupation and economic level, people are interested in sport, and sport continues to be a central fixture in society. Not too many years ago, the study of sport and the athlete's quest for proficiency was perceived as frivolous activity, whereas now it is considered a significant area of investigative inquiry. Furthermore, research conclusions made about striving for and achieving excellence in sport usually provide insights applicable to many endeavors and occupations beyond the sports world.

Health and exercise promotion also will receive more attention. From the exercise psychologist's perspective, the study of routine exercise involvement, as well as factors associated with avoidance and dropping out, leads to practical solutions. Researchers have identified potential psychological benefits of exercise, including improved body and self-concept, positive mood shifts, anxiety management, reduction in depression, and overall feelings of well-being (e.g., Berger & Motl, 2001; Landers & Arendt, 2001). These types of research findings will continue to be of importance to society and offer sport and exercise psychology the opportunity to expand its contributions, which have been traditionally thought of as mostly oriented to high-level competitive sport.

One direction in future research will involve determining more of the positive aspects of sport and exercise experiences. As suggested by Peterson (2000), optimism certainly could be one of the most important variables in the framework of positive psychology. For example, besides administering surveys that measure precompetitive state anxiety and competitive trait anxiety, sport psychologists may focus more on precompetitive state optimism and trait optimism (Burke, Joyner, Czech, & Wilson, 2000). Exercise psychologists will probably increasingly pursue a possible relationship between exercise participation and optimistic tendencies (Kavussanu & McAuley, 1995). Researchers may wish to further investigate how optimism may provide protective health benefits (Taylor, Kemeny, Reed, Bower, & Gruenewald, 2000). Other possible areas related to this focus on positive sport and exercise psychology could be happiness (Diener, 2000; Maddux, 1997; Myers, 2000), humor (Burke, Peterson, & Nix, 1995), flow experiences (Jackson, Ford, Kimiecik, & Marsh, 1998), disease prevention and health promotion (Gauvin & Spence, 1995), the study of experts (Bloom, Durand-Bush, & Salmela, 1997; Moritz, Hall, Martin, & Vadocz, 1996), and profiles of excellence (Silva, 1996).

Conceptual Approaches

Sport and exercise psychology research related to learning and performance has tended to be conducted within the cognitive psychology framework. Major contributions should continue in regard to the following areas of study: (a) understanding mental processes and functions, as well as cognitive strategies, associated with effective learning and performance; (b) formulating practical guidelines to help individuals use their mental processes to their advantage; (c) developing self-regulatory strategies to cope with stress and potential performance distractors, thereby enhancing achievement potential; and (d) determining techniques to enhance self-perceptions, self-efficacy, and other personal characteristics associated with achievement motivation.

The counterargument to cognitive psychology models is that traditional research approaches related to this kind of conceptualization are too contrived and do not account for the irregularity and unpredictability of human states and behaviors. Ecological and dynamical concepts (e.g., Cziko, 1992; Turvey, 1990) emphasize the continuing interaction of action and perception and offer alternative approaches to cognitive psychology and information-processing models for the study and understanding of movement behaviors. Presumably, these perspectives are more real-world-oriented and tend to view the larger picture of behavior. Whereas information-processing models depend to a great extent on isolated cognitive processes and a computer analogy, perception-action models are linked more closely to the biological sciences. Related to such approaches to understanding human behaviors are advances in understanding and applying principles that are based on the concepts of chaos, nonlinear dynamics, and self-organization (Barton, 1994). Although the ideas evolved primarily from investigators in the physical or natural sciences, these models are gaining the increased attention of psychologists.

Research Methodologies

Diverse approaches in the study of various topics in sport and exercise psychology are more readily accepted. A push will continue for more applied research, undertaken under realistic conditions, to contribute directly to practical knowledge and meaningful potential intervention services. The call will be for research to be directly useful to participants in sport and exercise programs. In other words, whereas traditional experimental designs and quantitative data guided research for several years, increasingly popular and acceptable are case studies, single-subject designs (Carboni, Burke, Joyner, Hardy, & Bloom, in press; Scruggs & Mastropieri, 1998; Shambrook & Bull, 1996; Swain & Jones, 1995), and qualitative methods. Although many scholars have endorsed these types of research designs, the prominent sport psychology research journals have not shown a proclivity to publish many articles of these sorts. We predict that the *Journal of Applied Sport Psychology*, *The Sport Psychologist*, the *International Journal of Sport Psychology*, and the *Journal of Sport and Exercise Psychology* will begin to publish more of these types of research investigations. It is possible that in the near future a sport and exercise psychology journal specifically devoted to such single-subject, case study, and qualitative designs may materialize.

As issues become more complex and sophisticated, they are best addressed with collaborative efforts from specialists in different fields (Singer, 1994). The depth of knowledge is impressive in different specializations as to substance and approaches to research. The trend is toward creating "working groups" in an informal manner or through centers and institutes identifying a common theme of interest. One way or another, the cross-fertilization of experts is desirable and will contribute significantly to the advancement of the sport and exercise psychology field.

Conclusion

The goals of establishing sport and exercise psychology as a scientifically based specialization advancing a strong body of knowledge, preparing students with legitimate credentials, and offering meaningful and effective services will be further realized in the future. The process is well underway for attaining such goals, as indicated by the increasing number of graduate students with excellent credentials and enthusiasm, the number of higher education institutions offering specializations in sport and exercise psychology, the number and quality of research articles being published, and the commitment by leaders in both kinesiology and psychology to advance the field. There is still a long road to traverse, but in many ways, the process of striving can be as exciting as that of realizing.

Sport and exercise psychology is emerging at a rapid rate all over the world as a legitimate scholarly specialization that offers valuable services (Weinberg & Gould, 1999). Establishing identity, respect, and recognition is not easy. Sport and exercise psychology will continue to take important steps in this regard, and in becoming recognized as a constructive, positive force in the new millennium.

References

American Psychological Association. (1992). Ethical principles of psychologists and code of conduct. *American Psychologist, 47,* 1597–1611.

Barton, S. (1994). Chaos, self-organization, and psychology. *American Psychologist, 49,* 50–14.

Berger, B. G., & Motl, R. (2001). Physical activity and quality of life. In R. N. Singer, H. R. Hausenblaus, & C. M. Janelle (Eds.), *Handbook of sport psychology, Second Edition* (pp. 636–671). New York: Wiley.

Bloom, G. A., Durand-Bush, N., & Salmela, J. H. (1997). Pre- and postcompetition routines of expert coaches of team sports. *The Sport Psychologist, 11,* 127–141.

Buceta, J. M. (1993). The sport psychologist/athletic coach dual role: Advantages, difficulties, and ethical considerations. *Journal of Applied Sport Psychology, 5,* 64–77.

Burke, K. L. (1999). Comments on Balague's 1997 A.A.A.S.P. conference keynote address. *The Sport Psychologist, 13,* 231–234.

Burke, K. L. (1994). Computerized consulting in sport psychology: Some experiences with youth baseball, softball, and teeball. *Perceptual and Motor Skills, 78,* 538.

Burke, K. L., & Johnson, J. J. (1992). The sport psychologist–coach dual role position: A rebuttal to Ellickson and Brown (1990). *Journal of Applied Sport Psychology, 4,* 51–55.

Burke, K. L., Joyner, A. B., Czech, D. R., & Wilson, M. J. (2000). An investigation of concurrent validity between two optimism/pessimism questionnaires: The Life Orientation Test–Revised and the Optimism/Pessimism Scale. *Current Psychology, 19,* 125–132.

Burke, K. L., Peterson, D., & Nix, C. (1995). The influence of humor on athletes' evaluations of their coaches. *Journal of Sport Behavior, 18,* 83–90.

Carboni, J., Burke, K. L., Joyner, A. B., Hardy, C. J., & Bloom, L. C. (in press). The effects of brief imagery on free throw shooting performance and concentrational style of intercollegiate basketball players: A single-subject design. *International Sports Journal.*

Cziko, G. A. (1992). Purposeful behavior as the control of perception: Implications for educational research. *Educational Researcher, 21,* 10–18.

Diener, E. (2000). Subjective well-being: The science of happiness and a proposal for a national index. *American Psychologist, 55,* 34–43.

Gauvin, L., & Spence, J. C. (1995). Psychological research on exercise and fitness: Current research trends and future challenges. *The Sport Psychologist, 9,* 434–448.

Howell, W. (1992, December). Field's scientific deficit will have dire effects. *APA Monitor, 23,* 21.

Jackson, S. A., Ford, S. K., Kimiecik, J. C., & Marsh, H. W. (1998). Psychological correlates of flow in sport. *Journal of Sport and Exercise Psychology, 20,* 358–378.

Kavussanu, M., & McAuley, E. (1995). Exercise and optimism: Are highly active individuals more optimistic? *Journal of Sport and Exercise Psychology, 17,* 246–258.

Landers, D. M., & Arendt, S. M. (2001). Physical activity and mental health. In R. N. Singer, H. A. Hausanblas, & C. M. Janelle (Eds.), *Handbook of Sport Psychology* (2nd ed., pp. 740–765). New York: Wiley.

LeUnes, A., & Hayward, S. A. (1990). Sport psychology as viewed by chairpersons of APA-approved clinical psychology programs. *The Sport Psychologist, 4,* 18–24.

Lidor, R., Morris, T., Bardaxoglou, N., & Becker, B. (2001). *The world sport psychology sourcebook* (3rd ed.). Morgantown, WV: Fitness Information Technology.

Maddux, J. E. (1997). Habit, health, and happiness. *Journal of Sport and Exercise Psychology, 19,* 331–346.

Moritz, S. E., Hall, C. R., Martin, K. A., & Vadocz, E. (1996). What are confident athletes imaging? An examination of image content. *The Sport Psychologist, 10,* 171–179.

Myers, D. G. (2000). The funds, friends, and faith of happy people. *American Psychologist, 55,* 56–67.

Peterson, C. (2000). The future of optimism. *American Psychologist, 55,* 44–55.

Petrie, T. A., & Watkins, C. E. (1994). A survey of counseling psychology programs and exercise/sport science departments: Sport psychology issues and training. *The Sport Psychologist, 8,* 28–36.

Sachs, M. L., Burke, K. L., & Schrader, D. (2001). *Directory of graduate programs in applied sport psychology* (6th ed). Morgantown, WV: Fitness Information Technology.

Scruggs, T. E., & Mastropieri, M. A. (1998). Summarizing single-subject research. *Behavior Modification, 22,* 221–242.

Seligman, M. E. P., & Csikszentmihalyi, M. (2000). Positive psychology: An introduction. *American Psychologist, 55,* 5–14.

Shambrook, C. J., & Bull, S. J. (1996). The use of a single-case research design to investigate the efficacy of imagery training. *Journal of Applied Sport Psychology, 8,* 27–43.

Silva, J. M. (1996). 1995 Coleman Roberts Griffith address: Profiles of excellence. *Journal of Applied Sport Psychology, 8,* 119–130.

Singer, R. N. (1989). Applied sport psychology in the United States. *Journal of Applied Sport Psychology, 1,* 61–80.

Singer, R. N. (1994). Sport psychology: An integrated approach. In S. Serpa, J. Alves, & V. Pataco (Eds.), *International perspectives on sport and exercise psychology* (pp. 1–20). Morgantown, WV: Fitness Information Technology.

Singer, R. N. (1995). Sport psychology: An overview. In K. Henschen & W. F. Straub (Eds.), *An analysis of athlete behavior* (pp. 3–23). Ithaca, NY: Mouvement.

Singer, R. N., Hausenblas, H., & Janelle, C. (Eds). (2001). *Handbook of sport psychology* (2nd ed.). New York: Wiley.

Singer, R. N., Murphey, M., & Tennant, L. K. (Eds.). (1993). *Handbook of research on sport psychology.* New York: Macmillan.

Swain, A., & Jones, G. (1995). Effects of goal-setting interventions on selected basketball skills: A single-subject design. *Research Quarterly for Exercise & Sport, 66,* 51–63.

Taylor, J. (1994). Examining the boundaries of sport science and psychology trained practitioners in applied sport psychology: Title usage and area of competence. *Journal of Applied Sport Psychology, 6,* 185–195.

Taylor, S. E., Kemeny, M. E., Reed, G. M., Bower, J. E., & Gruenewald, T. L. (2000). Psychological resources, positive illusions, and health. *American Psychologist, 55,* 99–109.

Turvey, M. T. (1990). Coordination. *American Psychologist, 45,* 938–312.

Waite, B. T., & Pettit, M. E. (1993). Work experiences of graduates from doctoral programs in sport psychology. *Journal of Applied Sport Psychology, 5,* 234–250.

Weinberg, R. S., & Gould, D. (1999). *Foundations of sport and exercise psychology* (2nd ed.). Champaign, IL: Human Kinetics.

Index

Navratilova, Martina, 429
NCAA. *See* National Collegiate Athletic Association
Needs assessment, 17–18
  and intensity, 100 (*see also* Intensity)
Negotiating of terms of consultation, 399–404
Networking, 490
Networks, referral, 330–331
NFF. *See* National Football Foundation
NFL. *See* National Football League
NFL/NFF Coaching Academy, 200–201
NGB (National Governing Boards), 397, 407
Niche development, 487
Nicklaus, Jack, 50
Norepinephrine and serotonin theory, on exercise therapy benefits, 234
Norms, group, 351–352
North American Society of Pediatric Exercise Science, 443
North American Society for the Psychology of Sport and Physical Activity (NASPSPA), 441, 442, 532, 533
  online address of, 452
Notes, imagery, 66

O

Observation, of self-talk, 86
Observational learning (modeling), 131, 147
  case studies in, 132–133, 144–146
  developmental issues in, 139–143
  and exercise, 190
  modifying physical skills and psychological responses through, 135–139
  in rehabilitation from sports injury, 143–144
  theoretical approaches to, 133–135
  tips on, 146
  in youth sport, 362
Older people, exercise therapy for, 237
Olympic athletes
  distractions for, 408
  and drug use, 311
  and goal setting, 29, 31
  imagery useful for, 50
  number of practitioners working with, 397

and positive self-statements, 82
psychological problems of, 160
women (1996, 2000), 418
See also Elite athletes
Olympic Committee, U.S., sport psychologists hired by, 451
Olympics for the Physically Disabled, 430
One-trial generalizations, 79
Operant techniques, in youth sport, 362
Organizations, professional, 441, 532
Osteoporosis, 309
Outcome evaluations, 284–285
Outcome expectations, 190
Outcome goals, 26, 38–39
Outcome orientation, 33
  and overintensity, 107
Overconfidence, underintensity from, 108
Overintensity, 106–107, 126
  regulation of, 112–115, 116–119

P

Pain
  hypnosis for, 162
  and referral, 328
  use of strategies to minimize, 171
Pairing phase, in cognitive restructuring, 80
Paralympics, 430
Parents in youth sports, 344–345
  parent-based interventions, 355–361, 365–366
  and performance anxiety, 343
  support from, 40
  See also Significant others
Passive relaxation script, 117
Payment source, for clinical practice, 496
Peak performance (psychological skills) training, 481–482
Pediatric Exercise Science, 443
Peer-assisted learning, 143
Peer models, 141–143
Perception
  of effort, 155, 157, 177
  and internal-imagery perspective, 61
Perfectionism, 78
  and drug use, 311

About the Editors

Judy L. Van Raalte received her PhD in social psychology from Arizona State University, Tempe. She is currently associate professor of psychology at Springfield College, Springfield, MA. As a certified consultant, AAASP, she has provided applied sport psychology services for several athletes and teams. She has also published broadly in the area of sport and exercise psychology.

Britton W. Brewer received his PhD in clinical psychology from Arizona State University, Tempe. He is currently associate professor of psychology and head men's cross country coach at Springfield College, Springfield, MA. His research is focused on psychological aspects of sport injury rehabilitation. He is a certified consultant, AAASP, and serves on the editorial boards of the *Academic Athletic Journal*, the *Journal of Applied Sport Psychology*, *Physical Therapy in Sport*, and *The Sport Psychologist*.